HUMANITY AT THE LIMIT

HUMANITY
AT THE LIMIT

*The Impact of the Holocaust
Experience on Jews and Christians*

Edited by Michael A. Signer

Indiana University Press
Bloomington and Indianapolis

This book is a publication of

Indiana University Press
601 North Morton Street
Bloomington, IN 47404-3797 USA

http://www.indiana.edu/~iupress

Telephone orders   800-842-6796
Fax orders   812-855-7931
Orders by e-mail   iuporder@indiana.edu

Library of Congress Cataloging-in-Publication Data

Humanity at the limit : the impact of the Holocaust experience on Jews and Christians / edited by Michael A. Signer.
    p.   cm.
    Includes index.
    ISBN 0-253-33739-9 (cl : alk. paper)
    1. Holocaust, Jewish (1939–1945)—Influence. 2. Judaism—Relations—Christianity—1945- 3. Christianity and other religions—Judaism—1945- 4. Holocaust, Jewish (1939–1945)—Moral and ethical aspects. 5. Holocaust (Jewish theology) 6. Holocaust (Christian theology) I. Signer, Michael Alan.

D804.3 .H85 2000
940.53'18—dc21
                                                        00-035031

1 2 3 4 5   05 04 03 02 01 00

Contents

Preface
Michael A. Signer

To ORGANIZE A scholarly conference on the Holocaust under the sponsorship of a Catholic university in America requires a unique perspective. Dozens of academic gatherings to analyze the destruction of European Jewry take place every year. Articles appear in newspapers and magazines with increasing frequency. Churches and synagogues throughout North America and Europe organize commemorations. It would seem that another collection of scholarly essays would only repeat conclusions reached by others. However, in 1998, when the Vatican Commission on Religious Relations with the Jewish People issued its long-anticipated document, *We Remember: Reflections on the Shoah*, the Notre Dame Holocaust Project faculty committee planning the conference saw this as a fortuitous occasion to bring scholars together under the auspices of one of America's oldest Catholic universities.

The controversies that the Vatican document provoked within both Jewish and Catholic communities about the role of the Church hierarchy and its members in promoting or preventing the destruction of European Jewry, as well as the role of the papacy and its relationship to Germany before and after 1939—topics that have long been subjected to scrutiny—will continue far into the future. The essays in this volume have a rather different focus. They do not aim specifically at an assessment of the Church or of Jewish activity, but have a much wider horizon, reflecting the title, *Humanity at the Limit: The Impact of the Holocaust Experience on Jews and Christians.*

Why did we choose the universal term "humanity" and link it with "Holocaust experience"? Knowledge of the destruction of European Jewry suggests that an inquiry into the Holocaust would more appropriately generate titles about "inhumanity" without any limits. The words of Victor Klemperer, born a German Jew and baptized as a Protestant, may provide an answer. In January 1937 he wrote, "Among the documents I have kept here there is now the new curriculum vitae . . . it is less emotional by several degrees, I am no longer capable of underlining my Germanness, the whole national ideology has gone to pieces for me." Four years after Hitler came to power Klemperer had lost faith in his "Germanness" (*Deutschtum*). No longer could he believe that Germany represented the height of cultural and ethical values that had been at the very center of his self-consciousness. Like so many others who were born into German Jewish families, to be "human" was to participate in the literature and ethos of Germanness and German culture. In four short years the basis of his life and values had been destroyed. The culture of Goethe and Schiller was sinking into "barbarism." All around him he observed that humanity had transgressed the boundaries of what he had known to be civilization. The limits of humanity were clear to him even before the death camps existed.

Half a century after the liberation of the death camps, many people are still seeking to understand the quirks of fate and history that permitted the totalitarian regime to usurp power in Germany through a democratic electoral process. Though more and more information is published, the appetite for comprehension remains unsatisfied. After years of silence, the past decades have witnessed a flood of publications about the Holocaust. This scholarly effort commenced with Raul Hilberg's massive *The Destruction of the European Jews,* which chronicled the administration of the horror. Other scholars have moved on to describe the details of daily human experience during the Shoah. While scholarly writing about the mechanisms of the perpetrators continues, new resources about the victims are coming to light. As the last generation of survivors of the war and camps is dying, testimonies pour forth, as both written memoirs and audiovisual recordings. Beyond the efforts of historians and those who document the experience of the survivors, literary creativity in poetry and prose adds to what we can learn about how men and women survived this horror. Despite Theodor Adorno's caveat, "No poetry after Auschwitz," many readers gain a more intimate sense of the horror from reading the novels of Elie Wiesel or Aharon Appelfeld than from the carefully constructed arguments of historians. Theologians, Jewish and Christian, have addressed questions about the nature of divinity that permitted the destruction of innocent children or the ethics of mass murder. Any effort to come to terms with the Holocaust must contend with the competing claims on human understanding that are offered by a variety of disciplines.

The sheer quantity of knowledge and thought that has been amassed produces an impulse to move beyond describing the realities of the horror. More than constructing a coherent narrative of the complex events of the Holocaust, it is urgent to discern the principal themes and broad perspectives that will enable our generation to go beyond banalities about goodness or evil that end with the slogan "Never again." The events that destroyed six million Jews and other victims of the Nazi terror will never happen again. However, in the past twenty years the cultures that lived through the Holocaust have seen countless instances of genocide in the Balkans, Africa, and Southeast Asia. If the Holocaust reflects such an unremittingly negative portrait of human nature, can we derive any redemptive themes from this tragic period? It would seem imperative that, having lived with such destruction, the generation that grew up immediately after the war should pass on to its children a legacy that might inoculate them against the human force impelling them toward violence.

We seem to be almost genetically encoded to discover the "lessons" of the Holocaust. In America and in Western Europe there is a growing sense that knowledge of this history will prevent future generations from perpetrating the horror again. However, Lawrence Langer, in his book *Preempting the Holocaust,* issues a strong warning against the attempt to discover universal lessons from the Holocaust. Langer argues that nothing redemptive can be learned from a world in which babies are capriciously torn to shreds before the eyes of their mothers. The Holocaust did not happen to universal humanity. It involved Jews, homosexuals, Slavs, Gypsies, and Germans. The evil of the Holocaust occurred under specific conditions in a specific time and place.

The essays in this volume attempt to avoid delineating redemptive or evil moments in ever sharper perspectives. Rather, they juxtapose good and evil behavior before, during, and after the Holocaust. The idea of juxtaposition, which was at the foundation of this conference, was proposed by Walter Benjamin, the Jewish philosopher and cultural critic, who wrote, "Juxtaposition is image at a standstill." By following Benjamin's maxim, the reader is led to perceive the complexity of human experience during the Holocaust. From the interplay of human experience refracted through the many academic disciplines represented here emerges an understanding of the claim that the Holocaust makes on Jews and Christians today.

Focusing on the theme, "Humanity at the Limit: The Impact of the Holocaust Experience on Jews and Christians," the authors start from the premise that the Holocaust was not beyond the boundary of humanity. Human beings committed acts of terror, but they also engaged in heroic deeds of goodness. One cannot enjoy the privilege of distance from those "beasts" who murdered any more than one can make the facile claim that in such a situation, one would have done the "good." The Holocaust, or Shoah, occurred among human beings. Moreover, the Holocaust pushed human experience to the very limits: life and death and the choices between them. The horizons of heaven and earth were obscured by the smoke of the crematoria.

The "humanity" of the Holocaust must not be understood only as an abstraction. The human beings who perpetrated the evil, stood by silently, or suffered belonged to national cultures. They were limited by time, location, and the pressures upon their societies. These human beings were also members of religious communities that, historically, imposed limits on the behavior of their members. Christians were and are enjoined by Scripture to follow the two great commandments: love of God and love of neighbor. Generations of Christians and Jews living together had experienced expulsions and violence, but not train transports and death camps. National Socialism catalyzed a reaction in the Christian populations of Germany and its conquered territories that transgressed the limits of their specific Christian humanity. The progressive deterioration of the condition of Jewish victims in the ghettos and camps produced the Musselman—the emaciated glassy-eyed inmate of the camps who became a modern icon of a human being pushed by starvation and cruelty far beyond any limit.

We thought these themes might best be explored by an international gathering of scholars. American audiences do not have ready access to scholarly analysis of Holocaust themes that emerge from conferences beyond their own boundaries. The Notre Dame Holocaust Project placed a high priority on inviting scholars from Germany, Eastern Europe, and Israel as well as from the United States and Canada.

The essays by German theologians who have been active in promoting Jewish-Christian relations in the land where the Holocaust occurred provide a moving testimony to the difficulties of helping that country confront its past. Both Hanspeter Heinz, a German, and John T. Pawlikowski, an American, raise questions about specific ideas in the Vatican document on the Shoah. Edna Brocke, an Israeli educator who has lived in Germany, shatters many stereotypes about the realities of educating Christians and Jews there about the Holocaust when she suggests that there is not "too little" education, but perhaps an oversaturation of the horrors. German youth become anesthetized to forget, and memory does not serve to develop a sense of responsibility. Austrian and Polish scholars provide their perspectives on the activity of the churches in their own countries before, during, and after the war.

Beyond the international perspectives offered by the participants, the conference was interdisciplinary. No single academic discipline encompasses a comprehensive explanation of the complex events and actions that constituted the Holocaust. Saul Friedländer points to the limits of historical studies, which can provide adequate accounts of the "how" but not the "why" of the Holocaust. His essay moves from the historical to the philosophical and theological themes of evil and the haunting question, "What is the nature of human nature?" Joan Ringelheim, writing from a philosophical perspective, also encourages a variety of approaches to understanding the Shoah. The reader will encounter the work of scholars from theology, history, art and artistic representation, as well as the history of science. Each area endeavors to offer new data and new perspectives. The authors do not always speak the same language, nor are they necessarily familiar with scholarship in other areas. Literary scholars often do not read historians, nor do historians of genetics familiarize themselves with theology. This printed version of the conference presentations cannot convey the excitement generated as scholars exchanged ideas and information with colleagues in other disciplines. We hope that the erudition reflected in these multidisciplinary contributions will lead readers to a more nuanced understanding of the Holocaust.

The issue of religion is central to this collection. The past fifty years have seen a monumental change in the approach of Christians to Jews and Judaism. Especially for Catholics, the Vatican II Council statement *Nostra Aetate* in 1965 provided the possibility for a serious re-evaluation of the consequences of the Church's anti-Jewish traditions. The establishment of the Secretariat for Religious Relations with the Jews in 1975 has enabled the Catholic Church to clarify its attitudes. Statements issued by this secretariat almost every decade have reflected a deeper understanding of Judaism. Protestant churches in both the United States and Europe have issued similar statements. Commemorating the fiftieth anniversary of the liberation of Auschwitz-Birkenau, Catholic episcopal conferences and Protestant synods in France, Germany, and Poland made strong pronouncements about their failure to protest or prevent the destruction of European Jewry.

The Jewish community's reception of these theological statements has been cautious. While Jewish theologians and scholars have actively engaged their Christian colleagues, the Holocaust has remained a stumbling block between them. Many Jewish theologians have seen a strong connection between the end of the Holocaust in 1945 and the founding of the state of Israel in 1948. Emil Fackenheim and Irving Greenberg have both articulated the significance of Israel for post-Holocaust Jewry. Indeed, many Jews have measured the progress of Christian attitudes by their degree of empathy for the Jewish state.

Despite the ongoing rapprochement between Christian and Jewish communities, issues relating to the Holocaust continue to provoke great tensions. The embrace of Kurt Waldheim by John Paul II and the controversy over the Carmelite convent in Auschwitz-Birkenau have taxed the limits of patience of both Jews and Christians. Remi Hoeckman urges both Christians and Jews to base their continuing dialogue on the trust that both communities are striving together to create a world of justice and compassion. Out of that trust emerges the strength to continue working toward reconciliation during moments of intense disagreement or misunderstanding of the motivations of either community.

Younger theologians represented in this volume point toward new directions for considering the Holocaust. Peter C. Phan opens the horizon of theological reflection to the worldwide Church. He demonstrates that in Asia, where few Jews had lived, the anti-Jewish traditions of the Church colored its theological teachings. On a more positive note, he reveals how Asian liberation theologians can contribute innovative paths toward reconciliation of deeply felt resentments. Robert A. Krieg discusses how an expanded notion of God's grace in the world enabled Romano Guardini, one of the great Catholic theologians, to move toward friendship with Martin Buber. The two essays by Jewish theologians reflect new areas of thought. Rachel Adler develops a feminist approach to a Jewish theology of the Holocaust. By utilizing the biblical genre of the psalm of lament and the teachings of the nineteenth-century Hasidic master Nachman of Bratzlav, she finds an appropriate voice for women and men to approach the theological void created by the Holocaust. Peter Ochs focuses on the "wounded but holy word" as a theological entry into the problem of discerning the divine in the darkness of the Holocaust. His use of the writings of the Talmudist David Weiss Halivni reveals the power of language in a world where the word was completely debased.

There remains the pleasant task of thanking those individuals who have contributed to this book. Betty Signer has worked diligently with all of the scholars who have written for this volume. The Notre Dame Holocaust Project would not have succeeded without her efforts. William Reilly, trustee of the University of Notre Dame, initiated the Notre Dame Holocaust Project and contributed material support. Gratitude is also due to many faculty colleagues who worked toward the success of our project.

In conclusion, perhaps the words of Peter von der Osten-Sacken's essay are most haunting: "I have visited concentration camps with Jewish friends. We walk on the same paths, but we are on very different journeys." It is our hope that this volume will contribute to a greater mutual understanding of both the paths and the different journeys.

HUMANITY AT THE LIMIT

Facing the Shoah
Memory and History
Saul Friedländer

O<small>N</small> J<small>ULY</small> 9, 1942, Henry Montor, the president of the United Palestine Appeal, asked Richard Lichtheim, the representative of the Jewish Agency in Geneva, to send him an article of fifteen hundred words reviewing the position of the Jews in Europe. "I feel at present quite unable to write a 'report,'" Lichtheim answered Montor on August 13, "a survey, something cool and clear and reasonable. . . . So I wrote not a survey but something more personal, an article if you like, or an essay, not of 1500 words but of 4000, giving more of my own feelings than of the 'facts.'" Lichtheim ends his accompanying letter with "all good wishes for the New Year to you and the happier Jews of 'God's own country.'" Lichtheim's essay, entitled "What Is Happening to the Jews of Europe," opens with the following two paragraphs:

> A letter has reached me from the United States, asking me "to review the position of the Jews in Europe." This I cannot do because the Jews of Europe are today no more in a "position" than the waters of a rapid rushing down into some canyon, or the dust of the desert lifted by a tornado and blown in all directions.
>
> I cannot even tell you how many Jews there are at present in this or that town, in this or that country, because at the very moment of writing thousands of them are fleeing hither and thither, from Belgium and Holland to France (hoping to escape to Switzerland), from Germany—because deportation to Poland was imminent—to France and Belgium, where the same orders for deportation have just been issued. Trapped mice running in circles. They are fleeing from Slovakia to Hungary, from Croatia to Italy. . . . At the same time, thousands are being shifted under Nazi supervision from the ghetto of Warsaw to forced-labor camps in the country further east, while other thousands just arrived from Germany or Austria are thrown into the ghettos of Riga or Lublin.

Whether, when he sent his "essay" on August 13, 1942, Lichtheim was privy to the information that five days earlier his Geneva colleague Gerhard Riegner had conveyed to the State Department and the Foreign Office, we do not know. In fact, the plan for a general extermination of European Jewry that Riegner transmitted to London and Washington had already been implemented months earlier, and by August 1942, close to a million and a half European Jews had been exterminated. And yet, even if Lichtheim's description of "what was happening to the Jews of Europe" was factually false because it missed the defining aspect of these events—total physical extermination—it conveys, in words not to be forgotten, something that defies direct expression: the sense of despair and doom of tens and tens of thousands of Jews fleeing "hither and thither" like "trapped mice running in circles," as well as—unreported by him, but sensed throughout his essay—the suffocating terror of the remaining millions.

"I am bursting with facts," Lichtheim went on, "but I cannot tell them in an article of a few thousand words. I would have to write for years and years. . . . That means I really cannot tell you what has happened and is happening to five million persecuted Jews in Hitler's Europe. Nobody will ever tell the story—a story of five million personal tragedies every one of which would fill a volume."

* * *

As strange as Henry Montor's demand for a fifteen-hundred-word report on the situation of the Jews in Europe may appear to us today, it can, in a way, be considered paradigmatic of most representations and commemorations of the Shoah; Lichtheim's answer expresses an opposite mode of evocation: on the one hand, the need for precise factual information, offered within strict limits and probably around a central idea that would give it coherence; on the other, an outburst of pain and despair that, in principle, rejects the possibility of order and coherence.

Over the last decades, the memory of the Shoah has crystallized around these two poles. Whereas the first one suggests a sense of closure, the second indicates the existence of an ongoing, open-ended process of remembrance. In other terms, the first is embodied in set rituals, in organized presentations ranging from textbooks to museums, from monuments to public commemorations. This public memory demands simplicity as well as clear interpretation; its aim, unstated and maybe unperceived, is the domestication of incoherence, the elimination of pain, the introduction of a message of redemption.

The second domain knows no rules. It is the sudden disruption of any set rendition among those who imagine this past—the immense majority now—and those who still remember it. In the testimonies of those who remember, both expressions of the past resurface: the organized, oft-rehearsed narration, on the one hand, and the uncontrolled and chaotic emotion, on the other.

In the long run, the memory of the Shoah will probably not escape complete ritualization. Yet, to this day, at least, an open-ended representation of these events seems present in the Western world and possibly beyond. Moreover, it appears to be growing as time goes on. After suggesting some interpretations of the paradoxical expansion of this memory and pointing to the complex interaction between the memory of the Shoah and the writing of its history, it is the challenges and responsibilities incumbent upon the historian that I would like to address in conclusion. In this domain there can be no credo, merely some reflections about compelling assignments and unresolved questions.

The Expanding Memory of the Shoah

The two decades following the war can be characterized as a period of virtual silence about the Shoah: The consensus was one of repression and oblivion. Adult contemporaries of Nazism still dominated the public scene. Even the survivors chose to remain silent, since very few people were interested in listening to them (even in Israel), and since, in any case, their own main goal was social integration and a return to normalcy.

In the mid-sixties, a first wave of debates shook these defenses. The generation born during or toward the end of the war was moving into the limelight; in Europe, primarily, the student unrest of the later part of the decade and its sequels called into question various aspects of contemporary culture as well as the lies and the obfuscation regarding the Nazi period. The major turmoil occurred in Germany, but the famous slogan of the French students, *"nous sommes tous des juifs allemands,"* intended to protest the expulsion of the Jewish student leader Daniel Cohn-Bendit, had more than one meaning; at the same time, in Marcel Ophuls's "The Sorrow and the Pity," France witnessed a first rift in the construction of the mythical self-representation of its history during the war years. However, this return of the past was quickly neutralized by theoretical abstractions about all-pervasive "fascism," produced mainly on the extreme left, and by the extreme politicization of the debates.

In the late 1970s and early 1980s, a second wave of controversies opened the way for a growing subjectivity and weakened the hold of some of the theoretical constructs of the previous decade. An expansion of autobiographical literature among both Germans and Jews, and of deeply probing and innovative films, as well as the quest for the history of everyday life under Nazism, created a new, more direct confrontation with the past. However, some of these endeavors, especially in Germany, also carried an unmistakable apologetic urge, and early postmodern representations of the Nazi era were not devoid of perverse fascination. Yet, strangely enough, it was a mass media event, the screening of the NBC miniseries *Holocaust* in 1978–79, that became a turning point of sorts all over the West, drawing increased attention to the extermination of the Jews as the defining event of the Nazi period. Over the last decade—particularly, it seems, for the third postwar generation, the "generation of the grandchildren"—this past became even more present following the fierce debates of the 1980s in Germany known as "the historians' controversy," and as an indirect consequence of the downfall of Communism and German reunification.

The duration of the phases varies in different national and religious contexts. For example, the period of "amnesia" may have been particularly lengthy and the passage to broader awareness quite abrupt in France and, even more so, Switzerland. In France, the surge of a national memory of Vichy's anti-Jewish policies found its first major expression some twenty years ago, first on the judicial level and then on the political and institutional level, as well as in the intellectual and artistic domains. As for the unexpected uproar over the role of Switzerland during the war, it has led to fierce public controversy about the material and financial exploitation and defrauding of Jewish victims, not only in that country, but throughout Europe. This debate, it has to be added, has contributed to the reappearance in Switzerland, and possibly elsewhere in Europe, of a kind of antisemitism that seemed to be a thing of the past: an antisemitism of the middle classes that is *salonfähig*—or, in other words, openly acceptable again.

The religious domain may prove to have an even more lasting impact than the national domain on the presence of the past. Establishing a Carmelite convent at Auschwitz was a minor matter compared to the storm that may erupt if Pius XII is beatified, as seems imminent. The entire set of controversies regarding the role of Christianity, its anti-Jewish teachings, and its traditional hostility toward the Jews—all of which provided the obviously involuntary but historically unavoidable background to their extermination—would reappear again. Thus the Holocaust is present in Western consciousness like some sort of lava rising ever closer to the surface and announced by ever stronger eruptions. Yet recognizing this growing presence of the past does not explain it. Let me turn to three possible interpretations: a generational factor, an ongoing demand for justice, and the transformation of Nazism into *the* metaphor of evil for our time.

* * *

The generational factor is the first explanation that comes to mind. The "generation of the grandchildren," mainly among Europeans (Germans in particular), but among Jews as well, has now achieved sufficient distance from the events in terms both of the sheer passage of time and of personal involvement to be able to confront the full impact of the past. Thus, the growing rise of the memory of the Shoah could in the first place be interpreted as the gradual lifting of collective repression, induced by the passage of time.

This interpretation could be understood, metaphorically speaking, as "working through," but also, possibly, as a collective "return of the repressed." Are we now ready to face the worst aspects of this past, or is the repressed returning, as the historian Dominick LaCapra expressed it, in the form of "renewed disavowal in certain quarters . . . and commercialized, politically tendentious, and self-interested (if not pornographic) representations in other quarters"?[1] In other words, are we witnessing primarily a gradual lifting of defenses, or could one argue that, simultaneously, the growing awareness of the past is also due to very different impulses, such as the fascination with the aesthetics of Nazism that flourished in the 1970s, or, more recently, the growing diatribes of negationists and the activism of radical right-wing groups?

Generations, it should be added, are not merely categories of time but also clusters of shared formative experience. The Germans who served in the Wehrmacht were far apart, in terms of experience, from adolescents only two or three years younger, who at the end of the war were only *Flakhelfer*, that is, manning anti-aircraft batteries. A single year could make a major difference. This issue would demand a long disquisition. Suffice it to mention here that, primarily in Germany, there is often an age-group (or generational) element in what I have called the return of the repressed.

In the 1980s, the "historians' controversy" took place among scholars, who, with the exception of two out of some twelve or fourteen, were all members of the HJ generation, and had all been adolescents in the Third Reich. Their positions were sharply divided, as we know, but the intensity of the debate manifestly stemmed, at least in part, from the impact of these long-buried experiences and their refraction through the prism of later political choices.

Last year, the signs of an age group were evident once more, in Martin Walser's outburst and the standing ovation that he received at the *Friedenspreis* ceremony in Frankfurt, and in the accolades from people such as von Dohnanyi and Augstein. Ignaz Bubis, however clumsily or angrily, expressed the outrage of a memory much less deflected or reinvested by time.

* * *

In a letter to Karl Jaspers, Hannah Arendt wrote on August 17, 1946: "The Nazi crimes, it seems to me, explode the limits of the law; and that is precisely what constitutes their monstrousness. For these crimes, no punishment is severe enough. It may well be essential to hang Göring, but it is totally inadequate. That is, this guilt, in contrast to all criminal guilt, oversteps and shatters any and all legal systems. That is the reason why the Nazis in Nuremberg are so smug. They know that, of course. And just as inhuman as their guilt, is the innocence of their victims. Human beings simply can't be as innocent as they all were in the face of the gas chambers. . . . We are simply not equipped to deal, on a human, political level, with a guilt that is beyond crime and an innocence that is beyond good and virtue."[2]

Arendt's letter is a *cri du coeur* that made much sense in 1946; yet I would argue that even today, many people would opt for such an absolute stand in regard to Nazi crimes. The present-day judicial process is for the most part no longer at issue (the Papon trial in France was possibly the last major court case to deal with Nazism and related crimes), but the demand for an absolute, uncompromising, and almost metaphysical justice remains, primarily in the community of the victims. It also appears in segments of European society somehow involved in the collaboration with Nazism. There it becomes a demand for distinctions between degrees of involvement, of responsibility and of guilt. And on all sides, the quest for justice focuses on the shaping of memory; it contributes to the growth of memory.

The demand for justice is also fueling fierce debates on comparative victimization within the Nazi system of terror and extermination itself, and among various terror and extermination systems—the Stalinist and the Nazi, for example. Over the last three decades or so, some of these debates have spread to the American scene. The growing demand of diverse ethnic minorities for the recognition of their own historical heritage, one that would offer a tale of suffering and triumph, is leading to overt confrontations about degrees of historical martyrdom. In this context, the Holocaust has become a focus of resentment, and the demand for justice fuses with increasingly acrimonious arguments about the historical comparability or exceptionality of the extermination of the European Jews. More than anything, the adoption of the Holocaust by popular culture has increasingly added a peculiar dimension to its image in the consciousness of vast sectors of American and Western society.

* * *

Nazism has become the central metaphor of evil in our time. It may well be that in our age of genocide and mass criminality, apart from its specific historical context, the extermination of the Jews of Europe is now perceived by many as the ultimate standard of evil against which all degrees of evil may be measured.

Such a perception of Nazism was present even before the war among the Allies, in occupied Europe, and even among resistance groups in Germany itself. After the war, Hannah Arendt identified Nazism with "radical evil"; her later notion of the "banality of evil" was no contradiction: In our epoch, radical evil is linked to the utter banality of its perpetrators, the Eichmanns of this world.

The most extreme insult that one can hurl against any brutal behavior is to compare it with Nazism; the worst tag that one can apply to a hated leader is a comparison with Hitler. And, incidentally, the only Christian name that may have disappeared from the repertory after 1945 is Adolf. In other words, Nazism and evil have become so naturally intertwined that this identification triggers an ongoing and expanding process of representation, but also of recall by association: *Schindler's List, Life Is Beautiful, The Reader;* Kosovo, Le Pen, Heider; gay bashing, mercy killing, abortion or anti-abortion, and so on. But doesn't that ever-spreading reference mean an ever-growing dilution, and ever-growing simplification, and ever-growing vulgarization? And is the process self-triggered, or does it fulfill a function of sorts in our society?

I wish to suggest here that the simplification in the representation of Nazism and of the Holocaust in popular culture and the function of this simplified representation in our society are linked. By function I do not mean to dwell again upon the politics of identity of various groups in this country, nor upon the diverse forms of instrumentalization of the Holocaust. More relevant would be the urge of the Catholic Church to make sure that believers today and in the future are convinced that at the time of its greatest challenge, the papacy was resolutely on the side of the victims, and that the Vicar of Christ stood undaunted *against* evil in our time.

The most basic function of this representation of evil is inherent to the self-image of liberal society as such.

Nowadays, liberal society is not faced with any concrete enemy; its existence was not threatened even before the demise of Communism. But in order to identify its own ideals and the nature of its institutions, any society needs to define the quintessential opposite of its own self-image. Owing to its unquestionable horror, to the immense number of its victims, to the heroic sacrifices demanded to achieve victory over it, Nazism did and does fulfill the function of the Enemy per se. This is true for the United States, but also, for different and no less obvious reasons, for present-day liberal, democratic Germany, and for the Western world more generally. In fact, few are the regimes since 1945 that would have chosen to identify with the Nazi model. . . .

The memory of the extermination—but also of the suffering and the agony imposed by Nazism, or of the fateful commitments demanded of those willing to resist it—remains a landscape of death, against the background of which choices were made that still appear to many as the most important ever made in modern times. In a world in which such choices have all but disappeared, the memory of the Shoah is paradoxically linked to a simplified, watered-down, yet real and probably deep-seated longing for the tragic dimension of life.

On Memory and History

It may have become evident, from what has been said until now, that the various facets of the expanding memory of the Holocaust may create a whole array of dilemmas in the writing of its history.

The impact of generational change on the transformation of the historiography of Nazism and the Shoah has often been mentioned.[3] The personal memories of those historians who were the contemporaries of Nazism do indeed find their expression in distinct forms of emphasis or avoidance.[4] More specifically, it has been argued that emotional involvement in these events precludes a rational approach to the writing of their history. The "mythic memory" of the victims has been set against the "rational" understanding of others. I certainly do not wish to open old debates, but merely to suggest that German and Jewish historians, as well as those of any other background, cannot avoid a measure of "transference" in regard to this past. Of necessity, such involvement impinges upon the writing of history. But the historian's necessary measure of detachment is not hindered, thereby providing the presence of sufficient self-awareness. It may indeed be harder to keep one's balance in the other direction; whereas a constantly self-critical gaze might diminish the effects of subjectivity, it could also lead to other, no lesser risks, those of undue restraint and paralyzing caution.

The main aspect of the interaction between the memory of the Holocaust and its historiography belongs to the moral dimension of the events—that is, to the demand for justice and to Nazism as a metaphor of evil. In the early 1980s, German historians seized upon the TV show *Holocaust* and similar media representations in order to criticize a black and white, so-called moralistic, representation of Nazism. In the unfolding "historians' controversy" and in the debate about the historicization of National Socialism, this "moralistic," "black and white" dimension of the representation of the events, and thus the limits of their historicization, was one of the themes at stake.[5] To this day, the intertwining between the writing of the history of the Holocaust and the unavoidable use of implicit or explicit moral categories in its interpretation and narration remains a major challenge. It is around these shared moral categories that history and memory must encounter one of their central differences. It may well be that the apparent dichotomy between a necessarily "detached" history of National Socialism and the no less unavoidable presence of a moral dimension in dealing with this epoch may find its resolution only in the sensitivity and creative intuition of the historian.

In the memory of contemporaries, and increasingly in present-day perception, the extermination of the Jews may have become one of the defining events of our time. Yet it seems impossible to situate its historical place. How can historical inquiry define the significance of Chelmno, Belzec, Sobibor, and Treblinka, sites whose sole function was *immediate* extermination?[6] Approximately two million victims were murdered at these sites alone within less than a year (between the spring of 1942 and that of 1943). How can the significance of such events be integrated into the interpretation of our epoch? After all, they influenced neither the course of the war nor any major trend in postwar history; and for many historians, so brief a span of time is but the foaming crest on the waves of long duration. Is the real impact of this history solely in the memory it has left?

Historical writing about the Holocaust has increasingly attempted to circumvent such problems by focusing on the mechanisms that led to the "Final Solution" within Nazism itself, or on the logistics, the technology, and the bureaucratic processes of its implementation, on the agencies of extermination and the behavior of the perpetrators. For example, in regard to his *The Destruction of the European Jews,* Raul Hilberg stated that he had focused on the "how" rather than the "why" of that history. Such historical inquiry into the mechanisms of the "Final Solution" is the very basis of our knowledge, and undoubtedly remains a primary task. But ultimately, the "why" overshadows all other concerns.

It goes without saying that major issues of interpretation, of historical roots, of historical categories, have also been addressed from the very beginning of this historiography. We all know at least some of these interpretations: the special course of German history, antisemitism (eliminationist or not), fascism, totalitarianism, modernity. It is at this level that a peculiar responsibility of the historian comes to the fore.

On the Historian's Responsibility

The historian cannot be and should not be the guardian of memory. The historian's gaze is analytic, critical, attuned to complexity, wary about generalizations. But the historian should not avoid the precise definition of interpretive concepts and categories in a domain so wide open to extraordinary flights of imagination or malicious denials. Moreover, on a very different level, historians should dare to challenge the complacency and routine already existing in their domain. Regarding the first issue, let me choose as a brief illustration the continuing debate about the comparability of Nazi and Stalinist crimes within the framework of two similar totalitarian regimes.

Totalitarianism as a key interpretive category is on the rise again. Decades ago, during the "Cold War," it was used to help fight Communism; today it is used to bury Communism historically, by trying to show that Stalin's crimes may have been worse than Hitler's. In Eastern Europe, first and foremost, but also in France and to a lesser degree in Germany, this revival of the "Greater Evil" theory has sometimes taken on strange emphasis. We are confronted not with Arendt's query into the origins of totalitarian systems but with a crusade of sorts, aiming to demonstrate that totalitarianism is the explanation for it all, and that on the scale of mass criminality, Stalin was in first place, Hitler merely in second. It certainly is a legitimate query, but one that demands, for example, that the following be considered.

In the fall of 1942, the Wehrmacht was about to cross the Volga at Stalingrad. Had the Germans succeeded, they probably would have brought about the military collapse of the Soviet Union; the war would have been significantly prolonged, Auschwitz would not have been liberated in January 1945, and the remnants of European Jewry would have been completely exterminated. Are there many people today who, notwithstanding their knowledge of Stalinist crimes, would declare, in retrospect, that they wish the Wehrmacht had crossed the Volga?

The majority that would still answer negatively remains, I believe, influenced by a vague intuition related to a historical-philosophical distinction most admirably expressed by the French-Jewish intellectual Raymond Aron.

Aron's anti-Stalinism was straightforward and uncompromising from the immediate postwar years onward, but he clearly perceived the difference between Nazism and Communism, as Arendt did in her "Questions of Moral Philosophy," and as many historians do to this day. Aron identified the quintessential difference between the two regimes at the conceptual level—and there indeed it lies: "For those who wish to 'save the concepts,'" Aron wrote, "there remains a difference between a philosophy whose logic *is* monstrous, and one that lends itself to a monstrous interpretation."[7]

It remains the historian's prime responsibility to probe the concrete aspects of such distinctions and to work through the details of related arguments. But therein lies the major challenge as well. In the face of simplified representations of the past, the historian's duty is to reintroduce the complexity of discrete historical events, the ambiguity of human behavior, and the indeterminacy of wider social processes. The task is daunting because of the difficulty of conciliating the nuanced results of scholarship and the necessary reference to historical, but also moral/philosophical, categories. In the face of a phenomenon such as Nazism, however, such tasks are not yet sufficient. There is, as mentioned, a run-of-the-mill history of the Holocaust that demands to be thoroughly questioned.

Some two years ago, the historian Thomas Laqueur wrote a highly perceptive critique of what he called the "business as usual" historiography of the Holocaust, one that "fails to confront both the particular moral breakdown these events imply and the subjective terror that they inspired."[8] For Laqueur, as for me, only the integration of the individual fate within the historical narration could eventually enable the historian to overcome the dichotomy between the unfathomable abstraction of the millions of dead and the tragedy of individual life and death in the time of extermination.

In other words, how can we render a history of the Holocaust that includes both the history of the victims as a collectivity and the narration of the events according to the victims' perceptions, as well as descriptions of their individual fate? Laqueur evoked the thousands of short biographical sketches and pictures of children deported from France collected by Serge Klarsfeld. These children could not speak in their own voices, but the little that could be found about the life and deportation of a boy of eight or a girl of three sufficed, precisely because it was so little.

Such testimonies cannot enlighten us about the internal dynamics of Nazi persecutions and exterminations, but they put Nazi behavior in its full perspective; they describe face-to-face encounters between the perpetrators and the victims during the persecutions, the deportations, and the killings. But more than anything, these testimonies are our only source for the history of the victims' path to destruction. They evoke, in their own chaotic way, the depth of these people's terror, despair, apathetic resignation—and total incomprehension.

The integration of the victims' voices radically widens the narrative span. It has to be complemented by the historian's effort to find correspondingly new concepts that would express, however inadequately, the breakdown of all norms and the dimensions of suffering that traditional historiography cannot easily deal with.

* * *

Wittlich (in the Mosel region), November 10, 1938. The synagogue has been set on fire, and the Jewish shops have been destroyed. Herr Marx, the butcher, like most Jewish men, has been shoved into a truck that is about to leave for a concentration camp. On the street, in front of the ruined shop, among jeering SA men, Frau Marx stands wailing: "Why do you do this to us? What did we ever do to you?" And on both sides of the street, the Marxes' lifelong German neighbors stand at their windows, watching her—in silence.

Was it fear, was it hatred, was it just plain human indifference to the despair of today's outcasts who had been yesterday's friends? The most elementary human ties had disappeared, and the tornado evoked by Lichtheim in his anguished letter had not even started.

NOTES

1. Dominick LaCapra, *Representing the Holocaust: History, Theory, Trauma* (Ithaca, N.Y.: Cornell University Press, 1994), 189.

2. Hannah Arendt and Karl Jaspers, *Correspondence 1926–1969* (New York: Harcourt Brace Jovanovich, 1992), 54.

3. See, in particular, Norbert Frei, "Farewell to the Era of Contemporaries: National Socialism and Its Historical Examination en route into History," *History & Memory* 9, nos. 1/2 (Fall 1997): 59ff.

4. See, in particular, Martin Broszat and Saul Friedländer, "A Controversy about the Historicization of National Socialism," in Peter Baldwin, ed., *Reworking the Past: Hitler, the Holocaust and the Historians' Debate* (Boston: Beacon Press, 1990).

5. The most profound comment on this debate and its implications is to be found in Jörn Rüsen, "The Logic of Historicization: Metahistorical Reflections on the Debate between Friedländer and Broszat," *History & Memory* 9, nos. 1/2 (Fall 1997): 113–144.

6. Arno Mayer, *Why Did the Heavens Not Darken?: The "Final Solution" in History* (London: Verso, 1988).

7. Tony Judt, *The Burden of Responsibility: Blum, Camus, Aron and the French Twentieth Century* (Chicago: University of Chicago Press, 1998), 154.

8. Thomas Laqueur, "The Sound of Voices Intoning Names," *London Review of Books,* June 5, 1997, p. 3.

PART I

The Impact of the Holocaust
An Interdisciplinary Approach

2 | Divine and Human Responsibility in the Light of the Holocaust
John T. Pawlikowski

In his presentation at the Notre Dame Holocaust Project conference, Saul Friedländer presented an insightful articulation of the major challenges that the Holocaust presents to humanity as we close this millennium. I especially appreciate his call for historians to go beyond the "how" of the Holocaust to probe the "why" of what has surely been one of the most evil realities known to humankind. It goes without saying that any approach to the Holocaust must be marked by sound research into documentation and testimonies from the period. That critical analytical work is the important work of historians. But we cannot stop with analysis that then claims total ambiguity in terms of meaning of the event for human action today. We may never be able to do justice to the victims of the Nazis, as Friedländer suggests, but we need to remember their victimization and continue to listen to their voices as a way to improve the quality of justice in the contemporary world. We need to recognize that the Holocaust presents a direct challenge to many modern ideologies and theologies, as Friedländer has emphasized. I particularly welcome his call for a re-examination of the nature of evil.

As a religious social ethicist I have long been interested in the issues Professor Friedländer has discussed in light of the Holocaust. I have addressed a number of them in previous writings.[1] I would like to focus here on the nature of human and divine responsibility. I believe that this represents one facet of the question of evil in our time. For a long time I have been convinced that coming to terms with evil will require a new understanding of how creation is to be directed if we are to see morality rather than chaos in our midst.

Back in the early 1970s two futurists introduced me to a fundamentally new reality with which religious ethics has yet adequately to grapple. Victor Ferkiss, a political scientist out of the Catholic tradition, and Hans Jonas, a social philosopher of Jewish background, served warning that humankind had reached a new threshold in its evolutionary journey. The human community now faced a situation whose potential for destruction was equal to its possibilities for new levels of human dignity and creativity. What path humanity would follow was a decision that rested with the next several generations. Neither divine intervention nor the arbitrary forces of nature would determine the choice in the end. And the decision would have lasting impact, well beyond the lifespan of those who are destined to make it. It would, in fact, determine what forms of life will experience continued survival.

Ferkiss's 1974 volume, *The Future of Technological Civilization,* put the late-twentieth-century challenge to humankind in these words: "Man has . . . achieved virtually godlike powers over himself, his society, and his physical environment. As a result of his scientific and technological achievements, he has the power to alter or destroy both the human race and its physical habitat."[2]

Hans Jonas, in a groundbreaking speech in Los Angeles in 1972 at a gathering of learned societies of religion and subsequently in published writings, conveyed essentially the same message as Ferkiss. Ours is the first generation to have to face the question of basic creational survival. In the past there was no human destructive behavior from which humankind could not recover. But today we have reached the point, through technological advancement, where this principle no longer holds. Humanity now seems increasingly capable of actions that inflict terminal damage on the whole of creation and raise serious questions about the future of human life itself.[3] Buckminster Fuller did not exaggerate the profundity of the choice before us when he asserted that contemporary humanity now stands poised on a threshold between utopia and oblivion.

For me, the Shoah represents perhaps the clearest twentieth-century example of the fundamental challenge now facing humanity as described by Ferkiss, Jonas, and Fuller. I have emphasized in a number of published essays[4] that in the final analysis I view the Shoah as inaugurating a new era in human self-awareness and human possibility, an era capable of producing unprecedented destruction or unparalleled hope. With the rise of Nazism, the mass extermination of human life in a guiltless fashion became thinkable and technologically feasible. The door was now ajar for dispassionate torture and the murder of millions not out of xenophobic fear, but through a calculated effort to reshape history, supported by intellectual argumentation from some of the best and brightest minds in the society. It was an attempt, Emil Fackenheim has argued, to wipe out the "divine image" in history. "The murder camp," Fackenheim insists, "was not an accidental by-product of the Nazi empire. It was its essence."[5]

The basic challenge of the Shoah lies in our changed perception of the relationship between God and humanity and its implications for the basis of moral behavior. What emerges as a central reality from the study of the Holocaust is the Nazis' sense of a new Aryan humanity freed from the moral restraints previously imposed by religious beliefs and capable of exerting virtually unlimited power in the shaping of the world and its inhabitants. In a somewhat indirect, though still powerful way, the Nazis had proclaimed the death of God as a governing force in the universe. In pursuit of their objective, the Nazis became convinced that all the "dregs of humanity"—first and foremost the Jews, but also Poles, Gypsies, gays, and people with disabilities—had to be eliminated, or at least their influence on culture and human development significantly curtailed.[6]

The late Uriel Tal captured as well as anyone the basic theological challenge presented by the Shoah. In his understanding the so-called Final Solution had as its ultimate objective the total transformation of human values. Its stated intent was liberating humanity from all previous moral ideals and codes. When the liberating process was complete, humanity would be rescued once and for all from subjection to God-belief and its related notions of moral responsibility, redemption, sin, and revelation. Nazi ideology sought to transform theological ideas into exclusively anthropological and political concepts. In Tal's perspective the Nazis can be said to have adopted a kind of "incarnational" ideology, but not in the New Testament sense of the term. Rather, for the Nazis, "God becomes man in a political sense as a member of the Aryan race whose highest representative on earth is the Führer."[7]

If we accept this interpretation of the ultimate implications of Nazism, we are confronted with a major theological challenge. How does the human community properly appropriate the genuine sense of human liberation that was at the core of Nazi ideology without surrendering its soul to massive evil? However horrendous their legacy, the Nazis were correct in at least one respect. They rightly perceived that some basic changes were underway in human consciousness. The impact of the new science and technology, with its underlying assumption of freedom, was beginning to provide humankind on a mass scale with a Promethean-type experience of escape from prior moral chains. People were starting to perceive, however dimly, an enhanced sense of dignity and autonomy that went well beyond what Western Christian theology was prepared to concede. This new sense of human autonomy is certainly critical to any effort to respond to Professor Friedländer's call for a new understanding of evil in our time.

Traditional theological concepts that had shaped much of the Christian moral perspective—notions such as divine punishment, divine wrath, and providence—were losing some of the hold they had exercised over moral decision making since biblical times. Christian theology had tended to accentuate the omnipotence of God, which in turn intensified the impotence of the human person and the rather inconsequential role played by the human community in maintaining the sustainability of creation. The Nazis totally rejected this previous relationship. In fact, they were literally trying to turn it upside down.

Numerous Jewish writers have attempted to respond to the fundamental implication of the Holocaust in terms of human and divine responsibility. The initial Jewish responses by Emil Fackenheim, Richard Rubenstein, and the late Arthur Cohen tried to forge a new understanding of the balance between divine and human responsibility. Even David Hartman, who has objected to focusing on the Holocaust in terms of Jewish religious identity today, has argued for an enhanced understanding of human co-creatorship within a framework rooted in the continuing biblical tradition of covenant. More recent attempts, such as those by David R. Blumenthal[8] and in the collected writings of Hans Jonas edited by Lawrence Vogel,[9] to probe the significance of the Holocaust for understanding divine governance over creation have likewise moved in the direction of heightening human responsibility as part of a more mature God-human relationship.

One of the more intriguing responses over the years has come from Irving Greenberg. His is a perspective with both theological and practical dimensions.

For Greenberg, the Holocaust has destroyed all further possibility of a "commanded" dimension to our understanding of the God-human community relationship. "Covenantally speaking," he says, "one cannot order another to step forward to die."[10] Any meaningful understanding of a covenantal relationship between God and humanity must be understood as voluntary. The voluntary nature of the post-Holocaust covenantal relationship unquestionably heightens human responsibility in Greenberg's eyes: "If after the Temple's destruction, Israel moved from junior partner to true partner in the covenant, then after the Holocaust, the Jewish people is called upon to become the senior partner in action. In effect, God was saying to humans: You stop the Shoah. You bring the redemption. You act to ensure that it will never again occur. I will be with you totally in whatever happens, but you must do it."[11] Based on this theological reversal in divine-human responsibility after the Shoah, Greenberg strongly argues for the assumption of power on the part of the human community. For Greenberg it would be immoral to abandon the quest for power. "Power inescapably corrupts," he writes, "but its assumption is inescapable after the Holocaust." The only option in the post-Shoah world that will enable us to avoid the repetitions of human degradation and evil of the Nazi era is to combine the assumption of power with what Greenberg terms the creation of "Better mechanisms of self-criticism, correction, and repentance." Only in this way can we utilize power "without being the unwitting slave of bloodshed or an exploitative status quo."[12]

I remain sympathetic to Greenberg's understanding of the heightened role of human responsibility in the governance of creation. I also concur with his position that such governance will require the assumption of power. In that context I find myself at odds with the unqualified pacifist position as well as the hard ecological vision, which tends to submerge humanity within creation as such. But I do feel that Greenberg has carried the theological role reversal too far. Imaging God as the "junior partner" renders God overly impotent. I would opt for a more co-equal relationship, though with a redefined sense of divine responsibility.

The language of "co-creatorship," developed mostly in Christian theological literature but also present in some Jewish writings, represents the most promising paradigm after the Shoah. While this notion of co-creatorship has roots in the biblical tradition, its full magnitude has become apparent only in light of events such as the Shoah, and, as theologian Philip J. Hefner (who has refined the notion as "created co-creatorship") has emphasized, "with our enhanced appreciation of the vast evolutionary process in which the role of human responsibility emerges as absolutely decisive."[13]

While I am aware that it is open to misuse, I do not agree with those ethicists, such as Stanley Hauerwas, who have strongly criticized Pope John Paul's appropriation of "co-creatorship" in his encyclical *Laborem Exercens*[14] on the grounds that it would lead to a Nazi-like mentality within the human community, nor with those who reject it out of hand, arguing that it would open the door to ecological destruction. Surely the affirmation of co-creatorship must be tempered by the notion that the Creator God retains a central role. Hence my rejection of Greenberg's "junior partner" status for God. And Hauerwas's call for "humility" in light of the Shoah sounds an important cautionary note for any co-creatorship paradigm. But as the prevailing motif for understanding the human/divine responsibility problematic, it would likely prevent humankind from assuming full governance of creation, a failure that might well entail economic, ecological, and nuclear disaster on a global scale. Unless we recognize that human responsibility has been raised to a new level in consequence of the Shoah and through our improved understanding of the evolutionary dynamic within creation, the human community will likely refrain from taking those decisive steps that will ensure the continuity of life at all levels of creation. To follow Hauerwas or the hard ecologists in terms of envisioning humankind's role in creational governance could result in people of faith becoming bystanders rather than central actors in human history. To ensure that the notion of co-creatorship does not wind up elevating human power to a destructive level, we need to re-affirm the role of divine responsibility, but in a refined sense. The paradigm of an all-powerful God who will intervene to halt human and creational destruction is dead after the Shoah and in light of our contemporary evolutionary consciousness. On this point the Nazi ideologues were perceptive. Where their vision was fatally flawed, and so humanly destructive, was in responding to the "death" of the interventionist God with an assertion, as theologian Michael Ryan has put it, "of all pervasive power for themselves."[15]

If we are successfully to curb the excessive use of human power in evil ways within a paradigm of co-creatorship, we must reintroduce into human consciousness, especially in our now highly secularized societies parented by the Enlightenment and the ideology of global capitalism, a deep sense of what I have called a *compelling God*. This experience of a compelling God, whom we must come to experience through symbolic encounter that is both personal and cultural, will result in a healing, a strengthening, an affirming that will bury any need to assert our humanity, to try to "overpower" the Creator God, through the destructive, even deadly, use of human power. This sense of a compelling Parent God who has gifted humanity, whose vulnerability for the Christian has been shown in the Cross (as Jürgen Moltmann has brilliantly articulated in *The Crucified God*[16]), is the indispensable foundation for any adequate paradigm of co-creatorship today.

Let me expand somewhat on Moltmann's view. Moltmann's reflections on the Holocaust began after a visit to the Maidenek concentration camp near Lublin, Poland. As he started to wrestle with the implications of his visit to the camp, he found strength in the closing words of Elie Wiesel's book *Night*: "Where is God? . . . He hangs there from the gallows." From there Moltmann goes on to interpret the Holocaust as the most dramatic revelation thus far of the basic meaning of the Christ Event: God can save people, including Israel, because through the Cross he participated in their very suffering. To theologize after the Holocaust would provide a futile enterprise in Moltmann's view,

> were not the *Sh'ma Israel* and the Lord's Prayer prayed in Auschwitz itself, were not God Himself in Auschwitz suffering with the martyred and murdered, every other answer would be blasphemy. An absolute God would make us indifferent. The God of action and success would let us forget the dead, which we still cannot forget. God as nothingness would make the entire world into a concentration camp.[17]

What emerges for Moltmann from the experience of the Holocaust is a "theology of divine vulnerability" that has roots in Abraham Heschel's notion of "divine pathos." He also argues that the idea of the suffering of God as the basic redemptive activity is consonant with rabbinic theology of the first century:

> The God who suffers in exile with Israel preserves the people from despair and fear. The realization of God's fellow-suffering impedes apathy, maintains sympathy for God in life, and holds hope for the future of God open.[18]

Moltmann adds that in rabbinic theology it is claimed that this suffering on the part of God is something he experiences at the very core of his being. God is not merely present where people are suffering; that suffering directly affects God. As Moltmann puts it, "God is not involved in history; history is in God himself."[19]

Moltmann's perspective has encountered resistance from the likes of the late A. Roy Eckardt, Francis Fiorenza, and the Jewish scholar Eugene Borowitz. In my judgment, these critiques, while they have value, are considerably overdrawn. A Christology of the Cross is a meaningful response to the Holocaust, at least in terms of the notion of divine vulnerability if it is integrated into a larger whole.

If we understand the ministry of Jesus as emerging from the heightened sense of divine-human intimacy that surfaced in Second Temple Judaism,[20] then Christological statements made by the Church in reflection on that ministry can be seen as attempts to articulate a new sense of how profoundly humanity is imbedded in divinity. The ultimate significance of Christology so understood lies in its revelation of the grandeur of the human as a necessary corrective to the demeaning paternalism that often characterized the sense of the divine-human relationship in the past. In this sense a major component of all authentic Christology is theological anthropology. Martin Luther understood this in *The Freedom of the Christian Man*. And Gregory Baum has stressed that in his first papal encyclical Pope John Paul II presented human dignity as integral to Christological doctrine.[21]

In my view the fear and paternalism associated in the past with the statement of the divine-human relationship were at least partially responsible for the Nazis' attempt to produce a total reversal of human meaning. Incarnational Christology can help the human person understand that he or she shares in the very life and existence of God. The human person remains creature; the gulf between humanity in people and humanity in the Godhead remains formidable. But it is also clear that a direct link exists; the two humanities can touch. The human struggle for self-identity vis-à-vis the Creator God, the source of the misuse of human power in the past, especially during the Holocaust, has come to an end in principle. Its full realization, however, still lies ahead. In this sense we can truly affirm that Christ continues to bring humankind salvation in its root meaning—wholeness.

With a proper understanding of the meaning of the Christ Event, men and women can be healed, they can finally overcome the primal sin, the desire to supplant the Creator in power and in status that lay at the heart of the Holocaust. Critical to this awareness is the sense of God's self-imposed limitation, God's vulnerability, manifested in the Cross. This is where Moltmann's theology can make a significant contribution. The notion of "divine vulnerability" can become a powerful Christological symbol[22] to remind us that one need not exercise power, control, and dominance to be "Godly." It also shows that God desires not simply to absorb humanity totally back into divine being, but rather to affirm its eternal distinctiveness. Douglas John Hall takes a position in the same vein when he writes that

> [w]hatever emphasis may be called for in the context where faith is confessed, the profession of faith always must entail the courage to affirm the reality of that which negates while at the same time insisting upon the gracious possibility of negating the negation. The profession of faith must do this because precisely the core of that upon which the disciple community meditates is a gospel which declares that the great negation by which creaturely life is continuously threatened has been entered into and is being overcome by a God who, by personally submitting to the aboriginal Nothingness, nullifies its power over us.[23]

But let me underline that if the notion of "divine vulnerability" is to serve in the above way it must be disassociated from direct linkages to Jewish sufferings above all, as well as the sufferings of other victims of the Nazis. From a theological perspective Jesus' suffering must be regarded as voluntary and redeeming. No such claim can be made in good conscience for the sufferings endured by Nazi victims. And on the human level, it is difficult to compare the depth of sufferings endured by the Gypsies, Poles, people with disabilities, gays, and others with that of Jesus, as painful as his sufferings no doubt were.

What I am claiming is that the Holocaust represents at one and the same time the ultimate expression of human freedom and of evil—the two are intimately linked. The ultimate assertion of human freedom from God in our time that the Holocaust represents may in fact prove the beginning of the final resolution of the conflict between freedom and evil. When humanity finally recognizes the destruction it can produce in totally rejecting dependence on its Creator, as was the case during the Holocaust, when it perceives that such rejection is a perversion and not an affirmation of human freedom, a new stage in human consciousness may be dawning. We may finally be coming to grips with evil at its roots, we may finally be answering the challenge, at least theologically, that Professor Friedländer has presented. The power of evil will wane only when humankind develops along with a profound sense of the dignity it enjoys because of its direct links to God a corresponding sense of humility occasioned by a searching encounter with the devastation it is capable of producing throughout creation when left to its own wits. A sense of profound humility evoked by the experience of the healing power present in the ultimate Creator of human power is critical to a resolution of the challenge of evil in light of the Shoah.

I remain convinced that the notion of a compelling God who is also a vulnerable God must be sustained both in our personal understanding and in our societal consciousness. This latter point is especially challenging for those of us who generally subscribe to the vision of church-state separation that is enshrined in Western democracies and that for Catholicism was raised to a level of theological principle at the Vatican II Council in its "Declaration on Religious Liberty."[24] Nonetheless we also need to take very seriously Vatican II's "Declaration on the Church in the Modern World," which strongly emphasized the centrality of culture in public morality. Unless a sense of a compelling God is integrated into Western communal consciousness, not in fundamentalist ways but as a true moral barometer, I fear that personal consciousness of a compelling God by itself will prove ineffective in guarding against the abuse of human co-creatorship. It could easily lead, as the church historian Clyde L. Manschreck warned some years ago, to "naked state sovereignty."[25] Today we might add as well, as Pope John Paul II did in his 1998 World Peace Day Message, the ideology of global capitalism.[26]

To sum up, the Shoah and our contemporary evolutionary consciousness force upon us a major reformulation of divine and human responsibility. It will need to be a reformulation that takes into account the prophetic words uttered by Catholic philosopher Romano Guardini soon after the Shoah:

> In the coming epoch, the essential problem will no longer be that of increasing power—though power will continue to increase at an even swifter tempo—but of curbing it. The core of the new epoch's intellectual task will be to integrate power into life in such a way that man can employ power without forfeiting his humanity, or to surrender to power and perish.[27]

I now turn to the recent Vatican document on the Holocaust, "We Remember,"[28] on which Professor Friedländer has commented. This document bears the mark of both sound research and a measure of internal Catholic politics. Clearly it acknowledges the Holocaust as a reality to which sinful Catholics contributed through their involvement in anti-Semitism both over the centuries and during the period of the Shoah. While the document speaks generically of "the sons and daughters of the Church" as being involved with anti-Semitism, this term certainly includes Catholic leaders. There is no possibility of Holocaust denial, or the denial of Catholic involvement, in light of "We Remember." The papal cover letter adds strength to the statement, especially in those parts of the Catholic world that had no direct involvement with the event in a historical sense. Anti-Semitism and the Holocaust are now on the international Catholic agenda. But I concur with Professor Friedländer that the document is incomplete, even disappoints, in several important areas. Let me now turn briefly to three of them.

The first has to do with the sinfulness of those Christians who espoused anti-Semitism. The document leaves the distinct impression that these Catholic Christians were misinterpreting authentic Church teaching. Hence the Church itself is to be seen as an unscathed institution. Behind this perspective lies a theology of the Church as a holy and spotless reality unaffected by the sinfulness we experience in human history. This is classical ecclesiology that not all Catholic theologians are willing to accept fully today. It is impossible to take up this theological issue in this response. But it is possible to say that even within such a transcendent ecclesiology the document could have emphasized that the sinfulness of certain Catholics was often the result of teaching and preaching sanctioned by institutional Catholicism over the centuries. Father Edward Flannery's classic volume *The Anguish of the Jews*[29] has brilliantly documented this. Many Catholics who harbored anti-Semitism did so because of what they heard and read in the *Church Fathers* and other Catholic documents.

Secondly, the document makes too sharp a distinction between Nazi ideology and classical anti-Semitism. True Nazi ideology was pagan at heart and eventually proposed the annihilation of Jews, not merely misery and marginalization (as bad as these were in terms of Jewish suffering). But many Catholics acquiesced or even collaborated with the Nazis because of the history of Christian anti-Semitism. "We Remember" makes a valuable point in not drawing a straight line between classical Christian anti-Semitism and Nazi ideology as some scholars do. Yet in overstating the dichotomy, the Vatican document fails to acknowledge that classical Christian anti-Semitism provided an indispensable seedbed for the growth of Nazism, especially on the popular level.

Finally, and perhaps most troubling from a scholarly point of view, is the footnote that defends the actions of Pius XII during the Shoah on the basis of several laudatory statements from important Jewish leaders of the time. For several years now I have argued that using the term "silence" relative to Pius XII is unjust at worst and misleading at best. It should be struck from our vocabulary in discussing his pontificate.[30] Certainly Pius XII chose to limit his efforts to the diplomatic rather than the public realm. This decision is definitely open to evaluation and critique, as is his overall record. He might well have done more through diplomatic channels, and earlier at that. We also need to hear more about how his contemporaries, both Catholic and Jewish, evaluated his efforts. In this context the positive statements referred to in "We Remember" need to be on the table. Too many people who simply accuse Pius XII totally ignore them. But to the casual reader the document leaves the impression that these Jewish commendations are the full story. They are not, whether in terms of Catholic perspectives (e.g., Jacques Maritain or Polish leaders) or Jewish ones (e.g., Gerhart Riegner of the World Jewish Congress). The research on Pius XII needs to continue. "We Remember" tends to leave the impression that the final verdict is in. This is simply not the case from the standpoint of sound scholarship.

In short, the new Vatican document, while significantly deficient in the areas highlighted above, does make Holocaust study and Holocaust education an important priority for Catholicism. For this I am grateful. The International Catholic-Jewish Liaison Committee, meeting at the Vatican shortly after the release of "We Remember," committed itself to continued study of the issues raised, however inadequately, in the document. It is to this challenge that I believe we must devote our attention.

NOTES

1. Cf. John T. Pawlikowski, "The SHOAH: Its Challenges for Religious and Secular Ethics," *Holocaust and Genocide Studies* 3, no. 4 (1988): 443–455; "Christian Ethics and the Holocaust: A Dialogue with Post-Auschwitz Judaism," *Theological Studies* 49, no. 4 (December 1988): 649–669.

2. Victor Ferkiss, *The Future of Technological Civilization* (New York: George Braziller, 1974), 88.

3. Hans Jonas, *The Imperative of Responsibility* (Chicago: University of Chicago Press, 1984).

4. Cf. John T. Pawlikowski, *The Challenge of the Holocaust for Christian Theology* (New York: Anti-Defamation League, 1982); "Christian Theological Concerns after the Holocaust," in Eugene J. Fisher, ed., *Visions of the Other: Jewish and Christian Theologians Assess the Dialogue* (New York/Mahwah: Paulist, 1994), 28–51.

5. Emil Fackenheim, *The Jewish Return into History* (New York: Schocken, 1978), 246.

6. Cf. John T. Pawlikowski, "Uniqueness and Universality in the Holocaust: Some Ethical Reflections," in Linda Bennett Elder, David L. Barr, and Elizabeth Struthers Malbon, eds., *Biblical and Humane: A Festschrift for John F. Priest* (Atlanta: Scholars Press, 1996), 275–289.

7. Uriel Tal, "Forms of Pseudo-Religion in the German *Kulturbereich* prior to the Holocaust," *Immanuel* 3 (1973–1974): 69.

8. David R. Blumenthal, "Theodicy: Dissonance in Theory and Praxis," *Concilium* 1 (1998): 95–106.

9. Hans Jonas, *Mortality and Morality: A Search for Good after Auschwitz*, ed. Lawrence Vogel (Evanston: Northwestern University Press, 1996).

10. Irving Greenberg, "The Voluntary Covenant," in *Perspectives*, no. 3 (New York: National Jewish Resource Center, 1982), 15.

11. Greenberg, "Voluntary Covenant," 17–18.

12. Irving Greenberg, "The Third Great Cycle in Jewish History," in *Perspectives*, no. 1 (New York: National Jewish Resource Center, 1981), 24–25.

13. Philip J. Hefner, *The Human Factor: Evolution, Culture and Religion* (Minneapolis: Fortress, 1993); also cf. John T. Pawlikowski, "Theological Dimensions of an Ecological Ethic," in Richard N. Fragomeni and John T. Pawlikowski, eds., *The Ecological Challenge: Ethical, Liturgical and Spiritual Responses* (Collegeville, Minn.: Liturgical Press, 1994), 39–51.

14. Stanley Hauerwas, "Jews and Christians among the Nations," *Cross Currents* 31 (September 1981): 34.

15. Michael Ryan, "Hitler's Challenge to the Churches: A Theological-Political Analysis of *Mein Kampf*," in Franklin Littell and Hubert G. Locke, eds., *The German Church Struggle and the Holocaust* (Detroit: Wayne State University Press, 1974), 160–161.

16. Jürgen Moltmann, *The Crucified God* (New York: Harper and Row, 1974).

17. Jürgen Moltmann, "The Crucified God," *Theology Today* 32 (1974): 13. Also cf. Jürgen Moltmann, *Jesus Christ for Today's World* (Minneapolis: Fortress, 1993).

18. Moltmann, "Crucified God," 13.

19. Ibid.

20. Cf. John T. Pawlikowski, *Jesus and the Theology of Israel* (Wilmington, Del.: Michael Glazier, 1989).

21. Gregory Baum, "The First Papal Encyclical," *Ecumenist* 17 (1979): 55.

22. On Christological symbols and the Holocaust, cf. Z. Amishai-Maisels, "Christological Symbolism of the Holocaust," *Holocaust and Genocide Studies* 3 (1988): 457–481.

23. Douglas John Hall, *Professing the Faith: Christian Theology in a North American Context* (Minneapolis: Fortress, 1993), 79.

24. Cf. John T. Pawlikowski, "Catholicism and the Public Church: Recent U.S. Developments," in D. M. Yeager, ed., *The Annual of the Society of Christian Ethics* (Washington: Georgetown University Press, 1989), 147–165; and "Walking with and beyond John Courtney Murray," *New Theology Review* 9 (August 1996): 20–40.

25. Clyde L. Manschreck, "Church-State Relations—A Question of Sovereignty," in

Clyde L. Manschreck and Barbara Brown Zikmund, eds., *The American Religious Experiment: Piety and Practicality* (Chicago: Exploration Press, 1976), 121.

26. John Paul II, "From the Justice of the Earth Comes Peace for All," *Origins* 27, no. 28 (January 1, 1998): 468.

27. Romano Guardini, *Power and Responsibility* (Chicago: Henry Regnery, 1961), xiii.

28. Vatican Commission for Religious Relations with Jews, "We Remember: A Reflection on the 'Shoah,'" *Origins* 27, no. 40 (March 26, 1998): 669, 671–675; also cf. "International Catholic-Jewish Liaison Committee Meets at Vatican," *Origins* 27, no. 42 (April 9, 1998): 701, 703–704.

29. Cf. Edward Flannery, *The Anguish of the Jews,* rev. ed. (New York: Paulist, 1985).

30. Cf. John T. Pawlikowski, "The Vatican and the Holocaust: Unresolved Issues," in Henry F. Knight and Marcia Sachs Littell, eds., *The Uses and Abuses of Knowledge* (Lanham/New York/London: University Press of America, 1997), 403–413; also cf. John T. Pawlikowski, "The Legacy of Pius XII: Issues for Further Research," *Catholic International* (Oct. 1998): 459–462.

Racism and Ethics
3 | Constructing Alternative History
Sidra DeKoven Ezrahi

IN HIS PRESENTATION at the Notre Dame Holocaust Project conference, Saul Friedländer suggested that "it may be that, beyond traditional religious categories . . . what our contemporaries are seeking to discover in the Shoah is a new definition of Evil." And, inevitably, a redefinition of the very "nature of human nature"—or, as he rephrased it, "the nature of *all of us*." This essay responds to that challenge. My fundamental working premise is that both the challenge and the response are compatible with a postmodern moral discourse that is constructed of radically new possibilities for empathic acts of imagination, for embracing "all of us."

Such a discourse is evolving in a polarized cultural environment that extends to every public space—literature, theater, cinema, commemorative rituals and sites, oral histories, and theory. The reverberations of this polarity are epistemological, aesthetic, and ethical. The examples I will draw upon here come almost exclusively from literature and the performing arts, primary nonpolitical sites in which secular societies negotiate their moral profile.

One extreme end of this polarity rests on the referential status of the Shoah as an—or *the—Event*, the place or entity to which our historiographic or artistic reflections do—or do *not*—correspond. (We never say *the Event* when referring to World War I or the French Revolution or the Civil War.) The Holocaust is represented by the exponents of this position as the epicenter of an earthquake or as the center of a volcano or as a black hole. It is the *unsayable*, that which swallows up all the words, all the colors, and even the instruments that would measure the damage. The many elaborations of this position take on a theological cast as the approach to the Center becomes a kind of pilgrimage. The closer one is to the Center—the place, the person, or even the story itself—the more authentic the representation. In its most extreme articulation, writing poetry or narrative constitutes a transgressive, barbaric activity to the extent that it takes place outside the vortex leading to the epicenter and maintains linguistic and conventional connections with the world beyond.

Let me acknowledge at the outset that in referring casually to "barbarisms" and "earthquakes" I am taking liberties with two of the most ubiquitous tropes in the critical discourse on representation of the Shoah. Loosely coopted by the culture industry they helped to define, T. W. Adorno and Jean-François Lyotard have provided the signposts for a symbolic geography in which the place that swallows up everything—all words, all life, all structures, all meaning—is indexed metonymically as "Auschwitz" or, more precisely, the *crematorium* of Auschwitz. Assuming that *any* language survives the earthquake, goes this reasoning, only the most transparent or positivistic writing would be adequate to the mandate to represent *that* place. All other forms of aestheticization occupy some barbaric space outside the consensual community of rememberers. This is of course a gross simplification of the profoundly ambiguous and dynamic elaborations of Adorno's and Lyotard's philosophies, which have been submitted elsewhere to more subtle critical analyses; I am deliberately focusing on this rarefied symbolic geography as the apocalyptic ground on which the most polemical expressions of the position I am describing rest.

At the other end of this polarity is a radically different landscape. Located in the periphery, *back turned toward Auschwitz,* it unfolds as a vast terrain punctuated with potentially infinite points of access. Words and stories that were "swallowed up" in the epicenter or black hole may appear in the "barbaric" periphery, in the place where fictive possibility may even defy historical representation. In their protean and mobile forms, they subvert any and all apocalyptic or redemptive schemes.

There is a constant, unresolved tension between center and periphery, between the gravitational pull of the black hole, of Chaos as a parody of the Sacred Center, and the cosmos-building of more distant places, local shrines, that manage to free themselves from the pull of the center and set up alternative sites and alternative scenarios. The distinction is between static and dynamic approaches to history and its moral and social legacies, between a premise of incommunicability and incommensurability on the one hand and communicability and commensurability on the other. And it revolves around the privilege granted to or withheld from those who are survivors—either because they didn't die or because they were *not there*—to write themselves (ourselves) into *and out of* the past.

I am attempting to explore here the ethical implications of a typology I developed elsewhere. In that essay I argued that one cluster of cultural impulses is absolutist and the other relativist in regard to the same historical stimuli:

> The absolutist approach locates a non-negotiable self in an unyielding place whose sign is Auschwitz; the relativist position represents the memory of that place as a set of strategies for an ongoing *re*negotiation of that historical reality. For those I will refer to as the "relativists," the immobility of the past is mitigated, at times undermined, by the very conventions mobilized to represent it. For those I will call the "absolutists," an invented language grounded in a sense of sustained "duration" or unmastered trauma prevents convention and commensurability from relativizing the absolute reality of the place.[1]

All works of historical representation and interpretation are being performed in the aftermath, at a distance, but it is distance itself that is at stake.

The language of the absolutists is frozen in a mythical replay of inexorable forces yielding either an empty and silent, or noisy and apocalyptic, vision. The psychological dimensions of this position were most explicitly defined by Lawrence Langer and have been adapted by those who refer to the "deep memory" that is inarticulable and incommensurable. One of the first writers to offer a model for "re-*present*-ing" Auschwitz was Tadeusz Borowski. In "This Way for the Gas, Ladies and Gentlemen," all mention of a world outside, beyond, before or after Auschwitz is effaced. "All of us walk around naked," is the way this story begins. Consider, further, Paul Celan's "black milk of daybreak": "we drink it at evening / we drink it at midday and morning." It is a world replayed *sub specie aeternitatis*.

The material expression of this frozen world can be found in the architecture of our memorial sites, most starkly in the reconstruction of Auschwitz and Birkenau and the various attempts to establish where IT happened (at the railroad platform? at the gate with its lacerating message like a wound on the human landscape? at the crematorium? in Birkenau II?). The paths leading inexorably to *that place* are reenacted kinetically in the railroad tracks in Claude Lanzmann's film *Shoah* and in the testimonies to the lives and the words that were swallowed up in its center. The presumption is that an aura of authenticity emanates from the gas chamber and the Sonderkommando who operated it. By extension, there are concentric circles of authenticity, stretching from the body of the survivor to his/her postwar family, and from there to the non-participants and non-witnesses, and for each of these circles there is an appropriate language, beginning with the witness or documentary report closest to the Event Itself.

An example of the other—the dynamic, centrifugal, or relativist posture built of the same materials—may be found in Primo Levi, as early as his *Survival in Auschwitz* and in his own survival *after* Auschwitz, the long productive years that followed his liberation and preceded his putative suicide. In the most celebrated chapter in his memoir, "The Canto of Ulysses," what is most significant is that there remains a world out there . . . not only a world of poetry and beauty encapsulated in the memory of Dante's verses, but also the *otherness* of the Christian vision of cosmic order.

I want to submit that it is only the relativist position that provides enough space to recreate a real moral discourse—a discourse based on the legitimacy of great acts of projection. Such attempts are more than a search for memory sites and points of origin and reference, something other than the locus of absolute, unspeakable, evil. They serve the effort to create points of departure for the construction of alternative histories, of a "history that might have been," in the language of Eric Santner: the identification for postwar Germans, for example, of moments where moral decisions might have been made and were not.[2] Of course, the artistic imagination is the only place where counter-histories, even counter-factuals, are legitimate. Although nodding acknowledgment of Aristotle's distinction between history and poetry is made by participants in the debate on the limits of representation—from Hayden White to James Young[3]—their emphasis on narrative forms and conventions and the subject-position of the witnesses and participants obscures the funda-mental license that free societies have always accorded their artists (and that totalitarian societies have always rescinded): to carry on the moral debate through *argument* with history and its "successes."

Literary examples of the construction of alternative sites of memory that prompt a new moral discourse include Shoshana Felman's provocative reading of Albert Camus's *The Fall* (the absences in the Jewish Quarter of Amsterdam as analogues of the unremarked suicide of an anonymous woman from a bridge in Paris—that is, revisiting the place where you personally or collec-tively failed to take a stand). Alternative scenarios for reengaging with the past take place *anywhere*, but the ghetto and even the concentration camp serve as common venues: the Lodz ghetto (in Jurek Becker's novel *Jacob the Liar*, and in its film adaptations), the Warsaw ghetto (in Jaroslaw Rymkiewicz's nar-rative *Umschlagplatz: The Final Station*), a generic concentration camp (in Roberto Benigni's film *Life is Beautiful*).

Alternative history is based on the presumption of a normative world out-side Auschwitz and an untouched "age of innocence" as primary references. In all of the above evocations of ghettos and camps as alternative sites of memory, children are the touchstone and target of major acts of "revisioning" history. Jacob the "Liar" engages in the most outrageous fabrications of a "better world" for the preservation of the innocence of his young ward, Lena, much as Guido does for his son in Benigni's film; in a verbal photomontage, Rym-kiewicz positions his own childhood self vis-à-vis the iconic boy in the Warsaw ghetto to give him respite from the burden of raising his arms for an eternity. Saul Friedländer's ability to reconstruct his childhood out of a cup of hot chocolate with his mother at the Café Slavia, out of his father's copy of Mey-rink's *The Golem*, is the counter-narrative to his more mature historical con-sciousness of imminent doom. He admits at the beginning of his memoir that he was born in Prague "at the worst possible moment, four months before Hitler came to power." But even if the historian acknowledges with nearly forty years' hindsight that "the way of life of the Jews in the Prague of my childhood was perhaps futile and 'rootless,' seen from a historical viewpoint," the child in him insists that "this way of life was ours, the one we treasured."[4] This is the beginning of all narrative, the "petite madeleine" of all memory banks, the platform for the victims' voices he will introduce in *Nazi Germany and the Jews*—and the points of departure that, however short, make every post-Holocaust journey possible.

Childhood becomes necessary as a nature preserve with no backshadows[5]— analogous, perhaps, at the individual level, to mediated access to faith in the Enlightenment ("the discourse of modernity," in Friedländer's words) at the collective level. We are presented in these cultural productions with another set of "concentric circles," with the *self* in the center, safe even for a brief moment in the bosom of family and nature—as counterpart to the concentric circles with Auschwitz at the center. The difference between those survivor memoirs and fictions with the protected self at the center, providing a ground of reference for the construction of postwar identity, and those for which the protected self is so occluded as to be missing as primary reference is the structural representation of the difference between the possibility and the impossibility of narrative itself and the construction of an ethical discourse on this subject at century's end.

This point is driven home dramatically if one considers how lionized Binjamin Wilkomirski was when his book *Fragments* first appeared; it may very well be that he provided the text that the absolutists were waiting for, the most harrowing of all texts to have emerged from the black hole. This self-declared memoir begins: "I have no mother tongue." It follows from this that the narrator has no *mother* either—no mother, or father, or nature preserve to which he can reliably refer:

> My earliest memories are a rubble field of isolated images and events. Shards of memory with knife-sharp edges, which still cut flesh if touched today. Mostly a chaotic jumble, with very little chronological fit; shards that keep surfacing against the orderly grain of grown-up life and the escaping laws of logic.[6]

The debate over the authenticity of Wilkomirski's narrative is as germane as the book itself to the argument I am making here. Whether or not this document is authentic, or some fantastic creation of a deranged mind, or simple fraud, it speaks a language for which the only possible "objective correlative" is Auschwitz, the *logically necessary* language of a survivor with no reference to a world beyond or before such total chaos. The apocalyptic landscape preempts any language of one's own, any private territory of the self, and any narrative that is not already invaded and fragmented by a trauma that began before one could formulate a nature preserve, before one could even construct a family album.

In the imaginative reconstructions represented in work as diverse as the "fictions" of Borowski, the testimonial film of Lanzmann, and the "memoir" of Wilkomirski, Auschwitz is the terminus of a *centripetal* imagination, wholly transcendent and therefore wholly unrepresentable. The *centrifugal* narrative, on the other hand, provides an infinity of mobile points of departure and access.

In conclusion, I would like to explore the ramifications of this argument in one arena in which a centrifugal, open-ended, ironic, and self-critical discourse is struggling against a centripetal, totalizing, formulaic, or mythic one: Israel in the aftermath of 1967. The three decades that have elapsed can be defined as an era in which fundamentalist and expansionist definitions of the collective self and absolutist definitions of excluded and inimical others have competed with inclusivist definitions of self and porous definitions of geographical and cultural boundaries; what have evolved are two diametrically opposed worldviews and political platforms. The more inexorable or absolutist the representation of the Holocaust becomes in the rhetoric and thinking of certain sectors of Israelis infected with toxic doses of "Post-Holocaust Stress Disorder," the more unyielding and archetypal the definition of the ongoing encounter between Israelis and Arabs and the more mythical the internal debate with "Jewish Destiny."

Y. H. Yerushalmi defined Jewish collective apprehension of historical events from the postrabbinic period till the modern period as a pattern of archetypes derived from biblical prototypes. While this position has been challenged by other historians and certainly deserves to be more inflected and nuanced when examining the intricacies of Jewish historical consciousness over many centuries, the logic that locks Israel into an internal theodicy between God and His chosen people has resurfaced in the essentially premodern attitudes of enclaves of contemporary Jews who perceive historical realities as replays of basic mythic patterns. The pageant that represents the Arab-as-Nazi-as-Amalek is the Jewish version of apocalyptic or absolutist thinking, of a discourse that totalizes, constituting its own form of "deep memory." It traps us in paradigms that are morally self-congratulatory and yield lethal forms of "repetition-compulsion." If Jew/Nazi is just the most recent incarnation of the eternal, inexorable enmity between Jews and Others, then by definition we remain stuck in a reductive pattern that can admit no free acts of moral imagination. Since it is unimaginable that the Jews could behave like Nazis, since the Jews are always already Jews—that is, victims—then the Arabs must be Nazis and everything we do is a form of at worst self-sacrifice and at best self-defense.

For a long time after the Shoah, representations of the Holocaust in Israeli literature banished the Nazis, making them either demonic ("Ha-German," in the words of the Hebrew poet Uri Zvi Greenberg) or invisible (effacement as a form of revenge—a curious reading of Deuteronomy 25:17: *"timheh et zekher amalek mi-tahat ha-shamayim"* [thou shalt blot out the remembrance of Amalek from under heaven]). Such representations allowed for essentially no open ethical debate. The literature that emerged through the 1960s was with few exceptions a literature of either elegy or trauma, but it fit too unfortunately into the theodicy of the Jews as God's eternal victims—a form of essentialism and predestination that today continues to gain strength among Israel's ultra-orthodox and many fellow-travelers who do not bother to examine its political and moral implications. The Nazis in this scheme are simply the agents of an eternal cosmic enmity.

"Imagining the Nazi" is the beginning of a new ethical rhetoric in the culture in Israel that is broadly referred to as "post-Zionist"; going so far into unexplored, unimaginable territory as to imagine the Jew as Nazi is to finally come to terms with the Jewish self in its most aggressive alterity. David Grossman's *See Under: Love* ponders "the Nazi within oneself" and fantasizes about "Sondar," the heroic leader of the "Commandos."[7] The imagination of alternative histories leaves narrative space in which the Jew can imagine him/herself as both hero and aggressor. One of the first poetic sites to reflect this was Dan Pagis's Cain and Abel poems, in which the two brothers serve as universal—and interchangeable—referents for fratricide, in place of Abraham and Isaac and the covenantal model (the Jew as the sacrifice that God wants, and the hand that wields the knife as incidental to the act).

In the 1980s and '90s this new relativism was largely manifested in the performative arts, challenging the rituals of consent in the commemorative spaces. The distance from commemorative to theatrical performances in Israel is the distance between the consensual, ritual affirmation of a relatively fixed, if largely secularized, theodicy and the ongoing reflexive encounter with the past as moving target. Examples of the latter include Arbeit Macht Frei [Acco Theatre group], Yehoshua Sobol's dramatic trilogy on the Lodz ghetto, and Shmuel Hasfari's play *Tashmad* (1984). Hasfari's drama focuses on the fantasies of a group of settlers living on the West Bank as their settlement is being emptied of its Jewish inhabitants by the Israeli army; the stage business employs the symbols and gestures of a swastika and a "Heil Hitler" salute. But the most powerful expression of this sensibility is Hanokh Levin's play *Ha-Patriot,* defined by the playwright as a "satirical cabaret." Mahmud, the Arab boy, assumes the iconographic capitulary pose of the little boy with hands raised in the Warsaw ghetto. Lahav, the main Israeli character, addresses his own mother while aiming his revolver at Mahmud's head:

> He will avenge your blood and the blood of our murdered family, as then, mother, when your little brother stood alone in front of the German at night, in the field, and the German aimed his revolver at his head, and your little brother, trembling with fear, said (and he sings as he aims the revolver at Mahmud):
>
> > Don't shoot.
> > I have a mother.
> > She is waiting for me at home.
> > I haven't eaten yet. Dinner. Don't kill me.
> > I am a child.
> > I am a human being like you.
> > What did I do?
> > What difference would it make to you if I yet lived?
> > (from the program notes of *Ha-Patriot*)[8]

The fate of this passage reflects the perceived threat that such daring acts of representation evoked in the Israeli public sphere: it was excised from the play by the board of censors (which was still operative in those years in Israel, under a code inherited from the British Mandate) and remained only in the program notes.

While performances like this inaugurated a new moral discourse, they were only the beginning of the process; with the Intifada, the Palestinians became subjects in history, in their own eyes as well as in the eyes of their Israeli "interlocutors." The representation of the Arab as "Jewish" object of history in Levin's play is, then, still part of an *interior* dialogue in which the Arab is a projection of the Israeli psyche. The decade that has elapsed since the Intifada, the era of the Peace Process, is one of greater parity between two subjects acting in and writing history.

All versions of monolithic memory and identity fixed either in the disconnected present or in the traumatic past deny the capacity of the human soul to regenerate after trauma and to contain past and present without killing either one. The price that Jews and especially Israelis pay as a collective when they are too obsessed with the past is that although the disembodied or bodiless victims, with their silences and their black holes, may provide great photo opportunities for the apocalyptically minded, they now stand in the way of present- or future-oriented, demystified meditations on the connection between collective trauma and collective power.

A "new definition of evil" in Israel would be an affirmation of a "universal" discourse that is external to the theodicy that explains Jewish history as an internal dialogue and a series of fixed archetypes. The license to imagine history as either an iconography with *interchangeable* players or as one scenario in an infinitude of *possible* histories could be the greatest contribution that free artistic representations of the Holocaust could make to the moral discourse that will cross the millennial divide.

NOTES

1. Sidra DeKoven Ezrahi, "Representing Auschwitz," *History and Memory* 7, no. 2 (Fall/Winter 1996): 122. Many of the cultural texts that are mentioned here in passing are analyzed in greater detail in that essay.

2. Eric Santner, *Stranded Objects: Mourning, Memory, and Film in Postwar Germany* (Ithaca: Cornell University Press, 1990), 152–153.

3. See their and other essays in *Probing the Limits of Representation: Nazism and the Final Solution*, ed. Saul Friedländer (Cambridge: Harvard University Press, 1992). For an overview and attempt at a different approach to this ongoing debate, see James E. Young, "Toward a Received History of the Holocaust," *History and Theory* 36 (December 1997): 25–26.

4. Saul Friedländer, *When Memory Comes* (N.Y.: Farrar, Straus and Giroux, 1979), 9. See on this Sidra DeKoven Ezrahi, "See Under: Memory," *History and Memory*, Special Festschrift in Honor of Saul Friedländer's Sixty-Fifth Birthday (Fall/Winter 1997): 364–375.

5. On "backshadowing," see Michael André Bernstein, *Foregone Conclusions: Against Apocalyptic History* (Berkeley: University of California Press, 1994).

6. Binjamin Wilkomirski, *Fragments: Memories of a Wartime Childhood* (N.Y.: Knopf, 1996), 3–4.

7. David Grossman, *See Under: Love,* trans. Betsy Rosenberg (New York: Farrar, Straus and Giroux, 1989), 29. The "Jewish self as Nazi" has already been explored in other cultural contexts, most notably in American fiction after the Eichmann trial.

8. Quoted in Sidra DeKoven Ezrahi, "Revisioning the Past: The Changing Legacy of the Holocaust in Hebrew Literature," *Salmagundi,* Special Issue on A Sense of the Past (Fall 1985–Winter 1986): 268.

4 | The Strange and the Familiar
Joan Ringelheim

W E ARE BORN strangers into the world. What we see, hear, touch, and feel is unfamiliar at birth. Few instincts accompany us at birth. Almost immediately, we begin to engage in a process of watching, learning, and experiencing the world around us. I have heard it said that if a piece of music is played over and over during pregnancy, it will be recognized by the child after she or he is born. Does the same apply to voices heard? to stories read? to television or radio programs? Even if it can be shown that some recognition is connected from the fetus to the baby, recognition is not equivalent to knowledge. What we know about the world—language, games, culture, law, etiquette, science, math, morality, and so on—is learned. Growing up, then, is a process of becoming at home in the world—at home with things, people, and ideas. If we as individuals are born strangers into our private lives, we as a generation are born strangers to our age. Consequently, it is not only as individuals in our private and personal lives that we try to become at home in the world, but also as members of various communities—cultural, religious, national, even international communities. We are engaged in a constant process of chronicling, narrating, assessing, and trying to understand ourselves in our private and public worlds—trying to move from the strange to the familiar.

Historians help us navigate that strangeness—help delineate it and make it known, or familiar, so that we can begin to understand who we were and who we are—begin to understand how we came to be what we are. The heart of the historian's task, as Simon Schama suggested, is to "negotiate between strangeness and familiarity"—the strangeness with which we are born and the familiarity we acquire.[1] The historian attempts to bring us closer to what is distant—distant in time, place, and culture—as well as to provide us with revisions of what we thought was familiar. Much as we might wish it, familiarity never fully overshadows strangeness. Just as life's moorings are never completely stable, our understanding of the past is always awaiting new interpretations. We are in a constant negotiation between a strangeness that never quite goes away and a familiarity that never quite takes hold even as we strive to acquire it.

As the historian delineates and narrates the past, we sometimes become more "at home" with ourselves as a people, as a culture, as a civilization, and, occasionally, as human beings.[2] Let us not be romantic, however; being "at home" in the world may include an understanding of the world, but not comfort with that world. Familiarity can breed not only contempt, but also shame, guilt, perplexity, and the like. In the case of the twentieth century, movement toward any form of familiarity means that we must examine what is most strange about us—our limits. So much of this century has been lived at the limits of technological and social progress and, paradoxically, at the limits of destructiveness—genocide and world wars. It is an irony of our time that our advances have been invariably linked to the excesses of our own destructive capacities.

The aim of this volume is to look at the landscape of the twentieth century and to consider these limits—indeed, to consider whether they are limits at all. What might it mean to be at home on this earth in the twentieth century? We have become familiar with genocide in the twentieth century. The history of the Holocaust and its successor genocides have become familiar patterns to many people—patterns we could not have predicted or understood prior to the Holocaust and the Second World War. If genocide has become familiar, if we are at home in a world that plans—even expects—genocide, what does this mean for and about humanity? Has humanity reached its limit, or have the limits of humanity been annulled?[3] Do the apparently familiar patterns also carry with them a strangeness we cannot seem to fathom? Is the familiarity only superficial and the strangeness very deep?

Given the extent and kind of destructiveness we find in the twentieth century, it is reasonable to suggest that humanity has not only reached, but also annulled, its limits. At the end of *Eichmann in Jerusalem,* Hannah Arendt warns us that what was "unprecedented, once it has appeared, may become a precedent for the future" and that the advent of nuclear energy makes it possible to construct and use "instruments beside which Hitler's gassing installations look like an evil child's fumbling toys, [and] should be enough to make us tremble."[4] In the midst of technological and scientific achievements as well as social progress, the twentieth century provides us with a history of death and destruction that is second to none. The twentieth century is thus far the "most productive *and* destructive century on record."[5]

Between 1500 and 1990, there were approximately 589 wars and more than 141,901,000 deaths.[6] Between 1900 and 1995 alone, there were more than 250 wars with approximately 109,746,000 deaths, 62 million of whom were civilians.[7] The twentieth century accounts for more than 75 percent of the war dead since 1500, more than 90 percent of the war dead since 1700.

The death toll during the Second World War was approximately 40,498,000: 20,779,000 civilian dead; 19,719,000 military dead. Of all those civilians who died or were murdered during the Second World War, between 25 and 29 percent were Jews, who were only about 1 percent of the total population in Europe. This is to say that between 5 and 6 million Jews either were killed or died during the Holocaust, as the Germans under the Nazi regime and their collaborators committed themselves to the most far-reaching genocide the world has ever witnessed or experienced.

Following the Second World War—between 1945 and 1992—there were 149 wars with approximately 23 million deaths, 15 million of whom were civilians, 7 million of whom were military.[8]

The most distinguishing feature of the twentieth century may not be just the numbers of the dead in massacres, wars, and genocides, but rather the proportion of these dead who were civilians. In the 1960s, 63 percent of the war dead were civilians; in the 1980s, 74 percent; in the 1990s, the rate is still higher, reaching the ninetieth percentile.[9] War and genocide have become intimate companions in the twentieth century.[10] Why?

One might think that this link between war and genocide, or at least the link between war and the huge rise in civilian deaths during war, has to do with some equivalent rise in human brutality, immorality, amorality, or a reduction of human sensitivity. It does not seem likely that the character of the human race is fundamentally different than it was even one thousand years ago. It may be risky to label any one factor as the most significant cause of the kind of destruction we have witnessed during the twentieth century. A plausible explanation for the twentieth century's destructiveness lies within two domains: (1) our scientific and technological achievements and (2) our belief that if we can make something powerful (whether a weapon or a vaccine), we should make it and use it. Our technology gives us the capacity to be more destructive than in previous centuries; and we have taken advantage of our newfound abilities. Even in the genocide in Rwanda (between April and June 1994), where machetes and rifles were the instruments of death, the radio was an essential means for organizing and exhorting the killers. Thus, in the twentieth century, we developed the technology and weaponry that could kill masses of people. Simultaneously we advanced policies and strategies to make it possible.

Between 1933 and 1945, a span of only twelve years, the world witnessed the nearly successful attempt of the Germans under National Socialism to destroy the Jewish population and culture in Europe as well as the possibility of the physical destruction of the human species through the use of the atomic bomb. At the same time that most of the world learned about the Holocaust, most also learned about omnicide. Then, within a few days after the first bomb was dropped on Hiroshima, the United States dropped a second nuclear bomb, this time on Nagasaki. Without question, the unprecedented quickly became a precedent. With regard to the trend that all things destructive have escalated in this century, Jonathan Schell commented that Nagasaki "is proof that, having once used nuclear weapons, we can use them again. It introduces the idea of a series—the series that, with tens of thousands of nuclear weapons remaining in existence, still continues to threaten everyone."[11]

Following the Holocaust and the Second World War, genocide itself has become a series, for example, Cambodia, Bosnia, Rwanda. If we ponder all the human destruction of the twentieth century, there can be no doubt that the limits of humanity have been annulled.[12] Perhaps this is one characteristic of being human—namely, straining at or stretching all limitations, even the limits of destruction. If limits and restraints have been annulled, then it may be that our ability to even comprehend the extent of destruction has become disabled. If we view what we thought were limits as bounded by a protective circle, once the circle has been broken we are in a world without signposts. It is as if we were walking down a flight of stairs without a banister.[13] The stairs may be familiar, but there is much unsteadiness without a banister on which to lean. A frame of reference has been removed. I believe that this is similar to our experience in the twentieth century. We are in a world that is uncanny—that is, a world that seems strange.

It is within this framework of limits—namely, the limits of our continually expanding destructiveness—that we have to locate the means for understanding the destructiveness of the twentieth century. Whether we are trying to understand the Holocaust, the phenomenon of genocide, or the reality of the atomic bomb, three questions arise: (1) How do we understand the Holocaust? (2) How do we understand Hiroshima and Nagasaki? (3) What constitutes understanding? It would appear that as we annul the limits of humanity, we also question our ability to understand the meaning of this annulment. The familiarity of genocide generates a strangeness we either can't or don't want to penetrate. Since the Holocaust is the centerpiece of this volume, I should like to quote several important thinkers who, in different ways and perhaps for different reasons, tell us that the limits that were either reached or annulled during the Holocaust cannot be understood.

First, Raul Hilberg. In the closing of his painful autobiography, Hilberg presents a letter written by H. G. Adler to a friend about the first edition of *The Destruction of the European Jews.* Upon reading the letter, Hilberg felt that Adler, whom he had never met, had somehow looked into his soul. Adler wrote: "At the end, nothing remains but despair and doubt about everything, because for Hilberg there is only recognition, perhaps also a grasp, but certainly no understanding."[14] Hilberg is telling us that he truly does not comprehend the Holocaust.

Saul Friedländer has said that there is an "opaqueness" that characterizes what we try to understand about the Holocaust, an opaqueness that creates an "unease" that defies all modes of "significant representation and interpretation."[15] He maintains that there is nothing in the Holocaust or in any of its interpretations that is relevant for understanding the history of humanity because the Holocaust resists any attempt to install meaning about itself. Thus there is nothing about the Holocaust that allows for any redemption of that past.[16] Friedländer is telling us that he doesn't get it.

Hannah Arendt claims that the Holocaust is incomprehensible because there is no possible crime that the victims could have committed that would justify the punishment meted out by the Nazis. For her, the incommensurability between the innocence of the victims and their punishment during the Holocaust is beyond understanding. Thus, the events that transpired during the Holocaust are beyond our capacity to comprehend. And without such comprehension the basis for the creation of history is destroyed. For these reasons she points out that "Human history has known no story more difficult to tell."[17] Indeed, it may be impossible. And with this, Arendt is telling us that she doesn't understand the Holocaust.

Finally, Susan Sontag, in her 1964 review of Rolf Hochhuth's *The Deputy,* adds to these sentiments:

> The supreme tragic event of modern times is the murder of the six million European Jews. . . . The murder of the six million Jews cannot be wholly accounted for either in terms of passions, private or public, or of error, or of madness, or of moral failure, or of overwhelming and irresistible social forces. Some 20 years after, there is more controversy about it than ever. What happened? How did it happen? How could it have been allowed to happen? Who are responsible? The great event is a wound that will not heal; even the balm of intelligibility is denied us . . . the event is, in some sense, incomprehensible. Ultimately, the only response is to continue to hold the event in mind, to remember it.[18]

Sontag is saying that she doesn't get it.

Most of us who have confronted the documents, stories, photos, documentary footage, artifacts, and narratives about the Holocaust shake our heads and don't get it. We have experienced the opaqueness, the incomprehensibility and inexplicability of which Hilberg, Friedländer, Arendt, Sontag speak. Still, we can't simply accept this standpoint without asking: Precisely to what are we referring when we claim that we don't understand? What exactly is opaque about the Holocaust? The opaqueness doesn't seem to be about what happened or about how it happened. We know more or less how it happened—that is, the mechanics of this complex set of events. Raul Hilberg, more than anyone, gave us this knowledge. Of course, we continually accumulate more details. Hans Mommsen has suggested that we have the complete outline and all we get now are the details. It is probably more accurate to say that the details offer us different perspectives on the outline we have; sometimes the details even change portions of that outline. What else, then, are we looking to understand about the Holocaust? What are Raul Hilberg, Saul Friedländer, Hannah Arendt, and Susan Sontag looking for?

The Holocaust may be opaque, but so is all experience. Language never captures experience. Language represents but does not replicate experience. This is true whether we are talking about the Holocaust, the death of a child, a piece of music, or a bird singing. When a young daughter or son dies of cancer, a mother wonders about and struggles with the question "Why?" She asks the doctor and gets a medical explanation. Her question may still remain because she is really looking beyond science, beyond an explication of how the child died. But where is she to find this other, perhaps deeper, answer? I don't think it can be found unless she is willing to accept some sort of philosophical, theological, or religious answer. When we wonder about the recent spate of school killings in the United States—children killing children as well as adults—we can easily get descriptions of how the events happened, even details as to why, apparently, the young boys decided to shoot at all. Still there is always a deeper "why," the answer to which usually remains elusive, no matter our need for its solace. Experience is always thicker than our ability to either represent or understand it. Nothing is a substitute for experience. If you don't play a musical instrument, can you imagine what it would be like to make music? There is a gap between experience and its representation. There is a gap between experience and our ability to understand it. If by "understanding" we mean to close that gap, we will fail.

This gap between experience and representation, between experience and understanding, is not unique to the Holocaust, or to genocides in Cambodia, Bosnia, Rwanda, or to the bombs dropped on Hiroshima and Nagasaki. The desire to close this gap is not only relevant to an exploration of the limits of humanity. That gap is threaded throughout all experience. In spite of this, does it mean that we can't understand "the otherness of the past, its obstinate unfamiliarity [and] the integrity of its remoteness"?[19] Does it mean we can't understand what was once completely strange and unfamiliar—for example, genocide or the Holocaust—even as they become, in some respects, more and more familiar? There is a language, however inadequate, for the death camps, for the ghettos, for starvation, for terror, and for the bombing of Hiroshima and Nagasaki. As a matter of fact, there are many languages: photos, film footage, survivor testimony, diaries and memoirs, poetry, novels, history books, and, of course, documents. They do not capture or encapsulate the experience. They only approximate it. We are capable of understanding within the limits of our languages and imagination. These means for approximating experience may not satisfy our deepest needs to understand, but they are all we can hope for as humans. To be able to understand, however, is not equivalent to locating meaning. To be able to understand the Holocaust, even if it were fully possible, would not redeem its place in history or create a way to construct redemptive meaning. The Holocaust remains meaningless in that sense. Still, it is crucial for us to know this set of events if we are to be at home with the twentieth century—if we are to know who, in some sense, we have become. There is no telling what becomes of this knowledge.

For now, all we can do is reconstruct the history and tell the stories of those who experienced it. In this way, we bear the past in the present and carry it for the future. In this way, we rescue what all history rescues—the "unbearable sequence of sheer happenings"[20]—and then we have the possibilities for understanding. All we can hope for is the possibility of more and more under-standing. As Shakespeare wrote:

> If thou didst ever hold me in thy heart,
> Absent thee from felicity awhile,
> And in this harsh world draw thy breath in pain
> To tell my story. (Hamlet)

And so I end where I began: We are born strangers into the world. Grow-ing up is a process of becoming at home in the world. If this is the case, what does it mean to be at home in the twentieth century—a century of unparal-leled destruction? Is the twentieth century still strange to us, or has it become familiar? Or is it somehow both? As for the limits of humanity, I believe we have annulled them. I wonder whether we still possess the capacity for re-straint.

NOTES

The views expressed in this paper are solely my own and do not necessarily represent the views of the United States Holocaust Memorial Museum.

1. Simon Schama, "Clio at the Multiplex," *New Yorker,* January 19, 1998, p. 40. Novelists, poets, playwrights, and others should certainly be in this characterization.

2. People read history for a variety of reasons. Some read history to learn lessons; others read history for the sheer pleasure of finding themselves in another place and another time. This discussion about "becoming at home" in the world does not claim to offer the full range of ways in which people relate to the study of history.

3. See Samuel Hynes, *The Soldier's Tale: Bearing Witness to Modern War* (New York: Allen Lane; Penguin Press, 1997), 270.

4. Hannah Arendt, *Eichmann in Jerusalem* (New York: Penguin Books, 1976), 273.

5. Ruth Leger Sivard, *World Military and Social Expenditures 1996* (Washington, D.C.: World Priorities, 1996), 7.

6. Ruth Leger Sivard, *World Military and Social Expenditures 1991* (Washington, D.C.: World Priorities, 1991), 20. "The rise in war deaths has thus far outstripped the rise in population . . . there have been over four times as many war deaths (between 1900 and 1990) as in the 400 years preceding." Armed conflicts since 1991 only add to these statistics.

There were 211 wars in the nineteenth century with 19.4 million dead; 55 wars in the eighteenth century with 7 million deaths; 36 wars in the seventeenth century with 6.1 mil-lion deaths; 60 wars in the sixteenth century with 1.6 million deaths.

7. *World Military Expenditures 1996,* 17–19.

8. Ruth Leger Sivard, *World and Military Expenditures 1993* (Washington, D.C.: World Priorities, 1993), 20–21.

9. *World Military Expenditures 1996,* 7.

10. It may well be that "genocide" is not the right word to apply here. Then again, the term "war" may also be inapplicable. If the dead in contemporary wars are primarily civil-ians, are we talking about war at all?

11. Jonathan Schell, "The Gift of Time," *Nation,* February 2/9, 1998, p. 60.

12. Hynes, 270: "Just as what troubles us most about the death camps is that in them human beings acted without humanity, as though the limits of human behavior had been

annulled, so at Hiroshima natural law seemed to have been altered and a new kind of disaster added."

13. See Richard Bernstein, *Hannah Arendt and the Jewish Question* (Cambridge, Mass.: MIT Press, 1996), 4. Bernstein writes that Hannah Arendt is trying "to think and judge without banisters."

14. Raul Hilberg, *The Politics of Memory: The Journey of a Holocaust Historian* (Chicago: Ivan R. Dee, 1996), 203.

15. Saul Friedländer, "The 'Final Solution': On the Unease in Historical Interpretation," in *Lessons and Legacies,* ed. Peter Hayes (Evanston, Ill.: Northwestern University Press, 1991), 35.

16. Friedländer, 23-35.

17. Hannah Arendt, "The Image of Hell," in *Essays in Understanding 1930-1954,* ed. Jerome Kohn (New York: Harcourt Brace, 1994), 199.

18. Susan Sontag, *Against Interpretation and Other Essays* (New York: Dell, 1966), 166. See also 124-125.

19. Schama, 41.

20. "The story reveals the meaning of what otherwise would remain an unbearable sequence of sheer happenings." Hannah Arendt, *Men in Dark Times* (New York: Harcourt Brace and World, 1968), 104. See also Arendt, "Image of Hell," 200: "Those who one day may feel strong enough to tell the whole story will have to realize, however, that the story *in itself* can yield nothing but sorrow and despair—least of all, arguments for any specific political purpose."

Against Redemption
5 | The Arts of Counter-Memory
James E. Young

The Anti-redemptory Aesthetic

Despite the brilliant example of his own work, *Nazi Germany and the Jews,* Saul Friedländer is still not convinced that an anti-redemptory historiography of the Holocaust is possible.[1] Even that narrative that integrates something akin to the deep, unassimilated memory of survivors as a disruption of "rational historiography" also seems to mend these same disruptions with the inexorable logic of narrative itself. The question arises: to what extent will the introduction of the survivors' memory into an otherwise rational historiography add a destabilizing strain to this narrative, and to what extent will such deep, unassimilable memory be neutralized by the meaning generated in any and all narrative? To a great extent, I believe Saul Friedländer has answered this question with his own work, a complex historical narrative that fluently, if paradoxically, resists its own tendency toward closure—a tremendous achievement.

With this example in mind, I would like to explore a few of the ways that the public art of memory itself has begun to resist the certainty of its monumental forms, the ways that a new generation of public memorial artists has begun to challenge the traditional redemptory premises of art itself. And even though I will concentrate here on what I believe is the anti-redemptory aesthetic of counter-monuments, I should also make clear that many other examples of this aesthetic can be found in the work of other postwar artists, architects, and musicians, such as Art Spiegelman, Christian Boltanski, Vera Frenkel, Rachel Whiteread, Daniel Libeskind, David Levinthal, and Steve Reich—among many others whose work I explore in a forthcoming book.[2]

Among the hundreds of submissions in a competition two years ago for a German national "memorial to the murdered Jews of Europe," one seemed especially uncanny for the ways it embodied the impossible questions at the heart of Germany's memorial process. Artist Horst Hoheisel, already well known for his negative-form monument in Kassel, proposed a simple, if provocative, anti-solution to the memorial competition: blow up the *Brandenburger Tor,* grind its stone into dust, sprinkle the remains over its former site, and then cover the entire memorial area with granite plates. How better to remember a destroyed people than by a destroyed monument?

Rather than commemorating the destruction of a people with the construction of yet another edifice, Hoheisel would mark one destruction with another. Rather than filling in the void left by a murdered people with a positive form, the artist would carve out an empty space in Berlin by which to recall a now absent people. Rather than concretizing and thereby displacing the memory of Europe's murdered Jews, the artist would open a place in the landscape to be filled with the memory of those who come to remember Europe's murdered Jews. A landmark celebrating Prussian might and crowned by a chariot-borne Quadriga, the Roman goddess of peace, would be demolished to make room for the memory of Jewish victims of German might and peacelessness. In fact, perhaps no single emblem better represents the conflicted, self-abnegating motives for memory in Germany today than the vanishing monument.[3]

Of course, such a memorial undoing will never be sanctioned by the German government, and this, too, is part of the artist's point. Hoheisel's proposed destruction of the *Brandenburger Tor* participates in the competition for a national Holocaust memorial, even as its radicalism precludes the possibility of its execution. At least part of its polemic, therefore, is directed against actually building any winning design, against ever finishing the monument at all. Here he seems to suggest that the surest engagement with Holocaust memory in Germany may actually lie in its perpetual irresolution, that only an unfinished memorial process can guarantee the life of memory. For it may be the *finished* monument that completes memory itself, puts a cap on memory-work, and draws a bottom line underneath an era that must always haunt Germany. Better a thousand years of Holocaust memorial competitions in Germany than any single "final solution" to Germany's memorial problem, I wrote at the time.[4]

Like other cultural and aesthetic forms in Europe and America, the monument—in both idea and practice—has undergone a radical transformation over the course of the twentieth century. As intersection between public art and political memory, the monument has necessarily reflected the aesthetic and political revolutions, as well as the wider crises of representation, following all of this century's major upheavals—including both First and Second World Wars, the Vietnam War, the rise and fall of communist regimes in the former Soviet Union and its eastern European satellites. In every case, the monument reflects both its socio-historical and aesthetic contexts: artists working in eras of cubism, expressionism, socialist realism, earthworks, minimalism, or conceptual art remain answerable to both the needs of art and official history. The result has been a metamorphosis of the monument from the heroic, self-aggrandizing figurative icons of the late nineteenth century, celebrating national ideals and triumphs, to the anti-heroic, often ironic and self-effacing, conceptual installations marking the national ambivalence and uncertainty of late-twentieth-century postmodernism.

In fact, Andreas Huyssen has even suggested that in a contemporary age of mass memory production and consumption, there seems to be an inverse proportion between the memorialization of the past and its contemplation and study.[5] It is as if once we assign monumental form to memory, we have to some degree divested ourselves of the obligation to remember. In the eyes of modern critics and artists, the traditional monument's essential stiffness and grandiose pretensions to permanence thus doom it to an archaic, premodern status. Even worse, by insisting that its meaning is as fixed as its place in the landscape, the monument seems oblivious to the essential mutability in all cultural artifacts, the ways the significance in all art evolves over time. In this way, monuments have long sought to provide a naturalizing locus for memory, in which a state's triumphs and martyrs, its ideals and founding myths, are cast as being as naturally true as the landscape in which they stand. These are the monument's sustaining illusions, the principles of its seeming longevity and power. But in fact, as several generations of artists—modern and postmodern, alike—have made scathingly clear, neither the monument nor its meaning is really everlasting. Both a monument and its significance are constructed in particular times and places, contingent on the political, historical, and aesthetic realities of the moment.

Unlike the utopian, revolutionary forms with which modernists hoped to redeem art and literature after World War I, much post-Holocaust literature and art is pointedly anti-redemptory. The post-Holocaust memory artist, in particular, would say, "Not only is art not the answer, but after the Holocaust, there can be no more Final Solutions." Some of this skepticism has been a direct response to the enormity of the Holocaust—which seemed to exhaust not only the forms of modernist experimentation and innovation, but also the traditional meanings still reified in such innovations. Mostly, however, this skepticism stems from these artists' contempt for the religious, political, or aesthetic linking of destruction and redemption that seemed to justify such terror in the first place.

Indeed, of all the dilemmas facing post-Holocaust writers and artists, perhaps none is more difficult, or more paralyzing, than the potential for redemption in any representation of the Holocaust. Some, like Adorno, have warned against the ways poetry and art after Auschwitz risk redeeming events with aesthetic beauty or mimetic pleasure.[6] Others, like Saul Friedländer, have asked whether the very act of history-writing itself potentially redeems the Holocaust with the kinds of meaning and significance reflexively generated in all narrative.[7] Though Friedländer also questions the adequacy of ironic and experimental responses to the Holocaust, insofar as their transgressiveness seems to undercut any and all meaning, verging on the nihilistic, he also suggests that a postmodern aesthetics might "accentuate the dilemmas." And even by Friedländer's terms, this is not a bad thing: an aesthetics that remarks its own limitations, its inability to provide eternal answers and stable meaning.

Works in this vein acknowledge both the moral obligation to remember and the ethical hazards of doing so in art and literature. In short, postmodern re sponses devote themselves primarily *to* the dilemmas of representation, their difficulty and their irresolvability.

For many artists, the breach itself between events and their art now demanded some kind of representation: but how to do it without automatically recuperating it? Indeed, the postmodern enterprise is both fueled and paralyzed by the double-edged conundrum articulated first by Adorno: not only does "[c]ultural criticism share the blindness of its object," he wrote, but even the critic's essential discontent with civilization can be regarded as an extension of that civilization.[8] Just as the avant-garde might be said to feed on the illusion of its perpetual dying, postmodern memory-work seems to feed perpetually on the impossibility of its own task.[9]

In Germany, once the land of what Saul Friedländer has called "redemptory anti-Semitism," the possibility that art might redeem mass murder with beauty (or with ugliness), or that memorials might somehow redeem this past with the instrumentalization of its memory, continues to haunt a postwar generation of memory-artists.[10] Moreover, these artists are both plagued and inspired by a series of impossible memorial questions: How does a state incorporate shame into its national memorial landscape? How does a state recite, much less commemorate, the litany of its misdeeds, making them part of its reason for being? Under what memorial aegis, whose rules, does a nation remember its own barbarity? Where is the tradition for memorial *mea culpa*, when combined remembrance and self-indictment seem so hopelessly at odds? Unlike state-sponsored memorials built by victimized nations and peoples to themselves in Poland, Holland, or Israel, those in Germany are necessarily those of the persecutor remembering its victims. In the face of this necessary breach in the conventional "memorial code," it is little wonder that German national memory of the Holocaust remains so torn and convoluted. Germany's "Jewish question" is now a two-pronged memorial question: How does a nation of former perpetrators mourn its victims? How does a nation re-unite itself on the bedrock memory of its horrendous crimes?

Nearly fifty years after the defeat of the Nazi regime, contemporary artists in Germany still have difficulty separating the monument there from its fascist past. German memory-artists are heirs to a double-edged postwar legacy: a deep distrust of monumental forms in light of their systematic exploitation by the Nazis and a profound desire to distinguish their generation from that of the killers through memory.[11] In their eyes, the didactic logic of monuments— their demagogical rigidity and certainty of history—continues to recall too closely traits associated with fascism itself. How else would totalitarian regimes commemorate themselves except through totalitarian art like the monument? Conversely, how better to celebrate the fall of totalitarian regimes than by celebrating the fall of their monuments? A monument against fascism, therefore, would have to be monument against itself: against the traditionally didactic function of monuments, against their tendency to displace the past they would have us contemplate—and finally, against the authoritarian propensity in monumental spaces that reduces viewers to passive spectators.

One of the most fascinating results of Germany's memorial conundrum has been the advent of its "counter-monuments": brazen, painfully self-conscious memorial spaces conceived to challenge the very premises of their being. At home in an era of earthworks, conceptual and self-destructive art, a postwar generation of artists now explore both the necessity of memory and their incapacity to recall events they never experienced directly. To their minds, neither literal nor figurative references suggesting anything more than their own abstract link to the Holocaust will suffice. Instead of seeking to capture the memory of events, therefore, they recall primarily their own relationship to events, the great gulf of time between themselves and the Holocaust. For this generation of German artists, the possibility that memory of events so grave might be reduced to exhibitions of public craftsmanship or cheap pathos remains intolerable. They contemptuously reject the traditional forms and reasons for public memorial art, those spaces that either console viewers or redeem such tragic events, or indulge in a facile kind of *Wiedergutmachung,* or purport to mend the memory of a murdered people. Instead of searing memory into public consciousness, they fear, conventional memorials seal memory off from awareness altogether; instead of embodying memory, they find, memorials may only displace memory. These artists fear rightly that to the extent that we encourage monuments to do our memory-work for us, we become that much more forgetful. They believe, in effect, that the initial impulse to memorialize events like the Holocaust may actually spring from an opposite and equal desire to forget them.

In the pages that follow, I would like both to recall a couple of the counter-monuments I have already discussed at much greater length elsewhere and to add a few more recent installations to the discussion. In this way, I might both refine and adumbrate the concept of counter-monuments in Germany, the ways they have begun to constitute something akin to a "national form" that pits itself squarely against recent attempts to build a national memorial to the "murdered Jews of Europe" in the center of the country's re-united capital, Berlin. As before, I find that the ongoing debate in Germany has been especially instructive in my own considerations of the monument's future in this decidedly anti-redemptory age.

The Counter-Monument

Widely regarded as two of Europe's most provocative artists of "erasure" and self-abnegation, Jochen Gerz and Esther Shalev-Gerz are still best known for their disappearing "Monument against Fascism" in Harburg-Hamburg, dedicated in 1986. It consisted of a twelve-meter-high lead-covered column that was sunk into the ground as people inscribed their names (and much else) onto its surface; on its complete disappearance in 1994, the artists hoped that it would return the burden of memory to those who came looking for it. With audacious simplicity, their "counter-monument" thus flouted a number of memorial conventions: its aim was not to console but to provoke; not to remain fixed but to change; not to be everlasting but to disappear; not to be ignored by its passersby but to demand interaction; not to remain pristine but to invite its own violation; not to accept graciously the burden of memory but to throw it back at the town's feet.[12]

In keeping with the bookish, iconoclastic side of Jewish tradition, such a monument also recalled that the first "memorials" to the Holocaust period came not in stone, glass, or steel at all—but in the narrative that filled spaces now empty of Jews. As the preface to one of the *Yizker Bikher* (Memorial Books) commemorating a lost Jewish community suggests, "Whenever we pick up the book we will feel we are standing next to [the victims'] grave, because even that the murderers denied them."[13] The shtetl scribes hoped that when read, the *Yizker Bikher* would turn the site of reading into memorial space. In response to what has been called "the missing gravestone syndrome," the first sites of memory created by survivors were thus interior spaces, imagined gravesites.[14]

In his next memorial installation at Saarbrücken, Jochen Gerz seems to have recapitulated not only this missing gravestone syndrome but also the notion of the memorial *as* an interior space. Celebrated in Germany for his hand in Harburg's vanishing monument, Gerz was appointed in 1991 as a guest professor at the School of Fine Arts in Saarbrücken. In a studio class he devoted to conceptual monuments, Gerz invited his students to participate in a clandestine memory-project, what he regarded as a kind of guerrilla memorial action. The class agreed enthusiastically, swore themselves to secrecy, and listened as Gerz described his plan: Under the cover of night, eight students would steal into the great cobblestone square leading to the Saarbrücken Schloss, former home of the Gestapo during Hitler's Reich. Carrying book bags laden with cobblestones removed from other parts of the city, the students would spread themselves across the square, sit in pairs, swill beer, and yell at each other in raucous voices, pretending to have a party. All the while, in fact, they would stealthily pry loose some seventy cobblestones from the square and replace them with the like-sized stones they had brought along, each embedded underneath with a nail so that they could be located later with a metal detector. Within days, this part of the memorial-mission had been accomplished as planned.[15]

Meanwhile, other members of the class had been assigned to research the names and locations of every former Jewish cemetery in Germany, over two thousand of them, now abandoned, destroyed, or vanished. When their classmates returned from their beer party, their bags heavy with cobblestones, all set to work engraving the names of missing Jewish cemeteries on the stones, one by one. The night after they finished, the memory-guerrillas returned the stones, each inscribed and dated, to their original places. But in a twist wholly consistent with the Gerzes' previous counter-monument, the stones were replaced face down, leaving no trace of the entire operation. The memorial would be invisible, itself only a memory, out of sight and therefore, Gerz hoped, *in mind.*[16]

But as Gerz also realized, because the memorial was no longer visible, public memory would depend on knowledge of the memorial-action becoming public. Toward this end, Gerz wrote Oskar Lafontaine, minister-president of the Saarland and vice president of the German Social Democratic Party, apprising him of the deed and asking him for parliamentary assistance to continue the operation. Lafontaine responded with 10,000 DM from a special arts fund and a warning that the entire project was patently illegal. The public, however, had now become part of the memorial, for once the newspapers got wind of the project, a tremendous furor broke out over the reported vandalization of the square; editorials asked whether yet another monument like this was necessary; some even wondered whether or not the whole thing had been a conceptual hoax designed merely to provoke a memorial storm.

As visitors flocked to the square looking for the seventy stones out of over eight thousand, they too began to wonder "where they stood" vis-à-vis the memorial: Were they standing on it? In it? Was it really there at all? On searching for memory, Gerz hoped, they would realize that such memory was already in them. This would be an interior memorial: as the only standing forms in the square, the visitors would become the memorials for which they searched.

Where the politicians stood was less equivocal. As Jochen Gerz rose to address the Saarbrücken Stadtverband to explain his project, the entire CDU contingent stood up and walked out. The rest of the parliament remained and voted the memorial into public existence. Indeed, they even voted to rename the plaza "Square of the Invisible Monument," its name becoming the only visible sign of the memorial itself. Whether or not the operation had ever really taken place, the power of suggestion had already planted the memorial where it would do the most good: not in the center of town, but in the center of the public's mind. In effect, Jochen Gerz's "2,160 Stones: A Monument against Racism" returns the burden of memory to those who come looking for it.

Nor is Gerz the only German artist to have adapted what might be regarded as Jewish memorial motifs to recall the nation's missing Jews. Having already designed a negative-form monument in Kassel to commemorate a pyramid fountain destroyed by Nazis in 1938 as "the Jews' fountain," Horst Hoheisel turned to the next generation with a new, more pedagogically inclined project.[17] With permission from the local public schools, Hoheisel visited dozens of grade-school classrooms of Kassel with a book, a stone, and a piece of paper. The book was a copy of *Namen und Schicksale der Juden Kassels* (The Names and Fates of Kassel's Jews). In his classroom visits, Hoheisel would tell students the story of Kassel's vanished Jewish community, how they had once thrived there, lived in the very houses where these schoolchildren now lived, how they had sat at these same classroom desks. He then asked all the children who knew any Jews to raise their hands. When no hand appeared, Hoheisel would read the story of one of Kassel's deported Jews from his memory book. At the end of his reading, Hoheisel invited each of the students to research the life of one of Kassel's deported Jews: where they had lived and how, who their families were, how old they had been, what they had looked like. He then asked these schoolchildren to visit Kassel's formerly Jewish neighborhoods and to meet the German neighbors of Kassel's deported Jews.

After this, students were asked to write short narratives describing the lives and deaths of their subjects. Then they wrapped these narratives around cobblestones and deposited them in one of the archival bins the artist had provided every school. After several dozen such classroom visits, the bins had begun to overflow, and new ones were furnished. In time, Hoheisel transported all of these bins to Kassel's *Hauptbahnhof,* where he stacked them on the rail platform whence Kassel's Jews were deported. It is now a permanent installation, what the artist is calling his *Denk-Stein Sammlung* (memorial stone archive).

This memorial cairn—a witness-pile of stones—marks both the site of deportation and the community's education about its murdered Jews, their absence now marked by an ever-evolving memorial. Combining narrative and stone in this way, the artist and students have thus adopted the most Jewish of memorial forms as their own—thereby enlarging their memorial lexicon to include that of the absent people they would now recall. After all, only they are now left to write the epitaph of the missing Jews, known and emblematized primarily by their absence, the void they have left behind.

In two further installations, one realized and the other as yet only proposed, artists Misha Ullmann and Rachel Whiteread have also turned to both bookish themes and negative spaces in order to represent the void left behind by the "people of the book." In order to commemorate the infamous Nazi book-burning of 10 May 1933, the city of Berlin invited Misha Ullmann, an Israeli-born conceptual and installation artist, to design a monument for Berlin's *Bebelplatz.* Today, the cobblestone expanse of the *Bebelplatz* is still empty of all forms except for the figures of people who stand there and peer down through a ground-level window into the ghostly white underground room of empty shelves Ullmann has installed. A steel tablet set into the stones simply recalls that this was the site of some of the most notorious book-burnings and quotes Heinrich Heine's famously prescient words, "Where books are burned, so one day will people be burned as well."

Indeed, the English sculptor Rachel Whiteread has proposed casting the very spaces between and around books as the memorial figure by which Austria's missing Jews would be recalled in Vienna's *Judenplatz*. Her winning proposal for Vienna's official Holocaust memorial—the positive cast of the space around books in an anonymous library, the interior turned inside-out—thus extends her sculptural predilection for solidifying the spaces over, under, and around everyday objects, even as it makes the book itself her central memorial motif. But even here, it is not the book per se that constitutes her now displaced object of memory, but the literal space between the book and us. For as others have already noted, Whiteread's work since 1988 has made brilliantly palpable the notion that materiality can also be an index of absence: whether it is the ghostly apparition of the filled-in space of a now demolished row house in London ("House" launched Whiteread to international prominence) or the proposed cast of the empty space between the book-leaves and the wall in a full-size library, Whiteread makes the absence of an original object her work's defining preoccupation.[18]

Given this thematic edge in all her work, it is not surprising that Whiteread was one of nine artists and architects invited to submit proposals for a Holocaust memorial in Vienna. As proposed, Whiteread's cast of a library turned inside-out measures ten meters by seven meters, is almost four meters high, and resembles a solid white cube. Its outer surface would consist entirely of the roughly textured negative space next to the edges of book leaves. On the front wall facing onto the square there would be a double-wing door, also cast inside out and inaccessible. In its formalization of absence on the one hand and of books on the other, it found an enthusiastic reception among a jury looking for a design that "would combine dignity with reserve and spark an esthetic dialogue with the past in a place that is replete with history."[19] Despite the jury's unanimous decision to award Whiteread's design first place and to begin its realization immediately, the "esthetic dialogue" it very successfully sparked in this place so "replete with history" eventually paralyzed the entire memorial process.

For like many such sites in Vienna, the *Judenplatz* was layered with the invisible memory of numerous anti-Semitic persecutions—a synagogue was torched here in a 1421 pogrom, and hundreds of Jews died in the autos-da-fé that followed. Though Whiteread's design had left room at the site for a window into the archaeological excavation of this buried past, the shopkeepers on the *Judenplatz* preferred that these digs into an ancient past also be left to stand for the more recent murder of Austrian Jews as well. And although their anti-Whiteread petition of two thousand names refers only to the lost parking and potential for lost revenue they fear this "giant colossus" will cause, they may also fear the loss of their own Christian memory of this past. For to date, the sole memorial to this medieval massacre was to be found in a Catholic mural and inscription on a baroque facade overlooking the site of the lost synagogue. Alongside an image of Christ being baptized in the River Jordan, an inscription reads: "The flame of hate arose in 1421, raged through the entire city, and punished the terrible crimes of the Hebrew dogs." In the end, the reintroduction into this square of a Jewish narrative may be just as undesirable for the local Viennese as the loss of parking places.

In either case, the debate in Austria remains curiously displaced and sublimated. Now lost in the debate are the words one of the jurors and a curator at New York's Museum of Modern Art, Robert Storrs, had used to describe what made Whiteread's work so appropriate in the first place. "Rather than a tomb or cenotaph," Storrs wrote,

> Whiteread's work is the solid shape of an intangible absence—of a gap in a nation's identity, and a hollow at a city's heart. Using an aesthetic language that speaks simultaneously to tradition and to the future, Whiteread in this way respectfully symbolizes a world whose irrevocable disappearance can never be wholly grasped by those who did not experience it, but whose most lasting monuments are the books written by Austrian Jews before, during and in the aftermath of the catastrophe brought down on them.[20]

Thus would Whiteread's design recall, indirectly, that which made the Jews of Europe a people: their shared relationship to the past. For it was this shared relationship to a remembered past through the book that bound Jews together, and it was the book that provided the site for this relationship. Though Whiteread is not Jewish, she has—in good Jewish fashion—cast not a human form but a sign of humanity, gesturing silently to the acts of reading, writing, and memory that had once constituted this people as a people.

The Holocaust as Vicarious Past

As his sole example of deep memory, Friedländer refers to the last frame of Art Spiegelman's so-called comic book of the Holocaust, *Maus: A Survivor's Tale,* in which the dying father addresses his son, Artie, with the name of Richieu, Artie's brother who died in the Holocaust before Artie was even born.[21] The still apparently unassimilated trauma of his first son's death remains inarticulable—and thereby deep—and so is represented here only indirectly as a kind of manifest behavior. But this example is significant for Friedländer in other ways, as well, coming as it does at the end of the survivor's life. For Friedländer wonders, profoundly I think, what will become of this deep memory after the survivors are gone. "The question remains," he says, "whether at the collective level . . . an event such as the *Shoah* may, after all the survivors have disappeared, leave traces of a deep memory beyond individual recall, which will defy any attempts to give it meaning."[22] The implication is that, beyond the second generation's artistic and literary representations of it, such deep memory may be lost to history altogether.

In fact, here I would like to end with a reflection on Art Spiegelman's *Maus,* not because it actually answers Friedländer's call for an integrated history of the Holocaust, but because it illustrates so graphically the very dilemmas that inspire Friedländer's call. At the same time, I find that by embodying what Marianne Hirsch has aptly termed an aesthetics of post-memory, it also suggests itself as a model for what I would like to call "received history"—a narrative hybrid that interweaves both events of the Holocaust and the ways they are passed down to us.[23] Like Hirsch, I would not suggest that post-memory takes us beyond memory, or displaces it in any way, but is "distinguished from memory by generational distance and from history by deep personal connection. Post-memory should reflect back on memory, revealing it as equally constructed, equally mediated by the processes of narration and imagination. . . . Post-memory is anything but absent or evacuated: It is as full and as empty as memory itself."[24] For like others in his media-savvy generation born after— but indelibly shaped by—the Holocaust, Spiegelman does not attempt to represent events he never knew immediately but instead portrays his necessarily hyper-mediated experience of their memory. This postwar generation, after all, cannot remember the Holocaust as it actually occurred. All they remember, all they know of the Holocaust, is what the victims have passed down to them in their diaries, what the survivors have remembered for them in their memoirs. They remember not actual events, but the countless histories, novels, and poems of the Holocaust they have read, the photographs, movies, and video testimonies they have seen over the years. They remember long days and nights in the company of survivors, listening to their harrowing tales, until their lives, loves, and losses seemed grafted indelibly onto their own life stories.

Born after Holocaust history into the time of its memory only, this media-conscious generation rarely presumes to represent events outside of the ways they have vicariously known and experienced them. Instead of attempting to portray the events of the Holocaust, they write and draw and talk about the event of its transmission to them—in books, film, photographs, and parents' stories. Instead of trying to remember events, they recall their relationship to the memory of events. "What happens to the memory of history when it ceases to be testimony?" Alice Kaplan has asked.[25] It becomes memory of the witness's memory, a vicarious past. What distinguishes many of these artists from their parents' generation of survivors is their single-minded knack for representing just this sense of vicariousness, for measuring the distance between history-as-it-happened and their own post-memory of it.

As becomes clear, then, especially to the author himself, Art Spiegelman's *Maus: A Survivor's Tale* is not about the Holocaust so much as about the survivor's tale itself and the artist-son's recovery of it. In Spiegelman's own words,

"*Maus* is not what happened in the past, but rather what the son understands of the father's story. . . . It is an autobiographical history of my relationship with my father, a survivor of the Nazi death camps, cast with cartoon animals."[26] As his father recalled what happened to him at the hands of the Nazis, his son Art recalls what happened to *him* at the hands of his father and his father's stories. As his father told his experiences to Art, in all their painful immediacy, Art tells his experiences of the storytelling sessions themselves—in all of their somewhat less painful mediacy.[27]

While Spiegelman acknowledges that the very word *comics* "brings to mind the notion that they have to be funny," humor itself is not an intrinsic component of the medium. "Rather than comics," he continues, "I prefer the word commix, to mix together, because to talk about comics is to talk about mixing together words and pictures to tell a story."[28] For unlike a more linear historical narrative, the "commixture" of words and images generates a triangulation of meaning—a kind of three-dimensional narrative—in the movement between words, images, and the reader's eye. Such a form also recognizes that part of any narrative will be this internal register of knowledge—somewhere between words and images—conjured in the mind's movement between itself and the page.

The narrative sequence of his boxes, with some ambiguity as to the order in which they are to be read, combines with and then challenges the narrative of his father's story—itself constantly interrupted by Art's questions and own neurotic preoccupations, his father's pill-taking, the rancorous father-son relationship, his father's new and sour marriage. As a result, Spiegelman's narrative is constantly interrupted by—and integrative of—life itself, with all its dislocutions, associations, and paralyzing self-reflections. It is a narrative echoing with the ambient noise and issues surrounding its telling. The roundabout method of memory-telling is captured here in ways unavailable to straighter narrative. It is a narrative that tells both the story of events and its own unfolding as narrative.

The result is a continuous narrative rife with the discontinuities of its reception and production, the absolutely authentic voice of his father counterpoised to the fabular images of cartoon animals. In its self-negating logic, Spiegelman's commix also suggests itself as a pointedly anti-redemptory medium that simultaneously makes and unmakes meaning as it unfolds. Words tell one story, images another. Past events are not redeemed in their telling but are here exposed as a continuing cause of the artist's inability to find meaning anywhere. Meaning is not negated altogether, but that created in the father's telling is immediately challenged in the son's reception and visualization of it.

In fact, the "story" is not a single story at all but two stories being told simultaneously: the father's story and Spiegelman's imaginative record of it. It is double-stranded and includes the competing stories of what his father says and what Artie hears, what happened during the Holocaust and what happens now in Artie's mind. As a process, it makes visible the space between what gets told and what gets heard, what gets heard and what gets seen. The father says one thing as we see him doing something else. Artie promises not to betray certain details, only to show us both the promise and betrayal together. Indeed, it may be Artie's unreliability as a son that makes his own narrative so reliable.

Throughout *Maus,* Spiegelman thus confronts his father with the record of his telling, incorporating his father's response to Art's record of it into later stages of *Maus.* Like any good postmodern memory-art, *Maus* thereby feeds on itself, recalling its own production, even the choices the artist makes along the way (would he draw his French wife who converted to Judaism as a frog or as an honorary *Maus?*). The story now includes not just "what happened," but how what happened is made sense of by father and son in the telling. At the same time, it highlights both the inseparability of his father's story from its effect on Artie and the story's own necessarily contingent coming into being. All of which might be lost to either images or narrative alone, or even to a reception that did not remark its own unfolding.

No doubt, some will see this as a supremely evasive, even self-indulgent, art by a generation more absorbed in their own vicarious experiences of memory than by their parents' actual experiences of real events. Some will say that if the second or third generation want to make art out of the Holocaust, then let it be about the Holocaust itself and not about themselves. The problem for much of Spiegelman's generation, of course, is that they are either unable or unwilling to remember the Holocaust outside of the ways it has been passed down to them, outside of the ways it is meaningful to them fifty years after the fact. As the survivors have testified to *their* experiences of the Holocaust, their children and children's children will now testify to their experiences of the Holocaust. And what are *their* experiences of the Holocaust? Photographs, film, histories, novels, poems, plays, survivors' testimony. It is necessarily mediated experience, the after-life of memory, represented in history's after-images: the impressions retained in the mind's eye of a vivid sensation long after the original, external cause has been removed.

Why represent all that? Because for those in Spiegelman's generation, to leave out the truth of how they came to know the Holocaust would be to ignore half of what actually happened: we would know what happened to Vladek but miss what happened to Art. But isn't the important story what happened to Vladek at Auschwitz? Yes, but without exploring why it's important, we leave out part of the story itself. Is it self-indulgent or self-aggrandizing to make the listener's story part of the teller's story? This generation doubts that it can be done otherwise. They can no more neglect the circumstances surrounding a story's telling than they can ignore the circumstances surrounding the actual events' unfolding. Neither the events nor the memory of them take place in a void. In the end, which is the more truthful account: that narrative or art which ignores the facts surrounding its own coming into being, or that which paints these facts, too, into its canvas of history?

"Why should we assume there are positive lessons to be learned from [the Holocaust]?" Jonathan Rosen has asked in an essay that cuts excruciatingly close to the bone of Spiegelman's own ambivalence. "What if some history does not have anything to teach us? What if studying radical evil does not make us better? What if, walking through the haunted halls of the Holocaust Museum, looking at evidence of the destruction of European Jewry, visitors do not emerge with a greater belief that all men are created equal but with a belief that man is by nature evil?"[29]

Rosen's ironic question also comes with a very clear judgment built into it: the Holocaust was an irredeemably terrible experience then, had a terrible effect on many survivors' lives, and endows its victims with no great moral authority now. Categories like good and evil remain, but they are now stripped of their idealized certainties.

From Friedländer's integrated historiography to the counter-monuments to Art Spiegelman's commix, these works succeed precisely because they refuse to assign singular, over-arching meaning to either events or our memory of them. This is the core of their anti-redemptory aesthetic. Such historians and artists continue to suggest meaning in history but simultaneously shade meaning with its own necessary contingency. In side-shadowing both the history and memory of the Holocaust in this way, not only do they resist the temptation for redemptory closure in their work, but they can make visible why such history is worth recalling in the first place.

NOTES

1. See Saul Friedländer, *Nazi Germany and the Jews,* vol. 1, *The Years of Persecution* (New York: Harper Collins, 1997).

2. For the purposes of this presentation, I have drawn from (and elaborated on) related articles I have published elsewhere, all parts of a forthcoming book, *At Memory's Edge: After-Images of the Holocaust in Contemporary Art and Architecture* (New Haven: Yale University Press, in press). In particular, see James E. Young, "Germany's Memorial Question: Memory, Counter-memory, and the End of the Monument," *South Atlantic Quarterly* 96, no. 4 (Fall 1997): 853–880; and "The Holocaust as Vicarious Past: Art Spiegelman's *Maus* and the Afterimages of History," *Critical Inquiry* 24, no. 3 (Spring 1998): 666–699.

3. This essay elaborates and expands on themes I first explored in "The Counter-monument: Memory against Itself in Germany Today," *Critical Inquiry* 18, no. 2 (Winter 1992): 267–296. Also see James E. Young, *The Texture of Memory: Holocaust Memorials and Meaning* (New Haven: Yale University Press, 1993), 27–48.

4. For a record of this competition, see *Denkmal für die ermordeten Juden Europas: Kurzdokumentation* (Berlin: Senatsverwaltung für Bau- und Wohnungswesen, 1995). For a collection of essays arguing against building this monument, see *Der Wettbewerb für das "Denkmal für die ermordeten Juden Europas": Eine Streitschrift* (Berlin: Verlag der Kunst, 1995).

On his proposal to blow up the Brandenburger Tor, see Horst Hoheisel, "Aschrottbrunnen—Denk-Stein-Sammlung—Brandenburger Tor—Buchenwald. Vier Erinnerungsversuche," in Nicolas Berg, Jess Jochimsen, and Bernd Stiegler, eds., *Shoah—Formen der Erinnerung: Geschichte, Philosophie, Literatur, Kunst* (Munich: Wilhelm Fink Verlag, 1997), 253–266.

5. Andreas Huyssen, "The Monument in a Post-modern Age," in James E. Young, ed., *The Art of Memory: Holocaust Memorials in History* (Munich: Prestel Verlag, 1994), 11.

6. T. W. Adorno, "Engagement," in *Noten zur Literatur*, vol. 3 (Frankfurt am Main, 1965), 125–127.

7. Saul Friedländer, *Memory, History, and the Extermination of the Jews of Europe* (Bloomington: Indiana University Press, 1993), 55.

8. Theodore W. Adorno, *Prisms,* trans. Samuel and Shierry Weber (Cambridge, Mass.: MIT Press, 1981), 27, 91.

9. For a brilliant elaboration on the "ever-dying" of the avant-garde, see Paul Mann, *The Theory-Death of the Avant-Garde* (Bloomington: Indiana University Press, 1991).

10. Friedländer, *Nazi Germany and the Jews,* 3.

11. For elaboration of this theme, see Matthias Winzen, "The Need for Public Representation and the Burden of the German Past," *Art Journal* 48 (Winter 1989): 309–314.

12. For a detailed discussion of the Harburg counter-monument, see James E. Young, *Texture of Memory,* 27–48. Also see Achim Konneke, ed., *Das Harburger Mahnmal gegen Faschismus/ The Harburg Monument against Fascism* (Hamburg, 1994).

13. From "Forwort," in *Sefer Yizkor le-kedoshei ir (Przedecz) Pshaytask Khurbanot ha'shoah,* p. 130, as quoted in Jack Kugelmass and Jonathan Boyarin, eds., *From a Ruined Garden: The Memorial Books of Polish Jewry* (New York: Schocken Books, 1983), 11.

14. On the "missing gravestone syndrome," see Joost Merloo, "Delayed Mourning in Victims of Extermination Camps," in Henry Krystal, ed., *Massive Psychic Trauma* (New York, 1968), 74.

15. For the details of this project, I am indebted to personal correspondence and conversations with Jochen Gerz, as well as these articles, among others: Barbara V. Jhering, "Duell mit der Verdrängung," *Die Zeit,* 14 February 1992; Amine Haase, "Mahnmale gegen Faschismus und Rassismus," *Kunst und Antiquitäten* 1, no. 2 (1992): 12–14; Jacqueline Lichtenstein and Gerard Wajeman, "Jochen Gerz: Invisible Monument," *artpress* (April 1993): E1–E6.

16. "Art, in its conspicuousness, in its recognizability, is an indication of failure," Jochen Gerz has said. "If it were truly consumed, no longer visible or conspicuous, if there were only a few manifestations of art left, it would actually be where it belongs—that is, within the people for whom it was created." From Doris Von Drateln, "Jochen Gerz's Visual Poetry," *Contemporanea* (September 1989): 47.

17. For more on Hoheisel's "negative-form" monument, see "The Counter-monument: Memory against Itself in Germany Today," noted above. For the details of this current project, I am indebted to conversations and correspondence with the artist, Horst Hoheisel.

18. See Fiona Bradley, ed., *Rachel Whiteread: Shedding Life* (London, 1996), 8. Other essays in this exhibition catalogue for the retrospective of Rachel Whiteread's work at the Tate-Liverpool Gallery by Stuart Morgan, Bartomeu Mari, Rosalind Krauss, and Michael Tarantino also explore various aspects of the sculptor's gift for making absence present.

19. *Judenplatz Wien 1996: Wettbewerb Mahnmal und Gedenkstätte für die judischen Opfer des Naziregimes in Österreich 1938–1945* (Wien, 1996), 94.

20. Ibid., 109.

21. Art Spiegelman, *Maus: A Survivor's Tale,* vols. 1 and 2 (New York: Pantheon, 1986, 1991), vol. 2, p. 135.

22. Friedländer, *Memory, History,* 41.

23. Marianne Hirsch, "Family Pictures: *Maus,* Mourning, and Post-Memory," *Dis-*

course 15, no. 2 (Winter 1992–93): 8–9. For an elaboration of "received history," see James E. Young, "Notes toward a Received History of the Holocaust," *History and Theory* (December 1997): 21–43.

24. Ibid.

25. Alice Yeager Kaplan, "Theweleit and Spiegelman: Of Mice and Men," in Barbara Kruger and Phil Marian, eds., *Remaking History: DIA Art Foundation Discussions in Contemporary Culture*, no. 4 (Seattle: Bay Press, 1989), 160.

26. From author's interview with Art Spiegelman, as well as from Art Spiegelman, "Commix: An Idiosyncratic Historical and Aesthetic Overview," *Print* (November/December 1988): 61.

27. For an extended working through of this proposition, see James E. Young, "The Holocaust As Vicarious Past: Art Spiegelman's *Maus* and the Afterimages of History," *Critical Inquiry* (Spring 1998): 666–699.

28. Spiegelman, "Commix," 61.

29. Jonathan Rosen, "The Trivialization of Tragedy," *culturefront* (Winter 1997): 85.

PART 2
Theology from the Depths
New Directions in Germany

Introduction
Four German Theologians
Robert A. Krieg

In *The White Crucifixion* (1938), Marc Chagall has portrayed Jesus of Nazareth as an observant rabbi. The painting depicts a pogrom, presumably *Kristallnacht:* a mob with axes and banners rushes in from the left, houses are aflame, gray smoke billows against a black sky, a man runs into a burning synagogue, and Jews flee, some in a boat and others on foot. In the center there is a large cross, on which hangs a victim wearing a *tallith.* Over the cross float three distraught Jews, who are listening to a fourth, a rabbi. A lit menorah stands near the cross. Breaking in from the upper right is a broad beam of white light, which flows around the cross and streams to the figures in flight. The painting is an invitation to remember: once again, the victims are Jews. Remembering is also a theme evident in the essays by four German theologians, of whom the first two are Catholic and the second two are Protestant.

Dr. Hanspeter Heinz, professor of pastoral theology at the University of Augsburg, has addressed the question of healing in his essay, "After Sixty Years—How Can We Speak of Guilt, Suffering, and Reconciliation?" He moves toward an answer by drawing a contrast between two stances within the Catholic Church toward the Shoah. One approach is interpersonal; it prompts Christians to enter into dialogue with Jews in order to appreciate their views of God and life, especially after the Shoah. This approach stays in touch with experience. Adopting this stance, Heinz recounts the "miracle" of how Jews and Christians in Germany since 1971 have set up a permanent discussion group within the Central Committee of German Catholics. Fruits of their conversations include written summaries of their joint insights. In 1988 they produced the document "After 50 Years, Reichskristallnacht 1938: How Can We Talk about Guilt, Suffering and Reconciliation?" Heinz also describes a second approach to the Shoah, a theoretical approach, which directs Christians to uphold long-standing views of the church, thereby implicitly distinguishing between the church itself and the actions of some of its members. In other words, it stresses the ideal, while admitting the actual failure of individuals and groups. This stance manifests itself in the Vatican's statement, *We Remember: A Reflection on the Shoah* (March 12, 1998). Without defending this statement, Heinz clarifies the set of ideas that undergirds it. In conclusion, Heinz recounts a recent visit to Auschwitz and its lessons concerning appropriate ways to remember. His anecdote shows the value of an ongoing encounter between Jews and Christians.

Reiterating Heinz's interpersonal approach, Dr. Hans Hermann Henrix, director of the Bischöfliche Akademie of the Diocese of Aachen, maintains in his essay, "In the Shadow of the Shoah: Being a Theologian in Germany Today," that the only way for Christians to keep alive the memory of the Shoah is to remain in dialogue with Jews. He gives three examples of encounters with Jews that have deeply influenced him. A conversation with Rabbi Zalman Schachter in 1980 brought him to realize that the Shoah is "a tumor in the human memory." Moreover, at a seminar with Professor Emil Fackenheim in 1983 he learned that "the scene of guilt also wants to be the scene of grace." Also, Professor Emmanuel Levinas taught him in 1981 that truly knowing someone brings with it a moral commitment: "With my life I vouch for the other being, I am his hostage." From these three meetings, Henrix discovered that when a person embraces a stranger, he or she may become attentive to the distance and presence of God in human life. With this thought, Henrix concludes: "A theological existence in the shadow of the Shoah—with the 'tumor in the memory'—is constantly anew *a theology from face to face.*"

Working within the theological tradition of Karl Barth, Dr. Bertold Klappert, professor of systematic theology at Wuppertal, has described a change in Christian theology in his essay, "An Alternative for Christian Substitution Theology and Christology after the Shoah." The conventional Christian view, namely that Jesus brought an end to God's bond with Israel, set a course that eventually led to Auschwitz. The churches have now disowned this substitution or displacement theory, and Karl Barth, H. J. Iwand, Rabbi Leo Baeck, and others have proposed an alternative understanding of the Christian covenant. In this perspective, God did not renounce his intimacy with Israel; rather God reformulated this relationship so that non-Jews could share in it. In other words, God has invited all peoples to join with "the chosen people," the Jews, in making the pilgrimage to Zion. This alternative view of the covenant has significant implications for Christians' reflections on Jesus and the church. Christians must not lose sight of the fact that Jesus was a Jew. Indeed, he was a Jew who invited non-Jews to walk with Israel to the new Jerusalem. Furthermore, Christians must not separate the church from its origins in biblical Israel. God's dwelling within the community of Jesus, namely the Christian churches, presupposes God's presence among the Jewish people. Recalling St. Paul's image in his letter to the Romans, Klappert concludes that the church is the branch grafted on to the vine, and as such, it must remain connected with its roots.

Dr. Peter von der Osten-Sacken, director of the Institut Kirche und Judentum at Berlin's Humbolt University, has highlighted a shift in the Christian mind in his essay, "The Revival of the Jewish People within the Christian Consciousness in Germany." Until recently, Christians usually represented Judaism as a moribund religion or as a belief that had become stifled by its own laws and practices. But Christians in Germany now see that such a representation was wrong: Judaism is alive, even after the Shoah. Given this new recognition by Christians, Jews around the world as well as those living in Germany may rightly ask, "Can we trust you now?" The author avers that it will probably take three or four generations before trust is even possible. Yet, as Emil Fackenheim has observed, there are instances in recent years when Jews and Christians are rising above, "as if by angels' wings," the mountain that has kept them apart.

These reflections by Germans who are deeply engaged in Jewish-Christian dialogue manifest the pain and the benefits of remembering—remembering together and yet out of distinct religious communities. For Christians such encounters are directing their attention to the history of Jews, including to Jesus the Jew. In this regard, the church historian Jaroslav Pelikan has made an insightful comment in his book *Jesus through the Centuries*. Commenting on Chagall's *The White Crucifixion,* Pelikan has posed a question to which the only answer is the pledge to keep the memory alive:

> Would there have been such anti-Semitism, would there have been so many pogroms, would there have been an Auschwitz, if every Christian church and every Christian home had focused its devotion on icons of Mary not only as the Mother of God and Queen of Heaven but as the Jewish maiden and the new Miriam, and on icons of Christ not only as Pantocrator but as *Rabbi Jeshua bar-Joseph,* Rabbi Jesus of Nazareth, the Son of David, in the context of the history of a suffering Israel and a suffering humanity?[1]

This question is appropriately answered by the authors of these four essays. Dr. Heinz, Dr. Henrix, Dr. Klappert, and Dr. von der Osten-Sacken are committed to remembering the Shoah. Furthermore, they represent the pledge of the churches today. These four theologians are widely respected in their believing communities and work closely with Catholic and Protestant leaders throughout Germany. On January 23, 1995, the German Catholic bishops' conference commemorated the fiftieth anniversary of the liberation of the Auschwitz concentration camp by issuing a statement in which they declared that "many times [in the Third Reich] there was failure and guilt among Catholics" and that German Catholics must "painfully learn from this history of guilt of our country and of our church as well." Protestant leaders have issued similar statements. There is reason to hope that miracles of dialogue and reconciliation similar to those recounted in these papers will become more common among Jews and Christians.

NOTE

1. Jaroslav Pelikan, *Jesus through the Centuries* (New Haven: Yale University Press, 1985), 20.

6 | In the Shadow of the Shoah
Being a Theologian in Germany Today

Hans Hermann Henrix

In 1998 Jews in Israel and the Diaspora celebrated the fiftieth anniversary of the foundation of the State of Israel. As far as Christians in Germany are concerned, the proper appreciation of half a century of national existence of the State of Israel calls for a scope of remembrance that reaches further back into the past. For it was the persecution and extinction of the Jewish people by Germany's National Socialists that contributed to the foundation of the State of Israel and thus the realization of an ancient Jewish longing, recognized ultimately by the community of nations. It is thus inevitable that the path of remembrance must lead back beyond the year 1948—most certainly as far back as the year 1938. The state-planned and meticulously carried out murder of the Jews casts its message on the wall during the *Reichskristallnacht* ("Night of Broken Glass")—so called by the Nazis themselves—between 9 and 10 November 1938. In the list of German dates of remembrance for 1998 the sixty-year anniversary of the *Reichskristallnacht* takes its place right beside the jubilee of the State of Israel.

The *Reichskristallnacht,* following 9 November 1938, indeed was a pogrom night. Hundreds of synagogues were devastated and went up in flames. Torah scrolls were flung into the streets, trodden underfoot, spat on, thrown into flames or rivers. Thousands of shops belonging to Jewish citizens were looted, destroyed, and burned down. Innumerable Jewish families were roused from their sleep, brutally manhandled, and robbed of their houses and property. What an embarrassment for many Jewish couples, to be suddenly confronted in the middle of the night and in their own bedrooms by rude strangers who were ready for senseless and blind destruction. More than 100 people were killed, nay, murdered. Over the following several weeks, 26,000 well-off Jewish men were tortured in the concentration camps of Dachau, Buchenwald, and Sachsenhausen, where hundreds of them perished or were murdered. Those were days and weeks of deliberately reneging all ideals embodied in German law and German culture. It paved the way for the planned intrusion of barbarity into social life in Germany—organized and enacted by the state authorities. The German Jews now began to realize that civic rights and legal entitlements did not apply to them any longer. German Jewry was put an end to, once and for all, with full intention and in the full light of publicity, right before everybody's eyes.[1] But the many ordinary citizens kept silent.

Even today, there are people in Germany who feel ashamed of what happened. So, in annual remembrance of the evil events of the *Reichskristall-nacht*, people still today gather to pray and exhort. When ten years ago Christian and Jewish men and women, the old and the young, pupils and students, came together in the city of Aachen to remember the fiftieth anniversary of the *Kristallnacht,* Klaus Hemmerle, Catholic Bishop of Aachen, who has since untimely passed away, found the following words of lamentation and prayer:

The House of my God was set aflame,
—and mine own have done it.
It was taken away from those who gave me the name of my God,
—and mine own have done it.
They were set out of their own homes,
—and mine own have done it.
They were deprived of all their belongings, their honor and their good names
—and mine own have done it.
Their lives were taken away,
—and mine own have done it.
They who pray to the Name of the same God,
have kept silent on all this
—yes, mine own have done it.

Some say: let's forget about it, and put an end to it.
But what has been forgotten returns, unexpectedly and unrecognized.
How can we put an end to what we forget?
Should I say: Mine own did it, not me?
—No, mine own did it.

What shall I say?
My God, have mercy on me!

What shall I say?
Preserve in me Thy name, preserve in me their names,
Preserve in me their memories, preserve in me my shame:
My God, have mercy on me![2]

This is a text of deep-felt lament, not of accusation. It contains great compassion, not merely words dissociating themselves from what happened. The text is a prayer that, though in a subdued tone, calls up in detail the historical events and at the same time invokes God's mercy to free us from our troubles. And it is a text that does not reject nor neglect the question of guilt that is handed down from one generation to the next, but consciously takes it up. Even if the misdeeds of a previous generation do not turn subsequent generations into perpetrators, the ties between successive generations cannot simply be cut. There is such a thing as generation-surpassing responsibility, which we have to bear and which may make us call out for the mercy of God.

On the fiftieth anniversary of the *Reichskristallnacht* not only such acts of remembrance occurred, but equally some of disremembrance. In a big German university, the divine service on opening the teaching term, held in the morning of 10 November 1988, gave no indication whatsoever as to the historical context of the day, even though the go-ahead for initiating the pogrom was issued from the hometown of this university. Apparently such a thing as an anamnestic culture cannot be considered a matter of course in Germany. It needs fostering, growing not least from live contacts with Jews and Judaism. Whoever lays oneself open to such living contacts makes oneself available to others and their ways of life.[3] Such a person gets in touch with a resisting memory. Such a person will enter into new commitments of life, which are bound to influence his sensitivity and thought. If that person is a Christian theologian, then he will hit upon new modes of perception with regard to his theological thought.

I have been asked to report on how this may come about. Experiences arising from the dialogue with Jewish partners, and their power to change entrenched theological thought, will have to be taken into account. I follow this request with some hesitation, though; a meeting with Emmanuel Levinas comes to mind. When in 1982 I fetched him from the station to take him to a symposium on his philosophy at my Aachen Academy, he immediately admitted to me, "I feel like someone standing in the sun, groping for his own shadow." I think he was telling me that he wanted to make a rather equivocal statement—saying among other things perhaps that philosophy cannot be reduced to mere biography. Being a theologian, I immediately interpreted this as "theology being more than mere biography." I therefore cannot deny harboring a certain uneasiness when mentioning a few experiences gained from meeting others and from the ensuing dialogues, experiences that are to help me to draw the outlines of a theological existence in Germany in this day and age.

The Shoah as "A Tumor in the Human Memory"

My first experience leads me back into the year 1980. In May of that year a group of about twenty Jewish and Christian students and teachers from Temple University in Philadelphia began a seven-week study period in Germany, including two conferences in our city of Aachen. The group had landed at Brussels Airport, whence they arrived by train at Aachen Main Station, where I picked them up, put their baggage in some cabs, and walked with them the few hundred yards to our conference center. On the way to the center where we were to have an unforgettable time together, Zalman Schachter, a senior member of the group, introduced himself as having been in Aachen once before, forty-two years ago. As a nineteen-year-old he had made his way right across Germany to cross the German-Belgian border and thus escape from the Nazis. He said he had engaged a tout, had arranged a place and time to meet that man in a forest near Aachen, and had handed over to him almost all the money he possessed. Zalman Schachter had of course been at the appointed meeting place on the set time—but the tout hadn't turned up. He had spent the night in great panic and fear of death, then crossed the border on the following day with the help of others, finally leaving Germany behind. Now, for the first time, he had returned to Aachen and Germany.

Listening to his story, I realized: The past will not pass away. The presence of this past appeals to me, ever anew, not to conduct a dialogue on Jewish questions that is based only on theoretical premises, while at the same time forgetting about the immediacy of the Jews dead and alive. The distress they suffered when they were caught up in the Shoah rose to utter desperation: those of them forced to despair were the loneliest beings imaginable; the silence enveloping them was absolute and exclusive. Since they had, as Levinas put it, "this tumor in their memory," forty-two years and more would not be able to change that.[4] To have this "tumor in the memory" since the time of the Shoah has been the life-destiny of many of the survivors and their relatives. This "tumor in the memory" of so many lifelong sufferers must effect a binding commitment on Christians not to forget Auschwitz and all that it stands for. Their theological understanding must be affected by that "tumor in the memory." Johann Baptist Metz has expressed this in his instruction "not to indulge any longer in theological thought which is directed towards possibly forgetting about, or in fact remaining untouched by the occurrence of Auschwitz."[5]

A theological form of existence that owns up to this commitment will not be able to turn its back on the sufferings of the Shoah. That theology will have to foster a theological consciousness that interprets the Hebrew Bible, the gospels of Jesus Christ, and the other scriptures of the New Testament, that analyzes the teachings of the Church, and that deals with the themes occupying the theological disciplines—all in a spirit of moral remembrance of Auschwitz. That is to say, such a consciousness will always be aware that theology at all times runs the danger of initiating, by way of polemics, a chain reaction of religious disqualification, which via social ostracism will lead toward physical threats of the worst kind.

The Scene of Guilt Also Wants to Be the Scene of Grace

A second experience occurred in November 1983, when "Jews and Christians," a discussion group in the Central Committee of German Catholics, had invited Jewish and Christian experts on philosophical and theological ethics—about twenty professors from different countries—to participate in workshop talks. Some of those who met in this select round of colleagues in order to discuss fundamental ethical questions knew each other only from the books they had written. The first round of talks therefore served as a mutual introduction. Very soon this rather distanced academic exercise became less stylized, indeed quite personal. Emil Fackenheim, who, in view of the experience of Auschwitz, in his religious existentialism fought for a renewal of the understanding of Jewish revelation, on this occasion was fighting back deep emotion. He pointed out that for the first time in forty-five years he was talking German in a circle of friends. The last address in German he had given as a student of rabbinical studies was a sermon to the Jewish congregation of Baden-Baden during the Yom Kippur service on 10 October 1938. One month later, in the wake of *Reichskristallnacht,* he ended up in the KZ Sachsenhausen. On returning to his hometown Halle after having been released from the concentration camp a few months later, he was invited to the home of his former teacher of Greek, who, as a non-Jew, urged him to leave the country, as worse times were to come and Germany was heading for a catastrophe. The teacher commented: "Fackenheim, when it's all over, though, you must return to take your share in constructing a new Germany." The former pupil said he replied: "After what I've seen and experienced in the concentration camp, that will be quite impossible for me to do. Others must help with that reconstruction, not me." And in our latter-day discussion Fackenheim added that, after all, that experience was only the beginning and that his return to Germany became even more impossible after what happened in Auschwitz.

Referring to this summary of life as a German Jew, his fellow Jew, Werner Marx, a regular member of the "Jews and Christians" group, introduced himself as a survivor who had lived and worked in the United States for fifteen years. There he wrote a book on Heidegger that earned him a call from Freiburg University to succeed that great philosopher. It took him a year and a half of being advised by friends and of pondering on whether as a Jew he was entitled to and indeed should accept this chair in Germany. Eventually he accepted the offer. Turning to Emil Fackenheim, he said: "Other answers are possible, too. I consider it the obligation of a survivor, his task indeed, to return to where he was taken from so as to achieve reconciliation and 'normalization' of matters. Every day of my life I live in view of the things that have happened. The others don't do that. To me it seems to be the easier alternative to stay away and say: 'I will not return to Germany.' But a Jew who lives in Germany has a great mission, that is to say, he is able to work towards overcoming the evil where it is rooted and whence it has started."

Although Emil Fackenheim's existential reply to life in Germany initially seemed utterly opposed to that of Werner Marx, in the ensuing discussion he nevertheless came quite close to the views of his fellow Jew. His analysis that technology derives from the common Jewish-Christian tradition, while anti-Semitism drew its full modern-age impact from Christian history, therefore made Fackenheim come to the therapeutic conclusion: "Wherever a problem originates from, it is where we have to look for its solution."[6] Or put in a more theologically versed form: "The scene of guilt also wants to be the scene of grace."[7]

The state of Christian-Jewish relationships in Germany will always be determined by the fact that Germany is the land of the Shoah. The burden of this fact and the extent of responsibility issuing from it can be summarized in that statement: "The scene of guilt also wants to be the scene of grace." This statement then also documents the measure of gratitude that we Christians owe to the Jews among us, such as Edna Brocke, Ernst Ludwig Ehrlich, Nathan Peter Levinson, and others who engage in this dialogue. The statement directly points to the task laid upon us as Christians and within our communities. If our Germany is to be, or to become, a place of grace, then continued efforts by many are needed—above all, the effort of analyzing what happened in the course of the Shoah and what role Christians and their churches played in that context, as well as the challenge of working for *teshuvah*. The need for *teshuvah* was admitted by the Catholic Church of Germany in the central text "Our Hope" of 22 November 1975, issued by the common Diocesan Synod:

> We are the country whose recent political history was darkened by the attempt to systematically exterminate the Jewish people. And in this period of National Socialism—despite the exemplary behavior of some individuals and groups—we were nevertheless as a whole a Church community who kept on living their life in turning their back too often on the fate of this persecuted Jewish people, who looked too fixedly at the threat to their own institutions and who remained silent about the crimes committed against the Jews and Judaism. Many became guilty from sheer fear for their lives. We feel particularly distressed about the fact that Christians even took active part in these persecutions. The practical sincerity of our will of renewal is also linked to the confession of this guilt and the willingness to painfully learn from this history of guilt of our country and even our Church: to the extent that our German Church in particular . . . is bound to accept special responsibility in respect of the encumbered relationship of the Church as a whole with the Jewish people and its religion.[8]

Urged by this obligation, I was able to contribute some of the groundwork needed by the German bishops to formulate, on the occasion of the fiftieth anniversary of the *Reichskristallnacht* in 1988 as well as that of the liberation of the concentration camps of Auschwitz and Auschwitz-Birkenau in 1995, the texts acknowledging the guilt and failings of Christians and the Church on the way to the Shoah and during the years of its occurrence.[9] Acting from the same sense of obligation, I accepted the assignment entrusted to me by Cardinal Edward Cassidy, president of the Vatican Commission for Religious Relations with the Jews, to compose a draft paper that might serve as a basis for a Vatican document on the topical area of "Anti-Semitism, Shoah and the Church."

Following the Vatican document *We Remember: A Reflection on the Shoah* of 16 March 1998,[10] my colleagues and I in the Conference of German Bishops working group "Questions of Judaism," after working three years at this draft, had to realize that our earnest endeavors were not accompanied by the hoped-for success.

Dogmatic under the Scrutiny of Ethics

The third experience that I want to cite cannot be pinned down to any specific moment or hour in the life of a theologian. It originated in meeting with Emmanuel Levinas and his work over an extended period. I met him for the first time in Israel in March 1981.

* * *

Levinas had been invited by the Central Committee of German Catholics to a seminar on the "Common Responsibility of Jews and Christians for the Future of Mankind" in Jerusalem. He gave a lecture on the topic of "Ethical Consensus and Ideology." As a young man, the philosopher had studied in Germany with Edmund Husserl and Martin Heidegger, and after the Shoah he vowed never to set foot again on German ground—a decision he stuck to until his death on 25 December 1995. Thus he expressly stated why as an outsider he had accepted the German invitation of actively participating in this seminar; among other things, he argued that scientists, theologians, and philosophers from Germany now

> are setting out on their way to the ancient Jewish people and its Bible, that these people are coming from the heart of old Europe, the cradle of the Occident, from that heart which had lived through so many climaxes of intellectual and spiritual life, yet at the same time had been marked by the greatest terrors it had been able to bear, a heart no less that was filled with sorrow and fear at the new uncertainties it was confronted with—if such a departure happens, I thought to myself, this is in keeping with the actuality of our times . . . the journey were to receive its full importance particularly because of the prospect of a dialogue on the question of what we Christians and Jews in view of the common sources of our ethics in the Holy Scriptures would be able and ought to do for the welfare of the humanity of tomorrow.[11]

He spoke of a suspicion that finds in every gift of altruism, in every selflessness, certain subjective interests and secret intentions. This suspicion he contrasted with the idea of eventual purification by means of constantly suspecting all forms of ideology: we are "now able to ascertain . . . that scientific discourse is not capable of exhausting and fully utilizing all manifestations of the reasonable. . . . Even from the depth of the most violent protest the value of the 'other human being' manages to surface: preemptive of the other person . . .

calling into question the own self . . . a responsibility for the other human beings."[12]

I intuitively recognized the unusual status of this thinker who with his personality seemed to form a living commentary on his philosophy. But listening to Levinas, I initially had not been able to fully grasp the entire scope of his thought. Only gradually it dawned on me that this was a mode of strictly philosophical thinking, which nevertheless did not negate its rootedness in biblical thought; what appeared to be meaningful to him in the first place was the ethical quality of any problem, although he never neglected to ask the ontological question. His progress of thought contained a motion toward the Messianic, though not holding out the promise of an approaching eschatological state. I increasingly began to notice a calling into question of my own tradition of thought, new-scholastic so-called critical realism, but also that of topical areas of Christian theology. I had learned that cognition was possible only when based on critical discourse and that it needed tangible evidence. The latter could at least be secured on the basis of the so-called judgment of consciousness, which assisted the cognitive subject in investigating cognitive contents of the "I think" mode and thus confirmed them with some certainty.

In my later examination of the work of Levinas, my philosophic tradition began to crumble away. I had further encounters with him. I was in charge of preparations for and the organization of a number of symposia and consultations, which took place on Dutch territory near Aachen.[13] Being exposed to his philosophy on these occasions, I felt increasingly alienated from my own school of thought, critical realism. To a growing extent I sensed more than ever before the provocative strength of his thought.

For Emmanuel Levinas, who returned home in 1945 from being directly confronted with the most menacing capabilities of Man, Western philosophical traditions had experienced their extreme crisis, indeed their *exitus*. Levinas had been face to face with a reality that appeared to be part and parcel of the tradition of Western philosophy and its ontology: cognition is thought of as the cognitive object being approximated, indeed assimilated to, the cognitive subject. Cognition is considered possible when the recognized object and the individual recognizing it have become congruent in the same theoretical imago. But such assimilation—this I had to learn to accept as a feature of Levinas's criticism—entails violence by the cognitive subject. Whatever is identified in turn loses its autonomy. Understanding works "in such a way that the otherness of the recognized being is extinguished in terms of cognitive existence."[14] Whatever is recognized obeys the imperatives of reason; it owes its meaning to the totality of all that exists, as this is the category in which it is embedded now. In the terminology of Levinas, this "theory which contains the understanding of all that exists deserves the title of ontology"—but it is an ontology that is unable to conceive of otherness, of the exteriority of the other one.[15]

In contrast to this, Levinas envisages a radically different solution to the elementary question of how cognition is possible and how sense reveals itself. He keeps looking for the concrete situation where something like Good becomes evident and meaningful. It is the other being who calls into question my carefree world ownership, my pleasure in all good things of life, as well as the concerned egocentricity of my structuring my own world around me.[16] Particularly—and here we are confronted with the spirit of the Bible within the philosophical discourse—the strange, the widow, the orphan is the other being. Because of his strangeness I am disturbed by his presence. Levinas, who doesn't want to analyze psychologically, but describes from a philosophical and phenomenological point of view, speaks of an "epiphany of the countenance,"[17] of an emergence of the countenance. The "epiphany of the countenance" manifests itself—as Levinas might also put it—in the scream of the other being. The scream of the other being transmits a twofold command to me: "Don't kill me!" and "Don't leave me alone."[18] In this moment Truth appears as Goodness, cognition as the ethical. I am called before a tribunal of immeasurable importance and significance. I am a hostage of the other being. Being a hostage of the other one is—as Levinas is also capable of saying—"a rough and dour term for love."[19] With my life I vouch for the other being; I am his hostage.

Bearing responsibility for my fellow-being is pre-deliberate "subjection to the other being."[20] I am asked to say "*Hineni*—Here I am." In the scream of the other being and in the citation to declare "*Hineni*—Here I am" the origin of ethics is embedded. The question asking for the meaning of life receives an answer from this source. The origin of justice also contains, or indeed is the origin of, that cognition. An exhortation, a call, an appeal occurs, in the course of which "God comes to mind," that is to say, God invades my mind, invades my thought.

Once theological thought is infected by this kind of philosophy, it can hardly rid itself of it. It cannot simply follow it either, but it is called to critically reflect upon it. It does not want to continue to speak about God, however, without listening to this philosophical voice. Theological thought finds itself urged to wrest an ethical meaning from whatever dogmatic term of Christian tradition and doctrine it encounters. Dogma is not simply turned into an ethical axiom, but it is somehow tested in order to avoid its slipping into the realm of the ideological. I want to clarify this tenet by adding a few brush strokes to that question which over the last fifteen years has been considered intensively in German-language theology.

Characteristically, the Jewish philosopher Hans Jonas (1903–93) started a theological discussion on the possibility of comprehending the might of God as almightiness. In his essay on "The Idea of God after Auschwitz," which he read in 1984 both to the Tübingen University Protestant Faculty of Theology and to the great gathering of German Catholics in Munich, he advocated a renunciation of the almightiness of God. If after Auschwitz one wanted to hold on to the idea of the goodness and understandability of God, then one would merely arrive at an affirmation of His powerlessness. This powerlessness had to be considered as a lack of power not that had become apparent in the course of history, but that was inherent in the creative act of God. But does not the departure from the idea of power, respectively of omnipotence as connected with God, leave a gap in the pledge we made to the sufferers of the past and the dead of the Shoah? Must we—I would want to ask—really dispatch with the idea of the omnipotence of God? Do we indeed have to renounce the desire for a powerful God? Do not those who in Auschwitz have shown themselves to be just and righteous, the Saints of the Shoah, testify to the fact that the desirable, that is, the omnipotence of God, is, in the words of Emmanuel Levinas, that which "(must) be kept separate, as a matter to be desired—close, yet separate—holy"? The almightiness of God awakens our desire for it, evokes a movement toward it; and yet at the very moment when that almightiness is most needed, it seems to turn toward the other being, toward fellow-man, toward a responsibility that, as far as the Saints of the Shoah were concerned, went as far as acting in proxy for the other being. This continued separation of God's omnipotence would mean as much as His absence. It would be an "intrigue" of the all-powerful God who entrusts fellow-man to me. This "intrigue" would mean a self-limitation of God, at the same time calling Man into an unlimited responsibility for his fellow-being.[21]

The very talk about the omnipotence of God and the desire embedded in it has to pass the acid test of ethical standards. This is its meaning with regard to each respective present, unless it aimed at being a mere ethical dispensation and unable to reject in a well-reasoned manner the reproach of being ideologically inclined.

At the same time the theological term, the omnipotence of God, contains the idea of a "beyond." This "beyond" or "extra" added to the ethical dimension extends to those who cannot be reached by my responsibility for those alive today: it extends to the suffering and dead of history. The idea of "omnipotence," beyond its ethical meaning, constitutes an appeal to God's power of saving Man. It appeals to Him to work effectively and powerfully for those who need saving. Christian theology does not let go of the notion of the powerful God. In doing so, it professes a desire toward the omnipotence of God. However, it is a desire that cannot do without the acid test of ethical demands. Christian theology is asked not to console itself in the certainty of its own ethical sufficiency but to bear witness to hope existing for the other beings.[22]

* * *

Life as a theologian in the Germany of today is overshadowed by the Shoah. The theology that the theologian answers for—I have to state this quite unequivocally—does not focus its work exclusively on the Shoah. That would indeed be asking too much. It would lead into abysmal meditation and speechlessness, a temptation that still today is exercised on the life and belief of all of us by the power of the dead of Auschwitz. What is at stake is rather the entirety of the themes offered by the Christian message. Christian belief, spirituality, and existence have to be represented responsibly in view of and in all openness toward Jewish tradition and existence, Jewish historical experience and resistance. If this happens, then the Christian-Jewish relationship can be considered—in the words that Franz Rosenzweig once used—as a "bond of community and non-community."[23] Theological biography or existence with the "tumor in the memory" then experiences in a dual manner closeness and strangeness, or confidence and contradiction. No comfort can be promised, but rather an ecumenical expanse that does not betray a Christian theologian's vocation, nor leave unconnected his identity as a Christian theologian. I was able to experience this in my friendship of many years with Jakob J. Petuchowski, of blessed memory (1925–91). He presented Judaism to me as an evocation as well a provocation, as a waking call and a jolting of the spirit. He talked about Jesus as his cousin and told me about the Holy One of Israel, whom in my diction I was able to talk about as the Father of Jesus Christ without making him feel hurt.[24] Our conversation made clear from what positions of differing identity we appreciated each other as Jew and Christian. Arguing the extent of our respective modes of theological thinking, we saw new approaches and avenues of theological ways of thinking opening up. A theological existence in the shadow of the Shoah—with that "tumor in the memory"—is constantly anew *a theology from face to face.*

NOTES

The text for this chapter was translated by Hagal Mengel.

1. See for the events of the "Night of the Broken Glass" or "Black Thursday" and the public response of American Jews to the *Kristallnacht,* Haskel Lookstein, *Were We Our Brothers' Keepers? The Public Response of American Jews to the Holocaust, 1938–1944* (New York: Hartmore House, 1988), 35–80.

2. Quoted from Klaus Hemmerle, *Gemeinschaft als Bild Gottes: Beiträge zur Ekklesiologie,* vol. 5 of *Selected Writings* (Freiburg: Herder, 1996), 316.

3. For this, cf. Johann Baptist Metz, "Wem gehört die anamnetische Vernunft?" *Orientierung* 57 (1993): 241–244, or "Athen versus Jerusalem," *Orientierung* 60 (1996): 59f.; Friedrich-Wilhelm Marquardt, *Von Elend und Heimsuchung der Theologie: Prolegomena zur Dogmatik* (München: Kaiser, 1988), 151ff.

4. Thus (translated) according to Emmanuel Levinas, *Eigennamen, Meditationen über Sprache und Literatur* (München/Wien: Hanser, 1988), 101–104, 102.

5. Johann Baptist Metz, "Ökumene nach Auschwitz," in Eugen Kogon and Johann Baptist Metz, *Gott nach Auschwitz* (Freiburg: Herder, 1979), 121–144, 138; and similarly in Metz's "Im Angesicht der Juden. Christliche Theologie nach Auschwitz," *Concilium* 20 (1984): 382–389, 384.

6. Emil Fackenheim, "Die menschliche Verantwortung für die Schöpfung: Zur Aktu-

alität der Thora nach Auschwitz," in Wilhelm Breuning and Hanspeter Heinz, eds., *Damit die Erde menschlich bleibt: Gemeinsame Verantwortung von Juden und Christen für die Zukunft* (Freiburg: Herder, 1985), 86–112, 100.

7. Ibid., 159.

8. Quoted from Rolf Rendtorff and Hans Hermann Henrix, eds., *Die Kirchen und das Judentum: Dokumente von 1945 bis 1985* (Paderborn/München: Bonifatius/Kaiser, 1988), 245.

9. See "Common Declaration of the Bishops' Conferences of the German Federal Republic, of Austria and of Berlin, on the Fiftieth Anniversary of the Pogroms against the Jewish Community on the Night of 9/10 November 1938: 'Accepting the Burden of History,'" *SIDIC* 22, no. 1/2 (1989): 36–42; "Statement of the German Roman Catholic Bishops on the Occasion of the Fiftieth Anniversary of the Liberation of the Extermination Camp of Auschwitz on 27 January 1995," *SIDIC* 27, no. 1 (1995): 24f.; and Hans Hermann Henrix and Wolfgang Kraus, eds., *Die Kirchen und das Judentum: Dokumente von 1986 bis 1998* (forthcoming).

10. Commission for Religious Relations with the Jews, *We Remember: A Reflection on the Shoah* (Vatican City: 1998).

11. Emmanuel Levinas, "Ethischer Konsens und Ideologie" (unpublished manuscript), 1–5.

12. Ibid., 1.

13. Publications resulting from these meetings with E. Levinas are Hans Hermann Henrix, ed., *Verantwortung für den Anderen und die Frage nach Gott, Zum Werk von Emmanuel Levinas* (Aachen: Einhard, 1984); Breuning and Heinz; Gotthard Fuchs and Hans Hermann Henrix, *Zeitgewinn: Messianisches Denken nach Franz Rosenzweig* (Frankfurt am Main: Knecht, 1987).

14. Emmanuel Levinas, *Totalité et Infini: Essai sur l'Extériorité*, 4th ed. (Phaenomenologica 8) (The Hague: Martinus Nijhoff, 1980), 12; German edition: *Totalität und Unendlichkeit: Versuch über die Exteriorität*, trans. Wolfgang N. Krewani, 2nd ed. (Freiburg/München: Alber, 1993), 49 (hereafter TU).

15. TU, 50.

16. Marcel Poorthuis draws to our attention that the description of the subject in its serene world ownership and of its needs of water, food, sun, etc. takes up about a quarter of the phenomenological description in TU; see Buber and Levinas, "From Dialogue to Substitution," *Annales de Philosophie* 15 (1994): 51–64, 53.

17. Cf. TU, 64, and others, e.g., *Die Spur des Anderen: Untersuchungen zur Phänomenologie und Sozialphilosophie*, 2nd ed. (Freiburg/München: Alber, 1987), 221.

18. Emmanuel Levinas, "Philosophie, Gerechtigkeit und Liebe: Ein Gespräch," *Concordia* 4 (1983): 48–62, 49f.

19. Quoted from Bernhard Casper, "Denken im Angesicht des Anderen," in Henrix, *Verantwortung*, 30.

20. Emmanuel Levinas, *Wenn Gott ins Denken einfällt: Diskurse über die Betroffenheit von Transzendenz* (Freiburg/München: Alber, 1985), 101.

21. The term "intrigue," which here is applied to the omnipotence of God, can be found in Emmanuel Levinas, "Gott und die Philosophie," in Bernhard Casper, ed., *Gott nennen: Phänomenologische Zugänge* (Freiburg/München: Alber, 1981), 81–123, 104ff.

22. Cf. the unfolding of this idea in Hans Hermann Henrix, "Machtentsagung Gottes? Ein Gespräch mit Hans Jonas im Kontext der Theodizee," in Johann Baptist Metz, ed., *"Landschaft aus Schreien:" Zur Dramatik der Theodizeefrage* (Mainz: Grünewald, 1995), 118–143.

23. Thus Franz Rosenzweig in his famous letter of 31 October 1913 to his cousin

Rudolf Ehrenberg, in Franz Rosenzweig, *Briefe und Tagebücher,* vol. 1, 1900–18, of *Der Mensch und sein Werk: Gesammelte Schriften* (The Hague: Martinus Nijhoff, 1976), 132–137, 137.

24. Cf. Jakob J. Petuchowski, *Mein Judesein: Wege und Erfahrungen eines deutschen Rabbiners* (Freiburg: Herder, 1992); Jakob J. Petuchowski, "Ferner lehrten unsere Meister . . . ," *Rabbinische Geschichten aus den Quellen neu erzählt und herausgegeben* (Freiburg: Herder, 1980); Hans Hermann Henrix, "Ein Cousin Jesu," in Rudolf Walter, ed., *Das Judentum lebt—ich bin ihm begegnet: Erfahrungen von Christen* (Freiburg: Herder, 1985); Hans Hermann Henrix, "Von der Nachahmung Gottes: Heiligkeit und Heiligsein im biblischen und jüdischen Denken," in *Erbe und Auftrag* 65 (1989): 177–187.

7 The Revival of the Jewish People within the Christian Consciousness in Germany

Peter von der Osten-Sacken

To REMEMBER BELONGS to the nature of Judaism and of Christianity as well, for both communities are based on holy scriptures and on the history that is passed on in these scriptures. The history that we discuss in this volume is no holy history. It is a history of defamation and discrimination, of persecution and murder. Jews and Christians can meet each other in the pain of the memory of this history, and maybe they can really meet only this way. Still, a strong and lasting difference remains. I have visited exhibitions on the Holocaust and a concentration camp with Jewish friends. It was the same feeling every time: We are walking next to each other and with each other, but nevertheless we are walking very different ways, because in remembering we belong to different communities.

There is a feeling of this kind—even if it is a different one—when you visit an exhibition like that with a Christian friend who is not German. I am pointing this out as well, because it helps us to get closer to reality. When we ask about the preconditions of the Holocaust and about its influence on Christians, our attention is directed to the whole history of Christianity from its beginnings. In this history, just as anywhere else, there is a close relation between thinking and talking and the consequent action. But from time to time there is a difference between them. And the bitter truth is this: the Holocaust originated in Germany and was done by Germans. Therefore, you cannot speak of a direct, unavoidable relation between Christianity and the Holocaust, though there is no doubt that the Holocaust would not have been possible without the traditional Christian hostility toward the Jews.

The question about the impact of the Holocaust on Christians therefore refers especially to the following questions: What image or what understanding of Judaism did Christians in Germany gain in the aftermath of the Holocaust, and what conclusions did they draw from this understanding?

* * *

In his article "Christianity" in the *Encyclopaedia Judaica*, R. J. Zwi Werblowsky described the *traditional* Christian image of Judaism as follows:

The doctrine that the "Law" . . . had now lost its validity; that in Christ it had been "fulfilled," i.e. terminated, surpassed, and to all practical purposes abrogated; and that the order of Grace had now [through Jesus Christ] come in place of that of the Law—all these combined with the Gospel accounts of Jesus' harsh attacks on the Pharisees as hypocrites or as representatives of a mechanical religion of outward devotion . . . [created] a climate of hostility and a negative Christian image of Judaism. The image implied that *theologically* Judaism was an inferior religion, *historically* the Jewish religion had played out its positive role, and *morally* the Jews were examples of stubborn blindness and obduracy. Even at its best, i.e. in its biblical phase, Israel had been rebellious and had persecuted its prophets, and its Law—albeit divine—was but a preparatory discipline . . . [To summarize, post-biblical Judaism was caricatured] as a dead, petrified, or fossilized religion without spiritual vitality and dynamism.[1]

Judaism as a dead and fossilized religion: it is this motif that leads to the theological core of the problem of Christian hostility toward the Jews. Thus, what characterizes the Christian attitude over centuries can be looked at as a kind of death sentence for Judaism. This death sentence appears in a form that qualifies Judaism only as a pure entity of the past, which has lost any significant presence. I would like to give a few examples.

Problematic beginnings can be found in the New Testament. The apostle Paul defines the service of Israel as "service of death."[2] Besides that, he also has a word of life and future for Israel.[3] But the leading word "death" has persisted in Christian tradition. In a depressing way this is expressed in the Easter sermon of the bishop Melito of Sardis in Asia Minor in the second century. In front of his Christian assembly, he accuses the Jewish community, in their absence, by saying: "You dashed down the Lord, [therefore] you were dashed down to the ground. And [now] you lie dead."[4]

A Bible illustration from the fifteenth century may stand for the Middle Ages. The image shows the funeral of the synagogue. It lies dead in a coffin, the tables of the covenant in its hand, surrounded by Jesus Christ and the crowned Ecclesia.[5]

Amy Newman found the same theme with Martin Luther in the sixteenth century and famous personalities of German history such as Kant, Schleiermacher, and Hegel in the eighteenth and nineteenth centuries. In an article entitled "The Death of Judaism in German Protestant Thought from Luther to Hegel" she shows how deeply the conception of Judaism as a dead entity had influenced the thinking of theologians and philosophers in eighteenth- and nineteenth-century Germany.[6] Such death sentences can be found up to the time of the rise of the Nazi regime. As late as 1929, a Protestant church leader welcomed the participants of a Jewish Mission Assembly with the words "The only Jew who has the right to exist before World History is the baptized Jew, the Jew who follows Jesus, but the Jew who rejects Jesus has no right to exist anymore."[7]

One may hope that this church leader was deeply scared when he later experienced what it meant when a group had no right to exist anymore. No matter how literally or symbolically he actually meant his words, the cited judgment shows clearly how flowing the transition is from religious hostility toward Jews to life-threatening anti-Semitism. Christians who were listening to those voices of Christian teachers and leaders had to get the impression that if something happened to the Jews, then they deserved it.

I would like to point out that there were examples of Christians and Jews living naturally as neighbors and that there were other Christian voices than those quoted above. They still existed when the Jewish Germans were beginning to be discriminated against by the government and had their rights taken away in 1933. One of these Christians was Marga Meusel, a leading social worker in the Protestant church. In 1935 she was asked by a dean of the Confessing Church to write a memorandum about the situation of the baptized Jews in Germany.[8] She did not limit the memorandum to the Christians of Jewish descent, but included all Jews in Germany. Contrary to the Nazi doctrine, she called the Jews a "part of our people." She labeled what had happened since 1933 a vehement persecution and a screaming injustice. Through this injustice, Marga Meusel wrote, the Christian-minded people had—already in 1935!—burdened themselves with a heavy guilt, which would last for generations. She proved with many examples from newspapers what she summarized: "In the name of blood and race, the atmosphere in Germany has constantly and strategically been poisoned for the last two years by hate, lies, defamation, humiliations of the lowest kind in speeches, proclamations, magazines, and daily press in order to turn people into willing tools of persecution."[9] Finally, she made demands about what had to be done. The memorandum was to be discussed in two synods of the Confessing Church. But it was left closed and undiscussed—probably for fear of governmental consequences.[10]

I did not choose this example for any apologetical reasons; just the opposite. It shows that there were a few who, as Christians, named the truth, although they remained unheard of. Marga Meusel later worked in the well-known Grüber office and died in 1953.

* * *

With that, I come back to the tradition that I call the Christian death sentence for Judaism. It is a characteristic of all of these judgments that they have nothing or nearly nothing to do with existing Judaism. Just the opposite: they are dogmatic or ideological judgments. They deny a legitimate presence of the Jewish people by declaring it dead in the name of the Christian message. It is this Christian attitude toward Judaism that kept Judaism from being perceived as an entity with its own rights and significance. Considering this, the Christian relationship to Judaism before and after the Holocaust can only be described as paradox, if not as absurd. For there was an extremely lively, diverse, and rich Jewish life in Germany. But only a few Christians realized the Jewish community in its significance as a living reality, as a factor that belonged to and carried society as others did. Only when in the years 1933 to 1945—as Paul Celan said—"Death proved to be a Master in Germany," only after all the mental and physical murders of this time, when there were almost no Jews left in Europe, only then people began to realize and accept the Jewish existence as a living reality of the present.

It is this context and this reality that I meant by the word "paradox." The title of my lecture, "The Revival of the Jewish People within the Christian Consciousness in Germany," relates to this context. This revival has different forms and contents. It includes the perception of the diverse life of the small Jewish communities in Germany itself. Revival of the Jewish people within the Christian consciousness also includes phenomena that are not directly related to the existence of a community in the neighborhood: a new approach to Jewish religion, culture, and history. It seems to be most important that a process of reversal has begun on the Christian side. The arrogant doctrine that God has rejected his people seems to be an idea of the past. It made room for the rediscovered certainty of the lasting election of Israel as God's people. To put it differently: Judaism is a community in its own right, which is not primarily to be perceived and judged by its attitude toward Christianity, even though Christianity has a special relationship to the Jewish people.

* * *

What I have said about the keyword of "revival"—is it reality or is it an idealization of Christian reality in Germany? Maybe it is close to the truth to say that there are a number of important statements issued by churches and denominations. There are important beginnings in respect to Christian-Jewish encounters. Particularly among the younger generations there is a significant religious rethinking and a recognizable wish to renew the Christian-Jewish relationship. During the last twenty years more than four hundred students of theology have studied a whole year in Israel within a program dedicated to the renewal of the relationship between Christians and Jews—to give just one example. At the same time, it is no secret that for the Jewish part, there are still many considerable deficits and disappointments. All in all: For a long time, what has to be done will be a lot more than what has already been done and achieved. Instead of naming further examples, I would like to go a different way.

I believe that as a Christian, one has to ask oneself a main question. How would I answer if Jews asked me the essential question: Can we trust you, can we trust you now? I think it will be possible only after three to four more generations to answer this question without hesitation, because the lasting verification of a different relationship between Christians and Jews is still ahead of us. Today, I would like to answer the question "Can we trust you now?" with a short text. One could call it a story of hope and silent grievance, and therefore it seems to fit particularly our situation. It is the end of an unpublished report written by Emil Fackenheim. He wrote it after he taught at different universities in Germany in 1997. At the end of this time, during the 6th Christian-Jewish Summer University held in Berlin, he lived in painful proximity to the place of the former Hochschule für die Wissenschaft des Judentums (College for the Science of Judaism). That is where he himself had studied and where he had seen many of his murdered college friends for the last time. Emil Fackenheim writes at the end of his report—and I thank him for his approval to let me cite these sentences:

> Two things will remain with me for whatever I shall still say or write. The first is the image of the Holocaust as a huge mountain between Jews and Germans. Faith is supposed to move mountains but this mountain needs to be picked up and thrown into the deepest of the sea and even God can't do that. Nor can we get around the mountain by changing the subject to the Gulag or anything else. But it happened to me a couple of times that, as if by angels' wings, I and a German flew over the mountain.
>
> The second thing is that I got clear on Jewish post-Holocaust theology: it cannot either trivialize God or trivialize the Holocaust victims. This will fragment Jewish faith for who knows how long, but I have yet to understand how a post-Holocaust Christian theology can fail to be equally fragmented.[11]

NOTES

Translated into English by my daughter Stella and Christoph Kock. Basic aspects of this essay can be found in expanded form in my article "Christliche Theologie nach Auschwitz," in M. Görg and M. Langer, eds., *Als Gott weinte. Theologie nach Auschwitz* (Regensburg: Verlag Friedrich Pustet, 1997), 12–29.

1. R. J. Zwi Werblowsky, "Christianity," in *Encyclopaedia Judaica*, vol. 5, 508, 513 (italics are mine).

2. 2 Cor. 3:7.

3. Cf. Rom. 9–11.

4. Melito of Sardis, *On Pascha and Fragments: Texts and Translations*, ed. St. G. Hall (Oxford: Clarendon Press, 1979), 57, §§ 99f., lines 743–745.

5. *Bible moralisée*, Paris, Bibliotheque Nationale, Cod fr 166, fol 40v; cf. *Katalog für die Ausstellung 'Judentum im Mittelalter' im Schloß Halbturn Burgenland* (Eisenstadt: Kulturabteilung des Amtes der Burgenländischen Landesregierung, 1978), fig. 26.

6. Amy Newman, "The Death of Judaism in German Protestant Thought from Luther to Hegel," *Journal of the American Academy of Religion* 61 (1993): 455–484.

7. Hans Schöttler, cited by E. Albert, "Eine für die Judenmission bedeutsame Tagung," *Der Messiasbote* (1929, no. 4): 3. Schöttler held high-ranking church positions in Königsberg (1912–17) and Magdeburg (beginning in 1917).

8. In fact, she was asked for two memoranda, the first for the Augsburg synod in June, the second for the Steglitz (Berlin) synod in September 1935. The short account above is related to the second one: M. Meusel, "Zur Lage der deutschen Nichtarier," in W. Niemöller,

ed., *Die Synode zu Steglitz: Geschichte—Dokumente—Berichte* (Göttingen/Zürich: Vandenhoeck and Ruprecht, 1970), 29–58. For biographical notes see H. Ludwig, "Die Opfer unter dem Rad verbinden. Vor- und Entstehungsgeschichte, Arbeit und Mitarbeiter des 'Büro Pfarrer Grüber'" (Habil.-Schrift, Humboldt-Universität, Berlin, 1988), 32ff. For the previous history of both memoranda, their "fate," and their recognition from a historical point of view cf. Ludwig, 32–34; W. Gerlach, *Als die Zeugen schwiegen. Bekennende Kirche und die Juden,* rev. and exp. ed. (Berlin: Institut Kirche und Judentum, 1993), 129–145, 156–159; and E. Röhm and J. Thierfelder, *Juden—Christen—Deutsche,* vol. 1: 1933–1935 (Stuttgart: Calwer Verlag, 1990), 337–346 (first memorandum); vol. 2, pt. 1: 1935–1938 (Stuttgart: Calwer Verlag, 1992), 44f., 188–196 (second memorandum).

9. Meusel, 31.

10. Cf. Gerlach, 158.

11. Emil Fackenheim, "Sum-Up about a Three Months' Visit in Germany" (unpublished report, 1997).

An Alternative for Christian Substitution Theology and Christology after the Shoah

8

Bertold Klappert

In 1966, Karl Barth, the leader of the Confessional Church during the Nazi era, who was expelled from Germany to Switzerland in 1935 and who drafted "The Barmen Declaration" in 1934, which Irving Greenberg characterized as "a system of absolute alternative values to the Nazi system,"[1] made a famous statement to the Vatican in Rome, one year after Vatican II: "There is only one great ecumenical question: our [the Church's] relationship with Judaism."

The Road to Auschwitz

The Tradition of Elimination and Substitution Christology

Since the second century C.E. the Church has developed and later implemented ways of dealing with Israel-Judaism that can be described in four short formulas:

(a) *The Church is the substitution of Israel:* the transcendental Christ of the Church stands in contrast to the Messianic hope of Judaism.

(b) *The Church integrates Israel:* the Church is grounded in Israel, but Israel's destiny is to be integrated into the Church (P. Althaus).

(c) *The Church is superior to Israel:* she is the new universal, spiritual and eschatological people of God, the spiritual Israel vis à vis the "Israel of the flesh" (M. Luther).

(d) *Israel serves as a negative foil to the Church:* the Church represents the gospel of grace ("Evangelium"), Israel is the image of failure and judgment ("Gesetz").[2]

Even after the horror of the Shoah, the Church continues to make use of this substitutional tradition. Arthur Rubinstein experienced this tradition when coming to Germany and meeting Probst Grüber after the war in 1961. In 1948, the Bekennende Kirche in Deutschland (Confessional Church in Germany) published a declaration concerning the "Jewish question."[3] This declaration summarized the results of genuine Protestant theology, because theologians were involved here who had fought honestly against Hitler and who had not belonged to the "Deutsche Christen" (German Christians). I will select some propositions from that document:

(a) "When the Son of God was born as a Jew, the election and destiny of Israel were fulfilled." The term "fulfillment" is used here in a substitutional way.

(b) "Israel, having crucified (Israel's) Messiah, rejected its election and destiny." That means: In contrast to the New Testament, it is said here, Israel crucified its Messiah and did this in full consciousness of what it was doing.

(c) "Since the coming of Christ and because of him, Israel's election has been passed over to the universal Church of humankind."

(d) After Auschwitz, German theologians still dare to say: "The judgment of God manifested against Israel till today is a sign of God's patience."[4]

That means: the Shoah is proclaimed to be God's judgment over Israel rather than being recognized as a tremendous sign of God's judgment against the Church.

As far as I know, there was, on the German Protestant side, only one early and sensitive theological echo to Auschwitz, which was put forward in 1947 in the German weekly *Die Zeit* (14 August 1947) on Eugen Kogon's book *Der SS-Staat*.[5] This book was summarized in a letter by Iwand, a close friend of the Rabbi R. R. Geis, which he wrote to the Czech theologian Josef Hromádka in 1959. Iwand professes and confesses there:

> Next to the other alarming failures of the Confessional Church vis à vis the social and the peace question, we have to name the Jewish question, which makes us restless until today. We didn't see clearly enough that the attack against the Jews was directed against Him, Jesus Christ Himself. Theologically, we were holding on to the *humanity of Jesus Christ,* but that this human being was *a Jew,* we declared (with Luther, Melanchthon, Hegel and Schleiermacher) to be irrelevant according to *a universal humanism.* We didn't realize that the uprooting of the Church from Israel means the Church's loss of ecumenism.

Iwand adds the question of the Church's and academic theology's guilt:

> Who is going to take this guilt away from us and our theological fathers— because there it started? . . . How can the German people that has initiated the fruitless rebellion against Israel and his God become pure? Do you understand that this question arises as soon as we start digging a little deeper?[6]

The Never-Renounced Covenant between God and Israel

The Church as Partaker of the Reformulated Covenant of Israel

In 1942, Karl Barth finished his *Doctrine of the Election,* which he published in the year of the Wannsee conference. In §34 of the *Church Dogmatics,* Barth puts forward the astounding thesis of the election of the *one* congregation in the two forms of Israel and the Church.[7] He published his doctrine of reconciliation in 1953. There he presents the brief thesis: "God's Covenant with His people of Israel is as such 'the fundament and condition for the reconciliation of the world in Christ.'"[8] The word "condition" must be understood here not just in the ordinary sense of the term but also axiomatically: the reconciliation of the world with God in Jesus Christ (God reconciling Israel and the world of the non-Jews, the reconciliation in Christ crucified) is based upon God's one uncanceled and undismissed Covenant with Israel.

Here is dismissed the early anti-Judaistic thesis of Barnabas (2nd century C.E.): "Israel's covenant is not ours" (Barnabas 4:6b–8). Here is repeated and rediscovered the more early confession of the New Testament Christianity: The never renounced and never canceled covenant between the God of Israel and the people of Israel is also ours![9]

This relationship of Israel and the Church from the perspective of the theology of the one Covenant has been continued after Auschwitz, on the Protestant side, by Walther Zimmerli and has especially been referred to in modern Catholic exegesis. I think of Erich Zenger's book *Das erste Testament* (The First Testament, 1991),[10] his article "Israel und die Kirche in dem einen Gottesbund" (Israel and the Church in the One Covenant of God),[11] and the book *Der niemals gekündigte Bund* (*The Never Canceled Covenant*) by Norbert Lohfink, published in 1989.[12]

The Old Testament scholars Lohfink and Zenger point out that the biblical concept of the Covenant offers a starting point to relate the Church to Israel. As examples, Zenger refers to the *Rheinische Synodalbeschluß* of 1980 and the Resolution of the *Reformierter Bund* (Reformed Church Alliance) of 1990, formulated by the Hebrew Bible scholar H.-J. Kraus, a close friend of R. R. Geis, German rabbi and student of Leo Baeck: "God did not dismiss His Covenant with Israel. We are beginning to realize: in Jesus Christ all of us— human beings from the world of non-Jesus, by our origin far away from the God of Israel and His people of Israel—are honoured and called to participate in God's Covenant with Israel (Eph 2:11ff)."[13]

While being transported to the concentration camp in Theresienstadt in 1943, Leo Baeck (1873–1956), "the Shepherd of the Persecuted,"[14] the impressive figure and representative of German Judaism during the Nazi period, wrote the following: "In the one Covenant, comprising all [humanity] (open for all [humanity]), valid for them all, the Jewish people stands on earth."[15]

Following this tradition of Leo Baeck, following his theology of God's *one* Covenant with Israel, open and opened also for the non-Jews, and following Irving Greenberg's reformulation of the covenant vis-à-vis the divine and human responsibility, in the sense of heightening the role of human responsibility, the Rhinish Protestant Synod confessed in 1980, in the presence of Prof. Y. Ashkenazy (Amsterdam), prisoner in Auschwitz, Zwi Werblowsky (Jerusalem), and E. Brocke (Essen):

- We confess with dismay the co-responsibility and guilt of the German Church for the Holocaust.
- We believe in the permanent election of the Jewish people as the people of God and realize that through Jesus Christ the church is taken into the covenant of God with His people.
- Therefore we declare:
  Throughout centuries the word "new" has been used in biblical exegesis against the Jewish people: the new covenant was understood in contrast to the old covenant, the new people of God as replacement of the old people of God. This disrespect for the permanent election of the Jewish people and its condemnation to non-existence marked Christian theology, the preaching and work of the church again and again right to the present day. Thereby we have made ourselves guilty also of the physical elimination of the Jewish people.[16]

A Christology of Jesus the Jew

A Christology of Teshuva

What does a christology of Teshuva mean? It means the Christian confession to Jesus the Jew.

In his extensive christological and eschatological concept (six volumes!) Fr.-W. Marquardt declares programmatically: "It is important that Jesus of Nazareth remains the only issue in christology. To keep that in mind we have decided to move Jesus as Jew to the centre of this christology."[17]

In his commemoration speech to remember the murdered and the liberation of the concentration camp of Auschwitz fifty-three years ago, Prof. Yehuda Bauer, the director of the International Research Institute for Holocaust Studies in Yad Vashem, Jerusalem, asked in the German Bundestag on 27 January 1998:

What is the uniqueness of the Shoah?
Is it the brutality and the sadism?
Is it the modern technology and bureaucracy?
Is it the genocide (look at the Armenian genocide!)?
No, I think for the first time in history all men and women, descending from—in this case Jewish grandfathers and grandmothers—were sentenced to death, simply because they were born as Jews. Simply being born was a dead-sin, which had to be penalized by death. This has never happened before!

This is the context of Marquardt's christology: the decision to move Jesus the Jew, simply because he was born as a Jew, into the center of christology.

The theology of the unrenounced, uncanceled, but nevertheless reformulated covenant (I. Greenberg) and the rediscovery of the confession to Jesus the Jew, who unites humankind, the non-Jews, with Israel, the chosen people of

God, suggest and imply (a) a christology of Teshuva on the one hand and (b) a christology of the pilgrimage of the non-Jews to Zion on the other hand.

A CHRISTOLOGY OF TESHUVA AWAY FROM A SUBSTITUTION CHRISTOLOGY

In 1980, the Synod of the Protestant Church of Rhineland, the biggest church of the member-churches in Germany, adopted a statement toward a renewal and renovation of the relationship of the Christians to the Jews:

> The Synod of the Evangelical Church in the Rhineland accepts the historical necessity of attaining a new relationship of the church to the Jewish people and is brought to this by four factors:
> (1) The recognition of Christian co-responsibility and guilt for the Holocaust—the defamation, persecution and murder of the Jews in the Third Reich.
> (2) The new biblical insights concerning the continuing significance of the Jewish people within the history of God (e.g. Rom. 9–11), which have been attained in connection with the struggle of the Confessing Church.
> (3) The insights that a) the continuing existence of the Jewish people, b) its return to the land of promise, and also c) the foundation of the state of Israel, are signs of the faithfulness of God towards His people.
> (4) The readiness of Jews, in spite of the Holocaust, to (engage in) encounter, common study and cooperation.

A CHRISTOLOGY OF THE PILGRIMAGE OF THE NON-JEWS TO ZION

If, with Leo Baeck, we speak of the one, never renounced, never canceled Covenant of Israel's God with His people of Israel, and if we speak, with L. Baeck,[18] D. Flusser, and C. Thoma,[19] of the New Testament christology located within the Jewish-Messianic hope, then consequences are implied and a task is given to us, which still lies ahead of us all and which is a test for a real Teshuvah that moves away from our tradition of a substitutional christology.

I am talking about the New Testament christology of the relation of the non-Jews to Israel, of "the pilgrimage of the Gentiles to Mount Zion." It is not—as expected by the Church and formulated by her theologians in general—a christology of the pilgrimage of the Synagogue into the universal Church of mankind (W. Pannenberg[20]). The Lutheran theologian Paul Althaus pointed out during the Nazi era: "It is the destiny of Israel to be incorporated into the Church."

A christology of Teshuvah confesses and hopes just the opposite: It is the destiny of the Church (Rom. 11:17, 25: remember the "eiselthein"!) to be re-rooted in Judaism and to practice and to teach a christology within the prophetic promise of the pilgrimage of the Gentiles to Zion.[21]

At this point, I am referring to a study and memorandum of the Evangelische Kirche in Deutschland (Protestant Church in Germany, EKD) from

1991. The decisive contribution within this memorandum was written by the Hebrew Bible scholar Rolf Rendtorff. He discusses the relationship between Israel and the nations according to the Hebrew Bible: "Israel *is* God's people."

According to Rendtorff and the Catholic scholar N. Lohfink, the main issue of the relationship between Israel and the non-Jews is the *promise of the pilgrimage of the Gentiles to Mount Zion:* "It is expected that one day the nations will join universally in Israel's service, to praise the God of Israel together with Israel, moving on to Mount Zion on a great universal pilgrimage to hear the Torah, the word of the true God" (Isa. 2:2–4).[22]

The God of Israel and the Torah of Israel

An Ecclesiology of Teshuva

As far as the New Testament is concerned, the God of Israel and the people of Israel are inseparable.

Israel's God is the God who lives among and with His people of Israel, who accompanies His people. Hence, all the nations are destined to join in the praise with Israel, praising Israel's God: "Praise God, all Gentiles, praise him along *with* His people" (Rom. 15:10 = Deut. 32:43, LXX). That is why all christological statements in the New Testament are ultimately completed by theocentric statements: Christ, the promised Messiah, serves Israel's God and His people (Rom. 15:7ff.); bowing the knees in the name of Jesus Christ ultimately serves the honor of Israel's God (Phil. 2:11). God's dwelling among His people of Israel—Christ's historical origins—leads Paul not to the praise of Jesus as God (Lutheran translation along with the Vulgate) but to the praise of Israel's God: "God who is over all be blessed forever! Amen!" (Rom. 9:5).

God's dwelling with and among His people of Israel[23] is the presupposition for God's indwelling in Christ (Col. 1:19).

"God in Christ—reconciling the world" (2 Cor. 5:19) therefore cannot be turned into "Christ is God." This is the border between a dangerous and problematic deification of Jesus on the one hand and the proclamation of God's indwelling and incarnation in Christ, the Son of God, on the other hand.

According to the Hebrew Bible, the Talmud, and the New Testament, Israel and the Church are God's witnesses to God's coming into the world. Together, Israel and the Church serve the coming of God's kingdom and His justice (Matt. 6:3), and, therefore, they both keep alive the hope for the coming kingdom (*olam ha ba*) and the new creation of heaven and earth, where justice dwells (2 Pet. 3:13). So we need not only a new definition of *evil,* as Saul Friedländer has argued deeply and convincingly in his contribution to this volume. We need also a new definition of *justice,* as M. Horkheimer said: that the murderer shall not triumph always and ultimately over his victim.

An ecclesiology of Teshuva toward the God of Israel and His chosen people of Israel implies at once the lasting relevance of the Torah, because the triad "God of Israel—people of Israel—Torah of Israel" is inseparable. Therefore, the relation of the Church as an ecumenical people of God consisting of all nations (Acts 15:14) to Israel as the remaining and first-chosen people of God (Rom. 9:4), is not possible without the question of the validity of the never canceled Torah. According to a midrash on Deuteronomy, the Torah was offered to all people. They all refused; only Israel accepted.[24]

If Christ must be seen not as the abrogation or substitution, but on the contrary as the fulfillment and establishment (Hebrew: heqim) of the validity of the Torah, then the demands of the Torah are also valid for the non-Jews (cf. Rom. 8:4; 10:4), then the Sermon on the Mount is an interpretation of the Torah for all the nations (Matt. 5–7; 28:16–20). What is good for Israel, that is, the Torah of Israel's God, is also good for the Church as the ecumenical people of all nations. What is good about the Torah, namely, the demands of justice and of love, should be memorized by the Church, in learning from and together with Israel. For the Church community to be on the way with Israel implies learning from Israel's Torah.

In his commemoration speech to remember the liberation of the concentration camp of Auschwitz fifty-three years ago, Prof. Yehuda Bauer said in the German Bundestag on 27 January 1998:

> In the Hebrew Bible are the ten commandments. Maybe, we should add three more commandments after the Shoah:
> 11. You, your children and grandchildren should never become *committers* (of such crimes),
> 12. You, your children and grandchildren should never become *victims* (of such crimes),
> 13. You, your children and grandchildren should never be passive *bystanders* of mass murder and genocide and on Holocaust-like tragedies.[25]

Therefore it is wrong—along with the Lutheran ecclesiastical and theological tradition—to define the "gospel as free from the law" (*gesetzesfreies Evangelium*). Rather, it is necessary to define the "gospel for the non-Jews as free from circumcision" (*beschneidungsfreies Evangelium*, K. Berger),[26] and at the same time it is necessary to learn from the Torah in the Hebrew Bible and in the Talmud. That is the way of discipleship: to ask about the sanctification of God's name and about the doing of the divine will of justice (Zedakah) as God's instruction for our entire life: "That we Christians cannot participate in Israel's Covenant with God free of charge, is something we should have known for a long time from the commentary on the Torah which Jesus gave through the Sermon of the Mount, and from his own biography" (E. Zenger).[27]

Epilogue: Do Not Forget the "With"!

The shadow of Christian and of the churches' anti-Judaism and anti-Semitism is long and also after the Shoah still present and imminent. Let me give a few examples:

- In 1995, thirteen professors of the Theological Faculty of the University of Göttingen issued a statement pleading for the Christian mission vis-à-vis the Jewish people (Plädoyer für die "Judenmission").
- A representative of the WCC and of a world-mission board to whom I spoke about my participation at this Holocaust conference said to me spontaneously: The Holocaust is to be blamed on the Jews during the Nazi era. Look at the policy of the State of Israel against the Palestinians up to today!
- An Old Testament scholar at the University of Bonn speaks and pleads for a theology of the broken covenant with the following argument: If the covenant between God and Israel is not broken (Leo Baeck speaks of the never renounced and canceled covenant between the God of Israel and the chosen people of Israel), we can't believe anymore and teach anymore the New Covenant in Christ.
- A declaration by the Lutheran churches (VELKD) and Protestant churches (EKU) in Germany in 1996—protesting against the Christian-Jewish dialogue on the basis of the never broken covenant of God with His people of Israel—not only speaks in the old anti-Judaistic categories of "law and gospel" ("Gesetz und Evangelium"), of the old and new covenant ("alter und neuer Bund"), but argues also that Jesus is *historically* speaking a Jew, but *theologically* relevant is only that he is the representative of humanity and humankind (vere homo, true and genuine human being instead of vere Judaeus). In other and drastic terminology: As the music of Beethoven is not based on the fact that Beethoven was born in Bonn, so the worldwide impact of Jesus on humankind and humanity is not related to the fact that Jesus was a Jew.

Hans Joachim Iwand, a theologian of the Confessional Church and a close friend of the German Rabbi R. R. Geis and of Karl Barth, was the first to summarize in a short Pentecost-meditation on Ephesians 2:11: "You non-Jews, do not forget the 'with'; you are implanted branches. How can you live without the root?" Do not forget the "with"![28]

That we—the ecumenical Church of all nations (as the Catholic scholar Fr. Mußner insisted, referring to Rom. 11:27)[29]—will become fellow heirs and partakers of Israel's (after the Shoah, reformulated) Covenant with the heightened role of the human partner and human responsibility (I. Greenberg), this would indeed be an alternative to our traditional substitution theology and substitution christology.

DO NOT FORGET THE "WITH"! Teshuva of the Church would imply this, and out of it could follow a new identity of the Church related to the Jews, not eliminating the Jews and the Jewish people.

This new identity of the Church could and would also have a big *social and political* impact on German society. The alternative, which Victoria Barnett mentioned for all our societies—based on a new relation of the Church to Judaism and based on the rediscovery of the relevance of the Torah of

Israel—is also very relevant for Germany: Does the German people try to find its identity in *ethnic terms* (a non-Jewish or non-Islamic orientation) or in *democratic and cultural* terms? The former German chancellor W. Brandt, Nobel Peace Prize winner, and our famous President G. Heinemann, member of the Confessional Church in Barmen in 1934, tried to teach and convince the German people to choose the democratic-constitutional and cultural option.[30]

NOTES

1. I. Greenberg, "Cloud of Smoke, Pillar and Fire: Judaism, Christianity, and Modernity after the Holocaust," in E. Fleischner, ed., *Auschwitz: Beginning of a New Era? Reflections on the Holocaust* (KTAV Publishing House, 1974), 29.

2. Bertold Klappert, *Israel und die Kirche: Erwägungen zur Israellehre Karl Barths*, Theologische Existenz Heute (München: Kaiser, 1980), 14ff.

3. Richard L. Rubinstein, *After Auschwitz* (New York: Macmillan, 1966), 46ff.; Rolf Rendtorff and Hans Hermann Henrix, eds., *Die Kirchen und das Judentum: Dokumente von 1945 bis 1985* (Paderborn/München: Verlag Bonifatius, 1988), 540–544.

4. Evangelische Kirche im Rheinland (ed.), *Handreichung Nr. 39* (Düsseldorf, 1980), S. 9.

5. Eugen Kogon, *Der SS-Staat: Das System der Deutschen Konzentrationslager* (Frankfurt am Main: Europäische Verlagsanstalt, 1946).

6. Hans Joachim Iwand, "Antwort. Ein Brief an Josef L. Hromádka," in *Frieden mit dem Osten. Texte 1933–1959* (München: Kaiser, 1988), 206.

7. Karl Barth, *Church of Dogmatics*, II/2 (Edinburgh: Clark, 1961–1971), 195. Hereafter cited as *CD*.

8. *CD*, IV/1, §57:1, 6.

9. K. Backhaus, *Gottes nicht bereuter Bund* (München: Gütersloh Verlagshaus, 1993); E. Busch, *Unter dem Bogen des einen Bundes. Karl Barth und die Juden, 1933–1945* (Neukirchen: Neukirchener Verlag, 1997).

10. Erich Zenger, *Das erste Testament. Die jüdische Bibel und die Christen* (Düsseldorf: Patmos, 1992).

11. Erich Zenger, "Israel und die Kirche in dem einen Gottesbund?" *Kirche und Israel. Neukirchener Theologische Zeitschrift* 6 (1991): 99–114.

12. Norbert Lohfink, *Der niemals gekündigte Bund. Exegetische Gedanken zum christlich-jüdischen Gespräch* (Freiburg: Herder, 1989).

13. Zenger, "Israel und die Kirche," 111.

14. Leonard Baker, *Der Hirt der Verfolgten. Leo Baeck im Dritten Reich* (Stuttgart: Kohlhammer, 1982).

15. Leo Baeck, *This People Israel: The Meaning of Jewish Existence* (New York: Holt, Rinehart and Winston, 1965), 71.

16. "Synod of the Protestant Church of Rhineland (Germany)," in World Council of Churches, ed., *The Theology of the Church and the Jewish People*, trans. F. H. Litell and B. Klappert (Geneva, 1982), 92ff., 93.

17. Fr.-W. Marquardt, *Das christliche Bekenntnis zu Jesus, dem Juden. Eine Christologie*, vol. 1 (München, 1990), 47.

18. Leo Baeck, *Das Evangelium als Urkunde jüdischer Glaubensgeschichte*, Bücherei des Schocken-Verlags, vol. 87 (Berlin: Schocken, 1938).

19. D. Flusser, "Der jüdische Ursprung der Christologie," in *Bemerkungen eines Juden*

zur christlichen Theologie (München: Christian Kaiser Verlag, 1984), 54–65; C. Thoma, *Das Messiasprodukt* (Augsburg: Pattloch Verlag, 1994), 134.

20. Wolfhart Pannenberg, "Church (of mankind) and Israel," in *Systematic Theology* (Grand Rapids, Mich.: W. B. Eerdmans, 1993), vol. 3, 509ff.

21. Bertold Klappert, "Eine Christologie der Völkerwallfahrt zum Zion," in *Jesusbekenntnis und Christusnachfolge,* Kaiser Traktate 115, ed. M. Stöhr (München: Kaiser, 1992), 65–93.

22. Evangelische Kirche Deutschland, ed., *Zur theologischen Neuorientierung im Verhältnis zum Judentum. Eine Studie der Evangelische Kirche in Deutschland, Christen und Juden,* vol. 2 (Gütersloh: Verlagshaus Gerd Mohn Gütersloh, 1991), 38.

23. Michael Wyschogrod, *The Body of Faith: Judaism as Corporeal Election* (New York: Seabury Press, 1983).

24. Jacob Josef Petuchowski, "Es lehrten unsere Meister," in *Rabbinische Geschichten* (Freiburg: Herder, 1979), 84ff.

25. *Des Parlament* no. 2, February 1998, Bonn S. 28.

26. Klaus Berger, "Heiden, Heidenchristentum," in *Evangelisches Kirchenlexikon,* vol. 2 (Göttingen: Vandenhoek and Ruprecht, 1989), 408.

27. Zenger, "Israel und die Kirche," 111.

28. H. J. Iwand, *Predigtmeditationen,* vol. 1 (Göttingen: Christian Kaiser Verlag, 1977), 20–23.

29. Fr. Mußner, *Traktat über die Juden* (München: 1979).

30. G. Heinemann, *Unser Grundgesetz ist ein großes Angebot. Rechtspolitische Schriften* (München: Christian Kaiser Verlag, 1989); idem, *Glaubensfreiheit—Bürgerfreiheit. Kirche—Staat—Gesellschaft. 1945–1975* (München: G. Heinemann, 1990).

WORKS CITED

Baeck, L. *Das Wesen des Judentums* [The Essence of Judaism]. 1926. *Leo Baeck-Werkausgabe,* Bd I, ed. A. H. Friedländer and B. Klappert. München: Gütersloh Verlagshaus, 1998.
———. *Dieses Volk. Jüdische Existenz 1955/1957-. Leo Baeck-Werkausgabe,* Bd II, ed. A. H. Friedländer and B. Klappert. München: G. Heinemann, 1996.
Bauer, Y. *Gedenkrede zur Befreiung des Vernichtungslagers Auschwitz (27.1.1945) im Deutschen Bundestag am 27.1.1998.*
Colijn, G. J., and M. Sachs Littell (eds.). *From Prejudice to Destruction: Western Civilization in the Shadow of Auschwitz.* Selected papers of the 1994 conference "Remembering for the Future II," Berlin, 13–17 March 1994, 1995.
Deselaers, M. *"Und sie hatten nie Gewissensbisse?" Die Biografie von Rudolf Höß, Kommandant von Auschwitz.* Leipzig: Benno, 1997.
Fleischner, E. (ed.). *Auschwitz, Beginning of a New Era? Reflections on the Holocaust.* New York: KTAV, 1976.
Geldbach, E. (Hg.). *Vom Vorurteil zur Vernichtung? "Erinnern" für morgen.* Munster: Lit, 1995.
Ginzel, G. B. (ed.). *Auschwitz als Herausforderung für Juden und Christen.* Heidelberg: L. Schneider, 1980.
Pollefeyt, D. (ed.). *Jews and Christians: Rivals or Partners for the Kingdom of God? In Search of an Alternative for the Theology of Substitution.* Louvain: Peeters Press, 1997.
World Council of Churches (eds.). *The Theology of the Churches and the Jewish People: Statements by the WCC and Its Member Churches.* Geneva: WCC, 1988.

9

After Sixty Years—How Can We Speak of Guilt, Suffering, and Reconcilation?

Hanspeter Heinz

As a German theologian, I consider it a precious gift to have as friends Jewish thinkers with whom I can explore Jewish and Christian history. I am thinking here primarily about the issues of guilt, suffering, and reconciliation. For me the most important place for learning about these issues has been the discussion group "Jews and Christians," founded in 1971 under the sponsorship of the Central Committee of German Catholics. The year 1988 was the fiftieth anniversary of the *Reichspogromnacht,* or *Kristallnacht.* The discussion group of Jews and Christians issued a declaration that received almost unanimous support. Our document was noticed by many state and church representatives and groups even outside the realm of the Church.

In my contribution, I will describe this group, whose chairperson I have been since 1974, and present a summary of our declaration. I will use our declaration as a point of entry into a broader discussion about the nature of guilt, reconciliation, and responsibility within the context of ecclesiology—the self-reflection of Catholics upon the nature of their community.

Presentation of the Discussion Group "Jews and Christians" under the Central Committee of German Catholics

The Central Committee of German Catholics is a body in which Catholic lay organizations have been working together on a national level for 150 years. Every other year it sponsors a nationwide "Katholikentag," which attracts approximately 100,000 people, especially young people. At the Katholikentag in 1970, for the first time there was a workshop entitled "The Parish and Fellow Jewish Citizens." After that workshop we sent a request to the Central Committee requesting that a permanent board be established to prepare programs about Jewish-Christian relations for every future Katholikentag. Because the Central Committee agreed to our request, thousands of Catholics and non-Catholics who attend these events meet their Jewish contemporaries and encounter the living reality of Jewish intellectual and spiritual life. Indeed, for many people who attend the Katholikentag, this is the first time in their lives that they meet Jews.

The Jewish-Christian discussion group has a membership of ten Jews and fifteen Catholics, both clergy and laity, among them two contributors to this volume: Edna Brocke and Hans Hermann Henrix. Beyond our responsibility for planning programs for biennial Katholikentage, our goals have been:

1. Promoting the appropriate image of Jews and Judaism through preaching, instruction, and education.
2. Making efforts to reveal and nurture the reality of the connection of the Church with the Jewish people by broadening our own experience. Because of the small number of Jews living in Germany, we have realized this goal by travel to meet with Jews and Christians in Israel, New York, Hungary and Poland.
3. Promoting reflection on basic philosophical-theological concepts by arranging seminars and conventions.
4. Writing statements about current issues for the president of the Central Committee; for example, a statement concerning the Vatican's recognition of the state of Israel.[1]

During the years of our committee's existence, the most difficult and challenging task was the process of formulating our declaration in 1988, "After 50 Years Reichskristallnacht 1938—How can we talk about guilt, suffering and reconciliation?" This text not only reflected the realization of the initial phase of our work, but also was an exciting moment of our mutual evolution as a discussion group of Jews and Christians.

In the course of our work together we discerned the subtle differences between what appeared to be identical concepts. We were then able to replace misleading comparisons with more appropriate ones. During our conversations we learned to distinguish between "forgiving" and "forgetting," between "reconciliation with God" and "reconciliation with fellow humans," between forgiveness by the victim and reconciliation between the communities of perpetrators and victims, between an appropriate request of someone and a coercive pressure on him or her, even if this pressure stems "simply" from a hopeful expectation.

We also had to learn to deal very cautiously with statements that began with the pronoun "we." Because guilt and suffering affect each group in different ways, we had to introduce many passages with the phrases "we Jews" and "we Christians." Moreover, since our discussions moved us to reject the concept of collective guilt, we had to differentiate between the experiences of those who lived through the Shoah and those who were born afterward. Only then could there be the hope that all Germans would learn together through our nation's and our church's history of guilt, and that later generations for their part "will help to reduce the mountain of estrangement and animosity that has grown up between us."[2]

When I think about the document that we wrote and the entire process of our deliberations, there are three ideas that stand out for me as a Catholic theologian living in Germany:

- We Christians have recognized that dialogue between Christians and Jews is never to be taken for granted or routine. Rather, it is almost a "miracle" when a Jew extends his hand in peace to a Christian after Auschwitz.
- Our Jewish partners in the dialogue came to the conclusion that "reconciliation does not mean a betrayal of the dead."[3]
- It has become clear to us Christians that the Shoah is a Christian problem not only with respect to Christians' relationship with the Jewish community; the Church also must work through this problem for its own sake, in order to face the God of history. The Shoah then becomes a problem for serious internal Christian theological reflection about the nature of the Church itself. This internal reflection by no means diminishes the significance of the Shoah as a problem in Christian-Jewish relations. Instead, it reveals new dimensions for the Church as the "people of God on the way."

I would like to turn my focus now to some basic considerations about why my Church still has such difficulties admitting its historical guilt, especially its complicity in the Shoah.

The Problematic Relationship between the Catholic Church and Its History

In *Tertio millenio adveniente* (from 10 November 1994) Pope John Paul II calls Catholics to a sincere remembrance of Christendom's history of guilt:

> Hence it is appropriate that as the second millennium of Christianity draws to a close the church should become more fully conscious of the sinfulness of her children, recalling all those times in history when they departed from the spirit of Christ and his Gospel and, instead of offering to the world the witness of a life inspired by the values of faith, [often] indulged in ways of thinking and acting which were truly forms of counter-witness and scandal.[4]

For this call of penitence, the Pope appeals to the Constitution of the Church of the Second Vatican Council, *Lumen gentium*: "The church, embracing sinners to her bosom, is at the same time holy and always in need of being purified, and incessantly pursues the path of penance and renewal."[5] In light of *Tertio millenio adveniente*, we can also analyze what appears to be the apologetic motif in the document *We Remember: A Reflection on the Shoah*, published on 12 March 1998 by the Commission for Religious Relations with the Jews. A reflection on this document illustrates how the leadership of the Catholic Church constrains itself from a sincere and open admission of its historical guilt. This text refers to the guilt of "some sons and daughters of the Church," but not to the guilt of the Church itself. The causes for this reluctance to speak of the Church as "guilty" or "sinful" are deeply rooted in Catholic theology and ecclesial piety. Let me now comment briefly on four ideas that create difficulties for a statement about ecclesiastical "sin" with respect to the Shoah.

The Sanctity of the Church

Our approach to the question of sin in the Church begins with the idea of "sanctity of the Church." I believe that this notion is based on what I call "mentality" rather than reflective theology. By the word "mentality" I mean a predisposition to a particular idea rather than a developed argumentation.

We can observe that already in patristic and medieval ecclesiology, the Church was primarily an object of spiritual meditation as a mystery of faith — the loving relationship between Jesus Christ and his bride, the Church. This spiritual perspective allows for the identification by the faithful with the Church despite all *their own* guilt and weakness. On a secondary level the reality of the Church for Catholics is an issue of theological reflection as the basis for reform.

According to the Second Vatican Council, the Church is a sacrament of salvation, a reality, while at the same time a symbol for the sovereign power of God. It is not only an instrument of redemption, but also a tangible sign of redemption. Catholics are therefore cut to the quick wherever a non-respectful critique is leveled against the Church, whether the criticism comes from inside or outside.

In the Credo Christians profess the "sancta Ecclesia" (Holy Church). It is my understanding that the sanctity of the Church is not to be interpreted ethically, as a freedom from sin, but as the experience of the continuing reality and witness of Jesus Christ in his Church. For Catholics, there is joy in the Word of God and in the celebration of the sacraments, especially of the Eucharist. They also find blessing in the Church hierarchy in spite of the weakness and the sins of the popes, bishops, and priests. The Council Fathers rejected the theological division proposed by reformation theologians between the believed essence of the Church and its reality as lived in the world.

For contemporary Catholics great dangers lie in this spiritual relationship to the Church: It may, on the one hand, lead Christians to do away with necessary reforms because they consider any "reform" of the Church unnecessary. In addition, it may cause Christians to refrain from any open statement about the Church's history of guilt, especially the guilt that Church leadership and official meetings of the hierarchy, such as synods or councils, might have brought upon themselves.

When Christians think about the Church in this way, the belief in the sancta Ecclesia may function as an exoneration from addressing honestly and conscientiously the burden of the past. The Second Vatican Council shows the way: as a "people of God on a pilgrimage" the Church is a community on the way into the promised kingdom of God with all other "people of his grace."[6] This allows one's joy in the Church always to grow stronger than one's frustration with it. An admission of guilt will come to the Church easier, the more it trusts in the promise that it cannot completely and finally fall from grace. It cannot loose the reality, despite any sin, of being the people of God.

A Centeredness on Christ

The second problem of the Church and its relationship to guilt and responsibility rests upon a Christocentric theology. The New Testament proclaims Jesus Christ as the Alpha and Omega of the entire history of salvation, as the Amen of all of God's promises. Typological exegesis concentrates all God's words and deeds in Jesus and at the same time evaluates everything earlier, later, or estranged from Christ as at most a proto-form of the real thing. Western systemic thinking—in the static form of scholasticism or in the dynamic-historical form of German idealism (Hegel)—fostered this tendency toward a closed view of the world and history, centered on Jesus Christ. In this grandiose order everything has its place: God and the Devil, Heaven for the saved and Hell for the damned. The abyss of evil at work in history and even in the Church is labeled and categorized by such systemic thought and therefore rendered harmless. In our own century this leads to a situation where Christians are rendered helpless when faced with the atrocity of the Shoah, which explodes the boundaries of thinking and systematization.

In Adorno's negative dialectics (where "the whole is the untrue") lies the end of all systemic thought, but Christian belief cannot be content with this. To renounce a logical synthesis of all reality does not release one from the necessity of an ethical commitment to the realization of the Shalom of the kingdom of God for the good of the endangered and deprived life. The reasonable answer lies in the theological patience that, despite all obstacles, trusts that God will bring his righteousness to triumph when and how he wills it. Resilient hope goes further than the so-called meta-perspective on eschatological perfection. Finally, a parting from systemic thinking allows us to dialogue about faith free from hesitation in interdenominational and interfaith relationships.

In our time, after Auschwitz, all systems have come to a crisis. We have entered a period of dialogue. Dialogue between people makes possible surprising new experiences, while the confrontation between systems always aims at the victory of one system—usually one's own. But where then is the Christian identity that stands and falls with the proclamation of Jesus as Christ? Christians believe in Christ as the only way to the Father, and it is through him in the end that the Jews come to the Father as well. But Jews do not believe this. Here "knowledge" stands against "lack of knowledge," as if Christians know that Jesus is the Messiah for all people and Jews do not know this. But here stands rather faith against faith, as a definitive meeting of our discussion group clarified. This clarification forbids, however, all threats of control and violence and any indoctrination through "compelling arguments." But we are still required by God's will to give witness to our faith and hope, even when it may be a provocation to others.

Authoritarianism

A third point in analyzing the relationship between guilt and the Church is the problem of submission under the authority of state and church.

Heribert Prantl writes in the *Süddeutsche Zeitung* on 21/22 March:

> The word "resistance" has found no echo in Germany. [. . .] To be peaceful is a citizen's first duty! Obedience is the Christian's honor. These are maxims from the Germans' collective consciousness. For many centuries these have been imprinted onto their minds. The Germans therefore showed themselves to be orderly especially at the low point of their history. [. . .] Good citizens have followed reprehensible instructions, simply because they were instructions; good soldiers have followed criminal commands simply because they were commands; good judges have followed unjust laws, simply because they were laws. They all followed without pangs of guilt, and they did this not only under a dictatorship.

I now quote from the pastoral letter of the German bishops five months after Hitler stepped into power: "We Catholics do not hesitate to appreciate freely the strong emphasis of authority in German politics and to submit ourselves with an attitude that is a supernatural virtue, because we see in each human authority a reflection of divine sovereignty."[7]

Catholic ecclesial piety of the last four centuries was a piety that glorified the hierarchical structure of the Church against the attacks from the reformers. This attitude found its parallel in the absolutism in the civil governments. To be obedient to the Pope and to the bishops was considered typically Catholic. The closed character of Catholicism was a strength especially during times when the Church had to defend itself. But it came at a price, the price of neglecting free speech and the formation of conscience, which Catholics must obey more than any outside authority. That one becomes guilty through deficient Christian or civil resistance to secular authorities was unthinkable in the Catholic Church before the war. Perhaps this is why we so often and so emphatically refer to few dissidents from our own numbers, who themselves found little support from their superiors.

This authoritarian obedience was criticized by the last Council. However, postconciliar debates illustrate that this old way of thinking has not been entirely overcome. While the "Catechism of the Catholic Church" de-emphasizes an obedience to the individual conscience, it emphasizes an obedience to the ecclesial magisterium. One necessary corrective measure has been the motto of the "Week of Brotherhood" this year, which adapts a saying from Hillel: "If not I, who else? If not now, when?"

Piety of Passion

Our fourth and final point for evaluating the relationship between the Church and sin is the piety of Christ's passion. "Piety of passion" is the veneration of Jesus during his period of suffering. For Christians this piety means the realized participation in these sufferings, their contrition for their own sins, and the readiness to offer themselves with Christ for the sins of the world.

Johann Baptist Metz thinks it a spiritual error that the Church has, for centuries, made the faithful occupy themselves with fear of Hell by threat of eternal damnation and the promise of eternal life in Heaven. In this way the Church has neglected the more important task of teaching the faithful to be sensitive to suffering, especially to the sort of suffering one person inflicts upon another. For in every person who suffers, even in every person who is guilty, a human being is threatened, violated, destroyed. And every person, so Michael Wyschogrod says, is created in the image of God, almost equal to God. Wyschogrod asserts that the Bible itself proclaims this sense of dignity not only in Abraham and his descendants, but also in Adam and his offspring. This terrifying insight about the trivialization of the suffering of others came to Metz in the face of the insensitivity and apathy revealed in the behavior of most Christians with respect to the fate of the Jews under Hitler.

In my opinion, the contrast between the sensitivity to sinfulness and the sensitivity to suffering has its spiritual roots, since the Middle Ages, in the piety of passion and its theological roots in the still older teaching of vicarious atonement. Since Jesus endured immense suffering and atoned for all the sins of the world, pious people were misled into simply concentrating all their feelings of pity, grief, and indignation over inhumane injustices on the suffering of the servant of God and into merging themselves with his suffering through acts of atonement on behalf of all humankind. Even so, they lost sight of the individual sufferers. They offered them no empathy. At best they prayed on Good Friday for the worst sinners of all, the "murderers of God." Sympathy for Jesus detracted from sympathy for fellow human beings and from the struggle against origins of human suffering that they could influence.

Thus a theology of vicarious atonement, a theology of sacrifice, and the piety of passion detracted from the horror, even the senselessness, of suffering, so that this suffering was also not seen as an unbearable outrage. The faithful looked to the cross for consolation and hope for themselves, but this piety leads to a lack of solidarity if it designates all suffering—especially others' suffering—as punishment or atonement. This warning applies especially to the extermination of the European Jewry.[8] The rash theological answer is not a witness of faith, but a scandal. My relationships with my Jewish friends have spoiled any appreciation of this piety for me.

Consequences

As a pastoral theologian I wish to practice this sensitivity for the suffering of others, especially regarding Auschwitz, where Christians murdered with the grossest insensitivity to suffering. Therefore three members of the discussion group and Michael Signer took a trip there last December to reflect with Manfred Deselaers and other Jewish and Christian friends upon the meaning and realization of a culture that remembers. The result of our four days of deliberation was not doctrines and directives, but a list of questions, from which I would like to pose two here:

What can we do to overcome the problematic alternative between Christianization or the secularization/atheisation of Auschwitz?

In our talks we heard the fears and outrage of Jewish voices. Many of them argued that through Christian symbols and religious acts (such as the celebration of the church service in the former camp) Auschwitz is becoming Christianized, becoming forged into a Christian cemetery, into a Christian place of pilgrimage. In their fear we also felt the mistrust of ecclesial and political authorities in Poland and those groups' desire to claim the symbolism of Auschwitz as a site of the genocide of the Polish people.

On the other hand, we observed the Polish Catholics' anxiety and outrage that Jewish Shoah survivors and international pressure were forbidding them to express reasonably their appreciation for their dead. They maintained through the power of their Christian faith their human dignity against the Nazis' desire to destroy them. For them, an apodictic prohibition of religious symbols in Auschwitz leads to an historicization and atheisation of the memorial site. In this confrontation we came to understand that one cannot by legal means regulate deep-seated anxieties and the lack of trust in the other side. These changes require patient work, time, and above all encounters that build trust between partners. Perhaps then in a few decades the situation will change, so that a number of symbols from different religions and ideologies can find legitimacy together. The symbolism of Auschwitz and the practice of placing religious symbols inside and near the camp are on shaky ground without a tangible human basis.

The second question:

What should be done to protect Auschwitz from banalization through the insensitivity of the visitors to the dignity of the victims or through the sensationalization of violence?

During our discussions we saw ourselves facing the fact that entire classes from Poland, Germany, Israel, and other countries visited the camp at Auschwitz-Birkenau daily. We asked ourselves: What kind of values and basic questions can be addressed by young people when visiting the camp? What is the result of such a visit to the camp for young people, who, by way of the mass media, are accustomed to a culture of violence? As difficult as these questions are, they cannot be set aside to be pondered for decades. Therefore the question arises: How can young people be helped to realize the reality of Auschwitz-Birkenau adequately, through education of the guides and through suitable brochures, and how can they go home from the camp as messengers of reconciliation and peace?

For me, especially owing to my experiences in the "Jews and Christians" discussion group, the words of the Sermon on the Mount in Matthew have pointed the way in striving to take seriously the fears, biases, and misunderstandings of others: "Blessed are those who hunger and thirst for righteousness, for they will be filled. Blessed are the merciful, for they will receive mercy. Blessed are the pure in heart for they will see God. Blessed are the peacemakers, for they will be called children of God. . . . Should anyone press you into service for one mile, go with him two miles" (Matt. 5:6–9:41).

NOTES

1. Declarations:
—Arbeitspapier, "Theologische Schwerpunkte des jüdisch-christlichen Gesprächs," vom 8. Mai 1979, in *Berichte und Dokumente,* published by Zentralkomitee der deutschen Katholiken, Heft 39 (Bonn, 1979), 6–19; also published in *Die Kirchen und das Judentum. Dokumente von 1945–1985,* ed. Rolf Rendtorff and Hans Hermann Henrix (Paderborn/München, 1989), 252–262. (Eng. title: Basic Theological Issues of the Jewish-Christian Dialogue.)
—Erklärung "Nach 50 Jahren—wie reden von Schuld, Leid und Versöhnung?" vom 6. Januar 1988, in *Berichte und Dokumente,* Heft 68 (1988), 16–46. (Eng. title: After 50 Years—How Can We Talk about Guilt, Suffering, and Reconciliation?)
—Erklärung "Kloster und Kreuz in Auschwitz?" vom 4. April 1990, in *Berichte und Dokumente,* Heft 75 (1990), 47–52. (Eng. title: A Covenant and Cross in Auschwitz?)
—Stellungnahme "Juden und Judentum im neuen Katechismus der Katholischen Kirche—Ein Zwischenruf" vom 29. Januar 1996. Diskussionspapier, ergänzt durch vier Stellungnahmen aus den USA (Eugene Fisher, James L. Heft, Alan Mittleman, Michael Signer), in *Berichte und Dokumente,* Heft 101 (1996), 1–40.
—Handreichung "Reise ins Heilige Land" vom August 1983, hrsg. vom Zentralkomitee der deutschen Katholiken und vom Katholischen Bibelwerk (Stuttgart, 1984); also in *Die Kirchen und das Judentum . . .,* 288–303. Also published in *Die Kirchen und das Judentum. Dokumente von 1945–1985,* ed. Rolf Rendtorff and Hans Hermann Henrix (Paderborn/München, 1989), 288–303.

Documentations of congresses and travels:
—Wilhelm Breuning/Nathan Peter Levinson, *Zeugnis und Rechenschaft. Ein christlich-jüdisches Gespräch* (Stuttgart, 1982), 78 pp.
—Wilhelm Breuning/Hanspeter Heinz (Hrsg.), *Damit die Erde menschlich bleibt. Gemeinsame Verantwortung von Juden und Christen für die Zukunft* (Freiburg/Basel/Wien, 1985), 190 pp.
—Dokumentation der Studienreise von Präsidium und Gesprächskreis "Juden und Christen" des Zentralkomitees der deutschen Katholiken vom 8.–16. März 1986 nach New York und Washington, in *Berichte und Dokumente,* Heft 63 (1987), 66 pp.

—Bericht über eine Reise des Präsidiums des Zentralkomitees der deutschen Katholiken und von Mitgliedern des Gesprächskreises "Juden und Christen" beim ZdK nach Ungarn (5. bis 10. April 1991), in *Berichte und Dokumente,* Heft 80 (1991), 1–32.

—Dieter Henrich/Johann Baptist Metz/Bernd Jochen Hilberath/Zwi Werblowsky, *Die Gottesrede von Juden und Christen unter den Herausforderungen der säkularen Welt. Symposion am 22./23. November 1995 in der Katholischen Akademie* (Berlin, Münster, 1997), 109 pp.

Projects initiated and supported by the Gesprächskreis:
—Günter Biemer/Ernst Ludwig Ehrlich (Hrsg.), *Lernprozeß Christen Juden,* 4 vols. (Düsseldorf/Freiburg, 1980).

The first publication is available in a French translation, the first three texts are available in Polish and Hungarian translations, the first four texts are available in English translations. All texts can be ordered by e-mail from zdkbonn@aol.com or via mail from Zentralkomitee der dt. Katholiken, Hochkreuzallee 246, D-53175 Bonn, Germany.

2. Gesprächskreis Juden Christen, After 50 Years Reichskristallnacht 1938—How can we talk about guilt, suffering and reconciliation?, 8.

3. Ibid., 5.

4. Pope John Paul II, *Tertio millenio adveniente,* no. 33.

5. Second Vatican Council, *Lumen gentium,* no. 16.

6. Luke 2:14.

7. Hirtenbrief des deutschen Episkopats vom 3. Juni 1933, in *Akten deutscher Bischöfe I,* bearb. v. B. Stasiewski (= Kommission für Zeitgeschichte, Reihe A: Bd. 5) (Mainz, 1968), 239–248, here 241.

8. In our declaration we have replaced the Greek word "Holocaust" (meaning a completely burnt offering) with the Hebrew word "Shoah" (meaning destruction), because one should not lend a religious sense to the insane, technically crafted murder of millions of innocent Jews by using the term "sacrifice," and also thereby veil its senselessness.

PART 3

The Limits of Covenant

Introduction
The Limits of Covenant
John K. Roth

How did the Holocaust take place? Why did the Shoah happen? Those two questions about the destruction of European Jewry and millions of other defenseless people during the Nazi period, 1933–1945, persist more than any others. Those questions, of course, assume some clarity about what the Holocaust was or what the Shoah continues to be, topics about which we are still learning. Nevertheless, one reason why *How?* and *Why?* will not go away is that historical inquiry—however critically pursued and meticulously documented it may be—does not put either of them to rest. Such inquiry does not, indeed cannot, do so because the question *How?* is both related to and different from the question *Why?* The following essays by Rachel Adler, Robert A. Krieg, Peter Ochs, and Peter C. Phan shed important light on aspects of these issues. Their writing does so by exploring themes that deal with a religious and theological problem. That problem can be called "The Limits of Covenant." To introduce their work, consider further the key Holocaust questions: *How?* and *Why?*

When we ask "How did the Holocaust take place?" what does that question mean? What do we want to know? At first, the kind of response one is after seems obvious. Building on awareness of what happened, we want to know the Holocaust's causes. Here *what* happened and *how* it happened mix and mingle: we want facts but also something more, an accounting of and for them that provides a coherent and trustworthy interpretation. We want to know—in ways that both name and relate—who was involved in it, what they did and did not do. We want to identify and integrate the political, social, psychological, economic, historical, philosophical, and religious factors that established the environment for such massive destruction. All along the way, we want to document and organize the details so that our understanding of what took place incorporates perspective that will tell how one thing led to another. Such telling, it seems, will give the responses to "How did the Holocaust take place?" that we seek.

The more one considers the responses that *How?* requires, the more daunting the task becomes to answer "How did the Holocaust take place?" Where can we turn to get the necessary responses to a question that is no sooner considered than it seems to spiral out of our control? First and foremost, we turn to historians—and rightly so. They gather the evidence, discover the details, retrieve and evaluate the testimony, preserve and study the documents, and develop the accounts that tell not only what happened during the Holocaust—an indispensable contribution—but also how the Holocaust happened. Without the historians' diligence, there can be no serious, let alone adequate, study of the Holocaust. Nevertheless, neither individually nor collectively are historians able to put to rest the question "How did the Holocaust happen?" They are not able to do so because the question *How?* is both related to and different from the question *Why?*

Human beings—particular persons living in specific times and places—made the Holocaust happen. That fact creates the link between *How?* and *Why?* How the Holocaust took place depends largely on why people acted as they did. Why people act as they do is a question that historical inquiry can answer only in part. Nothing that any historian will ever find can settle why a person acted as he or she did. History can tell us what happened and to a large degree how. It can even shed light on why people act as they do, but historical inquiry alone cannot master the range of human feeling, intention, reflection, choice—the scope of human experience—that enters into desires, motivations, yearnings, aims, hopes, and decisions. These ingredients are parts of *Why?* that relate to *How?* They are indispensable, in particular, for getting at the part of *How?* that is found when the question "How did the Holocaust take place?" emphasizes perpetrator-focused issues, such as "How *could* human beings act *that way* toward one another?" or issues focused on those who were targeted by the perpetrators, such as "How *could* human beings endure *those conditions?*" As far as study goes, disciplines in the social sciences and humanities different from but also related to history—psychology, philosophy, and religious studies, to name but three—have parts to play that are also crucial if we are to respond to the wide-ranging meanings contained in the question "How did the Holocaust take place?"

Even when all of these disciplines have their say, versions of *How?* will remain. Versions of *How?* will remain because *How?* leads to *Why?* These two questions, however, are not one and the same. Their relationship involves a difference that can be seen in one of the reasons why the question "Why did the Shoah happen?" will not go away. That question persists partly because historical inquiry will continue indefinitely. Historians might wish otherwise; presumably they would like to "get it right"—definitely, definitively, once and for all. Yet study of the Holocaust reveals that historical inquiry about that event is unlikely to reach closure. The Shoah remains so vast, its scope so immense, that new findings keep awaiting us. Even if they are unlikely to alter the basic facts that Holocaust studies have documented, we cannot be sure of that. Furthermore, it remains unclear that there ever will or can be a single "master narrative" to frame the basic facts in perpetuity. Historians keep writing different, however closely related, narratives about the Holocaust. That result is what one should expect. After all, historians—indeed all Holocaust scholars—are interpreters. Even the most reliable Holocaust interpretations are subject to correction as new evidence and freshly thoughtful criticism appear. Such interaction is what keeps interpretations reliable—nothing else can. Nevertheless, as they leave the *How?* unsettled, these continuing outcomes invite the question *Why?*

Another reason for the persistence of *Why?*—probably a more basic one—emerges from historical inquiry in a different way. Historian Saul Friedländer points it out when he observes that the smallest details raise the largest "whys." Those details—they involve the systematic but one-by-one murder of nearly six million Jews—show that Holocaust history is not history-as-usual. What happened in the Shoah stretches comprehension so far because it breaks down normal expectation too much. Thus, the question *Why?*, far from being put to rest (let alone satisfied), is likely to be intensified—silently if not openly. For new knowledge about the Holocaust, unfortunately, always seems to make the event worse, not better. The more detail we encounter, the more we know about the Shoah, the more devastating that event turns out to be.

The devastation will be intense because its roots are so deep. They trace back, at least in part, to forms of human understanding that have been as formidable as they are ancient. The idea of *covenant* is among them. Why did the Shoah happen? One of the correct responses has to involve the following line of thought: the Shoah happened *partly* because human communities—Jews and Christians—understood themselves in different but related ways to be in a special relationship with God. Entailing responsibilities between God and God's people, and also among those people and their relationships with other human groups, these covenantal understandings produced some of the greatest achievements of human civilization, but also deep-seated conflict and rivalry that helped to form the Holocaust's seedbed.

If no one—human or divine—had conceived the idea of a covenant between God and humankind, it is unlikely that the Shoah would have happened, for there would have been no Christian-Jewish rivalry to help spark the catastrophe that took place centuries later. Undeniably, the identity of the Shoah's victims, perpetrators, and bystanders was saturated, in one way or another, with the idea of *covenant*. Moreover, as the historian Victoria Barnett says, history does not stop when it is over. The idea of *covenant* does not and will not go away. It has to be encountered if we are to grasp *How?* and *Why?* more fully. It also has to be encountered because Jewish and Christian identities—personal and communal—remain after the Shoah, and in ongoing ways these identities are intertwined with the issue of what to make of the idea of *covenant* after Auschwitz. Those dilemmas point, among other things, to the limits of covenant. What shall be done with the idea of covenant, which is part of the Holocaust's origins and part of the Shoah's aftermath?

Developing a Jewish feminist perspective, Rachel Adler is a pioneer in advocating the importance of women's voices in the development of post-

Holocaust Jewish theology. Her essay explores the factors that have worked against the construction of feminist Jewish theology, especially post-Holocaust theology, and then it introduces a perspective that confronts what she calls "the incomprehensible violence of God." Resisting narratives of redemption, she urges "the recovery of lament for feminist theology." Using sources from the Bible and *midrash*, she weaves this theme into "the metaphor of the covenant as a marriage." Troubled though the metaphor and the reality of marriage may be, Adler thinks these ingredients offer "God and Israel an opportunity to grow into partnership" that persists "despite violence and betrayal."

A Roman Catholic theologian who focuses on Christology, Robert A. Krieg calls attention to the Jewish-Christian dialogue carried out by Martin Buber and Romano Guardini, two important philosophers and theologians—the former Jewish, the latter Catholic—who were in contact before and after the Shoah. Couching his discussion of Buber and Guardini in developments surrounding the Second Vatican Council, Krieg finds that the Buber-Guardini discussions not only "foreshadowed the development of the relationship between Catholicism and Judaism that has resulted from Vatican II," but also teach us that "Jews and Christians must deliberately enter into an interreligious dialogue that will enrich both faiths." Such discussion, Krieg suggests, cannot avoid encountering the meaning and limits of covenant.

Jewish philosopher Peter Ochs begins on a different note. "Do Jews and Christians," he asks, "share any covenant before *or* after the Shoah?" Ochs emphasizes that the issue of covenant *after* the Shoah is whether or how covenant can be a meaningful term when "an eluctable rupture" has taken place. Drawing on the life and thought of Talmudic scholar David Weiss Halivni, Ochs stresses that the meaning of covenant is not only a communal issue but also a topic that must not overlook or underestimate the experiences of individuals, especially those who have wrestled personally with the collision between traditional religious texts and teachings and the concrete particularity of the Holocaust's devastation. Halivni's experience is particularly instructive in this regard, Ochs shows, because it emphasizes "a continued but transformed Covenant, one that is not only Written-and-Oral but also Ruptured-and-in-the-Process-of-Restoration."

With particular reference to Asian perspectives, theologian Peter C. Phan assesses the strengths and weaknesses that the perspectives of "liberation theology" can bring to the discussion of post-Holocaust issues surrounding the idea of covenant. Unmasking ways in which liberation theology retains "vestiges of mostly unintentional anti-Judaism"—these elements, he emphasizes, can be especially harmful because they are unintentional and unconscious—Phan goes on to stress that Asian liberation theologians offer significant contributions that can help Jews and Christians to reconceptualize God after Auschwitz. In addition, Asian liberation theologians can be helpful, Phan contends, because "instead of focusing on a special election by and covenant with

God, they regard our common humanity and our shared struggle for its liberation from all forms of oppression as the basis for constructing an understanding of our relationship with God and with each other."

How did the Holocaust take place? Why did the Shoah happen? The authors of the essays that follow all agree that sound responses to those questions must take into account the idea of covenant and its limits. Their thinking diverges, however, about how to deal with covenant as a living and normative idea after Auschwitz. Nevertheless, none of them gives it up. To the contrary, each significantly reaffirms it—tentatively and in transformed ways, but substantively nonetheless. For them, the limits of covenant leave open, not unlimited but still varied, the ways in which Jews and Christians—indeed people everywhere—may relate to this troubled, troubling, and yet enduring idea. How and why the Holocaust happened, it seems, cannot be understood apart from the idea of covenant and its limits. As the essayists show, however, the idea of covenant and its limits prevent our understanding from being complete, because the Shoah makes us encounter, question, explore, even lament and wonder about them, again and again.

The Holocaust

10 | Reflections from the Perspective of Asian
Liberation Theology

Peter C. Phan

THE TRAUMA CAUSED by the systematic slaughter of six million Jews by the
Nazis from 1933 to 1945 was indelibly branded on the Jewish collective psy-
che. During the half century that separates us from the Holocaust (*Shoah* or
Churban), it has provoked a veritable avalanche of writings by both Jewish and
Christian thinkers exploring its implications for their faith and practice. As
Franklin Littell has argued, the Holocaust is as much a central event in Chris-
tian history as in Jewish history.[1]

Within the sphere of Christian theology, liberation theology, which has by
now moved beyond its original Latin American context and its Catholic home
to grow deep roots in other continents and in different ecclesial soils, can no
doubt be regarded as the most influential and challenging development in modern theology.[2] Yet, curiously enough, Johann Baptist Metz's dictum, whose
anti-bourgeois political theology has exerted a significant influence on liberation theology, that no future theological construction be unaffected by Auschwitz,[3] seems to have had no effect on liberation theology. No Latin American
Christian liberation theologian has so far dealt extensively with the Holocaust
as a theological theme, much less consciously shaped his or her theology in
the light of the Holocaust itself.[4] This observation is no less true of Asian
liberation theologians. By contrast, some Jewish theologians, such as Dan
Cohn-Sherbok and Marc Ellis, have attempted to bring insights of liberation
theology to bear on their understanding of Judaism and the state of Israel.[5]

In this essay I will attempt first to unmask vestiges of anti-Judaism in some
representative writings by Asian theologians; their anti-Judaism is all the more
pernicious as it is mostly unconscious.[6] Secondly, resources of Asian liberation
theology will be harnessed to address some of the issues raised by the Holocaust and Holocaust theology.[7] Finally, some suggestions will be made to further the conversation between Asian liberation theology and contemporary
Christian theology of Judaism.

Jews and Judaism in Asian Theology

Historical records show that Jews were present in East Asia when Christians moved out of the borders of the Roman empire, from West Asia into East

Asia.[8] If the *Acts of Thomas* can be trusted, the first convert of St. Thomas, "the Apostle to India," was a little Jewish flute girl at the court of the Indian king Gundaphar.[9] In Asia as elsewhere, the Jewish communities of the Second Diaspora were often the first focus of Christian evangelism. According to *The Doctrine of Addai,* written between 390 and 430, the missionary Addai, reputedly St. Thomas's disciple, when he came to Edessa, the capital of the tiny kingdom of Osrhoene, first sought out the Jewish community, lodging with "Tobias the son of Tobias." According to the same document, one of the four groups of people who accepted Addai's teaching—the others being the nobility and members of the royal family of Osrhoene, pagan religious leaders, and the common people—were Jews "skilled in the law and prophets, who traded in silk."[10]

When Matteo Ricci arrived in China, he found a colony of Jews in Kaifeng, but no Christians.[11] In 1595 he found pockets of Christians ("five or six families") in Nanjing and elsewhere in central China who seemed to have lost all their earlier beliefs, making their churches into temples and in many cases even converting to Islam. The only traces of the Christian faith among them were their rudimentary knowledge of the psalter and the sign of the cross, which they made over their food.[12] In 1602 Ricci was informed that in the northwestern regions of China, in the old kingdom of Xixia, there were "certain white men with flowing beards who had churches with bell towers, ate pork, worshiped Mary and Isa (as they called Christ our Lord) and adored the Cross."[13]

In Beijing, in the summer of 1608, Ricci received a visit from a Chinese Jew by the name of Ai Tian who had come to the capital to take the examinations for the doctoral degree. Assuming that Ricci was a Jew, Ai Tian told him that there were in his hometown ten or twelve families of Jews and a magnificent synagogue, which only recently they had renovated at the cost of ten thousand gold pieces, and that there was an even larger Jewish community in Hangzhou. Ricci was also told that in Kaifeng there were certain strangers whose ancestors came from abroad and who observed the religious custom of venerating a cross. About three years later Ricci dispatched a Jesuit Chinese lay brother to Kaifeng to verify his visitor's report about the presumed Christians. The brother confirmed the accuracy of the Jewish informant but said that these Christians, perhaps for fear of persecution, were reluctant to admit to being Christian.[14]

From his conversations with Chinese scholars, Ricci discovered that the Chinese word *huihui* referred not only to Muslims but also to scattered communities of Jews ("the *huihui* who reject the sinews"—a reference to Jacob's wrestling with the angel) as well as to the descendants of the Nestorian Christians ("the *huihui* of the cross").[15] A great stone discovered in 1623 at Xian, the ancient T'ang-dynasty capital Chang'an, with the inscription "A Monument Commemorating the Propagation of the Ta-ch'in (Syrian) Luminous Religion in China," speaks of the arrival of a Nestorian missionary in the Chinese capital in 635. The missionary's name was Alopen; he came carrying "the true Sutras" with him and was requested by King T'ai-tsung to translate the scripture into Chinese. With funds from the king's own treasury the first Christian church was built in China in 638.[16]

That the same word, *huihui,* was used during the Ming dynasty to refer to Jews, Christians, and Muslims alike implies that in Chinese eyes these three Western religions, with their belief in the one God, were basically the same. It may also indicate that the relationships among the followers of these three related religions in China, in contrast to the long history of mutual hatred in Europe, had been amicable, so that the Chinese did not have any reason to regard them as possessing separate or rival identities. Indeed, when the emperor Wanli saw the full-length portraits of the Jesuits in Beijing, he looked at them for a moment and pronounced: "They are *huihui.*"[17]

That relationships between Jews and Christians in China during Ricci's time were friendly is supported by the fact that when the lay brother was sent a second time to Kaifeng, this time to visit the head of the synagogue, with a letter from Ricci stating that he had at his house in Beijing all the books of the Old Testament as well as those of the New Testament, the rabbi gave the brother a very warm welcome. But he took exception to Ricci's affirmation that the Messiah had already come, saying that the Messiah would not come for another ten thousand years. Despite this difference of opinion, however, the head of the synagogue added that given Ricci's reputation and learning, he would confer upon Ricci the dignity of high priest of the synagogue if he would join the Jewish faith and abstain from eating pork.[18] Later, three other Jews, one of whom was the nephew of the first visitor, came from the same city to Beijing and were warmly received by the Jesuits. All three eventually decided to receive baptism after being convinced that the Messiah had come, in Jesus.

It is significant that Ricci, despite the fact that he had had first-hand experiences of Christians' hostility toward Jews, first in his hometown Macerata, then in Rome and in Goa, refrained from polemic with the Jews.[19] In his famous "catechism," *The True Meaning of the Lord of Heaven,* Ricci does not make any disparaging remark about the Jews.[20]

By contrast, anti-Judaism is unfortunately pronounced in a later influential catechism. When Alexandre de Rhodes, the Jesuit "apostle to Vietnam,"[21] wrote his *Cathechismus pro iis, qui volunt suscipere Baptismum, in Octo dies divisus,*[22] he transmitted to the East much of the centuries-long anti-Judaic heritage of Christian theology. Speaking of Jesus' performing of miracles, de Rhodes paints a very dark portrait of the scribes and Pharisees, highlighting their jealousy and hatred of Jesus:

> Among the Jews the Lord had many and very skillful enemies, because their works were evil. These were called *Scribae* and *Pharisaei.* . . . Many

powerful people hated the light the Lord projected in the holiness of his life as well as in his admirable doctrine because they were charged with various sins. As a result, people venerated him and abandoned the *Pharisaei* to follow him. This increased the jealousy of the *Scribae* and *Pharisaei* who sought to destroy the Lord's reputation in front of people by means of calumnies under the guise of piety and religion.[23]

After relating Jesus' healing of the man born blind, de Rhodes comments on the pride and spiritual blindness of the Pharisees: "Those who in their pride rely on their own wisdom and refuse to accept the Word of God, will fall into many sins; they become blind and finally fall into the precipice of eternal death. Thus, the *Pharisaei,* impious and proud they were, refusing to accept the light of the Lord Jesus manifested by so many miracles, became blind and finally fell into the ruin of eternal damnation."[24] At the end of the sixth catechetical day, de Rhodes urges his catechumens to embrace the Christian faith by rejecting the "hard-heartedness of the Jews": "Let us detest the hard-heartedness of the Jews, let us adore the Lord, and let us embrace ardently in our minds his divine teaching in order to be enlightened now, and to obtain eternal life later."[25]

In his narrative of Jesus' passion, de Rhodes repeatedly refers to "the Jews" as accomplices in the killing of Jesus and affirms that the destruction of Jerusalem by the Romans was God's punishment for this crime: "Because this crime of the Jews was the most atrocious since the creation of the world, it should not pass without receiving even in this life its punishment."[26] As evidence of the severity of divine punishment, he cites Flavius Josephus's "incredible and horrible story of a [Jewish] hungry mother who was suckling her child; she killed it with her own hands, cooked it, and ate it."[27] De Rhodes repeats the common view among Christians that all the calamities that happened to the Jews during the siege and destruction of Jerusalem were "divine vengeance against the evil Jews," whereas those who had accepted the Christian faith could escape them.[28]

It goes without saying that de Rhodes's remarks about the Jews and the Pharisees, blameworthy as they are, do not necessarily reflect a conscious anti-Judaism on his part. Rather, they are inherent in Christianity's "teaching of contempt" against Jews, which he inherited in his theological studies in Rome. Nevertheless, they are no less lethal, since they have seeped not only into catechesis in Asia but also into widespread popular devotions such as the way of the cross[29] and the passion play.[30]

While such a negative view of Jews and Judaism, deplorable as it is, may be excusable due to the lack of historical knowledge of the Judaism of Jesus' times in the seventeenth century, one is surprised to see the persistence of such a view in some contemporary Asian theologians. Like their Latin American counterparts, some Asian theologians tend to set in sharp contrast the difference between Jesus and his message about the kingdom of God on the one hand and various groups of Jews on the other. For example, Aloysius Pieris, an influential Sri Lankan Jesuit theologian, explains Jesus' baptism in the Jordan at the hand of John the Baptizer as a "prophetic gesture" and contrasts it starkly with other spiritualities of his time:

> I observe that Jesus was faced with several streams of traditional religiousness when he answered this prophetic call. Not every kind of religion appealed to him. From his later reactions we gather that the narrow ideology of the Zealot movement did not attract him. Nor did the sectarian puritanism of the Essenes have any impact on him. As for the Pharisaic spirituality of self-righteousness, Jesus openly ridiculed it. His confrontations with the Sadducees—the chief priests and elders—indicate that he hardly approved their aristocratic "leisure class" spirituality. Rather, it was in the ancient (Deuteronomic) tradition of prophetic asceticism represented by the Baptizer that Jesus discovered an authentic spirituality and an appropriate point of departure for his own prophetic mission. In opting for this form of *liberative* religiousness to the exclusion of others, which appeared enslaving, he indulged in a species of "discernment," which we Christians in Asia, confronted with a variety of ideological and religious trends, are continually invited to make.[31]

While one may agree with Pieris's characterization of Jesus' spirituality as prophetic and liberative, one must object to his labeling the spirituality of the Zealots as "narrow ideology," that of the Essenes as "sectarian puritanism," that of the Pharisees as "self-righteousness," and that of the Sadducees as "aristocratic, 'leisure class' spirituality." Pieris is of course within his right to contrast Jesus' spirituality with other ideal *types* of spirituality, but to attribute "narrow ideology," "sectarian puritanism," "self-righteousness," and " 'leisure class' spirituality" to specific historical groups and to stigmatize these spiritualities as "enslaving," especially when these groups have been maligned throughout Christian history, is historically inaccurate and perpetuates the worst caricatures of them.

Similarly, Choan-Seng Song, a prolific Presbyterian Taiwanese theologian, has repeatedly contrasted Jesus' behavior and attitude with those of "Jewish authorities."[32] Commenting on Job's theological struggle, Song argues that "it is a struggle to be liberated from the God of the traditional religion and become free for God in God's own self."[33] Again says Song: "Job's dialogue with his friends turns out to be not a dialogue at all. It becomes Job's struggle against the false God of religious traditions and theological orthodoxy. His real adversary is not his friends, but the false God they defend. To debunk that false God becomes his preoccupation. 'I am ready to argue with God,' says Job with determination—the God of my friends, the God of my religion, the God of my ancestors."[34] The God of traditional religions is, according to Song, "the God of retribution." It is true that Song's rejection of the God of retribution forms part of his critique of religion and religious traditions in general; still in this context it is the Jewish religion that is directly targeted ("the God of my friends, the God of my religion, the God of my ancestors").[35]

Furthermore, contrasting "the God of retribution" of Judaism and of religion in general with the "Abba" of Jesus, Song highlights the distance between them, especially on the cross. Commenting on Jesus' cry "My God, my God, why have you abandoned me?" Song argues against Jürgen Moltmann that Jesus' words do not refer to the separation between God the Father and God the Son in an alleged intra-trinitarian conflict.[36] Rather, in Song's understanding, they express the radical opposition between "the God of retribution," "the God portrayed in the story of the flood in the Hebrew Scriptures,"[37] "the God of legalism, the God of religious absolutism, the God of theological dogmatism"[38] on the one hand and Jesus' Abba, the God of "*karuna*" (compassion) on the other, the God to whom the cross of Jesus is itself "an act of shame, disgrace, and outrage committed by human beings, an act that offends and shocks the moral feelings of the human community and the heart of God, who loves Jesus and other human beings as Abba, as Parent."[39]

This same radical opposition between Jewish religious authorities and Jesus is carried by Song into his interpretation of Jesus' trial before the Sanhedrin. Using the categories of "official" and "popular" histories, the former being "stories told by the king, the ruler, the rich and the powerful . . . history taught in school, recited on official occasions, and preserved in the national archives and annals"[40] and the latter being "stories remembered and circulated by the ruled, the powerless, and the poor . . . by word of mouth, passed on in handwritten copies, and preserved not in national archives and records, but in the memories of people,"[41] Song suggests that what was on trial at the Sanhedrin was "popular history," that is, the history of Jesus and his friends: "Tried with him is a host of the women and men with whom Jesus has been associated—prostitutes, tax-collectors, sinners, people who are poor, men, women, and children who are socially and religiously discriminated against."[42] Over against this popular history stands the "official history" represented by the Sanhedrin and the Pharisee in Jesus' parable about the two men who went to the Temple to pray (Luke 18:10–14). The prayer of the Pharisee "does not radiate his own self-confidence only, however. It radiates the self-confidence of his proud tradition, the religious hierarchy, and the whole complexity of rituals and teachings. In other words, the prayer is the epitome of the entire official history."[43] Thus concludes Song:

> What we see at the supreme council of priests and teachers is the confrontation of the popular history of Jesus and the official history of the religious authorities. Much was at stake, especially on the part of the official history. It had to maintain its officiality. It had to defend its legitimacy. It had to assert its power and authority. In contrast the popular history that

Jesus carried with him to the trial had no officiality to maintain; its "popularity," its being of people, in itself made it more "official" than any other claim to officiality.[44]

In reading Song's interpretation of Jesus' trial and death one cannot help but be powerfully moved by his passion for justice and his solidarity with the poor and the oppressed. On the other hand, with the hindsight of the Holocaust, one cannot but reject the facile way in which Song associates "the God of retribution" with the religion of Job's ancestors, in contrast to the Abba of compassion of Jesus, and the way in which he associates the oppressive "official history" with the Sanhedrin and Jewish religious authorities, in contrast to the liberating "popular history" of Jesus and his marginalized people. As with Pieris, Song is within his right to contrast Jesus' understanding of God and behavior with other ideal *types* of understanding of God and behavior. But he runs the terrible risk of perpetuating the injustice, perpetrated throughout the history of Christianity, of stereotyping Judaism and different groups of Jews when he ascribes a legalistic concept of God to Judaism and an oppressive and hypocritical behavior to specific groups of Jews, such as the Pharisees and the members of the Sanhedrin.[45]

Asian Liberation Theology and Holocaust Theology

Despite these vestiges of mostly unintentional anti-Judaism, Asian liberation theology offers rich resources to address some of the issues confronting Holocaust theology.[46] Stephen R. Haynes has provided a useful definition of Holocaust theology as "any sustained theological reflection for which the slaughter of six million Jews functions as a criterion, whether the Shoah displaces or merely qualifies traditional theological criteria and norms such as Scripture, tradition, reason, and religious experience."[47] As mentioned above, to date no Asian liberation theologian has set out to develop his or her theology using the Shoah as its overarching criterion and norm. Nevertheless, a meaningful dialogue between Holocaust theology and Asian liberation theology is possible on the basis of what the latter has said about some of the issues that Holocaust theology considers pivotal. Among the many themes of Christian Holocaust theology, I will concentrate on four: the concept of God, covenant, christology, and the ethics of power.[48]

The God of Karuna: The Mute God

While Orthodox Jewish theologians have generally tended to minimize the negative impact of the Holocaust on the Jewish belief in God,[49] most Jewish and Christian Holocaust theologians maintain that the Holocaust has shattered the traditional belief in God, that is, a God who is both infinitely good and omnipotent. Richard Rubenstein claims that the Shoah destroyed any possibility of believing in a covenantal God of history and calls for a "paganism" in which human existence is lived within the confines of the material world, without any transcendence.[50] Emil Fackenheim is convinced that the image of God was destroyed during the Holocaust and urges a restoration of the divine image in which God's power is curtailed.[51] For Arthur Cohen the Holocaust as the *tremendum* erased the conventional image of God as an interventionist in human history and attempts to fashion a new image of God in which human freedom and rationality are recognized.[52] Irving Greenberg believes the Shoah removes the image of God as a "commanding" being in a covenantal relationship; rather, the covenant is now to be understood as a purely voluntary act that highlights human responsibility.[53]

Catholic theologian John Pawlikowski applauded these thinkers' attempts at reconceiving the divine-human relationship after the Holocaust, especially their rejection of any simplistic belief in an interventionist God in history. But he finds them ultimately unsatisfactory because "they would appear to have left humanity too much to its own whims after the *Shoah*. They have not adequately explored whether God continues to play a significant role after the *Shoah* in the development of a moral ethos within humanity that can restrain radical evil. The role they have in fact assigned to God is not potent enough."[54]

With their reflections on the human-divine relationship Asian liberation theologians can offer a significant contribution to the project of reconceptualizing God in a manner appropriate to our post-Holocaust time. As we have seen above, Choan-Seng Song rejects the "God of retribution" and argues for the God of compassion. Describing the compassionate God as "the speaking God" (sometimes in anger), "the listening God," and "the remembering God," Song goes on to speak of God as "the mute God." Jesus' Abba-God, who has spoken, listened, and remembered throughout Jesus' life, Song suggests, became the mute God when his Son died on the cross. More precisely, the God of Jesus was shocked into silence by grief: "The silence of Jesus' God must have been the silence of grief. God was grieved into silence. It must have been a deep grief. When grief is shallow, silence does not follow. . . . Shallow grief can make us talkative. . . . But deep grief renders us silent. It deprives us of the power of speech."[55] Was God silent during the Holocaust, not because God had abandoned God's covenanted people or was absent from them, but because God was shocked into silence by the horror of their sufferings?

But silence, Song points out, is not necessarily a sign of weakness; it can also be a "silence of protest." Just as Jesus' silence before the religious authorities and the Roman court was a silence of protest, God's silence at the cross was a silence of protest: "God did not respond to Jesus' cry, not because God had abandoned him, but because God's horror and grief must have turned into silent protest. 'Look!' God must have been filling the air with silent grief and protest saying, 'What have you human beings done to Jesus, "my beloved

Son"?"[56] Was God not protesting with horror and grief during the Holocaust: "Look! What have you human beings, Nazis and otherwise, done to Israel, my beloved and chosen people?"

Furthermore, God's silence is not just grief and protest. For Song, it is also "a silence of pity (*karuna*)":

> It is not just anger. It is not simply grief. It is not merely protest. It, above all, must be pity, *karuna,* the matrix, the womb, engaged in the creation of life and nourishment of it. In that silence of the womb, pity (*karuna*) struggles to empower the embryo of life for the day of fulfillment. That silence of God is like a womb enveloping Jesus on the cross, empowering him during the last moments of his life and nourishing him for the resurrection of a new life from the womb.[57]

Since the Holocaust, has God not been the God of *karuna* for the Jews, empowering and nourishing them, not merely for survival in a secular and militarily powerful state, but *"to serve as God's People upon whom the redemption of God's world and God's own name uniquely depends."*[58]

Lastly, the God of compassion is not an "omnipotent" God. Song laments the fact that "the answer of traditional theology to this world of power is a powerful God. It invokes a powerful God and prays to an omnipotent God for intervention. Power must be counteracted with power."[59] Rather, the God of compassion is the God who has "the power to love others and to suffer with them."[60] Song insists that "the cross of Jesus is the cross of God. The cross people have to bear is the cross of God too. The cross of Jesus and the cross of suffering women, men, and children are linked to God and disclose the heart of the suffering God."[61]

But Song is quick to point out that a suffering God alone is no help: "A God easily carried away by sentiments, offers no help in hell. That God would be too overwhelmed by the sight of pain and suffering to know what to do. . . . A tearful God may invite our sympathy but not our trust and confidence."[62] What is needed is the God of powerful grace: "To have the will to live in hell and to see the eternal light of hope in the midst of perpetual darkness, we need God's grace, not weak grace, but strong grace, not sentimental grace, but nononsense grace, not fragile grace, but *powerful* grace. This is the grace with which God created heaven and earth."[63] But this powerful grace, Song argues, is not available to us until in faith we become active participants in its working in history, until in faith we get involved in the struggle against the power that oppresses us. Ultimately, for Song, the God of compassion who suffers with us invites and empowers us to take up our own responsibility in freedom to liberate ourselves from those who oppress us.

In our post-Shoah time, God can no longer be an "omnipotent" God, carrying out his will without the collaboration of his creatures, totally transcendent to human history, and stranger to the suffering of people in the world. In the eyes of Asian liberation theologians, God bears the crosses of all women, men, and children. However, God does not simply suffer with those who suffer. On the contrary, if the cross of Jesus is any indication, God protests against their suffering, wants to remove it, and will vindicate those who suffer against their oppressors. But God removes suffering and vindicates the oppressed not by "intervening" from outside history, by himself, without their resources and collaboration, but with his powerful grace God calls forth and empowers those who suffer from oppression and injustice to take charge of their destiny and struggle for their liberation.

God's Covenant with All Nations and All Peoples

Intimately related to the question of God in post-Holocaust theology is the issue of election and covenant, and in connection with it, of the relationship between Israel and the church. As is well known, part of the Christian "teaching of contempt" against Jews and Judaism is the supercessionist or displacement doctrine, according to which God's covenant with Israel has been abolished and replaced by God's new covenant with the church. In contemporary theology various typologies or models have been proposed to understand the nature of the relationship between Israel and the church, and different categories have been put forward to express it.[64] With regard to the covenant, questions have been raised as to the number of this covenant, and in Christian-Jewish dialogue it is now customary to classify various Christian theologies of the covenant into three types: single-covenant, double-covenant, and multi-covenant perspectives.[65] The single-covenant view conceives of Jews and Christians as basically partners of an ongoing, integrated covenantal tradition lived out by each not so much in different contents as in different modes. In this view Gentiles can be saved only through linkage with the Jewish covenant, something made possible in and through the Christ event.[66] The double-covenant view emphasizes the distinctiveness of each tradition but insists that both are ultimately crucial for the complete emergence of the kingdom of God.[67] The multi-covenant perspective regards the Jewish and Christian covenants as two among an undetermined number of covenants that God makes with different religious traditions, among which none can claim universality and normativity for others.[68]

Asian liberation theologians have not directly dealt with the issue of the number of covenant(s), but their reflections on the relationship between God and Asian peoples throw a helpful light on it. Confronted with religious pluralism, which is the hallmark of Asia, Asian theologians have raised the question of how God is related to them. Leading the discussion is again Choan-Seng Song. In an effort to fashion what he calls a "transpositional theology," that is, a theology that is distinctly Asian in character, he attacks what he terms the "ethno-religious centrism" of Jewish and Christian theologies. By centrism Song means the attitude of both Judaism and Christianity to take themselves exclusively as the center, norm, and goal of human history.[69] Such a view, in his judgment, leads to rigidity, homogeneity, and above all exclusivism, which refuses to see God's presence and activity outside the boundaries of one's own community. Rather than election and covenant, which evoke privilege and particularism and create the "us" versus "them" mentality, Song prefers the symbol of "reign of God": "The reign of God, according to Jesus, is not an institution but people—people with dignity as human beings regardless of their backgrounds and entitled to freedom and justice, people affirming their full humanity and refusing to accept the conditions that belittle that humanity."[70] What unites Jews, Christians, and all other peoples is not a particular election by God but their common humanity and their shared struggle to defend it whenever and wherever it is threatened and oppressed. By shifting the emphasis from covenant to the reign of God, Song wants to avoid the theological exclusivism that has characterized certain types of theology of religion.[71]

This focus on the reign of God forces us, according to Song, to overcome our ethnocentric concept of God. Quoting with approval "The People's Creed," written by a Christian from Zimbabwe, Song says that God is "a color-blind God" who has created "technicolor people."[72] Overcoming religious "centrism" also allows us to recognize "the saving activity of God in the world of nations and peoples, in the community of people of other religions as well as in the community of Christians."[73]

This rejection of religious centrism is also espoused by some Asian feminist theologians, such as Kwok Pui-lan and Chung Hyun Kyung. Aware that the Bible has been used in the colonial discourse to legitimate belief of the inferiority of Asian peoples and the deficiency of Asian cultures and suspicious of the Bible's patriarchal bias, Kwok Pui-lan believes that the concept of election and hence covenant leads to exclusion of the Other. Following Cain Hope Felder, she affirms that "the explicit concept of Yahweh's preference for Israel over other nations and peoples developed into a religious ideology relatively late, that is, in the period of Deuteronomic history toward the end of the seventh century B.C.E."[74] Chung Hyun Kyung also sees a connection between the claim to a special election by God and colonialism practiced by the West upon Asia. Rather than starting from and relying on the history of the covenant of God with Israel and Christianity of which the Bible is the normative record, she urges that Asian women construct their theology on their own stories:

> The text of God's revelation was, is, and will be written in our bodies and our peoples' everyday struggle for survival and liberation. God did not come first to Asian women when Western missionaries brought the Bible to Asia. God has always been with us throughout our history, long before Jesus was born. The location of God's revelation is our life itself. Our life is our text, and the Bible and church tradition are the context which sometimes becomes the reference for our own ongoing search for God.[75]

Asian liberation theologians generally reject the Christian supercessionist doctrine with regard to God's covenant with Israel. By the same token, they also reject Christianity's claim to an exclusive and total possession of a new and perfect covenant with God. Rather they insist on God's no less real presence in other religions, with their own scriptures and rituals, and in other peoples, especially in those who are poor and suffer. Instead of focusing on a special election by and covenant with God, they regard our common humanity and our shared struggle for its liberation from all forms of oppression as the basis for constructing an understanding of our relationship with God and with each other. In this way, Asian liberation theologians broaden the perspective of the discussion among Holocaust theologians of the issue of God's election and covenant.

Christ, the Marginal Person Par Excellence

For Holocaust theology christology has become the *instantia crucis*. With rhetorical flourish Rosemary Radford Ruether declares that "anti-Judaism developed theologically in Christianity as the left hand of Christology. That is to say, anti-Judaism was the negative side of the Christian claim that Jesus was the Christ."[76] Naturally, then, post-Holocaust theologians have made special efforts to reformulate a christology that is free from anti-Judaism.[77]

Asian liberation theologians too have been busy shaping a christology that would make sense to their situation. Aloysius Pieris develops a portrait of Christ as a poor monk, Choan-Seng Song an image of Christ as the crucified people, and Chung Hyun Kyung a picture of Jesus as a suffering and liberating woman.[78] Here I will focus on the portrait of Jesus as a marginal person as developed by Jung Young Lee.[79]

Drawing upon his experiences as an immigrant and on the history of Chinese, Japanese, and Korean immigrants in the United States, Lee defines his and their experiences as being on the margin as opposed to being at the center. By "marginality" Lee does not mean only being "in-between," that is, the experience of the people-on-the-margin as described by those who dwell at the center. This classical understanding of marginality is one-sided because, framed by the central group, it emphasizes the negative effects of marginality, such as ambivalence, excessive self-consciousness, restlessness, lack of self-confidence, pessimism, and the like. It needs to be corrected and complemented by the self-understanding of the marginalized people themselves. Marginal people, according to Lee, see themselves primarily as being "in-both." As Asian-Americans, Asian immigrants are both Asian and American. To stress "in-bothness" means first of all affirming one's racial, cultural, and religious origins. Being on the margin, however, prevents this affirmation of ethnic, cultural, and religious particularity from being excessive, since the margins are where different worlds touch each other and merge into each other.

Being "in-between" and being "in-both" are not mutually exclusive; both have something true to say about being an immigrant. They need to be brought together in a holistic understanding of marginality. Lee suggests that being "in-between" and "in-both" are included in being "in-beyond." To be in-between and in-both the Asian and American worlds, the immigrant must be in-beyond them. And the symbol of being in-beyond is to be a hyphenated person.[80]

With this understanding of marginality, Lee rereads the incarnation, birth, life, death, and resurrection as stories of divine marginalization and develops a portrait of Jesus as a "new marginal person *par excellence.*"[81] To indicate this fact, Lee places a hyphen between Jesus and Christ: "I use a hyphenated 'Jesus-Christ' because Jesus is the Christ, while the Christ is also Jesus. In other words, Jesus as the Christ is not enough. He is also the Christ as Jesus. Just as 'Asian-American' means an Asian and an American. Whenever I say Jesus, I mean Jesus-Christ; whenever I say Christ, I mean Christ-Jesus. They are inseparable, two facets of one existence."[82] In particular, in his death and resurrection, according to Lee, Jesus becomes the new marginal person by embracing both total negation and total affirmation; Jesus becomes a new "creative core." This new creative core is the point of intersection between two worlds, between the center and the margin, and creates a new world, a new circle with Jesus as the new core or center. But this new core is not another center of centrality; in fact it marginalizes the old centers of marginality and turns the margins into the new creative core. The new core will not become another center of centrality, for it remains at the margin of marginality. In this way the new creative core can reconcile the center with the margin and vice versa. Jesus as the new creative core is the perfect new marginal person, "because in him every marginal determinant is nullified, and everyone can overcome his or her marginality. In the creative core of Jesus-Christ, racism is overcome, sexism is no longer in practice, the poor become self-sufficient, the weak find strength."[83]

Is it not possible that in this Asian christology, in which the claim of messianic fulfillment for Jesus is relativized, and yet in which Christ is granted the status of a new creative core reconciling the margin with the center and the center with the margin, Christians, who have relegated Jews to the margin of their circle, can bring Jews to their center? In this Asian christology, is it not possible that Jews, who have long occupied the margin of a Christian society, can be brought into a new center, not in order to relegate other groups, be they Christians or Palestinians, to the margin of their newly founded state, but to reconcile them with themselves in the new center?

Power or Release from Han?

Millennia of oppression leave indelible scars not only on the oppressed persons' bodies but on their souls as well. To overcome this state of helplessness and to prevent it from ever recurring, the oppressed people, once liberated, will establish all kinds of institutions to perpetuate the memory of their oppression. Their stories of oppression and suffering can produce even a religion *sui generis*. This is, according to Rabbi Michael Goldberg, what has happened to the Holocaust. There is now "the Holocaust cult": The Holocaust with its dogma of survival at any cost has replaced the Jewish faith in God and functions as "civil Judaism"; it has a cult in the observance of Yom Hashoah; it erects shrines and museums; and it has its own priesthood.[84] In particular, the Holocaust gave birth to the state of Israel, which in the eyes of some Jews and Holocaust theologians has acquired the status of an article of faith, totally immune from any possible criticism.

Asia, too, has its own holocausts, in the long past as well as in recent years, from centuries of political oppression and colonialism to the "Rape of Nanjing" to the "Killing Fields." Oppressed Asian peoples, too, have perpetuated their histories of suffering to make sure that their descendants and others will not forget them and that oppression will not be repeated. Among Asian liberation theologians, Korean theologians have devoted much attention to the theme of the suffering and oppression of the *minjung*. By *minjung*, a Korean word that literally means "the popular mass" but that is left untranslated, is meant "the oppressed, exploited and suppressed politically, economically, socially, culturally, and intellectually, like women, ethnic groups, the poor, workers and farmers, including intellectuals themselves."[85]

According to *minjung* theologians, a prolonged oppression and humiliation of the Korean *minjung* by foreign powers such as the Chinese and the Japanese and by their own dictators have produced in them a deep sense of *han*. *Han*, another Korean word that defies exact translation and is left untranslated, literally means anger, grudge, or sad resentment. It is defined by Hyun Young Hak as "a sense of unresolved resentment against injustice suffered, a sense of helplessness because of the overwhelming odds against, a feeling of total abandonment ('Why has Thou forsaken Me?'), a feeling of acute pain and sorrow in one's guts and bowels making the whole body writhe and wiggle, and an obstinate urge to take 'revenge' and to right the wrong all these constitute."[86] It is agreed by *minjung* theologians that Korean women constitute "the *minjung* of the *minjung*" and suffer from "the *han* of *han*."

There are two ways to deal with *han*. One is passively to accept and internalize it as one's fate, which leads to resignation and despair. The other is to refuse it and work toward eliminating it. The process of resolving *han* is called *dan*, literally meaning "cutting off." According to Kim Chi-ha, a Korean Catholic poet and activist, it takes place on both individual and collective levels. On the individual level, it requires self-denial or renunciation of material wealth and comforts. This self-denial will cut off the *han* from our hearts. On the collective level, *han* can work toward the transformation of the world by raising humans to a higher level of existence. This process, again according to Kim Chi-ha, is composed of four steps: realizing the presence of God in us and worshiping God, allowing this divine consciousness to grow in us, practicing what we believe about God, and struggling against injustice by transforming the world.[87]

Other more traditional and less militant ways to remove *han* include rituals, drama, mask dance, and shamanism. By means of these activities the participants achieve what is called "critical transcendence," through which past *han* is resolved and liberation achieved.[88]

The Holocaust has produced in the Jews a kind of *han*. Instead of internalizing it as their divinely ordained fate, most Jews believe it is incumbent upon them to remove it by securing power and using it against those who threaten their survival. One of the results of this effort of empowerment, together with the Zionist movement, is of course the founding of the state of Israel. But as is well known, the battered child will often grow up into a child batterer, and the oppressed, once they have achieved power, will turn into oppressors if driven by fear and forsaking moral norms. That the state of Israel has been guilty of abusing its power, especially in its treatment of Palestinians, is doubted by few. Even ardent Holocaust theologians have been critical of certain policies of the Israeli government vis-à-vis the Palestinians, especially during the *intifada*.[89] Furthermore, as Michael Goldberg has pointed out, the memory of the Holocaust has been used by some Jews as both a moral sword and a shield — "a sword of moral criticism with which to prick the consciences of others and a shield to deflect the sting of that selfsame criticism from their own consciences."[90] The rabbi feels obligated to remind his fellow Jews that "even victims can still sin."[91] Marc Ellis, a Jewish liberation theologian, has called for the de-absolutization of the state of Israel and of the Holocaust in working out a resolution to the Israeli-Palestinian conflict and a new Jewish theology.[92]

John Pawlikowski has persuasively argued that one of the theological challenges of the Holocaust is the question of the ethics of power. He agrees with Jewish Holocaust theologians such as Emil Fackenheim and Irving Greenberg that after the Shoah the Jews cannot rely on divine intervention in human history to protect them, even if they consider themselves a covenanted people, but must assume responsibility, through the use of power, for their survival.[93] But he hastens to quote Romano Guardini, warning that we must "integrate power into life in such a way that man can employ power without forfeiting his humanity, or to surrender his humanity to power and perish."[94]

It is here that *minjung* theologians' reflections on the process of resolving *han* will prove helpful. For, besides the struggle to bring about justice and freedom for themselves and to become subjects of their own histories, the oppressed people, according to *minjung* theologians, must practice, not as an alternative to the social and political struggle but as a necessary complement to it, a spiritual discipline that would bind them in solidarity with other victims and thus prevent their exercise of power from becoming abusive and repressive. Such spirituality has been described as "concrete and total," "creative and flexible," "prophetic and historical," "community-oriented," "pro-life," "ecumenical, all embracing," and "cosmic, creation-centered."[95] Ultimately, such a spirituality will lead one to recognize that oneself, a victim, has become a victimizer in one's turn and that to fully overcome injustice and suffering and to achieve freedom, one must make the painful journey from a self-absorbed obsession with one's own suffering to altruistic actions to redress injustices on behalf of one's fellow innocent sufferers, from self-righteous protestations of one's innocence to a humbling and humanizing encounter with the mysterious and free God, from an arrogant demand for satisfaction of one's rights to a grateful recognition of God's gratuitous love.[96] Michael Lerner, in developing an approach to Jewish liberation theology, insists on the same dynamics:

> The Torah screams out to the Jews a very different message: When you go into your land, do not re-create Egypt, *do not re-create a world of oppression.* You do not have to do so. Your own experience as people who were oppressed may create a psychological tendency to become oppressors, but it simultaneously has created another possibility: the possibility of remembering your experience, and using that as a basis for identifying with the oppressed, and not re-creating that oppression for others in the present.[97]

Furthermore, should this process not finally lead Jews and Christians to asking for forgiveness and granting forgiveness, and ultimately to mutual reconciliation?

> The reality of the Holocaust cannot be made to go away by continuing to weigh up guilt and responsibility. Such exercises, while not completely pointless, often come close to being obscene. Rather what we and the Jew must both do is to remember. But without forgiveness we Christians are tempted simply to forget, deny, or wallow in inaction; and Jews are tempted to lose their humanity in humiliation or vengeance. But if we are forgiven we have the chance to remember and to make this terrible event part of our common history so that we can together make a different human story for the future and look forward to the day when God's reign will come and we can embrace as brother and sister.[98]

Holocaust Theology and Asian Liberation Theology: The Continuing Dialogue

In 1995, fifty years after atomic bombs were dropped on Hiroshima and Nagasaki, Japan remembered not only Japanese victims of the war but Jewish victims as well. A Holocaust museum, dedicated to the memory of 1.5 million Jewish children murdered by the Nazis, was opened in June of the same year in Fukuyama, a city near Hiroshima. Anne Frank's diary, translated into Japanese, was also exhibited in Hiroshima's Peace Park.

Less known is what has been called the Fugu Plan, Japan's top-secret plan to create an "Israel in Asia." Conceived by Japanese diplomats, industrialists, and military leaders, this scheme involved offering displaced European Jews a safe haven in Japan-controlled Manchuria. Its purpose was twofold: (1) obtaining Jewish financial and technical resources in exchange for physical safety and (2) improving Japan's image with the United States and gaining the sympathy of America's most influential Jewish population. The plan was called "the Fugu Plan" because, though advantageous to Japan, if mishandled it would backfire badly—like the blowfish, delicious but deadly if badly cooked, called *fugu* in Japanese. Though this plan foundered with Japan's entry into the Tripartite Pact with Nazi Germany and Italy in 1940, it saved the lives of thousands of Jews from the Holocaust since they were issued Japanese transit visas and given wartime refuge in Asia.[99]

These two unlikely events symbolize the dialogue between Holocaust theology and Asian liberation theology. Conceived apart in different times and at different places but in the same womb, namely, the common faith in the God of Abraham, Isaac, and Jacob, they are brought together like long-lost twins in an unexpected reunion. As often happens between siblings, their relationships may not always be smooth, there may be misunderstanding and even rivalry, and sometimes ugly things are said, and in this case, by the younger against the elder.

Though dissimilar, these twin theologies have some identical genes. Both were born in the crucible of prolonged and bitter oppression and injustice. Because of their experience of innocent suffering, they are animated by a burning sense of justice. And in their struggle for liberation, both appeal to the Exodus, the founding event of both Judaism and Christianity, as the source of their empowerment. They put their faith and trust in a God who takes sides with the poor and the oppressed. To galvanize people of other faiths to the same struggle for freedom and justice, they also appeal to their common humanity and dignity.

But like twins they not only are blessed with similar strengths but also are susceptible to the same diseases. By insisting upon suffering and empowerment as well as on innocence and redemption,[100] both Holocaust theology and Asian liberation theology run the risk of romanticizing the people whose interests they serve, be they the state of Israel or the *minjung* or the women within the *minjung,* placing them beyond the realm of evil and turning them into new messiahs and idols. They run the risk of forgetting the real danger of yesterday's oppressed becoming tomorrow's oppressors. Furthermore, when the people they defend achieve independence and power, both theologies insist that they and their policies be judged according to the common standards of morality of the nations, opting for normalization rather than specialness, thereby losing their distinctive if not unique character as God's covenanted people, the Jews obscuring their prophetic legacy and the Asian Christians their Christian heritage vis-à-vis other religious communities.

Fortunately, these diseases are not fatal to these two theologies, since each possesses within itself antibodies to fight against them. However, their immunity will be much improved if in a continuing dialogue they share with each other their particular strengths and set up defenses against common dangers, just as the Japanese remembered not only their own victims of the atomic bombs but also the Jewish victims of the Holocaust, and as the architects of the Fugu Plan, even out of self-interest, attempted to save European Jews from the Nazi death camps.

NOTES

1. See Franklin Littell, "Christendom, Holocaust and Israel," *Journal of Ecumenical Studies* 10 (Summer 1973): 483–497, and *The Crucifixion of the Jews* (New York: Harper and Row, 1975). For helpful bibliographies on the Holocaust, see the massive work of Steven T. Katz, *The Holocaust in Historical Context*, vol. 1, *The Holocaust and Mass Death before the Modern Age* (New York: Oxford University Press, 1994), 583–677. Vol. 2, *The Holocaust and Mass Death in the Modern Age*, and vol. 3, *The Uniqueness of the Holocaust*, have been announced but have not yet appeared. Bibliography on the Jewish-Christian dialogue can be found in the following works: A. Roy Eckardt, "Recent Literature on Christian-Jewish Relations," *Journal of the Academy of Religion* 49, no. 1 (1981): 99–111; Eugene J. Fisher, *Faith without Prejudice: Rebuilding Christian Attitudes toward Judaism*, rev. and expanded ed. (New York: Crossroad, 1993), 195–205; Eugene J. Fisher, ed., *Visions of the Other: Jewish and Christian Theologians Assess the Dialogue* (New York: Paulist Press, 1994), 90–98; Eugene J. Fisher and Leon Klenicki, eds., *In Our Time: The Flowering of Jewish-Catholic Dialogue* (New York: Paulist Press, 1990), 107–161; James H. Charlesworth, ed., *Jews and Christians: Exploring the Past, Present, and Future* (New York: Crossroad, 1990), 242–248; Norman A. Beck, *Mature Christianity in the 21st Century: The Recognition and Repudiation of the Anti-Jewish Polemic in the New Testament*, expanded and rev. ed. (New York: Crossroad, 1994), 346–352; James F. Moore, *Christian Theology after the Shoah* (Lanham, Md.: University Press of America, 1993), 177–182; Peter von der Osten-Sacken, *Christian-Jewish Dialogue: Theological Foundations*, trans. Margaret Kohl (Philadelphia: Fortress, 1986), 203–207; Michael E. Lodahl, *Shekhina/Spirit: Divine Presence in Jewish and Christian Religion* (New York: Paulist Press, 1992), 223–231; Clark M. Williamson, *A Guest in the House of Israel: Post-Holocaust Church Theology* (Louisville: Westminster/John Knox Press, 1993), 317–335.

2. The writings of Latin American liberation theologians are already well known and need not be cited here. It is sufficient to mention the names of Gustavo Gutiérrez, Juan Luis Segundo, Leonardo Boff, Clodovis Boff, and Jon Sobrino. Works that present liberation theology from the global perspective include Curt Cadorette et al., eds., *Liberation Theology* (Maryknoll: Orbis, 1992); Alfred T. Hennelly, *Liberation Theologies: The Global Pursuit of Justice* (Mystic, Conn.: Twenty-Third Publications, 1995); and Priscilla Pope-Levison and John R. Levison, *Jesus in Global Contexts* (Louisville: Westminster/John Knox Press, 1992).

3. Metz's full statement reads as follows: "What Christian theologians can *do* for the murdered of Auschwitz and thereby for a true Christian-Jewish ecumenism is, in every case, this: Never again to do theology in such a way that its construction remains unaffected, or could remain unaffected, by Auschwitz. In this sense, I make available to my students an apparently very simple but, in fact, extremely demanding criterion for evaluating the theo-

logical scene: Ask yourselves if the theology you are learning is such that it could remain unchanged before and after Auschwitz. If this is the case, be on your guard!" See *The Emergent Church,* trans. Peter Mann (New York: Crossroad, 1981), 28.

4. It is significant that even in a book such as *On Job: God-Talk and the Suffering of the Innocent* (Maryknoll: Orbis, 1987), which deals with the possibility of believing in and speaking about God in the face of massive innocent suffering, Gustavo Gutiérrez does not discuss the Holocaust at all. Perhaps Gutiérrez may be excused by his intention to focus on "what it means to talk of God in the context of Latin America, and more concretely in the context of the suffering of the poor—which is to say, the vast majority of the population" (p. xviii). In the conclusion of his book, Gutiérrez maintains that in Latin America the question is not precisely "How are we to do theology after Auschwitz?" but rather "How are we doing theology *while Ayacucho lasts?*" since cruel murder on a massive scale is *still* going on (102).

A book edited by Otto Maduro, *Judaism, Christianity and Liberation: An Agenda for Dialogue* (Maryknoll: Orbis, 1991), contains essays by two Christian Latin American theologians, one by Pablo Richard entitled "Jewish and Christian Liberation Theology" (pp. 33–39), the other by Julio de Santa Ana entitled "The Holocaust and Liberation" (pp. 40–52). This volume deals with various aspects of the Jewish-Christian dialogue from the perspective of liberation theology. Even though Latin American liberation theologians have not written extensively on Judaism, their writings, especially their understandings of Jesus and his Jewish context, have been subjected to a stringent critique from the vantage point of contemporary Jewish-Christian dialogue. See Leon Klenicki, "The Theology of Liberation: A Latin American Jewish Exploration," American Jewish Archives 35 (April 1983): 27–39, and John T. Pawlikowski, *Christ in the Light of the Christian-Jewish Dialogue* (New York: Paulist Press, 1982), 59–73. Pawlikowski examines Gustavo Gutiérrez, José Miguez Bonino, Jon Sobrino, and Leonardo Boff.

Outstanding among feminist Christian theologians who have written extensively on liberation theology and Judaism is Rosemary Radford Ruether. See her book written together with her husband, Herman J. Ruether, *The Wrath of Jonah: Religion and Nationalism in the Israel-Palestinian Conflict* (San Francisco: Harper and Row, 1989).

5. See Dan Cohn-Sherbok, *On Earth as It Is in Heaven: Jews, Christians, and Liberation Theology* (Maryknoll: Orbis, 1987); Marc Ellis, *Toward a Jewish Theology of Liberation* (Maryknoll: Orbis, 1987); Marc Ellis, *Beyond Innocence and Redemption: Confronting the Holocaust and Israeli Power* (San Francisco: Harper and Row, 1990). For evaluations of Jewish liberation theology, see the essays in *Judaism, Christianity and Liberation* by Judd Kruger Levingston, "Liberation Theology and Judaism" (1–19), Michael Lerner, "Breaking the Chains of Necessity: An Approach to Jewish Liberation Theology" (55–64), Rosemary Radford Ruether, "False Messianism and Prophetic Consciousness: Toward a Liberation Theology of Jewish-Christian Solidarity" (83–95), Richard L. Rubenstein, "Jews, Israel, and Liberation" (96–109), and Norman Solomon, "Economics and Liberation: Can the Theology of Liberation Decide Economic Questions?" (122–39).

6. I use "anti-Judaism" rather than "anti-Semitism" because this hostility against Jews and Judaism was based primarily on theological motives rather than on racial ideologies and/or economic stereotyping.

7. By "Asian theology" I refer to the theology done by Indian, Japanese, Korean, Sri Lankan, and Taiwanese theologians with whose writings I am familiar.

8. For a history of Asian Christianity from the beginnings to 1500, see the monumental work of Samuel Hugh Moffet, *A History of Christianity in Asia,* vol. 1 (Maryknoll: Orbis, 1998). I am indebted to Moffet for information on the early history of Christianity in Asia and bibliographies related to it.

9. The two modern translations of the *Acts of Thomas* are: from the surviving Syriac

text, A. F. J. Klijn, *The Acts of Thomas: Introduction, Text and Commentary* (Leiden: Brill, 1962), and from a Greek text, G. Bornkamm, "The Acts of Thomas," in E. Hennecke, *New Testament Apocrypha*, vol. 2, ed. W. Schneemelcher, English ed. by R. M. Wilson (London: Lutterworth, 1965).

10. *The Doctrine of Addai* exists in two manuscripts, an early fifth-century one, discovered by Cureton in 1848 and published in 1864, and the other, more complete, dated to the sixth century, from the Imperial Public Library of St. Petersburg, translated and edited by George Phillips as *The Doctrine of Addai the Apostle* (1876). See W. Cureton, *Ancient Syriac Documents Relative to the Earliest Establishment of Christianity in Edessa and the Neighboring Countries . . .* (London: 1864; reprint, Amsterdam: Oriental Press, 1967).

11. See *Opere storiche del P. Matteo Ricci*, vol. 2, ed. Pietro Tacchi Venturi (Macerata: F. Giorgetti, 1913), 289–293.

12. See Pasquale M. D'Elia, ed., *Fonti Ricciane*, vol. 2 (Rome: Libreria dello Stato, 1942–49), 320.

13. See ibid., 141, n. 4.

14. See ibid., 323.

15. See Jonathan Spencer, *The Memory Palace of Matteo Ricci* (New York: Viking Penguin, 1984), 95.

16. On the first Christian mission to China, see Moffett, 288–323.

17. D'Elia, 130.

18. See ibid., 324–325.

19. For an account of Ricci's experiences of anti-Judaism, see Spencer, 108–111.

20. See Matteo Ricci, *The True Meaning of the Lord of Heaven*, trans., with introd. and notes, by Douglas Lancashire and Peter Hu Kuo-chen (St. Louis: Institute of Jesuit Sources, 1985). Indeed, in this work, Ricci does not mention the Jews at all, though he could have done so in the last chapter of his book, where he gives a brief account of God's plan of salvation, in particular of Mary and Jesus.

21. Alexandre de Rhodes (1593–1660) came to Cochinchina (Central Vietnam) in 1624, started his mission in Tonkin (North Vietnam) in 1627, and was expelled from there in 1630. He came back to Cochinchina in 1640 and worked there off and on until 1645. Again expelled from Cochinchina, he was sent to Rome to lobby for the establishment of a hierarchy in Vietnam. In 1654 he left for the mission in Persia, where he died in 1660. Besides producing many important historical works on the beginnings of Christianity in Vietnam and a Vietnamese-Portuguese-Latin dictionary, de Rhodes wrote a catechism, the first book written in the Romanized script. For the life and work of Alexandre de Rhodes, see Peter C. Phan, *Mission and Catechesis: Alexandre de Rhodes and Inculturation in Seventeenth Century Vietnam* (Maryknoll: Orbis, 1998).

22. The catechism was published in Rome in 1651 under the auspices of the Congregation of the Propaganda Fide. For an extensive discussion of this catechism, see Phan, *Mission and Catechesis*. For an English translation of this work, see ibid., 211–315. The book has also been translated into Thai.

23. Ibid., 278. De Rhodes's views of the Jews and the Pharisees are derived exclusively from the Gospel of John, upon which later Christian anti-Judaism depends heavily. For an excellent study of anti-Judaism in the Gospel of John, see R. Alan Culpepper, "The Gospel of John as a Threat to Jewish-Christian Relations," in *Overcoming Fear between Jews and Christians*, ed. James M. Charlesworth (New York: Crossroad, 1992), 21–43.

24. Ibid., 280.

25. Ibid., 282.

26. Ibid., 297.

27. Ibid., 297.

28. Ibid., 297–298. De Rhodes's implicit anti-Judaism is all the more poignant as he

was a descendant of Jews. The de Rhodes family was from Catalayud, Spain. Probably the family left for Avignon toward the end of the fifteenth century, when the Spanish Inquisition was getting very harsh against "converted" Jews. The family's original name was *Rueda,* written as *Rode* in provençal. "Rode" or "rouelle" means a small wheel, which Jews were required to wear on their clothes during the Middle Ages. The "de" was added to the name as an elegant way to hide the true ethnic origin of the family.

29. De Rhodes introduced a paraliturgical devotion called *ngam dung* (standing meditation). To enable Christians to participate in the liturgy of the Holy Week, in particular the Tenebrae, and to obviate their ignorance of Latin, de Rhodes composed in Vietnamese the mysteries of the passion in fifteen *ngam* (meditations). Each of the meditations is declaimed, with the accompaniment of drum and gong, by a member of the faithful, most often a man, who stands (*dung*) on a platform in the middle of the church. Behind the platform there is a crucifix and a fifteen-branch candelabrum. At the end of each meditation, a candle is extinguished, followed by the common recital of one Our Father, seven Hail Marys, and one Glory Be. This well-attended devotion, which resembles the classical theater (*cheo, tuong*), with its dialogues between the assembly and the declaimer and the use of drum and gong, is still celebrated in many parts of Vietnam on every Friday of Lent and each evening of the Holy Week. Needless to say, in these meditations there is no lack of disparaging statements against Jews and Judaism.

30. As is well known, passion plays are very popular in the Philippines. They are also widespread in Vietnam. Most probably they were introduced to Vietnam by Portuguese and Spanish missionaries in the seventeenth century. Needless to say, in these dramatizations of the passion a lot of negative stock ideas about Jews and Judaism are given a vivid form. On the dangers of dramatizations of the passion, see the excellent document issued by the Bishops' Committee for Ecumenical and Interreligious Affairs, *Criteria for the Evaluation of Dramatization of the Passion* (Washington, D.C.: NCCB, 1988).

31. Aloysius Pieris, *An Asian Theology of Liberation* (Maryknoll: Orbis, 1988), 46. One of Pieris's theological leitmotifs is that Jesus underwent a double baptism: at the river Jordan (prophetic religiousness) and on the cross (material poverty). He argues that Asian churches, if they are to become churches *of* Asia and not only *in* Asia, must immerse themselves in this double baptism, living the religiousness of Asian religions and struggling for the liberation of the poor. For an interpretation of Pieris's christology, see Peter C. Phan, "Jesus the Christ with an Asian Face," *Theological Studies* 57 (1996): 406–410. Other works by Pieris include: *Love Meets Wisdom: A Christian Experience of Buddhism* (Maryknoll: Orbis, 1988) and *Fire and Water: Basic Issues in Asian Buddhism and Christianity* (Maryknoll: Orbis, 1996).

32. Choan-Seng Song (b. 1929) is currently president of the World Alliance of Reformed Churches; professor of theology and Asian cultures at the Pacific School of Religion, Berkeley, California; and regional professor of theology at the South East Asia Graduate School of Theology in Singapore and Hong Kong. His publications include *Third-Eye Theology: Theology in Formation in Asian Settings* (Maryknoll: Orbis, 1979; rev. ed. 1990); *The Compassionate God* (Maryknoll: Orbis, 1982); *Tell Us Our Names: Story Theology from an Asian Perspective* (Maryknoll: Orbis, 1984); *Theology from the Womb of Asia* (Maryknoll: Orbis, 1986); *Jesus, the Crucified People* (New York: Crossroad, 1990); *Jesus and the Reign of God* (Minneapolis: Fortress, 1993); and *Jesus in the Power of the Spirit* (Minneapolis: Fortress, 1994). On Song's theology, see Peter C. Phan, "Experience and Theology: An Asian Liberation Perspective," *Zeitschrift für Missionswissenschaft und Religionswissenschaft* 77 (1993): 114–118; on his christology, see Phan, "Jesus the Christ with an Asian Face," 417–421.

33. Song, *Jesus, the Crucified People,* 44.

34. Ibid., 54.

35. Elsewhere Song explicitly criticizes Judaism's notion of God as a "high-voltage God," that is, as a being remote from and dangerous to the common people, in contrast to the God of Jesus, who is near and available to all, none excluded: "As the heir to the religion of the Old Testament, Judaism is a very high-voltage religion. The God of Judaism is carefully protected from unworthy men and women polluted with cares of this world. Persons in the street are unclean because the niceties of religious laws and rituals are just too remote from their daily lives. This God is even more remote from the pagans who have no pious blood, not even a drop of it, in their veins. They are thoroughly contaminated by sins and impiety. To all these persons the God of Judaism is a very dangerous God. They can only try to imagine what that God looks like from the outer court of the Temple. It is this high-voltage religion that Jesus dared to challenge. In the end Jesus was 'electrocuted' by that high-voltage religion." See his *The Compassionate God,* 110. It must be pointed out that Song applies the same critique to Christianity as well.

36. See Song, *Jesus, the Crucified People,* 98: "The cross is *not,* as some theologians would have us think, Jesus-God tearing away from God, the Son-God going through the pain of separation from the Father-God. The cross is not such a 'theo'-logical thing. It is not 'the Second Person' of the Trinity forsaken by 'the First Person' of the Trinity. Nor is it 'the Second Person' of the Trinity left in the lurch by 'the Third Person' of the Trinity. Such 'trinitarian' language makes little sense of the cross on which Jesus died. Highly abstract theological language such as this almost suggests a mutiny within God."

37. Ibid., 75.

38. Ibid., 122.

39. Ibid., 82. It is clear that Song does not limit the concept of the God of retribution to Judaism alone but thinks that it is also endemic to Christian theological tradition, indeed to any organized religion. The God of retribution is "the God of an organized religion and a religious hierarchy" (98).

40. Song, *Jesus and the Reign of God,* 190.

41. Ibid., 190.

42. Ibid., 197.

43. Ibid., 197.

44. Ibid., 205.

45. In general, Asian liberation theologians are not well acquainted with recent studies on the historical Jesus and on the Second Temple period in Judaism, in particular the Pharisees. This lack of proper knowledge is also present in many Latin American liberation theologians, as John Pawlikowski has correctly pointed out. Had they possessed this knowledge, liberation theologians would have avoided the approach of articulating the meaning of the Christ experience in terms of Jewish rejection and would have constructed a christology by incorporating Jewish cultural and religious values.

46. As was mentioned above, the Holocaust has radically challenged both Jewish and Christian theologies. Holocaust theologians claim that the Holocaust represents the "end point," "interruption," "crisis," "break," "rupture," and "paradigm shift" in both theologies.

47. Stephen R. Haynes, "Christian Holocaust Theology: A Critical Assessment," *Journal of the American Academy of Religion* 62, no. 2 (1994): 554. In this essay Haynes offers an informed and balanced critique of Christian Holocaust theologians (e.g., A. Roy Eckardt, Alice L. Eckardt, Franklin Littell, Harry James Cargas, Paul Van Buren, and Robert Willis), especially their unconditional support for the state of Israel, to which they assign a profound theological significance, raising it to the status of a "theological datum." See also Haynes, *Prospects for Post-Holocaust Theology* (Atlanta: Scholars Press, 1991), for his evaluation of Karl Barth, Jürgen Moltmann and Paul Van Buren.

48. Stephen R. Haynes lists eleven topics for post-Holocaust theology in the 1990s:

covenant, Jewish Monotheism vs. Christian Trinitarianism, Messianism, the church-Israel relationship, the theological significance of the Holocaust, the status of Christian anti-Judaism, the place of Scriptural and theological traditions in the church's revision of its understanding of Israel, Jewish desire to be left alone, Christian Zionism, the identity of a Jew, and secular vs. theological conceptions of Israel. See his *Prospects for Post-Holocaust Theology* (Atlanta: Scholars Press, 1991), 277–284. On the other hand, John T. Pawlikowski sees the challenges of the Holocaust for Christian theology in three areas: the concept of God, christology, and ethics (in particular the ethics of using power). See his "The Shoah: Continuing Theological Challenge for Christianity," in *Contemporary Christian Religious Responses to the Shoah,* ed. Steven L. Jacobs (Lanham: University Press of America, 1993), 140–165, and "Christian Theological Concerns after the Holocaust," in Fisher, *Visions of the Other,* 28–51.

49. David Hartman and especially Michael Goldberg refuse to take the Holocaust as the "master story" on which to interpret the history of Israel. Both regard the story of the Exodus and God's covenant with Israel at Sinai as the fundamental stories in which the meaning of Israel's survival is to be found and call for a renewed faithfulness to the covenant as a way to guarantee Jewish survival. See David Hartman, *A Living Covenant: The Innovative Spirit in Traditional Judaism* (New York: Macmillan, 1985), and Michael Goldberg, *Why Should Jews Survive? Looking Past the Holocaust toward a Future* (New York: Oxford University Press, 1995).

50. See Richard Rubenstein, *After Auschwitz: Radical Theology and Contemporary Judaism* (New York: Bobbs-Merrill, 1966).

51. See Emil Fackenheim, *The Jewish Return into History* (New York: Schocken Books, 1978). See also his *God's Presence in History: Jewish Affirmations and Philosophical Reflections* (New York: New York University Press, 1970), and *To Mend the World: Foundations of Future Jewish Thought* (New York: Schocken Books, 1982).

52. See Arthur Cohen, *The Tremendum: A Theological Interpretation of the Holocaust* (New York: Crossroad, 1981).

53. See Irving Greenberg, "The Voluntary Covenant," *Perspectives* no. 3 (New York: National Jewish Resource Center for Learning and Leadership, 1982), and also his magisterial essay "Cloud of Smoke, Pillar of Fire: Judaism, Christianity, and Modernity after the Holocaust," in *Auschwitz: Beginning of a New Era? Reflections on the Holocaust,* ed. Eva Fleischner (New York: Anti-Defamation League of B'nai B'rith, 1974), 7–55.

54. Pawlikowsli, "The Shoah: Continuing Theological Challenge," 149. Pawlikowski goes on to develop his notion of a "compelling" God by which one can "recover a fresh sense of transcendence to accompany our heightened sense of human responsibility after the *Shoah*" (149). He further suggests that this notion of a "compelling" God can be obtained only though sacramental celebration and prayer.

55. Song, *Jesus, the Crucified People,* 115.

56. Ibid., 116.

57. Ibid., 119.

58. Goldberg, 168.

59. Song, *Jesus in the Power of the Spirit,* 185.

60. Song, *Theology from the Womb of Asia,* 165.

61. Song, *Jesus, the Crucified People,* 122.

62. Song, *Jesus in the Power of the Spirit,* 188.

63. Ibid., 190. For Song's contrast between God's "power" and human dictatorship and totalitarianism, see his *Tell Us Our Names: Story Theology from an Asian Perspective,* 163–180. Song argues that the "power" of God leads to "people politics" (democracy) as opposed to "power politics" (autocratic rule). Moreover, Song also believes that "people politics" will lead to what he calls the "politics of the cross" of Jesus, but he immediately adds: "The powerless cross proves so powerful that throughout the centuries it has empow-

ered countless persons to struggle for justice and freedom. In the name of the cross Christians give witness to the God of love and mercy in a world of hate and conflict" (180).

64. For Bertold Klappert's eight models, see his *Israel und die Kirche: Erwägungen zur Israellehre Karl Barths* (Munich: Kaiser, 1980). Klappert speaks of "substitution," "integration," "typology," "illustration," "subsumation," "complementarity," "representation," and "participation" models. Klappert considers the first five as negative and the last three as positive. Marcus Barth summarizes four models: 1. Israel's replacement by the church; 2. partial continuity between Israel and church, which is the former's remnant; 3. schism in the one people of God, which brought out the "split people"; 4. complementarity between Israel and church. See his *The People of God* (Sheffield: JSOT Press, 1983).

65. See John Pawlikowski, *What Are They Saying about Christian-Jewish Relations?* (New York: Paulist Press, 1980), 33–67, and *Jesus and the Theology of Israel* (Wilmington, Del.: Michael Glazier, 1989), 15–47.

66. Pawlikowski argues that this position is held, of course with varying nuances, by Monika Hellwig, Marcel Dubois, Cardinal Carlo Martini, Michael Remaud, and Pope John Paul II among Catholics; by Bertold Klappert, Peter von der Osten-Sacken, Paul van Buren, A. Roy Eckardt, and J. Coos Schoneveld among Protestants. Among official church documents that tend toward this position are to be noted the Vatican's *Notes on the Correct Way to Present the Jews and Judaism in Preaching and Catechesis in the Roman Catholic Church* (June 24, 1985) [available in *In Our Time: The Flowering of Jewish-Catholic Dialogue,* ed. Dr. Eugene J. Fisher and Rabbi Leon Klenicki (New York: Paulist, 1990), 38–50]; The Synod of the Evangelical Church of the Rhineland's *Towards Renovation of the Relationship of Christians and Jews* (January 1980) [available in *The Theology of the Churches and the Jewish People: Statements by the World Council of Churches and Its Member Churches* (Geneva: WCC Publications, 1988), 92–94].

67. This position is held by Gregory Baum, Clemens Thoma, and Franz Mussner among Catholics, and by James Parkes and J. Coert Rylaarsdam among Protestants. Pawlikowski himself subscribes to the double-covenant view, though he confesses that "there are times I have been tempted to accept the invitation of Paul van Buren and others and shift over to a single covenant viewpoint" (*Visions of the Other,* 41).

68. This is the position of John Hick, Paul Knitter, Rosemary Radford Ruether, and "pluralists" in the theology of religion in general. For an evaluation of these covenant perspectives, especially with reference to Karl Rahner, see Peter C. Phan, "Karl Rahner in Dialogue with Judaism and Islam: An Assessment," in *Religions of the Book,* ed. Gerard S. Sloyan (Lanham: University Press of America, 1992), 129–150.

69. Song believes that centrism is best expressed by Arend van Leeuwen when he writes: "Israel and the land of Israel represent the whole earth, the whole of mankind. Israel herself is a new creation, and her land the token of a new earth which the Lord will create. For that reason the life of the whole earth hangs upon the promise that Israel is to return to her land. . . . The Lord reveals to Israel, his people, what his purpose is for the whole earth" (*Christianity in World History* [London: Edinburgh House, 1964], 104). Quoted in Song, *The Compassionate God,* 79.

70. Song, *Jesus and the Reign of God,* 44. For a discussion of the symbol of the reign of God for Asians, see Peter C. Phan, "Kingdom of God: A Theological Symbol for Asians?" *Gregorianum* 79, no. 2 (1998): 295–322.

71. For a discussion of the three types of theology of religion—exclusivism, inclusivism, and pluralism—see Peter C. Phan, "Are There Other 'Saviors' for Other Peoples? A Discussion of the Problem of the Universal Significance and Uniqueness of Jesus the Christ," in *Christianity and the Wider Ecumenism,* ed. Peter C. Phan (New York: Paragon House, 1990), 163–180.

72. Song, *Jesus and the Reign of God,* 45. The text "The People's Creed" is found in

Canaan Banana, *The Gospel According to the Ghetto* (Geneva: World Council of Churches, 1974), 8.

73. Song, *Jesus in the Power of the Spirit*, 226.

74. See Kwok Pui-lan, *Discovering the Bible in the Non-Biblical World* (Maryknoll: Orbis, 1995), 89–90. Kwok Pui-lan is also aware that the concept of election and covenant has been used by Christians to oppress Jews. Furthermore, though urging against anti-Semitism in feminist interpretation, she regards the Hebrew Scriptures simply as "one significant religious resource of humankind illuminating the human capacity to love, to struggle, to repent, and to cry in joy" (89).

75. Chung Hyun Kyung, *Struggle to Be the Sun Again: Introducing Asian Women's Theology* (Maryknoll: Orbis, 1990), 111. Chung also suggests that Asian women theologians "must move away from our imposed fear of losing Christian identity, in the opinion of the mainline theological circles, and instead risk that we might be transformed by the religious wisdom of our people" through the method of *"survival-liberation centered syncretism"* (113).

76. Rosemary Radford Ruether, "Anti-Semitism and Christian Theology," in Fleischner, 79. The responses of Walter Burghardt and Yosef Hayim Yerushalmi to Ruether's essay (93–107) offer important corrections to the latter's exaggerations.

77. Among these efforts to be noted are: Eugene B. Borowitz, *Contemporary Christologies: A Jewish Response* (New York: Paulist, 1980); Michael B. McGarry, *Christology after Auschwitz* (New York: Paulist, 1977); Pawlikowski, *Christ in the Light of the Christian-Jewish Dialogue;* and John Pawlikowski, *Jesus and the Theology of Israel* (Wilmington, Del.: Michael Glazier, 1989).

78. For studies of Asian christologies, see Phan, "Jesus the Christ with an Asian Face," 399–430, and *Asian Faces of Jesus,* ed. R. S. Sugirtharajah (Maryknoll: Orbis, 1993).

79. Jung Young Lee (1935–96) was an American-Korean theologian. Besides a portrait of Jesus as a marginal person, Lee also uses the *yin-yang* metaphysics to show that Jesus is the perfect realization of change. Among his many works see *God Suffers for Us: A Systematic Inquiry into the Concept of Divine Possibility* (The Hague: Martinus Nijhoff, 1974); *The Theology of Change: A Christian Concept of God from an Eastern Perspective* (Maryknoll: Orbis, 1979); *Marginality: The Key to Multicultural Theology* (Minneapolis: Fortress, 1995); and *The Trinity in Asian Perspective* (Nashville: Abingdon, 1996). For a discussion of Lee's christology, see Phan, "Jesus the Christ with an Asian Face," 410–417.

80. Lee contends that metaphysically, the situation of the immigrant as being "in-between," "in-both," and "in-beyond" corresponds to the dipolar reality of *yin* and *yang,* and epistemologically, it corresponds with the inclusive position of both-and and neither-nor as opposed to that of either-or.

81. Lee, *Marginality,* 71.

82. Ibid., 78.

83. Ibid., 98.

84. See Goldberg, 41–59.

85. Chung Hyun Kyung, "'Han-pu-ri': Doing Theology from Korean Women's Perspective," in *We Dare to Dream: Doing Theology as Asian Women,* ed. Virginia Fabella and Sun Ai Lee Park (Hong Kong: Asian Women's Resource Centre for Culture and Theology, 1989), 138–139. Chung is quoting from David Kwang-sun Suh, mentioned below. For discussions of *minjung* theology, see *An Emerging Theology in World Perspective: Commentary on Korean Minjung Theology,* ed. Jung Young Lee (Mystic, Conn.: Twenty-Third, 1988); David Kwang-sun Suh, *The Korean Minjung in Christ* (Hong Kong: Christian Conference of Asia, 1991); Commission on Theological Concerns of the Christian Conference of Asia, *Minjung Theology: People as the Subjects of History* (Maryknoll: Orbis, 1983); and Phan, "Experience and Theology," 118–120.

86. Hyun Young Hak, "Minjung: The Suffering Servant and Hope," a lecture given at James Memorial Chapel, Union Theological Seminary, New York, April 13, 1982, p. 2, quoted in Chung, *Struggle to be the Sun Again,* 42. Moon Hee-suk gives another description of *han* as "the anger and resentment of the minjung which has been turned inward and intensified as they become objects of injustice upon injustice." See his *A Korean Minjung Theology: An Old Testament Perspective* (Maryknoll: Orbis, 1985), 1–2. James Cone, a proponent of Black theology, suggests that the equivalent of *han* is the "blues" in Black experience in North America.

87. See Lee, *An Emerging Theology,* 10–11. Besides Kim Chi-ha two other prominent proponents of *minjung* theology are Professor Suh Nam-dong and Professor Ahn Byung-mu.

88. Korean feminist theologians highlight the role of women as priestesses in shamanistic rituals (*mudang*) as a way to liberate them from their manyfold bondage. See Chung Hyun Kyung, "Opium or Seed for Revolution? Shamanism: Women-Centered Popular Religiosity," in *Theologies of the Third World: Convergences and Differences,* ed. Leonardo Boff and Virgilio Elizondo (Edinburgh: T. and T. Clark, 1988), 96–104.

89. See Irving Greenberg, "The Ethics of Jewish Power," *Perspectives,* no. 3 (New York: National Jewish Resource Center for Learning and Leadership, 1988): 1–27. For other critics of Israeli policies, see Ellis, *Beyond Innocence and Redemption,* 56–94.

90. Goldberg, 126.

91. Ibid., 128.

92. See Ellis, *Toward a Jewish Theology of Liberation* and especially *Beyond Innocence and Redemption.*

93. See Pawlikowski, "The Shoah: Continuing Theological Challenge," 161–163.

94. Ibid., 164.

95. See Chung, *Struggle to Be the Sun Again,* 91–96.

96. This is the suggestion made by Gustavo Gutiérrez in his *On Job: God-Talk and the Suffering of the Innocent.* Gutiérrez speaks of the "language of prophecy" and the "language of contemplation" required in dealing with the evil of innocent suffering. For a discussion of these two languages, see Peter C. Phan, "Overcoming Poverty and Oppression: Liberation Theology and the Problem of Evil," *Louvain Studies* 20 (1995): 3–20.

97. Lerner, 57.

98. Stanley Hauerwas, "Resurrection, the Holocaust, and Forgiveness: A Sermon for Eastertime," in *Removing Anti-Judaism from the Pulpit,* ed. Howard Clark Kee and Irwin J. Borowski (New York: Continuum, 1996), 119–120.

99. See Marvin Tokayer and Mary Swartz, *The Untold Story of the Japanese and the Jews during World War II* (New York: Paddington, 1979).

100. According to Marc Ellis, these are the two themes of early Holocaust theology, represented by Elie Wiesel and Emil Fackenheim. The third theme is specialness and normalization, which is embodied in the writings of Irving Greenberg. See *Beyond Innocence and Redemption,* 2–6.

11 | Martin Buber and Romano Guardini
Case Study in Jewish-Catholic Dialogue

Robert A. Krieg

THE INTERRELIGIOUS dialogue is not only a desire stemming from Vatican Council II and fostered by the present pope. It is also a necessity in the present situation of the world."[1] So declared the Vatican's International Theological Commission in a statement issued in English in August 1997. In its statement, "Christianity and the World Religions," the Commission has tried to follow through on Vatican II's *Nostra Aetate,* the Declaration on the Relationship of the Church to Non-Christian Religions. It has succeeded in this effort by re-affirming God's universal love. Yet, the Commission has not fully realized its intention, for its statement lacks *Nostra Aetate*'s spirit of discovery. The statement neglects to say that Catholics may learn something new about God and their Christian faith by meeting with representatives of other religions. For example, the Commission could have noted that Catholics may become better Catholics by speaking with Jews—speaking with Jews about the God of Abraham and Sarah and also about the Holocaust. Such is an insight of the Second Vatican Council: namely, that interreligious dialogue can help Christians grasp their own faith more fully, while also deepening their appreciation of other religious traditions.[2]

This kind of enrichment, in fact, occurred in the collegial relationship between the Jewish scholar Martin Buber and the Catholic scholar Romano Guardini. Because of Buber's outreach to Guardini during the 1920s, Guardini awakened to the riches of the Jewish faith. Further, as a result of his respect for Buber, Guardini began to question the then conventional theological view that God's covenant in Jesus Christ had "displaced" God's covenant with Israel. It was this questioning by Guardini as well as by other Catholics that set the stage for *Nostra Aetate*'s declarations that "the Jews remain very dear to God for the sake of the patriarchs, since God does not take back the gifts he bestowed or the choice he made" and that "the Jews should not be spoken of as rejected or accursed as if this followed from holy scripture."[3]

I wish to view the collegial relationship between Martin Buber and Romano Guardini as a case study in Jewish-Catholic dialogue.[4] I will proceed in three steps. First, a review of the friendship between Buber and Guardini will show that Buber's many initiatives toward Guardini bore fruit after the Second World War. Second, a consideration of Guardini's christological writings will highlight how their view of Judaism conflicted with Guardini's growing respect for Buber and Judaism. Third, an examination of Guardini's personal reflections during the 1950s and 1960s will show that the tension between Guardini's new experience of Judaism and his inadequate theology of Judaism motivated him to seek a fresh paradigm for God's covenant with Israel. This case study of Buber's influence on Guardini will lead to the conclusion that the International Theological Commission could have assumed a more adventuresome perspective on interreligious dialogue, especially by acknowledging the important role of paradigms in religious belief.[5]

The Evolving Friendship between Buber and Guardini

Martin Buber was born in Vienna in 1878. He was a professor at the University of Frankfurt am Main from 1924 until 1933 and at the Hebrew University in Jerusalem from 1938 until 1951. He died in Jerusalem in 1965.[6] Romano Guardini was born in Verona, Italy, in 1885, grew up in Mainz, Germany, and was a professor at the University of Berlin from 1923 until 1939, when the Third Reich forced him to resign. After the war, Guardini taught at the universities of Tübingen and Munich until his death in 1968.[7] A review of the correspondence and contacts between these two religious thinkers shows that Buber's efforts to communicate with Guardini during the 1920s led to Guardini's change in his stance to Buber and implicitly to all Jews, though sadly after the Shoah.

Martin Buber first contacted Romano Guardini in late 1918 or early 1919. After reading Guardini's *The Spirit of the Liturgy* (1918), Buber wrote to the young priest, congratulating him on his phenomenological analysis of worship.[8] Buber contacted Guardini again in the spring of 1922, when he attended a lecture by Guardini in Bonn and stayed afterward to speak informally with him. Concerning this first meeting, Buber wrote to the Protestant theologian Friedrich Gogarten on December 9, 1922, that Guardini welcomed the opportunity to speak with Buber, and yet in the following weeks (apparently in an exchange of letters) Guardini seemingly backed away from Buber. In Buber's words: "I have also met Guardini at the lecture which I heard. In our conversation he drew close to me, however subsequently withdrew to the distance of [an] assured sense of church."[9]

However, Buber did not lose interest in Guardini. He invited the Catholic theologian to a Jewish-Christian dialogue in Frankfurt am Main in the spring of 1923. It is not known whether Guardini actually attended this gathering, although he said he would be there. In any case, Guardini wrote to Buber, thanking him for the invitation and praising his book, *I-Thou* (1923). He said: "I have been reading your book for a long time. I am filled with respect, for it is well done. Perhaps I will come [to the conference in order] to tell you what I have questions about. However, these [questions] are entirely within my positive regard [for your work]."[10]

The last known prewar contact between the scholars occurred in 1928, when they agreed to hold a joint lecture, entitled "Religion and Authority: Form and Freedom," at Stuttgart's Jüdisches Lehrhaus. But Guardini withdrew from the engagement for an unknown reason, and his friend Herman Hefele, professor at the University of Tübingen, participated in his place.[11]

It appears that Buber and Guardini had little or no communication with each other from the mid-1930s until the spring of 1952. Then Romano Guardini gave a public lecture at the University of Tübingen on May 23, 1952, on Germans' need to become reconciled with Jews. Entitling his talk "Responsibility: Thoughts on the Jewish Question," the Catholic theologian explained that if Western civilization's most creative minds, such as Plato, Augustine, Mozart, and Leibnitz, could be brought to Auschwitz, they would be horrified and ask, "Where at the time was conscience? Where was honor? Indeed, where was . . . reason?"[12] Although no answer would suffice, it could be said that "[h]ere something has come out of the dark underpinnings of human beings: the barbarian, the animal in humanity." Further, this subhuman force had used the most sophisticated technology of the day to attain its goal: the extermination of Jews. This goal would shock Plato and other great minds because it violates a value that Western civilization has come to cherish: the dignity of the human person. In the aftermath of this outrage, Guardini asked, what should Germans do? First, they must honestly and publicly admit what occurred. Second, they must recognize their common humanity with Jews and assume moral responsibility for the Holocaust. This responsibility required that Germans find ways to assist the Jewish people. Outreach to Jews was important for Germans themselves as well as for Jews, for Germans would be acting as persons, thereby restoring in themselves what Adolf Hitler had deliberately set out to destroy.

Soon after giving this lecture Guardini sent a copy of it to Martin Buber in Jerusalem. On December 12, 1952, Buber wrote to Guardini that Guardini's statement indicated to Buber that Buber could now reestablish ties with his colleagues in Germany. Referring to Guardini's lecture, Buber said that "[w]hile reading it, I noticed that something had changed for me. It was again possible for me to speak publicly in Germany."[13] Indeed, from this point on Martin Buber returned to Germany for visits, lectures, and awards.[14] Moreover, Guardini's talk showed not only that something had changed for Buber but also that something had changed for Guardini himself. Before 1952 the theologian had been passive in his collegial relationship with Buber; but after his lecture Guardini initiated numerous contacts with Buber.

On June 17, 1953, the German Book Publishers announced that they would award their prestigious Peace Prize to Martin Buber.[15] Guardini immediately invited Buber to give a lecture in Munich when he came to Germany in the autumn to receive the award. Declining the invitation to lecture, Buber said that he would gladly visit with Guardini in Munich.[16] This informal meeting took place in Guardini's apartment on August 9. A few weeks later, on September 27, 1953, the German Book Publishers bestowed their Peace Prize upon Martin Buber.[17] And Guardini, who had received this award in the previous year, deliberately joined Buber for the ceremony.[18]

Guardini and Buber stayed in touch with each other during the late 1950s. For instance, after Guardini informed Buber that he would be teaching a new course on the philosophy of language in the autumn of 1958, Buber asked for a copy of Guardini's syllabus. Guardini immediately sent the Jewish philosopher this material, along with a lengthy letter in which he clarified some aspects of his syllabus.[19]

Finally, in 1963, on the occasion of Buber's eighty-fifth birthday, Guardini was among the German benefactors who donated funds so that the Martin Buber Forest could be planted in Israel's Kibbutz Hazorea. Further, although he rarely engaged in public projects, Guardini also assisted the fund-raising committee in locating donors.[20] Accompanying the gift to the State of Israel was a public statement written by Guardini:

> Martin Buber reached his eighty-fifth birthday on February 8, 1963. This fact makes a claim on our attention, for Buber is a man to whom we owe a debt of gratitude. In our day when material things have become overpowering, he has thought about the reality of the spirit. Against the danger which threatens us in the impersonal character of machines and organizations, he has called to consciousness the significance of the person and personal relationships. In a time which experienced the absurd event of the persecution of the Jews, he has given us a new translation of the Hebrew Bible out of which the sound of the ancient [divine] revelation impacts us with fresh originality. He accomplished this difficult project by working initially with friend Franz Rosenzweig and then alone.[21]

Guardini's statement continues with an explanation of why Buber's German friends had chosen to give trees in honor of Buber. In short: "The symbol of the tree belongs to that which arises out of the essence of things and is therefore always valued." This tribute to Buber sums up Guardini's postwar respect for the Jewish scholar. It prompts such questions as: Why did it take the Shoah to ignite Guardini's awareness of Buber and Judaism? Why had Guardini remained distant from Buber during the 1920s? One answer is that the conventional theology of displacement had obscured Guardini's view of Buber and Judaism.

Guardini's Theology of Judaism

The inadequacy of Guardini's theology of Judaism is evident in two of his christological books: *The Lord* (published in German in 1937) and *The Humanity of Christ* (published in German in 1958).[22]

Guardini wrote *The Lord* from 1932 to 1937 on the basis of "meditations" on the life of Christ that he offered as homilies at Masses in Berlin and at Burg Rothenels. In other words, he worked on this book while German Jews suffered from the Third Reich's boycott of their businesses (April 1, 1933), the Aryan Laws (April 7, 1933), and the Nuremberg Laws (1935). Yet, this persecution of the Jews seemingly made no impact on Guardini's "meditations." In *The Lord* he wrote in reference to the Jews of Jesus' day: "But the Jewish people did not believe. They did not change their hearts, so the kingdom did not come as it was to have come."[23] Further: "The failure of the Jewish people to accept Christ was the second Fall, the import of which can be fully grasped only in connection with the first."[24] Also, he observed that when Christians see Jews, "[t]he whole heritage of sin with its harshness and distortion looms at us. . . . Their wisdom is both divine gift and fruit of long human experience; knowledge, cleverness, correctness. They examine, weigh, differentiate, doubt; and when the Promised One comes and prophecy is fulfilled, . . . they cling to the past with its human traditions . . . and their great hour passes them by."[25]

Twenty years later, Guardini expressed a similar view in *The Humanity of Christ*. He stated that Jesus "claimed for himself the promises that had been made to David."[26] To be sure, Guardini recognized the ties between Jesus and Judaism. For example, he observed that Jesus "firmly upheld the Law and held scrupulously to the place which his Father had assigned him in history." Nevertheless, Guardini left no doubt that God's covenant in Jesus Christ had superseded God's covenant with Abraham: "What the Jewish people should always have done, but actually did so seldom, i.e., ascend by faith above immediate, tangible nature to the realm of the mind and spirit so as to become what God desired them to be, had finally been accomplished in Christ."[27] It may be significant, however, that in this postwar text Guardini remained uncharacteristically ambiguous on one point, namely, whether God has withdrawn his covenant from the Jews. Insofar as this lack of clarity is intentional, it gives an indication that Guardini was rethinking his theology of Judaism.[28]

In summary, a disparity existed between Guardini's new stance toward Buber and Judaism, on the one hand, and his conventional theology of Judaism, on the other hand. While Guardini had attained a breakthrough in his relationship with Buber in the 1950s, he did not come to a new theology of Judaism. Guardini's way of life was ahead of his theology; or, to put it another way, his *praxis* preceded his theory. But is not this kind of delay common in the history of ideas, as one paradigm shows itself to be increasingly inadequate while a new paradigm has not yet emerged?

Guardini's journey toward a fuller understanding of God's covenant with Israel is, I propose, an instance of what Thomas S. Kuhn has demonstrated in *The Structure of Scientific Revolutions* (1962, 1970). According to Kuhn, a paradigm is "an entire constellation of beliefs, values, techniques, and so on shared by the members of a given community."[29] The search for truth uncovers new data, neglected phenomena, and anomalies, with the cumulative effect of the erosion of the mental framework within which scholars are working. Eventually, there emerges a new way of making sense of things; a case in point is the Copernican revolution. This view of change in intellectual inquiry best explains what happened in Guardini's view of Judaism from the end of the war until his death in 1968.[30]

Toward a Change of Theological Paradigms

Guardini's entries in his diary during the 1950s and 1960s disclose that he felt the dissonance between his growing respect for Martin Buber and Judaism, on the one hand, and his inadequate theology of Judaism, on the other.

After Buber visited with Guardini in Munich on August 9, 1953, Guardini commented on the visit in his diary: "Martin Buber was here today for tea. He will [soon] receive the Peace Prize from the German Book Publishers; [he] has spoken at different universities and wishes to rest somewhat from now until the conferral of the Prize in Frankfurt. It was lovely to be together with him. He is wonderfully informed, wise and venerable."[31] These words of admiration for Buber lead Guardini to ask some questions of himself: "What keeps someone in the [Christian] faith? What brings it about that someone, as in a breath, all at once no longer understands, so that everything is gone? From time to time an anxiety burdens me. . . . We are capable of understanding so little."[32] These statements indicate, I believe, that Buber challenged Guardini to consider anew the character of the Christian faith and its relationship to the Jewish faith. At tea with the Jewish scholar, the Catholic scholar had sensed their spiritual kinship. Yet, this experience clashed with Guardini's theology of Judaism, and Guardini longed for a new coherence between his experience and his theory.

Guardini took another step toward understanding Martin Buber's faith when in June 1957, he set out to read the new translation of the Hebrew Bible into German by Martin Buber and Franz Rosenzweig.[33] Six months later (February 1958), as Guardini was making his way through 2 Samuel, he wrote in his diary: "I am reading 2 Samuel in the translation by Buber. By means of it, everything attains a new forcefulness."[34] Why was Guardini rereading the Hebrew Bible at this time? Surely, he wanted to see Buber's work. Moreover, he was likely rethinking the relationship between the Jewish and Christian faiths.

Two further indications of Guardini's new questioning about Judaism occurred in the mid-1960s. First, Guardini wrote a series of meditations on the Psalms, *The Wisdom of the Psalms,* which he published in 1963. (At the request of the German Bishops' Conference, he had produced a new translation of the Hebrew Psalms, *Deutscher Psalter,* in 1950.) Second, in letters to his friend Pastor Josef Weiger he mentioned that he was rethinking his theology.

In particular, he was considering how he could shift from a christocentric orientation to a theocentric orientation. Such a shift would have permitted Guardini to recognize the validity of Judaism.[35]

Romano Guardini was on the verge of a new view of the relationship between Jewish and Christian faiths during the last years of his life. Having finally recognized the inadequacy of his earlier theology of displacement, he had not yet attained an insight on how to conceive of God's covenant with Abraham and Sarah. Vatican II's *Nostra Aetate* offered this new paradigm in October 1965, shortly after Buber's death (June 13, 1965) and three years before Guardini's death. As noted earlier, the council declared in *Nostra Aetate:* "The Jews remain very dear to God." With this single sentence, the Second Vatican Council rejected the theology of displacement and laid the cornerstone for a new paradigm of God's eternal covenant with Israel.

Interfaith Dialogue and Theological Paradigms

In conclusion, I wish to return to the International Theological Commission's statement, "Christianity and the World Religions." Although the Commission spoke of the approach to interreligious dialogue that works with the category of paradigm, it quickly set aside this approach, implying that it necessarily leads to relativism.[36] The Commission could have benefited from the work of the theologian Avery Dulles. Dulles, who has worked with images, models, and paradigms of Christian belief, has observed that such an approach can bring about a deeper grasp of the truths of Christian faith. In his words: "The new scientific paradigms have been accepted because, without sacrificing the good results attained by previous paradigms, they were able in addition to solve problems that had proved intractable by means of the earlier models."[37] In this perspective, Vatican II's discussion of God's covenants in *Nostra Aetate* not only safeguards the teachings of Christian revelation but also provides a fuller understanding of God's covenant in Jesus Christ than was available in the theology of displacement. At the same time, the council illumined the truth about God's eternal covenant with Israel. In short, Vatican II brought about a shift in Catholic paradigms of Judaism.

On his eightieth birthday, Guardini explained his vision of theological inquiry as the mediating point in a dialogue between Christian faith and the contemporary world. He said that "on the basis of Christian faith, there should open a view of the world, a glimpse of its essence, an assessment of its values, that is otherwise not possible." At the same time, the culture and issues of the day should enrich Christians' understanding of their faith, for "from the world and its problems questions are posed to divine revelation which brings its otherwise silent content to speech. In this ever new, changing encounter, there is attained a fruitful illumination of Christian existence."[38] This statement makes sense when one approaches it with an appreciation of the crucial role of paradigms in intellectual inquiry. In this statement, Guardini himself has implicitly affirmed the value of paradigm shifts in theology. Further, it is accurate and beneficial to speak of Guardini's change toward Judaism within the language of paradigms because this language permits an appreciation of how Guardini could have recognized the need for change on an experiential level before seeing its implications on a conceptual level. Moreover, the language of paradigms permits the recognition that Guardini could revise the model within which he viewed Judaism, while at the same time not abandoning the valid insights and values contained in the unfortunate theology of displacement.

These reflections on the collegial relationship between Buber and Guardini lead to a simple conclusion. As the new millennium approaches, Catholics must meet with Jews not for the sake of the Jews but for the sake of Catholics. They must approach Jewish-Catholic dialogue as an opportunity for discovery, for a journey of faith. In this endeavor, Catholics may hear anew the sacred words in the Book of Genesis: "Now the Lord said to Abram [and Sarai], 'Go from your country and your kindred and your father's house to the land that I will show you. I will make of you a great nation, and I will bless you, and make your name great, so that you will be a blessing. I will bless those who bless you, and the one who curses you I will curse; and in you all the families of the earth shall be blessed'" (Genesis 12:1–3).

NOTES

1. International Theological Commission, "Christianity and the World Religions," *Origins* 27 (August 14, 1997): 150–166, 162. I am indebted to Mary C. Boys, Susannah Heschel, and Michael A. Signer for some of this essay's ideas.

2. See *Nostra Aetate*, articles 2 and 4, and *Gaudium et Spes*, articles 3, 35, 40, 44, and 92, in Paul VI, *Vatican Council II*, ed. Austin Flannery (Northport, N.Y.: Costello Publishing, 1996).

3. *Nostra Aetate*, article 4.

4. The collegial relationship between Buber and Guardini is discussed in greater depth in Robert A. Krieg, "To *Nostra Aetate*: M. Buber and R. Guardini," in Marshall Lee, ed., *Lessons and Legacies IV* (Evanston, Ill.: Northwestern University Press, forthcoming).

5. Jacques Dupuis recognizes the important role of language for religious experience in his *Jesus Christ at the Encounter of World Religions*, trans. Robert R. Barr (Maryknoll: Orbis Books, 1991).

6. See Maurice Friedman, *Martin Buber's Life and Work: The Early Years 1878–1923* (New York: E. P. Dutton, 1981); *Martin Buber's Life and Work: The Middle Years 1923–1945* (New York: E. P. Dutton, 1983); and *Martin Buber's Life and Work: The Later Years 1945–1965* (New York: E. P. Dutton, 1984).

7. See Robert A. Krieg, *Romano Guardini: A Precursor of Vatican II* (Notre Dame: University of Notre Dame Press, 1997); Robert A. Krieg, ed., *Romano Guardini: Proclaiming the Sacred in a Modern World* (Chicago: Liturgy Training Publications, 1995); Hanna Barbara Gerl, *Romano Guardini 1885–1968* (Mainz: Matthias Grünewald, 1985).

8. See Friedman, *The Later Years*, 111.

9. This letter is quoted in Gerl, *Romano Guardini*, 133 n. 38. See also Haim Gordon

and Jochanan Bloch, *Martin Buber: A Centenary Volume* (New York: KTAV Publishing House, 1984), 446; Martin Buber, *Briefwechsel aus sieben Jahrzenten,* vol. 2 (Heidelberg: L. Schneider, 1973), 114.

10. See Gerl, *Romano Guardini,* 133–134.

11. Ibid., 298; also, see Buber, *Briefwechsel aus sieben Jahrzenten,* vol. 2, 326.

12. See Romano Guardini, *Verantwortung: Gedanken zur jüdischen Frage* (Munich: Kösel, 1952).

13. See Friedman, *The Later Years,* 111. This letter is available in Archive #870 of the Romano Guardini Archives at the Katholische Akademie in Bayern, Munich. I am grateful to the Archives' director, Dr. Hans J. Mercker, for making this letter and other documents available to me.

14. See Maurice Friedman, "Martin Buber's 'Narrow Ridge'," in *Martin Buber and the Human Sciences,* ed. Maurice Friedman (Albany: State University of New York Press, 1996), 3–25, 11.

15. See Michael Keren, "Martin Buber's Impact on Political Dialogue in Israel," in *Martin Buber and the Human Sciences,* 283–294, 287.

16. See Buber's letter (July 13, 1953) to Guardini, Archive #870, Romano Guardini Archives.

17. See Martin Buber, "Genuine Dialogue and the Possibilities of Peace," in *Martin Buber, Pointing the Way,* ed. Maurice Friedman (New York: Harper and Brothers, 1957), 232–239.

18. See Gerl, *Romano Guardini,* 354; Friedman, *Martin Buber's Life and Work: The Later Years,* 118.

19. Guardini's letter to Buber is dated November 22, 1958; see Archive #871, Romano Guardini Archives.

20. See Friedman, *Martin Buber's Life and Work: The Later Years,* 397; Nahum N. Glatzer and Paul Mendes-Flohr, eds., *The Letters of Martin Buber,* trans. Richard and Clara Winston and Harry Zahn (New York: Schocken Books, 1991), 657.

21. In the Romano Guardini Archives, the telegram is located in Archive #871 and the statement on Buber is located in Archive #1309. For the full text of the telegram, see Krieg, "To *Nostra Aetate.*" Soon after writing this telegram, Guardini wrote at greater length concerning the tree as a symbol of life; see Romano Guardini, "Die Bäume von Isola Vicentina" (October 12, 1963), in Romano Guardini, *Stationen und Rückblicke* (Würzburg: Werkbund Verlag, 1965), 35–40.

22. For constructive proposals that move Christian thought away from the notions of supersessionism and displacement, see the essays in Katharine T. Hargrove, ed., *Seeds of Reconciliation* (North Richland Hills, Tex.: BIBAL Press, 1996).

23. Romano Guardini, *The Lord,* trans. Elinor Briefs (Chicago: Henry Regnery, 1954), 40.

24. Ibid., 98.

25. Ibid., 268.

26. Romano Guardini, *The Humanity of Christ,* trans. Ronald Walls (New York: Pantheon Books, 1964), 78; see also 10–13.

27. Ibid., 79.

28. See Romano Guardini, *Jesus Christus: Meditations,* trans. Peter White (Chicago: Henry Regnery, 1957), 20–21, 59–62, 93, 99.

29. Thomas S. Kuhn, *The Structure of Scientific Revolutions,* 2nd ed., enlarged (Chicago: University of Chicago Press, 1970), 175.

30. The use of the category of paradigm in theological inquiry is discussed in Hans Küng and David Tracy, eds., *Paradigm Change in Theology,* trans. Margaret Köhl (New York: Crossroad, 1989).

31. Romano Guardini, *Wahrheit des Denkens und Wahrheit des Tuns* (Paderborn: Ferdinand Schöningh, 1985), 50.

32. Ibid.

33. On the new translation of the Hebrew Bible into German that Martin Buber and Franz Rosenzweig undertook, see Klaus Reichert, "ZEIT IST'S. Die Bibelübersetzung von Franz Rosenzweig und Martin Buber im Kontext," in *Trigon 6,* ed. Guardini Stiftung (Berlin: Dreieck Verlag, 1997), 163–190.

34. Guardini, *Wahrheit des Denkens,* 108.

35. See Romano Guardini, *Theologische Briefe an einen Freund* (Paderborn: Ferdinand Schöningh, 1976), 59–61.

36. International Theological Commission, "Christianity and World Religions," 152.

37. Avery Dulles, *Models of the Church,* expanded ed. (New York: Doubleday, 1987), 31.

38. Romano Guardini, "Wahrheit und Ironie" (1965), in *Stationen und Rückblicke,* 43.

12 | Wounded Word, Wounded Interpreter

Peter Ochs

Covenant after Shoah?

Do Jews and Christians share any covenant before *or* after Shoah? Are there one or two covenants? The Jewish philosopher Franz Rosenzweig offered a two-covenant theory. The Christian theologian of scripture Paul Van Buren (whose passing we still mourn) framed a complex form of one-covenant theory. Some of us, who call themselves "Jewish textual reasoners," hope to extend his thesis, from a Jewish perspective, offering what we might call a one and a half (or at least one plus a little) covenant theory. There are covenantal elements that Judaism and Christianity share, but there are also some that we do not share. Before exploring such subtleties, however, we must address a painful preliminary question. As the Catholic theologian John Pawlikowski put it in his remarks at the conference on Humanity at the Limits: What is the Jewish Covenant now after Shoah? IS there ANY such Covenant? I offer these remarks to respond to his question, describing the life and textual theology of the Talmudist David Halivni as an illustration of how, indeed, the Jews may maintain their covenant in this awful time. This will leave for other occasions and other voices the question of whether Christians might now join this covenant and in what way.

I begin with a list of assumptions that underlie this particular approach:

First, the question of Covenant should not be oversimplified. I believe that questions about "THE" Jewish covenant may be oversimplified, or rendered too conceptual. The issue is of a relationship with God, of how that relationship is characterized in the Torah, and of the consequences of what the Torah says for Israel. I therefore understand Covenant as that which binds the people of Israel to each other by way of God and to God by way of each other, and I understand the "that which" and the "way of" in this phrase to refer to the Word of God, *dibbur.* Furthermore, I understand this Word, as it binds Israel, to be synonymous with Torah. Torah thus appears as the binding of one to the other, and as the way to and of God. To study Torah, Word, or Covenant would therefore be to study a mode of relationality: for example, to study a social grouping or community.

While we may speak, in these terms, of there being one Jewish covenant and thus one form of relationality in a formal sense, the Torah writes of a Brit

(Covenant) established in different ways at different times: for the Avot and Imahot (patriarchs and matriarchs), for Moses, for David. We must consider the plurality of specific covenantal traditions and texts from one perspective, and what we consider the enduring, single Covenant from another perspective.

We must also bear in mind the evolutionary relationship among text traditions of the various covenants, particularly as they are marked by Israel's response to various catastrophes in its relation to God—for example, enslavement in Egypt, wars against the Philistines and the establishment of kingship, the First Destruction and Galut, and the Second Destruction and Galut. Each catastrophe conditions Israel's re-evaluation of the character of its Covenant with God.

Furthermore, we must consider the hermeneutical contexts for referring to these covenants. The primary context is rabbinic Judaism's distinction between the *torah she b'chtav* (the Written Torah) and the *torah she b'al peh* (the Oral Torah). The distinction is itself a mark of Israel's response to the Second Destruction (illustrated in Mishnah Avot) and, as the rabbis suggest, also the First (illustrated, as we will see, in rabbinic characterizations of Ezra). For the sake of Jewish-Christian dialogue, it is critical to bear in mind that, following Destruction, the Oral Torah is the primary vehicle of Israel's understanding of its Covenant. Too often, comparisons are drawn between the Written Torah and the New Testament, rather than between the Oral Torah and the New Testament as two different responses to the Written Torah. The dominant question for Jews today is the status of the Oral Torah as vehicle of the Covenant after Shoah.

Next, I must set a few definitions for this essay. Besides the general uses of the terms Brit, Torah, and Israel, the essay will presuppose some more specific interpretations for the sake of this exercise:

- The vehicle of Covenant is always Torah, understood as the tangible vehicle of relationship between God and Israel, who are the covenant partners at issue here.
- The Covenant with Israel is understood as not excluding God's covenants with other nations. We are speaking of a verbal relationship with the God of Israel, not a statement of the character of "Being" or some such thing, nor of the ontological status of Israel relative to other nations. This, we could say, is an intensive covenant; within this essay, detailed questions of other nations are simply bracketed. As for the question of another essay on Christian-Jewish relations: this would be treated not under the category of "other nations," but under the category of "other attachments to the written Torah of Israel"—a verbal/linguistic/hermeneutical issue first, rather than an ontological issue.
- A distinction will be introduced between the enduring Covenant between God and Israel and the specific covenants that emerge within this Covenant.

As a means of interpreting Halivni's writing, the enduring Covenant will be considered "Infinite" (or of the Infinity of God), the specific covenants finite.

- The dominant issue will become the status of the Oral Torah as a finite or non-finite Covenant of Israel.

Finally, I must also make some specific assumptions about the role of individual Jews in the Covenant with B'nai Yisrael:

- The enduring Covenant is with a people, Israel, not directly with individual Jews AS individuals. Therefore the individual Jew's consciousness and conscious understanding or observance of the Covenant is not a *primary* datum *about* the Covenant. This implies that it may become a datum by way of interpretation.
- In the modern context, where individual Jews often seek to re-evaluate the Covenant individually, individual Jews' responses to the Covenant may be assigned the status of finite elements of specific, finite covenants of the enduring Covenant.

The primary issue before us, however, is how the enduring Covenant withstands or does not withstand Israel's catastrophes and her ensuing re-evaluation of the Covenant. In this context, the individual Jew's experience acquires greater significance, since, while a covenant is a corporate entity, the *rupture or interruption* of a covenant is an individual event. A defense of this claim would be too technical for these remarks, so I will simply offer the claim as an assumption: that, within the Covenant(s) of Israel, individual Jews as individuals represent places where covenantal crises are articulated, where ruptures in the Covenant are suffered visibly, one could say, or where complaints against the Covenant are uttered.

To respond to the question, "Is there Covenant after Shoah?" I will therefore turn to one case study of the individual Jew's response to Covenant: Halivni's memoirs of Talmud study before and after Shoah. This will become a case study, in particular, of challenges to the Oral Torah as finite or non-finite Covenant of Israel. What do Halivni's memoirs suggest about the status of Oral Torah during and after Shoah, and thereby, the status of the infinite Covenant and of this finite Covenant after Shoah?

Halivni's Covenant after Shoah

In the phrase "Covenant after Shoah," I understand the "after" to mean after an ineluctable rupture; "rupture" refers to that which breaks a relationship; the act of "breaking a relationship" refers to a wholly singular event, an individuated phenomenon. I understand individual human beings qua individuals to represent places where the breaks in human community are embodied and, in that sense, re-membered; and individual Jews qua individuals to represent places where the ruptures in Israel's Covenant are embodied. Following these definitions, "Covenant after Shoah" is something to be studied first in individuals, where the rupture is re-membered. In this context, the term "Brit" may appear ironic: a Covenant is cut; after Shoah this cut is ruptured.

My remarks are therefore intensive, or focused on the individual, before being extensive, or focused on the relational. The individual subject is David Halivni, the noted Talmudist, as he remembers himself in the Holocaust memoir *The Book and the Sword*.[1] Those who know a little about Halivni may already anticipate where my remarks may lead. Here is a man whose scholarship lives inside of the rabbis' Oral Torah, as the Torah by way of which Jews live or embody the Written Torah. According to the definitions offered above, we would say that Halivni's scholarship inhabits the oral Covenant by way of which Jews embody the written Covenant; and the oral Covenant makes itself known, in historical time, through the transmission or evolving tradition of interpreting Torah. As an individuated event, his scholarship marks and embodies a break in that evolving tradition, and his personal memoir from out of the Shoah marks a narrative of this embodiment of breakage. The wonder and puzzle of the narrative is that Halivni is Talmudist, or student of the Oral Torah, after Shoah as well as Talmudic prodigy before. Either our definitions are faulty—Shoah does not refer to a breakage in the oral Covenant—or else Oral Torah, or Talmud, may already embody rupture as well as relationality.

To examine this puzzle, my remarks come now as a commentary on Halivni's Holocaust memoir. By way of illustration, I will select and comment on five of the memoir's vivid images.

1. Halivni's memoir begins with an "anonymous" midrash of his own.

> The sword and the book came down from heaven tied to each other. Said the Almighty, "If you keep what is written in this book, you will be spared this sword; if not, you will be consumed by it" (Midrash Rabbah Deuteronomy 4:2). We clung to the book, yet we were consumed by the sword.

Comment: Halivni sets his memoir immediately within the rhetorical patterns of the rabbis' Oral Torah, in which God remains an actor. Halivni has innovated, however; he is behaving like one of the sages of the Talmud (the *amoraim*). This implies either that the Oral Torah remains alive and open in his work or that he is performing some subversion, or some third reading that is neither of the Written nor of the Oral Torah per se. As evidence, we may note that he begins with a rabbinic-like assertion; then he offers a proof text in the manner of the classic midrashim—except that the Oral and not the Written Torah is cited as a proof text! Then he adds a third element after the proof text, that is, after the point at which the rabbinic midrash would end. Judging by the rhetorical structure of his anonymous midrash, Halivni would appear to inhabit a post-Talmudic voice. And the voice itself is ironic: we clung yet were consumed. The Torah remains, but contested.

2. Halivni then prefaces his first chapter with an "anonymous" aggadah of his own crafting, this time directly out of a narrative of the Shoah:

> When the sound of the closing of the door, after the first child was shoved into the crematorium, reached heaven, Michael, the most beneficent of angels, could not contain himself and angrily approached God. Michael asked, "Do You now pour out Your wrath upon children? In the past, children were indirectly caught up in the slaughter. This time they are the chief target of destruction. Have pity on the little ones, O Lord." God, piqued by Michael's insolence, shouted back at him, "I am the Lord of the Universe. If you are displeased with the way I conduct the world, I will return it to void and null." Hearing these words, Michael knew that there was to be no reversal. He had heard these words once before in connection with the Ten Martyrs. He knew their effect. He went back to his place, ashen and dejected, but could not resist looking back sheepishly at God and saw a huge tear rolling down His face, destined for the legendary cup which collects tears and which, when full, will bring the redemption of the world. Alas, to Michael's horror, instead of entering the cup, the tear hit its rim, most of it spilling on the ground—and the fire of the crematorium continued to burn.

Comment: Now Halivni imitates the mythopoetic imagination of the rabbis, once again both extending and either subverting or supplementing rabbinic theodicy. Halivni's memoir, it appears, may have a relation to the Oral Torah analogous to the Oral Torah's relation to the Written Torah. The Covenant remains, but somehow ruptured.

3. The narrative, "magid," begins with childhood life in the town, then the ghetto of Sighet. Halivni begins, "I do not remember when I came to Sighet for the first time to live with Grandfather. But I do remember what I was learning. I was learning Chumash, the Pentateuch, with Rashi's commentary, and that means I was about four years old." The dominant image of these childhood years is of Halivni's studying Talmudic texts. He was an *iluy,* a natural genius in textual study. The text came easily to him—memorizing it, interpreting it—and he soon gained a reputation from town to town as a child prodigy. Sighet was a Chasidic town. While Halivni never cultivated a sense for Chasidic practice, his grandfather's and his readings were always touched by some dimension of spirituality appropriate to this setting: as he writes in a later chapter, his Chasidic background leaves its mark in the intensity of his prayer. But the dominant image of this period comes in this phrase: "from all my troubles in Sighet I found relief in learning" (35).

Comment: What strikes me most is Halivni's coming to age from inside the text. In the terms of my earlier definitions, Halivni came to age already within the written Covenant of Israel by way of his role as reader of the rabbi's

Oral Torah. There is yet no distance from that oral discourse, however, only the comfort of being nestled within it.

4. *Sighet becomes a ghetto, then a place emptied of Jews.* Halivni writes:

> Even though I knew that the murderers were out there in the streets, . . . I shut them out, drew an imaginary wall and continued to do what I had done all those years, linking myself to the past and continuing to study the same material I had studied since the age of four (46–47).

> That all changed on the fateful day of May 14, 1944. . . . We were told on that day that we had to leave our house . . . and wait in the street for transport. . . . At that time . . . I lost my home and my imaginary life stopped. I stopped learning . . . I had no desire or ability to study Torah amid people ready to kill us. I did not learn on the train and did not resume formal learning until months after liberation . . . (47).

> In their wildest imagination the people of the ghetto could not have imagined what ultimately happened . . . that they would be gassed . . . including young children (57).

Comment: Note the contrast of imaginations. Halivni's childhood life inside the Oral Torah was a life of counterfactual imagination—counter to whatever everyday life he lived—except for his immediate familial relations and communal ethics. But there was a limit to what that textual life could resist: it was a life of positive sanctity, after all, and not mere escape; there was a degree of profanity before which that sanctity could not be opened. That degree of profanity would be one that also exceeded the bounds of folk imagination. Halivni's Oral Torah, in other words, was a haven only from an imaginably profane or obscene world; it withdrew from before the unimaginably obscene. In this sense, it withdrew from before the Infinite; what had the appearance of the infinitely evil, as well as from before the One who alone is really Infinite. I find an allusion here to Halivni's attraction to the plain sense, in both his religiosity and his hermeneutic: he appears to seek direct encounter with realia—with God, with God's active word in Torah, and with the effects of specific human acts of receiving that word. This may not be a matter of propositional literalness—an epistemological desire for full disclosure (as in what some label Cartesian or Lockean intuitionism). It may instead be a desire for direct testimony (without epistemological reduction, a desire for witness and evidence) and for direct experience (again, not in an atomistic sense, but nonetheless in a sensual, cognitive, and relational sense). He wants to be there, where the other is, and this desire carries with it an expectation that humans can and in cases should do this; the other and the Other can be known directly, and without reduction to the atomism or propositionalism that the Lockeans may associate with direct knowledge. This means that relations can be known.

In other words, Halivni's attraction to the plain sense may display what philosophers would call a realism: in this case, not a Platonic one, but the kind of scholastic, and call it relational, realism one sees in Duns Scotus, in Scotch common sense, and most of all in C. S. Peirce and in Franz Rosenzweig.

While Halivni flees to the text and encounters it in the space of imagination, the realist knows that imagination is a medium of encounter with relational realia. This is not the imagination of metaphor and fancy, but of analogy, mathematics, and divine speech. Later in the memoirs, in fact, Halivni claims that "from early childhood, I combined devotion to scholarship ki'pshuto— study according to the literal meaning . . . which is the basis of scientific, critical study—with intense Jewish living" (151). This study was not so critical as to detach him from the inner world of Oral Torah, but critical in the sense that it inclined him to cut through the mere appearances of the everyday or of the text to find what is really there rather than to create there some space of his own making. When the really horrible—the almost infinity of evil—ruptures the everyday, Halivni is therefore indisposed to turn from it to inner realms. The turn within, it appears, is not a negation of, or turning the back on, the perceptual realm, but a way of tracing certain movements from the perceptual realm to what is beyond it. I am led to this hypothesis, at any rate, by Halivni's leaving most horrible details out of his account of Auschwitz and Ebensee and by his report that he has not allowed himself to remember these details consciously. My reasoning is that he must sense that if he feeds his imagination precisely on what appears perceptually, rather than by the avoidance of it, then dwelling perceptually on these too horrible perceptions would corrupt his imagination more than train or wizen it. It would make of his imagination a space for a holocaust world before which too much that is good in everyday life and in rabbinic spirituality and in Torah learning and in halakhah would be weakened or corrupted. There is room for certain degrees of rupture, but not for any and all degrees. The human vessel of God's presence remains a human vessel, and to forget that would be, in the face of such trials, to risk destroying the vessel rather than perfecting it.

While Halivni's "intense Jewish living" may tempt the scholar to approach such risks, his work also implies that the halakhic life of Oral Torah brings protections. As a "fence around the Torah," the halakhah may be considered armor for the human vessel's dangerous flight of mediation between divine presence and profane context. Such mediation is a dimension of covenant. One way in which the *chorban* (Destruction) threatened the Covenant, we may say, is that it brought the halakhah of the Written Torah into question, rendering Israel less protected against the dangers of direct divine presence. The Shoah threatens Israel's Covenant in a comparable way, now bringing the halakhah of the Oral Torah into question. Without the protection of its halakhah, we may say, Israel's imagination becomes an unprotected and thus too fragile vessel of mediation between the divine presence and an obscene world. The present risk is therefore not merely human discomfort; human mediation of God's presence in the world is itself threatened. If so, as we will see, Halivni's efforts to repair the Oral Torah may have profound theological and ontological implications.

4x. Excursus: In a recent conversation,[2] Halivni explains that the goal of his work is to reduce the distance between the plain sense of Torah (*peshat*) and its applied meaning (*derash*). He says that the *gemara* (the *amoraic* discussion in the Talmud) seeks to understand the Written Torah; discovering "maculation" (some form of inadequate representation) in it, the *gemara* then seeks, by way of the midrash, to address the distance between what is written, unclearly, in the written text and what it should mean. Citing Talmudic sources, Halivni argues that the prophet/scribe Ezra received a maculate text: the Written Torah was not properly maintained in every detail through the biblical period of the monarchy and Temple. Anticipating the *gemara*, Ezra sought direct knowledge of what the Written Torah was supposed to say; receiving this, he corrected the text, in part by making textual emendations (*tikkunot*) and in part by transmitting a tradition of oral interpretation through which the distance between the apparent text and correct plain sense would be reduced. Halivni then explains that he works after the model of Ezra, but addressing the text of the Oral Torah itself, rather than that of the Written Torah. After all, he says, citing a rabbinic tradition, the Written Torah is naked if addressed independently of the *mitzvot*, or the actual enactment of the Oral Torah. But the text of the Oral Torah is maculated as well, and Halivni's concern is to reduce the distance between the correct text of the Oral Torah and the text we have—just as Ezra and the rabbis sought to reduce the distance, in several instances, between the Bible text's plain sense and its midrashic correction.

Comment: We could say that, like Ezra, Halivni receives and seeks to restore a maculated text of Torah from out of the fire—this time, the text of the rabbis' Oral Torah and the two fires, metaphorically, of modernity and, literally, of the Shoah. In one sense, we may say that, analogous to the Israelites of the monarchy, the Jews of late medieval and modern times have not properly maintained the Oral Torah: its texts are blemished and their corresponding interpretations are confused in places. In a second sense, we may say that, analogous to the Jews after the *chorban*, Jews after the Shoah question the oral Covenant, both as law, or means of protecting their access to God, and as mediator of the divine presence on earth. Halivni inherits and responds to both challenges. Inheriting both the halakhic practices of the oral Covenant and the academic-analytic practices of late medieval/modern Judaism, he has, in these years after and yet of the Shoah, introduced a form of scholarship-and-religious-life that is irreducible to the explicit rules of either of these practices. As illustrated in his book, *Revelation Restored,*[3] he practices a form of "depth" (or "transcendent") historiography that at once corrects the plain sense of the rabbis' Oral Torah and exceeds the limits of the academician's "plain sense historiography." We might best label this a uniquely Jewish practice of historical-critical reading: an alternative to the modern practices of either applying some generic Western academic method to the dissection of sacred Jewish texts or seeking to conduct the rabbis' Oral Torah as if modernity and the Shoah raised no challenges to it.

5. The story of a bletl.

> After Passover we were taken to the ghetto; later, to Auschwitz. . . . Soon after . . . I was taken from Auschwitz and found myself in one of the camps in Gros-Rosen. (60)

Halivni describes his work cutting stones, then working in the mines. One day a guard, with whom he had some silent relationship, was eating a sandwich wrapped in what he noticed was "a page of *Orach Chaim,* a volume of the *Shulchan Aruch* . . . , the Jewish Code of Law. . . . The page was from the laws of Passover. . . . The question on the page deals with whether an agent can nullify the leavened bread of a household before Passover" (67–68).

> Upon seeing the wrapper, I instinctively fell at the feet of the guard. . . . With tears in my eyes, I implored him to give me this bletl, this page. . . . He gave me the bletl, and I took it back to the camp. On the Sundays we had off [when Halivni gathered fellow mates for study], we now had not only Oral Torah but Written Torah as well. The bletl became a visible symbol of a connection between the camp and the activities of Jews throughout history. . . . The bletl became a rallying point (69).

The page was entrusted to a Mr. Finkelstein, who kept it in his clothes—at great personal risk. On Passover 1945, months later, after he had moved to another camp and lost contact, Halivni again met Mr. Finkelstein, who still carried the bletl with him. Mr. Finkelstein asked him to teach him the "exact formulation of the sacrifices performed in the Temple service of old and recited in the Musaf [additional morning] prayer. Sacrifice was on Mr. Finkelstein's mind. How appropriate! He himself was a sacrifice, so were we all" (72).

> Subsequently I heard from the Betlamer Rav that soon after we parted, Mr. Finkelstein collapsed. Before there was time to remove the bletl from his body, he was taken away to the crematorium. When Mr. Finkelstein's body went up in smoke, the bletl went with him. (72).

Comment. Once again, here is an analogy to Ezra's retrieving the Written Torah from the fires of the first *chorban* and, again, to the rabbis' retrieving the written TaNaKh from the fires of the second *chorban*. Once again, the retrieval accompanies a rupture in Israel's covenant relation with God. Is there Covenant after Shoah? Halivni's restoration of the Oral Torah is an instrument of his efforts at a more extensive *tikkun* (repair). Following Ezra's and the rabbis' patterns, Halivni's mode of repair is not literally to return to a previous text-practice, but to begin, through a subsequent practice, to restore what is missing in it—or, in his terms, to "narrow the gap" between the plain sense, *peshat*, and the interpreted text, *derash*. As anticipated earlier, however, we may note that what counts as Written Torah now includes the text of the rabbis' Oral Torah as well: discovering the bletl, he writes, meant bringing "Written Torah" as well as Oral Torah into his group's study sessions in the camps. This implies that the relationship between the Written and the Oral is only illustrated by, rather than literally limited to, the relationship between TaNaKh and rabbinic literature. And this would imply that Halivni's restorative scholarship would have the kind of relation to the rabbinic literature that this literature had to the Bible: in each case, fidelity to the deep meaning of the antecedent writings would accompany a radically reformatory relation to what we may call the surface meanings of those writings. In other words, if the rabbis were "Torah-true" in their acquiring a capacity to interpret and legislate beyond the literal bounds of the Written Torah, then Halivni is Torah-and-Talmud-true in his capacity to read and reconstruct Talmudic texts beyond their literary bounds. While Halivni enacts his Oral Torah fully within the bounds of the rabbinic halakhah and, in that sense, of the oral Covenant, we who study his work have reason to interpret his practice, for us, as at the same time the mark of another covenant. We might label this the neither written nor oral Covenant of religious academic Jews after the Shoah.

On the basis of this claim, we could then make sense of another, explicit claim of Halivni's:[4] that, to narrow the gap between *peshat* and *derash* would, at the same time, be to narrow the gap between the world, *briyat olam,* in its present, ruptured state, and what the world would be when the *peshat* and the *derash* were one. In this view, Halivni's effort at textual restoration is at the same time his effort at *tikkun olam* (repair of the world) after Shoah.

Since he seeks to restore a primordially literal sense of Torah through previously unused technologies, Halivni's effort has certain parallels to the kabbalists' efforts to reduce the polyvalence of the primary texts as we have them and, thereby, to disclose and uphold the direct intentions of the creator of the world. Unlike the kabbalists, however—or, to mention another parallel, the Qumran communities—Halivni explains that his method makes reference to its own inadequacies. Less optimistic, less self-certain than these other reformers, he agrees that the gap between *peshat* and *derash* must be bridged, but he does not agree that it can all be bridged now, all at once. While he does not relish deferral for its own sake, his interpretations retain vagueness and polyvalence because the messiah has not yet come.

And, in the meanwhile? We may conclude that this meanwhile is the place of Halivni's Third Covenant: that is, the Covenant after Shoah that is neither merely written nor oral, but also a third something whose defining character is not yet fully apparent, but about which we may make some preliminary observations.

Some Emergent Characteristics of a Third Covenant

At the outset, I suggested that we must, indeed, examine the status of a Jewish Covenant after Shoah before considering questions about what covenant Jews and Christians may or may not now share. I suggested, furthermore, that in a time of rupture the story of a people's covenant with God must be told first through the stories of the individuals in whose suffering the rupture is re-membered. Halivni's autobiographical narrative has provided one such individual story. In it, a child prodigy in the traditional study of Talmud emerges from the Shoah as participant in a continued but transformed Covenant, one that is not only written-and-oral but also ruptured-ánd-in-the-process-of-restoration. While it speaks only for itself, the story thereby carries broad implications—for those who want to draw them—about how the Covenant may continue after Shoah. Here, in closing, is a list of some of these implications: a suggestive, but inconclusive, list for now, since it is too soon to have any clear idea of how Jewish, and also Christian, thinkers may respond to this perspective on Halivni's example:

(a) If Halivni's work marks the appearance of a Third Covenant, what would be the status of the Oral Torah in such a covenant? To conceive of a Third Covenant may be to conceive of each covenant of this kind as a finite (that is, de-fined) life of the Infinite Covenant, conceived as the eternal but minimally describable relation between God and Israel. Referring to each covenant as finite in this sense would enable Halivni or others both to acknowledge the shattering effect of the Shoah for the Covenant of Israel and to maintain the infinite Covenant.

Just as traditions of the Written Torah precede canonization of the Written Torah and as traditions of the Oral Torah (from Ezra and Ezekiel) precede the rabbis' declaration of the Oral Torah, so too Halivni's claim (as extrapolated here) is already anticipated by the character of centuries of scholarly commentary on the Talmud and other rabbinic texts from medieval times forward. Halivni is not introducing a new post-Talmudic mode of "restoring" Talmud, but is, rather, articulating a long tradition of such restoration in a more overt way than many predecessors. His response to the Shoah forces a moment of taking stock of previously implicit distinctions. The taking stock is critical now, not as a challenge to the Oral Torah, but precisely as a means of protecting the tradition of Oral Torah in the face of the present consequences of Shoah. The Oral Torah is protected now as a second dimension of Written Torah, subject to restorative scholarship.

(b) Halivni's restorative scholarship belongs to a third genre of study, to be distinguished both from the methods of Oral Torah itself AND from the methods of historical-critical *Wissenschaft des Judentums* in its customary practice in the academy.

Halivni's restorative scholarship presupposes preliminary studies within the methods of Oral Torah, determining both the texts of the plain sense of Talmud, opening subsequent dimensions of reading, and also introducing the interpretive context for depth historiography.

His restorative scholarship includes a layer of academic, historical-critical *Wissenschaft* as a means of determining the plain sense historiography of the rabbinic texts. However, his scholarship adds to this a second layer of depth historiography, which offers workable hypotheses about dimensions of textual meaning that lie beyond the high probabilities of the plain sense historiography. Depth historiography is employed in two complementary but different ways: (i) as a vehicle for reconstructing and thus restoring the texts of Oral Torah (the work of *Mekorot uMesorot*)[5]—a deeper/imaginative dimension of historical-critical literary inquiry; (ii) as a vehicle for reconstructing a theological and mythopoetic rabbinic worldview to accompany the Talmudic reconstructions of a Third dimension of Torah (the work of Halivni's English writings)—a critical/academic dimension of rabbinic oral text study.

(c) Both of these uses of depth historiography serve the pragmatic function of preparing and securing the work of the community of Jewish scholars who participate in the enduring Covenant of Israel by way of a third dimension of Torah, as vehicle for interpreting the written traditions of Oral Torah.

This community is unique within rabbinic tradition, since its normative work emerges from out of the academy, rather than from out of either the yeshivot OR the seminaries of the established movements of rabbinic Judaism. The community is unique within Jewish academic tradition, since its critical, scientific work is placed in the service of the religious activity of restoring Torah.

(d) This interpretation of Halivni's memoirs is introduced, in sum, as an individual illustration of how the Covenant of Israel may be maintained by rabbinic scholars after Shoah. The rupturing effect of the Shoah is displayed in the transformation of Oral Torah into a written tradition subject to the restorative work of a third dimension of Torah. Through the rupture of a finite covenant of Israel, Israel's Infinite Covenant is thereby wounded but maintained.

(e) What would be the implications of a Third Covenant for Jewish-Christian relations? By way of introduction, alone, I may predict this much: that neither a simple two-covenant or one-covenant model would be adequate to accommodate this study's depiction of a Third Covenant of Israel. Both Israel and the Church might be seen as sharing in a finite covenant of the Written Torah, and they might be seen as offering contrasting (at times conflicting, at times complementary) traditions for interpreting the Written Torah—the Oral

Torah or the New Testament. But what relation would the Church have to a third dimension of Torah? First, we must ask what covenant of its own the Church declares after Shoah. If there is a third covenant of the Church that repairs the anti-Jewish elements of the covenant of the New Testament, then we have introduced grounds for a fruitful dialogue on this subject. Such a dialogue might proceed along several dimensions:

- recognizing a shared dimension of Written Torah;
- recognizing ways in which the Oral Torah and the New Testament display contrasting but parallel dimensions;
- recognizing shared academic resources for the historical-critical study of our written traditions;
- discussing the mutual benefits of nurturing "depth-historiographic" sub-communities of Jewish and of Christian scholars within the academy. These are elsewhere termed "postcritical" communities;
- discussing the relation between such sub-communities and the implications of that relation for relations between these their finite covenants.

NOTES

1. David Weiss Halivni, *The Book and the Sword: A Life of Learning in the Shadow of Destruction* (Boulder: Westview Press, 1996).

2. Personal conversation, April 24, 1998, about David Halivni's theses in *Revelation Restored*.

3. David Weiss Halivni, *Revelation Restored: Divine Writ and Critical Responses* (Boulder: Westview Press, 1997).

4. In conversations similar to the one mentioned in note 2.

5. David Weiss Halivni, *Mekorot uMesorot* [Sources and Traditions], 5 vols. (Jerusalem: Jewish Theological Seminary, 1975–98 and continuing).

13 Pour Out Your Heart Like Water
Toward a Jewish Feminist Theology of the Holocaust
Rachel Adler

Why Has There Been No Feminist Holocaust Theology?

Scholars sometimes ask why feminist Jews have produced no Holocaust theology, especially since the two theological movements developed concurrently. When, after twenty years of silence, Holocaust theology began in the late sixties and seventies, it was an elite conversation among exclusively male rabbis and professors of Jewish philosophy. At that same time, feminist Judaism emerged, intent not upon questions of the divine nature and the evils of the Jewish past but upon Jewish women's pressing concerns with the structures of Jewish community, law, and text. It is because we succeeded both in developing basic theological tools and in becoming full participants in the Jewish conversation that feminist theologians can now turn to confront the Shoah. My task in this essay will be first, to explore what impeded or discouraged the construction of feminist Jewish theology, and second, to propose some ways to begin.

Another reason for early feminist Judaism to avoid the issue of the Shoah was that Holocaust guilt was a weapon of feminism's adversaries. They compared the injustices of which feminists complained to the Holocaust and dismissed them as trivial. They blamed feminist "selfishness" for women's reluctance to assume the single most important task incumbent upon them: to replace the six million dead by bearing additional "mitzvah" children. They accused feminists of handing Hitler a posthumous victory by threatening the fragile stability of the Jewish people with division and controversy. These tactics were capable of wounding, precisely because American Jewish attitudes toward the Holocaust are complex, guilt-ridden, sentimental, and, as Jacob Neusner has argued, *constitutive* of American Judaism.[1] The two central foci of American Judaism, Neusner charged, are a catastrophe that did not happen to us and a country in which we do not live.[2]

Neusner's point is that a viable Diaspora Judaism must look neither to the past nor across the sea for its salvation, but rather must invest its energies in building a sustaining Jewish thought and praxis for its own time and place—precisely the challenge feminist Judaism took up. If American Judaism were firm upon its own foundations, perhaps it would know how to situate itself in relation to the unfathomable catastrophe that passed over it and the rebuilt Zion it does not call home. Guilt and confusion about Israel are assuaged by an often uncritical Zionism, but the questions of who American Jews are in relation to the Shoah and how they are to address it remain unresolved. Were we, as some scholars have charged, auxiliary murderers standing idly by as our people's blood was shed? Are we part of a collective victim, a mangled amputee now missing one third of its body? Or a collective survivor staggering under an unfulfillable ancient obligation to remember what is too vast, too fragmented, too inarticulate, too terrifying to be inculcated as communal memory?[3] Complicity and guilt, disjunction and mutilation, an obsessive obligation to remember that can be neither remitted nor fulfilled, distinguish Jewish responses to the Shoah. A fledgling feminist Judaism was unequipped to confront these explosive issues.

Feminist Holocaust Discourses

Accordingly, feminist Jews have made their first entry into Holocaust discourse in two areas: literature and history. The American Jewish canon of Holocaust literature is heavily male, while women's literature about the Shoah is marginalized. Even Nobel Prize–winning Holocaust poet Nellie Sachs receives little attention in this country. Two prominent examples of feminist poets who address the impact of the Shoah upon their own identities and upon the classical Jewish categories of exile and home are Irena Klepfisz and Melanie Kaye-Kantrowitz. In her recent book, *Jews and Feminism: The Ambivalent Search for Home*, Laura Levitt discusses the theological implications of their poetry.[4] But both Klepfisz and Kaye-Kantrowitz have been ghettoized; only other feminists discuss their work.

In contrast, the efforts of feminist historians have provoked considerable protest. By marshaling evidence of women's distinct vulnerabilities and victimizations, their coping styles, social organization, and patterns of leadership in ghettoes and camps, feminist historians correct and qualify the hegemonic masculine images that claim to be universal representations. Most recently, in *Commentary* magazine, Gabriel Schoenfeld published a devastating review of a new collection, *Women in the Holocaust*, edited by Dalia Ofer and Lenore Weitzman, comprehensively attacking feminist historians' efforts to apply the variable of gender to Holocaust experience as expressions of "a naked ideological agenda" whose goal is "to sever Jewish women, in their own minds, from their families as well as from the larger Jewish community."[5] His diatribe, reproduced on the op-ed page of the *Wall Street Journal*, was indignantly countered by a symposium of feminist scholars in *Lilith* magazine.[6] Opponents of feminist Holocaust scholarship behave as if gendering the catastrophe blasphemed the sacred. But what is this sacred that has been blasphemed?

Sidra DeKoven Ezrahi maintains that all representations of the Holocaust presume that it is unrepresentable, a black hole or a mountain of the inarticulable.[7] "I want to submit," she writes, "that the positioning of both the writer and the audience in relation to this mountain or this defiled center functions much as does the positioning of the pilgrim vis-a-vis the holy mountain or the sacred center; in what closely approximates a theological quest."[8] Sacred mountains attract not only pilgrims but priesthoods, however, and Judaism has traditionally both limited women's access to the sacred mountain—Sinai or Zion—and excluded them from its priesthood. Now, once more, a priesthood seeks to reserve its sacred mountain, its unsayable about which *so much* has been said, for another holy community in which women are subsumed by men.

Intrinsic Problems for a Feminist Theology of the Holocaust

Thus far, I have talked about external conditions inhospitable to a feminist Jewish theology of the Holocaust, but feminist theology has had intrinsic reasons as well for avoiding the Holocaust. Like the other liberal Jewish theologies of modernity, feminist theologies are optimistic. Little has been written on theodicy.[9] Nature is generally depicted as ordered and harmonious except when it is defiled by human greed.[10] Social justice is emphasized by many of the theologies, and humanity and society are viewed as perfectible.[11] Pain, sickness, grief, and death do not figure prominently in these theologies.[12] Only for Laura Levitt are unease and discord the central topics.[13]

The darkness of the Holocaust confronts our theologies with questions that will brook no more evasions: How do theologies that emphasize the need for women to become full contractors of the covenant justify covenanting with a God who did not save? Having learned how easily normal people can murder and how easily starvation, pain, and terror can dehumanize their victims, can we be so confident of human and social perfectibility? How do we account for disorder, rupture, atrocity? What is our response to the theological principle Irving Greenberg sets forth: that one ought not to make any theological statements that could not be made in the presence of babies burning alive in a crematorium?[14] Will we draw upon Sidra DeKoven Ezrahi's critique of approaches to the Shoah that absolutize it rigidly, make Auschwitz its single monopolistic sign, and reject metaphor, declaring the Holocaust utterly inarticulable, a single static event closed to interpretation?[15]

Finally, a serious consideration of the Shoah would expose the latent essentialism of the feminine God-language feminist Judaisms have worked so hard to establish, in which God is depicted as peacefully imminent in an idealized, harmonious nature. Especially beloved in this God language is the imagery of God as the good mother, the nourisher, the protector, the repository of "basic trust." But the God who is implicated in the Shoah is no nurturing mother, no Lady Wisdom. What language will we use in situations where we experience God as violent, abandoning, enigmatic?[16]

The Shoah demands to be assimilated into the collective memory of the Jewish people, into forms and norms, rituals, stories, interpretation. This time, for the first time, women and men bear equally Judaism's ancient obligation, to shape memory and to let ourselves be shaped by what we remember. For the first time, feminist theologians are both equipped and invited to ask the questions about theodicy, sociodicy, and anthropodicy that the Shoah arouses, to ask what resonances these new stories and images haunting our consciousness impart to sacred texts and words of prayer. I am unequal to this task, but I want to assume my obligation to make a beginning. If I approach my subject obliquely with the beginner's fearful and averted glance, if I am ignorant, or neglectful or clumsy, please forgive me.

What follow are jottings toward a theology, a rough map of some of the places I have gone in order to begin. With apologies to Ezrahi, I must begin with silence. I do not know whether mine is the enforced silence with which we are taught to confront the absolutized Holocaust or the epistemic silence that afflicts women excluded from discourse, but it is the only place from which I can begin.[17]

Toward a Feminist Theology of the Holocaust

The beginning is silence. The beginning is the void that is beyond language. This place where the alphabet of creation has no place, says Rabbi Nahman of Bratzlav, is the black hole of negation where rationality and its perplexities lie dissolved in silence.[18] Look in and your gaze is riveted; you fall, you drown. Only one like Moses can look into the void unscathed, says Nahman, the wordless one, *k'vad peh u'kh'vad lashon* (Exod. 4:10), his silence facing its silence. And how does Rabbi Nahman know this? He cites a strange and terrible talmudic midrash.[19]

The midrash is embedded in a technical discussion of malformed or missing letters that render a Torah scroll invalid for public reading. In the case that precedes the midrash, the leg of the letter vav in the word *va-yaharog,* "he killed," has been perforated and severed. This specific verb form occurs just once in the Pentateuch. The killer is God: "The Lord killed every first born in the land of Egypt" (Exod. 13:15).

The midrash goes like this: "Rav Judah said in the name of Rav, When Moses ascended on high [to receive the Torah] he found the Holy One adding ornamental crowns to the letters." Moses asks the purpose of this fancy calligraphy, and God replies, "There will be a man after many generations named Aqiba ben Yosef who will derive heaps and heaps of laws from every single flourish [*qoz*]." Moses, suitably impressed, asks to see the future wordsmith. "Turn around," says God, and, turning, Moses finds himself in the academy of Rabbi Aqiba, where he takes a seat at the end of the beginners' row. The midrash continues, "but he could not understand what they were discussing and was utterly abashed [*tashash koho*].[20] But then [Rabbi Aqiba] came to a certain legal matter[21] and the disciples asked, Rabbi, what is the source? He said, 'It is a law of Moses from Sinai,'" and Moses was comforted.

Thus far, we might read the midrash as a comic defense of the rabbinic doctrine that Oral Law has equal status with the Written Law. The hypothetical non-believer objects, "You can't derive laws from calligraphic flourishes," and the rabbinate responds, "God himself added those flourishes for that very purpose." The non-believer argues, "If Moses heard your legal discussions, he wouldn't understand a single word," and the rabbinate responds, "That's true, but he acknowledges the Torah's capacity to unfold into meanings unimaginable." The cream of the jest is that the category that Aqiba invokes, "a law of Moses from Sinai," means a law for which no scriptural basis exists, a law whose sole source of authority is that it is believed to have been revealed to Moses orally.[22] Yet instead of despairing in the presence of the Aqiba's alien and incomprehensible Torah, Moses is comforted. Thus far the story both disarms and seduces. Its outrageous anthropomorphisms, time traveling, and self-referential rabbinic jokes invite interpretation.

The word *qotz*, however, foreshadows darker lessons. *Qotz* has two discordant meanings: a flourish, or stroke, and a thorn. The stroke connects and makes intelligible. The thorn disrupts connection, perforates, wounds. Ultimately, Aqiba, master of the strokes, will become the stricken. He will die lacerated, mutilated, like the perforated vav in the legal case preceding the midrash. The meanings so smoothly and wittily unfolding for the reader will be punctured as well.

Moses, who withstands the first shock of the incomprehensible in Aqiba's classroom, asks the question that will transfer that shock to the reader. "Master of the Universe, if you have a man like this, why are you giving the Torah through me?" The response is brutally abrupt. "Silence," says God. "So it was planned." This ominous transformation in a deity who has been so lavish with information seems not to register with Moses. Like the rube enthralled by the circus magician, he begs the time machinist for another trick. "Master of the Universe, you have shown me his Torah, now show me his reward." "Turn around," God repeats. But the final show is not comedy but horror. "[Moses] turned and saw them weighing out [Aqiba's] flesh in the meat market. He cried, 'Master of the Universe, this is his Torah and this is his reward?' 'Silence,' said God, 'So it was planned.'"[23]

What Moses sees is not the martyrdom of Aqiba. This martyrdom, narrated in tractate Berakhot and elsewhere (b. Berakhot 61b), depicts Aqiba's victory over the nomos-destroying effects of torture and his invitation into Paradise, proclaimed by a divine voice.[24] Here, there is no Aqiba. There are only anonymous collops of meat for sale in an ordinary shop.[25] If the image seems hyperbolical, consider this quote from the Israeli documentary "Healing By Killing": In the film, a former concentration camp doctor recalls a chef's request to use the crematorium to replenish scarce meat supplies. "I didn't think it was unethical to take that human meat," says the doctor, "since it was lying around anyway." In our midrash as in the doctor's perception of Holocaust victims, the cultural meanings attached to martyrdom are inapposite. The victim's comportment in dying is as irrelevant as a cow's comportment before butchering. There are no revelations, no exhortations, no promises, no words. Silence: an alphabet lies dismembered.

The midrash is ruthless. It charms me, disarms me, then shocks me, wounds me, leaves me baffled. The Torah it shows me is the familiar scholars' playground, whose letters may be spun kaleidoscopically into world upon world of exegesis and law. Yet the transformation of the Torah of Moses into the Torah of Aqiba—the revolution in revelation, if you will—is ultimately mysterious. Some fundamental Why lingers in silence. Aqiba, master-maker of a dazzling world of Torah, will himself be violently unmade, cannibalized. And the Why of this terrible end will also remain in silence: It is the way it is, and so God planned it. In the classroom of Aqiba, Moses faces an unintelligible Torah. In the meat market he faces an unintelligible God.

The God of this midrash both is and is not recognizable as the God of the covenant. God-as-Torah-Scribe is a conventional rabbinic representation of the covenant partner who blesses the enterprise of law. What I mean by law here is Robert Cover's extended sense of the term—Law as the creative process by which interpretive communities translate foundational stories into a nomos, a normative world to be inhabited.[26] But at the end of the midrash, we glimpse a God who seems utterly beyond law, beyond justice, beyond compassion, a God who will not honor his promise to reward his covenant partners with protection, who accepts responsibility for appalling injustice but offers no explanation.

A reference to the next world, a cornerstone of the rabbinic belief system, would justify the divine plan, relieve the unbearable opacity of the story. But the midrashist refuses to move to the narrative of redemption. He will neither explain nor alleviate what, for lack of any better term, I must call the incomprehensible violence of God. The text leaves me with an intractable problem: How do I negotiate between my hunger for promised redemption and the integrity that forbids me to subsume the outrage of injustice?

Silence, Rabbi Nahman maintains, is the one true response to the abyss where a reasoning faith is drawn to its destruction. But the commandment to remember cannot be fulfilled by silence alone. Even the moving Yom Ha-Shoah ritual in the State of Israel, where sirens inaugurate two minutes of utter stillness, is dependent on some prior transmission of memory that authorizes and informs the silence. For such memories to become established, somehow the broken alphabet must be reconstituted. Some portal must be found by which we reenter the realm of language and speak about the unspeakable, some portal that will be for us a *petah tiqvah,* a doorway to hope.

Pain, says Elaine Scarry, unmakes the universe, expunging thought and feeling, self and world, "all that gives rise to and is in turn made possible by language."[27] "Conversely," she observes, "to be present when the person in pain rediscovers speech is almost to be present at the birth or rebirth of language."[28] The portal through which language is reborn is lament. In this genre the boundary between the made and unmade universe is thinnest, for it is the cultural form closest to the disordered and proverbial howl of pain.

The text to which I turn is the paradigmatic lament text: the Book of Lamentations, three of whose five chapters begin with the scream *eikha—How!*—which is the book's Hebrew name. The liturgical performance of Lamentations is the centerpiece of a mimesis of unmaking and remaking. Hauntingly chanted on the Ninth of Av, it commemorates the destructions of the Temple and other catastrophes of Jewish history. Ashkenazic tradition surrounds its recitation with graphic representations of a dead covenant and a bereaved community. The synagogue locus of the ordered nomos is deliberately disordered. The Holy Ark is shrouded like a corpse. Chairs on the altar are overturned, and fasting worshippers sit on the ground. The following Sabbath, the community rises to recontract the covenant as the Ten Commandments are read. The liturgical performances that frame Lamentations both present and overcome the terrifying possibilities of cosmic disorder and covenantal rupture.

The Book of Lamentations quite explicitly reconstitutes the alphabet. Four of its five chapters are alphabetical acrostics. Order is imposed by alphabetical sequence and the patterning of poetic language on content that is logically disordered. The poet and the two speakers, the woman Zion and the man who has known affliction, pour out a torrent of personal and collective woe: physical torment, humiliation, pity, self-blame, accusations hurled at a violent and predatory God, dreadful tableaus of jeering enemies, starving children, cannibal mothers, slave laborers, slaughtered bodies, pleas for mercy, pleas for bloody revenge.

This disturbance of narrative is consonant also with descriptions of Holocaust memory. Borrowing Hannah Arendt's phrase "the unbearable sequence of sheer happenings," postmodern ethnographer Ruth Linden contends that the accounts of the women survivors she records contain precisely these: fragments of "sheer happenings" whose senselessness and arbitrariness are falsified by ordering in narrative.[29] One repository for "sheer happenings" that are distorted by narrativization is lament. Lament's capacity to represent a prenarrative or non-narrative state gives it a unique capability to preserve what is irreducible and inexplicable about evil, curbing narrative's tendency to assign causes and meanings, to use storytelling to mend the unmendable.

The theological work of lament is to embody not only grief but indignation, not only acceptance but challenge. Walter Bruggeman contends that lament is a form of protest that "shifts the calculus and redresses the distribution of power between the two parties, so that the petitionary party is taken seriously and the God who is addressed is newly engaged in the crisis in a way that puts God at risk."[30] Rather than presenting a compliant false self, the lamenter confronts God with the immediacy of suffering in a way that renders retribution unjustifiable. The lamenter accuses God not of injustice but of compassionlessness. The woman Zion, urged by the poet to mobilize herself in defense of her little ones, to pour out her heart like water and lift up her hands to God, responds not with a plea but with a challenge. "See O God, look well (*habita*) at whom you have so brutalized. *l'mi 'ollalta ko*" (Lam. 2:20).

The work of lament in the book of Lamentations is initiated by a feminine persona because lament was originally a women's genre, composed not of wordless wails as popularly supposed, but of poetry.[31] Hence, God commands Jeremiah: "Call the lament-singing women, let the wise women come" (Jer. 9:16–17). The formal structures of lament and their performance by female artists are familiar to the rabbis of the Talmud. "What is meant by 'chanting' [*innui*]?" asks the Mishnah. "When all the women sing in unison. And lament [*qinah*]? When one speaks and all respond after her."[32]

Yet the recovery of lament for feminist theology cannot be an uncritical reappropriation. Citing the ubiquitous trope representing the nation as a woman and conquest as the violation of the body politic, Maeera Shreiber proposes that women are cast as the ideal speakers of loss and rupture because, in the gender code of these ancient texts, that is the condition they embody.[33] Drawing on Alan Mintz's finely nuanced reading of the Book of Lamentations, Shreiber concludes,

> According to the poem's discursive codes, the woman can both represent and articulate loss, but she cannot fix what has been broken—for that is her own essential condition. In this sociology of the text, only the male has recuperative agency; only the male can speak as an individuated subject with the authority to restore order.[34]

While I do not question Mintz's or Shreiber's taxonomy of the gender code, I think the power of the two personified lamenters and their respective modes has shifted for contemporary readers.

The Deuteronomic theodicy of retribution, repentance, and restoration invoked by the masculine persona ceased to be theologically viable in the time of the Crusades, although Holocaust theologians routinely resurrect it in order to beat it to death once more, while Zion's concrete indignation, her challenges of God and calls for redress are much more compelling.[35] The concluding chapter, where gendered personifications merge into a communal "we," is poised between hopeful reconciliation and the reiterated testimony of violation and abandonment—exactly my dilemma in reacting to the midrash. It is the liturgical tradition that tips the balance in favor of restoration, by insisting that the penultimate verse, "Take us back O God and we will turn back. Renew our days as of old," must be repeated after the final verse "for truly you have rejected us, bitterly raged against us." Applying the Mintz-Shreiber code, this last word would appear to be the anti-recuperative voice of Zion.[36] If I were orchestrating a performance of Lamentations, I would draft a powerful soprano to sing that last verse over the congregation's repetition of "take us back," "renew our days," to restore the textual tension that forbids easy recuperation.

Lamentations draws upon the metaphor of the covenant as a marriage, although in less elaborated form than in many of the prophets. That metaphor is itself violent and troubled, as many feminist theologians have pointed out.[37] Yet it is the one covenant metaphor that offers God and Israel an opportunity to grow into partnership, to begin to recognize the Other as separate from self and yet intimately bound to self. The one we hurt, the one with whom reconciliation is nevertheless possible. The metaphor of the sacred marriage whose participants persist despite violence and betrayal is applicable to human, political dilemmas as well. In South Africa, Rwanda, Cambodia, America, where civil covenants were intolerably violated, human, political beings struggle with conflicting impulses. Like the violent God of the prophets, we are caught between the unslakable passion for just retribution and the bitter compassion that counsels us to pardon the unpardonable, to mediate and mend the broken covenant. Rabbi Nahman of Bratzlav is famed for having said, "The wholest heart is a broken heart." After the Shoah, after genocide follows genocide to the very end of this bloody century, we had better break our hearts, for that is the only wholeness we can hope for.

NOTES

1. Jacob Neusner, *Strangers at Home: "The Holocaust," Zionism and American Judaism* (Chicago: University of Chicago Press, 1981), 1–11, 82–91.

2. Ibid.

3. Yosef Hayyim Yerushalmi, *Zakhor: Jewish History and Jewish Memory* (New York: Schocken, 1989), 5–26, 93–102, describes how events selected and reshaped for their normative value are inculcated in the form of communal memory by means of ritual.

4. For a theological discussion of these poets, see Laura Levitt, *Jews and Feminism: The Ambivalent Search for Home* (New York: Routledge, 1997), 135–162.

5. Gabriel Schoenfeld, "Auschwitz and the Professors," *Commentary* 105, no. 6 (June 1998).

6. Deborah E. Lipstadt, "Why is the *Wall Street Journal* Now Devaluing Women's Holocaust Experiences?" and Paula E. Hyman, Lenore J. Weitzman, Dalia Ofer, Marion Kaplan, and Lore Segal, "Women Scholars Speak Up," *Lilith* 23, no. 3 (Fall 1998): 10–13.

7. Sidra DeKoven Ezrahi, "Representing Auschwitz," *History and Memory: Studies in Representation of the Past* 7, no. 2 (Fall/Winter 1996): 121–154.

8. Ezrahi, 121.

9. See, however, Ellen Umansky, "Jewish Feminist Theology," in *Contemporary Jew-*

ish Theology, ed. Elliot N. Dorff and Louis E. Newman (New York: Oxford University Press, 1998), 144–145. Judith Plaskow, "Facing the Ambiguity of God," *Tikkun* 6 (Sept./Oct. 1991): 70, 96.

10. Marcia Falk, *Book of Blessings* (New York: HarperSanFrancisco, 1996), see for example 34–39.

11. Judith Plaskow, *Standing Again at Sinai* (San Francisco: Harper Collins, 1990); Rebecca Alpert, "Another Perspective on Theological Directions for the Jewish Future," in *Contemporary Jewish Theology,* 494–497; Rachel Adler, *Engendering Judaism* (Philadelphia: Jewish Publication Society, 1998), 21–59.

12. Marcia Falk's *Book of Blessings* (San Francisco: Harper, 1996), has a section on "Sustaining Life, Embracing Death." In it, death is construed as part of the life cycle but depicted without violence, pain, or terror (193–202).

13. Levitt.

14. Irving Greenberg, "Cloud of Smoke, Pillar of Fire: Judaism, Christianity, and Modernity after the Holocaust," in *Auschwitz: Beginning of a New Era?* ed. Eva Fleischner (New York: Ktav, 1977), 7–55.

15. Ezrahi, 122–123, 134–136.

16. The prophets offer such language, and it is conceptually feminine although grammatically masculine. Hosea's God declares, "Like a bear robbed of her young [*dov shakul*] I attack them/ and rip open the casing of their hearts. I will devour them there like the lioness [*levia*]." Variations on this trope in Job, Ezekiel, and elsewhere suggest that when the male speaker of Lamentations declares, "He is a lurking bear to me, a lion in hiding," he too is referring to a female predator. This trope, God as the ferocious female predator who is outside language and its appeals to reason and compassion, outside culture and its law courts and temples, parallels the trope of the cannibal human mother of Lamentations who reingests what she has brought forth.

17. Mary Field Belensky, Blythe McVicker Clinchy, Nancy Rule Goldberger, and Jill Mattuck Tarule, *Women's Ways of Knowing: The Development of Self, Voice and Mind* (New York: Basic Books, 1986), 17–20, 23–34.

18. Nachman of Bratzlav, *Liqutei Maharan* (Brooklyn: Hasidei Breslav, Moriah Offset Co., 1976). Offset from the original printing of Morenu Ha-Rav Shemuel ben Issachar ben Ber Siegal, 1808, Sermon on *Parshat Bo,* ch. 64, p. 70.

19. My own translation follows.

20. The expression *tashash koho* is literally translated "his strength was weakened" or "his power was exhausted." Judging from context, the expression seems to describe being paralyzed by shame. The same expression is used in a midrashic depiction of Moses' argument with God over the Golden Calf in b. Berakhot 32b, where God tells Moses that now that Israel has sinned, Moses is of no use to God. *Tashash koho,* the midrash relates, and he was unable to assert himself to respond until God gave him a hint.

21. The word *davar* has many meanings, but Rabbi Aqiba's response indicates that in this passage the term refers to a *davar halakha,* a legal matter.

22. Adin Steinsaltz, *The Talmud: A Reference Guide,* trans. Rabbi Israel V. Berman (New York: Random House, 1989), 183.

23. *kakh ala bamahshava,* literally, "Thus it rose to thought/plan/intention." For Rabbi Nachman, the phrase means "This is higher than or beyond thought." The second type of heresy, which inheres in the *hallal ha-panui,* the void, cannot be answered because it partakes of the silence of the void, in which there is neither conceptualization nor language. The void is, as it were, empty of divine presence. The silence of Moses or of one who partakes of the character of Moses can withstand the void and even rescue those who have fallen into its futile complexities, because such a person opposes to the void a faith equally empty of con-

ceptualization and language. Nachman of Bratzlav. See also "Silence," *The Encyclopedia of Hasidism,* ed. Tzvi M. Rabinowitz (Northvale, N.J.: Jason Aronson, 1996), 461.

24. b. Berakhot 61b, y. Berakhot 9:5, y. Sotah 4:5.

25. Janet Maslin, "Putting the 'Nazi' into Doctors," review of *Healing by Killing, New York Times,* Wed., April 22, 1998.

26. Robert M. Cover, "The Supreme Court 1986 Term: Forward: *Nomos* and Narrative," *Harvard Law Review* 97, no. 4 (November 1983).

27. Elaine Scarry, *The Body in Pain: The Making and Unmaking of the World* (Oxford: Oxford University Press, 1985), 30.

28. Scarry, 172.

29. R. Ruth Linden, *Making Stories, Making Selves: Feminist Reflections on the Holocaust* (Columbus: Ohio State Press, 1993), 9, 17–18.

30. Walter Bruggeman, "The Costly Loss of Lament," *Journal for the Study of the Old Testament* 36 (1986): 59.

31. Jer. 9:19 exhorts the elegy-makers to teach their daughters the craft because the devastation will require so many lamenters. See also Amos 5:16. On women as communal elegists see S. D. Goitein, "Women As Creators of Biblical Genres," *Prooftexts* 8, no. 1 (1988): 1–33.

32. M. Moed Qatan 3:9. In b. Moed Qatan 28b some verses of women's lament songs are cited.

33. Maeera Shreiber, "'Where Are We Moored?': Adrienne Rich, Women's Mourning, and the Limits of Lament," in *Dwelling in Possibility: Women Poets and Critics on Poetry,* ed. Yopie Prins and Maeera Shreiber (Ithaca: Cornell University Press, 1997), 23–41.

34. Shreiber, "Where Are We Moored?"

35. For example, Richard Rubenstein, *After Auschwitz: Radical Theology and Contemporary Judaism* (Indianapolis: Bobbs-Merrill, 1966), 66, 134–136.

36. Alan Mintz, *Hurban: Responses to Catastrophe in Hebrew Literature* (Syracuse, N.Y.: Syracuse University Press, 1996), 91–93.

37. For an extended discussion of this topic see Rachel Adler, "The Battered Wife of God: Violence, Law and the Feminist Critique of the Prophets," *Review of Law and Women's Studies* 7, no. 2 (Spring 1998): 171–201. Some major examples of the literature of feminist critique are: Gracia Fay Ellwood, *Batter My Heart* (Wallingford, Penn.: Pendle Hill Pamphlets, 1988); T. Drorah Setel, "Prophets and Pornography: Female Sexual Imagery in Hosa," in *Feminist Interpretation of the Bible,* ed. Letty Russell (Philadelphia: Westminster Press, 1985), 86–95; Renita J. Weems, "Gomer: Victim of Violence or Victim of Metaphor?" *Semeia* 47 (1989): 87–104, and *Battered Love: Marriage, Sex, and Violence in the Hebrew Prophets* (Minneapolis: Fortress, 1995); Naomi Graetz, "The Haftarah Tradition and the Metaphoric Battering of Hosea's Wife," *Conservative Judaism* 45, no. 1 (Fall 1992): 29–42. Fokkelien Van Dijk-Hemmes, "The Metaphorization of Woman in Prophetic Speech: An Analysis of Ezekiel xxiii," *Vetus Testtesmentum* 43 (1993): 162–170. See also Susan Brooks Thistlethwaite, "Every Two Minutes: Battered Women and Feminist Interpretation," in *Weaving the Visions,* ed. Judith Plaskow and Carol Christ (San Francisco: Harper and Row, 1989), esp. 312. In response to Naomi Graetz, see Benjamin Edidin Scolnic, "Bible-Battering," *Conservative Judaism* 45, no. 1 (Fall 1992): 43–52.

PART 4

Racism and Ethics
The Social Uses of Science

Introduction
Eugenics and the Social Uses of Science: Non-religious Factors in the Genesis of the Holocaust
Phillip R. Sloan

In Vasily Grossman's oceanic novel on World War II, *Life and Fate,* an issue is posed that seems to reach deeply into the inquiries of this volume.[1] He speaks of various levels of anti-Semitism. First there is "everyday anti-Semitism" that "merely bears witness to the existence of failures and envious fools." Second there is social anti-Semitism, a phenomenon that he sees, curiously enough, as primarily a product of democratic states; third there is totalitarian State anti-Semitism, in which the State capitalizes on the ignorance of the superstitious and the anger of the hungry, and transforms this into an ideology of party and state. In this form it was able to move through the level of overt discrimination—dismissal from positions, sanctions, wearing of stars—to outright extermination.

Whether this schema does any justice to the historical issues I leave to Holocaust scholars. But it does highlight a question that bears repeated asking: how did the first two orders of anti-Semitism, both with long histories before 1930, become transformed into high-technology, state-sponsored, bureaucratized extermination programs that created the Holocaust?

If this section of the volume cannot claim to answer these questions in detail, it can insert into a discussion that might otherwise focus on theological issues surrounding anti-Semitism in the Christian West some consideration of the complex role of science, and particularly the relatively new science of genetics and heredity studies, in the historical causation of these events. It is on this terrain that we can gain at least partial insight into the reasons why the events that played out in sequence from the German sterilization laws of 1933 to Auschwitz assumed the technological efficiency that they did.

All the essays in this section focus in some way on the importance of the eugenics movement of the 1920s and '30s in preparing the ground for some of the events that transpired in Nazi Germany. This history calls attention to the existence of a large international community of scientists, enthusiasts for science, and social reformers from all ends of the political spectrum who were enamored with the new science of genetics and the possibilities a genetic understanding of human beings promised for the social improvement of the human species. This widespread ideology, seeing in genetic science a solution to social questions, was readily available to the totalitarianism of National Socialism to use for the ends of State-sponsored anti-Semitism.

A large body of writing, including important studies by the two main contributors in this section, Peter Weingart and Daniel J. Kevles, along with the works by such individuals as Kenneth Ludmerer, Paul Weindling, Robert Proctor, Martin Pernick, Diane Paul, and several others, has clarified for us the details of the complex history of the eugenics movement in the decades since Darwin's *Origin of Species* and *The Descent of Man*[2] and has illuminated some of the linkages with the eugenics of the Nazi state.

Two generalizations seem to emerge from these historical studies. The first is that we cannot dismiss the social applications of genetics to society in the 1920s and '30s as the product of "crank" and disreputable science. Such judgment has the advantage of retrospective hindsight, but cannot do justice to the way these issues were perceived at the time. Too many reputable scientists were involved in aspects of this movement to allow this easy exit. The implications of the Nazi use of *compulsory* means to realize the eugenic measures that many had been publicly advocating become apparent only slowly to leaders of the eugenics movement. The German eugenics laws, when instituted in 1933, seemed to many to be only applied common sense. To accompany the English translation in 1933 of the German sterilization laws, the editor of the mainline American *Journal of Heredity* made a comment that highlights this point:

> The policy of the present German government is therefore to gather about it the recognized leaders of the eugenics movement, and to depend largely on their counsel in framing a policy which will direct the destinies of the German people, as Hitler remarks in *Mein Kampf,* "for the next thousand years." Whether this policy will be carried through successfully, of course remains to be seen. At best, mistakes will be inevitable. But the Nazis seem, as this scientific leadership becomes more prominent in their councils, to be avoiding the misplaced emphasis of their earlier pronouncements on race, and to be proceeding toward a policy that will accord with the best thought of eugenicists in all civilized countries.[3]

A second point needs emphasis, particularly in the context of a volume concerned with the religious and theological dimensions of the Holocaust. It is perhaps imperfectly raised in the recent Vatican document *We Remember,* but it points to the role of non-religious currents of thought that were able to utilize religious anti-Semitism for other ends. This concerns the profound "biologizing" of human beings that most dramatically accompanied the scientific triumph of Darwinism, but more generally represented the culmination of a process of naturalization that reached back into the "natural historical" approach to human beings of the Enlightenment. This naturalism both subverted a traditional theological view of human nature and also undermined the universalism that had served to replace theological reference points for much of eighteenth-century moral and political reflection.[4] In the wake of these developments of the eighteenth century, the categories of race, biological heredity, and historical evolution by natural forces were able to become for significant portions of the scientific community the defining framework in which human beings were to be understood. Darwinism only added a more convincing scientific basis to support these pre-existing developments; it did not initiate them.

When evolutionary naturalism was coupled with theories of the "hard" genetic determination of inheritance through the combination of Mendelian genetics and Weismannian germ-plasm theory in the early decades of the century,[5] many founders of the eugenics movement found it scientifically warranted to conclude that human beings were generally determined by unalterable biological properties passed on by inheritance. Carrying with them the authority of science, these attitudes were able to affect more popular understandings of genetics and public assumptions about genetic health and its implications for the body politic, which National Socialism could readily draw upon. We will see aspects of these questions elaborated in the papers in this section.

The issues raised for discussion are not only historical issues. As we proceed in the current international effort to analyze and eventually manipulate the most basic levels of human inheritance through the work of the international Human Genome Project, we are faced with enormous issues concerning the responsible and restrained use of our scientific and technological knowledge in its application to human beings. It will be technically possible to realize in the future the utopian programs of many of the eugenicists of the early decades of this century. Many observing the Genome Project have therefore feared the rise of a "new" eugenics as a likely consequence of this internationally based research effort. The U.S. Congress, at the suggestion of scientists themselves, has therefore set aside 3 percent of the total budget of the Genome Project for the ongoing assessment of the ethical and legal consequences of this scientific enterprise. Whether such safeguards are sufficient is an issue that concerns several critics of the project.

If we are to avoid new kinds of catastrophes created by efforts to achieve utopian social ideals by the application of genetic science to society, it seems vitally important that we learn from past history how popular consciousness, politics, and scientific ideas functioned in the genesis of the German nightmare. In many quarters there is currently considerable unease, a "fear of Frankenstein,"[6] about what biological science is doing behind the scenes. The public media currently bombard us with claims about genetic explanations of human behavior, society, ethics, consciousness, sexuality, and aggression and any number of claims about our biological existence. The effect of this discourse of genetic determinism and reductionism on popular and public consciousness is uncertain. But we can see how in the past popular social perceptions of scientific ideas were transformed into powerful ideologies that did affect legislation and helped define the meaning of "defectiveness" in ways that had political significance outside Germany.[7]

As we look forward from this point into our biotechnological future, the challenge is to see how we can use more carefully the promethean fire of our new genetic and biological science for positive ends, to extract, as Rabbi Moshe Tendler said recently, the "honey" from the bee of modern biotechnology, while avoiding its considerable potential for a "sting."[8] Retrospective study of the scientific dimensions of the Holocaust as well as prospective reflection both seem vitally necessary.

The essays and comments in this section address these questions from several perspectives. The first essay, by historian of science Daniel J. Kevles, sets a larger historical scenario for the eugenics movement in the period after Darwin and Galton, displaying in particular the character of this movement in North America. The next essay, by sociologist of science Peter Weingart, examines these issues from a more specifically German context. Three comments on the essays follow. The first is by legal scholar Roberta M. Berry. She has looked at the interactions of genetics, law, and society from both a historical and also a contemporary perspective, and has recently studied the famous *Buck v. Bell* case, which encouraged sterilization of defectives in the United States.

Reflections by anthropologist Jonathan Marks follow. His fundamental study of race theory appeared in 1995 as *Human Biodiversity: Genes, Race and History*. He examines these issues with some concern for the future directions of our contemporary biological research.

The final contribution is from Belgian moral theologian Didier Pollefeyt, who has written widely on the issue of ethics after the Holocaust. He comments on historical questions and looks ahead to the ambiguities of the Human Genome Project.

NOTES

I wish to acknowledge the valuable advice and assistance of my colleagues Susan Sheridan, Maura Ryan, Hillary Cunningham, and Harvey Bender for the conception and planning of this section. I also am thankful for the encouragement of John D. Reilly and the support of the John J. Reilly Center for Science, Technology, and Values, at Notre Dame, in the sponsorship of this component of the Holocaust conference.

1. Vasily Grossman, *Life and Fate*, trans. Robert Chandler (New York: Harper and Row, 1985), 486–487.

2. Peter Weingart, Jurgen Kroll, and Kurt Bayertz, *Rasse, Blut und Gene: Geschichte der Eugenik und Rassenhygiene in Deutschland* (Frankfurt am Main: Suhrkamp, 1988); Daniel Kevles, *In the Name of Eugenics* (Berkeley: University of California Press, 1985); Kenneth M. Ludmerer, *Genetics and American Society: A Historical Reappraisal* (Baltimore: Johns Hopkins University Press, 1972); Paul Weindling, *Health, Race, and German Politics between National Unification and Nazism, 1870–1945* (Cambridge: Cambridge University

Press, 1989); Robert Proctor, *Racial Hygiene: Medicine under the Nazis* (Cambridge, Mass.: Harvard University Press, 1988); Martin Pernick, *The Black Stork: Eugenics and the Death of "Defective" Babies in American Medicine and Motion Pictures since 1915* (New York: Oxford University Press, 1996); Diane R. Paul, *The Politics of Heredity: Essays on Eugenics, Biomedicine, and the Nature-Nurture Debate* (Albany: State University of New York Press, 1998). For an overview of the literature see Philip Pauly, "The Eugenics Industry—Growth or Restructuring?" *Journal of the History of Biology* 26 (1993): 131–145.

3. Paul Popenoe, "The German Sterilization Law," *Journal of Heredity* 24 (1933): 257–60, 260. For a picture of the complex makeup of the international eugenics community at this period, it is instructive to survey the proceedings of the International Congresses of Eugenics that commenced with the Paris meeting in 1913, with the second and third meetings in New York City at the American Museum of Natural History in 1921 and 1932. The first American meeting was coordinated by a subcommittee appointed by the National Research Council. A useful history of the meetings and participants is to be found in the Proceedings of the Third Congress, *A Decade of Progress in Eugenics* (Baltimore: William and Wilkins, 1934).

4. I have explored some of the early roots on this in my "The Gaze of Natural History," in *Inventing Human Science: Eighteenth Century Domains,* ed. C. Fox, R. Wokler, and R. Porter (Berkeley: University of California Press, 1996), 112–151.

5. See Kevles, chs. 1, 3.

6. See Jon Turney, *Frankenstein's Footsteps: Science, Genetics and Popular Culture* (New Haven: Yale University Press, 1998).

7. See Martin Pernick, "Defining the Defective: Eugenics, Esthetics, and Mass Culture in Early Twentieth-Century America," in *Controlling Our Destinies: Historical, Philosophical and Ethical Perspectives on the Human Genome Project,* ed. P. R. Sloan (Notre Dame: Notre Dame University Press, 1999), 131–152.

8. Moshe Tendler, "Comments on Cloning" (AAAS Forum on Cloning, Washington, D.C., June 25, 1997). Available on videotape from the American Association for the Advancement of Science.

The Ghost of Galton
Eugenics Past, Present, and Future

I4

Daniel J. Kevles

In April 1991, an exposition opened in the hall atop the great arch of *La Defense*, in Paris, under the title *La Vie en Kit*—Life in a Test Tube—*Éthique et Biologie*. The biological exhibits included displays about molecular genetics and the human genome project. The ethical worries were manifest in a catalogue statement by the writer Monette Vaquin that was also prominently placarded at the genome display:

> Today, astounding paradox, the generation following Nazism is giving the world the tools of eugenics beyond the wildest Hitlerian dreams. It is as if the unthinkable of the generation of the fathers haunted the discoveries of the sons. Scientists of tomorrow will have a power that exceeds all the powers known to mankind: that of manipulating the genome. Who can say for sure that it will be used only for the avoidance of hereditary illnesses?[1]

Eugenics has no more powerful association than with the Nazis. During the Hitler years, Nazi bureaucrats provided eugenic research institutions with handsome support. Their research programs were expanded to complement the goals of Nazi biological policy, exploiting ongoing investigations into the inheritance of disease, intelligence, and behavior to advise the government on its sterilization policy. One of the German eugenics institutes had the prominent geneticist Otmar von Verschuer on its staff. It trained doctors for the SS in the intricacies of racial hygiene and analyzed data and specimens obtained in the concentration camps. Some of the material—for example, the internal organs of dead children and the skeletons of two murdered Jews—came from Josef Mengele, who had been a graduate student of Verschuer's and was his assistant at the Institute. In Germany, the eugenics movement prompted the sterilization of several hundred thousand people and helped lead to anti-Semitic programs of euthanasia and ultimately, of course, to the death camps.

The association of eugenics with the Nazis is so strong that many people were surprised at the news last year that between the 1930s and the 1970s Sweden had sterilized some sixty thousand people, most of them women. The sterilizations were carried out under laws originally intended in part to achieve the eugenic purpose of reducing the births of children suffering from genetic diseases and disorders, particularly of a mental kind.[2] The fact of the matter is that after the turn of the century, eugenics movements, including demands for sterilization of the unfit, blossomed in the United States, Canada, Britain, and Scandinavia, not to mention elsewhere in Continental Europe and parts of Latin America and Asia. Eugenics was thus not unique to the Nazis. It could—and did—happen everywhere.

Historians have long known that eugenics was not unique to the Nazis, but many writers on eugenics have tended to view pre-Hitler eugenics in and out of Germany through the lens of the Holocaust. Any number of books and articles tend to emphasize the race and class bias of early eugenic doctrine, the shoddy science on which the doctrine rested, and the state interference with reproductive rights to which the doctrine led, primarily through eugenic sterilization programs of the allegedly unfit. The Holocaust orientation of this historiography is well justified, but in recent years a new wave of historical inquiry into eugenics has begun to take hold. It reflects contemporary concerns with developments such as the rush of progress in the understanding and diagnosis of genetic disease, the advent of the new reproductive technologies and the emphasis on reproductive rights, and the cultural shift in attitudes toward sexuality and women. To illustrate these issues in eugenics past, present, and future, I propose here to focus on eugenics in North America and to deal with both the way the eugenics movement adumbrated the Nazis and the way it foreshadowed much that vexes us today in the arena of gender and reproductive rights.

Race and Class in Anglo-American Eugenics

Eugenics in Britain, the United States, and Canada had its roots in the social Darwinism of the late nineteenth century, with all its metaphors of fitness, competition, and inequality. A key proto-eugenic theme was that social measures interfered with natural selection and thus fostered the multiplication of the unfit, a trend that was said to lead to social degeneration. Proto-eugenicists on the western side of the Atlantic knew about and admired Galton. They took him as their patron saint, embracing his ideal of improving the human race by, as he put it, getting rid of the "undesirables," multiplying the "desirables," and encouraging human beings to take charge of their own evolution.[3]

In North America, Galton's eugenic ideas took broadly popular hold after the turn of the twentieth century. Adherents of eugenics were united by an absorption with the role of biological heredity in shaping human beings. Most eugenicists in the United States and Canada believed that human beings were determined almost entirely by their "germ plasm," their inheritable essence, which was passed on from one generation to the next and which overwhelmed environmental influences in shaping human development. Their belief was reinforced by the rediscovery, in 1900, of Mendel's theory that the biological makeup of organisms was determined by certain "factors," which were later identified with genes. Human beings, who reproduce slowly, independently, and privately, are disadvantageous subjects for genetic research. Nevertheless, since no creature fascinates us as much as ourselves, efforts were mounted and institutions established in the early twentieth century to explore human inheritance, especially eugenically relevant traits.

In North America, the most important such institution was the Eugenics Records Office, which was affiliated with, and eventually became part of, the biological research facilities that the Carnegie Institution of Washington sponsored at Cold Spring Harbor, on Long Island, New York, under the directorship of the biologist Charles B. Davenport. Eugenic research included the study of the hereditary transmission of medical disorders—for example, diabetes and epilepsy—not only for their intrinsic interest but because of their social costs. A still more substantial part of the program consisted of the analysis of traits that involved qualities of temperament and behavior that were alleged to make for social burdens. A major object of scrutiny was mental deficiency—then commonly termed "feeblemindedness"—which was often identified by intelligence tests and was widely interpreted to be at the root of many varieties of socially deleterious behavior.

Typically for eugenic scientists, Charles B. Davenport concluded that patterns of inheritance were evident in insanity, epilepsy, alcoholism, "pauperism," and criminality. Such findings were widely disseminated in popular books, articles, and lectures, and they made their way into common culture. A chart displayed at the Kansas Free Fair in 1929, purporting to illustrate the "laws" of Mendelian inheritance in human beings, declared, "Unfit human traits such as feeblemindedness, epilepsy, criminality, insanity, alcoholism, pauperism, and many others run in families and are inherited in exactly the same way as color in guinea pigs."[4]

Davenport helped introduce Mendelism into the influential studies of "feeblemindedness" that were conducted by Henry H. Goddard, the psychologist who brought intelligence testing to the United States. Goddard speculated that the feebleminded were a form of undeveloped humanity: "a vigorous animal organism of low intellect but strong physique—the wild man of today." He argued that they lacked "one or the other of the factors essential to a moral life—an understanding of right and wrong, and the power of control" and that these weaknesses made them strongly susceptible to becoming criminals, paupers, and prostitutes. Goddard was unsure whether mental deficiency resulted from the presence in the brain of something that inhibited normal development or from the absence of something that stimulated it. But whatever the cause, of one thing he had become virtually certain: it behaved like a Mendelian character. Feeblemindedness was "a condition of mind or brain which is transmitted as regularly and surely as color of hair or eyes."[5]

Feeblemindedness was not only inherited; it was also said to be increasing at a socially menacing rate. Between 1918 and 1922, a survey of mental deficiency in seven Canadian provinces was conducted under the auspices of the Canadian National Committee on Mental Hygiene (CNCMH). It found that in all seven the incidence of feeblemindedness was high and a threat to society on grounds that feeblemindedness was a primary cause of poverty, crime, and prostitution. In 1920, Helen MacMurci.y, an energetic advocate of public health coupled to eugenics, published *The Almosts: A Study of the Feebleminded*. Addressed to laypeople, the book contended that feebleminded Canadians cost higher taxes because of their need for care and clogged the hospitals and reformatories. While they represented only 3 to 5 percent of the population, they accounted for half or more of alcoholics, juvenile delinquents, and unmarried mothers, not to mention perhaps as many as 97 percent of prostitutes.[6]

The backbone of the North American eugenics movement comprised people drawn from the white middle and upper middle classes, especially professional groups. Its supporters included prominent laymen and scientists, particularly geneticists, for whom the science of human biological improvement offered an avenue to public standing and usefulness. The eugenics leadership also included a number of medical practitioners, especially those who worked with people suffering from mental diseases and disorders.

Much of eugenics belonged to the wave of progressive social reform that swept through the United States and Canada during the early decades of the century. For progressive reformers, eugenics was a branch of the drive for social perfection that many reformers of the day thought might be achieved through the deployment of science to good social ends. Eugenics, of course, also drew significant support from social conservatives, concerned to prevent the proliferation of lower-income groups and save on the cost of caring for them. The progressives and the conservatives found common ground in attributing phenomena such as crime, slums, prostitution, and alcoholism primarily to biology and in believing that biology might be used to eliminate these discordances of modern urban, industrial society.

Eugenics in North America was distinguished from its counterpart in several other nations—notably Britain, the Scandinavian countries, and even Germany—by its emphasis on race. By "race," eugenicists of the day did not mean primarily differences between blacks and whites. They meant differences between white Anglo-Saxon or Nordic peoples and the immigrants flooding into North America during the period from Eastern and Southern Europe. Like eugenic scientists elsewhere, many American eugenicists held different national groups and "Hebrews" to represent biologically different races and express different racial traits. Davenport found the Poles "independent and self-reliant though clannish"; the Italians tending to "crimes of personal violence"; and the Hebrews "intermediate between the slovenly Servians and the Greeks and the tidy Swedes, Germans, and Bohemians" and given to "thieving" though rarely to "personal violence." He expected that the "great influx of blood from Southeastern Europe" would rapidly make the American population "darker in pigmentation, smaller in stature, more mercurial . . . more given to crimes of larceny, kidnapping, assault, murder, rape, and sex-immorality."[7]

Such observations were based upon crude, often anecdotal anthropological data, but IQ studies by Goddard and others had it that feeblemindedness occurred with disproportionately high frequency among lower-income and minority groups—notably recent immigrants in the United States from Eastern and Southern Europe. The seemingly deleterious impact of immigration acquired further authoritative backing after World War I, upon analysis of the IQ tests that had been administered to the thousands of draftees in the U.S. Army.

The psychologist Robert Yerkes, the head of the testing program, and others claimed that the tests were almost entirely independent of the environmental history of the examinees and that they measured "native intelligence"; but the tests were biased in favor of scholastic skills, and test performance thus depended on the educational and cultural background of the person tested. A postwar testing vogue generated much data concerning the "intelligence" of the American public, yet the volume of information was insignificant compared with that from the wartime test program, which formed the basis of numerous popular books and articles about intelligence tests and their social import. According to a number of popular analyses of this data, almost four hundred thousand draftees—close to one-quarter of the draft army—were unable to read a newspaper or to write letters home. Particularly striking, the average white draftee—and, by implication, the average white American—had the mental age of a thirteen-year-old.[8]

The psychologist Carl Brigham, one of the wartime Army testers, extended the analysis of the Army data in 1923, in his book *A Study of American Intelligence*. The Army data, Brigham said, constituted "the first really significant contribution to the study of race differences in mental traits." Brigham found that according to their performance on the Army tests the Alpine and Mediterranean "races" were "intellectually inferior to the representatives of the Nordic race." He declared, in what became a commonplace of the popular literature on the subject, that the average intelligence of immigrants to the United States was declining.[9] The IQ test results reinforced the overall eugenic perception that "racial degeneration" was occurring in the United States and that a good deal of the trend was attributable to the immigrants flooding into the country from Eastern and Southern Europe.

Eugenicists did not concern themselves much, if at all, with blacks. To be sure, the IQ surveys indicated that the average intelligence of black Americans appeared to be just as low as most white Americans had long liked to think it. The Army test data and various test surveys disclosed that blacks accounted for a disproportionately large fraction of the feebleminded; according to the Army test data, the average black person in the United States had the mental age of a ten-year-old. Blacks nevertheless did not foster eugenic anxieties, largely, it seems, because eugenicists did not count them as contributors to the quality of American civilization. Or more important, one might say, as threats to that quality. The segregation of American society kept blacks isolated and under control. Eugenics in the Deep South illustrates the point. The large majority of blacks lived in the Southern region of the United States, but blacks were not objects of interest to southern eugenicists, where the social control of them was stringent. The South also had few recent immigrants. The overall aim of southern eugenicists was the preservation of the quality of the white population, and its target was the region's white native "rubbish," in the phrase of an Atlanta pediatrician.[10]

American eugenicists fastened on British data that indicated that half of each succeeding generation was produced by no more than a quarter of its married predecessor and that the prolific quarter was disproportionately located among the dregs of society. Before the war, leading eugenicists in the United States had warned that excessive breeding of the lower classes was giving the edge to the less fit. The growth of IQ testing after the war gave a quantitative authority to the eugenic notion of fitness. The vogue of mental testing not only encouraged fears regarding the "menace of the feeble-minded," it also identified the source of heedless fecundity with low-IQ groups, especially immigrants, and it equated national deterioration with a decline in national intelligence.

Canadian eugenicists also identified the "menace of the feebleminded" partly with the immigration of "defective aliens." Drawing on the work of Goddard, MacMurchy estimated that Canada was admitting more than one thousand feebleminded immigrants a year. Like analysts of immigrants in the United States, Canadian analysts held that mental defectiveness was disproportionately present among immigrants from Eastern and Southern Europe and that it was mostly inherited. The CNCMH survey typically found that the recent wave of Slavic immigrants to Alberta was marked by a high incidence of feeblemindedness. It was claimed that some 70 percent of patients in the mental hospitals of Alberta were foreign born, that there were more people in the mental hospitals of Canada than in all the general hospitals put together, and that hard-working taxpayers were having to support these human drains on the public welfare.[11]

By permitting the immigration of mentally deficient aliens to continue unabated, Canada was said to be committing "race suicide." It was not only the absolute numbers of the immigrants that worried Canadian eugenicists; it was also that the newcomers seemed to proliferate to excess, bringing the threat of the differential birth rate to Canada. In Canada, as elsewhere in Anglo-American eugenic circles, the differential birth rate was often attributed to high sexual drive coupled with an irresponsibility that was thought to be inherent among immigrants—the same high degree of eroticism that was alleged to make many of them turn to prostitution. Whatever the cause of the differential birth rate, eugenic reasoning went that if immigrant deficiencies were hereditary and Eastern European immigrants out-reproduced natives of Anglo stock, then inevitably the quality of the Canadian population would decline.[12]

Eugenic Measures

In a preliminary act passed in 1921, then in a final one passed in 1924, the United States severely restricted immigration from Eastern and Southern Europe. It had broad public support. Although it would have passed without the support of eugenicists, they provided a biological rationale for the measure. But in other arenas eugenicists were more decisive. Early in the century, an Alabama eugenicist remarked that it was "essentially a state function" to restrain "the procreative powers" of the unfit. The idea was to decrease the frequency of socially bad genes in the population primarily by the passage of eugenic sterilization laws. In the United States, by the late 1920s some two dozen American states had framed compulsory eugenic sterilization laws, often with the help of the Eugenics Record Office, and enacted them.[13]

Eugenic sterilization was not uniformly adopted in the United States. More than a third of the states of the union declined to pass sterilization laws, and most of those that did pass them did not enforce them. In regional terms, relatively few states in the Northeastern United States passed these laws. Only three states in the Old South did. In the Northeast and to some degree elsewhere, including Louisiana, the passage of sterilization measures was effectively resisted by Roman Catholics. Catholics strongly opposed sterilization, partly because it was contrary to Church doctrine and partly because Catholics made up a very high fraction of recent immigrants to the United States and were thus disproportionately placed in jeopardy of the knife. Passage was accomplished largely in the Middle Atlantic states, the Midwest, and California, the champion of them all. As of 1933, California had subjected more people to eugenic sterilization than had all other states of the union combined. Wherever they were passed, the laws reached only to the inmates of state institutions for the mentally handicapped or mentally ill. People in private care or in the care of their families eluded them. They thus tended to work discriminatorily against lower-income and minority groups. California, for example, sterilized blacks and foreign immigrants at nearly twice the per-capita rate as the general population.[14]

Like their counterparts in the United States, Canadian eugenicists also agitated for immigration restriction and sterilization of the mentally deficient. The CNCMH argued for guarding the gates against the insane and the feebleminded, and in 1924, the convention of the United Farm Women of Alberta established a committee to seek to prohibit entry into Canada of immigrants who were feebleminded, epileptic, tubercular, dumb, blind, illiterate, criminal, or anarchistic. Apparently, the movement for immigration restriction failed.

But the drive for sterilization was another story. Agitation for sterilization began before World War I, with its advocates explaining that segregation of feebleminded people was insufficient; destruction of their capacity to reproduce would be far more economical, since then they would no longer have to be housed at state expense. Helen MacMurchy contended, "We must not permit the feeble-minded to be mothers of the next generation." A bill to authorize sterilization of the mentally deficient was introduced into the Ontario legislature in 1912 but failed.[15]

Resistance to sterilization laws was strong in the Eastern provinces of Canada, not least because Catholics there were politically powerful. But in the Western provinces, which had many fewer Catholics, support for sterilization grew after World War I. A look at the Alberta case illuminates the forces at work. Sterilization acquired increasing advocacy from highly respected members of society like Emily Murphy, a suffragist, pioneer as a female police magistrate in Alberta, and member of the board of visitors to Alberta's mental institutions. In addresses to women's organizations, she spoke energetically in favor of sterilization of the feebleminded, declaring that 75 percent of the cause of feeblemindedness and insanity was heredity, warning of the threat that the differential birth rate posed, and quoting Henry Goddard to the effect that "every feebleminded person is a potential criminal." In 1924, the results of the CNCMH survey, together with an initiative from the United Farmers of Alberta (UFA), prompted the first introduction of a measure in the Alberta legislature to sterilize mental patients, and in 1925, the UFA endorsed compulsory sterilization of the mentally deficient. President Margaret Gunn of the United Farm Women of Alberta argued that the procreation of derelicts who would "lower the vitality of our civilization" had to be prevented. Responding to opposition that sterilization would violate the civil liberties of inmates, she declared that "democracy was never intended for degenerates."[16]

The pro-sterilization forces received a substantial boost from a Royal Commission on Mental Hygiene that was established under the chairmanship of Dr. E. J. Rothwell in 1925 and delivered a preliminary report in 1927 and a final report in March 1928. Intended to examine the issue of mental deficiency in British Columbia, it nevertheless appears to have played an important role in advancing the issue in Alberta. Its views were authoritative, since the Commission obtained evidence from experts in Eastern Canada and in the United States. It concluded that the growth in the frequency of mental deficiency had been exaggerated, but it did find that facilities for care of people with mental diseases and disorders were increasingly overcrowded. It was apparently divided on what causes mental problems, with some of its witnesses having argued that they were fundamentally psychodynamic, while others held that they were mainly hereditary. Nevertheless, the principal remedy it advanced was sterilization, which it argued for as an economic necessity for coping with rising institutional costs. Witnesses from California testified that sterilization programs were highly successful there. With sterilization, patients could enjoy the greater liberty of living relatively normal lives in the community. Proponents of the operation claimed that sterilization was morally beneficial for the mentally deficient, fostering greater order and self-control in their lives. The Commission thus endorsed sterilization for people in mental institutions who consented to the procedure and who "might safely be recommended for parole from the institution and trial return to community life, if the danger of procreation with its attendant risk of multiplication of the evil by transmission of the disability to progeny were eliminated."[17]

On March 25, 1927, George Hoadley, the minister of health in the United Farmers of Alberta government, introduced a bill that would authorize the sterilization of people who suffered from mental deficiency or disorders and who resided in state institutions for their care.[18] The bill provoked a long and bitter debate. The measure was denounced as a violation of the patients' civil liberties. It was attacked on grounds that the coupling of discharge from the institution to consent to undergo the operation made a mockery of the idea of freely given consent; Laudas Jolly, a UFA member from St. Paul, noted that the measure offered "mutilation as the price of liberty for inmates of mental hospitals." The bill was also opposed as without scientific foundation and as an offense to moral and religious principles. Nevertheless, the bill had broad support from medical practitioners and laypeople alike, including the UFA and the United Farm Women of Alberta, the women's section of the Dominion Labor Party in Calgary, the Canadian Mental Hygiene Society, the Women's Christian Temperance Union, and the College of Physicians and Surgeons. Premier Brownledd called sterilization far more effective than segregation and insisted that "the argument of freedom or right of the individual can no longer hold good where the welfare of the state and society is concerned." In March 1928, the measure passed by a solid majority of 34–11.[19]

During the 1930s, the economic depression strengthened support for eugenic sterilization in Canada and the United States—largely, one is inclined to think, so that the state homes for the mentally handicapped could release more inmates and thus save money. Madge Thurlow Macklin, a geneticist at the University of Western Ontario, an organizer of the Eugenics Society of Canada, and an outspoken advocate of eugenic sterilization of the feebleminded, warned against the differential birth rate, raising fears that Canadian society, including its public schools, was being swamped by people with mental deficiency. She declared, "We care for the mentally deficient by means of taxes, which have to be paid for by the mentally efficient." She insisted that sterilization was warranted on grounds of "incontrovertible scientific facts." In 1937, Macklin visited Germany, surveyed the Nazi programs for the mentally ill, and returned to Canada with her support for sterilization undiminished.[20]

In the United States and Canada during the 1930s, sterilization rates climbed. In 1930, a Eugenics Society of Canada was founded, its membership heavy with medical doctors. Its treasurer, in a publication called *Sterilization Notes*, pointed to the "successes" of the sterilization programs already under way in California and Germany as well as in Alberta. He stressed sterilization as a mean of reducing the burdens of relief, and an official of the Edmonton Public School Board held that further sterilization of defectives would save considerable money in the costs of crime and unemployment.[21] Perhaps not surprisingly, Eastern European immigrants and the Métis were sterilized under the Alberta program at a far higher rate than their proportion in the population would have warranted.[22]

In the United States, the eugenic sterilization laws were declared constitutional in the 1927 U.S. Supreme Court decision in the case of *Buck v. Bell,* in which Justice Oliver Wendell Holmes delivered himself of the opinion that three generations of imbeciles were enough. The case had originated in Virginia. In the course of hearing it, the Virginia Board was presented with evidence that Carrie Buck, the patient who was proposed for sterilization, was feebleminded and that her feeblemindedness was hereditary in the Buck line. The gathering of this evidence satisfied the requirements of the law. It also satisfied the requirements of the U.S. Constitution, according to Justice Holmes. He observed in his opinion for the majority: "There can be no doubt that so far as procedure is concerned the rights of the patient are most carefully considered, and as every step in this case was taken in scrupulous compliance with the statute after months of observation, there is not doubt that in that respect the plaintiff in error has had due process of law."[23]

Virginia was not alone in its attention to at least the form of protecting individual rights in its sterilization law. In 1932, a review of sterilization laws in other states concluded that they all provided for reasonable notice to the person for whom sterilization was proposed and provided that person an opportunity for self-defense. In the mid-1930s, when twenty-eight states had eugenic sterilization laws on their books, a student (and enthusiast) of them noted:

> There is a growing tendency also for the statutes to define more specifically the criteria by which the courts shall decide that the particular individual falls within, or without, the sterilization category. The qualities of the individual, his own case history, and where possible to secure them, the description of natural qualities of his nearest blood-kin, are essential. Provisions for hearing both sides of the case, and ample provisions for appeal to higher courts are made so that there is continuously less danger that the State will make unjust decisions in the proposed sterilization of a particular defective individual.[24]

In retrospect, it is evident that what was legal and constitutional left a good deal to be desired measured against standards of human rights. The scientific evidence concerning Carrie Buck's feeblemindedness was flimsy and would not have stood close scrutiny by a scrupulous geneticist or psychologist even in the 1920s. The American sterilization laws were drawn in form to protect the rights of individuals, but in substance and practice they failed to do so. The Alberta law provided no such protection even in form after it was modified in 1937 to eliminate the requirement that the patient or the patient's guardian give consent for the procedure.

Gender and Eugenics

Eugenics was not a uniform, monolithic movement. To be sure, eugenicists were bound together by a common belief that human qualities—behavioral and moral as well as physical—were rooted in biology; but beyond that, they were disparate in numerous ways, not least in that they comprised a coalition of conservative, progressive, and radical adherents. And while they might be progressive on some issues, many were conservative on others, notably those concerning gender.

Not that women were absent from the eugenics movement. On the contrary, they played a highly influential role in North American eugenics. Like their male counterparts, they were largely middle to upper middle class, white, Anglo-Saxon, predominantly Protestant, and educated. Though not rich, they tended to be well-to-do. They had the time and inclination to attend lectures and debates, interest themselves in public affairs, and keep abreast of science and to set their social compasses by the new discoveries. In the United States and Canada, women played a prominent role in local groups and constituted a large part of the eugenics audience.

Eugenics, concerned ipso facto with the health and quality of offspring, focused on issues that, by virtue of biology and prevailing middle-class standards, were naturally women's own. Many women became involved in eugenics by virtue of their involvement with the progressive reform movements that flourished early in the century. They visited factories and the homes of factory workers, saw how the other half lived, and concluded that lower-income groups needed a variety of protections and assistance. To this end, they advocated, for example, child labor laws, school improvement, and measures for public and maternal health. They also advocated eugenics as a way of promoting reductions in the burdens both on lower-income women and on society. Like the campaigns against alcoholism, prostitution, and pornography, eugenics brought women into the domain of public affairs and provided them with a respectable avenue of social activism. It also brought women, as social activists if not as researchers, into direct involvement with the world of science, from which they were otherwise largely barred.

Although many women in the eugenics movement were progressive in their advocacy of state intervention on behalf of child and maternal welfare, they were socially conservative on issues of gender and sexuality. Eugenics complemented—and perhaps in part grew out of—the late-nineteenth-century social-purity movement. That movement had proposed to work a moral re-form of a society given to prostitution and the like. Mixing standard medical texts with moral prescriptions, it had tended to deny that women's sexual energy matched that of men, and it had insisted upon the reduction of male sexual expression to the female level and the replacement of male lustfulness by female tenderness, spirituality, and moral concern. It had thus encouraged women to take greater control over their marital sex and, in consequence, over the frequency with which they would bear children. Honoring motherhood, the movement aimed to make motherhood voluntary, an achievement that it claimed not only would benefit women but would promote the eugenic interest of the race.[25]

The conservatism of many eugenicists on what was called "the woman question" led them to oppose the use of birth control, often termed "preven-tive checks." Contraception, if provided to the lower classes, would obviously enable them to reduce their birth rate, thus making for healthier families and diminishing what eugenicists took to be the dysgenic effects of higher fertility among lower-income groups. Sexual conservatives, however, feared that the availability of birth control would permit the separation of passion from the responsibilities of procreation, and thus foster licentiousness. The British eu-genicist Leonard Darwin—one of Charles Darwin's sons—kept the subject of birth control out of the deliberations of the Eugenics Education Society and the pages of the *Eugenics Review.* It was not simply that so many members of the society found the subject distasteful but that they considered birth control "racially" devastating. Although contraceptive methods might in principle help halt the proliferation of lower-income, less-educated groups, they tended in practice to be ignored in those sectors of the population; instead, they were used disproportionately by the upper classes—precisely those groups whose declining fecundity alarmed so many eugenicists.[26]

Within both English and American conservative eugenics, it was a morally injunctive commonplace that middle- and upper-class women should remain at home, hearth, and cradle—that it was their duty, as Theodore Roosevelt trumpeted, to marry and bear children (four per marriage was the number thought necessary to maintain a given stock). Edwin Grant Conklin, profes-sor of embryology at Princeton University and one of the prominent biolo-gists of his day, declared in 1915 that the feminist movement was "a benefit to the race" insofar as it brought women greater intellectual and political free-dom, but insofar as it demanded "freedom from marriage and reproduction it is suicidal."[27]

The sexual conservatism of eugenics was implicit at the least in the move-ment's concern with feeblemindedness. Feeblemindedness lumped together mental and moral capacities. Often women who bore illegitimate children were taken to be ipso facto feebleminded. Eugenicists were divided about the sexual drives of feebleminded males, but there was no dispute about that of feebleminded women. They were reputed to be sources of debauchery, licentiousness, and illegitimacy. Mary Dendy, one of Britain's leading workers with the mentally deficient in the decade before the First World War, remarked: "the weaker the Intellect . . . the greater appears to be the strength of the reproductive faculties. It is as though where the higher faculties have dwindled the lower, or merely animal, take command."[28]

For all the scientific theorizing, there was a good deal of circularity to the analysis. Immoral behavior was taken ipso facto as evidence of feeblemindedness, which in turn was claimed to produce immoral behavior. The circularity arose from the tendency of eugenicists to identify as depravity most sexual expression that fell outside the bounds of prevailing middle-class standards. One critic proposed that "some of these pseudoeugenicists would, if they had the power, castrate or sterilize every man or woman who is not strictly moral according to their standard of morality, who smokes, drinks a glass of beer, indulges in illicit sexual relations, or dares to doubt the literal veracity of the Bible."[29]

It seems indisputable that socially conservative women eugenicists were perhaps even more eager than their male counterparts to regulate the sexual behavior of other women, particularly those in lower-income groups. Sterilization appealed to eugenicists not only because it would prevent lower-income women from reproducing but also because—so it was thought—it might also reduce their sex drive. The prevailing popular tendency seems to have been to confuse sterilization with castration and to assume that sterilization reduced sexual energy. According to a 1932 study of sterilization laws in the United States by Jacob H. Landman—a lawyer who had earned a doctorate for his investigation of the subject—sexual offenses or moral degeneracy figured explicitly in the grounds for sterilization found in almost half the state statutes then on the books. In the rest of the sterilization statutes, sexual license was implicitly covered in the provisions concerning "feeblemindedness." A review in 1938 of sterilizations at the Virginia Colony for Epileptics and Feebleminded noted that two-thirds of the inmates sterilized had been in trouble with the law, with sexual infractions ranking third among the offenses committed by the males and first among those committed by the females. In California, three out of four of the sterilized women had been judged sexually delinquent prior to their institutional commitment.[30]

After the Holocaust

Paradoxically, even while sterilization rates were rising, opinion was turning increasingly against eugenics, not least because of its association with the Nazis. In Alabama, for example, attempts to pass a sterilization law in the mid-1930s prompted a Methodist newspaper to warn that the "proposed sterilization bill is a step" toward the "totalitarianism in Germany today." There the "state is taking private matters—matters of individual conscience, and matters of family control—in hand, and sometimes it's a rough hand, and always it's a strong hand." Governor Bibb Graves put the issue more succinctly: "The great rank and file of the country people of Alabama do not want this law; they do not want Alabama, as they term it, Hitlerized."[31]

Scientific opinion had started turning against eugenic doctrine in the 1920s because of the shoddiness that colored its theories of human heredity, and by the 1930s the scientific critique was growing increasingly forceful and convincing. Psychologists held that the diagnosis of mental deficiency depended too heavily upon the results of intelligence tests. Mental-health professionals learned from experience that a number of people committed to institutions as feebleminded on the basis of the Binet-Simon tests were capable of leading successful independent lives. One might be slow at lessons but possess more than adequate common sense and be a useful member of society. By the late 1920s, Henry H. Goddard himself had, as he said, gone over "to the enemy," conceding that only a small percentage of the people who tested at mental ages of twelve or less were incapable of handling their affairs with ordinary prudence and competence. By the 1930s, the growing consensus of scientific opinion was that the alleged menace of the feebleminded was a myth, a speculation totally without foundation.[32]

Conclusions about the genetics of mental deficiency were undercut by the fact that the children of men and women admitted to asylums often did not themselves appear to be similarly afflicted. Some deficiencies were in fact inherited, but matings between mentally deficient people did not necessarily produce deficient offspring in the numbers predicted by Mendel's laws as eugenicists used them. In the speculation of geneticists, the reason was that many traits were polygenic in origin—that is, the result of many genes. Then, too, the mental deficiency suffered by one parent might originate in a different set of genes from that found in another. In sum, by the 1930s just what genetic combinations made for mental deficiency were, to say the least, unclear. Mental deficiency was found in many forms. Complex in its expression, it was presumably diverse in its causes.

Science aside, after World War II, eugenic sterilization also became offensive to moral sensibilities in most regions of the Western world because of its association, now revealed, with the Nazi death camps. The Eugenics Society of Canada died around the end of World War II. Sterilizations continued in several American states through the early 1960s, and in Alberta until 1972, but eugenics had become a dirty word in North America.

Yet even as eugenics fell completely out of fashion, genetic research was raising the curtain on a new, potentially revolutionary era in the control of heredity, including the human variety. Rapid progress in human cytogenetics—particularly the recognition in 1959 that Down's syndrome arises from a chromosomal anomaly—soon made prenatal diagnosis possible, with the option of abortion for women at risk of giving birth to children with severe chromosomal disorders. The unveiling of the structure of DNA, in 1953, opened the door to the discovery of how genes actually control the development (and misdevelopment) of organisms. By the mid-1960s, it was understood that genes embody a code, written into their chemical structure, that instructs the cell what specific proteins to manufacture. Finding proteins associated with diseases made it possible to identify flaws in DNA that generated illness and to detect disease genes in recessive carriers and fetuses homozygous for illnesses such as Tay-Sachs disease and sickle-cell anemia. The working out of the genetic code even inspired Galtonian visions on the part of some biologists that human beings might at last really take charge of their own evolution.[33]

Many commentators have cautioned that the onrushing advance of molecular genetics is likely to foster a revival of negative eugenics. Since it will in principle be easy to identify individuals with deleterious genes of a physical (or presumptively anti-social) type, the state may intervene in reproductive behavior so as to discourage the transmission of these genes in the population. In July 1988, the European Commission, which is the Brussels-based executive arm of the European Community, proposed the creation of a human genome project for the Community under the rubric "predictive medicine," which was taken to imply eugenic goals because such goals inhered in the intention of protecting people from contracting and transmitting genetic diseases. In the view of the Commission, however, the genome proposal would enhance the quality of life by decreasing the prevalence of many diseases distressful to families and expensive to European society.[34]

Economics may well prove to be a powerful incentive to a new negative eugenics. Undoubtedly, concern for financial costs played a role in the eugenics movement. In the early twentieth century, social pathologies were said to be increasing at a costly rate. At the Sesquicentennial Exposition in Philadelphia, in 1926, the American Eugenics Society exhibit included a board that, in the manner of the population counters of a later day, revealed with flashing lights that every fifteen seconds a hundred dollars of your money went for the care of persons with bad heredity, that every forty-eight seconds a mentally deficient person was born in the United States, and that only every seven and a half minutes did the United States enjoy the birth of "a high-grade person . . . who will have ability to do creative work and be fit for leadership." Thus it was reasoned, eliminate bad genes from the gene pool and you would reduce what are nowadays called state and local welfare costs, by reducing public expenditures for "feeblemindedness" in its public institutional settings—that is, state institutions and state hospitals for the mentally deficient and physically disabled or diseased. Perhaps indicative of this reasoning is that in California and several other states, eugenic sterilization rates increased significantly during the 1930s, when state budgets for the mentally handicapped were squeezed.[35]

In our own day, the more that health care in the United States becomes a public responsibility, payable through the tax system, and the more expensive this care becomes, the greater the possibility that taxpayers will rebel against paying for the care of those whom genetics dooms to severe disease or disability. It is likely that even a national health system like that in Britain or France might, on grounds of cost, seek to discriminate between patients, using the criterion of how expensive their therapy and care might be. Public policy might feel pressure to encourage, or even to compel, people not to bring genetically affected children into the world—not for the sake of the gene pool but in the interest of keeping public health costs down.

All this said, however, a number of factors are likely to offset a scenario of socially controlled reproduction, let alone a revival of a broad-based negative eugenics. Analysts of civil liberty know that reproductive freedom is much more easily curtailed in dictatorial governments than in democratic ones, the threats to *Roe v. Wade* notwithstanding. Eugenics profits from authoritarianism—indeed, almost requires it. The institutions of political democracy may not have been robust enough to resist altogether the violations of civil liberties characteristic of the early eugenics movement, but they did contest them effectively in many places. The British government refused to pass eugenic sterilization laws. So did many American states, and where they were enacted, they were often unenforced.

What makes contemporary political democracies unlikely to embrace eugenics is that they contain powerful anti-eugenic constituencies. Awareness of the barbarities and cruelties of state-sponsored eugenics in the past has tended to set most geneticists and the public at large against such programs. Most geneticists today know better than their early-twentieth-century predecessors that ideas concerning what is "good for the gene pool" are highly problematic. Then, too, handicapped or diseased persons are politically empowered, as are minority groups, to a degree that they were not in the early twentieth century. They may not be sufficiently empowered to counter all quasi-eugenic threats to themselves, but they are politically positioned, with allies in the media, the medical profession, and elsewhere, including the Roman Catholic Church—a staunch opponent of the past eugenics movement—to block or at least to hinder eugenic proposals that might affect them. Then, too, the constitutional definition of due-process protections has been greatly expanded since *Buck v. Bell;* the invasion of privacy inherent in mandatory sterilization would appear now to be constitutionally prohibited.

A typically anti-eugenic coalition rose up in response to the European Commission's proposal for a human genome project after it went to a committee of the European Parliament for consideration. The committee attacked any genome project that aimed to be an enterprise in preventive medicine, noting that the application of human genetic information for such purposes would almost always involve decisions—fundamentally eugenic ones—about what are "normal and abnormal, acceptable and unacceptable, viable and non-viable forms of the genetic make-up of individual human beings before and after birth."[36]

The Parliament urged modifications to the program—particularly complete excision of the purpose of predictive medicine—that drew support from both Green Party members and conservatives on both sides of the English Channel, including German Catholics. The Parliament's action prompted Filip Maria Pandolfi, the new European commissioner for research and development, to revise the Community's genome program, explaining that "when you have British conservatives agreeing with German Greens, you know it's a matter of concern."[37]

In 1990, the European Community adopted a genome program without the goal of predictive medicine, and committed itself in a variety of ways—most notably, by prohibiting human germ line research and genetic intervention with human embryos—to avoid eugenic practices, prevent ethical missteps, and protect individual rights and privacy.[38]

Beyond the Shadow

The near-term ethical challenges of human genetics lie neither in private forays in human genetic improvement nor in some state-mandated program of eugenics. They lie in the grit of what the project will produce in abundance: genetic information. They center on the control, diffusion, and use of that information within the context of a market economy, and they are deeply troubling.

The advance of human genetics and biotechnology has created the capacity for a kind of "homemade eugenics," to use the insightful term of the analyst Robert Wright—"individual families deciding what kinds of kids they want to have."[39] At the moment, the kinds they can select are those without certain disabilities or diseases, such as Down's syndrome or Tay-Sachs. Most parents would probably prefer just a healthy baby, if they are inclined to choose at all. But in the future, some might have the opportunity—for example, via genetic analysis of embryos—to have improved babies, children who are likely to be more intelligent or more athletic or better looking (whatever those comparative terms mean).

Will people pursue such opportunities? Quite possibly, given the interest that some parents have shown in choosing the sex of their child or that others have pursued in the administration of growth hormone to offspring who they think will grow up too short. The key report to the European Parliament on the human genome project noted that the increasing availability of genetic tests was generating increasingly widespread pressure from families for "individual eugenic choice in order to give one's own child the best possible start in a society in which heredity traits become a criterion of social hierarchy." A

1989 editorial in *Trends in Biotechnology* recognized a major source of the pressure: " 'Human improvement' is a fact of life, not because of the state eugenics committee, but because of consumer demand. How can we expect to deal responsibly with human genetic information in such a culture?"[40]

The increasing availability of human genetic information challenges individuals with wrenching decisions. Purely for personal reasons, people may not wish to obtain their genetic profiles, particularly if they are at risk for an inheritable disease for which no treatment is known. Still, genetic testing, prenatal or otherwise, can be liberating if it reveals to individuals that either they or their newly conceived children are free from some specific genetic doom. A young woman tested and found to be without the gene for Huntington's declared, "After 28 years of not knowing, it's like being released from prison. To have hope for the future . . . to be able to see my grandchildren."[41]

The problems and opportunities of individual choices aside, challenges to systems and values of social decency will arise from the torrent of new human genetic information coupled with the new reproductive technologies, such as artificial insemination by donor and in vitro fertilization. In recent years, these new reproductive technologies have provoked vigorous objections from radical feminists. Michelle Stanworth, for example, acknowledges that these technologies contribute to a trend toward fewer pregnancies and healthier children, but she stresses that "the view that reproductive technologies have given women control over motherhood—and thereby over their own lives—simply will not do." Emphasizing that some can give rise to adverse health effects, she stresses that they can be oppressive to women and akin to a forced draft of women's bodies, a subordination of them to purposes that are not their own. She holds that "by removing eggs and embryos from women and implanting them in others, medical practitioners will gain unprecedented control over motherhood itself." Stanworth adds, "Infertile women are too easily 'blinded by science'; they are manipulated into 'full and total support of a technique which will produce those desired children'; the choices they make and even their motivations to choose are controlled by men." The Canadian novelist Margaret Atwood's *Handmaiden's Tale* goes so far as to suggest indirectly that men are bent on exploiting the reproductive capacities of women by enslaving them. Some radical feminist critics also contend that the new reproductive technologies are degrading, that they relegate women to mere baby-making machines installed in a kind of "reproductive brothel," to be exploited for profit or perhaps in the service of the eugenic state.[42]

In practice, the new reproductive technologies have been exploited for neither neo-eugenic ends nor male domination. They have been tamed, just as birth control was tamed from the 1920s onward, to permit women privately to control their sexual and reproductive lives, pursing them in all the ways that contemporary moral and legal standards permit. Most women do not reject these technologies out of hand. Many are using them. Most appear to welcome them—because they empower women to have or not have children, and to have a better chance at bearing healthy children.

The new reproductive technologies are assisting women to have families, and to have healthy families, in numerous ways. One may quarrel with the costliness of in vitro fertilization; it is nevertheless a procedure that thousands of otherwise infertile women seem to want and that they have insisted on including among the benefits of medical insurance. Surrogate motherhood, stripped of the commercial and contractual problems that first beset its use, has become an uncontroversial commonplace. Artificial insemination by donor is equally accepted and resorted to. Dr. Wayne Decker, of the Fertility Research Foundation of New York, remarked to a reporter in 1974: "A lot of things we wouldn't do a few years ago, we no longer think twice about. For instance, I do forty or fifty artificial inseminations a week, whereas a few years ago we would do ten or twelve a year. The repellent connotations of artificial insemination are almost nonexistent now. Couples not only accept it but seem often to regard it as more natural than adoption."[43]

Artificial insemination seemed to a growing number of women a natural and attractive way to become a single parent. Among them was Afton Blake, a Los Angeles psychologist and the second woman to have a baby with the assistance of Robert Graham's Sperm Bank. Blake wanted, she explained, to raise a child "without conflict from a spouse," adding, "An unborn child should be guaranteed the best genetic material."[44]

Like birth control, the new reproductive technologies have not been used primarily, if at all, for eugenic purposes. What the future may hold, however, is anyone's guess. Human cloning seemed a part of the science-fiction future in the 1960s; it no longer seems quite that now. In 1978, the first test-tube baby, Louise Brown, was nurtured in her mother's womb as all other children were and born without any specially eugenic endowment. But now the genetic selection of embryos is possible, and the genetic manipulation of them seems closer. The new reproductive technologies could lead to some sort of new eugenics.

Concerning the larger society, much of the discussion about the information to come from the genome project has rightly emphasized that employers may seek to deny jobs to applicants with a susceptibility—or an alleged susceptibility—to disorders such as manic depression or illnesses arising from features of the workplace. Life and medical insurance companies may well wish to know the genomic signatures of their clients, their profile of risk for disease and death. Even national health systems might choose to ration the provision of care on the basis of genetic propensity for disease, especially to families at risk for bearing diseased children.

The eugenic past has much to teach about how to avoid repeating its mistakes—not to mention its sins, including the ghastly sins of the Holocaust. But the vast majority of issues raised by the advance of human genetics fall outside those of the Holocaust. It is important not to become absorbed with exaggerated fears that the advance of human genetics will necessarily foster a drive for the production of superbabies, or the callous elimination of the unfit, or the subordination of women. It is essential to focus on the genuine social, ethical, and policy challenges—some of them already evident—that human molecular genetics and the new reproductive technologies raise, and to respond to them by creating codes of law and conduct for their use.

NOTES

1. Monette Vaquin, *La Vie en Kit: Éthique et Biologie* (Paris: L'Arche de la Defense, 1991), 25. "Aujourd'hui, stupéfiant paradoxe, la génération qui suit le nazisme donne au monde les outils de l'eugénisme au-delà des rêves hitlériens les plus fous. Comme si l'impensé de la génération des pères hantait les découvertes des fils. Les scientifiques de demain auront un pouvoir qui excède tous les pouvoirs connus dans l'humanité: celui de manipuler le génome. Qui peut jurer qu'il ne servira qu'à l'évitement des maladies héréditaires?"

2. Gunnar Broberg and Nils Roll-Hansen, eds., *Eugenics and the Welfare State: Sterilization Policy in Denmark, Sweden, Norway, and Finland* (East Lansing: Michigan State University Press, 1996), 77-150.

3. Francis Galton, *Inquiries into the Human Faculty* (London: Macmillan, 1883), 24–25; Karl Pearson, *The Life, Letters, and Labours of Francis Galton*, 3 vols. in 4 (Cambridge: Cambridge University Press, 1914-1930), vol. 3A, 348.

4. Daniel J. Kevles, *In the Name of Eugenics: Genetics and the Uses of Human Heredity* (Cambridge, Mass.: Harvard University Press, 1995), 62.

5. Henry H. Goddard, *Feeble-mindedness: Its Causes and Consequences* (New York: Macmillan, 1914), 4, 7-9, 14, 17-19, 413, 504, 508-509, 514, 547.

6. Angus McLaren, *Our Own Master Race: Eugenics in Canada, 1885-1945* (Toronto: McClelland and Stewart, 1990), 25-41, 93.

7. Charles B. Davenport, *Heredity in Relation to Eugenics* (New York: Henry Holt, 1911), 216, 218-219, 221-222.

8. Mark Haller, *Eugenics: Hereditarian Attitudes in American Thought* (New Brunswick: Rutgers University Press, 1963), 109-110, 123; U.S. War Department, *Annual Reports, 1919* (Washington, D.C.: Government Printing Office, 1920), I, 2791.

9. Henry H. Goddard, "Mental Tests and the Immigrant," *Journal of Delinquency* 2 (September 1917): 244, 249, 268; "Two Immigrants Out of Five Feeble-minded," *Survey* 38 (September 15, 1917), 528-529; Carl Campbell Brigham, *A Study of American Intelligence* (Princeton: Princeton University Press, 1923), xx, 197; Stephen Jay Gould, *The Mismeasure of Man* (New York: W. W. Norton, 1981), 164-168.

10. Edward J. Larson, *Sex, Race, and Science: Eugenics in the Deep South* (Baltimore: Johns Hopkins University Press, 1995), 1, 9, 93.

11. McLaren, 50-51, 99; Tim Christian, "The Mentally Ill and Human Rights in Alberta: A Study of the Alberta Sexual Sterilization Act" (Faculty of Law, University of Alberta, n.d.), 14-15.

12. McLaren, 50-51, 72.

13. *Buck v. Bell,* 274 U.S., 201-207.

14. Larson, 37-38.

15. McLaren, 38-43, 64; Christian, 10-12.

16. Christian, 8-12.

17. McLaren, 96–98.

18. Christian, 20–22, 124–125.

19. Christian, 2, 13, 15, 20–22.

20. McLaren, 136–147.

21. Christian, 27; McLaren, 114–121, 157.

22. Christian, 76, 81, 85, 90, 118–21.

23. *Buck v. Bell.*

24. Harry H. Laughlin, "Further Studies on the Historical and Legal Development of Eugenical Sterilization in the United States," *American Association on Mental Deficiency, Proceedings,* 41 (May 1–4, 1936), 100; Jacob H. Landman, *Human Sterilization: The History of the Sexual Sterilization Movement* (New York: Macmillan, 1932), 16–17.

25. Kevles, 64–65.

26. Ibid., 88–89.

27. Edwin Grant Conklin, *Heredity and Environment in the Development of Men* (Princeton: Princeton University Press, 1915), 484–485.

28. Kevles, 107.

29. Ibid.

30. Ibid., 108; Jacob H. Landman, *Human Sterilization* (New York: Macmillan, 1932), 56–93.

31. Larson, 146.

32. Kevles, 148.

33. Robert Sinsheimer, "The Prospect of Designed Genetic Change," *Engineering and Science* 32 (April 1969): 8.

34. Commission of the European Communities, *Proposal for a Council Decision Adopting a Specific Research Programme in the Field of Health; Predictive Medicine: Human Genome Analysis (1989–1991),* COM (88) 424 final-SYN 146 (Brussels: Commission of the European Communities, 20 July 1988), 1, 3, 10, 12, 20, 30.

35. Kevles, 62–63; Philip R. Reilly, *The Surgical Solution: A History of Involuntary Sterilization in the United States* (Baltimore: Johns Hopkins University Press, 1991), 91–93. The last state eugenic sterilization law was passed in 1937, in Georgia, partly in response to conditions of overcrowding in the state's institutions for the mentally handicapped. Edward J. Larson, "Breeding Better Georgians," *Georgia Journal of Southern Legal History* 1 (Spring/Summer 1991): 53–79.

36. European Parliament, Committee on Energy, Research, and Technology, *Report . . . on the Proposal . . . for a Decision Adopting a Specific Research Programme in the Field of Health: Predictive Medicine: Human Genome Analysis (1989–1991),* 23–28.

37. *London Financial Times,* April 5, 1989. Copy in BioDoc: a collection of documents on biotechnology, European Economic Community, DG-XII, Brussels; Dirk Stemerding, "Political Decision-Making on Human Genome Research in Europe" (paper delivered at Harvard University workshop on the Human Genome Project, Cambridge, Massachusetts, June 15, 1990), 2.

38. European Community, *Common Position Adopted by the Council on 15 December 1989 . . . Programme in the Field of Health: Human Genome Analysis (1990–1991)* (Brussels: Commission of the European Community, Dec. 14, 1989 [sic]), 10619/89; "Council Decision of 29 June 1990, adopting a specific research and technological development programme in the field of health, human genome analysis (1990–1991)," *Official Journal of the European Communities,* No. L 196/8, (26 July 1990), (90/395/EEC).

39. Robert Wright, "Achilles Helix," *New Republic* 203 (July 9 and 16, 1990): 27.

40. Jane E. Brody, "Personal Health," *New York Times,* Nov. 8, 1990, p. B7; Barry Werth, "How Short Is Too Short?" *New York Times Magazine,* June 16, 1991, pp. 15, 17,

28–29; European Parliament, 25–26; John Hodgson, editorial, "Geneticism and Freedom of Choice," *Trends in Biotechnology* 7 (Sept. 1989): 221.

41. Jerry E. Bishop and Michael Waldholz, *Genome: The Story of the Most Astonishing Scientific Adventure of Our Time—The Attempt to Map All the Genes in the Human Body* (New York: Simon and Schuster, 1990), 274.

42. Michelle Stanworth, "The Deconstruction of Motherhood," in Michelle Stanworth, ed., *Reproductive Technologies: Gender, Motherhood and Medicine* (Minneapolis: University of Minnesota Press, 1987), 14–17; Gena Corea, "The Reproductive Brothel," in Gena Corea et al., *Manmade Women* (Bloomington: Indiana University Press, 1987), 38; Barbara Katz Rothman, *In Labor: Woman and Power in the Birthplace* (New York: W. W. Norton, 1989).

43. Kevles, 299.

44. Ibid.

15 Eugenics and Race-Hygiene in the German Context
A Legacy of Science Turned Bad?
Peter Weingart

Why Eugenics Haunts Science

The history of eugenics, race-hygiene, and race-biology has, perhaps after an undue delay, become a heavily tilled field in the history of science. It
attracts attention as does perhaps no other historical episode. The reason for
this otherwise inexplicable attraction must be other than just antiquarian cu-
riosity, usually identified with historians' reconstruction of outdated systems
of knowledge. The history of the applied science of eugenics, or race-hygiene,
as it was called in Germany and the Scandinavian countries, has been identified with racism, and due to its history, so has its heir, human genetics. Racism,
in particular anti-Semitism, although having many roots, has become identified with "scientific racism," that is, with race-biology and race-hygiene. The
most ominous link is undoubtedly the use of elements of race-biology and
race-anthropology in Nazi ideology, so much so that the scientists working in
this area labeled National Socialism "applied biology." However, there is also
a different tradition implied with eugenics, that of preventive social medicine.
It too, primarily because of the Nazi experience, has become identified with
social discrimination or "social racism." This legacy of the past haunts today's
human genetics and its most recent technological advances in the mapping of
the human genome.

Eugenics—and not, as is usually assumed, nuclear physics—is the field of
science that, by having been put into practice, has demonstrated to the world
that the unity of science and morality is a chimera. The atom bomb explosions
over Hiroshima and Nagasaki, which may have given Oppenheimer and the
more sensitive among his colleagues the feeling of "having known sin," have
remained strangely abstract, more like threatening machines that distance the
operator from the horror they create. Eugenics and race biology are "soft technologies," they involve concrete persons' actions, and they are implicated in
the greatest crime of human history: the Holocaust.

The history of eugenics has been told many times.[1] The focus of interest
here is on the ways scholars deal with this history and what that tells us about
science and its relation to political practice and moral judgment, for it appears
that this may be one key to better understanding both what role eugenics (as
science) played in the Holocaust and why the specter of eugenics haunts science

and political discourse to this day. Two types of discourse deal with the role of science (eugenics/race science) in connection to the Holocaust: (1) a *scholarly* discourse situating the story in the history of science and aiming at understanding the intellectual development in a particular social and political context; (2) a *moral* discourse, which is a discourse of maintaining the identity of (morally good) science, and thus of a dividing line between good and evil supported by science. The two are being conflated in writings about the subject; that is, the arguments of one are being weighted in the context of the other.

The conflation has its roots in two firmly institutionalized beliefs intimately connected with science and political thought:

1. the belief that good science is also morally good. This belief goes back to the early days of modern science, when the experimental philosophers renounced all claims to political reform, and the objectivity of knowledge itself became identified with its supposed social and political value.[2] The Enlightenment reinforced this belief, and it was reiterated during World War II and the Cold War;
2. the belief and practice that political action be legitimated not only by delegation of power but also by knowledge. This belief can be traced back to Machiavelli and then also to the Enlightenment.[3]

The story of eugenics and race-biology is troubling because it shatters these beliefs and thus the identities for which they provide the foundations.

Mario Biagioli, in a thoughtful analysis of the then current scholarly literature on the historiography of German medicine and life sciences in the Nazi period, has unraveled the mostly unconscious argumentative strategies employed by the respective authors. He shows that the involvement of (medical and biological) science, ranging from the legitimation and implementation of the Nazis' racial policies to the so-called Final Solution, is treated as "a major anomaly within the history of science" resulting in different ways of "bracketing" Nazi science.[4] While these strategies of *setting aside as an exception* may serve to preserve the identities at stake, in particular that of science as a moral institution, they are both historically wrong and misleading. They are misleading because they provide us with the wrong foundations for judging present-day developments. In particular, it is misleading to suggest that we may find consolation in some unexplainable aberration of science that has since been corrected once and for all. They are wrong because they imply a temporal, intellectual, and social *discontinuity* between "science under the Nazis" and "science afterward and everywhere else," which simply does not stand up to a test. The various strategies of "bracketing" eugenics/race-hygiene can be said to have failed the test if it can be shown, at the very least:

- that eugenics/race-hygiene was current and "up to date" research rather than quackery,
- that the eugenic discourse was not limited to a particular group of

people identifiable by nationality or more importantly by political conviction,

- that eugenicists and race biologists were not forced into their positions, censored, or otherwise abused by a totalitarian régime,
- that *genealogically* there is a continuity of research that creates *structurally* very similar moral dilemmas, that is, today's dilemmas implied
in the knowledge and technologies derived from mapping the human
genome.

I wish to emphasize that my focus is on the role of *science* in legitimating
and implementing policies that ultimately led to the Holocaust. To demonstrate the points mentioned means neither to exonerate individual scientists of
crimes nor to make the understanding of the Holocaust easier. On the contrary. It means that the strategy of bracketing, of appealing to unaccounted
forms of perversion of particular disciplines or their practitioners, or blaming
"bad" disciplines gaining undue influence over "good" disciplines, is judged
inadequate.[5] As long as we can continue to ask meaningful questions and be
dissatisfied with explanations, anything short of pressing on for further explanations amounts to mystification and prevents learning for the future.

An increasing volume of recent historiographic work uncovers facts from
the Nazi period and reveals ambivalences of personal, organizational, and political involvement with the régime and its criminal practices. The results of
this work are eroding unambiguously drawn lines and the myths connected
with them. The argument has been made that the generation or two after the
end of the war needed clear "black-and-white" differentiations in order to
come to terms with the horror and to (re-)establish their identity and that only
the later generations are able to "re-discover" ambivalences and thereby begin
to understand. From the vantage point of the moral discourse this attempt at
understanding runs the risk of relativizing and historicizing an event that, for
moral reasons, does not permit such an exercise. Here, I want to walk that fine
line of trying to understand by uncovering the myth of "good science being
morally good" while at the same time respecting the need to maintain threatened identities.

Race and Hygiene: The Discourse on Eugenics in Germany

The early history of eugenics is instructive with respect to the two traditions that merged in the movement and eventually separated again: the anthropological and the medical. When eugenics was inaugurated in Germany by
Alfred Ploetz in 1895, his book alluded to both "the fitness of our race" and
the "protection of the weak," thereby revealing the two traditions that were
to merge in the new movement but that would eventually be separated again.[6]
The concepts of "race" and "people" were not clearly distinguished; the use

of "race" ranged from morphological type ("Nordic race") to species ("physical and intellectual racial fitness"). Ploetz's and then Schallmayer's concepts of race-hygiene, as they termed eugenics, emerged in the context of a discourse on "race" that, again, was made up of two components. Anthropology in Germany and on the continent in general was physical anthropology and had become primarily the anthropometric study of racial "types." Physical anthropology in Germany had, in contrast to the French and American schools in the period of 1860–1890, an explicitly anti-racist, liberal-humanitarian orientation best exemplified by the outspoken attacks by eminent leaders of the field such as Virchow and others against both anti-Semitism and the *völkisch* ideology of Pan-Germanism. After the turn of the century it came increasingly under the impact of the tide of conservative nationalist circles' Aryan racism. With Gobineau, Lapouge, Chamberlain and many other less well-known authors engaging in popular nationalist and anti-Semitic writings glorifying the Aryan race, humanists, linguists, archaeologists, and lay writers had created an influential discourse extending far beyond the realm of academia. It was to gain considerable influence in an area that was otherwise dominated by physicians and natural scientists.[7]

In order to understand the subsequent developments, the political and the scientific contexts have to be seen in their conjunction. The increasing fear of degeneration that plagued the latter part of the nineteenth century was not only fed by the most visible repercussions of unmitigated capitalism in European urban industrial centers. It was also given focus by the new science of descendance: Darwin's theory of development and selection became the foundation for the eugenicists' interpretation of the assumed degeneration but also contained the hope that it was not an immutable fate. The diagnosis of degeneration counted as the basis for therapy.[8] Degeneration, however, was a vague concept, and consequently therapy could not be more precise. Criteria of degeneration ranged from perceived broad "racial" features, reflecting uncritical amalgams of ideals of classical beauty and parochial perceptions of their threats, to behavioral patterns like alcoholism and more focused common diseases.[9] The fear of degeneration had its parallel in the obsession with racial impurity, and both were amplified by the perspective of the theory of heredity. For the same reason the early race-hygienic movement considered itself a broadly based reform movement, linking up with temperance groups, vegetarians, proponents of country life, social-hygienists, physicians, and many others. Darwin himself had set the stage by linking the health and development of the human species to the logic of selection. Now the search for hereditary traits was on, and it was given focus and urgency by Weismann's theory of the continuity of the germ plasm. Although controversial for many years, Weismann's selectionism gained prominence over Lamarckism, especially among the eugenically oriented. As both a developed social science and scientifically based knowledge about human heredity were lacking, existing schemes of social welfare suddenly appeared questionable. Under the impact of Weismannism, eugenics developed into a hermetic deductive *social biology* with far-reaching schemes to eliminate counter-selective social institutions.[10]

The advent of the new science of genetics after the rediscovery of Mendelian inheritance theory, although gaining ground only slowly, opened new technological and political perspectives to the practitioners. The theory of heredity constituted a revolution in the sterile anthropometric research program, but it also gave focus to the hitherto diffuse fears of degeneration and the effects of racial mixing. In 1913 Eugen Fischer published his *Rehobother Bastards* and with it became the leading young anthropologist in the country, having demonstrated the fruitfulness of the new theory in its application to the study of racial miscegenation. The search for unambiguous criteria of racial differentiation and delineation seemed a promising research program when moved to the level of genetics and blood groups. "Biological anthropology" now appeared as the research strategy superior to anthropometrical and statistical surveys, and when the heritability of "traits" such as eye, hair, and skin pigmentation as well as blood groups was found, the supposed *reality* of "races" became more compelling.[11]

Until genetics was put on a more cautious base by the experimental Morgan school in the United States and subsequent reception of this school's findings in Germany, the German race-hygienists' more speculative approach to heredity left ample room for political value judgments to enter their policy recommendations.

Thus, the link between the debates about racial mixture in anthropology and degeneration in social-hygiene and medicine was provided by the new genetics, or theory of heredity, as it was still called. This was the scientific modernization that made it appear an attractive contender in demography and social medicine. The neo-Darwinian and Mendelian selectionist biologism represented by the new generation of anthropologists and biologists like Fischer, Reche, and Lenz gradually delegitimated neo-Lamarckism and thereby, for the time being, *narrowed* the spectrum of political valuations that could be supported by scientific knowledge. The more fundamental opposition to Aryanism and Nordicist and related racist ideas had lost its base both in terms of scientific theories and in people to support them. While the crude race theories of the nineteenth-century authors could be branded as "superseded," a "refined" *scientific* concept of race gained more credibility. In the light of the theory of human heredity, fear of a degeneration of certain "racial features" and fear of an increase of certain heritable diseases appeared to be similar and led to the same selective logic of their therapy: the control and direction of human reproduction.

In spite of its pervasiveness, this "racist" component of the discourse on race was not without criticism among eugenicists. This remains an important criterion of the difference both between the popular and the scientific discourses and between race-biology and eugenics even in light of the many connections. Schallmayer, although a social Darwinist by today's standards, not only ridiculed the "Nordic" movement but also rejected in clear terms their goal of purifying the race or giving priority to the "Nordic elements" as a legitimate objective of eugenics.[12]

A clear indication of the parallel and ultimately conflicting constellation of the anthropological and the medical components of eugenics is the development of the respective scientific and professional organizations and their programs. In 1925 a competitor to the German Association for Race-Hygiene was founded (*Deutscher Bund für Volksaufartung und Erbkunde*), which had its membership base among the civil servants of the registry offices. Several of its officers worked in responsible positions in the Prussian Welfare Administration. The eugenicists themselves spoke of the division of the movement into a conservative, race-hygiene-oriented "Munich" faction and a more moderate eugenics-oriented "Berlin" faction. When the two societies merged in 1931, the original goal to "improve the race" had been reformulated to the more mundane "eugenic formation of family and Volk."

Similarly, the 1927 foundation of the Kaiser Wilhelm Institute for Anthropology, Human Heredity and Eugenics, which was to become the most important research site in the field in Germany, was supported by declarations from scientists and policymakers alike that it would stay aloof from the nationalist and racist leanings that had been associated with the race-hygiene movement before and during World War I.[13] The suggestive equation between the anthropological race-hygiene orientation and the political right on the one hand and the medical eugenic orientation and the political left on the other hand, however, uses today's political categories (not reliably stable either) as an interpretive framework and thereby oversimplifies the picture.

An overview of the scholarly debate in Germany, and to some extent internationally, shows that from about 1923 on, the scientific foundations of race-hygiene were no longer contested in principle. Criticism became technical in nature and concerned the practicability of eugenic measures (such as health certificates as a precondition for marriage licenses and sterilizations). The main issue became the genetic basis of eugenic/race-hygienic claims and policy measures. One of the few outspoken critics raised his voice at the Fifth International Congress of Hereditary Science in Berlin, 1928. Raymond Pearl, himself a eugenicist and geneticist, submitted a paper in which he castigated the class and race biases rampant in eugenics and called for a fair but critical analysis of eugenic propaganda on the part of the genetics community.[14] Pearl's article signaled the distancing of Anglo-Saxon geneticists from eugenics, but this movement was by no means unanimous. Herman J. Muller, also a eugenicist and geneticist, hailed the 1931 American translation of the German "charter" of eugenics, *Menschliche Erblichkeitslehre und Rassenhygiene* (Human Heredity and Race-Hygiene), authored by Baur, Fischer, and Lenz, as the "best work on the subject of human heredity," and lauded Baur and Lenz as leading geneticists in Europe. His criticism was directed to the second part of the book, in which Fischer and Lenz had forgone science to support the crassest popular biases.[15] Other critics within Germany were too marginal to make an impact. Viewed from the outside, the remaining differences among the scientists were within the realm of normal scientific controversy. At the dawn of Hitler's ascent to power, German genetics, although organizationally and financially weak, was internationally recognized. With its more holistic orientation to hereditary processes, however, it differed from the reductionist approach of the Morgan school in the United States.

The Lure of Race-Hygiene as an Applied Science: From Enthusiasm to Opportunism

Parallel to the virtual scientific consensus on the feasibility of eugenics, the eugenic credo also cut across the entire political spectrum, foreclosing a fundamental normative critique. The spectrum of the German eugenic discourse in the mid-1920s extended from, on one end, race-oriented research into specific mental traits and abilities and suggested policy measures of racial purification to, on the other, medically oriented research into the heredity of specific diseases as well as measures of reproductive control such as sterilization. The scientific base of the former was more tenuous, and its affinity to the political right closer than the latter's. The social and political environments had a decisive influence as to which elements of the scientific discourse would diffuse beyond the narrow confines of academia into the realm of public discourse and politics and find support.

The scientific and collectivist dispositions of the political left made it receptive to the promises of the modern social technology of eugenics. Bebel and Kautsky welcomed the perspectives of a biological liberation of the working class. Julius Moses, a social-democratic member of the Reichstag, expressed his hope that the new Kaiser Wilhelm Institute for Human Heredity would be instrumental in advancing a scientifically sound eugenics. In the Soviet Union eugenics was advanced by the geneticists from 1921 onward until "bourgeois genetics" fell into disrepute at the end of the 1920s.[16]

The often anti-Semitic overtones of race-hygiene tracts, against which the political left formulated its anti-racist criticisms, did not even prevent an impressive number of Jewish physicians and researchers from following the lure of the eugenic promise, although most of them later became its victims. One reason for this support was undoubtedly the fact that they represented a sizable group within the German medical profession and shared its values. Among the great names of eugenicists of Jewish origin are Richard Goldschmidt, Heinrich Poll, and Curt Stern as geneticists; Wilhelm Weinberg (co-author of the Hardy-Weinberg law) as statistician and Felix Bernstein as mathematician;

Magnus Hirschfeld, Albert Moll, Max Hirsch, Max Marcuse, and others as physicians and sexologists. All of them had actively participated in the eugenic discourse and published more or less radical proposals of eugenic measures for the control of human reproduction.[17]

The eugenic credo was also pervasive across the Western industrial societies and even beyond.[18] This is perhaps best exemplified by the "Geneticists' Manifesto," published on the occasion of the Seventh International Congress of Genetics in Edinburgh in 1939, immediately before the outbreak of World War II. Signed by the most eminent geneticists of England and the United States (among them declared Marxists like Muller and Haldane), it criticized the Nazis' racial policies but otherwise emphatically advocated positive and negative measures of control of the reproductive process whose scientific modernity and social radicalism reached beyond anything realized by the National Socialists. With their manifesto the geneticists had, in fact, linked the eugenic utopias to the scientifically more timely, anti-fascist vision of human genetics, but it was a scientistic vision of a eugenic improvement of mankind nonetheless.

The liberal and welfare-minded mid-Weimar years were not particularly receptive to the selectionist arguments that were advanced by race-anthropologists and race-hygienists. This changed rather suddenly with the world economic crisis. In Germany, the drop of the GNP by 25 percent within four years and the rise of unemployment from 1.8 million in 1929 to 5.6 million in 1932 prepared the ground for a high receptivity to cost-saving schemes in the public health sector. Comparative cost-benefit analyses of different strategies, notably sterilization, became common. Their targets were patients with physical or mental disabilities believed to be hereditary. Soon alcoholics, criminals, and whoever fell into the category of "socially unfit" were included.

Likewise, in an atmosphere of rapidly disappearing tolerance, the anthropological discussion about racial mixture linked up with the growing anti-Semitism and played on its political leverage. Social and racial discrimination, although distinguishable in terms of their disciplinary origins and their targets, had the same methodological basis and profited from the same political climate.

The interest of the state medical administration in race-hygiene as a preventive strategy coincided with a paradigm shift in public medical care. Arthur Gütt, its main proponent, called for a shift from what he deemed to be an exaggerated individual and social-hygiene-oriented system of medical care to one that would be based on heredity (genetics), race-hygiene, and demographic policy.[19] This fundamental re-orientation of the system of medical care implied its reorganization from a diversified communal to a unified state administration. When the National Socialists assumed power in 1933, Gütt became the most influential medical administrator and the architect of a new law unifying the public medical care system, in which heredity and race-care (Erb- und Rassenpflege) were integral parts. The law, put into effect in 1934, provided the framework for the infamous "Nuremberg Laws" passed in 1935, which contained the core provisions of the National Socialist race policy.

Until very recently, historians who were probably unaware of the history of anthropology and eugenics and who all too readily believed accounts of the supposed ad-hoc character of the Nuremberg Laws did not realize that these laws were merely the implementation of more than twenty years of discussion in the two fields.[20] Far from inventing these ideas, the Nazis (or rather Hitler himself) had only translated race-hygienic and race-anthropological postulates into the party program. The "Law for the Protection of German Blood and German Honor" reflected concerns about racial purity and prohibited marriage and sexual intercourse (Blutsgemeinschaften) between Germans and members of foreign races. The "Law for the Protection of Hereditary Health of the German People," in turn, was supposed to put marriage under a eugenically motivated state control through the issuing of marriage permits. This law was intended to complement the sterilization law of 1934, which had been written under the previous government but passed with a significant alteration, the abolition of consent, by the new National Socialist régime.[21] While the implementation of the eugenic control of marriages ultimately failed, the "protection of German blood" was one of the several steps toward the Holocaust.

The Nazis thereby had put into practice a program of eugenic measures whose drastic intervention into human privacy and health relied heavily upon an autocratic government such as the National Socialist régime and whose scientific base, in retrospect, was more than shaky. These two aspects characterize quite well the nature of eugenics/race-hygiene as an applied science and at the same time focus on the special relationship the scientists concerned had with the "new state." Several factors can explain the race-hygienists' eagerness to become involved in policy making and thus their susceptibility to the offerings of the new rulers:

(1) Eugenics/race-hygiene was a relatively new discipline still in search of professional recognition. Although the eugenicists probably did not consciously employ strategies to increase the fear of degeneration, they crystallized that fear and gave it scientific focus. They were a fairly small group but had a larger number of sympathizers looking for coherence. The expectation was that a National Socialist state would authorize them to assume eugenic functions in the health system that would amount to the establishment and increase of professional control far beyond anything the medical profession had at that point.

(2) The large majority of eugenicists/race-hygienists were physicians. Conservative in their social and political values as a profession to begin with, they faced a severe downward mobility toward the end of the 1920s, when thousands were unemployed. The percentage of members of the NSDAP among

physicians was the highest in any professional group. The ousting of the Jewish physicians, who in some large cities like Frankfurt and Berlin made up more than 50 percent of all medical doctors, is the result of a competition that could assume such crass form only because it was sanctioned by the state.

(3) There was an affinity between the eugenicists/race-hygienists and the National Socialists, which because of the points mentioned above ranged from a mutually utilitarian relationship to a deeper ideological affinity. Fritz Lenz, one of the leading German geneticists and race-hygienists, had explicitly and correctly claimed an "essential relationship" (*Wesensverwandtschaft*) between race-hygiene and the "Fascist idea of the State." He took pride in the fact that Hitler had taken many of his ideas from Lenz's own writings.[22] Although he did not share Hitler's radical anti-Semitism, he applauded him as the "first politician of great influence who has recognized race hygiene as the central task of politics and who wants to throw his full weight behind it."[23] It is, thus, no accident that the race-hygienists welcomed and supported the Nazis, even though not all of them were quite as enthusiastic as they had been before the Nazis' rise to power. This cautionary stance turned into often enthusiastic willingness to collaborate soon after the January 1933 takeover. No one forced Ernst Rüdin, the prominent psychiatrist and leading race-hygienist, to eulogize Hitler in 1934: "The importance of race hygiene has become evident to all aware Germans only through the political work of Adolf Hitler, and only through him has our more than thirty-year-old dream become reality: to be able to put race hygiene into action."[24]

Was (good) science politically suppressed or corrupted? The answer is not a simple yes or no. The Nazis took control of the German Society for Race Hygiene (Eugenics), that is, the professional society, by forcing its officers (Fischer, Muckermann, and Ostermann) to step down. Rüdin was named *Reichskommissar* and was directly responsible to the minister of the interior. This procedure was the political *Gleichschaltung* practiced in all sensitive sectors of society. In effect, the political authorities *selected* among different factions within the pertinent scientific community; they chose those theories and their representatives that were closer to their political views and provided the adherents with privileges, which is not an uncommon practice. Many race-hygienists were removed from their positions for "racial" (in the case of Jews) or political reasons *regardless* of their agreement on eugenic issues. In the case of the firing of Jewish physicians and eugenicists, theories and political views did not even matter, as the criterion was "race" as defined in the laws governing the "Reconstitution of the Civil Service" and the Nuremberg Laws.

Even if one assumes that political pressure played a role in the early phase, after the change of power the ensuing cooperation and active support of the race-hygiene policies on the part of the scientists suggest unambiguously that the new arrangement was to their liking. They profited from it directly. Fischer and Rüdin put their institutes in the service "of the new necessities of the state" in July 1933.[25] They were followed by virtually the entire eugenics/race-hygiene community.

It is usually assumed that the political authorities are monolithic in their attempts at suppressing science or selecting between factions within science. That, too, is an unwarranted simplification. Within the Party moderates and radicals, pragmatists and ideologues were battling for influence, and their respective fortunes shifted even as the Nazis' power consolidated and they began to prepare for war.[26]

The other side of this is the opportunism of those scientists who found themselves profiting from the arrangement. As numerous accounts from other disciplines and even from other countries show, the pattern is a common one, and whether political pressure is successful or not is a question of the collaboration or resistance of the scientists concerned. But in the case of eugenics/race-hygiene, resistance was not at issue. Being an integral part of the party's program, it shared some of its popularity. Books on race sold hundreds of thousands of copies, and many less qualified authors jumped on the bandwagon of the "heredity" fad. The wave of publications was so great, in fact, that race-hygienists deplored it and the NSDAP felt compelled to authorize the publication of "literature guides."[27] The affinity between National Socialism and eugenics/race-hygiene rested on ideological agreement—an anti-individualist, "gene-pool" (in today's terms) orientation—and on the mutuality of interest, that is, scientific legitimation of race policies and state authorization of professionalization. This affinity was supported, for a time, by popular consent. Only this particular constellation can explain why, in Germany, political authorities and scientists embarked on a eugenic and race policy whose goals surpassed its available, scientifically based means by far and whose ethical unacceptability was swept aside.

The Legacy of Eugenics/Race-Hygiene, Euthanasia, and the Holocaust

So far it has been shown that eugenics was not "bad science" carried out by crooks, nor was it limited to a particular nationality or identifiable exclusively with the political right. And it was demonstrated that the German eugenicists/race-hygienists were not forced into their research but were rather enthusiastic and opportunist in their collaboration. This latter aspect is particularly relevant and leads to the question of the relations between race-hygiene and the Holocaust.

Most historical accounts of eugenics and race-hygiene in Germany draw a direct line from the Nuremberg Laws to the Holocaust and, thus, hold (a corrupt or perverted) science responsible for the genocide.[28] Their evidence is the direct personal involvement of psychiatrists in the euthanasia activity and of physicians in the medical experiments at the concentration camps, that is, the involvement of the same people who were active race-hygienists. The most prominent and revolting case is, of course, that of Josef Mengele and his murderous research at Auschwitz.[29] However, the link is not as direct and unilinear as the involvement of individuals suggests. To this day historians have not found conclusive evidence of an actual order from Hitler initiating the Holocaust, but all available evidence suggests that it is highly unlikely that he and the bureaucracy that implemented the mass murder were driven by scientific, that is, eugenic and race-hygienic, motivations.[30] There is also another reason why the link between eugenics/race-hygiene and the Holocaust is not a direct one: neither the euthanasia of mental patients nor the murder of Jews, Sinti, and Roma has a systematic place in the selectionist logic of eugenics.

In 1920 a book appeared with the ominous title *Allowing the Destruction of Life Unworthy of Living (Freigabe der Vernichtung lebensunwerten Lebens)*, which started the debate over euthanasia.[31] Its authors were a lawyer and a physician, not race-hygienists, and the debate they had initiated took place outside the eugenic discourse. It was an economic debate, and the motives were criticized by the race-hygienists, with the obvious argument that the issue of selection was not one of the death of individuals but of the number and hereditary value of their offspring.[32] If one accepted the eugenic and race-hygienic goals of protecting heredity and "race," was the argument, the measures of sterilization and marriage permits would suffice to meet them.

The more important link between the first mass killings (the so-called T4-Aktion) in the psychiatric clinics (sanctioned by psychiatrists) and the race-hygienic discourse lies on a different level. The central elements of eugenic/race-hygienic thought served to delegitimate established social values of humanity: the "biologization of the social," the selectionist terminology of social Darwinism, the reduction of ethnic, religious, and cultural differences as well as of social patterns of behavior to immutable biological differences, the abstraction from the individual in favor of a biologically conceived *Volkskörper* ("gene pool" in today's terminology), which was to be kept "racially clean" and hereditarily "healthy." All these culminated in de-humanizing terminology, represented in such concepts as "life not worth living" (*Lebensunwertes Leben*) and a differential valuation of "races," which ranked Jews as a "completely inferior race."[33] The mental models expressed in this terminology fit the utilitarian perspective on the costs of psychiatric patients, of the homeless, and of prison inmates, which toward the end of the 1920s, under the pressure of the world economic crisis and mass unemployment, became rampant in popular propaganda. As we know today this thinking even prevailed over ethical considerations where they should have been held most firmly: among representatives of the Church and its institutions. Thus, it is questionable to claim that the mass murder through euthanasia and the Holocaust were *legitimated* by science.[34] The role of science (i.e., the fields involved) was rather one of preparing the ground for it by creating and entertaining a discourse whose scientistic fervor blurred the ethical boundaries that had hitherto remained unquestioned.

This points to a further indirect link between eugenics/race-hygiene and euthanasia and the Holocaust, a link that implicates science as an *institution*. The case of the notorious cooperation of Otmar von Verschuer, then director of the Berlin Anthropology Institute and successor of Fischer, with Josef Mengele, who worked in a "medical" capacity in Auschwitz, though perhaps in the extreme, stands for all those physicians, psychiatrists, anthropologists, race-biologists, race-hygienists, and eugenicists who in one form or another took part in criminal experiments on humans in clinics and in the concentration camps or whose research profited from such experiments. The far-reaching network of research related to problems of human heredity profited from the accessibility of "material," that is, bodies, organs, skeletons, and pertinent data, which would have never been available under other circumstances. Although it was never proved before a court, von Verschuer is said to have sent Josef Mengele to Auschwitz in order to utilize the "unique opportunities for race-biological research" that it offered.[35] The daughter of psychiatrist and race-hygienist Ernst Rüdin, after the war when defending her father's collaboration with an SS funding organization, stated: "He would have sold himself to the devil in order to obtain money for his institute and his research."[36]

The reference to "unique opportunities of accessibilities" and the metaphoric use of the Faustian bargain are apt descriptions of the mentality fostered by science, which cannot be attributed to an aberration of the particular psyche of the individuals involved. The message behind this thinking is unambiguous: science and ethics are separate and different and not, as the strategies of bracketing imply, integral parts of the same. The search for knowledge, if left to itself, is not constrained nor guided internally by ethical concerns. The psychiatrists and physicians who took part in committing crimes against humanity in the process of research carried the Baconian dream of power to its extreme. They demonstrated the modernist *instrumentality* of knowledge, that is, the strict separation between the circumstances under which it is obtained and its uses.[37] This, then, is one of the legacies of eugenics/race-hygiene and their relation to euthanasia and the Holocaust.

The Transition from Eugenics to Modern Human Genetics: Continuities and Discontinuities

When at the end of the war the full extent of the horror committed in the name of race-biology and race-hygiene became publicly known, the political tide turned against "biologistic" thinking in general and against the concept of race as a legitimate term for policymaking in particular. At least the West witnessed a revulsion against authoritarianism and its glorification of the state above the individual, the essence of the different brands of fascism. Together with National Socialism, eugenics and race-biology now lost their legitimacy. In conjunction with the overwhelming moral indictment, the crucial factor was the restoration of the rights of the individual and not, as is often claimed by the scientific community, the prevalence of "good science" over "bad science" or the end of the "abuse" of science by corrupt political regimes.

The episode of the UNESCO Statement on Race and the scientists' attitudes toward sterilization and other eugenic measures after the war is compelling evidence of the sudden shift in political values. In 1949 UNESCO resolved to abolish racial discrimination with a statement on the state of research on race. In retrospect this enterprise illustrates the continuity of the scientific discourse and the inability particularly (but not exclusively) of the German race-hygienists to face their political involvement and to comprehend the value changes that had occurred in the political arena. A first version of the declaration formulated by social scientists, suggesting the replacement of the concept of "race" by that of "ethnic groups," met with resistance from geneticists and anthropologists. A second attempt to find a consensus initiated a heated debate among the geneticists now leading the effort and revealed the reluctance of some members to abandon the race concept. They clung to the fear of racial mixture and objected to the human rights formulation that all men were created equal. The document that was finally published contained the modern population geneticists' definition, according to which "races" can only be sensibly defined as populations that differ in the frequency of one or several genes. But this was not yet the consensus among the genetics and anthropology communities. Only the change in the political context had suddenly rendered the supposed dangers of racial mixture unimportant.[38] The reluctance of the anthropologists and geneticists to give up their morphological race concept had its parallel in the eugenicists' reluctance to relinquish their reliance on state surveillance and control of the reproductive process and the schemes of eugenic social technology. The profession was slow to adapt to the transition from a state interventionist and gene-pool-oriented eugenics, which relied on an authoritarian political order, to a disease-focused human genetics, based on individual choice more in line with modern democracies. The adaptation took place over a decade and a half.[39]

The human geneticists continued to express fear about the quality of the gene pool, which, in essence, was the translation of the old eugenic creed into modern scientific categories. The persistence of this creed and the resulting ambivalence in this time of transition were expressed, for example, by Lee Dice, the director of the first Heredity Clinic in the United States. Dice saw the difference between the old eugenics and the new practice in the "voluntary cooperation of the citizen," and he expressed the geneticists' slowly growing trust in the rationality of individuals' choices. But the quality of the gene pool remained high on his mind. Human geneticists, in his view, were interested not only in the "decrease of harmful genes, but also in the increase of desirable ones."[40] Likewise, Muller's diagnosis of a rising load of mutations due to the effects of modern medicine and the increasing radiation in the environment also fueled the fear regarding the quality of the gene pool and revived older eugenic themes.[41] As late as 1960 such leading scientists in the human genetics community as J. B. S. Haldane, Frederick Osborne, Ernst Mayr, James F. Crow, and Francis Crick gave Muller supportive comments for his explicitly eugenic vision of "germinal choice" by "artificial insemination." One of the few critics of his "benevolent utopia" was the geneticist Leslie C. Dunn, who pointed to the "historicity" of the value judgments implied in any breeding concept. Indeed, there was one important difference from the old eugenic schemes: the dysgenic effects Muller diagnosed were devoid of all categories of class and race.[42]

The subsequent "medicalization" of human genetics made possible by the advances in genetics provided the focus, the lack of which had haunted the field for so long: research concentrated on severe disorders and diseases, where it could find its legitimacy under the protection of the medical profession.[43] But the same techniques that provided the potential for therapy also posed the dangers of preventive medicine with their specific ethical dilemmas, and opened the perspective for new eugenic visions. It is evident that this development, which took shape in the mid-1960s, still characterizes the situation in human genetics today.

The rapid expansion of diagnostic capabilities, which allowed the diagnosis of hitherto unknown, rare, and less serious disorders, has continued to test the troubled demarcation between "medicalized" human genetics and eugenics. Prenatal diagnosis by amniocentesis triggered among human geneticists the debate over the classic eugenic problem of modern medicine's neutralizing selective mechanisms and thus contributing to the gradual degeneration of the gene pool. Implementation of routinized screening programs, first applied to "inborn errors of metabolism," revealed the context-dependency and value-laden nature of this technique as well as the political naiveté of the scientists involved. Screening for sickle-cell anemia failed in the quagmire of race politics because the genetic defect appears primarily among blacks and other groups that are on average socioeconomically underprivileged and that had not been involved in the preparation of the program. All of this demonstrates how thin the line between preventive medicine and eugenic policies can be, given a particular constellation of minority politics, values, and identities.

Like any other new technology, and especially those in the realm of medicine, the DNA-recombination techniques and their prospect of genetic manipulation increase the number of options available to the individual but therefore also call for decisions. The entire set of the new reproductive techniques, such as prenatal diagnosis, genetic screening, in-vitro fertilization, and ultimately genetic engineering, entail options that have eugenic implications if interpreted in such a way. Human genetics has never been able to escape the suspicion that it is motivated by eugenic strategies, not least because the memories of its abuse are very much alive. The genetic and medical technologies do not determine the uses to which they are being put, be it medical therapy or eugenic strategy. Thus, at a time when there is no reason to accuse democratic governments of eugenic conspiracies, let alone of authoritative imposition of such policies, it is still impossible to rely on an in-built constraint that would bar science from transgressing the boundary into the territory of eugenics. Such a barrier, moral and political in nature, has to be erected from outside, that is, by the polity. This was the case when in 1983 orientation to the quality of the gene pool was delegitimated as a value reference.[44] At about the same time a poll of the German human-geneticists' community showed a clear trend toward a consensus to refrain from eugenic, in favor of individual-oriented, counseling concepts, reflecting the value change that had taken place over the last four decades.[45]

The Human Genome Project and the Specter of Eugenics

The most recent incidence of eugenic ambivalence in the area of human genetics is in relation to the Human Genome Project, which, initiated at the end of the 1980s, has triggered a continued public debate. The criticisms launched against the project invariably appeal to the past experiences with eugenics, translated into more modern forms of social discrimination.[46] A proposal of the EC-Commission came into rough waters when a committee of the European Parliament reminded the Commission of the past experience with eugenics and stated that "clear pointers to eugenic tendencies and goals inhered in the intention of protecting people from contracting and transmitting genetic diseases." The ensuing amendments that the committee's report demanded from the Commission produced a series of changes—prohibition of human germ-line research and genetic intervention with human embryos—which were designed to assure that eugenic practices be avoided.[47]

These debates demonstrated that the structure of the problem has not changed in principle, only in detail, and that ambiguities that were previously avoided reappear. It is evident to all actors in the "Human Genome" game that the project will result in an "enormous expansion of information" about the human genetic makeup, which, in turn, will provide cheaper and more efficient screening methods for all kinds of genetic dispositions, many of which will not be covered by current concepts of disease. It is easy to predict that this type of information will continue to fuel the dynamics of social definitions of disease and will open an entirely new arena of interpretation about "normality"—one that is highly dependent on the actors and interests involved.

It is ironic that the new knowledge will provide precisely the means that the old eugenics was lacking but would have needed to be realized. The ability to diagnose genetic diseases before their becoming expressed, or even to find just carriers of recessive defects, is crucial to any effective eugenic program. The diagnosis of disorders for which there is no therapy in sight calls for eugenic elimination of the genetic material in question. The claim of relevance goes into the realm of multigenetic defects and more common diseases that have a strong environmental component. The rationale here is more ambiguous: since it is improbable that environmental risk factors can be controlled, let alone eliminated, it appears desirable to know as much as possible about factors of genetic predisposition in order to identify endangered individuals and to avoid transfer of their dispositions to subsequent generations.[48] As research on the human genome continues, new options will appear, new types of decisions will have to be made, and new ethical dilemmas will be posed. Recently, the first successful cloning of a sheep has renewed discussions about the prospects of cloning humans, and the first signs of a softening of the ban on cloning humans, provided it be couched in medical strategies, are apparent.[49]

The fit of this knowledge with the old eugenic programs thus seems compelling. This structural affinity between the logic of research on human heredity that was the basis of the old eugenics and the Human Genome Project that is the basis of predictive medicine and human genetics makes it untenable to bracket the former as bad or pseudo-science. The difference between the two must be established on different criteria.

The Human Genome Project is in one important respect different from its predecessor. In spite of the enormously increased knowledge in human genetics and its almost certain expansion in the near future, for two reasons it is not likely to result in eugenic uses in the style of the 1920s and 1930s. First, the knowledge proper has become more complex and does not lend itself to the same primitive social categorizations for which it was used during the first half of the century. Scientific knowledge does not give legitimacy to the discrimination of races, ethnic groups, and social deviants. And second, even when overzealous scientists cross that borderline, another check is in place: the political context and the associated value system today prevent unwarranted "biologization" of social categories. Many experiences during the past decades show that the political sensitivity about eugenic uses of new genetic technologies is high. In Germany, where the historical experience with eugenics is most vivid, public awareness and press coverage reveal an unusual level of information, given the esoteric nature of the subject.[50] In other words, the fit that existed between eugenics and the racist political value system in the 1930s exists no longer. But given the scientific profession's insatiable quest for new knowledge, its application, and the lure of social control that it confers, a certain amount of whistle-blowing may be a good check on technocratic expansionism.

Two paradoxes emerge in the debate on the Human Genome Project, which throw light on the ambivalence of scientific progress and provide focus for its assessment in light of the historical legacy of eugenics/race-hygiene. First, critics frequently point out that the genetic individual-oriented predictive approach forecloses social and ecological problem solutions. This is, indeed, one implication. But another one may be less comfortable to admit. The critics' implicit appeal to far-reaching social and ecological solutions is an appeal to political authority that would be in the position to exert power very similar in magnitude to that assumed by the earlier eugenics movement: on the basis of a selectionist "social biology" it had envisaged the reform of a host of social institutions in order to achieve a healthy gene pool.[51] Second, the slow transition of the genetics community from an authoritarian eugenics to an individualist human genetics, with its abdication to the gene pool as a legitimate concern and its reliance on individual decisions, may have population effects because of common value orientations about health and physical fitness. Thus, the paradoxical outcome of the "democratization" of human genetics may well be that the consumer orientation toward reproductive technologies and genetic therapies could lead to the realization of eugenic ideals. Only this time they would reflect the societal value system, an outcome of individual choices on a population scale.

NOTES

Several short passages of this text have been taken from P. Weingart, "The Thin Line between Eugenics and Preventive Medicine," in *Identity and Intolerance: Nationalism, Racism, and Xenophobia in Germany and the United States*, ed. N. Finzsch and D. Schirmer (New York: Cambridge University Press, 1998), 397–412.

   1. Daniel J. Kevles, *In the Name of Eugenics* (New York: Knopf, 1985). Peter Weingart, J. Kroll, and K. Bayertz, *Rasse, Blut und Gene, Geschichte der Rassenhygiene und Eugenik in Deutschland* (Frankfurt: Suhrkamp, 1988). Paul Weindling, *Health, Race and German Politics between National Unification and Nazism, 1870–1945* (Cambridge: Cambridge University Press, 1989).

   2. For an account of that historical compromise and its critique cf. E. Mendelsohn, "Science, Power and the Reconstruction of Knowledge," in *Knowledge and Higher Education*, ed. G. Bergendahl, Studies in Higher Education in Sweden no. 2 (Stockholm: Almquist and Wiksell, 1982), 49–71.

   3. Yaron Ezrahi, *The Descent of Icarus: Science and the Transformation of Contemporary Society* (Cambridge, Mass.: Harvard University Press, 1990).

   4. Mario Biagioli, "Science, Modernity, and the 'Final Solution,'" in *Probing the Limits of Representation. Nazism and the "Final Solution,"* ed. Saul Friedländer (Cambridge, Mass.: Harvard University Press, 1992), 185–205, 371–377.

   5. This refers to the literature reviewed by Biagioli to make his point: Michael K. Kater, "The Burden of the Past: Problems of a Modern Historiography of Physicians and Medicine in Nazi Germany," *German Studies Review* 10 (1987): 31–56; M. K. Kater, *Doctors under Hitler* (Chapel Hill: University of North Carolina Press, 1989); Bruno Müller-Hill, *Murderous Science* (Oxford: Oxford University Press, 1988); Robert J. Lifton, *The Nazi Doctors* (New York: Basic Books, 1986). As a recent example one may add M. Berenbaum, *The World Must Know, The History of the Holocaust As Told in the United States*

Holocaust Memorial Museum (Boston: Little Brown, 1993), who states that "the teaching of medicine, biology, history, anthropology, and sociology was *perverted* to support the *pseudo-science* of racial theory" (31, my italics).

6. Alfred Ploetz, *Die Tüchtigkeit unserer Rasse und der Schutz der Schwachen* (Berlin: S. Fischer, 1895).

7. The popularization of the discourse was effectively achieved by various nationalist associations as well as by Ludwig Woltmann's *Politisch-Anthropologische Revue*. This part of the discourse shaped its distinctly nationalist racist expressions. Incidentally, Aryomania was not a product of German biology, nor was it limited to Germany, but pervaded most of the European nations as well as the United States to a greater or lesser extent. The best detailed account of the early history and subsequent "shift" of physical anthropology is given by Benoit Massin, "From Virchow To Fischer. Physical Anthropology and 'Modern Race Theories' in Wilhelmine Germany," in *"Volksgeist" as Method and Ethic, Essays on Boasian Ethnography and the German Anthropological Tradition,* ed. George W. Stocking Jr., vol. 8 of *History of Anthropology* (Madison: University of Wisconsin Press, 1996), 79–153.

8. Wilhelm Schallmayer, *Vererbung und Auslese. Grundriss der Gesellschaftsbiologie und der Lehre vom Rassedienst,* 3rd. ed. (Jena: Gustav Fischer, 1918), IX.

9. Several popularizing tracts of race biology and its teaching compared Greek and Roman *statues* with individuals from, among other groups, Bushman tribes. Cf. Weingart, Kroll, and Bayertz, 95.

10. Peter Weingart, "Biology as Social Theory: The Bifurcation of Social Biology and Sociology circa 1900," in *Modernist Impulses in the Human Sciences 1870–1930,* ed. Dorothy Ross (Baltimore: Johns Hopkins University Press, 1994), 255–271.

11. Cf. Massin, "From Virchow To Fischer," 124.

12. Schallmayer, 375.

13. Weingart, Kroll, and Bayertz, 239.

14. Raymond Pearl, "Eugenics," in *ZIAV,* suppl. 1 (proceedings of the 5th International Congress of Hereditary Science, Berlin, 1928), 261–282. The article was later published in the U.S.A.

15. Herman J. Muller, "Human Heredity," in Herman J. Muller, *Studies in Genetics: The Selected Papers of H. J. Muller* (Bloomington: Indiana University Press, 1962), 541–543, 541.

16. On the reception of eugenics among the political and scientific left, see Diane Paul, "Eugenics and the Left," *Journal for the History of Ideas* 45 (1984): 567–590; Loren Graham, "Science and Values: The Eugenics Movement in Germany and Russia in the 1920s," *American Historical Review* (1977): 1133–1164.

17. Some of the names I owe to Benoit Massin in a private communication. On the involvement of Jewish scholars in physical anthropology and later in race-hygiene as well as their concern with Jews as a "race," cf. John M. Efron, *Defenders of the Race* (New Haven: Yale University Press, 1994), esp. ch. 2, pp. 19, 29.

18. Stefan Kühl, *Die Internationale der Rassisten. Aufstieg und Niedergang der internationalen Bewegung für Eugenik und Rassenhygiene im 20. Jahrhundert* (Frankfurt: Campus, 1997).

19. Alfons Labisch, Tennstedt, Florian, *Der Weg zum "Gesetz über die Vereinheitlichung des Gesundheitswesens" vom 3. Juli 1934. Entwicklungslinien und momente des staatlichen und kommunalen Gesundheitswesens in Deutschland,* Schriftenreihe der Akademie für Öffentliches Gesundheitswesen in Düsseldorf, Bd. 13, 1.2. (Düsseldorf, 1986).

20. Weingart, Kroll, and Bayertz, 498.

21. On the inherent link between "protection of blood" and "protection of heredity," cf. Gisela Bock, *Zwangssterilisation im Nationalsozialismus* (Opladen: Westdeutscher Verlag, 1986), 101; Weingart, Kroll, and Bayertz, 502.

22. Fritz Lenz, *Menschliche Auslese und Rassenhygiene (Eugenik)*, 3rd ed. (Munich: J. F. Lehmann Verlag, 1931), 451.

23. Fritz Lenz, "Die Stellung des Nationalsozialismus zur Rassenhygiene," *Archiv für Rassen- und Gesellschaftsbiologie* 25 (1931): 300–308, 308.

24. Ernst Rüdin, "Aufgaben und Ziele der Deutschen Gesellschaft für Rassenhygiene," *Archiv für Rassen-und Gesellschaftsbiologie* 28 (1934): 228–231, 228.

25. Protocol of the meeting of the *Kuratorium*, 5 July 1933, KWG Generalversammlung, KWI Anthropologie, MPG Archiv, Sign. 2404, 11. Max Planck, then president of the KWG, submitted to the political pressure and informed Minister Frick July 1933 that the KWG was willing to "put itself systematically in the service of the Reich as regards race hygiene research." Ibid. Cf. for a detailed account of the adaptation of the institute Peter Weingart, "Eugenics between Science and Politics," *OSIRIS* 5, 2nd series (1989): 260–282.

26. For an account of the party's controversial treatment of a "misfit" race researcher, L. F. Clauss, cf. Peter Weingart, *Doppel-Leben* (Frankfurt: Campus, 1995). Another pertinent though less dramatic case is that of the Catholic priest and eugenicist Eugen Muckermann. Cf. Weingart, Kroll, and Bayertz, 385. My thesis of political *selection* among scientific factions and the opportunism of scientists is corroborated by the stories of "German physics," "German chemistry," and to an extent the establishment of psychology. Cf. A.D. Beyerchen, *Scientists under Hitler* (New Haven: Yale University Press, 1977); Ulrich Geuter, *Die Professionalisierung der deutschen Psychologie im Nationalsozialismus* (Frankfurt: Suhrkamp, 1984).

27. On details cf. Weingart, Kroll, and Bayertz, 390; on the popularity of writings on race cf. also Weingart, *Doppel-Leben*.

28. Cf. Müller-Hill, *Murderous Science*; B. Müller-Hill, "Genetics after Auschwitz," *Holocaust and Genocide Studies* 2, no. 1 (1987): 3–20. Both are not professional historical accounts but typical for the argumentative pattern. Other works concentrate not directly on the Holocaust but on euthanasia: cf. Ernst Klee, *"Euthanasie" im SS-Staat. Die "Vernichtung unwerten Lebens"* (Frankfurt: Fischer 1983).

29. The most authentic reports remain: Alexander Mitscherlich and Fred Mielke, *The Death Doctors* (London: Elek, 1962); Mikos Nyiszli, *A Doctor's Eyewitness Account* (New York: Fell, 1960). Nyiszli, a prisoner, served as an assistant to Mengele. Mengele worked for Verschuer at the Berlin Institute of Anthropology.

30. One indication is the conflation of pragmatic political and scientific reasoning, also controversial *between* different ministries, over the issue of "Mischlinge," i.e., whether to "exclude" the ca. 300,000 individuals considered in "racial" terms to be of mixed Jewish and German descent from the "reproductive community" or to "absorb them into the German *Volkskörper.*" This issue already arose with the operationalization of the "Law on the Protection of Blood" (*Blutschutzgesetz*) and brought race-hygienists and bureaucrats into debate. Cf. Weingart, Kroll, and Bayertz, 505. It has to be mentioned that the race-biological considerations did, indeed, form the frame of reference for these debates but that the problem was the implementation of a respective law, not the fate of millions of Jews from all over Europe two years into the war.

31. Karl Binding, Alfred Hoche, *Die Freigabe der Vernichtung lebensunwerten Lebens* (Leipzig: Meiner, 1920).

32. Some argued selectionist: Karl H. Bauer, *Rassenhygiene: Ihre biologischen Grundlagen* (Leipzig: Quelle and Meyer, 1926), 207; others put forth ethical considerations: Lothar Loeffler, "Ist die gesetzliche Freigabe der eugenischen Indikation zur Schwangerschaftsunterbrechung rassenhygienisch notwendig?" *Deutsches Ärzteblatt* 63 (1933): 368–369, 369; on the whole debate cf. Weingart, Kroll, and Bayertz, 523.

33. Wilhelm Stuckart and Rolf Schiedermair, *Rassen- und Erbpflege in der Gesetzgebung des Dritten Reiches* (Leipzig: Kohlhammer, 1939), 10. The authors were jurists com-

menting on race legislation and contradicting their own claim that the issue was "difference in kind" (*Andersartigkeit*), not "difference in value" (*Anderswertigkeit*).

34. Thus J. Weinstein and N. Stehr, "The Power of Knowledge: Race Science, Race Policy, and the Holocaust" (ms., 1997). Noting the difference between the eugenic discourse and euthanasia but pointing to the conceptual links is B. Massin, "L'Euthanasie psychiatrique sous le IIIe Reich. La question de l'eugénisme," *L'Information Psychiatrique*, no. 8 (1996): 811–822.

35. Otmar von Verschuer, Nachlaß, Universität Münster, cited in B. Müller-Hill, *Tödliche Wissenschaft* (Reinbek: Rowohlt, 1984), 112.

36. The psychiatrist Zerbin-Rüdin, cited by Müller-Hill, *Tödliche Wissenschaft*, 131.

37. That message should be evident from the discussion that erupted in the early '80s in the United States and Canada on whether to use and cite the data of the hypothermia studies carried out by the infamous SS doctor Rascher. Cf. R. M. Martin, "Using Nazi Scientific Data," *Dialogue* 25, no. 3 (1986): 403–411. L. Martin, in defending use of the data, argues that the irreproducibility of the experiments cuts both ways, not just raising doubts as to their accuracy but on the other hand making "consideration of their results even more important, since they might provide all the information (of a certain sort) we can get" (ibid., 411). The debate arose because of "accessibility" of data being at issue. For detailed treatment of the problematic cf. Peter Weingart, "Science Abused?—Challenging a Legend," *Science in Context* 2 (1993): 555–568.

38. The episode is described from the viewpoint of the American geneticists by William B. Provine, "Genetics and the Biology of Race Crossing," *Science* 182 (1973): 790–796. For the reactions of some German race-hygienists cf. Weingart, Kroll, and Bayertz, 602.

39. On the steps taken by American geneticists cf. Herman J. Muller, "Progress and Prospects in Human Genetics," *American Journal for Human Genetics* 1 (1949): 1–18; Herman J. Muller, "Our Load of Mutations," *American Journal for Human Genetics* 2 (1950): 111–176. The development is described in more detail in Weingart, Kroll, and Bayertz, ch. 7.

40. Lee R. Dice, "Heredity Clinics: Their Value for Public Service and for Research," *American Journal for Human Genetics* 4 (1952): 1–13, 6.

41. Muller, "Our Load of Mutations," 111–176.

42. Herman J. Muller, "Germinal Choice: A New Dimension in Genetic Therapy," *Proceedings of the 2nd International Congress of Human Genetics* (Rome, Sept. 6–12, 1961), 1968–1973; Leslie C. Dunn, "Cross Currents in the History of Human Genetics," *American Journal for Human Genetics* 14 (1962): 1–13.

43. Victor A. McKusick, "The Growth and Development of Human Genetics as a Clinical Discipline," *American Journal for Human Genetics* 27 (1975): 261–273.

44. President's Commission for the Study of Ethical Problems in Medicine and Biomedical and Behavioral Research, "Screening and Counseling for Genetic Conditions" (Washington, D.C., 1983).

45. Maria Reif and Helmut Baitsch, *Genetische Beratung* (Berlin: Springer, 1986), 14.

46. Neil A. Holtzman and Mark A. Rothstein, "Invited Editorial: Eugenics and Genetic Discrimination," *American Journal for Human Genetics* 50 (1992): 457–459.

47. The so-called Härlin report cited in Daniel Kevles, "Out of Eugenics: The Historical Politics of the Human Genome," in *The Code of Codes: Scientific Issues in the Human Genome Project*, ed. D. J. Kevles and Leroy Hood (Cambridge, Mass.: Harvard University Press, 1992), 32.

48. Kommission der Europäischen Gemeinschaften, *Vorschlag für eine Entscheidung des Rates über ein spezifisches Forschungsprogramm im Gesundheitsbereich: Prädiktive Medizin: Analyse des Menschlichen Genoms (1989–1991)* (Brussels, 1988), 3.

49. Cf. Susan Wright, "After Dolly, a Slippery Ban on Human Cloning," *Christian Science Monitor,* June 23, 1997, p. 19.

50. Büro für Technikfolgenabschätzung beim Deutschen Bundestag, *TA-Projekt "Genomanalyse." Chancen und Risiken genetischer Diagnostik—Endbericht* (Bonn, 1993), 183.

51. Cf. Weingart, "Biology as Social Theory," 255–271.

16	*Eugenics after the Holocaust* *The Limits of Reproductive Rights*

Roberta M. Berry

I WILL BEGIN BY recounting briefly a few of the important points about the history and future of eugenics that Professors Kevles and Weingart develop in their essays. I will then comment on those points and offer my own opinion as to the future of eugenics in America. I will argue that we have reason to be concerned about potential eugenic applications of the new genetics in the twenty-first century, that reflection upon the early-twentieth-century eugenics movement and upon the Holocaust can inform us about these potential dangers, and that the regime of reproductive rights that has evolved in the late twentieth century is an insecure safeguard against these potential dangers, and in fact may contribute to them.

Professors Kevles and Weingart provide insightful historical analyses of the early-twentieth-century eugenics movement. Professor Kevles offers a revealing account of the movement in Britain and North America.[1] It was far from monolithic. Progressives and conservatives could and did find reason to support the eugenic goal of reducing the numbers of the "unfit," despite differing ultimate goals. Reducing the numbers of the "unfit" would propel society toward a perfectionist vision, on the progressive account, and would reduce the drag of those who could not carry their own weight, on the conservative.[2]

But there was another, deeper affinity among the participants in this far-flung movement, an affinity that explains this convergence upon the instrumental eugenic goal of reducing the numbers of the "unfit." Most eugenic reformers shared a set of convictions that was rooted in the biological and evolutionary science of the day. They believed that the fundamental characteristics of human beings—not just their eye color and their height, but their intelligence, their character, their tendency toward criminal conduct or alcoholism or promiscuity—were biologically based and heritable. They also believed that evolution was at work in human society as elsewhere in nature, that evolution entailed selection in favor of the "fittest," and that social measures should support and advance this evolutionary process. Hence their shared conviction that a program of eugenics could and should reduce the "unfit" among us.[3]

Professor Weingart carries us inside the community of eugenic science in Germany and several other nations before the Holocaust.[4] He carefully traces the anthropological and medical strands that merged in the eugenics movement. He describes the impact of the successive absorption of Darwinism, Weismann's theory of the germ plasm, and Mendel's work, and how the "theory of heredity" brought together the anthropological and medical strands in common cause. Concerns about racial degeneration as well as concerns about heritable disease seemed to require the same treatment: the assertion of control over human reproduction.[5] We learn from Professor Weingart's account that the social and political movement committed to the biological perspective on human life, and to the eugenic implications of this perspective, cut across the political spectrum in Germany as it did in North America. And the devastating economic crisis of the early 1930s helped expand the appeal of the eugenicists' agenda in Germany.[6]

Professor Weingart asks that we not delude ourselves about the role of science in German eugenics. He points out how badly mistaken and misleading is the myth that the relationship between science and the Holocaust is simply a story of exceptionalism, a story about the temporary hijacking of science to serve evil ends or about an alliance between an evil regime and the quack science of its own invention. As Professor Weingart points out, science and morality are not a unity. We should not assume that good science is inherently morally good—an assumption that underlies the exceptionalist account. He illustrates this point with a careful historical account of the relationship between eugenic science and the Holocaust. As Professor Weingart points out, favor granted by a political regime can aid the scientific endeavor, and some practitioners of science will welcome this aid, regardless of the methods and goals of the regime that is its source.[7]

In addition to the moral abuses that may arise in the conduct of science or in the uses to which scientific results are put, there is a more insidious danger that comes clear in Professor Weingart's account as well. The relationship between the agenda of eugenic science and the Holocaust was complex, but probably the most important influence of eugenic science was, as Professor Weingart recounts, its delegitimation of established social values, its "biologization of the social," its reductionism, its abstraction from the individual to the gene pool. Science can displace our moral vocabulary, substituting concepts and language that disable our capacity to discover and defend moral truth.[8]

Professors Kevles and Weingart also analyze the demise of the early-twentieth-century eugenics movement. Professor Kevles concludes that the North American eugenics movement eventually was undermined by two developments. First, the scientific underpinnings of the movement were wrenched out of alignment with its political agenda. If we were no longer confident that our standardized tests accurately identified those with mental handicaps and if the heritability of mental handicap was now called into question, there was no progressive perfectionism to be achieved and no utilitarian cost savings to be realized by a program of forced sterilization. Second, the horror of the Nazi death camps came to be known. If this could be the culmination of a program of eugenics, then abandonment of the program was the only possible response.[9] Professor Weingart also recounts the postwar response to the horror, in Germany and in other nations. The political tide turned against "biologist" thinking and state authoritarianism, the two pillars of state-sponsored eugenics. The postwar political culture rejected racism and the notion of racial hygiene, and embraced the concept of individual rights.[10]

Assessing the future of eugenics, Professor Kevles argues that the new genetics falls outside the shadow of the Holocaust. Increased scientific sophistication precludes a return to the simplistic eugenic notions of the past, and social and political changes—including a regime of constitutionally assured reproductive rights as well as the empowerment of the disabled and other constituencies—have generated some insulation against the virulent form of state-sponsored eugenics of the past. Professor Kevles concludes that a resurgent eugenics movement is unlikely, but urges us to anticipate a variety of other potential harms from the new genetics. He also notes the possibility that future parents may press for the opportunity to apply genetic technologies to determine the genetic features of their children.[11] Professor Weingart offers observations along similar lines and draws similar conclusions. He urges us to reflect upon a final paradox: the potential accomplishment of the eugenic goals of an earlier generation by means of consumer choice exercised by parents of future generations.[12]

* * *

First, I would like to note that, as Professors Kevles and Weingart point out, participants in the eugenics movement—otherwise quite diverse in their intellectual and social commitments—were quite homogeneous in one respect: they looked upon their fellow beings from a biological perspective, that is, they understood human beings as fundamentally biological and they understood human society as fundamentally concerned with the evolutionary selection of the biologically superior. Professors Kevles and Weingart provide a vivid account of the social programs that emerged in the first half-century following the synthesis of Darwinism and reductionist biology that yielded this biological perspective on human life. The picture that emerges from their account, obviously, is profoundly disturbing.

The advent of this biological perspective in the early twentieth century is a remarkable development in the history of human thought.[13] The pervasiveness of this perspective in the present day is equally remarkable.[14] Consider the fact that just a century or so ago this perspective would have been utterly unintelligible to anyone, while today all of us understand this perspective, even if we don't share it. None of us is surprised by claims about human nature and social policy that invoke the findings of biological and evolutionary science, even if we are unsure about how we should evaluate these claims and even if we appreciate that many of these claims are hugely controversial. Perhaps our children will be shy, or will get breast cancer, or will have perfect pitch because of the genes they inherit from us. Perhaps criminal conduct and mental disease have genetic bases we can and should identify and correct. Perhaps social welfare policy must take into account our evolutionarily developed social mores. The list goes on.

The sudden advent, pervasiveness, and persistence of the biological perspective are reasons for concern about the future. As the new genetics continues to expand our understanding of the biological aspects of human life, the biological perspective may settle in even deeper. Given the awful failures to harmonize this biological perspective with the most fundamental moral tenets of human conduct in the not-so-distant past, we should be wary of its destructive potential for the future.

My second comment concerns Professor Weingart's observation about the myth of good science as being inherently morally good science. I think this myth persists; its persistence is evidenced, in part, by the enormous authority that science and scientists enjoy in our culture, an authority that far exceeds that of politicians or philosophers or theologians. Perhaps this myth persists because modern scientists have been so enormously successful in expanding our understanding of the natural world; we want to attribute to them virtues beyond the scientific in the same way we want to attribute to our star athletes and artists virtues beyond the athletic and the artistic.[15]

Beyond this, perhaps our deep desire to know what is right and to know how we should conduct ourselves and organize our society makes us want to place our faith in those who seem to enjoy privileged access to truth and who appear, at times, to be able to offer us certain guidance. In our eagerness to know, we may tend to conflate the scientific and the moral enterprises, to assume that the results of scientific inquiry about the natural world will yield answers to our moral questions in a direct and unproblematic way. We may then want to assume that the successful pursuit of scientific truth will itself ordinarily be morally unproblematic, else we are caught in a frustrating circularity in which we can find no secure beginning point to anchor our search for moral answers. So we assume that scientists who contribute to moral catastrophes either must have participated under coercive duress or must have been engaged in quack science, not good science.

In any event, in our continuing effort to contemplate fully the meaning of the Holocaust, we must resist the myth, as Professor Weingart urges. We must not delude ourselves into thinking that our vigilance should be directed only at evil regimes seeking to hijack science, or that the demarcation between good science and quack science is the significant moral battle line. Good science everywhere and always can be conducted in morally good or evil ways to serve morally good or evil ends.

Furthermore, our vigilance must extend beyond review of scientific conduct and the ends to which science is put; the very doing of science often requires the adoption of a language and a set of concepts that unavoidably are controversial and fraught with potential moral significance.[16] For example, the meaning of the word "gene" has constantly evolved and continues to do so, reflecting the evolving theoretical commitments of those scientists who use the concept in their work.[17] Beyond this, scientists disagree about what we will know when we know what genes are, in the sense of knowing the sequence of bases that constitutes the genetic code; some think we will know what human life essentially is, and others disagree profoundly.[18] In addition, scientists routinely use words such as "aberrations," "variations," and "abnormalities" in referring to certain sequences in genetic material; the appropriate referents of these words may become increasingly controversial, especially in an era when human beings enjoy ever-increasing capacity to direct and control human reproduction at the genetic level.[19]

We have seen in the past, as Professor Weingart recounts, how scientific discourse can be used as a corrosive acid—an acid that dissolves the moral language and concepts that are our most important resources for discovering and acting upon moral truth. We must be aware that the concepts and language employed in scientific discourse inevitably reflect certain theoretical commitments and value-laden assumptions about the world. Given the enormous authority that science and scientists enjoy, and our past experience of how readily the scientific vocabulary lends itself to abuse in the service of political agendas, we must exercise vigilance to protect our very capacity to engage in moral discourse.

My third and final comment concerns the implications of the new genetic science and technology for the next century. In the early twentieth century, the biological perspective on human life and the scientific discourse associated with it encouraged the "scientific" judgment of human worth, which in turn supported political judgments of who should reproduce and who should not—and, finally, who should live and who should not. The biological perspective on human life is, if anything, more pervasive now than ever before, in part due to the influence of the new genetics. Although policymakers as well as the scientific community have invited ethical examination of the implications of genetic research,[20] the vastly expanded knowledge and power that the new genetic knowledge and technique will yield will place very heavy demands upon our capacity for vigilance. In light of these facts, do we have reason to be concerned about eugenics in the twenty-first century?

Perhaps Professors Kevles and Weingart are right to conclude, for the reasons they cite, that we face no imminent threat of a return to the government-sponsored eugenics of the past. In addition, I should say that I think we have much to gain from the new genetics and that I very much favor the pursuit of genetic knowledge and the employment of this knowledge to cure disease and to relieve suffering. But I also think that we do have reason to be concerned about future eugenic applications of the new genetics and that our experience in the first half of the twentieth century is instructive with respect to what we should be concerned about in the next century.

It is true that today's genetic science is far more sophisticated than the genetic science of several decades ago, and today's science could not be invoked in support of the crude eugenic policies of that era. But it is also true that today's science is always in the process of becoming yesterday's science, and some portion of yesterday's science is always in the process of being qualified, if not discredited altogether. In the bright light of hindsight, the scientific theory left behind suddenly appears obviously mistaken, and the influence of personal prejudices and misunderstandings in the formulation of the abandoned theory—and in the formulation of the political agenda founded on the theory—appears painfully obvious.

But, unfortunately, we must always view the present by today's dim light. And for every political agenda item undercut by today's new scientific theory, a new agenda item, equally troublesome, may take root in the fresh and congenial soil of the new scientific theory. Thus, scientific advance introduces a complex dynamic into the social and political realm, a dynamic of constantly delegitimating the old and legitimating the new.

This dynamic further challenges our capacity to be vigilant; the scientific endeavor, the claims that it yields, and the social and political uses of science are constantly changing in complex ways, and in ways that may pose new dangers. While we have left behind the social and political agenda that rested on the crude genetic science of the past, we have not left behind the biological perspective on human life, the myth of morally good science, the drive for scientific discovery that encourages self-deception or moral compromise among scientists, and the assorted prejudices and misunderstandings that often find opportunity for expression in some sort of political agenda. And there are other factors at work as well—factors that may complicate and heighten the danger posed by the new genetic science.

Consider, for example, the current trend in thinking about human cloning and about genetic "enhancement" of our children—"enhancement" being the attempt to improve our children's looks, intelligence, skills, or dispositions by altering their genetic endowments before birth.[21] Although there does not appear to be, as yet, a consensus as to whether cloning or genetic enhancement should be permitted, there does appear to be a gathering consensus as to what sorts of claims should or will count in deciding these questions.[22] These claims center upon the safety and efficacy of the practices, the predictable benefits and harms in consequence of the practices, and the reproductive rights of individuals.[23] If these claims are the only ones that count, these practices might very well join the roster of reproductive technologies that currently are available,[24] thanks to an alliance of those who would favor this result for one or more reasons.

Those who hold the biological perspective on human life may believe that cloning and genetic enhancement are morally acceptable or even desirable because selection of biologically preferable characteristics in our offspring likely will yield highly desirable consequences, both for the parents and children involved and for society as a whole.[25] Others may not subscribe to this view, but may conclude that the calculus of predictable benefits and harms—to potential parents, future children, and society—of these practices, if appropriately regulated, would yield a net plus.[26] Others may believe that freedom of choice with respect to whether and how to reproduce is a fundamentally important principle of social relations. On this view, we should respect the freedom of others to clone themselves or to enhance their offspring, whether or not we personally believe these practices to be morally acceptable or reprehensible, provided that these practices are subject to regulations that protect the interests of future children and society.[27] Thus, if the safety and efficacy hurdles are cleared, an alliance of those who hold any one or more of these views might successfully resist efforts to prohibit or restrict[28] these practices, and parents of the future would be free to produce genetic replicas of themselves if they liked, or to bestow upon their children the best genetic endowments that modern genetic science could provide.

This result, however, would challenge certain strongly and widely held moral beliefs about the nature of parenting and the parent-child relationship. These beliefs derive from reflection upon our personal and cultural experiences of parenting and our religious and secular traditions. Many of us look upon children as gifts to be received as they are and nurtured by their parents according to the age-old dialectic of parental effort met by resistance, followed by renewed effort refined, met by resistance and accommodation.

On this view, medical science should be used to relieve suffering in children that is caused by disease or disability, not to replicate ourselves genetically or to breed for the best in our children as we now breed for the best in our ornamental plants and show dogs. On this view, there should be limits to the control parents may exercise with respect to their children, and genetically designing children to fit their parents' conceptions of what kind of people they should be would fall outside those limits. We should not presume to know the particulars of the genetic constitutions that would be best for our children or us or the world, just as we should not presume to know the details of the life paths they should follow. We should not attempt to exercise control before birth that extends to designing their genetic constitutions, just as we should not attempt to exercise control after birth that extends to depriving them of access to other parents or to an adequate education. On this view, the cloning and genetic enhancement of human beings would constitute the latest failure to harmonize the synthesis of Darwinism and reductionist biology with our most fundamental shared moral convictions, convictions that we have good reason to believe are correct.

Of course, reasonable people can and do hold differing views, and I hope we will have a spirited public debate on the points of dispute among these views and about the reasons for believing one view or another to be right. But I fear that we may not have such a debate. This is not due to lack of public interest or concern, but rather to our increasing incapacity or unwillingness to engage our moral vocabulary—to make forceful presentations of claims that derive from reflection upon our experience and our traditions—in our public-policy debates. A number of factors contribute to this trend.

For one, both safety-and-efficacy claims and benefits-and-harms claims about cloning and genetic enhancement purport to refer to features of the natural world—to biological entities, genes, and their expression in the human organism—and to quantifiable or probabilistically measurable consequences of our conduct. Claims of this sort are seen as grounded in real features of the world and amenable to assessment and verification. In contrast, the moral vocabulary does not purport to refer to features of the natural world or to events and processes that lend themselves well to scientific measurement and expression. Instead, the moral vocabulary may refer to how and why parents conceive of their children as gifts, how parents treat their children in light of this conception, what significance the resulting relationship holds for parents and children, and how religious and secular traditions embrace the significance of these relationships. Claims constructed from the moral vocabulary often are seen as subjective, sectarian, and not amenable to assessment or verification.[29] While claims constructed from this vocabulary might appropriately serve as local norms for a like-minded community, they are viewed as inappropriate candidates for transcription into legal norms for the polity.[30]

What explains this peculiar discounting of the referents of our moral vocabulary and, hence, of the claims constructed from this vocabulary? Why is it assumed that human experiences and traditions are less real and knowable than genes, or that the results of our reflection upon them are less trustworthy than the results of our study of the expression of genes in the human organism and of the predicted consequences of human practices? Why is it claimed that public debate and policy making proceeds to truer, more reasonable, or better results if claims constructed from the moral vocabulary are either not counted or not heard in the public-policy debate?

One explanation for the excessive faith placed in claims framed in the scientific vocabulary may be the continuing myth of good science as morally good science. Even with all that we have learned about the complexity of the relationship between the scientific and the moral, we continue to cling to the myth, to hope that from the methods and claims of successful science we can derive good moral answers in an unproblematic way. While science surely can inform our moral understanding, it does not in itself answer our moral questions, and reflection upon other experiences and traditions surely informs our moral understanding as well—often in fundamentally important ways. Facing the reality of the Nazi death camps, for example, can carry us directly to the door of moral truth in a way that scientific inquiry in itself cannot.[31]

Another explanation may be the far readier transcription of the scientific vocabulary into the political and legal vocabulary that dominates the large modern bureaucratic state and its political branches, a vocabulary that is largely consequentialist and pragmatic and, hence, readily incorporates reference to the "real" and quantifiable.[32] Claims framed in the moral vocabulary simply cannot be processed in the same fashion as safety-and-efficacy claims and benefits-and-harms claims; hence they are deemed inappropriate inputs.

And the discounting of claims framed in the moral vocabulary may also be one consequence of the heavy demands that certain public-policy issues impose upon our capacity to communicate, persuade, and reach resolutions across divides of strongly held religious and secular beliefs. In these cases, we may want to resort to the "neutral" language of scientific discourse or to the "neutral" language of "rights" and "choice."[33]

This final resort, to claims framed in terms of rights, may yield paradoxical results in the realm of eugenics. While it is true that a strong social, political, and legal commitment to reproductive rights provides good assurance against the return of governmentally sponsored eugenics, the assurance is less than perfect, and the very commitment to rights can contribute to, as well as protect against, the dangers we face from the new genetics.

With respect to governmentally sponsored programs of eugenics, in the 1927 case, *Buck v. Bell,*[34] Supreme Court Justice Oliver Wendell Holmes and all but one of his fellow justices approved the involuntary sterilization of Miss Carrie Buck, a young woman who had been committed to an institution for the "feebleminded." In his opinion for the Court, Justice Holmes famously justified his finding that the Virginia statute at issue—which authorized the involuntary sterilization of persons determined to be unfit and likely to give birth to unfit offspring—was constitutional by invoking the sacrifices that could be demanded of American citizens under exigent circumstances:

> We have seen more than once that the public welfare may call upon the best citizens for their lives. It would be strange if it could not call upon those who already sap the strength of the State for these lesser sacrifices, often not felt to be such by those concerned, in order to prevent our being swamped with incompetence. It is better for all the world, if instead of waiting to execute degenerate offspring for crime, or to let them starve for their imbecility, society can prevent those who are manifestly unfit from continuing their kind. The principle that sustains compulsory vaccination is broad enough to cover cutting the Fallopian tubes. . . . Three generations of imbeciles are enough.[35]

Buck v. Bell was issued during the heyday of the American eugenics movement and at a time when we did not have a well-established commitment to reproductive rights. Yet, a regime of rights is always subject to restrictive interpretation. In *Korematsu v. United States,*[36] a case decided in 1944, the United States Supreme Court sanctioned the placement of tens of thousands of Japanese Americans in military camps without any individualized suspicion or finding of disloyalty. These citizens were deprived of their most basic liberties—to live in their homes and to come and go freely—purely on the basis of their Japanese ancestry. At the outset of its opinion in *Korematsu,* the Court declared "immediately suspect" any laws that curtailed the civil rights of a racially defined group, and claimed that such laws must be subject to "the most rigid scrutiny."[37] But the protection afforded by this constitutional standard proved paper thin. In language strikingly similar to that in *Buck v. Bell,* Justice Hugo Black invoked the exigencies of war:

> All citizens alike, both in and out of uniform, feel the impact of war in greater or lesser measure. Citizenship has its responsibilities as well as its privileges, and in time of war the burden is always heavier. Compulsory exclusion of large groups of citizens from their homes, except under circumstances of direct emergency and peril, is inconsistent with our basic governmental institutions. But when under conditions of modern warfare our shores are threatened by hostile forces, the power to protect must be commensurate with the threatened danger.[38]

Constitutional rights are only as secure as the moral sensibilities of those who interpret them. Under circumstances perceived as exigent—whether due to war or economic crisis or concerns about public health—constitutional rights will always be vulnerable to restrictive interpretation. This will be true particularly if our capacity for moral discourse erodes to the extent that we cannot muster telling arguments in opposition to abuse, or cannot persuade others to listen to them if we can muster the arguments. If, for example, criminal conduct were to surge, and genetic enhancement had been declared safe and effective in reducing the incidence of genetic endowments associated with antisocial behavior, perhaps the threat posed to our national well-being would be considered sufficient to justify public-health measures aimed at eliminating "antisocial genotypes" from the next generation.

This scenario, though, is quite unlikely. Any threat of coercive eugenic intervention in any American society we can envision in the future surely would galvanize a powerful alliance in opposition. The alliance would include those who object to the moral implications of eugenics generally, those reproductive-age individuals who are targeted by the intervention, and those who object to coercive governmental intervention in people's private lives whatever the occasion of it.

Far more likely, however, is the advent of a new consumer-driven eugenics. In this scenario, reproductive rights no longer would serve as a shield deflecting governmental efforts to impose a program of eugenics. Rather, those holding commercial interests in the practices of cloning and genetic enhancement would wield these rights as a sword to strike down efforts to prohibit or substantially restrict these practices. Their efforts would be supported by those who hold the biological perspective on human life, those who believe that the predictable benefits of these practices would outweigh their harms, and those who simply believe that we must respect the private choices of parent-consumers to employ safe and effective reproductive technologies. Such a scenario is not at all far-fetched, especially in an era in which we are no longer willing, or perhaps able, to bring into the public arena arguments framed in the moral vocabulary. It is in this way that we might well suffer the consequences of our inability to translate into public policy our most basic shared moral convictions about the dangers of the new genetics.

NOTES

I wish to thank Professors Kevin McDonnell, John H. Robinson, and Phillip R. Sloan for their helpful comments on this essay.

1. Daniel J. Kevles, "The Ghost of Galton: Eugenics Past, Present, and Future," in this volume.

2. Ibid.

3. Ibid.

4. Peter Weingart, "Eugenics and Race-Hygiene in the German Context: A Legacy of Science Turned Bad?" in this volume.

5. Ibid.

6. Ibid.

7. Ibid.

8. Ibid.

9. Kevles, "Ghost of Galton."

10. Weingart.

11. Kevles, "Ghost of Galton."

12. Weingart.

13. See generally Peter J. Bowler, *Evolution: The History of an Idea* (Berkeley: University of California Press, 1989), 282–332.

14. Edward O. Wilson, a leading proponent of the project to uncover the biological bases of moral conduct and codes, writes:

> The empiricist argument holds that if we explore the biological roots of moral behavior, and explain their material origins and biases, we should be able to fashion a wise and enduring ethical consensus. The current expansion of scientific inquiry into the deeper processes of human thought makes this venture feasible.

Edward O. Wilson, "The Biological Basis of Morality," *Atlantic,* April 1998, p. 54. See also Edward O. Wilson, *Consilience: The Unity of Knowledge* (New York: Knopf, 1998); Bowler, 328–332.

15. This attribution of special virtues to scientists has historical roots traceable to the beginning of the modern era. Historian of science Thomas Hankins describes the eulogies prepared for deceased members of the French Academy of Sciences by Bernard le Bovier de Fontenelle, long-time secretary of the Academy during the early Enlightenment period:

In addition to the virtues of the pastoral convention [simplicity, humility, austerity, want of ambition, and love of nature], Fontenelle endowed them with those virtues that Plutarch ascribed to the great men of the Roman world, the Stoic virtues of fortitude, duty, courage, and resolution.

Thomas L. Hankins, *Science and the Enlightenment* (New York: Cambridge University Press, 1985), 7.

16. In questioning the model of neutrality in genetic counseling, Karen Grandstrand Gervais surveys arguments regarding the inevitable theory-ladenness of scientific observation and the inevitable value-ladenness of theory choice. She then considers the evaluative content of the very language employed in scientific discourse:

The philosopher W. V. Quine has argued that there are no clear lines along which to distinguish the meaning of language from the beliefs members of a given community hold about it [citing W. V. Quine, *Word and Object* (1960)]. Words cannot predictably play a simply descriptive function because of the collateral information associated with them in the minds of both speaker and hearer. To the extent that collateral information is evaluative, the use of language is evaluative. Since the meaning of language is inextricably linked to the beliefs of language users, actual communication between persons relies on a sharing or identification of surrounding beliefs, some of which are inevitably evaluative in character.

Karen Grandstrand Gervais, "Objectivity, Value Neutrality, and Nondirectiveness in Genetic Counseling," in *Prescribing Our Future: Ethical Challenges in Genetic Counseling*, ed. D. Bartels, B. LeRoy, and A. Caplan (New York: Aldine de Gruyter, 1993), 119 and 127.

17. See Petter Portin, "The Concept of the Gene: Short History and Present Status," *Quarterly Review of Biology* 68 (1993): 173; and Philip Kitcher, "Genes," *British Journal for the Philosophy of Science* 33 (1982): 337.

18. Journalist Sandra Blakeslee reports some of the differing views of scientists interviewed about what we will know when we know the genetic code:

"Knowing the sequence of individual genes doesn't tell you anything about the complexities of what life is," said Dr. Brian Goodwin, a theoretical biologist at Schumacher College in Devon, England, and a member of the Santa Fe Institute in New Mexico.

"A gene makes a protein and that's about it," Dr. Goodwin said in a recent interview. "It doesn't tell you how proteins interact, how cells and tissues communicate, how organs come into being, how an immune system forms, or how evolution works." . . .

The alternative to reductionist and genocentric thinking is called wholism, said Dr. Scott Gilbert, a developmental biologist at Swarthmore College in Pennsylvania. Wholists believe that the whole is greater than the sum of its parts; even if you know all the properties of each part, you will still not understand the whole because something is missing, he said. That something includes special properties that emerge from the interacting parts that, in turn, affect the whole.

Proponents of reductionism are unabashed by such criticism. Modern biology has produced stunning successes using its reductionist approach, said Dr. Lewis Wolpert, a professor of anatomy at University College London in England. The notion that so-called emergent properties are required for understanding living organisms is "a bunch of yak, all talk and nothing more," he said. . . .

"All the talk about the need for different levels of organization offers us absolutely nothing," Dr. Wolpert said in an interview.

"People say there are 100,000 genes in each cell and how are we going to integrate all that information? Well, it's going to be jolly hard, but I don't think we need a new science to do it. Reductionism continues to be amazingly productive. We don't have all the details but the principles are absolutely clear."

Sandra Blakeslee, "Some Biologists Ask 'Are Genes Everything?'" *New York Times,* September 2, 1997, p. B7.

19. See for example Friedrich Vogel and Arno G. Motulsky, *Human Genetics: Problems and Approaches,* 3d ed. (New York: Springer, 1997), 658, discussing the evidence for a genetic influence in homosexuality, and Jonathan Tolins, *Twilight of the Golds: A Play in Two Acts* (New York: S. French, 1994), a play premised on the possibility of prenatal testing for a "gay" gene.

20. The United States Congress has allocated substantial funds for the study of the ethical, legal, and social implications of the Human Genome Project, a federally funded research program to map and sequence the human genome. See Daniel J. Kevles, "Out of Eugenics: The Historical Politics of the Human Genome," in *The Code Of Codes: Scientific and Social Issues in the Human Genome Project,* ed. Daniel J. Kevles and Leroy Hood (Cambridge, Mass.: Harvard University Press, 1992), 3 and 16; Walter Gilbert, "A Vision of the Grail," in *Code of Codes,* 83–84; Institute of Medicine, Division of Health Sciences Policy, Committee on Assessing Genetic Risks, *Assessing Genetic Risks: Implications for Health and Social Policy* (Washington, D.C.: National Academy Press, 1994), 3:

> The establishment of the Ethical, Legal, and Social Implications (ELSI) Program in the Human Genome Project (HGP) and the set-aside of the first 3 to 5 percent of the HGP research budget for the study of ethical, legal, and social issues is unique in the history of science. This support gives us the opportunity to "worry in advance" about the implications and impacts of the mapping and sequencing of the human genome, including several thousand human disease genes, before wide-scale genetic diagnosis, testing, and screening come into practice, rather than after the problems have presented themselves in full relief.

See also Roberta M. Berry, "From Involuntary Sterilization to Genetic Enhancement: The Unsettled Legacy of Buck v. Bell," *Notre Dame Journal of Law, Ethics and Public Policy* 12 (1998): 401, regarding the ethical issues associated with genetic enhancement; Roberta M. Berry, "The Genetic Revolution and the Physician's Duty of Confidentiality: The Role of the Old Hippocratic Virtues in the Regulation of the New Genetic Intimacy," *Journal of Legal Medicine* 18 (1997): 401, regarding the implications of genetic information for physician-patient confidentiality; Roberta M. Berry, "The Human Genome Project and the End of Insurance," *University of Florida Journal of Law and Public Policy* 7 (1996): 205, regarding the implications of genetic information for health, disability, and life insurance.

21. In December 1997, journalist and author Gina Kolata reported the trend in thinking about the prospect of human cloning and of genetic enhancement in connection with it:

> Just nine months have passed since an astonished world got its first glimpse of Dolly the lamb, the first animal cloned from a cell taken from an adult. It was a feat that science had declared impossible.
> In the hubbub that ensued, scientist after scientist and ethicist after ethicist declared that Dolly should not conjure up fears of a Brave New World. There would be no interest in using the technology to clone people, they said.

They are already being proved wrong. There has been an enormous change in attitudes in just a few months; scientists have become sanguine about the notion of cloning and, in particular, cloning a human being.

Some infertility centers that said last spring they would never clone now say they are considering it. A handful of fertility centers are conducting experiments with human eggs that lay the groundwork for cloning. Moreover, the Federal Government is supporting new research on the cloning of monkeys, encouraging scientists to perfect techniques that could easily be transferred to humans. Ultimately, scientists expect cloning to be combined with genetic enhancement, adding genes to give desired traits, which was the fundamental reason cloning was studied in animal research.

Gina Kolata, "On Cloning Humans, 'Never' Turns Swiftly into 'Why Not,'" *New York Times,* December 2, 1997, p. 1.

22. Harvard law professor Laurence Tribe explains why he no longer believes that sufficiently good reasons have been advanced for prohibiting human cloning:

Some years ago . . . I was among those who urged that human cloning be assessed not simply in terms of concrete costs and benefits, but in terms of what the technology might do to the very meaning of human reproduction, child rearing and individuality. I leaned toward prohibition as the safest course.

Today, with the prospect of a renewed push for sweeping prohibition rather than mere regulation, I am inclined to say, "Not so fast. . . ."

I certainly don't subscribe to the view that whatever technology permits us to do we ought to do. Nor do I subscribe to the view that the Constitution necessarily guarantees every individual the right to reproduce through whatever means become technically possible.

Rather, my concern is that the very decision to use the law to condemn, and then outlaw, patterns of human reproduction—especially by invoking vague notions of what is "natural"—is at least as dangerous as the technologies such a decision might be used to control. . . .

[A] society that bans acts of human creation for no better reason than that their particular form defies nature and tradition is a society that risks cutting itself off from vital experimentation, thus losing a significant part of its capacity to grow. If human cloning is to be banned, then, the reasons had better be far more compelling than any thus far advanced.

Laurence H. Tribe, "Second Thoughts on Cloning," *New York Times,* December 5, 1977, p. A31.

23. In February 1997, in response to the news of the successful cloning of Dolly, President Clinton requested that the National Bioethics Advisory Commission prepare a report and recommendations regarding human cloning. In June 1997, the commission recommended temporary moratoria on efforts to clone humans and on federal funding for these efforts. Although the commission considered a wide range of religious, ethical, and legal issues surrounding human cloning, it cited only safety issues in justifying its recommendations. See National Bioethics Advisory Commission, *Cloning Human Beings: Report and Recommendations of the National Bioethics Advisory Commission* (Rockville, Md.: N.B.A.C., 1997). See also Brian A. Brown, "Cloning: Where's the Outrage?" *Wall Street Journal,* February 19, 1998, p. A22, lamenting the fact that the standard objections to human cloning center on safety and efficacy issues and nightmarish scenarios of cloned armies and organ donors—objections that will disappear when the safety and efficacy issues are resolved and

the nightmarish uses are outlawed; John A. Robertson, "Liberty, Identity, and Human Cloning," *Texas Law Review* 76 (1998): 1371, considering policy reasons—and potential constitutional reasons—for permitting human cloning under certain circumstances if the practice is safe and effective; John A. Robertson, "Genetic Selection of Offspring Characteristics," *Boston University Law Review* 76 (1996): 421, examining policy and constitutional reasons for permitting parental selection of offspring characteristics under certain circumstances.

24. As Gina Kolata notes:

> Although a Presidential ethics commission [the National Bioethics Advisory Commission] has recommended a limited ban on cloning humans, only California has enacted a law making it illegal, and those who are intrigued by the idea argue that it is no worse, morally, than creating custom embryos from sperm and egg donors. After all, it is an American tradition to allow people the freedom to reproduce in any way they like.

Gina Kolata, "'Why Not,'" p. 1. See also Gina B. Kolata, *Clone: The Road to Dolly, and the Path Ahead* (New York: Morrow, 1998); Lee M. Silver, *Remaking Eden: Cloning and Beyond in a Brave New World* (New York: Avon, 1997).

25. Philosopher Jonathan Glover, in his 1984 book anticipating potential cloning and genetic enhancement technologies, writes:

> The idea of "human nature" is a vague one, whose boundaries are not easy to draw. And, given our history, the idea that we must preserve all the characteristics that are natural to us is not obvious without argument. Some deep changes in human nature may only be possible if we do accept positive genetic engineering. It is true that our nature is not determined entirely by our genes, but they do set limits to the sorts of people we can be. And the evolutionary competition to survive has set limits to the sorts of genes we have. Perhaps changes in society will transform our nature. But there is the pessimistic thought that perhaps they will not. Or, if they do, the resulting better people may lose to unreconstructed people in the evolutionary struggle. On either of these pessimistic views, to renounce positive genetic engineering would be to renounce any hope of fundamental improvement in what we are like. And we cannot yet be sure that these pessimistic views are both false.

Jonathan Glover, *What Sorts of People Should There Be?* (New York: Penguin, 1984), 53–54.

26. See for example Nicholas Agar, "Designing Babies: Morally Permissible Ways to Modify the Human Genome," *Bioethics* 9 (1995): 1, arguing that genetic enhancement that expands rather than limits the range of opportunities available to a child should be permitted; John Harris, "Is Gene Therapy a Form of Eugenics?" *Bioethics* 7 (1993): 178, arguing generally that genetic therapy that improves health or capacities should be permitted; David Resnick, "Debunking the Slippery Slope Argument against Human Germ-line Gene Therapy," *Journal of Medicine and Philosophy* 19 (1994): 23, arguing that genetic enhancement should be permitted if psychological harms to future generations and social injustices arising from its uneven availability can be prevented or reduced.

27. Law Professor John Robertson writes concerning this view:

> One need not accept human cloning as a morally acceptable way of family formation. But personal moral opposition alone is not an adequate basis for laws that prohibit others from using a technique that enables them to achieve legitimate

goals of having and rearing biologically related children. Given the general presumption in favor of reproductive freedom, a ban on safe and effective human cloning in all circumstances is not justified.

Robertson, "Liberty, Identity, and Human Cloning," 1441.

28. Restrictions on genetic enhancement might limit its use to circumstances in which the motivation for enhancement would be to prevent suffering caused by genetically influenced disease or disability.

29. Philosopher Bernard Williams claims there is a fundamental distinction between the scientific and the ethical:

> The basic idea behind the distinction between the scientific and the ethical, expressed in terms of convergence, is very simple. In a scientific inquiry there should ideally be convergence on an answer, where the best explanation of the convergence involves the idea that the answer represents how things are; in the area of the ethical, at least at a high level of generality, there is no such coherent hope. The distinction does not turn on any difference in whether convergence will actually occur, and it is important that this is not what the argument is about. It might well turn out that there will be convergence in ethical outlook, at least among human beings. The point of the contrast is that, even if this happens, it will not be correct to think it has come about because convergence has been guided by how things actually are, whereas convergence in the sciences might be explained in that way if it does happen. This means, among other things, that we understand differently in the two cases the existence of convergence or, alternatively, its failure to come about.

Bernard Williams, *Ethics and the Limits of Philosophy* (Cambridge, Mass.: Harvard University Press, 1985), 136–137.

30. Law Professor John Robertson writes:

> When carefully analyzed, the alleged harms of cloning tend to be highly speculative, moralistic, or subjective judgments about the meaning of family and how reproduction should occur. Such choices are ordinarily reserved to individuals, free of governmental coercion or definition of what provides reproductive meaning.

Robertson, "Liberty, Identity, and Human Cloning," 1441.

Law Professor Robert Rodes writes of the modern liberal conception of the subjectivity of values:

> The basic liberal approach, as I see it, is to extract from the medieval and classical philosophical synthesis its broadly attractive principles of personal autonomy, dignity, and worth, while leaving behind its more controversial and therefore more divisive principles regarding the ultimate destiny and purpose of human beings. Those who seek a philosophical basis for this split generally find it in an epistemology that refuses to attribute objective truth to anything that is not either empirically verifiable or logically inferable from self-evident principles.
>
> This doctrine naturally cuts the ground from under any objective standards of value we may wish to adopt. It makes judgments of good and evil, judgments of right and wrong, into personal preferences comparable to liking or not liking parsnips.

Robert E. Rodes Jr., *Pilgrim Law* (Notre Dame, Ind.: University of Notre Dame Press, 1998), 66–67.

31. See for example Alexander Mitscherlich and Fred Mielke, *Doctors of Infamy: the Story of the Nazi Medical Crimes* (Ann Arbor, Mich.: University Microfilms, 1975), detailing the horrors perpetrated by physicians during the Nazi regime.

32. T. M. Scanlon writes of the pervasive consequentialism in modern moral philosophy:

[Utilitarianism] occupies a central place in the moral philosophy of our time. It is not the view which most people hold; certainly there are very few who would claim to be active utilitarians. But for a much wider range of people it is the view towards which they find themselves pressed when they try to give a theoretical account of their moral beliefs. Within moral philosophy it represents a position one must struggle against if one wishes to avoid it.

T. M. Scanlon, "Contractualism and Utilitarianism," in *Utilitarianism and Beyond,* ed. Amartya Sen and Bernard Williams (New York: Cambridge University Press, 1982), 103. See also Frank Hahn, "On Some Difficulties of the Utilitarian Economist," in *Utilitarianism and Beyond,* 187, describing the pervasiveness of utilitarianism in public policy making; Rodes, 61–62, 132–134, discussing the marginalization of transcendent values in the managerial society.

33. See generally Mary Ann Glendon, *Rights Talk* (New York: Free Press, 1993), discussing reliance upon rights to the exclusion of other values. See also Rodes, 67–68, discussing the irreconcilability of our conceptions of freedom and equality in the absence of values to govern the inevitable conflicts and contradictions that will arise among them.

34. 274 U.S. 200 (1927).

35. Ibid., 207.

36. 323 U.S. 214, 65 S. Ct. 193, 89 L. Ed. 194 (1944).

37. Ibid., 216.

38. Ibid., 220–221.

17 Heredity and Genetics after the Holocaust

Jonathan Marks

I WRITE THIS essay not as an historian of science, but as a biological anthropologist, and one keenly aware of my intellectual lineage. My intellectual ancestors were measuring skulls and determining racial allocations on that basis,[1] and even if they were critical of Nazi anthropology, it is nevertheless difficult in retrospect to distinguish Nazi physical anthropology from American physical anthropology of the same era. The history of science is vital for understanding where we are as scientists, how we got here, and what mistakes we've made, so we don't make them again.

The themes that jump out at me from Professors Weingart's and Kevles's essays involve the general questions "What good is history?" and "What are the responsibilities of scientists?" As both essays point out, we live in an age that has transcended the eugenics era in some ways—no one is talking about sterilizing the poor on account of their genes any more. But of course, there are still contemporary social discourses concerning heredity and class, as 1995's best-seller *The Bell Curve* showed.[2] What is interesting about *The Bell Curve* is that it included no genetics, but did contain an appeal to heredity as an explanation for the lot of the poor. And significantly, when invited to invoke their authority to critique the work, the American genetics community was exceedingly reluctant.

In other words, there is still politics of heredity and still social consequences in politicizing heredity.

Heredity and Genetics

The first of three general points I will raise, then, is that we need to recognize the existence of parallel discourses about heredity. The one that both papers focus on is the scientific genetics of blots, bands, and gels—the hard science of genetics.

But as *The Bell Curve* shows, there is another form of hereditary discourse out there, one that has no recourse to the blots, bands, and gels of modern genetics, but speaks in idioms from another era. For example, a recent issue of the *Atlantic Monthly* featured a cover article by a distinguished Pulitzer Prize–winning entomologist, Edward O. Wilson of Harvard.[3] It was provocatively called "The Biology of Morality." Professor Wilson, writing from the standpoint of sociobiology, writes glibly about the genetic basis of xenophobia—hatred of aliens, or foreigners, or those different from you. You'll find similar things in recent books called *Demonic Males,* by a distinguished primatologist named Richard Wrangham,[4] and *The Third Chimpanzee* by another Pulitzer Prize winner, Jared Diamond.[5]

Now, the genetic basis for "xenophobia" is like the genetic basis for "feeble-mindedness" of the 1920s in being wholly imaginary, but unlike it in being ostensibly a pan-human universal, not a factor that ostensibly some people have and others lack.

So it is not about blots, bands, and gels, but rather, it represents the vocabulary of modern genetics grafted onto archaic, essentialized speculations about human nature.

But talking about genes for xenophobia like genes for cystic fibrosis or hemoglobin raises some unsettling questions of relevance to this conference. In Diamond's *The Third Chimpanzee,* you will find an interesting discussion of genocide—as merely a manifestation of those bad genes we all possess for xenophobia.

Now of course, one needs to tread a delicate line here. One does not want to celebrate or glorify martyrdom and victimization, for that serves to parochialize the experience and limit its meaning. But at the same time one does not want to trivialize it, which is precisely what I think the genetic explanation does.

The argument presented in sociobiology—and it is very likely being taught as biology and as science in your university—is how easy it is to hate and want to kill others unlike you. But I think that's a trivial observation, because it presupposes a natural difference between the two groups, the oppressors and the victims.

Of course, alienness is a construction, not a fact of nature. The greatest hatreds are between the peoples who are biologically the most similar: Hutu and Tutsi, Bosnian and Serbian, Israeli and Palestinian, Huron and Iroquois, German and Jew, English and Irish.

The lesson of the Holocaust, I think, resides not so much in the attempt on the part of one group to destroy another, which is indeed a recurrent tragic theme of human global history; but rather in the recognition that it was carried out by Europeans against themselves and that it took place in an age in which some form of enlightenment was thought to have existed.

What we learn from presupposing genes for it is unclear—except in entailing the absolution of responsibility. "It wasn't our fault, it was just human nature"—which is certainly a perverse use of genetics.

The reason I raise this point is to ask the question: Where is the genetics community here? Where is their critique of *The Bell Curve,* and of sociobiology and of its offshoot, so-called evolutionary psychology, which appropriate their vocabulary and proceed to use it in ways unfamiliar to geneticists themselves? Where are their withering critiques of the behavioral genetics laboratory that claims to have discovered the genes for homosexuality, novelty-seeking, and worry?[6] The answers to this question are complex, but are suggested in Professor Weingart's essay in relation to the 1930s, when he notes the motives of opportunism and profit for the geneticists to collaborate with the Nazi political machine.

That brings up a second point: Where do a geneticist's economic interests lie? The answer may sound cynical, but it's a crucial connection between the 1920s and the 1990s: *It is in a geneticist's interests to have you believe that everything significant in life is genetic.* The revolutionary difference between the social Darwinists and the eugenicists (aside from the fact that the social Darwinists wanted *less* government and the eugenicists wanted *more*) is that the eugenicists claimed to frame their ideas around the science of heredity.

The Responsibilities of Geneticists

We need the geneticists to distinguish the sound inferences about heredity from simple quackery. For if they don't, who can? But it is unclear that they can or that they will. Why? There are two reasons. In the first place, geneticists share the same cultural values and ideologies as other members of their society, class, and era. One's own cultural prejudices are almost always invisible. And in the second place, why would anyone expect them to kill a goose that lays golden eggs?

One of the juiciest epigrams in the world of genetics, widely quoted, was a line of James Watson's (co-discoverer of the structure of DNA) in *Time* magazine in 1989. Said Watson, "We used to think our fate was in the stars. Now we know, in large measure, our fate is in our genes."[7]

Now there are at least three ways to read that statement. First, it might be a scientific statement, subject to empirical test. We may have fates, they may be localized to our cellular nuclei, and genetics may indeed be like astrology, only presumably more accurate.

Second, it obviously articulates a social philosophy, one that would be easily recognizable to Charles Murray, author of *The Bell Curve,* as an explanation of why poor people are poor: their fate was in their genes. And one to which he would naturally be sympathetic.

But third, and most importantly, the statement is a grant proposal. It was a public appeal in *Time* magazine to fund the study of genetics.

Now it is very important to give Watson credit for having introduced the allotment of a small percentage of the Human Genome Project's budget for the study of Ethical, Legal, and Social Implications (ELSI). But at the same time, we have to examine the rhetoric very carefully. The times change, the victims change, the technologies change, the issues change. What remains the same is the invocation of science, of progress—as an institutionalized authoritative tool for victimization.

What are the responsibilities incurred here by biologists and geneticists? They were very slow to criticize the genetic rhetoric of the 1920s; they are no faster now. The critics of eugenics in America were people like anthropologist Franz Boas and lawyer Clarence Darrow, defenders of civil liberties. Darrow, for example, published a wonderfully eloquent critique called "The Eugenics Cult" in 1926.[8] In so doing, he evolved from biology's chief defender in the 1925 Scopes trial to its chief basher a year later. There was as yet no biologist on public record critical of the movement, willing to challenge the major players. Raymond Pearl of Johns Hopkins would be the first, with an article in the same magazine (his friend H. L. Mencken's *American Mercury*), called "The Biology of Superiority."[9] To have a major geneticist break ranks was newsworthy, and indeed, the publication of Pearl's article was widely reported by the Associated Press on October 25, 1927.

This issue may require a bit of amplification. The eugenics movement in America had a broad base of appeal, but its principal validation came from geneticists. In the late 1920s, for example, virtually every leading geneticist in America could be found on the Advisory Council of the American Eugenics Society (which was incorporated in 1925). One exception was Thomas Hunt Morgan, whose office was located in the same building as that of Franz Boas, in Schermerhorn Hall at Columbia University. Boas had been criticizing the movement since 1916, and wrote a scathing review of Madison Grant's *The Passing of the Great Race* in *The Nation* that year. Morgan, on the other hand, declined to review the book, and limited his criticisms of eugenics to some softly sarcastic comments in articles and books published in the mid-1920s. The other exception was Herbert Spencer Jennings of Johns Hopkins, who had reanalyzed the eugenic data purporting to identify a gradient in criminality among U.S. immigrants, increasing from northwest Europe to southeast Europe, thus justifying the immigration restriction laws. Jennings found the analysis to be flawed and wrote to the president of the American Eugenics Society, Yale economist Irving Fisher. When no action was taken as a result of his findings, Jennings resigned in 1924. Even then, he was Fisher's choice to succeed him as president of the American Eugenics Society in 1926, an honor that Jennings declined.[10]

The interesting question is, who *remained* on the "Advisory Board" of the American Eugenics Society, permitting their names to be used below or alongside such infamous demagogues as Madison Grant (*The Passing of the Great Race*, 1916) and Lothrop Stoddard (*The Rising Tide of Color*, 1927)? The answer is: nearly all major biologists and geneticists—E. G. Conklin of Princeton, William Castle and Edward East of Harvard, Michael Guyer of Wisconsin, Herbert Walter of Brown, A. Franklin Shull of Michigan, C. C. Little of the Jackson Laboratory, Samuel J. Holmes of California-Berkeley, Horatio Hackett Newman and Sewall Wright of Chicago.

There are no genetics textbooks from the 1920s that fail to advocate eugenics. Perhaps the most illustrative case is that of *Principles of Genetics,* written by E. W. Sinnott and L. C. Dunn (who would later become an outspoken critic of racist biology). In their first edition, they included a fairly standard chapter on eugenics, recommending to college biology students the sterilization (or worse?) of the poor: "[E]ven under the most favorable surroundings there would still be a great many individuals who are always on the border line of self-supporting existence and whose contribution to society is so small that the elimination of their stock would be beneficial."[11] Their second edition was published in 1932, after the market crashed and *everyone's* stock was eliminated, and so was that entire chapter, and the word "eugenics" has but a single referent in the index. The word does not even appear in the index of the third edition of 1939, nor in the fourth edition of 1950, now with Theodosius Dobzhansky as co-author.

But neither do those later editions contain a critique or an admission. There's just a burial of history, which obviously entails a failure to confront it, and raises the possibility of re-living it.

The point is, can we really expect anything different today, without changing the cost/benefit ratio for the geneticists? If Watson's rhetorical excess is good for business, it won't be criticized by the genetics community, and that will be the same mistake they made in the 1920s. If one cannot serve both God and Mammon, can we really fault modern geneticists for choosing Mammon?

The Cutting Edge of Bioethics

The last point I want to make concerns the silver lining to come out of the institutionalized scientific racism of the 1920s and '30s, namely the origin of modern bioethics, in the Nuremberg Code.

The bad news is that it is not widely part of the education of geneticists, so its ideas are still precarious. The ways in which that is so again relate to the universalizing theme behind this volume. We need to remember that the people who occupied "our" space five hundred years ago were not "our" lineal ancestors. They were someone else's ancestors.

The Human Genome Project articulated its goal early on, over a decade ago, to sequence the human genome. What did that mean? Within the framework of a medicalized view of the human genetic structure, each gene comes in one widespread normal form and a few rare, deviant forms leading to disease. Most people have the normal cystic fibrosis gene; the few that don't, have cystic fibrosis. Most people have the normal Tay-Sachs disease gene; the few that don't, have Tay-Sachs disease. Extrapolating that over the tens of thousands of genes we have, we might imagine building up a library of the structure of the normal genes and thereby the normal human genome.

That was criticized very quickly for its implicit conception of normality, which took all variation as effectively pathological. If you take as your model not the cystic fibrosis gene, but the gene for blood type—where all human populations have type A, most have type B, and all have type O, and they all are normal—you realize there is a different pattern there than the one assumed in the formulation of the medical genetics of the Human Genome Project.

Thus in 1991, a group of population geneticists led by Stanford's Luca Cavalli-Sforza, whose liberal credentials were unimpeachable, began to push for an augmentation to the genome project, namely a human genome *diversity* project.[12] The problem was that they articulated a strange goal, namely, to open the veins of the indigenous peoples of the world and bring their blood back to Palo Alto to be studied by geneticists.

The fact is, such studies had been conducted on a small scale for decades, but this was being proposed with the Genome Project as a springboard— big science, big press, big money—and somewhat unexpectedly, big accountability.

And here is where the Nuremberg Code fails. The Code specifies that a scientist must receive "voluntary consent" from the subject. Obviously that assumes efficient communication, a shared idea system, between the parties. Those of us who actually teach human genetics to elite first-world college students know it is hard enough to get *them* to understand the ideas. Imagine trying to get the voluntary informed consent of a non-literate Khoisan forager in Botswana, who has entirely different ideas about heredity, about the body, about medicine, about reproduction, about the nature of the blood, than you do.

It is axiomatic in anthropology that blood is never "just" blood. Blood is invariably powerfully vested with magic and surrounded by taboos. Consequently, it's not too easy to talk other people out of their blood, so you need to be very persuasive.

The supporters of this project framed it publicly in terms of a need to study peoples on the verge of extinction.[13] But they quickly had their priorities questioned; if the people were on the verge of extinction, saving their DNA seemed to be a perverse priority. Moreover, the supporters represented the very colonial powers that had decimated these peoples. One could hardly fault the project's intended subjects for thinking, "You took our land, eliminated our lifeways, killed our people, and now you want our blood." So by the mid-'90s, the project had come to be known as the Vampire Project, evoking an image of scientists lusting after the veins of indigenes, with ice water in their own.[14] The population geneticists responded by emphasizing their benign "purely scientific" goals, but when it came to light in 1994 that other scientists had recently obtained a patent on a cell line derived from a New Guinea tribesman, it became clear that there were issues of economic exploitation at stake. In a free market of bio-prospecting, the blood of natives was the mother lode.[15]

The most interesting claim made on behalf of the Diversity Project is that it will permit us finally to know the ultimate micro-phylogeny of the human species—who is related to, and descended from, whom. As I heard one of their spokesmen say to an audience of bioethicists, "We're going to tell these people who they really are." I'm happy to report that the audience was more sensitive to the issues of identity construction and identity politics, and the assumption of authority, than the geneticists appeared to be.

History confers identity, and identity is political, and identity politics is an arena in which geneticists are uniquely unqualified to work. As one Native American responded, "You want our assistance to tell us that our ancestors are not really our ancestors. You must be crazy."

The next step, given the difficulties in establishing honestly the repository they dreamed of, was to piggyback the collection of the material. A population geneticist at Yale, active in the Diversity Project, bragged to me last year that he had a new source of Nigerian blood. What was it? A local physician was studying schizophrenics, and doing blood tests, and agreed to send the population geneticist a bit of each sample. Of course, the subjects had not consented to the use of their blood for this other study, but he got his samples. On the other hand, his victory was Pyrrhic: the Human Genome Diversity Project itself has been derailed by a report from the National Research Council, which found it poorly conceptualized and bioethically untenable as presented.[16]

* * *

There are indeed continuities between genetics of the 1930s and the 1990s. In a post-Shoah civilization that aspires to the implementation of universal human rights, the exceedingly technological training of modern geneticists leaves them largely unschooled in those very humanistic values that constitute the advancement over their own predecessors. It should be no surprise, then, to find genetic subjects objectified and exploited, and often interpreted in racialized narratives. And I will just note in this context the Diversity Project's claim in the scientific literature that the European gene pool is composed of 65 percent Asian genes and 35 percent African genes[17]—a claim so laden with archaic assumptions that to the eye of the modern anthropologist it might as well have been printed in cuneiform.[18] And even more important, metaphysical genetic arguments are still invoked in support of public policy issues, while geneticists themselves sit quietly, either in agreement, or just cynically calculating the benefits that widespread belief in the genetic basis of xenophobia, altruism, homosexuality, intelligence, crime, and personality will have for their next grant proposal.

When geneticists today aver that social issues are rooted in the hereditary constitutions of circumscribed groups, or fail to deny it, they have the same conflict of interest that their predecessors had. That is why I find the sound bites of geneticists generally unreliable—I have no way to know whether they are speaking from their knowledge or from their pocketbooks.

That poses a dilemma for the rest of us that non-geneticists of the 1920s and '30s also faced. The greatest success of the eugenics movement was its ability to identify itself with science, biology, genetics, evolution, modernity, progress. To call into question the racism, the curtailment of human rights, the worst elements of science that eugenics also represented with the same zeal and the same authority—to question it was to position yourself against genetics, science, evolution, progress. How do we tease apart the folk ideologies of heredity from science, and use it to help people rather than to stigmatize them?

Today the universe of geneticists who could identify Charles Davenport or Eugen Fischer is a small one. It is a dual tragedy that the history of genetics is more widely perceived as threatening than liberating—a tragedy both for geneticists and for society. For if a lesson of the Shoah is that the world must never forget, how tragic indeed would it be if the scientific ideologues, Darwin's willing executioners, were allowed to forget.

Notes

1. E. A. Hooton, "Methods of Racial Analysis," *Science* 63 (1926): 75–81.
2. R. Herrnstein and C. Murray, *The Bell Curve* (New York: Free Press, 1995).
3. E. O. Wilson, "The Biology of Morality," *Atlantic Monthly,* April 1998, pp. 53–70.
4. R. Wrangham and D. Peterson, *Demonic Males* (New York: Houghton Mifflin, 1997).
5. J. Diamond, *The Third Chimpanzee* (New York: HarperCollins, 1994).
6. D. Hamer and P. Copeland, *Living with Our Genes: Why They Matter More Than You Think* (New York: Doubleday, 1998).
7. L. Jaroff, "The Gene Hunt," *Time,* March 20, 1989, pp. 62–67.
8. C. Darrow, "The Eugenics Cult," *American Mercury,* no. 8 (1926): 129–137.
9. R. Pearl, "The Biology of Superiority," *American Mercury,* no. 12 (1927): 257–266.
10. H. S. Jennings Papers, American Philosophical Society.
11. E. W. Sinnott and L. C. Dunn, *Principles of Genetics* (New York: McGraw-Hill, 1925), 406.
12. L. L. Cavalli-Sforza, A. C. Wilson, C. R. Cantor, R. M. Cook-Deegan, M.-C. King, "Call for a Worldwide Survey of Human Genetic Diversity: A Vanishing Opportunity for the Human Genome Project," *Genomics* 11 (1991): 490–491.
13. L. Roberts, "A Genetic Survey of Vanishing Peoples," *Science* 52 (1991): 1614–1617; R. Lewin, "Genes from a Disappearing World," *New Scientist,* May 29, 1993, pp. 25–29.
14. J. C. Gutin, "End of the Rainbow," *Discover,* November 1994, pp. 70–75.
15. A. T. P. Mead, "Genealogy, Sacredness, and the Commodities Market," *Cultural Survival Quarterly* 20 (1996): 46–53.
16. C. MacIlwain, "Diversity Project 'Does Not Merit Federal Funding.'" *Nature* 389 (1997): 774.
17. A. M. Bowcock, J. R. Kidd, J. L. Mountain, J. M. Hebert, L. Carotenuto, K. K.

Kidd, and L. L. Cavalli-Sforza, "Drift, Admixture, and Selection in Human Evolution: A Study with DNA Polymorphisms," *Proceedings of the National Academy of Sciences, USA,* 88 (1991): 839–843.

18. J. Marks, "The Human Genome Diversity Project: Good for If Not Good As Anthropology?" *Anthropology Newsletter* 36 (1995): 72.

WORKS CITED

Bowcock, A. M., J. R. Kidd, J. L. Mountain, J. M. Hebert, L. Carotenuto, K. K. Kidd, and L. L. Cavalli-Sforza. 1991. "Drift, Admixture, and Selection in Human Evolution: A Study with DNA Polymorphisms." *Proceedings of the National Academy of Sciences, USA,* 88: 839–843.

Cavalli-Sforza, L. L., A. C. Wilson, C. R. Cantor, R. M. Cook-Deegan, M.-C. King. 1991. "Call for a Worldwide Survey of Human Genetic Diversity: A Vanishing Opportunity for the Human Genome Project." *Genomics* 11: 490–491.

Darrow, C. 1926. "The Eugenics Cult." *The American Mercury* 8: 129–137.

Diamond, J. 1994. *The Third Chimpanzee.* New York: HarperCollins.

Gutin, J. C. 1994. "End of the Rainbow." *Discover,* November, pp. 70–75.

Hamer, D., and P. Copeland. 1998. *Living with Our Genes: Why They Matter More Than You Think.* New York: Doubleday.

Herrnstein, R., and C. Murray. 1995. *The Bell Curve.* New York: Free Press.

Hooton, E. A. 1926. "Methods of Racial Analysis." *Science* 63: 75–81.

Lewin, R. 1993. "Genes from a Disappearing World." *New Scientist,* May 29, pp. 25–29.

MacIlwain, C. 1997. "Diversity Project 'Does not Merit Federal Funding.'" *Nature* 389: 774.

Marks, J. 1995. "The Human Genome Diversity Project: Good for If Not Good As Anthropology?" *Anthropology Newsletter* 36: 72.

Mead, A. T. P. 1996. "Genealogy, Sacredness, and the Commodities Market." *Cultural Survival Quarterly* 20: 46–53.

Pearl, R. 1927. "The Biology of Superiority." *American Mercury* 12: 257–266.

Roberts, L. 1991. "A Genetic Survey of Vanishing Peoples." *Science* 252: 1614–1617.

Sinnott, E. W., and L. C. Dunn. 1925. *Principles of Genetics.* New York: McGraw-Hill.

Wilson, E. O. 1998. "The Biology of Morality." *Atlantic Monthly,* April, pp. 53–70.

Wrangham, R., and D. Peterson. 1996. *Demonic Males.* New York: Houghton Mifflin.

18 The Significance of Nazi Eugenics for Medical Ethics Today

Didier Pollefeyt

How SHOULD HUMAN genetics today deal with the legacy of Nazi eugenics? What is the significance of Nazi medicine for contemporary medical ethics? From my point of view, this is the basic question with which both Peter Weingart's and Daniel J. Kevles's essays are profoundly wrestling. Implicitly, they both criticize a common understanding of National Socialism as a major anomaly of human history, as a barbarous regression into pre-modern history, as a unique, sudden, incomprehensible, or "typical German" manifestation of demonic evil. This last, very popular, representation of Nazism often gives pretext to two different, even opposite, uses of Nazi medicine in ethical reflection on contemporary human genetics.

On the one hand, the "abnormalization" of Nazism as a demonical aberration in Western culture can be used today by scientists to establish a complete intellectual and social discontinuity between Nazi and contemporary science. Weingart's observations are particularly insightful here, since he uncovers the self-defensive character of the bracketing so often used when referring to Nazi "science." By creating a clear difference between then and now, medical scientists hope to find consolation and to restore their scientific identity and ethical integrity. How strongly people in general hang on to this comforting position of discontinuity becomes obvious in reactions to such situations as the revelation that countries like Sweden had eugenic projects of sterilization, even into the 1970s.

On the other hand, ethicists sometimes use the medical practices of the Holocaust to discredit the entire contemporary enterprise of human genetics, or of some aspects of it, such as prenatal diagnosis, or even the application of the personalistic notion of "quality of life."[1] In deontological reasoning, especially in Catholic moral theology, we sometimes find very moralizing references to Nazism in order to argue for the "absolute evil" of some current medical technique. Abortion, for example, is often referred to as a "modern day holocaust" by those who would prohibit the practice. Killing millions of innocent Jews in the Shoah is represented as morally equivalent to killing millions of innocent fetuses in abortion clinics in the United States. "Genetics and medicine become Hitlerized" is an often heard, simple, but sometimes successful slogan, since public opinion more easily turns against such medical practices when they are associated with the "diabolical" evil of Nazism.[2] As Kevles remarks in his essay, "Eugenics has become a dirty word in North America."

In short, many of the references made to the actions of Nazi doctors and scientists are based on a demonic (re)presentation of the Holocaust. That this is misleading can be shown only if the actions of the Nazis are carefully historically situated and analyzed. The strength of both essays is that they search with a great sense for historical detail into Nazi medical science and its relation with pre- and post-Holocaust medicine. As an ethicist, I appreciate their tendency toward "normalization" of the different aspects of the historiography of the Holocaust, because an adequate "ethics after Auschwitz" can be based only on this kind of appropriate historical-critical analysis, and not on mythology or ideology.

The historical complexity and ambiguity that their research brings to light, however, does not make it any easier for an ethicist to draw relevant moral conclusions. On one side, Kevles and Weingart convincingly show that eugenics was not unique to the Nazis. It could and did happen elsewhere. What the Nazis did stood in continuity with the eugenic intentions and practices in other countries before the war. In Europe, the United States, and Canada, "ordinary men" (Browning) believed in shaping human beings and society by taking charge of their biological heredity. Eugenics is not typically German, but a universal human possibility. Indeed, it would be absurd to argue that eugenics is bad only *because the Nazis did it*. Furthermore, both scholars show the structural affinities between the logic of research on human heredity, which was the basis of old eugenics, and the Human Genome Project, which is the basis of contemporary predictive medicine and so-called negative eugenics. Weingart particularly indicates that *genealogically* there is a continuity of research that creates *structurally* similar moral dilemmas, such as discrimination between patients on genetic grounds or a growing receptivity to cost-saving schemes in the public health sector.

On the other side, next to the continuity, both authors reveal the historical discontinuity between Nazistic and pre- and especially post-Nazistic genetic science, referring to the different sociopolitical contexts. Kevles argues that reproductive freedom is more easily diminished in dictatorial governments than in democratic ones. "Eugenics profits from authoritarianism—indeed, almost requires it," he says. Weingart indicates that the pre-Nazi eugenic debate was one not about the death of individuals, but about the number and hereditary value of their offspring. The measure was not genocide; sterilization and marriage prohibitions were sufficient. Both authors underline the difference between the sociopolitical value systems at work then and now. It sometimes seems as if a sound (democratic) political context would be enough to ensure that human genetics is ethically acceptable. Accordingly, both authors end with rather comforting conclusions. Weingart says that "the fit that existed between eugenics and the racist political value system in the 1930s exists no longer." Also, quoting from Kevles's contribution: "It is important not to become absorbed with exaggerated fears that the advance of human genetics will necessarily foster a drive for the production of superbabies."

The complexity both authors uncover of both continuity and discontinuity between Nazi eugenics and pre- and post-genetic medicine, between the universality of genetics and the uniqueness of Nazi eugenics, is very important. Nevertheless, even if I agree that the *slippery slope* from eugenics to Nazi genocide has often been used all too easily, my concern as an ethicist is that both authors in the end use the complex fact of continuity and discontinuity too facilely, in a comforting way, in favor of contemporary genetic medicine. I would not agree so readily that today, because the political context has changed, we should not be apprehensive of the individual and social desire for superbabies and that this desire has nothing structurally associated with values similar to Nazi values. Weingart, who is most aware of the historical continuity of genetic research, writes: "[T]he slow transition of the genetics community from an authoritarian eugenics to an individualist human genetics . . . could [paradoxically] lead to the realization of eugenic ideals similar to those that the eugenicists of the early twentieth century had in mind. Only this time it would be in consonance with our value system." If, however, people today support individualist, non-authoritarian human genetics, and if their position would be in consonance with their own value system, I'm not so sure that it would not also be fundamentally in consonance with crucial elements of the Nazi value system.

Therefore, I think we are in need of a more intricate hermeneutic for understanding the complex relation between continuity and discontinuity and, from the ethical point of view, for developing an even greater sensitivity to the fundamental continuity between "Nazi values and our own,"[3] even if the sociopolitical context is very different. In his paper, Weingart argues that the Holocaust was not *legitimated* by science. The role of science was rather one of *preparing* the ground for the Holocaust. This reasoning reminds me of the way the recent Vatican document on the Shoah, *We Remember,* uses in an analogous way the "correct" historical fact of continuity *and* discontinuity between anti-Judaism and anti-Semitism as an apologetic instrument in favor of the Catholic Church in the question concerning its responsibility for the Shoah, arguing that Christian anti-Judaism only *prepared* the ground for Nazi anti-Semitism, but did not *legitimate* it (and even criticized it). Quoting the Vatican document: "The Shoah was the work of a thoroughly modern neo-pagan regime. Its anti-Semitism had its roots *outside* of Christianity."[4] In Kevles's essay, I read analogically: "The eugenic past has much to teach about how to avoid repeating its mistakes—not to mention . . . the sins of the Holocaust. But the vast majority of issues raised by the advance of human genetics fall outside those of the Holocaust." Just as the Church is finally assigning responsibility for the Holocaust to modern eugenic racism, so in both papers it would seem as if the responsibility for the Shoah *ultimately* resides outside of human genetics, resting in particular upon the immoral (authoritarian) political system in which (Nazi) eugenicists worked and lived. In short, discontinuity finally wins out.

I would argue, however, that just as anti-Judaism and anti-Semitism are more deeply and complexly related than the Vatican document *We Remember* admits, from an ethical-hermeneutical point of view, there is also more that connects Nazi eugenics with contemporary genetic medicine than it seems at first glance, even if the sociopolitical context is very different. This likewise brings us to the question why, on what grounds, Nazi eugenics was wrong and contemporary genetic applications can be considered acceptable, or at least debatable?

What strikes me most in the analysis of Kevles and Weingart is the continuous *ethical* justification of genetic medicine, before, during, and after the war. From its origin, eugenics was understood as a way of taking moral responsibility for the evolution of society and humanity. It was and still is considered a movement of individual perfection and social reform, of promotion of individual well-being and welfare of state and society. It is striking that in pre-Nazi times, American defenders of eugenics were morally concerned that the availability of birth control would permit the separation of passion from the responsibility for procreation. In prewar Germany, also a great number of Jewish researchers believed in the promises of eugenics. As Peter Haas has convincingly shown,[5] eugenics was a moral good for the Nazi doctors. In fact, they tried to create a scientific Utopia by eliminating the bad genes from the gene pool. In the medical profession many became perpetrators of genocide in good conscience because they saw themselves as selectively killing in order to preserve the life and health of the larger client population. The Nazis used the existing eugenic theories, and put them together in a new way. For Haas, the intellectual jump was to see the nation (the genetic pool) as a single social body that was sick and could be cured in the same way as a real body could be cured: through the application of selectively applied death. After the war, even as eugenics lost its credibility, genetic research grew spectacularly in its search for controlling heredity in the name of an individual or social good.

Is there continuity in this history? The Nazi (eugenic) scientists and the contemporary genetic scientist both have a commitment to medical research, with its fundamentally good objective of discovering ways to improve human health by learning more about human illness and defects.[6] They are both part of the human drama to make sense of difficult times and control destiny. And they both live in the context of modernity, seeing the application of modern, scientific principles as the most responsible way to proceed. As Zygmunt Bauman has asserted,[7] these eugenicists represented the *mentalité* of modernity: modern human beings as subjects who represent an objective world in their own image. This absolutism of the subject, which is the hallmark of modernity, is not bad in itself, but is the fundament from which a leader could emerge whose sovereign will determines what constitutes and who possesses a life worthy or unworthy of living. This modern subject constitutes the continuity from pre- to post-war genetics. There is, of course, no identity between one as modern subject and one as the creator of the Holocaust, but there is a dialectal relation, in which the former can be easily transformed into the latter, especially in the name of ethics.

The rejection of certain people as subhumans thus need not be restricted to Nazism. Rather, this danger is inherent in modernity itself, even in a democratic setting. A growing risk of the development of contemporary preventive medicine and prenatal diagnosis, for example, is that couples who deliberately choose the birth of a disabled child will be accused of immoral and asocial behavior and will be financially and socially discriminated against. This development can give living disabled persons the impression that their life is subhuman and only a burden upon society, even if they live in a so-called post-Nazistic, non-totalitarian world.

The dividing line between good and evil is thus thin, and does not run between Nazi values and our own values. The absolute fury of the modern subject toward the Other, toward alterity itself,[8] is a risk of every modern society, and Nazi society reveals the endpoint of a possibility that is and remains intrinsic to modernity itself.

In his *Heidegger and "the jews"* Lyotard writes "the jews" in quotation marks and lower case to distinguish them from the real Jews.[9] For Lyotard, "the jews" are the embodiment of alterity, the Other, murdered as such, who are sometimes real Jews, as in Nazi-occupied Europe, and sometimes not. It is not because we live in a non-authoritarian political context that the rights of the Other cannot be violated. Today, the "jew" might well be the prenatal diagnosed fetus who is not the superbaby its procreators dreamed about and who is destroyed out of "ethical" concerns.

In Weingart's essay, we read that "it is still impossible to rely on an in-built constraint that would bar science from transgressing the boundary into the territory of eugenics. Such a barrier . . . has to be erected from outside, that is, by the polity." I would counter-argue that even in a democratic society the political majority can violate the Other, *with* its codes and laws. Moreover, I am not that sure that there are no in-built constraints in human beings against the violation of the Other. What I miss in both papers is an analysis not only of Nazi *eugenics,* but also of Nazi *eugenicists.* In his outstanding studies,[10] Lifton shows how eugenics involved what he calls "psychic numbing" among those who planned and administered eugenic programs. In this process one disassociates oneself from the consequences of actions that one might otherwise find deplorable. Dehumanizing, biological language facilitated that process.[11] In this process of fragmentation, one makes oneself invulnerable to the Other, even if one knows the Other is violated. Fragmentation is always self-deceptive![12] Ethics is always susceptible to manipulation by self-deception. In the end, the bracketing of Nazi "ethics" is therefore necessary. Next to the political codes and laws, I would appeal for the integration of the Holocaust in professional ethics for individual scientists. It is too easily said that the Nazis politicized science and that much of what went wrong under the Nazis can be traced to this politicization.[13] The question is why so many scientists were so willing to serve in this context, even if they could have refused to cooperate without sanctions. Professional ethics could cultivate a sensibility in scientists that would replace a dissociated mind-set with an integrated one, characterized by openness for the Other.[14] Such professional ethics must go further than modern utilitarian calculation, and should engage scientists critically in the search for new ways to symbolize our world. At this point science, ethics, and even theology can meet in a common enterprise to set free the best of the human mind, with its gifts and vulnerabilities.

NOTES

1. See C. B. Cohen, "'Quality of Life' and the Analogy with the Nazis," in *Quality of Life: The New Medical Dilemma,* ed. J. J. Walter and T. A. Shannon (New York: Paulist Press, 1984), 61–77.

2. A. L. Caplan, "How Did Medicine Go So Wrong?" in *When Medicine Went Mad: Bioethics and the Holocaust,* ed. A. L. Caplan (Totowa, N.J.: Humana Press, 1992), 53–92, esp. 60–61 ("The Nazi Analogy in Contemporary Bioethics").

3. H. Ofstad, *Our Contempt for Weakness. Nazi Norms and Values—and Our Own* (Gothenburg: Almqvist and Wiksell International, 1989).

4. Commission for Religious Relations with the Jews, *We Remember: A Reflection on the Shoah* (Vatican City: Libreria Editrice Vaticana, 1998).

5. P. J. Haas, *Morality after Auschwitz: The Radical Challenge of the Nazi Ethic* (Philadelphia: Fortress Press, 1988).

6. F. E. Katz, *Ordinary People and Extraordinary Evil: A Report on the Beguilings of Evil* (Albany: State University of New York Press, 1993), 60.

7. Z. Bauman, *Modernity and the Holocaust* (Cambridge: Polity Press, 1989).

8. A. Milchman and A. Rosenberg, "The Unlearned Lessons of the Holocaust," *Modern Judaism* 13 (1993): 177–190, esp. 186.

9. J.-F. Lyotard, *Heidegger en "de joden"* (Kok: Kampen, 1990), no. 136b, p. 110.

10. Especially R. J. Lifton, *The Nazi Doctors: Medical Killing and the Psychology of Genocide* (New York: Basic Books, 1986).

11. C. Koonz, *Genocide and Eugenics: the Language of Power,* in *Lessons and Legacies. The Meaning of the Holocaust in a Changing World,* ed. P. Hayes (Evanston: Northwestern University Press, 1991), 155–177, esp. 176–177.

12. D. Pollefeyt, "Auschwitz or How Good People Can Do Evil: An Ethical Interpretation of the Perpetrators and the Victims of the Holocaust in Light of the French Thinker Tzvetan Todorov," in *Confronting the Holocaust: a Mandate for the 21st Century?* ed. G. J. Colijn

and Marcia L. Littell, Studies in the Shoah 19 (New York: University Press of America, 1997), 91–118.

13. R. N. Proctor, "Nazi Biomedical Policies," in *When Medicine Went Mad*, 23–42, esp. 41.

14. R. J. Lifton and E. Markusen, *The Genocidal Mentality: Nazi Holocaust and Nuclear Threat* (New York: Basic Books, 1990), 223.

PART 5

History, Coexistence, and Conflict
Gentiles and Jews in East Central Europe

Introduction
Challenging History: Reflections on the Holocaust in Austria, Germany, and Poland
Doris L. Bergen

THE ESSAYS IN this section represent some of what is best in contemporary writings about the Holocaust and history. For one thing, they are the products not only of historians but of scholars of literature, religion, German, and Jewish Studies. Interdisciplinarity has been key to the study of the Holocaust since a political scientist, Raul Hilberg, published the foundational history almost forty years ago.[1] Of course many historians have made enormous contributions to the field—Saul Friedländer, Yehuda Bauer, Leni Yahil, Henry Friedlander, Sybil Milton, Richard Breitman, Christopher Browning, Omer Bartov—the list could continue. But their efforts have been complemented by the works of sociologists such as Nechama Tec, philosophers such as Joan Ringelheim and John K. Roth, journalist Gitta Sereny and psychologist Dori Laub, Richard Rubenstein and other scholars of religion, experts in Jewish Studies, Germanists, and anthropologists.

A past as complex as the period of the Shoah has to be approached from all angles. Its study needs the restless stimulation of new ideas and different methodologies. At least some of its students find that they cannot sustain a head-on approach. The novelist and survivor Aharon Appelfeld has said that thinking about the Holocaust is like gazing at the sun. Too long, too direct a look, and one is blinded.[2] One needs the relief of squinting or glancing to the side without looking away. And one assembles one's knowledge patiently, in fragments, through filters, and from photographs taken by others. So it is no coincidence that this section on history includes contributions by scholars who would not label themselves historians—Sander L. Gilman, Victoria J. Barnett, Monika Adamczyk-Garbowska—as well as by others who likely would: Gerhard Botz, J. Robert Wegs, and Michael C. Steinlauf.

The contributions cross other kinds of boundaries too. Their geographic range includes Austria, German-speaking Europe, and Poland. Until recently most of the scholarship available in English and German on the Holocaust focused on Nazi Germany. It paid little attention to Poles, Ukrainians, and others and relegated Germany's occupied territories in the east to backdrops—sites of slaughter and graveyards. In a sense Daniel Goldhagen's argument about uniquely German eliminationist anti-Semitism is symptomatic of a scholarly tradition that neglected the Holocaust's transnational nature.[3] Other scholars, like Thomas Sandkühler with his work on Galicia, remind us to consider the "periphery" as well as the core.[4] Moreover, territories away from Germany were crucial not only because Nazi functionaries initiated actions there, but because local populations exercised their own agency and struggled for ways to preserve their interests—or at least their lives. Gerhard Weinberg has shown the transformative power of considering World War II in its widest contexts.[5] The Holocaust was part of that global war, and it too demands broad, synthetic, inclusive study.

These essays, in particular those by Michael C. Steinlauf and Monika Adamczyk-Garbowska, help open discussion across national and linguistic boundaries. They also constitute a reply, although still preliminary, to calls to re-evaluate the past in post-Communist Europe. Indeed, neither Steinlauf's research nor Adamczyk-Garbowska's response would have been possible just over a decade ago. And even today the situation, like Adamczyk-Garbowska's moving essay, is open-ended. She closes with a question: was Krzysztof Kieslowski's description of the permanent "stain" of Polish anti-Semitism an "ominous prophesy?" Or will it be a warning heeded?

Changes in eastern Europe also feature largely—and much less ambiguously—in Sander L. Gilman's wide-ranging analysis. Indeed his entire argument about the "complex revitalization of Jewish communal and cultural life" in German-speaking Europe depends on the realities of Russian immigration. Victoria J. Barnett is less sanguine; she mentions the challenges to German identity "because of unification and the large numbers of ethnic German immigrants from eastern Europe." Gerhard Botz describes as a "decisive step" Austrian chancellor Franz Vranitzky's acknowledgment of at least some Austrian responsibility for the crimes of the Third Reich. Yet Botz remains concerned. Could it be, he asks, that with the "opening of the eastern borders" anti-Semitism in Austria may simply have taken second place to other hostilities: toward Gypsies, Serbs, and Romanians? All of the papers remind us how firmly rooted in the present is our understanding of the past—and how tenaciously elements of that past cling to us.

In different ways these essays acknowledge a need—cynics might say a fashion—in Central and Eastern Europe to discover (or invent) a pluralist past. Gilman points to "the bizarre neo-romantic German notion of Yiddish culture in Eastern Europe as klezmer and bagels." Steinlauf's observation about Poles since the late 1980s might apply just as well to Austrians and Germans too: "Raised in a monochromatic world of cultural and ethnic uniformity," they sift the past "for a myth of diversity and color."

For a long time Raul Hilberg's categories of "perpetrators, victims, and bystanders" have helped organize study and teaching about the Holocaust.[6] But useful as this scheme is, it can sometimes suggest a clarity that is misleading. The Italian Jewish writer Primo Levi talked about the "gray zone," an area of ambiguity between these groups; in the gray zone killers could also be rescuers, and criminals were sometimes victimized.[7] Historians have generally been more reluctant than writers of fiction, film makers, and poets to explore the gray zone. That terrain raises issues of identity, agency, and morality that are uncomfortable, inappropriate, or even taboo.

In different ways the work here ventures into the gray zone. Botz does not linger; he discounts Austrian gentiles' claims of victimhood, rejects assertions that they suffered just like the Jews, and establishes a clear line between perpetrators and victims. Gilman moves much further beyond familiar categories, above all by rejecting a kind of permanent victim status for European Jews. The Jews he discusses are active: they speak out, publish, disagree, and disrupt other people's stereotypes. By refusing to accept labels or categories imposed on them by the past, they open up new possibilities for the present. Steinlauf's position is even more complicated. Polish gentiles really were victims of Nazi German aggression, he points out. But they were also witnesses to genocide—and often its beneficiaries. Steinlauf's recognition of the coexistence of suffering and guilt that characterized the Polish experience of the war is perhaps his essay's most poignant achievement. And by risking the confusion of the gray zone Steinlauf, like Gilman, is able to raise new questions and find new places to look for answers.

Whatever one might think of Daniel Goldhagen's *Hitler's Willing Executioners,* one cannot deny that it sparked a great deal of discussion. Much of the debate has dealt with the issue of anti-Semitism: was it, as Goldhagen claims, the sole cause of the Shoah? Did the Germans embrace a unique and particularly deadly strain of Jew-hatred? Of the papers in this section, only Gilman and Barnett address Goldhagen directly. And both these writers are more interested in analyzing Goldhagen's reception in Germany than they are in confirming or refuting parts of his argument. Nevertheless, all of the papers make some significant claims about anti-Semitism. Either explicitly or implicitly, all six writers reject the notion that Nazi racial anti-Semitism was sharply distinct from older religious or economic hatreds. Anti-Semitism, these authors show, is dynamic, always mutating, reacting, and adapting. It is the intersections that interest these observers—the points where gentile attitudes toward Jews meet economic stresses, housing shortages, professional resentments, and myths about meaning. Unfortunately none of the contributions explores the intersections of gender and anti-Semitism, although the potential for such analysis is immense.

The authors included in this section are all sensitive to links between Christianity and hatred of Jews, although they show that such connections have taken very different, sometimes paradoxical, forms. In the assessments of Botz and Wegs, Christian anti-Jewishness was the constant that sometimes served to reproach more radical, racist hatreds but more often ended up legitimating them. Gilman uses Daniel Ganzfried's novel *Der Absender* (The Sender) to juxtapose the physical, religious markers of baptism and circumcision. Barnett insists that it is above all Christians who face the challenge of understanding anti-Semitism, and Steinlauf shows how Christian images and language have supported a Polish national memory that erases Jewish suffering. Adamczyk-Garbowska notes a dearth of sermons in Poland "in which priests remind the faithful about the evils of anti-Semitism." Such sermons, she suggests, "would have a much greater impact than hundreds of articles written by intellectuals for intellectuals."

In their chronological sweep all of the papers reveal some depressing continuities. Here Robert Wegs's matter-of-fact formulation has relevance beyond Austria: "The fact that Vienna's Jewish population fluctuated between only 5,000 and 8,000 Jews during the entire postwar period indicates that Jews did not and still do not find Vienna a very hospitable environment." These authors extend their gaze beyond 1945 and see no "zero hour." The legacy of the Shoah remains. Botz and Wegs lament the failure of many Austrians even now to face up to their past; Gilman shows how young European Jews continue working through themes from the Nazi past: anti-Semitism, betrayal, "the Jew's" body. Steinlauf depicts the guilt and shame of the Polish generation of witnesses to murder, and Adamczyk-Garbowska speaks of unmourned ghosts. In each case the enormity of the crime committed is reflected decades later by the magnitude of raw pain left in its wake.

In his entry for 10 December 1940, the German diarist Victor Klemperer made this terse observation: "*Lingua tertii imperii: the* Jew, *the* Englishman— nothing but collectives, no individual counts."[8] Klemperer was no historian, but he recognized the deadly power of language and the dehumanizing potential of labels. By complicating the categories, challenging familiar assumptions, and resisting closure, perhaps the contributions in this section help restore some humanity to the past they explore.

NOTES

1. Raul Hilberg, *The Destruction of the European Jews* (Chicago: Quadrangle Press, 1961; rev. ed., 3 vols., New York: Holmes and Meier, 1985).

2. Aharon Appelfeld, "Individualizing the Holocaust" (delivered at conference on the Holocaust, Stern College for Women, New York, 1993).

3. Daniel Jonah Goldhagen, *Hitler's Willing Executioners: Ordinary Germans and the Holocaust* (New York: Alfred A. Knopf, 1996).

4. Thomas Sandkühler, *Endlösung in Galizien: Der Judenmord in Ostpolen und die Rettungsinitiativen von Berthold Beitz* (Bonn: Dietz, 1996).

5. Gerhard Weinberg, *A World at Arms: A Global History of World War II* (Cambridge: Cambridge University Press, 1994).

6. Raul Hilberg, *Perpetrators, Victims, Bystanders: The Jewish Catastrophe, 1933–1945* (New York: Harper Collins, 1992).

7. Primo Levi, "The Gray Zone," in *The Drowned and the Saved,* trans. Raymond Rosenthal (New York: Vintage International, 1989).

8. Victor Klemperer, *I Will Bear Witness: A Diary of the Nazi Years, 1933–1941,* trans. Martin Chalmers (New York: Random House, 1998), 364.

19 | Non-Jews and Jews in Austria before, during, and after the Holocaust
Gerhard Botz

Vienna, however, was and remains the toughest, though also the most thorough, schooling of my entire life. [. . .] There I learned the fundamentals of a *Weltanschauung* in general, as well as a way of looking at political affairs in particular, which I later needed to augment only in certain details." Thus confessed Hitler in 1925.[1]

We have absolutely no reason to fundamentally doubt the autobiographical truth of these words or similar passages in *Mein Kampf* regarding his "position on Jewry." Hitler's anti-Semitism was molded in Vienna, and evolved out of the racial concepts of "Pan-German" Georg von Schönerer and radical *völkisch* sectarians[2] of the period after the turn of the century. This kind of anti-Semitism was a racist doctrine that regarded itself as "scientific" and can be regarded as "modern."[3] It tended to be espoused by a minority comprising for the most part academicians and students. Over the course of the subsequent decades, however, it began to influence wider circles and to permeate older forms of anti-Semitism.

Much more important at the turn of the century and in the interwar period, though, was a more widespread anti-Semitism of an economic and religious nature, which is connected with the name of Karl Lueger and his Christian Social Party.[4] This type of hostility toward Jews served Lueger's Catholic petit bourgeois movement as a means to promote political mobilization and played on centuries-old Christian stereotypes of Jews as the murderers of Christ. Even among the ranks of the Social Democratic Party's workers, and despite the fact that many of its leaders were Jewish intellectuals, there existed anti-Jewish prejudices, which most often appeared bearing the outer trappings of anti-capitalism.[5]

Just as young Hitler came to hate Jews during his Vienna years, there were relatively few non-Jews who were not either unfavorably disposed to Jews or fiery anti-Semites in the late Habsburg Monarchy and in the tiny Republic of Austria, which emerged in 1918 from its former provinces in the German-speaking regions along the Danube and in the Alps.[6] Thus, Arthur Schnitzler in his novel *Der Weg ins Freie* (The Road to the Open) could quite justifiably have one of his characters pose the merely rhetorical question:

Do you believe that there exists somewhere a Christian—and though he be the noblest, the most righteous and most loyal man on earth—a single one who, if his best friend, his beloved, or his wife were a Jew or of Jewish descent, in some moment of resentment, of annoyance, of rage, would not throw up to them the fact of their Jewishness—at least deep down inside?[7]

Since the end of the era of emancipation and political liberalism in Austria in the 1880s, the attitude toward Jews here—and similarly in Germany—was a sort of cultural code,[8] which played a determinative role in the country's political culture. Both non-socialist socio-political "camps" and the national identity of most German-speaking Austrians defined themselves to a large extent according to their position with respect to the Jews. To put it bluntly: the values of enlightenment, civil rights, religious tolerance, social reform, artistic modernity, and the like stood for "the Jews"; their opposites for the values and attitudes of non-Jews, as highly diverse as they might have been.

With the onset of large-scale waves of immigration from Eastern and East-Central Europe, the Jewish proportion of the population in the metropolis of the Habsburg Empire increased, and after 1900 remained rather constant at approximately 9 percent. As late as 1934 in Vienna, there were 176,000 members of the Jewish faith out of a total of 1.8 million inhabitants.[9] A considerable portion of the Jewish population—particularly the lower classes and the most recently arrived immigrants—was concentrated in a few districts along the Danube Canal and in the inner city, so that a culturally diverse, specifically Jewish milieu could develop there, especially in the district of the Leopold-stadt, the so-called *Mazzesinsel* (matzo island).[10]

This image, depicting the stark segregation of Viennese Jews, is repeated at the level of German-speaking Austria as a whole. Only one Jew out of ten lived in the Alpine and Danube-valley provinces. There, in contrast to the Habsburg metropolis, Jews formed only a tiny minority. In this respect the life of Austrian Jews differed from that of Jews in Germany. Most of them seem to have been less culturally integrated, were submitted to stronger social pressures for cultural integration, and displayed a relatively strong tendency toward assimilation and religious conversion.[11]

Thus, the "world of the Jews" in Vienna remained largely separated from the socio-cultural sphere of the Christians. But Jews in the rest of the territory of present-day Austria and those segments of Viennese Jewry who had climbed the social ladder to the bourgeoisie and the upper middle classes lived less segregated. They were particularly strongly represented in the professions, in commerce and finance, and among private employees. To refer to Steven Beller's hypothesis, these Jews who were favorably disposed to assimilation constituted, in fact, Vienna's "liberal bourgeoisie."[12] The world-renowned cultural and scientific innovators of *fin de siècle* Vienna also emerged from this group. In a rapidly modernizing, multinational society that continued to be strongly dominated by conservative values, anti-Judaism, and barriers separating the estates making up the social hierarchy, this was practically the only way open to Jews to attain enhanced social status and to assume a new identity following their break with the *shtetl* and their traditional way of life.[13]

Anti-Jewish prejudices and social impediments had at least formally been held in check by means of the civil rights that had been formally granted by the Austro-Hungarian monarchy in 1867 and through the symbolic figure of the old emperor, Kaiser Franz Joseph. To many Austrian Jews, the prejudice and impediments appeared to be handicaps but not a direct threat. The Christian anti-Semitism of Lueger and his mass movement seemed—and also was in many respects—politically opportunistic and economically instrumental; Schönerer's *Radau* anti-Semites were initially little more than a "lunatic fringe."[14]

Thus, despite the looming signs of danger that are clearly apparent to us in retrospect, the Jews of Vienna could also feel a certain degree of assurance under the slightly changed circumstances of the Republic after 1918. Despite all verbal anti-Semitic aggressiveness, anti-Jewish politics was mitigated by the imagination of the traditional "estate" society, which put every group into its "appropriate" place. Thus, there existed mostly a kind of uneasy coexistence between non-Jews and Jews in late Habsburg Austria.[15] More difficult, indeed, was the situation of that tenth of Austrian Jewry that lived as a minority of 1 percent, at most, outside of Vienna in the small and medium-sized provincial towns in which the Christian Social and German Nationalist sub-cultures dominated political life. With the exception of Burgenland, Jews here were confronted by much stronger opposition, which is why settling in such areas was never highly attractive.[16]

Nevertheless, anti-Semitism and discrimination against Jews could also be clearly perceived in the relatively protected urban center of the Habsburg state ever since the late nineteenth century. For this reason, the Jewish Community of Vienna issued publications and organized groups to combat anti-Semitism[17]—a struggle to achieve full social equality that found no support among non-Jews. An even more radical reaction to these new manifestations of hostility toward Jews, evident not only in Austria but in France and Eastern Europe as well, was that of Theodor Herzl, who propagated a novel type of "politics in a new key" (C. Schorske) as opposed to the new mass-level politics of the anti-Semites and the Marxist labor movement.[18] His response to the failure of emancipation and the end of the path to assimilation were the efforts to establish "the Jewish State" (1896) and Zionism,[19] but it was not until the 1930s that the proponents of Herzl's ideas attained a (relative) majority even in the Jewish Community of Vienna.

* * *

The social and economic crises during and after the First World War further aggravated the latent crisis that already existed in the relationship of non-Jews and Jews. The upheavals that shook the old political landscape, the collapse of the moral order, the sense of insecurity that undermined the national identity of German-speaking Austrians, revolutionary movements, Eastern European Jewish refugees and immigrants, economic calamities, and catastrophic unemployment produced or intensified widespread xenophobia and anti-Semitism. Even leaders of the Social Democratic Party, who were themselves frequently denounced as a "Jewish protective troop," called for the expulsion of the *Ostjuden,* whose numbers (about twenty thousand) were highly exaggerated by the anti-Semites.[20]

The Christian Social Party openly declared to combat the "domination of destructive Jewish influence in spiritual matters and economic affairs."[21] Many of its leading politicians, like I. Seipel and L. Kunschak, as well as Catholic newspapers, went even further, calling for restrictive hiring policies for Jews seeking public positions, for quotas to limit Jews at the universities, for special discriminatory laws, even for Jews to live in ghettos or to be interned.[22] Public discourse on the subject of Jews not only resorted to old Christian anti-Semitic images and modern racist concepts, it also assumed an openly threatening, violent tone toward Jews. However, racism and the readiness to resort to violence were especially manifest among the proponents of German nationalist extremism, *völkisch* groups, and the first National Socialists of the early 1920s. For them, the German *Volk*—the national identity now espoused by the majority of the inhabitants of the new Republic of Austria after 1918—defined itself first and foremost in contrast to "international Jewry," the cause of all economic and political evils.

The upshot was repeated attacks, vicious demonstrations, and anti-Jewish acts of violence, which, however, did not yet reach the proportions of 1938. The ruling political elite, even though they were to a large extent anti-Semitic, had to consider Austria's political and financial dependence on West European support, and so inhibited the outbreak of widespread anti-Semitic violence. But a Jewish writer and propagator of sexual liberty, Hugo Bettauer, whose novel *City without Jews* dramatically depicted the negative consequences of this wish of most non-Jews, fell victim to a Nazi assassin in 1925, an act that hardly any non-Jews saw fit to condemn in public. Further Nazi attacks of that kind led to similar reactions.[23]

The emergence of anti-Semitism during this first wave of anti-Jewish hate after 1918 and the subsequent events were not necessarily connected to the presence of Jews. After all, anti-Semitism also existed outside Vienna, in places where hardly anyone was personally acquainted with Jews or had ever even seen one. This was a case of direct recourse to potent religious roots, and was strongly characterized by provincial anti-modern and anti-Viennese emotions. The handful of Jews living in these regions were not infrequently subjected to public harassment, and a number of resort areas instituted policies—contrary to their own economic interests—to exclude Jewish vacationers.[24]

On the whole, this was a sign indicating an insidious trend toward segregation of non-Jews and Jews in interwar Austria. An increasing number of athletic clubs and alpinist associations introduced provisions in their constitution restricting membership to "Aryans," a practice that had previously been limited to *völkisch* gymnastic clubs and college fraternities. Many Austrian Jews took a stand against this trend, organizing protest demonstrations, establishing their own associations, and sometimes turning to the state and successfully obtaining the assistance of government institutions that were by no means favorably disposed to them and their cause. Even Christian Socialists and German Nationalists were forced to tone down their anti-Semitism once they had attained positions in the government—due in no small part to the unavoidable consideration of the financial support of Jewish industrialists and bankers as well as of Western governments, upon which the continually financial-crisis-ridden Austria was dependent. Thus, the wave of anti-Semitism receded during the economic and political consolidation phase in the mid-1920s.[25]

Anti-Semitism—in words and in deeds—increased once again in conjunction with the global economic crisis and the growth of National Socialism in the early 1930s. On one hand, Hitler's takeover of power in Germany provided a model as well as concrete support for the plans of radical anti-Semites in Austria; on the other hand, certain "moderate" anti-Jewish Christians distanced themselves from National Socialist anti-Semitism. The pastoral letter of Bishop J. M. Gföllner reflects these tendencies to replace *völkisch* anti-Semitism with a religious form of it, and to take the wind out of the Nazi sails by means of a Christian anti-Jewishness.[26]

Even the authoritarian regime of Christian Social Chancellor Dollfuss, which had established itself in Austria during the crisis of 1933, maintained an ambivalent attitude with respect to Jews. Discriminatory measures aimed at Jews and anti-Semitic rhetoric were combined with political policies that accepted the social and economic positions of the Jews and accorded a place to organizations representing Jewish interests within the Catholic model of a corporatist state.[27] Conversely, there were also many Austrian Jews who regarded a type of government-guaranteed "apartheid policy" as a last bulwark to hold back the unbridled anti-Semitism of the Nazis. Jewish intellectuals like Karl Kraus were thus strengthened in their turn to conservatism, and heads of Jewish organizations and Jewish business leaders supported the Austrian corporatist state to the very end.[28]

In light of this long tradition of anti-Semitism and anti-Judaism in Austria, it is a surprising but nevertheless well-documented finding of recent scholarly research that many of the Jews who were driven out of this country indicate in retrospect that they had suffered little if at all from hostility toward Jews before 1938,[29] and had not even been aware of anti-Semitism until the 1930s.

The historian Albert Lichtblau explains these circumstances by pointing out that a high proportion of Austrian Jews, despite all of their involvement in Austrian cultural life, had very few if any non-Jewish friends and went through life by maintaining a clear distance from their non-Jewish surroundings. "The majority of the Jews in Austria lived in the protected sphere of Vienna, the capital city governed by the Social Democrats, where, in light of the size of the Jewish community, exclusionary efforts on the part of non-Jews could not have the same painful effects as they could in cities or towns with smaller Jewish communities."[30] All of this—the objective situation as well as the subjective perception of it—changed quite suddenly with the *Anschluss* in March 1938. After that, many Austrian Jews who before had not considered themselves as Jewish were thrown by anti-Semitism into a Jewish identity.

* * *

Even before the Nazis had fully completed the process of assuming power in Austria, pogrom-like incidents had begun to take place—for the most part in Vienna.[31] These went far beyond anything that had gone on during the takeover of power in Germany. Open season on Jews was declared in a primal outbreak of popular hate for the Jewish; an outpouring of pent-up economic and political frustration was rained down upon them by a petit bourgeoisie and middle class seeking, at the expense of the Jews, material and social indemnification and compensation for intellectual inferiority complexes.

The chief initial manifestations were vicious slurs, humiliations, mistreatment, and arbitrary arrests. Jews, old and young alike, were impressed into "cleaner groups" and forced to wash off the painted slogans of the old regime from sidewalks and building walls as crowds of gleeful hecklers looked on, to paint over storefronts with anti-Semitic slogans, to commit acts of sacrilege. Those responsible were not only convinced Nazis; opportunistic hangers-on and totally "apolitical" individuals carried out nothing less than a campaign of plunder, directed at the private property and business assets of Jews, which went on for several weeks—sometimes with, sometimes without the formal authorization of the Nazi Party. Already in the spring of 1938, thousands of "acting administrators" had taken over Jewish stores and businesses; Nazis and other non-Jews excluded Jews from their workplaces, confiscated apartments belonging to Jews, and looted cash, jewelry, treasures of art, carpets, furniture, pianos, and other goods.[32]

Overnight, many previously unobtrusive non-Jewish neighbors and even some former friends were suddenly transformed into enemies of the Jews, longtime business partners or house servants mutated into unscrupulous "Aryanizers," government and police officials who had previously been loyal to the state revealed themselves to be Nazi sympathizers. Even more than the so-called "wild Aryanizations," it was the public rituals of humiliation that left behind severe trauma on the part of many Austrian Jews. Many of them were driven to suicide; others, who survived the Holocaust abroad, could never forget how quickly the "Viennese heart of gold" had suddenly turned into one of open hate and sadism. In almost all of the oral and written accounts of this time, as well as in works of literature dealing with it, this experience plays a central role in the memory of Austrian Jews after 1945.[33]

During the weeks following the *Anschluss,* Nazi authorities attempted to gain control of the spontaneous expressions of hate for Jews and the most severe acts of violence. A systematic purge of Jewry in the Nazi sense called for proceeding in an orderly fashion because of a number of considerations, not the least of which was international public opinion. The spontaneous persecution of the Jews was transformed into a "legal" process. Through the introduction of the Nuremberg racial laws and by means of administrative discrimination, the group of persecuted persons was clearly defined and distinguished from the non-Jewish population, which made possible the subsequent process of reverse solidarity.

Thus began as well a step-by-step, progressive process of exclusion of Jews from social life,[34] which proceeded much more quickly and thoroughly in Austria—and above all in Vienna—than it did in the so-called old Reich. In the "Ostmark," Austrian Nazis and bureaucrats conceived and tested new procedures and organizational innovations, which soon came to serve as models for those implemented by other German administrative hierarchies and by the SS. Eichmann and other Austrians such as Kaltenbrunner, Seyss-Inquart, Globocnik, and Franz Stangl, who later operated the machinery of the "final solution" throughout Europe, first began to develop their respective talents in Vienna, the starting point of their ignominious careers in the Third Reich.[35] The "Central Office for Jewish Emigration in Vienna," set up by Eichmann, carried out the initial development of that perfect system of bureaucratic coordination and the inclusion of the persecuted in the process of their own persecution, which would later be characteristic of the methods of mass extermination. In a much quicker and more comprehensive fashion than was the case in Germany, they also succeeded in inducing tens of thousands of Austrian Jews to "emigrate" before the war began; their personal property was systematically expropriated, and they thus financed their own expulsion. The expropriation of Jewish business assets proceeded with comparable "success"; in Vienna, this attained the proportions of a veritable social revolution and became a model for "de-Judaization" in all of Germany.[36]

Assets whose value exceeded that of the total Austrian state budget (for 1938) were confiscated from small, medium-sized, and large businesses, stock holdings, real estate, and other assets belonging to Jews. Within a matter of a few months, the antiquated Viennese commercial structure received a major impetus toward increased efficiency and greater concentration—above all, at the cost of the Jews—which served to further the economic preparations for war and provided Göring's Four Years' Plan with an occasion to express admiration for Austrian Nazi leaders and economic experts. These measures were carried on with increasing speed following the so-called *Reichskristallnacht*.

In Austria and particularly in Vienna, the pogrom of November 1938 was probably more intense and more violent than in many regions of Germany.[37] Incited by Goebbels, members of party organizations, the SA, and the Hitler Youth participated in this pogrom in such a high-spirited fashion that some German Nazis and even Gestapo officials voiced concern about the expediency of anti-Jewish campaigns such as this. It was not the destruction of synagogues and plate glass windows, the plundering of stores and apartments, or the mass arrests of Jews that evoked sympathy on the part of some onlookers; rather, it was the "very rough treatment" of the Jews, manifesting itself "usually in the form of brutal beatings," though not stopping short of rape and murder. In the words of an internal Gestapo report: "Sympathy for the fate of the Jews was voiced almost nowhere. In cases where someone dared—no matter how modestly—to bring forth such expressions, the crowd immediately and energetically stood up to the individual. A few persons expressing overly-friendly sentiments toward Jews were arrested." The report went on to say: "Whereas the broad general public permits itself to be led by its natural instinct with respect to its attitudes toward the measures being implemented, and therefore perceives them as a form of liberation, the intellectual upper classes in most cases express concerns of an economic [and] of an emotional nature."[38]

Basically, an appropriate description of the attitudes of the non-Jewish population toward the later phases of the persecution of the Jews is a "mixture of indifference, mute sympathy and, here and there, active help"[39]—in the best case. Only a very few provided active help, as substantiated by the mere handful of Jews who were able to survive hidden in Austria with the help of non-Jews; according to Erika Weinzierl these numbered only six hundred.[40] Moreover, the various forms of intervention and assistance offered by the Catholic Church concentrated on baptized Jews and those living in mixed marriages. On the contrary, the majority of the non-Jewish population of Vienna may well have had a direct interest in the elimination of the Jews. (This by no means applies to regions outside of Vienna, which had already been "cleansed of Jews" in 1939.)[41]

In the metropolis, there were 26,000 enterprises (each with a value of over 5,000 RM) that had originally belonged to Jews. This represented a quarter of all businesses, and it was toward these that the greed of the Nazis and their anti-Semitic followers was directed. Through the expropriation of these commercial assets, many Viennese hoped to improve their economic lot or even to take the first step up the ladder to the petit bourgeoisie. From the very beginning, Nazi leaders had been promising their cohorts in Vienna a piece of this profit resulting from the persecution of Jews, or spread a corresponding mood through the rank and file: "The Jew's gotta go, but his dough stays here!"[42] This age-old motif of popular Viennese anti-Semitism also contributed to the popularity in the city of the Aryanizations and the theft of art and other assets from Jews.[43]

Another powerful driving force behind the further radicalization of the persecution was the housing shortage. In 1938, the Jews of Vienna occupied approximately seventy thousand apartments, and many Nazis had their eyes on them. If one considers the fact that this number is even somewhat greater than the total of all the living units created by the famous residential building policy of "Red Vienna" between 1923 and 1933, then one can more readily gauge the social significance of this type of Nazi policy.[44] In various different ways—through direct pressure, diverse administrative measures, or simply forced emigration—the Aryanization of this property was carried out within a few months and several years. The Jews were subsequently concentrated into ever closer quarters, so that unofficial "quasi-ghettos" came into existence in various Viennese neighborhoods. After further Jewish emigration had become impossible as a result of the war, an increasing number of Viennese Nazi Party members began calling for the remaining Jews to be sent to labor camps, which were to be erected in the vicinity of Vienna, and to subsequently be deported to the *general government*. Hitler himself took this view under consideration and gave the deportation of Viennese Jews to the "East" ever higher priority.[45]

In several waves, which had already begun in October 1939, though initially without great success, over 48,000 Austrian Jews were deported from Vienna to the extermination camps in 1941 and 1942. Up to 1945, a total of at least 65,000 Austrian Jews died at the hands of their persecutors; a mere 5,700 were able to survive in Vienna due to a variety of different circumstances. The number of Jews who were driven out of Austria and found refuge, most often in North and South America, England, Palestine, and Shanghai, came to about 126,000. National Socialism was thus capable of bringing about in radical fashion what Austrian anti-Semites had already conceived, expressed, and demanded decades before. Vienna became a "City without Jews," which, practically speaking, it would also remain after 1945.[46]

* * *

In the reborn Republic of Austria, Jews were—and continue to be—an extremely tiny minority. Their numbers fluctuate between 5,000 and about 8,000, most of whom are members of the Jewish Community re-established in 1945. Even in the 1980s, membership was not increased substantially as a result of the 5,000 Soviet emigrants who remained in Austria. As was the case before the Holocaust, virtually all of the few Austrian Jews live in Vienna.

Along with the Jews who survived in Austria and who initially composed this postwar minority, there were about 4,500 Jewish emigrants who returned to Vienna from abroad; a large proportion of these came from Palestine, though there were also many from Shanghai and other "exotic" lands of refuge. Indeed, many of these returning emigrants were not able to cope with conditions in the new Austrian society, whose climate continued to be anti-Jewish, so that a significant fluctuation was displayed in the number of Jews in Austria up to the end of the 1950s. The social gap separating Jews from non-Jews was at least as deep as it had been before 1938. Many Jews considered their stay in Vienna after 1945 as only a temporary stopover but then remained there nevertheless, which gave rise to a completely different relationship to non-Jews as well as Jews from abroad. Gradually, the Jews from Eastern and East-Central Europe came to constitute the majority of the members of Austrian Jewish communities.[47] They had not experienced the deadly torment of the Jews here; for them, Vienna still radiated some of the splendor of the old imperial capital, and they were able to draw a certain identification with Austria out of the nostalgic recollection of the Austria of the past—which, however, the more critically oriented younger generation no longer wished to share.[48] And there were also the mental barriers, political differences, and ancient prejudices between the Jews who had previously lived in Austria and the newly arrived *Ostjuden,* as the film maker Ruth Beckermann has shown.[49] Furthermore, as the work of Helga Embacher has brought out, the founding of the state of Israel was also a source of tensions within the Jewish communities that had not been present before 1938, resulting from the "double loyalty" of a simultaneous sense of connectedness to both Israel and Austria.[50]

Enormous currents of migrating human beings, many of them former slave laborers and concentration camp prisoners from scores of different countries trying to return to their native lands after the war, flowed right through Austria during the second half of the 1940s. Repulsed by conditions in the Eastern European countries that had turned communist and by the pogroms then going on, more than 100,000 Jewish refugees from Eastern Europe once again crossed through Austria. There were also a great number of Jews among the hundreds of thousands of displaced persons, many of whom were attempting—often under the most hazardous circumstances—to emigrate to Palestine/Israel or to the West.[51] The non-Jewish population held them responsible for foodstuff shortages, black market dealings, and contagious diseases, and not infrequently made them the targets of verbal and physical anti-Semitic attacks.[52] Less dramatic was the situation in the 1970s and 1980s, when once again approximately 360,000 Jewish emigrants from the Soviet Union passed through Austria on their way to Israel or the United States.[53]

Post-1945 Austrian politicians offered support neither to Jewish re-migrants nor to refugees; rather, these were met with popular rejection and anti-Semitic prejudice, which was also openly expressed within government circles not only by Catholic Conservatives, but by Social Democrats as well.[54] And it was precisely these men who generally opposed the return of Jewish exiles from among their own party ranks, with the argument that this would only serve to revive the old anti-Semitic accusations leveled at the "Jew-ified Social Democracy." And Austrian officials made just as little effort to enable survivors of the Holocaust—not a few of whom had been responsible for significant scientific and artistic achievements abroad—to return to their homeland, a policy that remained in effect almost until the present day and one to which some historians have attributed responsibility for manifestations of provincialism in the Second Republic. Furthermore, the issue of indemnification of damages suffered at the hands of the Nazi regime went undiscussed for quite a long time.[55] It was only hesitantly and halfheartedly that the Republic of Austria provided Jews with symbolic and material recognition of their status as victims of National Socialism. It was not until fifty years after 1945 that a satisfactory state of affairs was reached with the establishment of a "National Fund" for the victims of Nazi persecution.

This incapability on the part of Austria to acknowledge its shared responsibility for the persecution of the Jewish victims of the Nazis was officially based upon the Second Republic's preferred depiction of Austria as merely the "victim of Hitler's Germany." In this matter, it was the Allies themselves who had already provided the key catch phrase in their Moscow Declaration of 1943, though the political elite of the Second Republic made a determined effort to conveniently forget the fact that this declaration had at the same time quite explicitly cited Austrian complicity.[56] If Austria and (non-Jewish) Austrians had been nothing but victims of National Socialism, then they found themselves in the same situation as the Jews. "Both are victims of national socialism," as conservative Austrian Chancellor Julius Raab declared in 1962 to President Nahum Grossmann of the World Jewish Congress during negotiations for compensation.[57] Therefore, there also were no grounds for Austria either to make any form of compensation payments or to critically confront and come to terms with its own Nazi past, as was taking place in the Federal Republic of Germany. Similar to the case of the communist German Democratic Republic, which historically fended off its responsibility for National Socialism, postwar Austria—with its emerging Austrian consciousness—spatially shifted its share of the blame to the Germans. It remains an open question whether the dissociation from pan-Germanic thinking and Austrian nation building could have been paralleled by a simultaneous process of mental de-nazification, in post-1945 Austria.[58] Simon Wiesenthal's efforts to expose Nazi criminals thus encountered tremendous handicaps for a long time in Austria. The Austrian government as well made the effort to limit to as great an extent as possible the return of real estate, businesses, apartments, art objects, and other such assets that had been confiscated from Jews.[59] Their concerns would quite well have had to do with the large number of former

Austrian Nazis and the many Austrians who had directly profited from the expulsion and the extermination of Jews.

The majority of the Austrian population—in which, immediately after 1945, strong German nationalist and pro-Nazi feelings were still widespread—also gradually began to believe in the Victim Myth that was being propagated by the political elite. The result of this was a lower level of motivation in comparison to Germany to carry out the process of de-nazification, as well as a less critical attitude toward manifestations of anti-Semitism. Thus, in schools, in public life, and in opinion polls, the old anti-Jewish prejudices could still be candidly expressed—unbroken by consciousness of co-responsibility for the Holocaust. Into the 1980s, even leading Austrian politicians could repeatedly get away with openly anti-Semitic "slips of the tongue." Likewise unbroken was the ongoing veneration in a small Tyrolian village of the victim of a purported medieval "ritual murder" as a Catholic martyr.[60] Thus, on the occasion of internal political conflicts such as the demonstrations against an anti-Semitic professor in Vienna in 1965 or during the crisis surrounding Kurt Waldheim's military service during the Second World War, otherwise latent anti-Semitism has repeatedly come to the surface.[61]

Even in the middle of the 1970s, when Social Democrat Bruno Kreisky, a man of Jewish descent, was chancellor and displayed a conciliatory attitude toward former Nazis, results of representative opinion polls indicated anti-Semitic attitudes of considerable proportions. For instance, 8 percent of respondents stated that they felt aversion to shaking hands with a Jew. In addition to these virulent anti-Semites, there were an additional 25 percent whose anti-Semitism was moderate. At that time, only 15 percent of Austrians displayed no anti-Semitic attitudes.[62] Other polls yielded similar results. Thus, 64 percent of respondents held the opinion that Jews exerted excessive influence on international finance and business, and 45 percent said that Jews had too much influence in Austria.[63] In the 1990s as well, such "anti-Semitism without Jews" has not disappeared, though it has certainly weakened somewhat.[64] One of the factors that may be responsible for this is that with the opening of the eastern borders, anti-Semitism has been shifted somewhat into the background and replaced by other forms of xenophobia—above all, hostility toward Gypsies, Serbs, and Rumanians.[65]

It had to wait for the arrival of the 1990s for an Austrian chancellor, Franz Vranitzky, to be able to state before the Austrian Parliament, and shortly thereafter in Israel as well, that on the one hand Austria as a state was not responsible for the deeds of the German Reich, as she had ceased to exist, and as there was a persecution and resistance of her political elite. On the other hand, "many Austrians [had been] involved in the repressive measures and persecutions of the Third Reich [. . .] and, indeed, in prominent positions," so that modern-day Austria cannot shirk its "shared moral responsibility" for the deeds of its citizens during the Nazi era.[66] Without a doubt, a decisive step had been taken—late but taken nevertheless—to rework the relationship of non-Jewish Austria to Austrian Jews, a relationship that is still oppressed by the burdens of history and its human and material losses.

NOTES

1. Translated from Adolf Hitler, *Mein Kampf* (Munich, 1938), 137.
2. Friedrich Heer, *Der Glaube des Adolf Hitler* (Munich, 1968), 51ff., 165ff.; Andrew G. Whiteside, *Georg Ritter von Schönerer* (Graz, 1981); Wilfried Daim, *Der Mann, der Hitler die Ideen gab* (Munich, 1958); recently also Brigitte Hamann, *Hitlers Wien* (Munich, 1996).
3. Peter G. J. Pulzer, *The Rise of Political Anti-Semitism in Germany and Austria* (New York, 1964); Albert S. Lindemann, *Esau's Tears. Modern Anti-Semitism and the Rise of the Jews* (Cambridge, 1997), 182ff.
4. John Boyer, *Political Radicalism in Late Imperial Vienna* (Chicago, 1995); Albert Lichblau, *Antisemitismus und soziale Spannung in Berlin und Wien 1867-1914* (Berlin, 1994); see also John Weiss, *Ideology of Death. Why the Holocaust Happened in Germany* (Chicago, 1996).
5. Robert S. Wistrich, *Socialism and the Jews: The Dilemmas of Assimilation in Germany and Austria-Hungary* (London, 1982), and "Sozial Democracy, Antisemitismus and the Jews of Vienna," in *Jews, Antisemitism and Culture*, ed. Ivar Oxaal, Michael Pollak, and Gerhard Botz (London, 1987), 111-120 (enlarged German ed., Gerhard Botz, Ivar Oxaal, and Michael Pollak, eds., *Eine zerstörte Kultur. Jüdisches Leben und Antisemitismus in Wien seit dem 19. Jahrhundert* [Buchloe, 1990], 169-180); Leopold Spira, *Feindbild "Jud"* (Vienna, 1981), 21ff.
6. Bruce F. Pauley, *From Prejudice to Persecution: A History of Austrian Anti-Semitism* (Vienna, 1992); see also George E. Berkeley, *Vienna and Its Jews* (Lanham, Md., 1988); John Bunzl, "Zur Geschichte des Antisemitismus in Österreich," in John Bunzl and Bernd Marin, *Antisemitismus in Österreich* (Innsbruck, 1983), 9-88.
7. Arthur Schnitzler, *Das erzählerische Werk*, vol. 4 (Frankfurt am Main, 1978), 203; see also Ruth Kluger, "The Theme of Anti-Semitism in the Work of Austrian Jews," in *Anti-Semitism in Times of Crisis*, ed. Sander L. Gilman and Steven T. Katz (New York, 1991), 177ff.
8. Shulamit Volkov, "Antisemitism as a Cultural Code: Reflexions on the History and Historiography of Antisemitism in Imperial Germany," reprinted in *The Nazi Holocaust*, vol. 2, ed. Michael R. Marrus (London, 1989), 307-328.
9. Michael John and Albert Lichtblau, *Schmelztiegel Wien—einst und jetzt* (Vienna, 1990), 145ff.
10. Marsha L. Rozenblit, *The Jews of Vienna, 1867-1914: Assimilation and Identity* (Albany, N.Y., 1983); for a partly contrasting interpretation see Ivar Oxaal, "The Jews of Young Hitler's Vienna," in *Jews, Antisemitism and Culture*, 11-38; Ivar Oxaal and Walter R. Weitzmann, "The Jews of Pre-1914 Vienna. An Exploration of Basic Sociological Dimensions," in *Leo Baeck Institute Year Book*, vol. 30 (1985).
11. Albert Lichtblau, *Antisemitismus und soziale Spannung in Berlin und Wien 1867-1914* (Berlin, 1994), 38ff.
12. Steven Beller, *Wien und die Juden* (Vienna, 1993), 65ff. (English ed., *Vienna and the Jews 1867-1938* [Cambridge, 1989]).
13. Michael Pollak, *Vienne 1900: Une identité blessée* (Paris, 1984).
14. Peter Pulzer, "Spezifische Momente und Spielarten des österreichischen und Wiener

Antisemitismus," in *Eine zerstörte Kultur,* 121–140; Wolfgang Häusler, "Toleranz, Emanzipation und Antisemitismus. Das österreichische Judentum des bürgerlichen Zeitalters," in Anna Drabek et al., *Das österreichische Judentum* (Vienna, 1974).

15. Cf. Albert Lichtblau, "Macht und Tradition: Von der Judenfeindschaft zum modernen Antisemitismus," in *Die Macht der Bilder: Antisemitische Vorurteile und Mythen,* ed. Jüdisches Museum der Stadt Wien (Vienna, 1995), 212–229.

16. Albert Lichtblau, "Antisemitismus—Rahmenbedingungen und Wirkungen auf das Zusammenleben von Juden und Nichtjuden," in *Handbuch des politischen Systems Östereichs. Erste Republik 1918–1933,* ed. Emmerich Talos et al. (Vienna, 1995), 461.

17. Walter R. Weitzmann, "The Politics of the Viennese Jewish Community, 1890–1914," in *Jews, Antisemitism and Culture,* 127.

18. Carl E. Schorske, *Fin-de-Siècle Vienna: Politics and Culture* (Cambridge, 1981), 146ff.

19. Adolf Gaisbauer, *Davidstern und Doppeladler* (Vienna, 1988), 82ff.

20. Albert Lichblau, "Partizipation und Isolierung: Juden in Österreich in den 'langen' 1920er Jahren," in *Archiv für Sozialgeschichte,* vol. 37 (1997), 231–253.

21. 1926 Christian Social Party program, quoted from Klaus Berchtold, ed., *Österreichische Parteiprogramme 1868–1966* (Vienna, 1967), 376.

22. Anton Staudinger, "Christlichsoziale Judenpolitik in der Anfangsphase der Republik," in *Jahrbuch für Zeitgeschichte 1978* (Vienna, 1979), 11–48; Anton Staudinger, "Katholischer Antisemitismus in der Ersten Republik," in *Eine zerstörte Kultur,* 256ff.

23. Gerhard Botz, *Gewalt in der Politik: Attentate, Zusammenstösse, Putschversuche, Unruhen in Österreich 1918 bis 1938,* 2nd ed. (Munich, 1983), 133ff., 258ff.

24. Lichtblau, "Antisemitismus," 465ff.

25. Günther Fellner, *Antisemitismus in Salzburg 1918–1938* (Vienna, 1979); Marko M. Feingold, ed., *Ein ewiges Dennoch: 125 Jahre Juden in Salzburg* (Vienna, 1993).

26. Staudinger, "Katholischer Antisemitismus in der Ersten Republik," 264ff.

27. Anton Pelinka, *Stand oder Klasse? Die christliche Arbeiterbewegung 1933 bis 1938* (Vienna, 1972), 220ff.; Sylvia Maderegger, *Die Juden im österreichischen Ständestaat, 1933–1938* (Salzburg, 1973).

28. Richard Thieberger, "Assimilated Jewish Youth and Viennese Cultural Life around 1930," in *Jews, Antisemitism and Culture,* 174–184; Peter Eppel, *Zwischen Kreuz und Hakenkreuz: Die Haltung der Zeitschrift Schönere Zukunft zum Nationalsozialismus* (Vienna, 1980).

29. Christian W. Haerpfer, "Israelische Bürger österreichischer Herkunft," in *Vertreibung und Neubeginn,* ed. Erika Weinzierl and Otto D. Kulka (Vienna, 1992), 461.

30. Lichtblau, "Antisemitismus," 463f.

31. For a general account see Herbert Rosenkranz, *Verfolgung und Selbstbehauptung. Die Juden in Österreich 1938–1945* (Vienna, 1978); Emmerich Talos, Ernst Hanisch, and Wolfgang Neugebauer, eds., *NS-Herrschaft in Österreich 1938–1945* (Vienna, 1988); Karl Stuhlpfarrer, "Antisemitismus, Rassenpolitik und Judenverfolgung in Österreich nach dem Ersten Weltkrieg," in Drabek et al., *Judentum,* 141–164.

32. Gerhard Botz, *Nationalsozialismus in Wien,* 3rd ed. (Buchloe, 1988), 51ff.; Hans Safrian and Hans Witek, *Und keiner war dabei: Dokumente des alltäglichen Antisemitismus in Wien 1938* (Vienna, 1988), 17ff.; see also Jonny Moser, "Das Unwesen der kommissarischen Leiter," in *Arbeiterschaft—Faschismus—Nationalbewußtsein,* ed. Helmut Konrad and Wolfgang Neugebauer (Vienna, 1983), 89–97; Elisabeth Klamper, "Der 'Anschlußpogrom,'" in *Der Pogrom. Judenverfolgung in Österreich und Deutschland,* ed. Kurt Schmid and Robert Streibel (Vienna 1990), 25–33.

33. George Clare, *Last Waltz in Vienna* (London, 1983); H. Hilsenrad, *Brown Was the Danube* (New York, 1966); Jüdische Schicksale. Berichte von Verfolgten, ed., *Dokumenta-*

tionsarchiv des österreichischen Widerstandes (Vienna, 1992), 90ff.; Ruth Klüger, *Weiter le-ben: Eine Jugend* (Göttingen, 1992); Raul Hillberg, *The Politics of Memory: The Journey of a Holocaust Historian* (Chicago, 1996); see also Carl Zuckmayer, "Hexensabbat das Pöbels," in his *Als wär's ein Stück von mir* (Frankfurt am Main), 57–81.

34. For this and the following see Gerhard Botz, "The Jews of Vienna from the *Anschluss* to the Holocaust," in *Jews, Antisemitism and Culture*, 185–204.

35. Hans Safrian, *Die Eichmann-Männer* (Vienna, 1993), 23ff.; Götz Aly and Susanne Heim, *Vordenker der Vernichtung* (Frankfurt am Main, 1993), 33ff.

36. Helmut Genschel, *Die Verdrängung der Juden aus der Wirtschaft im Dritten Reich* (Göttingen, 1966); Susanne Heim and Götz Aly, "Die Ökonomie der 'Endlösung,'" in *Sozialpolitik und Judenvernichtung,* ed. Susanne Heim et al. (Berlin, 1983), 83ff.; Gerhard Botz, "Experimentierfeld 'Ostmark': Pogrom-Antisemitismus und organisatorische Invention," in *Arisierungen in Österreich,* ed. Peter Schwarz (Klagenfurt, 1998).

37. Above all see the contributions to *Der Pogrom.*

38. Quoted from Tuiva Friedmann, "Die Kristall-Nacht" (unpublished ms., Haifa, 1972), 18.

39. Karl R. Stadler, *Österreich 1938–1945 im Spiegel der NS-Akten* (Vienna, 1966), 117.

40. Erika Weinzierl, *Zu wenig Gerechte: Österreicher und Judenverfolgung 1938–1945,* 2nd ed. (Graz, 1985), 85.

41. Michael John, "Modell Oberdonau? Zur wirtschaftlichen Ausschaltung der jüdischen Bevölkerung in Oberösterreich," *Österreichische Zeitschrift für Geschichtswissenschaften* 3, no. 2 (1992): 208–234; Gretl Köfler, "Tirol und die Juden," in *Tirol und der Anschluß,* ed. Thomas Albrich, Klaus Eisterer, and Rolf Steininger (Innsbruck, 1988), 169–182; Robert Streibel, *Plötzlich waren sie alle weg* (Vienna, 1991); August Walzl, *Die Juden Kärntens und das Dritte Reich* (Klagenfurt, 1987).

42. Quoted from Gerhard Botz, "'Arisierungen' und nationalsozialistische Mittel-standspolitik in Wien (1938 bis 1949)," *Wiener Geschichtsblätter* 29, no. 1 (1974): 126.

43. Botz, *Nationalsozialismus in Wien,* 328ff.; Hans Witek, "'Arisierungen' in Wien," in Talos et al., *NS-Herrschaft,* 199–216; Irene Etzersdorfer, *Arisiert* (Vienna, 1995), 23ff.

44. Gerhard Botz, "National Socialist Vienna: Antisemitism as a Housing Policy," *Wiener Library Bulletin,* no. 29, new series no. 39/40 (1976): S. 50; Herbert Exenberger, Johann Koß, and Brigitte Ungar-Klein, *Kündigungsgrund Nichtarier: Die Vertreibung jüdischer Mieter aus den Wiener Gemeindebauten in den Jahren 1938–1939* (Vienna, 1996).

45. Gerhard Botz, *Wohnungspolitik und Judendeportation in Wien 1938 bis 1945: Zur Funktion des Antisemitismus als Ersatz nationalsozialistischer Sozialpolitik* (Salzburg, 1975).

46. Gabriele Anderl, "Flucht und Vertreibung," in *Auswanderungen aus Österreich,* ed. Trude Horvath and Gerda Neyer (Vienna, 1996), 235–275; Jonny Moser, "Österreich," in *Dimensionen des Völkermords: Die Zahl der jüdischen Opfer des Nationalsozialismus,* ed. Wolfgang Benz (Munich, 1991), 67–94.

47. Friederike Wilder-Okladek, *The Return Movement of Jews to Austria after the Second World War* (The Hague, 1969).

48. Matti Bunzl, "Counter-memory and Modes of Resistance. The Uses of *Fin-de-siècle* Vienna for Present-Day Austrian Jews" (conference paper, Chicago, 1996); cf.: Hilde Spiel, *Vienna's Golden Autumn: 1866–1938* (London, 1987).

49. Ruth Beckermann, *Unzugehörig: Östereicher und Juden nach 1945* (Vienna, 1989), 100ff.

50. Helga Embacher, *Neubeginn ohne Illusionen: Juden in Österreich nach 1945* (Vienna, 1995), 84ff.

51. Thomas Albrich, "Brichah: Fluchtwege durch Österreich," in: *Überlebt und unterwegs: Jüdische Displaced Persons im Nachkriegsdeutschland,* ed. Fritz Bauer Institut (Frankfurt am Main, 1997), 207–228.

52. Embacher, *Neubeginn ohne Illusionen,* 66ff.

53. Dalia Ofer, "Emigration and Aliyah," in *Terms of Survival: The Jewish World since 1945,* ed. Robert S. Wistrich (London, 1995), 76.

54. Robert Knight, ed., *"Ich bin dafür, die Sache in die Länge zu ziehen"* (Frankfurt am Main, 1988).

55. Brigitte Bailer, *Wiedergutmachung kein Thema. Österreich und die Opfer des Nationalsozialismus* (Vienna, 1993).

56. Gerald Stourzh, *Geschichte des Staatsvertrages 1945–1955,* 2nd ed. (Graz, 1980), 214.

57. Quoted from Beckermann, 46; see generally Helga Embacher and Margit Reiter, *Gratwanderungen: Die Beziehungen zwischen Österreich und Israel im Schatten der Vergangenheit* (Vienna, 1998), 68ff.

58. Gerhard Botz, "Janus-Headed Austria: Transition from Nazism as Restoration, Continuity and Learning Process," in *Modern Europe after Fascism 1943–1980s,* vol. 1, ed. Stein Ugelvik Larsen and Bernt Hagtvet (Boulder, Colo., 1998), 360ff.

59. Recently: Anton Pelinka and Sabine Mayr, eds., *Die Entdeckung der Verantwortung. Die Zweite Republik und die vertriebenen Juden* (Vienna, 1998).

60. Andreas Maislinger and Günther Pallauer, "Antisemitismus ohne Juden—Das Beispiel Tirol," in *Voll Leben und voll Tod ist diese Erde,* ed. Wolfgang Plat (Vienna, 1988), 171–187, esp. 181ff.

61. Ruth Wodak et al., eds., *"Wir sind alle unschuldige Täter:" Diskurstheoretische Studien zum Nachkriegsantisemitismus* (Frankfurt am Main, 1990); Richard Mitten, *The Politics of Antisemitic Prejudice: The Waldheim Phenomenon in Austria* (Boulder, Colo., 1992). Critically: Christian Fleck and Albert Müller, "Front-Stage and Back-Stage: The Problem of Measuring Post-Nazi Antisemitism in Austria," in *Modern Europe,* vol. 1, 436–454.

62. Hilde Weiss, *Antisemitische Vorurteile in Österreich* (Vienna, 1984), 105ff.

63. Robert S. Wistrich, "Anti-Semitism in Europe after 1945," in *Terms of Survival,* 285.

64. In addition, Bernd Marin, "Ein historisch neuartiger 'Antisemitismus ohne Antisemiten'?" in: Bunzl and Marin, *Antisemitismus,* 171–192.

65. *Journal für Sozialforschung* 32, no. 1 (1992): 95ff.

66. Reprinted in Gerhard Botz and Gerald Sprengnagel, eds., *Kontroversen um Österreichs Zeitgeschichte: Verdrängte Vergangenheit, Österreich-Identität, Waldheim und die Historiker* (Frankfurt am Main, 1994), 574ff., 577ff.

20 | *Jews and Non-Jews in Austria*
J. Robert Wegs

GERHARD BOTZ, well known for his pioneering and perceptive studies of Austrian anti-Semitism, attempts in the preceding pages to provide readers with an understanding of Austrian attitudes toward the Jews before, during, and after the Holocaust. His essay does not then intend to break new ground, but rather to provide a deft summation of existing knowledge, much of it provided by Botz in his previous monographic works.

In the debate concerning the nature of nineteenth- and twentieth-century anti-Semitism, Botz disagrees with a dominant view that a basic religious opposition to the Jews had held sway until the late nineteenth century, when it was replaced by a racist, "scientific," secular dislike of the Jews. While Botz believes that Hitler and some who influenced him were driven by this latter view, he believes that a "more widespread anti-Semitism of an economic and religious nature" played a more important role in the twentieth century and was more deadly, since it influenced a much larger portion of the population. Examples of this are, according to Botz, the religiously based anti-Semitism of Christian Socialism and the anti-Jewish prejudices of even some Austrian Social Democrats, who associated Jews with capitalism. He believes that there were "relatively few non-Jews who were not unfavorably disposed to Jews or fiery anti-Semites" in the turn-of-the-century Habsburg monarchy or in the Austrian Republic that emerged after World War I. Austrian political culture was divided, much as Germany's was, between those who supported "the values of the enlightenment, civil rights, religious tolerance, social reform, artistic modernity, and the like" (the Jews) and those opposed to these values (non-Jews).

In assessing the levels of anti-Semitism in Germany and Austria, Botz believes conditions in Austria led to a more extreme dislike of Jews but relatively less persecution. Since Jews were more segregated, compared to Germany, they had fewer encounters with non-Jews and therefore suffered less. Botz cites Albert Lichtblau's study[1] of this separation that limited Jewish contact with non-Jews and, therefore, also reduced the humiliations and physical assaults meted out by the Nazis elsewhere. Some, as we will discuss later, did not begin to suffer until after the Nazi takeover in 1938. Jews lived primarily in a few districts in Vienna, where they developed "a culturally diverse, specifically Jewish milieu." Few Jews lived outside Vienna, and those who did, Botz argues, were, in comparison to German Jews, "less culturally integrated" but "were subjected to stronger social pressures for cultural integration and displayed a relatively strong tendency toward assimilation and religious conversion." This description begs for additional information and evaluation, since it would be logical to assume that Austrian Jews would have been more integrated since they were more heavily pressured to integrate.

Although there is overwhelming scholarly agreement that Vienna was an extremely anti-Semitic environment, a recent study by Brigitte Hamann[2] disagrees with Botz's assessment that Hitler's anti-Semitism "was molded in Vienna." Her assessment that his anti-Semitism did not originate in Vienna is based upon the viewpoint that Hitler adopted anti-Semitism in 1918–1919 because it was politically profitable to do so. She contends that he defended Jews during these years in Vienna and even had Jewish friends. Yet her acknowledgment that the anti-Semitism he eventually used had been learned in Vienna seems to seriously weaken her argument and support Botz's.

So, why did many Jews find Vienna a tolerable environment? According to Botz, they had been protected by Emperor Franz Josef and the civil rights granted by the Habsburg monarchy in 1867, which assigned every group its "appropriate" place (except for the Jews outside Vienna). Also, before World War I, extreme anti-Semitic groups remained small and ineffective, and the anti-Semitism of the Christian Socialists under Karl Lueger was more "politically opportunistic and economically instrumental." Finally, a large number of assimilated Jews became cultural leaders in Vienna. Botz refers in passing to Steven Beller's hypothesis that those "Jews who had climbed the social ladder to the bourgeoisie and the upper middle classes" and who "were favorably disposed to assimilation constituted, in fact, Vienna's 'liberal bourgeoisie.' "[3] It is unfortunate that space did not permit him to comment more fully on what is a disputed viewpoint. Marsha Rozenblit has argued that the fact of the small number of such Jews combined with Beller's narrow definition of this group, which eliminated the section of the middle class that was not "liberal," seriously undermines his argument that assimilated Jews were responsible for the cultural outpouring that characterized Vienna at the turn of the century.[4] She claims that the small number of Jews, only 175,000 in 1910, precluded their domination of Vienna's middle class.

Interwar economic and social problems brought increased hostility between Jewish and non-Jewish inhabitants. Even Social Democratic leaders, who had been among the few protectors of the Jews, called for the expulsion of the *Ostjuden* (Eastern European Jews). The Christian Socialists demanded an end to the "domination of destructive Jewish influence in spiritual matters and economic affairs." Some, including leaders such as the cleric Ignaz Seipel, called for restrictive hiring practices for Jews in public offices, quotas for Jews in the universities, and even internment. But even more destructive were the Austrian extremist nationalist groups, *völkisch* groups and Nazis who identified national identity with the German *Volk* and defined themselves "first and foremost in contrast to 'international Jewry.'" The fact that an extreme anti-Semitism existed outside Vienna, where few Jews existed, Botz ties directly to older Christian anti-Semitic images and provincial anti-modern and anti-Viennese feelings.

Some athletic clubs and alpinist associations joined with extremist *völkisch* groups and college fraternities to restrict membership to Aryans. Botz believes these actions would have gone further except that even the ruling elite needed support from Jewish industrialists and bankers as well as Western governments in the 1920s.

Opposition to Jews split in the 1930s between a "moderate" anti-Jewish Christian and a National Socialist *völkisch* anti-Semitism. Some anti-Jewish Christians attempted to counter the deadly *völkisch* anti-Semitism with a more moderate form of it that would steal the thunder from the Nazis. For example, even Jews found protection against Nazi attacks in Chancellor Dolfuss's authoritarian state. Although it carried out discriminatory measures against Jews, it "accepted the social and economic positions of the Jews and accorded a place to organizations representing Jewish interests within the Catholic model of a corporatist state."

Only with the Nazi *Anschluss* in 1938 did this situation change. Botz blames the outbreak of humiliations, deadly attacks, and confiscations of property that "went far beyond" anything that took place in Germany on the pent-up economic and political frustrations of a "petit bourgeoisie and middle class seeking, at the expense of the Jews, material and social indemnification and compensation for intellectual inferiority complexes."

Botz's previous research has shown that the Viennese violence was earlier and less orchestrated by Nazi officials. He contends, and there is little evidence to the contrary, that German Nazis had to control these chaotic attacks on the Jews in order not to rile international public opinion. Here, a fuller explanation of the difference between Austria and Germany would have been helpful. Were these economic and political frustrations so different? To what extent did "intellectual inferiority complexes" guide attacks on Jews?

Here and elsewhere Botz argues that Austrian bureaucratic procedures and organizations served as models for the Third Reich. Austrians pioneered bureaucratic coordination and the use of the persecuted in the process of their own destruction. Forcing Jews to emigrate and seizing their assets became a model for the Third Reich. One of the main motives was the confiscation of commercial assets of Jews (one-quarter of all businesses, and assets that exceeded the 1938 Austrian state budget). But perhaps more important in Botz's estimation was using Jewish-owned apartments to help solve a severe housing shortage in Vienna. Botz has argued convincingly in a previous work that the 70,000 Jewish-owned apartments in Vienna amounted to more housing units than those built from 1923 to 1933 by the "Red" Viennese government intent on solving the housing crisis. It would have been instructive had Botz had the space to comment more thoroughly on the social background of those involved in the confiscations. At one point he argues that they were the petit bourgeoisie and middle class, but at another point, those who wanted "to take the first step up the ladder to the petit bourgeoisie."

Viennese Nazi Party members were the first to advocate that Jews be deported to the *Generalgouvernement* in Polish-occupied territory when the war blocked further Jewish emigration. Adolf Eichmann's "Central Office for Jewish Emigration in Vienna," which combined bureaucratic coordination with the participation of the victims in their own destruction, proved to be the forerunner of the institutions of mass destruction in the Third Reich. In Austria, about 65,000 Jews died at Nazi hands, while another 126,000 fled. The inconsistency in the two figures Botz provides for the number of survivors in Vienna—600 or 5,700—undermines little his argument that Jews received limited protection in Austria. Even the Catholic Church directed its attention only to baptized Jews and those living in mixed marriages. Vienna became a city without Jews and remained so after the war.

Many of the 4,500 Austrian Jews who returned to Austria after the war could not tolerate the still-existing animosity among non-Jews. The "social gap separating Jews and non-Jews, which was as deep as it had been before 1938," persuaded many of these to leave Austria again. The Jewish community became primarily Jews from East-Central Europe, who had not experienced the anti-Jewish hostility of the prewar and wartime period. Botz believes that the public humiliations more than the confiscations of property persuaded Jews not to return to Austria. Not only the public, but Austrian politicians, including some Social Democrats who had protected Jews previously, met Jewish remigrants and refugees with rejection and anti-Semitism. Some Social Democrats claimed that the return of Jewish party members would "revive the old anti-Semitic accusations leveled at the Jewified Social Democracy." They must have been aware of the continued anti-Semitism among the masses and how this would play out politically. Botz shows that opinion polls indicated a strong anti-Semitism in the 1970s and 1980s, with a slight decline in the 1990s. Here it would have been helpful to have some comparative data with Germany and perhaps the United States. Although this is again asking Botz to do more than was possible in a short space, such a comparison would have indicated more clearly the extent of Austrian anti-Semitism. That this postwar hostility toward Jews had substance can be gleaned from Botz's data: over 100,000 Jewish refugees from Eastern Europe and countless displaced Jews passed through Austria, rather than remaining there. In the 1970s and 1980s another 360,000 Soviet Jews passed through Austria. Neither Austrian politicians nor the public, according to Botz, offered Jews any support. Social Democrats joined Catholic conservatives in an open rejection of efforts of Jews, including victims of the Holocaust, to return to Austria. The fact that Vienna's

Jewish population fluctuated between only 5,000 and 8,000 Jews during the entire postwar period indicates that Jews did not and still do not find Vienna a very hospitable environment.

This continuing postwar anti-Semitism, combined with Austria's long re- fusal to discuss indemnification for damages and to take responsibility for its role in the Holocaust, provides ample evidence of the continued hostility toward the Jews. Not until fifty years after 1945 was indemnification offered in the form of a National Fund for the victims of Nazism. Austria's claim of "victim" status made it possible, even necessary, to avoid making indemnifica- tion and to refuse to face their responsibility for their complicity. This "vic- tim" status, or convenient historical forgetting, made it more difficult for Aus- trians to accept the complicity of their postwar leaders in Nazi atrocities. When President Kurt Waldheim failed to remember his wartime experience in the Nazi SS, much of the public defended him and viewed the attack on him as being orchestrated by a Jewish-dominated world press. Only in the 1990s did an Austrian chancellor, Franz Vranitzky, admit Austrian responsibility for its role in the Nazi attacks on the Jews. Botz infers that such a change may be the result of Austrians' displacing their hatreds to other groups by "other forms of xenophobia—above all, hostility toward Gypsies, Serbs, and Rumanians." The recent growth of support for the xenophobic Freedom Party, led by Jörg Haider, supports Botz's observation concerning Austrian fears about increased immigration following a possible incorporation of Poles, Czechs, and Hungarians after the planned European Union expansion. Inter- estingly, Vranitzky's apology stated that Austria as a state was not responsi- ble for the deeds of the German Reich since it had ceased to exist and that there was persecution of and resistance by Austrian political elites. Botz rightly sees this statement as only a beginning step in repairing the relationship that "is still oppressed by the burdens of history and its human and material losses." One could see it further as a return of history, in that Austrians are now having to face up to their historical involvement in the Nazi Holo- caust.

For someone wishing to gain an outstanding introduction to and under- standing of the relationship between Jews and non-Jews in Austria, Botz's es- say, given the space limitations, would be an excellent place to start. After reading this essay, I would direct them to his other articles and books that have provided many of us with our understanding of Austrian anti-Semitism and National Socialism.

NOTES

1. Albert Lichtblau, *Antisemitismus und soziale Spannung in Berlin und Wien 1867–1914* (Berlin: Metropol, 1994).

2. Brigitte Hamann, *Hitler's Vienna: A Dictator's Apprenticeship*, trans. from German by Thomas Thornton (New York: Oxford, 1998).

3. Steven Beller, *Vienna and the Jews 1867–1938* (Cambridge: Cambridge University Press, 1989).

4. Marsha Rozenblit, *The Jews of Vienna 1867–1914: Assimilation and Identity* (Albany: State University of New York Press, 1983).

Who Is Jewish?
The Newest Jewish Writing in German and Daniel Goldhagen

Sander L. Gilman

Is There a "Jewish" Cultural Renaissance Today?

Recently, a rather pessimistic literature has appeared on the market, heralding the death of Diaspora Jewry in Europe. Typical of it is Bernard Wasserstein's study of European Jewry since the Shoah.[1] In a number of books and essays I have made an equally optimistic counter-argument, that Jewish culture in German and in Germany is establishing itself (again) as one of the most potent forces in the German cultural sphere.[2] I have stated that German Jewry is at the beginning of a radical explosion in terms of its cultural importance. It is evident, depending on how you define "the Jews" and "Jewish culture," that European Jewry is either vanishing or expanding.[3] Wasserstein and analogous critics create a sense of panic through their definition of "the Jews." I create a sense of positive development through my definition. The problem at the very beginning of this essay then must be—if I claim there is an expansion of Jewish culture in Germany, who are the Jews and what is the "Jewish culture" I am taking about?

"The Jews of Germany are vanishing." Soon, there will be no Jews left at all. They are intermarrying and they are immigrating. They have a very, very low birthrate and are not reproducing themselves. This is not only the thesis of Bernard Wasserstein's book; it was also the claim of the Jewish physician Felix Theilhaber in his *The Decline of the German Jews* (*Der Untergang der deutschen Juden*).[4] Written well before Oswald Spengler, but with the notion of decline firmly in place, Theilhaber's book was a best seller, as were the numerous books about the decline of the birthrate in France, England, Germany, and so on. What all of these discussions of the declining birthrate and the vanishing races did, of course, was to (1) label the group under discussion as victims under biological siege and (2) define them in a way that essentially limited who belonged to the group. Certainly the Jews in Germany before World War I were not vanishing—indeed, the only thing that was in debate in Theilhaber's books was, who is a Jew? And as an example of early Berlin Zionist rhetoric this book made sense. The "Jews" that Theilhaber saw were "vanishing" were the German Jews (in his definition); the Eastern European Jews living in Germany (his bête noire) were thriving, as he himself admits.

Let us begin, however, with the counter-argument to the present case as presented by Wasserstein. His is an odd book; it is what happens when one aspect of Jewish history, the history of disaster, becomes the dominant thread weaving through all Jewish history. Wasserstein has written a competent history of all of the bad things that happened to Jews in Europe after 1945 — what is missing is any evaluation of what is "bad" and whether some good things have been omitted from the narrative. His frame is the claim that the Jews of Europe are vanishing, and he compares them in his conclusion to the tiny community of Jews at Kai-fend, who were literally assimilated into Chinese culture over a thousand years. And yet even today their descendants still have some sense of themselves as different, perhaps even as Jews, given their claims for such an identity within the ethnic politics of the People's Republic of China.

Better, Wasserstein should have taken the case of the Jews of the Spanish peninsula, who were expelled in the fifteenth century—there, too, he would have found descendants who have only a vague sense of their difference. In Mexico there are still individuals who light a candle in a closet on Friday evening because it is a family tradition, but don't know from whence this tradition came. But there is also the world of Sephardic Judaism, ranging from secular ethnic Jews to ultra-orthodox ones. It is exploring the spectrum of Jewish experience that is important, not focusing on one aspect to the exclusion of all others. Here one can also draw an analogy to the difficulties of the Jews of the German-speaking world. If one narrowly describes the history of post-Shoah German-speaking Jewry, it seems a history of collapse and dissolution. Certainly the immediate postwar history seems to prefigure this model[5]—that is, if one defines "Jewry" only in ritual (halachic) terms. Who is a "Jew" is an important question in Germany, and the answer is virtually as complex as that of the Jews of the Spanish Diaspora.

Wasserstein prefaces his account with a tabulation[6] that computes the number of Jews in Europe. The commentary to this table—on which all of Wasserstein's argument rests—says that these numbers are of "varying reliability and in some cases are subject to a wide margin of error and interpretation." Wasserstein and I were just in Budapest at a meeting and had dinner with one of the community leaders there. According to Wasserstein's table in 1994 there were 56,000 Jews in Hungary, down from 80,000 in 1967. When I asked the community leader how many Jews there are in Budapest (where most of the Jews of Hungary now live), he said anywhere from 60,000 to 120,000—depending how you define who a Jew is. This is the crux of such arguments. They really should read: MY JEWS ARE VANISHING! For it is the definition of what is Jewish that is at the heart of Wasserstein's book. Even though he is aware of this problem and discusses it in the opening pages of the book, he falls back on crude biologism; a Jew is that person who is biologically/halachically (ritually) Jewish. And sadly, Wasserstein even uses the odd quasi-biological argument to buttress his thesis. He provides the argument that Anglo-Jewish women marry later[7] and marry out[8] to account for their "particularly low reproduction rate." He says similar things about French Jewry.[9] But marrying out decreases the number of Jews only if a strict religious definition of "Jewish" is taken, and even then the offspring of Jewish *women* are always Jewish!

The Jews of Europe are not vanishing! And certainly the Jews of the German-speaking world are not vanishing! Their numbers were reduced after the Shoah because of emigration to Israel and because of persecutions in Eastern Europe, but other (perhaps smaller) groups moved to Europe over time. The North African Jews moved to France, and the Russian Jews (no matter how defined) are now moving into the Federal Republic of Germany. Indeed, there is now a notable Israeli presence (Diaspora) in Europe, including in the Federal Republic. Russian immigration to Germany (and elsewhere in Europe) has meant a complex revitalization of Jewish communal and cultural life in even the small urban areas of the German-speaking world. And this world extends from the Federal Republic to Austria to German-speaking Switzerland. Jewish cultural visibility in mass and high culture there is at its highest point since the beginning decades of the century. Jewish culture in Germany is complex, self-contradictory, difficult—but exploding—and not just in terms of a romanticization of the Eastern European Jewish past or a "necrophilia" (a term that is used in Wasserstein's book and in the general discourse in today's Germany) for the victims of the Shoah and their culture.

Wasserstein, by the way, shares the bizarre neo-romantic German notion of Yiddish culture in Eastern Europe as klezmer and bagels. He sees it as "sentimental drama; haunting folk-songs and a dynamic newspaper press."[10] Where is Yiddish literary modernism, such as I. J. Singer, where is the political Yiddish culture of the Bund (which he even discusses), where is the complexity of Eastern European Yiddish life and culture in contact with the mainstream of Western European culture before the Holocaust?

The German situation is, in regard to the evocation of a romanticized Jewish past, even more complex. Michal Bodemann has argued that Jews in Germany are, or at least were for decades, virtual Jews; that is, there was such a need to imagine a Jewish presence in both the BRD and the GDR that the culture "created" a new Jewish identity separate from the actual presence of Jews.[11] But for non-Jewish and Jewish Germans, the model for this new Jewish identity was as much the American and Israeli experience of Jewish life as it was the German Jewish past. But Bodemann, like Erica Burgauer, recognizes that since the mid-1980s something has shifted in the presence and awareness of German culture (especially after reunification) concerning an active Jewish cultural presence.[12] What they seem to draw into question is the "authenticity" of this experience. It is the question of who determines what an authentic Jewish experience is (and who the "authentic" Jews are) that stands at the center of this discussion.

Wasserstein is not alone in creating the Jews he needs. I was sitting on a plane to Budapest in the summer of 1996, next to the leading Jewish bookseller in Germany. Her annual bibliographies form the core of any scholar's handy list of Jewish writers. We were talking about a wide range of writers, many of whom we both knew well. When I turned to the subject of one of them, a well-known and widely read woman playwright and novelist, she snapped at me: She's not Jewish—she doesn't even have a Jewish grandparent!

There lies the rub. If "Jewish" is defined by ritual and by practice, one set of discussions can be generated; if "Jewish" is defined by identity and self-understanding as well as reception, a totally different discussion takes place. Thus if one author has a Jewish mother and identifies herself as Jewish, there seems to be no problem. If another has a Jewish father and does the same, he is seen as somehow inauthentic. And if this identification is generations earlier, it is somehow even more inauthentic. In religious circles one of the major debates has to do with mixed marriages. The key word is that in mixed marriages the children are "lost" to their Jewish origins. Given the rejection of children of mixed marriages by the religious establishment, this is of little wonder. It is of even greater wonder (to me) that such children do sometimes come back and learn to understand and cherish their Jewish identity. Germany is a space (at least after 1989) where the badge of a Jewish identity has, at least in some circles, an added cachet. One can make an analogy to the "gain from illness" that the sociologists of medicine describe. The positive value of the status of the victim after the fact is part of the construction of the idea of the Jew in the German-speaking world. *And yet it is the very victim status that provides a critical edge for the cultural products dealing with being Jewish in the contemporary world, written by those who self-label or are labeled as Jews.* It has been striking (and now more scholars than myself recognize this) that there has been an explosion of such cultural manifestations of Jews in Germany, Austria, and Switzerland. Here it is the self-definition as Jews in the public (cultural) sphere through the creation of a Jewish persona of oneself as a writer, film maker, artist, or photographer and the dedication to the creation of artifacts that deal with what Dan Diner so insightfully called the "negative symbiosis" of being Jewish in Germany.[13]

The Goldhagen Debate: Setting the Stage

The debates about Jewish "authenticity" in the German-speaking world can be framed by the complex relationship of this world to the very notion of the Jews. Nowhere was this more clearly differentiated than in the initial German critical response to Daniel Goldhagen's *Hitler's Willing Executioners* before its publication in German in August of 1996.[14] This reception seems to be a litmus test of the new permissiveness that exists since reunification concerning public expression regarding aspects of the Shoah and the image of the Jews in Germany. The ability to talk about Jews in contemporary Germany as part of a contested present and in a complex and self-contradictory manner related to the past provides a frame for the images of today's Jews. The fact is that, as before the publication of the German translation in August 1996, there were more articles in *Die Zeit* (six) than in the *New York Times* (four). This is a mark of this new German fascination with the ability to finally expound in public about the Jews, here defined as *American* Jewish scholars, and their "preoccupation" with the Shoah. This is the context in which the most recent Jewish writing in German must be read. In the reception of Goldhagen's book it is not the "Jews" in general who bear the brunt of these attacks but "American Jews," defined in such a way as to define the absolute location of corruption and evil.

The linguistic taboos in place in the academy about Jews in general have been loosened since German reunification. When one German historian/historian of Germany who is non-Jewish (Hans Mommsen) can call another German historian/historian of Germany who is Jewish (Julius Schoeps) a "well poisoner" (*Brunnenvergifter*)[15] in the passion of a public debate about Goldhagen's book, one knows the standards have shifted. "Well poisoner" is an ancient libel about Jews and their general danger to the healthy non-Jewish body politic. And indeed, the debates about Daniel Goldhagen in Germany seem to permit the unvarnished use of a language of defamation rarely if ever heard in the halls of the German academy since 1945.

I find that the new polemical discussion about Daniel Goldhagen's American Jewish identity (rather than his book) reveals much more about the ability of the German academic public sphere to face up to their own long-term sense of intellectual and moral inferiority to their American colleagues than about any inherent desire to confront the issues raised by Goldhagen. As Goethe wrote, "America, you have it better"—at least you do not have to ask what your profession—the writing of history—did during the Holocaust! German scholars' claims that Goldhagen's book is "unscientific" because it arises out of his biography show the anxiety about the claims of objectivity and scientificity that haunt the writing of history in Germany (East and West) after the Shoah. Eberhard Jaeckel, professor of history at Stuttgart, makes this charge in his condemnation of Goldhagen's book as using "the most primitive of stereotypes" and reverting back to the primitive age of German historiography from the 1950s.[16] If the debates in the 1950s about the meaning and the origin of the Shoah were centered about the question of "collective guilt," they were also about the role that intellectuals and professionals played in the world of the Nazis. "What did you do in the war, Daddy?" "I wrote history, my son."[17]

Biography seems to be quite important in Germany during the discussion on Goldhagen's book, and it is "biography" that defines the role of the Jewish writer in contemporary German-language writing. You write what you experienced, and you therefore have a claim to a personal identity as a Jew but not a professional identity as a historian. What strikes me is that the discourse about Goldhagen concerns the constructed image of American Jews, not the "Jews" in general. And this theme reappears in an interesting way in modern Jewish writing in German. Perhaps here we have living proof of Dan Diner's point in his book on the German image of the Americans, in which he argues that America becomes a surrogate for the "Jews" in the nineteenth and twentieth century.[18] In this debate the "American Jew" becomes the locus of anxiety in a complicated way.

We can begin with the *enfant terrible* of German right-wing culture, Frank Schirrmacher, who, in two pieces in the *FAZ*,[19] condemned Goldhagen's book as creating a biologically essential image of the "Germans," which he certainly does not do. This clear misreading is strangely echoed by Eberhard Jaeckel's rather comic assumption that Goldhagen's evocation of an "anthropological" model is a biological one.[20] Since, as everyone knows, "anthropology is a sub-specialty of biology, which studies the inherited and not the acquired qualities of the human being," all anthropology is physical anthropology, because, of course, that is what the anthropology of race was in Germany before 1945. No other versions of anthropology seem to exist for Eberhard Jaeckel. (Actually Ingrid Gilcher-Holtey, professor of history at Bielefeld, quietly corrects this amazing gaff in her intelligent and sober discussion of Goldhagen's book as a prime example of the history of images, *mentalité,* in *Die Zeit.*)[21]

But it is necessary for Schirrmacher and Jaeckel to turn Goldhagen into — what? By accusing him of using a biological model for the writing of history, he is transformed into "Daddy" — those Nazi historians who truly did use a (for them completely "scientific") biological model to explain the glories of the Third Reich and the inherent inferiority of the Jews. The American Jew Daniel Goldhagen becomes the figure all historians of Jaeckel's generation fear — the "objective" Nazi historian, their own teachers and intellectual fathers. Goldhagen imagined as the new Jewish-American Nazi is a fascinating moment in the projection of a generation's anxieties. (It is also nothing new. "The Jews," then the Israelis, were labeled the new Nazis after the massacres in the refuge camps in Lebanon and during the Iraq war!)

If Goldhagen is the new "Nazi," who are his compatriots? Who is at fault for the popularity of Daniel Goldhagen's book? Frank Schirrmacher attributes the popularity of the book to "Jewish" critics in the United States. Here he joins the owner and editor of *Der Spiegel*, Rudolf Augstein, who wrote about the "mostly Jewish columnists" who were fueling the American debate on the book.[22] His article was titled "The Sociologist as Executioner," inverting the image of victim and murderer, and a picture of Goldhagen was subtitled "Hangman" Goldhagen. Who are these "American Jewish murderers," and why are they conspiring together against the "Germans"?

I have before me the typescript of the distinguished historian Hans-Ulrich Wehler's review/critique of Goldhagen's book.[23] I am a great admirer of Wehler's work. Unlike Schirrmacher, Wehler, professor of history at Bielefeld, is a serious historian of modern German history, whose scholarship is the basis for research throughout the world. Yet, given that, or precisely because, I admire Wehler's mind, I can read his essay as a space where the "American Jews" are indeed defined in ways similar to that of Schirrmacher.

Let me begin by noting that each of us creates the stereotype of the Jews she/he needs. Secular Jews such as myself tend to dismiss reactionary religious definitions and religious Jews contemptuous of cultural notions of Jewishness. Non-Jews create as many different Jews—smart Jews, national Jews, evil Jews, rapacious Jews—as they need. Such stereotypes are an extension of our way of organizing the world and reveal our sense of its inherent order. But what sort of "American Jews" do the most recent critics in Germany need to have?

First, they are conspiratorial and vindictive.

Second, they lie.

These are trademarks of classical anti-Semitism. It seems to be impossible to construct the "Jews" without evoking such tropes. Let us look at Wehler's presentation of this argument. Seeing Goldhagen as a prototypical vengeful Jew (Shylock with a Harvard degree), he writes:

> Should we not attempt to explain the almost complete extermination of the North American Indians from various different conditions and motives? Or should we capitulate and allow a young Navajo historian to derive everything from the tradition of "American murderers" beginning with the puritan branding of the red-skinned "children of Satan"—leading to My Lai?

> [Sollten wir die nahezuvollendte Ausrottung der nordamerikanschen Indianer nicht wenigstens aus sehr unterschiedlichen Bedingungen und Motiven zu erklären versuchen, sondern gleich aufgeben und es einem jungen Navajo-Historiker überlassen, alles aus dem Tradition "amerikanischen Killertums" seit der puritanischen Brandmarkung der rothäutigen "Kinder des Satans" abzuleiten—mit Folgerungen für My Lai?][24]

This passage is remarkable in its construction of the vindictive American Jew as "Indian." It is only because his Jewish nature is colored by his experience, by the prejudice he feels, that he feels himself constrained to act out. He is a historian, but only, of course, in name. Real historians have objective reasons for selecting their objects. The only possible reason for such a personal and vindictive approach to the "murderers" is personal history. One of the most interesting questions one must ask of every historian is how he/she selects a topic. Each historian or critic selects objects that are meaningful for her/him—not only Jewish historians of the Holocaust. Even German historians of the Holocaust.

But even more, for me, is the selection of the Native American image as the basis for Wehler's analogy—for it is not the Sabra and the Palestinians who are evoked in this passage but the American Jew. It is not that Wehler is creating a "you are as bad as us" scenario. He is too smart for that. But he does imply that the American Jew is as little a part of the "real" American Holocaust, the murder of the native Americans, as he is part of the "real" Shoah. The American Jew was spared the Holocaust, as Philip Roth has shown over and over again, and now desires to have the gain from the status of victim that the "real" victims have. It is not just that Goldhagen has the "blessings of a late birth," but that that birth was in the United States, where, unlike the Native American, he cannot claim victim status.

This trope reappears in odd places in the Goldhagen reception in Germany. Thus in the issue of *Der Spiegel* whose cover story is devoted to Goldhagen, the German Jewish gadfly Henryk Broder writes:

> If Daniel Goldhagen had been the child of a Texan cattle breeder and if he had gotten his doctorate writing about the Holocaust as others have writing about the American Civil War, things would be simpler. But he is the son of a Jewish intellectual, who would most probably have been a German professor had Hitler not intervened.

> [Wäre Daniel Goldhagen der Sohn eines texanischen Rinderzüchters und hätte er über den Holocaust promoviert, so wie andere über den amerikanischen Bürgerkrieg, wäre die Sache einfach. Aber er ist der Sohn eines jüdischen Intellektuellen, der wahrscheinlich ein deutscher Professor geworden wäre, hätte Hitler nicht interveniert.][25]

The move from native American to American cowboy is only a slight displacement. But it is a necessary one. This comes to be a Jewish reading of the Goldhagen "problem" in a German context. Are American Jews real Jews? Or are they inauthentic because they are neither Shoah survivors nor Israelis? Are they really just like cowboys or Indians? Is the survivor's child different, as the Native American historian would be different, not because of his own experience, but because of his identification with the history of his father, who is a survivor? Why the Wild West analogies anyhow?

Here the "German" construction of the American Jew is shared by Jew and non-Jew alike in Germany. It is Karl May's *Amerika*, with toy pistols and over-sized cowboy hats. But this Wild West is read differently by Wehler and by Broder. And yet for both the American Jew becomes the powerful surrogate for the *Amis*—the intellectual occupying power that dominated (and dominates) German historical consciousness in its every manifestation, from pop culture to academic discourse. And it is the American historian who must, therefore, be seen as corrupt and as unscholarly for German historiography to again lay claim to the objective writing of the history of—the perpetrator. Here too is a further violation of the taboo. Goldhagen has the temerity to write as a Jew about the murderers—not as he "should" about the victims. He becomes in this discourse the American as corrupt Jew, as Dan Diner has argued, and therefore, the perfect enemy.

American Jews lie, and in that way they fulfill the expectations of the anti-Semitic trope. Wehler puts Daniel Goldhagen in the same camp as other "false" Jewish American academics such as David Abraham, whose published dissertation on the roll of capital in the funding of the Nazis was dismissed as being based on invented documents, or Liah Greenfeld, whose comparative study of European nationalisms was denounced because it evoked the specter of the German *Sonderweg*. And now Daniel Goldhagen is on Wehler's list of— what is this a canon of? Certainly not bad historical scholarship by graduate students—that list would have to include too many German dissertations. It is not the canon of bad or evil scholarship on the Shoah—that list would have to begin with David Irving, and would need to continue through a very long list of works from French historians before it came to the trinity of Abraham, Greenfeld, and Goldhagen. What, oh what, could these three young AMERI-CAN JEWS have in common? They lie, of course, for lying is the special skill of the Jew in this rhetoric. They seem to be smart. They go to Harvard or teach at Princeton. But their intelligence is simply a mask for their mendacity. They are smart Jews within the age-old calumny that claims that Jewish superior intelligence is simply a cleverness designed to trick unsuspecting non-Jews.[26]

Wehler's selection is unconscious. He underlines this by including in his list of good historians of the Shoah Jews such as Alex Bein, George Mosse, Shulamit Volkov, Leon Poliakov, and the like. But there is not one "American Jew" on his list. German Jewish émigrés, Israelis, but not one American Jew is to be found among a longer list of good, non-Jewish historians. Now George Mosse is, of course, more American than anyone else I know. He has shaped the study of Germany in the United States for five decades, and I am in his deepest debt, as are all American historians of Germany. But for Germans, as can be seen in Irene Runge's long interview with him, he remains a *German* Jew.[27] The canon of lying Jews are all American Jews in this construction.

The German response to Daniel Goldhagen's book is a clear attempt to break with the hegemony that America has had in defining the "Germans." It is not just that the book is controversial but that it permits a discussion to take place that has been lacking over the past four decades. How are the Americans seen? Are they indeed dominated by the Jews, as German right-wing propaganda has said all along? Why does the *New York Times* seem always to have a "German" page in which anti-Semitic or xenophobic incidents are next to essays on German accomplishments? We know—and we can see how Jewish writers began to relate to this set of anti-Semitic tropes well before Goldhagen's work appeared on the scene.

Three Young Jews Writing

Such a frame of cultural projection on the part of Diaspora Jews who find the re-emergence of Jewish culture an imponderable and on the part of contemporary German intellectuals who are now able to localize and articulate their anxiety about Jews and Jewishness can frame the complexity of Jewish writing in contemporary Germany—and not surprisingly a few of its themes. In this section I will turn to look at three first books by some of the youngest authors in German to make the claim of a Jewish identity and articulate it in their writing. Not by accident they represent three quite "different" national voices: that of Austria (read: Vienna), Switzerland (read: Zurich), and East Berlin (that artifact now called one of the "new states," Berlin, but still truly the mirror of West Berlin). All three have specific tales to tell, and all use a voice that is authentic and appropriate for their own fantasy of what it means to sound Jewish. All three of them are men. A variation on this theme is to be found if one looks (as I have done in my earlier publications on this theme) at first books by Jewish women writers who are writing on the negative symbiosis of the Jews in contemporary Germany.

One place to begin is with the first novel of the new Jewish writing in German Switzerland. Daniel Ganzfried's first novel, *Der Absender* (The Sender), appeared in 1995.[28] Ganzfried was born in Israel in 1958 and grew up in Wabern near Bern. His novel recapitulates the theme of America as the topography (and antithesis) of Jewish identity in the contemporary world. The first strand of the novel is that the protagonist, having grown up in Zurich, now finds himself in New York, working for a new Holocaust museum beginning to be developed in the city. His job is to listen to audio tapes made by survivors of the Shoah and use them to document the history of that event. One tape recounts the life of a Hungarian Jew from his childhood through his experience of the Shoah. The protagonist is convinced that he is listening to the life story of his estranged father. The second strand in the novel is the autobiography of the anonymous Hungarian Jew from his carefree childhood through the end of the Shoah. A third strand of the novel evolves as the son persuades the writer of the autobiography to come to New York and confronts him on the observation deck of the Empire State Building. We never learn whether the "Absender" of the title was the father after all.

It is clear that Ganzfried is using "America" as the foil for the false consciousness of modern Jewry. The obsessive yet distanced relationship of his "America" to the Shoah (as opposed to the real relationship of European Jewry) forms the central theme of the novel's first strand. America does have it better—it is the superficiality and trendiness of American Jews that form the clear antithesis to the world of the Swiss Jews who are the children of survivors. American Jewish consciousness is represented by the planned Holocaust Museum in a city that never experienced the Holocaust except by viewing *Schindler's List.* Indeed the meeting at the top of the Empire State Building is taken from one of the classic 1990s romantic products of Hollywood, *Sleepless in Seattle,* which concludes with the reunion of the lovers on the observation deck of that building. The iconography of Hollywood *kitsch* is transformed into the unresolved meeting of father and son, survivor and seeker. Authentic Jewish experience is that of the displaced European (whether displaced to America or elsewhere in Europe), not the experience of "America."

One can contrast this text with other examples of the older Swiss-Jewish writing. There is a tradition of Diaspora writing in Swiss Jewish writing, perhaps best exemplified by the work of André Kaminski, especially his novel *Kiebitz*.[29] Like the work of Edgar Hilsenrath, Kaminski's comic novels use the world of the Jew in exile as their theme. Kaminski, who was born in 1923 and died in 1991, lived in Poland from 1945 to 1968, when he was expelled. Following his expulsion he lived in Israel and both northern and southern Africa. For the final years of his life he lived in Zurich and produced a wide range of work using the figure of the Eastern European Jew in the western European Diaspora as his theme. *Kiebitz* is written as a dialogue in letters between a Swiss German psychiatrist and Gideon Esdur Kiebitz, a Polish Jew living in Switzerland, who has lost the power of speech.

What is striking about both Kaminski's novel of 1991 and Ganzfried's novel of 1995 is how they deal with precisely the types of stereotypes that dominate the response to the Goldhagen affair. Certainly the central trope of the Goldhagen affair is that Goldhagen claims to be a smart Jew but is in fact a lying Jew. Kaminski bemoans the fact that God has damned the Jews as smart Jews:

> It is Jewish bad luck, he moaned. Yes, we are a chosen people, the luckiest in the history of the world. God always distinguishes us. He makes pianists out of us, chess world masters, Noble Prize winners in physics and medicine. But have you every heard of a Jewish boxing champion? A Jewish shooting king? Are we ready for war? Naturally not.

> [Ein wahrhaft jüdisches Pech, stöhnte er. Dabei sind wir doch ein auserwähltes Volk, die Glückspilzeder der Weltgeschichte. Gott zeichnet uns unetwegt aus. Pianisten macht er aus uns, Schachweltmeister, Nobelpreisträger der Physik und Medizin. Aber hat man je einen jüdischen Meisterboxer gesehen? Einen jüdischen Schützenkönig? Sind wir denn für Kriegszeiten gerüstet? Natürlich nicht.][30]

Or in an exchange with a non-Jew:

> "I said something, Ariel."
> "What?"
> "That you Jews always know more than we do."
> "Naturally."
> "Why naturally?"
> "That is our secret."

> ["Ich hab' was gesagt, Ariel."
> "Was?"
> "Daß ihr Juden immer mehr wißt als wir."
> "Natürlich."
> "Warum ist das natürlich?"
> "Das ist unser Geheimnis."][31]

"Smart Jews" is a trope from the complex vocabulary of the world that fears and thus stereotypes the Jews. Daniel Ganzfried's comment reverses this theme. He describes the narrative of the anonymous taped speaker's schooling in Hungary and his teacher's conviction that there are "two kinds of Jews: either the very smart or the very dumb. Sadly, I couldn't figure out what he was talking about, because of the Jews I knew none could have been placed in one or the other group" [zwei Arten von Juden, die es gebe: entweder sehr gescheiten oder sehr dummen. Leider konnte ich mir darauf keinen Reim machen, denn von den Juden, die ich kannte, hätte ich niemanden eindeutig einer der zwei Gruppen zuordenen können].[32] The naiveté of the schoolboy immediately deflates the claims of the smart (and stupid) Jew. For being smart, as Ganzfried knows, is not a form of praise but of difference and of opprobrium.

Ganzfried plays with the complexity of a Jewish child's dislocation in trying to fit the model of the smart Jew to the experiences of his world. He is aware of the complex history of the meaning of Jewish difference, specifically the meaning of the circumcised male body. Again, the anonymous narrator on the tape recounts his baptism as a child by a Christian nanny, which he is quite aware does not change him. His Christian friend, following a sports hour in school, has him pull down his gym pants and remarks: "Now look, not a trace of a Christian!" [Na seht ihr, keine Spur von Christ!]. His circumcision remains unrecuperated through the baptism. He remains a Jew no matter what his religion.[33] Such a biological argument is the sort of image that Jaeckel sees in his image of Jews and anthropology. It is an affirmation that such models are to be dealt with only retrospectively and still need to be undermined.

Thus the biological model of the Jew as a race is closely related in the 1930s and 1940s to the parallel image of the Jews as the source of social and societal disease. Ganzfried's taped narrator, embedded in the discourse of the 1940s, turns this image about. When the Hungarian Jews are forced to wear the Yellow Star, "I bore the mark as if it were a deformation from a terrible illness" [ich trug die Marke wie eine Entstellung aus schwerer Krankheit].[34] It is the Yellow Star that is the sign of disease, and it deforms the healthy Jews. Ganzfried is quite aware that the world of the past, with all of its pitfalls, is parallel to the world of the present. The tape exists as an artifact of the present, not of the past. And the complex question of memory and identity raised by the anonymous narrator and his story needs to be the bridge through which father and son are to be reconciled. Ganzfried uses these images taken from the German discourse of the past, but present in the German discourse of the present, to highlight that continuity and the "negative symbiosis" that Jews experience (even) in the world of Swiss Jewry.

The Viennese parallel to Ganzfried's text is that of Doron Rabinovici, whose volume of short stories, *Papirnik,* appeared in 1994.[35] Rabinovici stands very much in the tradition of the contemporary Viennese Jewish writing best repre-

298 | *Sander L. Gilman*

sented by the work of Robert Schindel (to whom the volume is co-dedicated) and Robert Manesse. Born in Israel in 1961, he came to Vienna in 1964 and did doctoral work in history there. This volume finds its authentic space not in America but in Vienna, a Vienna virtually completely masked in these tales but appearing with bits of local color, as in the image of the statue of the anti-Semitic mayor of Vienna, Karl Lueger, or the plague column in the middle of Vienna that haunts the text.

The distinction between an authentic space (Zurich, Vienna) and an in-authentic space is important to these young Jewish writers in German. And the inauthentic space is, simply put, America. In the very beginning of the most telling of these tales, "Der richtige Riecher" (The Right Smeller), a complex tale about smart Jews and Jewish noses, the Austrian Jewish protagonist, Amos, is confronted by a group of neo-Nazis, who taunt him with the line: "If you don't like it go to Israel—or to New York" [Wenn es euch hier nicht paßt, dann geht doch nach Israel—oder nach New York].[36] "New York is more fun," he is later told in English by a Jewish professor from Columbia University, but Amos wants to do his *Matura* (high-school-leaving certificate) in Israel, not New York. For Israel is the authentic place of Jewish experience. Israel, the Jewish professor from New York says, is indeed the place of purification for American Jews, who can travel to Israel to escape the conflicts in Brooklyn, where the Jews hate the Blacks, to Israel, where the Jews can hate the Arabs "with still better reasons" [mit noch besseren Gründen].[37] This ironic sense of an American Jewish inauthenticity highlights the reality of Vienna as the place of testing of "real" Jews.

Central to this story is the trope of the "smart Jew." For part of this image is the antithesis between "intelligence" and "strength." If you are smart, the trope has it, you cannot be strong. You must use your mind, not your fists. Who, as Kaminski's character notes, has ever heard of a Jewish boxer? (Many of us have, from Daniel Mendoza to Barney Ross, but that is not the point.) Amos does not make *aliyah*. He remains in Vienna and is forced to confront the anti-Semites on a daily basis. "We don't hate the Jews," they say, "the Jews hate us."[38] This constant overt anti-Semitism presents quite a different tone than does Ganzfried's sense of the Swiss world that his narrator leaves for New York. When a fellow student, Helmut, tells Amos that they should have gassed him in Mauthausen, Amos's response is to talk rationally to him. Amos's mother's reaction is that he should beat him up. But he doesn't want to do so, he wants to rely on rational means, discussion and argument. He wants to be a smart Jew, not a tough Jew.

His non-Jewish "friend" Peter, tall and handsome, observes to him that not all Jews stink, only Polish Jews, and when Amos says that his mother is a Polish Jew, Peter's response is "Oh, I am so sorry" [Oh, das tut mir leid].[39] Anti-Semitic comments are the stuff of daily exchange in this masked city of Vienna. On his walk through the Viennese pedestrian zone, Amos is confronted with the plague column representing the medieval black death and thinks of the Jews driven from the city because of the accusation that they had poisoned wells and caused the plague. The well poisoners, as we saw in the discussion of Goldhagen, today come again to be the Jews.

When Peter continues the quasi-liberal, anti-Semitic line, saying that while anti-Semitism is "naturally not to be excused, but when I look at the orthodox: why must they always separate themselves so? They don't have to run around looking like that. Also: why do they only accept those who are circumcised?" [natürlich unentschuldbar, aber wenn ich die Orthodoxen sehe: Warum müssen sie sich immer so absondern? Sie müssen nicht unbedingt so herumlaufen. Außerdem: Warum akzeptieren sie nur, wer beschnitten ist?],[40] here the line has finally been crossed. As in Ganzfried's text, it is the response to these classic anti-Semitic tropes that the narrator uses to set his discourse apart from that of the past. At this moment, Amos finally stops his rational responses and punches Peter in the nose: "the classic straight line which had up to then marked his organ of smell was forever changed and bent" [Die klassische Geradlinigkeit, die sein Riechorgan bisher ausgezeichnet hatte, war dahin und genickt] and Amos becomes the hero of his family "with a single blow" [mit einem Schlag].[41] Peter's classic Aryan profile becomes a marked one, marked not with the Jewish nose, but with the physical mark of his anti-Semitism. In a visible way Amos has marked him as an anti-Semite.

Rabinovici uses a very different style than does Ganzfried. Where Ganzfried adopts a pseudo-realistic tone, Rabinovici uses the language of the young German Jewish short-story writer Maxim Biller, always on the edge of a surreal moment. Space especially becomes the point of contention. And yet in both the realms of Ganzfried's New York and Hungary and Zurich and the almost Borges-like image of Rabinovici's Vienna, the question of an authentic space for the expression of a Jewish narrative in German stands at its center. America may be "fun," but the experiences there (and perhaps also in Israel) are not those that confront the daily topography of the Shoah on its own grounds. This is the authenticity that Ganzfried and Rabinovici claim for themselves, for their characters, and for their readers, whether Jewish or not.

In Benjamin Stein's first novel *Das Alphabet des Juda Liva* (The Alphabet of Juda Liva), published in 1995, the response to ideas of Jewishness and narrative space are overt.[42] Stein was born in 1970 in East Berlin and now lives in Berlin and Munich. He has won a number of fellowships, including the prized Alfred-Doeblin Fellowship of the Academy of the Arts. His novel is seemingly shaped by the discourse of Latin American magic realism. It moves, through the creation of a Jewish narrator, from contemporary Berlin (after reunification) to late medieval Prague. The frame is that the protagonist hires a story teller to come on weekly passes and provide his wife with an ongoing tale. It is story-telling in a Jewish vein that is at the center of this tale. The language of this novel seems to be shaped by the vocabulary of the kabbalah, indeed so much so that, following the model of many "Jewish" works of contemporary German fiction, it concludes with a glossary of terms for its evidently non-Jewish audience. Here the authenticity of the fictive topography seems to be guaranteed by the authenticity of the language of the narration.

But the "Jewishness" of this voice is suspect specifically because it makes such demands on the very idea of authenticity. Stein's novel stands in a narrative tradition of the German Democratic Republic, which is being continued here with a massive dose of Jewish mysticism. Beginning with Johannes Bobrowski's brilliant and original *Levins Mühle* (1964), written by an avowed Lutheran writer in the GDR, it continues through the first "Jewish" novel in the GDR, that is, a novel with a Jewish protagonist written by a Jewish writer, Jurek Becker's *Jakob der Lügner* (Jacob the Liar) (1969). In both of these texts we have complex narrative strands that demand the presence of a palpable "Jewish" voice in the text. What makes the voice "Jewish" is its claim to stand in a narrative tradition of a folkloric, Yiddish narrative, such as that of Sholem Aleichem. Indeed, it is the musical *Fiddler on the Roof,* in its Felsenstein version at the East Berlin *Komische Oper,* that has stood midwife to this novel as much as anything else.

Stein's novel, with its magical movements between levels of narrative, uses a self-combusting narrator who moves from contemporary Berlin to medieval Prague through his tale. He picks up these GDR traditions of representing a Jewish discourse. But physically the narrator also picks up on the image of the Jewish body and that of the smart Jew. For like the protagonist of Becker's novel, the narrator (not Jacob) is the smart Jew, insightful into the past and knowledgeable about the present. But Stein's narrator is also physically marked as the Jew of the anti-Semite's nightmares. He is described by the narrator as "neglectedly bearded and bow-legged" [verwahrlost bärtig und O-beinig][43] when we are first introduced to him. Again it is the physicality of the Jew that marks his difference and is used in the novel to delineate Jewish particularity.

Stein's novel uses in a more complex narrative form the idea of an internal Jewish narrative form taken from kabbalah, but it reveals itself to be a German literary response to the world. Here it is Prague that is the antithesis of Germany. The space of non-authenticity is Germany; that of authenticity for Jewish discourse remains Prague. It would seem that the antithesis between modernity and the past, between Berlin and Prague, escapes the "American" curse. But it is actually a trope taken from American Jewish writing of the 1980s. Both Philip Roth (*The Prague Orgy*) and Saul Bellow (*The Dean's December*) place the search for Jewish authenticity in the present in Prague.[44] Thus the Prague that Stein's novel represents is not only that of *Der Golem* (both Gustav Meyrink's 1915 novel and Paul Wegener's 1920 film), but also the American recapitulation of this theme in the 1980s, the notion of Prague as the Jewish space of experience as seen from the world of American Jewish letters. The authenticity of Prague is a place of Jewish trial. This is certainly the case in Stein's novel, even with its movement into the Middle Ages as a contrast to the Berlin of post-reunification Germany.

America, you have it better—certainly these three writers reverse this claim while honoring it. America is fun for the Jews—they become powerful, win Nobel prizes, and engage in the building of cultural institutions such as a video archive of the Holocaust. They are smart Jews, but they are not tough Jews. They have it easy. Superficial and not engaged in the reconstitution of a new Jewish culture, for "Jewish" culture in America has become mainstream culture. Since the American Jewish culture has never been destroyed, these young writers in Zurich, Vienna, and Berlin/Munich confront the literary tradition of American Jewry as well as the anti-Semitism present in their own culture. These three first books show a new level of awareness among the youngest Jewish writers in German of the complex world of images and texts in which they live and which they employ in complex ways in their texts. Is there a new Jewish culture developing in the German-speaking world? Evidently so!

NOTES

1. Bernard Wasserstein, *Vanishing Diaspora: the Jews in Europe since 1945* (Cambridge, Mass.: Harvard University Press, 1996).

2. See Sander L. Gilman and Karen Remmler, *Reemerging Jewish Culture in Germany: Life and Literature since 1989* (New York: New York University Press, 1994), and Sander L. Gilman, *Jews in Today's German Culture,* Schwartz Lectures (Bloomington: Indiana University Press, 1995).

3. Thomas Nolden, *Junge jüdische Literatur: Konzentriertes Schrieben in der Gegenwart* (Würzburg: Königshausen und Neumann, 1995).

4. Felix Theilhaber, *Der Untergang der deutschen Juden: eine volkswirtschaftliche Studie* (Munich: E. Reinhardt, 1911).

5. Michael Brenner, *Nach dem Holocaust: Juden in Deutschland 1945–1950* (München: Beck, 1995).

6. Wasserstein, viii.

7. Ibid., 73.

8. Ibid., 74.

9. Ibid., 243.

10. Ibid., 6.

11. Y. Michal Bodemann, *Gedächtnistheater: die jüdische Gemeinschaft und ihre deutsche Erfindung* (Hamburg: Rotbuch Verlag, 1996); Y. Michal Bodemann, ed., *Jews, Germans, Memory: Reconstructions of Jewish Life in Germany* (Ann Arbor: University of Michigan Press, 1996).

12. Erica Burgauer, *Zwischen Erinnerung und Verdrangung—Juden in Deutschland nach 1945* (Reinbek bei Hamburg: Rowohlts Enzyklopadie, 1993).

13. The term is from Dan Diner, "Negative Symbiose: Deutsche und Juden nach Auschwitz," *Babylon* 1 (1986): 9–20. On its applicability in the present context see Jack Zipes, "Die kulturellen Operation von Deutschen und Juden im Spiegel der neueren deutschen Literatur," *Babylon* 8 (1990): 34–44; Klaus Briegleb, "Negative Symbiose," in *Gegenwartslit-*

eratur seit 1968, ed. Klaus Briegleb and Sigrid Weigel (Munich: Hanser, 1992), 117–152; Hans Schütz, *Juden in der deutschen Literatur* (Munich: Piper, 1992), 309–329.

14. Daniel Goldhagen, *Hitler's Willing Executioners: Ordinary Germans and the Holocaust* (New York: Knopf, 1996.)

15. *Frankfurt Allgemeine Zeitung,* June 6, 1996.

16. *Die Zeit,* May 17, 1996.

17. To frame any discussion of the meaning of the Jews in the cultural life of the new Germany, such projections and attitudes on the part of the German intellectuals must be taken seriously. However, let me begin by stating my own views about the various theses represented by Goldhagen's book, and then, I hope, my "hidden agenda" will become evident. Like Goldhagen, I believe that mass education can inculcate negative images or stereotypes into various cultural groups and that individuals in such groups can respond to these images. However, I believe that the response can be either affirmative or critical. Thus the universal presence of negative images can potentially create as much resistance as it does advocacy, but it rarely does. Unlike Goldhagen, I believe that there is a complicated history of anti-Semitism (for me a blanket term for Jew Hatred) in the Christian West that is different from simple ubiquitous xenophobia. I see this as stemming from the very origins of Christianity and its constant need to distance itself from Judaism and the Jews. What Goldhagen views as eliminationist anti-Semitism is present in the early Church. Yet given the specificity of the self-conscious construction of a *Staatsnation* (in the sense of Friedrich Meinecke) in the place of a *Kulturnation* and the movement from the status and power of religious anti-Semitism to the new status of scientific racism at the close of the nineteenth century, the function of anti-Semitism in Germany is different from that in France or Austria. The *Sonderweg* debate, of whether Germany and "the Germans," however defined, were different in their specificity at the end of the nineteenth and beginning of the twentieth centuries, whether in their understanding of colonialism or the "Jewish Question," is not resolved. Indeed, comparative studies are beginning to pinpoint specifically the function of such stereotypes in understanding "German" culture, in contrast with other self-consciously constructed national and local cultures in Central Europe. This is not to say that nineteenth- and early-twentieth-century "German" culture in its construction of "Germanness," the "Germans," and the "Jews" was better or worse than in other national cultures, only that it fulfilled a different function. All of this means that, in my reading, the presence of what Goldhagen labels "eliminationist" (rather than exclusionist) anti-Semitism in Germany was necessary, but not sufficient, for the Shoah to take place.

18. Dan Diner, *America in the Eyes of the Germans: An Essay on Anti-Americanism* (Princeton, N.J.: Markus Wiener Publishers, 1996).

19. *Frankfurt Allgemeine Zeitung,* April 15 and April 30, 1996.

20. *Die Zeit,* May 17, 1996.

21. *Die Zeit,* June 7, 1996.

22. Rudolf Augstein, "The Sociologist as Executioner," *Der Spiegel* 16 (1996): 4.

23. *Die Zeit,* May 24, 1996.

24. Unpublished.

25. *Der Spiegel* 21 (1996): 59.

26. *Smart Jews: The Construction of the Idea of Jewish Superior Intelligence at the Other End of the Bell Curve,* Inaugural Abraham Lincoln Lectures (Lincoln: University of Nebraska Press, 1996).

27. George Mosse, *"Ich bleibe Emigrant": Gespräche mit George L. Mosse/Irene Runge, Uwe Stelbrink* (Berlin: Dietz, 1991).

28. Daniel Ganzfried, *Der Absender* (Zurich: Rotpunkt, 1995).

29. André Kaminski, *Die Garten des Mulay Abdallah: neun wahre Geschichten aus Afrika* (Frankfurt am Main: Suhrkamp, 1983); *Herzflattern: neun wilde Geschichten* (Frank-

furt am Main: Suhrkamp, 1984); *Nachstes Jahr in Jerusalem* (Frankfurt am Main: Insel Verlag, 1986); *Schalom allerseits: Tagebuch einer Deutschlandreise* (Frankfurt am Main: Insel, 1987); *Kiebitz* (Frankfurt am Main: Insel, 1988); *Flimmergeschichten* (Frankfurt am Main: Insel, 1990); *Der Sieg uber die Schwerkraft und andere Erzählungen* (Frankfurt am Main: Insel-Verlag, 1990).

30. Kaminski, *Kiebitz*, 99.

31. Ibid., 231.

32. Ibid., 79.

33. Ibid., 88–89.

34. Ibid., 147.

35. Doron Rabinovici, *Papirnik* (Frankfurt am Main: Suhrkamp, 1994). The stories are "Papirnik," "Ein Prolog," "Die Bank," "Noemi," "Sechsneunsechssechsneunneun," "Der richtige Riecher," "Ich schreibe Dir," "Uber die Säure des Regens," "Die Exekution," "Der Schauer und die Seherin," "Lola," "Ein Epilog".

36. Rabinovici, "Der richtige Riecher," 61.

37. Ibid., 63.

38. Ibid.

39. Ibid., 71.

40. Ibid., 72.

41. Ibid., 72–73.

42. Benjamin Stein, *Das Alphabet des Juda Liva* (Zurich: Ammann, 1995).

43. Ibid., 11.

44. Saul Bellow, *The Dean's December* (New York: Harper and Row, 1981); Philip Roth, *The Prague Orgy* (London: Cape, 1985), also as the epilogue to *Zuckerman Bound* (New York: Farrar Straus Giroux, 1985), comprising: *The Ghost Writer, Zuckerman Unbound, The Anatomy Lesson,* Epilogue: *The Prague Orgy.* See also Sepp L. Tiefenthaler, "American-Jewish Fiction: The Germanic Reception," in *Handbook of American-Jewish Literature: An Analytical Guide to Topics, Themes, and Sources,* ed. Lewis Fried, Gene Brown, Louis Harap (Westport, Conn.: Greenwood, 1988), 471–504.

22 What Is Cultural Identity?
Victoria J. Barnett

In REPLYING TO Sander Gilman's essay, I would like to open with Theodor Adorno's insight that the key to understanding anti-Semitism is not to study the Jews but to analyze the anti-Semites. "It is they," wrote Adorno, "who should be made conscious of the mechanisms that provoke their racial prejudice."[1] This is an especially useful exercise for Christians.

In Holocaust studies, the focus is often on Christian theology and teachings about Judaism. Today I would like to focus on another aspect: what the theologian Miroslav Volf has called the "sacralization of cultural identity."[2] In Volf's view, this means more than just church nationalism or the church's tradition of alignment with state authority. Perhaps the key word for our discussion is not "sacralization" but "cultural identity." The issue of cultural identity was at the heart of the so-called "Jewish question," which, of course, was really a "German question." In seeking to define themselves nationally, ethnically, culturally, and politically, Germans used the "Jewish question" as a way of defining who they were not. The role of "the other" in this situation is clear, as the work of numerous scholars, including Sander Gilman, has shown.

A number of issues arise here, but a central one in the historical context concerns the issue of assimilation. Who was "German?" How did they become "German?" It is interesting (some would say no coincidence) that the discussion about these questions in Germany intensified at the very time when many of the boundaries excluding Jews were being erased. Emancipation laws throughout Europe had altered the status of Jews and the educational and professional possibilities open to them. As more paths opened to them, many Jewish Germans embraced German culture and the notion of *"Bildung."*

During the same period, however, "racialized" thinking gained influence among scholars in a number of fields, in Germany and elsewhere. Anthropologists and medical professors began to measure skulls and noses, and scholars in many fields made pseudo-ethnic assumptions about things like the music, literature, and culture of different peoples.

This was the historical moment when, as Hannah Arendt put it, Judaism was replaced by "Jewishness."[3] Theories about "Jewishness" were mainstream society's retaining wall against full assimilation. Thus, even if Jews converted or became secularized, they remained "Jewish"—that is, not truly German.

Yet assimilation was a double-edged sword. For Jews, it required that they abandon their own identity in order to become part of a culture that devalued that identity. "Jewishness" was something to be discarded. Yet, when Jews actually did this, their readiness to assimilate was viewed as evidence of their poor moral fiber. In the late nineteenth century, German anti-Semites like Adolf Stoecker reserved their strongest attacks for secular Jews, not religiously observant ones.[4] What kind of people, he asked, would abandon the faith of their ancestors? — although that is precisely what mainstream German society was asking them to do. The result was a process that Volf describes as "exclusion by assimilation."[5]

Genuine assimilation was impossible because of the underlying prejudices that remained. In her study of the German village where she was born, Canadian anthropologist Frances Henry observes:

> Two aspects of integration led some Jews to the erroneous belief that they were as German as everybody else: their participation in the institutional structures of German society, particularly their entry into high-status occupations, and their belief in and subscription to the values of Germanness. Their social marginality, however, was indicated by their exclusion from social networks. . . . By maintaining not only their religious affiliations but also their traditional economic institutions, they perpetuated their identity as an ethnic group and were thus perceived, categorized and labeled as such by their Gentile neighbors. Both Jews and Gentiles observed their ethnic boundaries, reinforcing Jewish status as an observable, identifiable ethnic group.[6]

But the ramifications of this for Jews throughout Germany were painfully clear. One of the most successful German Jews was Walter Rathenau, who rose through the political ranks to become Weimar foreign minister before his assassination in 1922 by right-wing extremists. Yet even at the pinnacle of his career, Rathenau wrote:

> In the youth of every German Jew there is a painful moment that he remembers all his life: when for the first time he becomes fully aware that he came into the world as a second-class citizen, and that no amount of ability and no personal merit can free him from this situation.[7]

This factor, I think, helps explain the attention that Daniel Goldhagen's book *Hitler's Willing Executioners* received in Germany. In looking specifically at anti-Semitism, Goldhagen pinpointed its centrality in a way that hadn't been done before in Germany, despite the great effort and time many Germans have devoted to wrestling with their past. Moreover, Goldhagen's book appeared at a time when Germans were confronting the issue of identity anew because of unification and the large numbers of ethnic German immigrants from eastern Europe who have moved to Germany in the past ten years.

The problem is that Goldhagen doesn't really address the deeper question of how prejudice works, of how we become who we are because of our prejudices, and of how our sense of social self develops. What factors empower prejudice? What factors disarm it? One of the factors is certainly the issue of "identity"—as our talk of things like "assimilation" and "otherness" shows. It is intriguing to observe how, in the decades since the Holocaust, those previously defined as the "other" now insist on defining their identity themselves, in many cultures throughout the world. In a way, we live in an age of identity as self-defense. This is not just a legacy of the Holocaust, but of the aftermath of colonialism, of the impact of feminism and the civil rights movement in the United States, and of similar political developments throughout the world. It is what Octavio Paz once described as "revolt as the criticism of masks, the beginning of genuine dialogue, the creation of our own faces."[8] This liberating process, of course, was intended to *undo* the "sacralization of cultural identity"—but it hasn't quite worked out that way. Miroslav Volf, who writes about this, offers examples from his native land of Yugoslavia. But we can find examples throughout the world—from Sri Lanka, from Rwanda, and, to a less horrifying degree, from the United States—that all show that we are confronting the old question of how to achieve, in the words of South African theologian Charles Villa-Vicencio, "a unity that both recognizes and transcends our differences."[9]

All these questions may seem abstract. But, as the fate of six million European Jews shows, they are very existential questions, and when we discuss them, we are not dealing in abstractions.

NOTES

1. Theodor Adorno, Else Frenkel-Brunswik, Daniel Levinson, and R. Nevitt Sanford, *The Authoritarian Personality* (New York: Harper and Brothers, 1950), 128.

2. Miroslav Volf, *Exclusion and Embrace. A Theological Exploration of Identity, Otherness, and Reconciliation* (Nashville: Abingdon Press, 1996), 49.

3. Cited in Zygmunt Bauman, *Modernity and the Holocaust* (Ithaca: Cornell University Press, 1989), 59.

4. See Eberhard Bethge, "Adolf Stoecker und der kirchliche Antisemitismus," in *Am gegebenen Ort: Aufsätze und Reden 1970–1979* (Munich: Christian Kaiser Verlag, 1979), 202ff.

5. Volf, 75.

6. Frances Henry, *Victims and Neighbors: A Small Town in Nazi Germany Remembered* (South Hadley, Mass.: Bergin and Garvey, 1984), 164.

7. In Monika Richarz, ed., *Jewish Life in Germany* (Bloomington: Indiana University Press, 1991), 25.

8. Octavio Paz, *Alternating Current* (New York: Viking Press, 1973), 202.

9. Charles Villa-Vicencio, "Telling One Another Stories," in *The Reconciliation of Peoples,* ed. Gregory Baum and Harold Wells (Maryknoll, N.Y.: Orbis Books, 1997), 31.

23 | Poland and the Memory of the Holocaust

Michael C. Steinlauf

NEITHER PERPETRATORS OF the Holocaust nor its victims, Poles were its ultimate, paradigmatic witnesses. Certainly, a handful of Poles saved Jews, some Poles blackmailed, denounced, even murdered Jews, but what characterized Polish experience as a whole was witnessing, and this even as Poles themselves were the objects of intense persecution. It is Poles who saw the ghetto walls go up and watched their neighbors imprisoned behind them. Poles watched the ghettos burn, saw their neighbors herded into sealed trains, watched the "transports" arrive at their destination, smelled the smoke of the crematoriums, witnessed the hunting of escapees. Individual impressions were confirmed by the accounts of family and friends and by the underground press. It should not have been difficult for Poles to conclude that they were witnessing the attempt to murder every Jew in Poland, perhaps every Jew in Europe.

Should it surprise us that this experience was not easily comprehended, not fully witnessed? The inability to accept, to assimilate, to grasp, that is, truly to witness the events of the Holocaust as they were occurring was not unique to Poles. It was inherent in the incredulous response of Americans who read the news of death camps, printed only in the corners of their newspapers because the editors, in turn, had found the information too "unbelievable" to put on page one; it was true of many of the perpetrators, the bureaucrats who did not want to know and were systematically kept from knowing the truth, carefully cloaked in euphemisms; it applied to Jews in the ghettos, who assumed that making themselves useful to the Germans would guarantee survival, and later, when they entered gas chambers believing they were showers; and it was true of the survivors, who typically questioned whether they could bear witness to themselves, much less to the world, about what they had experienced.[1]

If the failure to witness the Holocaust was common to all its contemporaries, then its surviving victims, perpetrators, and bystanders have all, in the years since the Holocaust, had to cope with the consequences of this failure. As we are only now beginning to understand, the unwitnessed event haunts us all; long after its historical terminus, its imprint remains in our consciousness and behavior, affects the shape of our politics and culture.[2]

How to approach the Polish experience of the Holocaust, this case of witnessing in extremis? Here I have found particularly useful the work of Robert

Jay Lifton, who has devoted decades to studying the effects of massive, traumatic exposure to death in various contexts, including the Holocaust. In his work of synthesis, *The Broken Connection: On Death and the Continuity of Life,* Lifton summarizes several "characteristic themes" or "struggles" within the survivors of massive death trauma. First is what he terms the "death imprint." This is "the radical intrusion of an image-feeling of threat or end to life." The more extreme, protracted, grotesque, absurd, or otherwise unacceptable is the image of death, the more unassimilable is the death imprint and the more anxiety it evokes. Second is "death guilt." It arises from the encounter with a situation in which the possibilities for physical and even psychic response are non-existent. "One feels responsible for what one has not done, for what one has not felt, and above all for the gap between that physical and psychic inactivation and what one felt called upon . . . to do and feel." What Lifton calls "the heart of the traumatic syndrome" is "psychic numbing." These are strategies, often involuntary and unconscious, that diminish the capacity to feel, that is, to witness. They include images of denial as well as, for example, the strategy of "interruption of identification ('I see you dying, but I am not related to you or to your death')." Psychic numbing severs the self "from its own history, from its grounding in such psychic forms as compassion for others, communal involvement, and other ultimate values. . . . [Since it] undermines the most fundamental psychic processes . . . we can speak of it as the essential mechanism of mental disorder." Psychic numbing is characteristically accompanied by anger, rage, and violence, through which the survivor attempts to regain some sense of vitality. It is also accompanied by a symptom that Freud first noted and termed the "repetition compulsion." Unable fully to witness the traumatic experience, the survivor obsessively repeats images and even behavior associated with it. Ultimately, the survivor struggles toward what Lifton calls "formulation," a restructuring of the psyche, its values and symbols, that includes the traumatic image. This, ideally, is a process that ends in psychic and moral renewal. But what happens if this healing is blocked? Our own century offers examples of entire societies that have experienced massive death trauma without the opportunity for renewal. The consequences have been a reinforcement of guilt, denial, anger, and aggression, what Lifton calls "a vicious circle of unmastered history."[3]

Now to apply this paradigm to Polish history, we have to modify it in several ways, which, however, seem to reinforce it. This above all concerns the role of guilt. For Poles, the sense of guilt in witnessing the destruction of the Jews not only was the result of helplessness before the machinery of murder, of "death guilt," but also was evoked by two factors rooted in the specific history of Polish-Jewish relations.

First was the Polish attitude to Jews before the war.[4] By the 1930s and continuing throughout the war, the great majority of Poles, to put it most simply, did not like Jews. Whether this dislike was the result of prewar Jewish economic power or Jewish sympathy for Bolshevism, whether it emerged out of Church doctrine or the ideology of exclusivist nationalism or Nazi propaganda, whether or not, in short, it depended on anything the Jews actually did, does not matter in this respect. What does matter is that this dislike did not as a rule mean that Poles wished to see the Jews murdered. On the other hand, this dislike did mean that many Poles wished that Jews would simply disappear. This is borne out by the widespread popularity in Polish society and politics, both before the war and during it as well, of mass emigration as a solution to the so-called Jewish question.[5]

Second, the fate of the Jews proved economically profitable for the Poles. The single contemporary Polish reference to the consequences of this that I have been able to find is in the work of the literary critic Kazimierz Wyka, who published the following in 1945:

> From under the sword of the German butcher perpetrating a crime unprecedented in history, the little Polish shopkeeper sneaked the keys to his Jewish competitor's cashbox, and believed that he had acted morally. To the Germans went the guilt and the crime; to us the keys and the cash box. The storekeeper forgot that the "legal" annihilation of an entire people is part of an undertaking so unparalleled that it was doubtless not staged by history for the purpose of changing the sign on someone's shop. The methods by which Germans liquidated the Jews rest on the Germans' conscience. *The reaction to these methods rests nevertheless on our conscience.* The gold filling torn out of a corpse's mouth will always bleed, even if no one remembers its national origin.[6]

Neither for the Polish shopkeeper occupying his competitor's premises (shortly to be dispossessed in turn by communist bureaucrats), nor for the millions of Poles moving into what had been Jewish homes, offices, synagogues, and communal institutions, making use of land, factories, warehouses, money, jewelry, furniture, clothing, dishes, and linen that had belonged to Jews, would it be simple morally or psychologically to accept this new order of things. To dislike one's neighbor, to wish him gone; then to observe his unprecedented total annihilation; finally to inherit what had once been his: such a sequence of events can only add immeasurably to the guilt occasioned by the trauma itself. The resulting self-accusation is all the more powerful for being unrelated to any actual transgression. In this respect the postwar German situation was less complicated: a small portion of the guilty could be punished, the crime could thereby be symbolically expiated, and the society, for better or for worse, could attempt to move on. But as witnesses Poles had committed no crime; there was nothing to expiate. Yet Polish history had loaded the act of witnessing the Holocaust to spring a psychological and moral trap from which there was no apparent exit. The unacceptable, unmasterable guilt could only be denied and repressed, thereafter to erupt into history in particularly distorted forms.

To this we must add a final factor whose importance cannot be overestimated: forty-five years of communist rule that either imposed silence on all these issues or manipulated them for political purposes. The memories of Polish witnessing of the Holocaust, what the war had seared into Polish consciousness, memories that, as nowhere else in postwar Europe, cried out for an airing, were therefore driven underground to fester and explode into history at moments of particular crisis.

I will devote the remainder of this essay to the examination of three such moments. The first is the immediate postwar period, until the consolidation of communist rule in 1948.[7] These were years that confirmed the worst fears of the most pessimistic Polish observers. The West had written off Poland and thereby validated the perspective of Polish right-wing nationalists: Poles could trust no one but themselves, it seemed; the rest of the world was either indifferent or hostile to Polish interests. Historically associated with such Polish attitudes beginning in the mid-nineteenth century was the figure of the Jew, perennially available as a trope for alien hostility to Poland and Poles. But now the figure emerged in a new form, that of the communist oppressor, the so-called *Żydo-Komuna*. This term has a history as well; before the war it was a staple of Polish nationalist and Catholic rhetoric.[8] During the war the association was rooted in a kernel of truth, the fact that for Jews Stalin was infinitely preferable to Hitler. Poles liked to emphasize that Jews had only one enemy during the war, while Poles had two. Supposed Jewish collaboration with the Russian occupiers of Poland east of the Bug River from 1939–41 inspired tales of "what they [the Jews] did to us on the other side of the Bug."[9] Here was another incarnation of the ancient myth of Jewish vengefulness. Now the belief became widespread that the *Żydo-Komuna* had finally come to power, especially that Jews controlled the security apparatus and were therefore responsible for the torture and murder of Polish patriots. Here too there were kernels of truth: Stalin's efforts to place minorities in the security apparatus of the emerging "people's republics," and the fact that in the turmoil of the postwar years, only the new Polish government could be counted on to defend the physical safety of Jews.

The postwar years were filled with violence so pervasive that many called it civil war; 20,000 people were killed as a host of armed groups fought the government, the Red Army, and each other. This was the world in which Jewish survivors began to emerge from concentration camps and places of refuge.[10] Hundreds of them were murdered, most killed as they returned to their home towns to discover the fate of families and friends, some in pogroms, the most notorious of which occurred in Kielce in July 1946 and claimed 42 lives.[11] In addition to the violence, Jewish sources uniformly attest to the pervasive mixture of surprise, derision, and animosity, punctuated by the inevitable refrain "What? You're still alive?" with which survivors were greeted.[12] There is also the reappearance in postwar Poland of the blood libel, the belief, dating back to the Middle Ages, that Jews used the blood of Christian children for their rituals. The majority of pogroms, including the one in Kielce, began with rumors about the disappearance of Polish children.

Finally, and perhaps most troubling of all, is the widespread hostility directed not just at Jews, but at Poles who had saved Jews. The historian Michał Borwicz, writing in 1958, recounts what happened when, just after the war, he attempted to publish accounts of Poles who had saved Jews:

> I began to receive paradoxical visits. People cited by name (and this as saviors!) arrived dispirited, complaining that in publishing their "crime," which consisted in aid rendered at the risk of their life, we exposed them as prey for their neighbors' vengeance. In turn, with similar complaints, certain Jews who had been saved began to appear, sent to us by those who saved them. Still others (the authors of written but as yet unpublished testimonies) came "preventively," to prohibit the future publication of their names. There were cases in which—at the demand of those who saved them—certain individuals refused permission to publish their testimonies at all, even without citing the relevant names, since "from other details (the name of the locality, etc.) their neighbors might guess who was meant."[13]

In the introduction to a collection of testimonies of child survivors published just after the war, the editor writes as follows:

> In this book, in many testimonies those who saved Jewish children are mentioned by name, but in others only initials are used. Why—if the names are known? I don't know if anyone beyond the borders of Poland will absorb and comprehend the fact that saving the life of a defenseless child hunted by a murderer can cover someone with shame and disgrace, or make trouble for him.[14]

A confidential memorandum written in February 1946 to a U.S. Embassy counselor in Poland recounts the plight of Jewish children who had been saved by Poles in Krakow: "Until this very day those children are kept in the garret of the house, hidden away from the neighbors for fear that the neighbors discover that the Christian family saved the Jewish children and vent their vengeance on the whole family, and this one year after liberation."[15]

What is the source of such bizarre hatreds, of behavior that seems to undermine our most elementary assumptions about humanity, behavior apparently triggered by little more than the appearance of a handful of survivors of the worst slaughter in history? Making use of the paradigm I have sketched, we can say that the image of the Jew in postwar Poland was weighted with an extraordinary psychic load. Transformed into Bolshevik minister and security policeman, the "Jew" attracted hostility that conveniently substituted for other, politically inadvisable, aggression. But this hostility was also rooted in the Polish experience of the Holocaust, in the new accusatory death-tainted image of the Jew that infused the traditional stereotype. With no hope of healing within the growing frost, Poles could only move from passive victimized to active victimizers, while nevertheless retaining the image of themselves as victims.

Let us now turn to the period 1968–70. Polish historiography correctly views these years as a turning point in postwar history.[16] The events repeated the pattern of previous political crises, but for the last time in Polish history. In March 1968, protesting Warsaw University students were set upon by police in an attack that soon extended to all efforts at political reform. Entirely separately, two years later, worker protests over price increases were smashed, but not before they had toppled the government of the so-called national communist Władysław Gomułka. In the aftermath of the events of "March," as they have come to be called, two historic shifts of allegiance transformed the nature of the Polish political struggle. The first was a gradual rapprochement between the intelligentsia, shorn of its belief in "socialism with a human face," and the Church. The second was a rapprochement between the intelligentsia and Polish workers. The events of March, in other words, witnessed the origin of those possibilities that would lead to the Solidarity movement; they were the birth of the death of communism, so to speak.

But the same two years also witnessed a powerful anti-Semitic campaign that forced some 20,000 Jews out of their jobs, primarily in the government, and then out of the country.[17] Conventional Polish historiography has seen this so-called anti-Zionist campaign as a pretext: evidence of the regime's ability to stoop to any means to discredit the political opposition, as well as a way of making room in the state bureaucracy for a new generation of apparatchiks.[18] But I would suggest that the Jewish issue was hardly a pretext in 1968. The memory of the Jew and, above all, the memory of the Jew's destruction were essential issues in the events of March.

The forces of repression in 1968—those responsible both for smashing the reform movement and for the anti-Semitic campaign—were mobilized by a group within the Polish Communist Party, the so-called Partisans led by Gen. Mieczysław Moczar. Moczar and his forces solidified an alliance between authoritarian communism and chauvinist nationalism. They did this by claiming to speak in the name of the Polish nation as a whole, of its proletarians and its fighters, as they put it. Key to their message was the need for Poles to regain and celebrate the memory of Polish sacrifice during the war years. With few exceptions, until 1968 the communists had been wary of telling the full story of Polish resistance to the Nazis. This is because the AK (*Armia Krajowa*), the Polish Home Army, the leading resistance organization, had been anticommunist. The heroic Warsaw Uprising of 1944, the work of the AK, had been de-emphasized in official history, and was generally missing in commemorations of the war.

But now, as their name suggests, the Partisans claimed to speak in the name a new kind of unity, one based in a common memory of the war years.

Moczar and his forces took over the Warsaw office of the International Auschwitz Committee and the High Commission to Investigate Nazi Crimes in Poland. Most important of all was Moczar's leadership of the veterans' association ZBoWiD (*Zwiazek Bojowników o Wolności Demokracjæ*). This organization, with a membership of 300,000, claimed to speak for all Polish veterans of the Second World War regardless of their politics. For the first time ever, tens of thousands of former members of the AK found it possible to come out of the closet, so to speak, and step proudly into the public arena. Moczar transformed them from outcasts into freedom fighters, and thereby assured himself their undying allegiance. The support of ZBoWiD, in turn, gave Moczar and his associates popular legitimation to appropriate the entire heritage of anti-Nazi resistance. Moczar could speak in the name of the generation most closely identified with the war years, those who had come of age during the war and immediately after.

Thus situated, Moczar was in a perfect position to lead a populist-style anti-intellectual campaign in the name of all "fighting Poles," all those, regardless of political allegiance, who had sacrificed for the fatherland during the World War, and now confronted a crafty and implacable foe that once again sought Poland's humiliation and defeat. Who was this adversary? Poland, according to the Partisans, was under siege by an international conspiracy that was overseen by American imperialism, but implemented by enemies much closer to home: Germans and Jews. The ultimate nature of the threat was always somewhat nebulous; while it doubtless included the restoration of capitalism, most of what was said turned on two other issues. The first was West German "revanchism," the supposed German desire to regain the territories that Poland had annexed after the war. The second was the alleged effort by Jews, both in Poland and abroad, to disfigure the memory of the war years. Such claims took pseudo-rational forms, as when they focused, for example, on the supposed anti-Polishness of works such as Leon Uris's *Mila 18* and Jerzy Kosinski's *Painted Bird*. The campaign as a whole, however, entered the realm of magical thinking. And here above all we detect the traces of the Polish experience of the Holocaust.

In the fully elaborated belief system of Moczar and the Partisans, we confront a paranoid vision of reality: the notion of a worldwide conspiracy against Poles and Poland whose agents are West Germans and Zionists. Their weapons are revanchism and historical revisionism, their goals the mutilation of the nation's borders and memory, its body and soul. In a host of contexts, victims and victimizers, as well as past and present, are conflated. Not only is Germany said to support Israel's "genocide" in the Middle East, not only are the Israelis *like* Nazis, they *are* Nazis. The public was informed that one thousand ex-Nazis were advising the Israeli army, that Moshe Dayan was actually a disguised Nazi war criminal, that Martin Bormann was hiding in Golda Meir's apartment, and that Dayan's daughter Yael "reminds us" of Ilse Koch, the Buchenwald commandant's wife reputed to have had lampshades made of human skin.[19] Moreover, this alliance between Nazis and Jews extended back into the past. Zionists, it was alleged, who needed the Holocaust in order to build support for a Jewish state, collaborated with the Nazis, as did Jewish communal leaders in the ghettos. Who then within this labyrinth were the real victims? Clearly, Poles, and doubly so, in the present and in the past. For the current conspiracy of Germans and Jews against Poland was intended to deny Polish victimhood in the past, to deny the martyrdom of the Polish nation during the war, and more: to exonerate the Germans of the murder of the Jews and pin the blame for it on the Poles.

The Holocaust, in other words, has been transformed affectively into a German-Jewish conspiracy against Poles. In this extraordinary reversal, we recognize the unacceptable, unmasterable substratum of guilt connected to Polish witnessing of the Holocaust. This was an anguish most powerfully rooted precisely in those who had come of age during the war years, whose identity was directly shaped by them. Festering for twenty years, repressed psychologically in the individual psyche and politically in the public arena, this anguish was now channeled by Moczar and his followers into a system of belief that denied facts but not feelings. Twenty years after the event, the anti-Zionist campaign, in all its irrationality, suggested that the murder of the Jews had become an obstacle that stood between Poles and their own past, preventing them from repossessing that past as a narrative of their own exemplary martyrdom. The meaning of the Holocaust had become Polish victimization *by* the Holocaust.

Let us now turn briefly to the Solidarity era of the 1980s.[20] Just as Solidarity was inconceivable without March '68, so a new Polish relationship to the Holocaust and the Jewish past was impossible without the anti-Zionist campaign. In the aftermath of that campaign, into the 1970s and beyond, it was widely believed that there were no more Jews in Poland. This was even the case abroad; the *American Jewish Yearbook* for several years simply stopped reporting from Poland. Within Poland, an absolute silence, publicly but even in private contexts, descended on Jewish matters. Finally, a new generation began to assume political and cultural leadership. If March '68 and the anti-Zionist campaign were the repressive work of the generation whose formative years were directly shaped by the war, that is, whose memory of Jews was a product of watching them murdered, then Solidarity was a product of the generation born after the war, who had never seen "real Jews," and above all had not witnessed their destruction. And therefore the memory of the Jew, having first been denied and then expelled from public consciousness, could now begin to be reconstructed. This, of course, was key to the larger project of Solidarity, a contest with the communists over history and memory, an attempt to repossess a Polish national past that had been defaced by the communists.

The past that Solidarity wanted to repossess was, by and large, not a chauvinist past but a pluralist one. Within this movement, a group of young Jews also emerged.[21] These young "Jews," "half-Jews," spouses of Jews, and sympathetic non-Jews were above all Poles whose primary identification was with the emerging opposition movement. They knew nothing of Jewish religious practices, languages, or history. They were entirely cut off from the tiny official Jewish community in Poland, whose elderly members might have served as a link to Jewish tradition, however attenuated; but so long as communism reigned, they would remain cut off from them, regarding the official community as hopelessly compromised. Their increasing involvement in Jewish culture could therefore assume the form of a voyage of pure discovery, the exploration of a lost continent. It was an approach premised on discontinuity and silence, an approach that was only possible in the aftermath of the anti-Zionist paroxysm. For this small group of seekers and the many more that followed in the 1980s, the expulsion of the "last" Jews of Poland was an exorcism that enabled them, as representatives of the postwar generation, to begin to reinvent a Jewish past. This Jewish quest was profoundly Polish, of course, for it was an integral part of the larger movement to regain the Polish past. But as part of the larger Polish enterprise, it marked it in a crucial way, confirming it as inherently pluralist. The Jew would increasingly appear as a legitimate and even honored representative of the new Polish past.

By the late 1980s, a new relationship to the Jewish past had begun to infuse increasing portions of Polish society as a whole. Raised in a monochromatic world of cultural and ethnic uniformity, Poles sifted the past for a myth of diversity and color. There they discovered the image of the bearded, black-garbed Jew, supremely exotic yet nevertheless an immemorial neighbor, rooted in the prewar landscape of a Poland that, like the Jew, no longer existed. This new image of the Jew could thereby begin to perform a new symbolic function as a focus of longing for a many-hued Old Poland, a Poland of the multi-national Commonwealth, of the *kresy* (eastern borderlands) and the *shtetl*. Rooted in the needs of the young, the image also permitted older Poles a nostalgic return to an idealized prewar youth. These were the sources of the "fashion for Jews" increasingly noted by contemporary observers, the popularity of Jewish songs and music, of *Fiddler on the Roof*, even of Jewish food. Gefilte fish, known as *ryba po zydowsku* (fish Jewish-style), became a restaurant staple.[22]

At the same time, the attempt to deal with real Jews often proved problematic. At issue for Poles in the bitter struggle over the presence of a Carmelite convent at Auschwitz was how to commemorate a place of martyrdom of both Poles and Jews, or in other words, how to admit the memory of the murdered Jew into Polish national memory.[23] This conflict, which peaked in 1989 with the expulsion of American Jewish protesters from the grounds of

Auschwitz, shared the front pages of the newly freed Polish press with news of the first free Polish elections in fifty years. It is no coincidence, I would submit, that the Auschwitz conflict accompanied the Polish transition to democracy.

NOTES

For a fuller discussion of the subject of this essay, including additional sources, see my book *Bondage to the Dead: Poland and the Memory of the Holocaust* (Syracuse: Syracuse University Press, 1997).

1. For some of the diverse material on these subjects see David S. Wyman, *The Abandonment of the Jews: America and the Holocaust, 1941–1945* (New York, 1984); Deborah E. Lipstadt, *Beyond Belief: The American Press and the Coming of the Holocaust, 1933–1945* (New York, 1986); Raul Hilberg, *The Destruction of the European Jews,* 3 vols., rev. ed. (New York, 1985); Yisrael Gutman, *The Jews of Warsaw, 1939–1943: Ghetto, Underground, Revolt* (Bloomington, Ind., 1982); Primo Levi, *The Drowned and the Saved* (New York, 1988). On the problematics of witnessing the Holocaust, see also Shoshona Felman, "The Return of the Voice: Claude Lanzmann's Shoah," in Shoshana Felman and Dori Laub, *Testimony: Crises of Witnessing in Literature, Psychoanalysis, and History* (New York and London, 1992), 204–283; in the same volume, see also Dori Laub, "An Event without a Witness: Truth, Testimony and Survival," 45–92.

2. Here it is appropriate to note several recent studies that probe comparable issues for other nations: Charles S. Maier, *The Unmasterable Past: History, Holocaust, and German National Identity* (Cambridge, Mass., 1988); Henry Rousso, *The Vichy Syndrome: History and Memory in France since 1944* (Cambridge, Mass., 1991); Saul Friedländer, *Memory, History, and the Extermination of the Jews of Europe* (Bloomington, Ind., 1993); Tom Segev, *The Seventh Million: The Israelis and the Holocaust* (New York, 1993); David Wyman, ed., *The World Reacts to the Holocaust: 1945–1992* (Baltimore, 1996). See also the important theoretical essay by Pierre Nora, "Between Memory and History: *Les Lieux de Mémoire,*" *Representations* no. 26 (Spring 1989): 7–25.

3. Robert Jay Lifton, *The Broken Connection: On Death and the Continuity of Life* (New York, 1979), 169, 171, 173, 175, 176, 295.

4. On Polish-Jewish relations in interwar Poland, see Ezra Mendelsohn, *The Jews of East Central Europe between the World Wars* (Bloomington, Ind., 1983), 11–83; Joseph Marcus, *Social and Political History of the Jews in Poland, 1919–1939* (Berlin, 1983); Yisrael Gutman, Ezra Mendelsohn, Jehuda Reinharz, and Chone Shmeruk, eds., *The Jews of Poland between Two World Wars* (Hanover, N.H., 1989); and Jerzy Tomaszewski, "Niepodlegla rzeczpospolita," in Jerzy Tomaszewski, ed., *Najnowsze dzieje Żydów w Polsce w zarysie (do 1950 roku)* (Warsaw, 1993).

5. See, for example, Jan Rzepecki, "Organizacja i dzialanie Biura Informacji i Propagandy (BIP) Komendy Glownej AK: Zakończenie," *Wojskowy Przeglad Historyczny,* no. 4 (1971): 147–153.

6. Kazimierz Wyka, "The Excluded Economy," in *The Unplanned Society: Poland during and after Communism,* ed. Janine Wedel (New York, 1992), 41. For the Polish text see "Gospodarka wylaczona," in *Zycie na niby; Pamietnik po klesce* (Kraków, 1984), 157; the essay bears the date 1945 and was first published in this version in 1959.

7. The major work on this period is Krystyna Kersten, *The Establishment of Communist Rule in Poland, 1943–1948* (Berkeley, 1991).

8. See the important new book by Ronald Modras, *The Catholic Church and Anti-semitism: Poland, 1933–1939* (Chur, Switzerland, 1994).

9. See Jan T. Gross, *Revolution from Abroad: The Soviet Conquest of Poland's Western Ukraine and Western Belorussia* (Princeton, N.J., 1988).

10. On Jews in Poland in the immediate postwar years, see S. L. Shneiderman, *Between Fear and Hope* (New York, 1947); Bernard D. Weinryb, "Poland," in Peter Meyer et al., *The Jews in the Soviet Satellites* (Syracuse, N.Y., 1953), 207–326; Lucjan Dobroszycki, "Restoring Jewish Life in Postwar Poland," *Soviet Jewish Affairs* (London) 3, no. 2 (1973): 58–72, and *Survivors of the Holocaust in Poland: A Portrait Based on Jewish Community Records, 1944–1947* (Armonk, N.Y., 1994); Yisrael Gutman, *Ha-yehudim be-Polin aharei milhamat ha-olam ha-shniya* (Jerusalem, 1985); Józef Adelson, "W Polsce zwanej ludowej," in *Najnowsze dzieje Żydów w Polsce w zarysie (do 1950 roku)*, ed. Jerzy Tomaszewski (Warsaw, 1993), 387–477; David Engel, *Beyn shihrur li-veriha: Nitsolei ha-Shoah be-Polin veha-maavak al hanhagatam, 1944–1946* (Tel Aviv: Am Oved, 1996).

11. The most comprehensive documentation is in Bożena Szaynok, *Pogrom Żydów w Kielcach 4 VII 1956 r.* (Warsaw, 1991).

12. Memorial books (*yizker bikher*) for Jewish communities destroyed in the Holocaust contain many such accounts, as do Jewish memoirs. Among the latter, see Dovid Sfard, *Mit zikh un mit andere* (Jerusalem, 1984), 160; and Hersh Smoliar, *Oyf der letster pozitsye, mit der letster hofnung* (Tel Aviv, 1982), 29; both were leaders of the postwar Jewish community in Poland. For further sources, see David Engel, "Palestine in the Minds of the Remnants of Polish Jewry," *Journal of Israeli History* 16, no. 3 (1995): 229 n. 34.

13. Letter to the Editor, *Kultura* (Paris), no. 11/133 (November 1958): 147.

14. Maria Hochberg-Mariańska, *Dzieci oskarżają* (Kraków, 1947), xxxii; this book has been translated as *The Children Accuse* (Portland, Ore., 1996).

15. David Engel, "The Situation of Polish Jewry as Reflected in United States Diplomatic Documents, Dec. 1945–July 1946," *Gal-Ed: On the History of the Jews in Poland* (Tel Aviv) 14 (1995): 120. The author of the memorandum was Samuel Margoshes, a former editor of the New York Yiddish daily, *Der Tog*.

16. See for example Jerzy Eisler, *Marzec 1968* (Warsaw, 1991).

17. English sources include: *The Anti-Jewish Campaign in Present-Day Poland: Facts, Documents, Press Reports* (London, 1968); Paul Lendvai, *Anti-Semitism without Jews: Communist Eastern Europe* (Garden City, N.Y., 1971); Josef Banas, *The Scapegoats: The Exodus of the Remnants of Polish Jewry* (London, 1979); Michael Checinski, *Poland: Communism, Nationalism, Anti-Semitism* (New York, 1982).

18. Some have also argued for the influence of the Soviets on the Polish anti-Zionist campaign; these include M. K. Dziewanowski in his *Communist Party of Poland: An Outline of History* (Cambridge, Mass., 1976), 299–301. But the Soviet anti-Zionist campaign did not originate, as once assumed, immediately after the Six-Day War, but rather only as a response to the subsequent growth of the Jewish national movement in the Soviet Union. The "opening salvo" in this campaign was an article published in *Pravda* on November 30, 1969. See Jonathan Frankel, "The Soviet Regime and Anti-Zionism: An Analysis," in *Jewish Culture and Identity in the Soviet Union*, ed. Yaacov Ro'i and Avi Beker (New York, 1991), 332.

19. Banas, 83; Lendvai, 159.

20. There is a large literature in English on Solidarity. Excellent journalistic accounts of its origins are Neal Ascherson, *The Polish August: The Self-Limiting Revolution* (New York, 1982); Lawrence Weschler, *Solidarity: Poland in the Season of its Passion* (New York, 1982); Timothy Garton Ash, *The Polish Revolution: Solidarity* (New York, 1984). Analyses include Abraham Brumberg, ed., *Poland: Genesis of a Revolution* (New York, 1983); David Ost, *Solidarity and the Politics of Anti-Politics: Opposition and Reform in Poland since 1968*

(Philadelphia, 1990); Roman Laba, *The Roots of Solidarity: A Political Sociology of Poland's Working-Class Democratization* (Princeton, N.J., 1991).

21. See, for example, Michel Wieviorka, *Les Juifs, la Pologne et Solidarność* (Paris, 1984), 11–67, 149–190.

22. For an excellent example of the "fashion for Jews," see Michael T. Kaufman, *Mad Dreams, Saving Graces; Poland: A Nation in Conspiracy* (New York, 1989), 175–177. On the subject of Jews and the memory of the Holocaust in Poland in the 1980s, see also Iwona Irwin-Zarecka, *Neutralizing Memory: The Jew in Contemporary Poland* (New Brunswick, 1989), and "Poland, after the Holocaust," in *Remembering for the Future: Working Papers and Addenda*, vol. 1, ed. Yehuda Bauer et al. (Oxford, 1989), 143–155; Antony Polonsky, "Polish-Jewish Relations and the Holocaust," *Polin: A Journal of Polish-Jewish Studies* 4 (1989): 226–242; Andrzej Bryk, "Polish Society Today and the Memory of the Holocaust," *Gal-Ed: On the History of the Jews in Poland* (Tel Aviv) 12 (1991): 107–129; and James E. Young, *The Texture of Memory: Holocaust Memorials and Meaning* (New Haven, Conn., 1993), 113–208.

23. On the controversy see Carol Rittner and John K. Roth, eds., *Memory Offended: The Auschwitz Convent Controversy* (New York, 1991); and Wladyslaw Bartoszewski, *The Convent at Auschwitz* (New York, 1991).

24 Poland and the Holocaust
Monika Adamczyk-Garbowska

In a nonfiction story by Hanna Krall (b. 1937), the narrator and Thomas Blatt, a survivor of Sobibór concentration camp, drive through little towns in the Lublin region. Blatt mentions the names of the Jews who lived and perished there. "Why is nobody sad?" he asks. The sun is setting. "Everything became even uglier and grayer," we read. "Perhaps because ghosts are circling around. They do not want to go away when people do not regret their absence, when they are unmourned. All this grayness comes from the unmourned ghosts."[1]

The grayness of Polish shtetls after the war was not only the result of the absence of Jews but also one of the effects of the Communist economy imposed upon the country. Today a number of towns and villages look perhaps less gray, but it does not change the message of the story, namely the fact that Jews were not mourned enough in Poland.

As we all know, for forty-five years after World War II, history in Poland, as in other countries of the former Communist Bloc, was the least independent subject, constituting a hotbed for manipulation. The selection of facts and, above all, their interpretation had precisely defined ideological dimensions. In the case of Jewish topics, their very absence, or their incidental and distorted presentation, made Jews almost a taboo issue, which could not be discussed openly. The resulting "mystery" around these questions made people either indifferent and ignorant or susceptible to biased opinions. A problem of equal importance is that up to 1989 very little attention was given to the long presence of Jews in Polish history. Most often they would appear in connection to the Holocaust and quickly disappear again.

As others have noted, in Polish-Jewish relations after the war a kind of martyrdom rivalry can be observed. Each side believes that emphasizing the sufferings of the other may decrease the scope of its own tragedy. Such a situation has to a large degree resulted from and been intensified by the fact that for many years one was not allowed to speak openly about numerous painful and/or controversial issues. Poles, who in the majority did not consider the end of World War II as a liberation of Poland, but as a transition to Soviet occupation, devoted inordinate attention to their own heroism and suffering, often forgetting about the suffering of other nations. Due to a substantial ideologization of school curricula, outside of school in many homes a different version of history was given to young generations. Nevertheless both the official and unofficial versions aimed at shaping patriotism, but patriotism understood narrowly and one-sidedly, forgetting that wise patriotic education has nothing to do with nationalism and uncritical acceptance of one's history.

Therefore some paradoxical situations and myths have survived until today, including the one about Jewish domination of or influence in Poland. For example, according to one of the latest opinion polls (1996), 37 percent of Poles think that Jews have too great an influence upon the Polish economy, 39 percent have a similar opinion as to their influence upon political life, and 28 percent believe that they have too much power in the media. Every third person among the examined group believed that 250,000 to 1 million Jews live in Poland today, while in fact the Jewish community is estimated as 5,000 to 20,000 people. This part of the society, although not actively anti-Semitic, can be especially susceptible to the nationalist rhetoric in which Jews appear in the form of "freemasons," "Euroliberals," or even *"katolewica"* (the Catholic Left) and seem to pose a threat, if not of causing the "fifth partition" or "colonization" of Poland, at least of dominating its economy and placing it in foreign hands. One can only hope that together with the strengthening of the democratic system in Poland, such views will find an ever-ebbing response.

Michael C. Steinlauf has made a number of very important points. I fully agree with his historical analysis. As to the modified version of Lifton's theory, I would say that in a sense, the conviction that a feeling of guilt has really existed among Poles and has had a relatively mass character is an optimistic viewpoint. Undoubtedly a number of works written by Polish writers of the older generations, who were the witnesses of the Holocaust, as well as by representatives of younger generations, who might be called potential witnesses, are a testimony to their experiencing the death stigma and to their full consciousness of that fact. But did that phenomenon have a mass character? It seems that very often there was not enough reflection upon what had happened, or that the very need for such reflection was completely erased from memory, not necessarily because of the feeling of guilt, but because of the lack of sensitivity. (Moreover, as Professor Steinlauf has written, Poles had many other problems immediately after their "liberation," which distorted their perception of the past.) As a result, quite often in Poles' statements referring to the Holocaust one can see not openness, a willingness for dialogue and admitting of one's own transgressions, but the somewhat competitive and obstinate attitude I have referred to.

One of the main problems in the dialogue is the fact that Poles most often take a defensive stand; even when admitting their own transgressions, they mention some transgressions of Jews, or, even more often, they give examples of anti-Semitism in other countries. One of the typical arguments is that of French anti-Semitism: "Why Poles? Weren't the French much worse?"

The evidence of how deep-rooted are both some stereotypes and the feeling that one should solve one's problems at home, without revealing them to the public, is visible in one of the reviews of Michael Steinlauf's book in a Polish-American newspaper. In it the reviewer, while seemingly praising the book, poses an argument quite typical in its irrationality: why is a Jew writing about the reactions of Poles instead of focusing on the reactions of Jews, especially American Jews, to the Holocaust of their brethren. The reviewer then suggests that Steinlauf should have waited patiently until "a reliable and competent Polish author" takes on this topic and only then "display his cards," since these are the principles of "fair play."[2]

Especially in the face of the recently published Vatican documents, a question must be raised about the role of the Catholic Church in this issue. Catholics in Poland are as polarized in this respect as the rest of the society, and in general I would say the scene is far from being satisfactory. It is true that various documents have been issued on Polish-Jewish relations, including the pastoral letter of the Polish episcopate in 1990, but they have entered and grown roots in public consciousness only to a very small degree. It is very rare to hear an ordinary Sunday sermon in which the priest takes a personal stand against anti-Semitism. (I use the word "ordinary" because you can certainly hear such sermons, but always on some special occasion, e.g., during a Jewish Culture Week, a Day of Judaism, etc.) I am not implying that the rare occurrence of such sermons has to be a result of ill will or widespread anti-Semitic views among the clergy. It may rather be a result of a lack of preparation, insensitivity, or inability to realize that such a need exists, or—even worse—a fear of how the faithful would respond.

In spite of appearances, the Church in Poland has not analyzed deeply and openly their attitudes towards Jews. For example, American Catholic theologian Ronald Modras's book *The Catholic Church and Antisemitism: Poland, 1933-1939*[3] has passed unnoticed—as far as I know—in Church circles, and I think (I would like to be wrong) that it would not have a chance to be published in Poland by any publisher directly or indirectly connected with the Church. Some ways of reasoning that the Catholic Church has abandoned in other countries still linger in Poland.

Quite often in the context of postwar Polish Jewish history Julian Tuwim's words come to my mind. (Julian Tuwim, 1894-1953, was an outstanding Polish poet from an assimilated Jewish family.) On the first anniversary of the Warsaw ghetto uprising he wrote from America in his manifesto "We, Polish Jews":

> Upon the armbands which you wore in the ghetto the star of David was painted. I believe in a future Poland in which that star of your armbands will become the highest order bestowed upon the bravest among Polish officers and soldiers. . . . And there shall be in Warsaw and in every other Polish city some fragment of the ghetto left standing and preserved in its present form in all its horror of ruin and destruction . . . and every day we

shall twine fresh live flowers into its iron links, so that the memory of the massacred people shall remain forever fresh in the minds of the generations to come, and also as a sign of our undying sorrow for them.[4]

Unfortunately, this was idealistic and naive reasoning. Another Polish poet of the same generation, also an assimilated Jew, Antoni Slonimski (1895–1976), understood the whole matter more accurately (and was richer in the experience of the first postwar years), as he showed in the last stanza of his "Elegy to Shtetls," written in 1947:

Gone are the little shtetls, passed into shadow
And this shadow shall lie between our words,
Ere two nations fed on centuries of suffering
Will draw near and unite anew.[5]

Undoubtedly the "shadow" lasted for long years largely due to the political system, which hindered any free exchange of ideas. Sharing Tuwim's hopes, I am trying to imagine that somewhere in Poland one can hear sermons in which priests remind the faithful about the evils of anti-Semitism, in which they say that Christians should be grateful that in the face of what befell Jews during the war there is still a Jewish community in Poland, a community that is trying to enable a small group of religious Jews to live in accordance with the principles of Judaism, and that there are in Polish political and cultural life assimilated Jews who often do a lot of good—as other Jews, assimilated and not, have done in the past history of the country. Such sermons, I suppose, would have a much greater impact than hundreds of articles written by intellectuals for intellectuals.

Polish society has always been very polarized, and one can see this polarization even today—and one place it exists is in different attitudes to the Holocaust. For example, the recent controversies over the cross at Auschwitz revealed some negative sentiments, but in a statement made before the 10th March of the Living, the Polish episcopate expressed their intention to join in spirit in the sufferings of the Jewish people. Also, the fact that the prime ministers of Israel and Poland headed the march together, and Polish Christians participated in it as well, is a positive sign. Generally, educated people, especially of younger generations, are less prone to prejudices and more capable of understanding and empathy.

I often turn to quotations from literature, not only because my field is literature rather than history, but because artists, it seems, sometimes can express more aptly and in a more condensed form ideas for which others need long treatises. As Michael Steinlauf has observed, it was the literary critic Kazimierz Wyka (1910–1975) who, when the war was ending, wrote the prophetic words about the "gold filling torn out of a corpse's mouth,"[6] and it was the poet Czeslaw Milosz (b. 1911) who more or less at the same time, in his oft-quoted poem "A Poor Christian Looks at the Ghetto," evoked the image of the "guardian mole."[7] Besides, poets and writers have always played a very important role in Poland, serving as the voice of collective conscience and taking a stand when the majority were silent. This is also true today. One of the most sensitive recent analyses of the discussed problem has been given by Andrzej Szczypiorski (b. 1924), a well-known Polish writer (his novel about the Holocaust, *Poczatek* [The Beginning], was published in English as *The Beautiful Mrs. Seidenman*) who states among other things that "Jews have the right to come to terms with their past, but Christians do not have such a right. Jews can even allow themselves to forget about the Holocaust. Christians are not allowed to do this." He states explicitly that Christians who do not realize the scope of Jewish suffering "do not have God in their hearts."[8] While Wyka's voice was isolated in his time, Szczypiorski represents a much larger group of people, including leading Polish artists and scholars.

I will close with a statement by another artist, the film maker who first became known as a representative of the Polish Cinema of Moral Concern and later gained international renown. Referring to the anti-Semitic campaign in 1968, Krzysztof Kieslowski (1941–1996) said:

> Anti-Semitism and Polish nationalism are a stain on my country which has remained to this day and I don't think we'll ever be able to get rid of it.[9]

I would like to read his words as a warning rather than as a fact or an ominous prophecy. The more people in Poland realize that anti-Semitism is a stain, the greater will be the chance that the ghosts evoked in Hanna Krall's story will be able to "rest in peace."

NOTES

1. Hanna Krall, "Portret z kula w szczece" [A Portrait with a Bullet in the Jaw], in *Taniec na cudzym weselu* (Warszawa: Polska Oficyna Wydawnicza "BGW," 1994), 94.

2. See Wojciech A. Wierzewski, "Michael Steinlauf spoglada na 'biednych Polaków'" [Michael Steinlauf Is Looking at "Poor Poles"], *Dziennik Zwiazkowy*, May 30–June 1, 1997, p. A 21.

3. (Shur [Switzerland]: Harwood Academic Publishers 1994).

4. Julian Tuwim, *My Zydzi polscy/We, Polish Jews*, ed. Ch. Shmeruk (Jerusalem: Magnes Press, 1984), 19.

5. Antoni Slonimski, "Elegia miasteczek zydowskich," in *Poezje* (Warszawa: Czytelnik, 1955), 356. Translation mine. Another translation can be found in *Stranger in Our Midst: Images of the Jew in Polish Literature*, ed. Harold B. Segel (Ithaca: Cornell University Press, 1996), 363.

6. See Kazimierz Wyka, "The Excluded Economy," in *The Unplanned Society: Poland during and after Communism*, ed. Janine Wedel (New York: Columbia University Press, 1992), 41. Quoted in Michael Steinlauf, *Bondage to the Dead: Poland and the Memory of the Holocaust* (Syracuse, N.Y.: Syracuse University Press, 1997), 59.

7. See Czeslaw Milosz, "A Poor Christian Looks at the Ghetto," in *The Collected*

Poems, 1931–1987 (New York: Ecco Press, 1988), 64–65. Both this poem and another one on a related topic, "Campo di Fiori," were written in 1943 in response to the destruction of the Warsaw ghetto.

8. Andrzej Szczypiorski, "Marzec i Polacy" [March 1968 and Poles], *Gazeta Wyborcza*, March 28–29, 1997, pp. 10–12.

9. *Kieslowski on Kieslowski*, ed. Danusia Stok (Boston: Faber and Faber, 1993), 38.

PART 6

Lost Hope and Betrayal
The Survivors

Introduction
"Reading" the Holocaust

Arnold J. Band

THE HISTORIOGRAPHY DEALING with the Holocaust has developed so rapidly over the past generation that it is in itself a subject for serious scholarly research and, consequently, the subject of academic conferences and seminars. What is less known even among Holocaust scholars is that the study of *literature* about the Holocaust has also advanced vigorously over the past few decades. Ironically, even while less-informed critics still begin their considerations with the by now well-worn cliché originating with Theodore Adorno's partially understood statement, it is an undeniable fact that the writing of fiction, poetry, and plays about the Holocaust is now a vast field with truly significant achievements. And just as problems of representation beset the historiography of the Holocaust, similar—or even more acute—problems are generated by Holocaust fiction. This literary output has, in turn, spawned a considerable critical literature, of varying degrees of sophistication, to be sure, but still a formidable body of critical writing.

Foremost in this field since the 1970s has been the work of Lawrence Langer, who, in essay after essay, studies the wide range of literary works that attempt to render some expression and, perhaps, understanding of the atrocities of the Nazi period. His essays have set a standard of sensitivity and rigor against which all other studies can be measured. His influence obviously transcends literary criticism of the Holocaust; it affects the study of the literature of atrocity in other cultures. When I was called upon to assist in the direction of a doctoral dissertation dealing with the literature of the Armenian massacres, I had the student immerse herself in Langer as a model of what to do.

In his essay "Opening Locked Doors: Reflections on Teaching the Holocaust," Lawrence Langer raises several interesting questions regarding the teaching of the Holocaust, or, more specifically, literature about the Holocaust. He argues persuasively that fifty years from now, when knowledge of the historical context of the Holocaust might be less than it is today, it will be very difficult to teach this material to students, since the cluster of ideas and tropes of Holocaust literature will be so foreign to the average readers that they will not understand the texts under consideration. This argument follows Langer's contention, advanced in essay after essay over almost three decades, that Holocaust literature by its very nature raises formidable problems of representation. These essays, in fact, have set a high standard for critical thinking about Holocaust literature, a standard by which one can measure the success or failure of this critical literature, since it is obvious to anybody who has worked in this field that Langer not only was a pioneer in the field, but has been the consistently trenchant voice of conscience and common sense with the publication of his first three books of essays: *The Holocaust and the Literary Imagination* (1975), *The Age of Atrocity* (1978), and *Versions of Survival* (1982).

This ambivalence about Holocaust literature was exacerbated by the late 1980s as Langer began to work in the Yale archives of Holocaust testimonies. One begins to sense in his later essays a growing realization that works of the imagination seem inadequate in the presence of the testimonies of Holocaust survivors. Nevertheless, there remains a persistent assertion that there is a cardinal value to this literature, that, as he says, "Holocaust literature is a major goad urging us to reimagine atrocity and to rewrite the text of suffering in contemporary terms." As we move further and further from the horrible years of World War II and have fewer and fewer living survivors in our midst, it shall become clear how important this literature is—and, consequently, how important the work of Lawrence Langer has been in teaching us how to read and think about these texts.

25 | Damaged Childhood in Holocaust Fact and Fiction

Lawrence Langer

ANYONE FAMILIAR WITH the stories of Jewish children during the Holocaust understands that it is inaccurate to describe their trying to stay alive outside the ghettos and camps as if they shared identical experiences. Normally childhood proceeds in an uninterrupted rhythm from infancy through youth to the vestibule of maturity. Theirs did not. The Germans assaulted Jewish identity before they attacked Jewish life, so that children were forced to practice public concealment even when they were not literally in hiding. Those trying to pass as Christians with forged papers were under a constant strain to deny their true selves, to pretend to be who they were not; slowly an external charade became a pressing internal performance. Anne Frank could comfortably affirm her Jewishness to her diary, but those existing under a camouflaged identity had to develop daily strategies to prevent a disclosure that might imperil their lives. All lived in fear of discovery, though the intensity of that fear was governed by the differing circumstances of each particular child.

The archetypal account of a hidden child is Anne Frank's *Diary of a Young Girl*, but readers who restrict their interest in the subject to that familiar work gain little insight into the complex and disruptive quality of the ordeal as it was experienced by others. Because Anne did not survive her hiding, her story remains unfinished, an aborted narrative that omits the consequences of her confinement in later life. Even what remains of her story is atypical, because very few hidden children had the "luxury" of living in concealment with an intact family, as she did. Generations of students project their image of seclusion from Anne's chronicle, and as a result gain scarcely a glimpse of the ceaseless tension that eroded the security and contaminated the innocence of tens of thousands of other threatened children.

We can reconstruct the distress of these thousands a voice at a time, weaving a tapestry of erratic patterns that only confirm the scarcely communicable privacy of the event. "I grew up without images of my home town," says Mira B., "no streets, no parks, only the interiors of apartments and hiding places." She was born in 1938, and when she was five her parents threw her over a wall of the Bendzin ghetto, where by pre-arrangement the sister of a former family servant picked her up and took her home. Her mother said she would come for her soon; instead, her mother was deported to Auschwitz. "But the days passed and my mother didn't come," Mira recalls. "She had promised me. I felt abandoned." Her Polish rescuer dyed Mira's hair red and passed her off as a relative from the country. But as so often happened with Jewish children taken in by Christian families, Mira's potential salvation proved to be a mixed blessing. Within a year, the woman died of a sudden illness, and the five-year-old Mira was left with the woman's husband, a Polish nationalist who himself was in hiding from the Nazis. He taught her to read and write, but he was a strict disciplinarian, and when she faltered in her learning, he whipped her. (He also whipped his own children, often more severely.) "Buried beneath my childhood memories," Mira later remembered, "was a dark sense that I myself was to blame for what happened to me after I was rescued." The legacy of guilt did not easily dissipate even when normal family life was restored. Mira was more fortunate than most: both of her parents survived, and returned to reclaim her. But she is not alone in reporting confusion rather than joy as a strong component of her reunion with her mother: "She looked very different. But it was clearly my mother. And yet for years after the war I had this fantasy that I was adopted, that my parents weren't my real parents."[1] When norms of being are radically disrupted, as they were for children during the Holocaust, they are not so quickly revived.

Indeed, as soon as we scrutinize the idea of the hidden child, it explodes into fragments, never to be repaired. There is no more an archetypal hidden child than there is a survivor syndrome. Those hidden "externally," like Nechama Tec, whose appearance and knowledge of Polish enabled her to circulate openly while her Yiddish-speaking parents were forced to remain indoors in the house of the Christian family hiding them, faced crises different from those encountered by children hidden "internally," cut off from contact with others and daily fearing discovery. The only way to illuminate the hardship is to listen to as many viewpoints as possible, with the recognition that few models may emerge to justify some legitimate generalizations.

For those in "external" hiding, the first problem was the immediate split in one's sense of self. It was unsafe to be who you really were, and even more dangerous to forget who you were supposed to be. Nechama Tec describes the psychological impact of the dilemma:

> Our daily existence was tied to two closely connected requirements: giving up our Jewish identity and silence. Giving up our identity meant playing a part, becoming someone else. The better we played the role, the safer we were. Sometimes we were so caught up in the new part that we actually forgot who we really were. Though helpful, this temporary forgetfulness was emotionally costly. For many of us, giving up our true identity created an emotional void and made us feel anxious, worried that we would never recapture our past. We also felt ashamed for giving up what had been cherished by our parents, those we loved.[2]

At a time when most children were seeking to strengthen their egos, Tec and others like her were forced to shun that development. The results were often bizarre, as Tec describes in her memoir of the period, *Dry Tears,* where she tells of having to ignore her Polish friends' antisemitic comments without flinching in order to maintain her Christian persona.

We can only speculate about what this must have done to the personality of an adolescent like Tec. "An extra layer of secretiveness," she relates, "combined with a fear of discovery, became part of my being. All my life revolved around hiding; hiding thoughts, hiding feelings, hiding my activities, hiding information. Sometimes I felt like a sort of fearful automaton, always on the alert, always dreading that something fatal might be revealed."[3] The gradual displacement of self that resulted is difficult to imagine. "A slow transformation was taking place in me," Tec writes. "It was as if in certain circumstances I lost track of who I really was and began to see myself as a Pole. I became a double person, one private and one public. When I was away from my family I became so engrossed in my public self that I did not have to act the part; I actually felt like the person I was supposed to be." The ensuing guilt and embarrassment made her feel like a traitor: "It was as if, as I gave up my old self, I was giving up my family as well."[4] The question of divided loyalties is an exasperating issue that continues to bedevil interpreters of the Holocaust experience. Unlike Mira B., Nechama Tec was not physically separated from her parents during the war, so that part of the time she could reinforce the family bond and confirm her status as the offspring of a stable domestic unit. But at other moments she became the family breadwinner, even engaging in illegal black market activities, reversing her role by risking her freedom and turning into a kind of custodian for her parents.

The Tec family survived intact, but this does not mean that they faced an undamaged future. Nechama's abnormal childhood is a paradigm for the uncertainty that continued to disturb survivors after the war. Reclaiming one of his factories upon returning to Lublin, her father aroused the hostility of a dissident Polish underground group, and only through the help of a double agent were the police able to foil an assassination scheme at the last moment. The Tecs abandoned hope of resuming a normal existence and chose to emigrate. Exile from home thus followed exile from childhood, and in her adult scholarly works Nechama Tec returns to the site of her early ordeal to explore the forms of rescue and resistance that enabled her family to survive at the price of her normal adolescence.

Intact families, of course, were the exception rather than the rule. Although like Nechama Tec, Yehuda Nir speaks of his lost childhood in the title of his memoir, his experience was in most ways the exact opposite of hers. In July 1941, a few weeks after the Germans occupied Lwów, the eleven-year-old Nir watched a column of men, including his father, being marched out of town. His father gave him a faint smile; Nir waved back, but couldn't catch his eye. He never saw his father again. Years later he learned that the men had been taken to a forest outside Lwów and shot. But during the preceding interval he always expected his father to return. "My father never died," he says, repeating a sentiment often expressed by survivors; "he just faded away, was carried off into nowhere. It was as if he were dead and alive at the same time. Even after the war, in 1945, when we found out that he had definitely been killed on the day of his arrest in July 1941, we continued to search for him through the Red Cross."[5] Although a fragment of the family unit remained— Nir still had his older sister and his mother—they could not resume normal life. Traditional roles disappeared; age and experience ceased to matter as what Nir called the brutal game of survival displaced the familiar routines that had governed their existence before the war.

The notion of being alive and dead at the same time, especially as it affects the imagination of a child, is a complex but widely cited idea to emerge from Holocaust testimonies, though it has never been sufficiently studied. In a terse short story called "The Key Game," Ida Fink—who as a teenager survived the war moving from hiding place to hiding place with her sister in Poland— condenses the issue into a painful dramatic moment of family role reversal that explodes the notion of mutual support usually associated with the situation she depicts. The "brutal game of survival" isolates family members from each other and makes of the child in the narrative a helpless victim even before the Germans have assigned him that role. Because the Jewish father in this family appears to be at greatest risk and his three-year-old son less vulnerable, the child and his mother play a game called "searching for the key" while the father scrambles into a tiny prepared hiding place in the bathroom. The mother mimics the sound of a doorbell announcing the arrival of the Germans while the child pretends to look for the key that his mother, away at work, will have put somewhere, all the while calling out to the Germans theoretically waiting on the other side of the door that he will find the key "in a minute." Meanwhile, the father disappears into his very real hiding place. After a few moments he reappears, complaining that he needs more time, that his son—three years old, we remember—must spend more time "looking" for the key. Terror for his own safety has displaced his paternal instinct, though his wife, reminding him of that role, urges him to say something, and he mechanically intones, "you did a good job, little one, a good job."[6]

The mother, more sensitive to the child's needs, remembers her role, though her tender words of reassurance are filled with a wrenching irony rarely available to the authors of autobiographical memoirs about similar situations: " 'That's right,' the woman said, 'you're really doing a wonderful job, darling— and you're not little at all. You act just like a grown-up, don't you?' " The fictional milieu allows Fink to shift from character to character, uniting innocence and fear in a sinister alliance that ultimately confuses the meaning of each. Asked what he would say if someone were *really* to ring the doorbell, the child engages in the following exchange:

"Mama's at work."

"And Papa?"

He was silent.

"And Papa?" the man screamed in terror.

The child turned pale.

"And Papa?" the man repeated more calmly.

"He's dead," the child answered and threw himself at his father, who was standing right beside him, blinking his eyes in that funny way, but who was already long dead to the people who would really ring the bell.[7]

When the Nazis violated traditional family hierarchies among their own citizens by inviting members of the Hitler Youth to report any disloyal sentiments they might overhear in household conversations, they redefined the bond linking children to their parents. They substituted a covenant between the citizen and the state for the earlier domestic intimacy, offering a form of psychological security that members of the organization could share with each other. But for their Jewish victims the Germans provided no such new external support. The child in Fink's story, obedient, bewildered, terrified, and betrayed, leaves us, like himself, searching for a key that does not exist, the key to the enigma of how the self should behave when threatened by extinction. The very effort to preserve identity by staying alive, or helping to keep someone else alive, simultaneously erodes identity, leaving a painful legacy to be unraveled when and if normal family relations return. Childhood is not the time for children to be custodians of their parents.

Many witnesses who were children during the Nazi era speak in their testimonies of their dilemma without offering any evidence that it has ever been resolved. Rachel G. was born in Brussels in 1934. In 1941, after the Germans had occupied Belgium, she was taken by a priest to a convent, where she was hidden along with several other Jewish girls. On her seventh birthday her father paid her a secret visit there; she never saw him again. Her name was changed, and during the war she was moved from convent to convent, finally being sent to a childless Catholic family living near the French border. They raised her as their own daughter, and she stayed with them until the liberation. Meanwhile, she learned that her parents had been deported to Auschwitz. Interviewed as an adult, Rachel G. speaks of the dual heritage from her childhood. She remembers both a loss of security and a transfer of security. Shifting loyalties at an impressionable age, she gradually "forgot" her real family and established emotional ties with whoever was protecting her at a particular time. Between the ages of seven and eleven, as the memory of her parents grew dim, she adapted to the life of a Jewish girl pretending to be a Catholic.

What emerges gradually from this testimony is the story of *two* childhoods, the one Rachel G. was born to but lost and the one she experienced with adults other than her parents. On the one hand, she is pained by having to describe the childhood she *had* rather than the one she missed. The absence of the latter leaves a lacuna in her life. But when she is asked how she feels about being Jewish today (1981), since she was raised as a Catholic, she replies that every time she sees a priest or a nun, she wants to kiss them. After the war, the couple who had been taking care of her wanted to adopt her, but Belgian law required a ten-month waiting period, to ensure that neither of her parents had returned from the camps. She was sent back to her original convent and attended school there as a Catholic. Just before the waiting period was up, a nun entered the classroom one morning and looked at her. "I knew my mother was outside," says Rachel G.

But instead of describing a joyful reunion, she speaks of her resentment toward her mother for having abandoned her. "I didn't want to go to my mother," she says. "I was too angry at her." For the moment, she recalls, she was hostile, even though her mother had been in Auschwitz for three years. Her father did not return. She admits that it took her a long time to realize that her parents' decision to send her into hiding is what saved her life. Yet she speaks more fondly of the nuns than of her mother, and the dual parental experience remains locked in her memory, leading to a heritage of divided loyalties that she cannot escape. She has raised her children to be Jewish, but they are confused by her confusion, since she speaks so enthusiastically about her childhood among the priests and the nuns.[8]

Even more disconcerting is the narrative of Menachem S. Born in 1938, he recalls moving to the Krakow ghetto in 1942 when he was four, then to the Plaszow labor camp the following year. In 1943, when he was five, his parents bribed a guard to allow the little boy to leave, tied a scarf around his neck, and pinned on his jacket an address, which turned out to be a brothel. He realizes years later that the choice was a shrewd one, since his parents hoped that among the many women there might be some who would be willing to care for him. His mother gives him her high school ID card, "just in case you need to recognize me when we come," and they promise to return for him after the war. He then offers a harrowing tale of how he drifted around as an "adult" rather than a child between his fifth and seventh years, among street gangs of orphaned or abandoned children, staying in the brothel at night until things got "hot" and he was taken in by a family in an outlying village. His parents survived as Schindler Jews, and in the summer of 1945 they came back to Krakow to seek him out. But when he sees them they are so emaciated that they are unrecognizable. His father, more than six feet tall, weighs 88 pounds, and his teeth are hanging loosely from his gums. They are utter strangers, and for a long time, he says, he addressed them as Mr. and Mrs. S. He makes no mention of joy, relief, pleasure, or satisfaction at finding the family unit intact. For five years he was unable to manage a transition back to normal reality. Instead, when he tried to become their child again, his pain intensified, and his life disintegrated into a constantly recurring cycle of disabling nightmares.

The coda to his testimony is filled with a rueful amusement. When his first child was born, he went on a buying spree, spending hundreds of dollars on toys, many of which, like electric trains and a bicycle, were inappropriate for a newborn infant. Perplexed at first by his behavior, he only slowly realized after his wife's prompting that he was buying the toys for himself, in commemoration of the buried youth that he never experienced. But it took him twenty-five years to speak about this to his children, because he feared transferring to them the anxieties that continued to plague him. Wounded memory operates like a parasite on the consciousness of some adult survivors long after they have passed beyond adolescence; it ambushed Menachem S. repeatedly after the liberation, culminating in the return to the traumatic time of his deprived childhood at the very moment when he became a father himself.

The temptation to romanticize the experience of hiding or passing and to idealize the rescuers is very strong, especially among those who are reluctant to face the boredom and the terror, to say nothing of the shattered identity, that afflicted the youthful victims. It is a vision that bears little resemblance to the truth. Anne Frank inadvertently contributed to the myth when she wrote in her diary, "I look upon our life in hiding as an interesting adventure, full of danger and romance." It is unlikely, had she survived, that she would have confirmed this sentiment after Westerbork, Auschwitz, and Bergen-Belsen. Edith H., a Dutch contemporary of Anne's, spent three years in hiding in Holland, partly alone, partly with her mother, and partly with both her parents. All survived, together with a sister who was in hiding elsewhere. Yet she complains bitterly in her testimony, "I didn't have any life from thirteen to [nearly] seventeen," mourning her lost childhood, a time she can never recover.[9] Marcel Proust's internal pursuit of the traces of lost time is based on a remembered chronology, not its abnormal disruption. The difference between the two is neatly captured by the testimony of Ely M., another Dutch Jewish girl who between the ages of ten and thirteen hid in various Christian homes, separated from her family. "You hear so often," she says, "that people start a new life and so on and how wonderful everything is. I personally . . . my feeling is that the after-effects are very hard for a child. When you come out of the war you don't want to be with your mother because you're estranged from your mother—for me it was [that way]."[10] Contrast this with the nostalgic pleasure with which the initial narrator of Proust's *Remembrance of Things Past* summons up the memory of his mother's leaving her party downstairs to come up to give him a goodnight kiss. The absence of such memories in the consciousness of so many child survivors leaves a void that the passage of time cannot replace. Philosopher Charles Taylor argues that the "full definition of someone's identity . . . usually involves not only his stand on moral and spiritual matters, but also some reference to a defining community."[11] But Ely M.'s "defining community" is a dead community, or more precisely, an exterminated one. In addition, during her years of hiding any stand she might have taken on moral and spiritual values was secondary to the more urgent necessity of keeping herself alive, a process that forestalled any meaningful expression of those values. We will never understand the concept of "damaged childhood" until we understand the feeling of estrangement that Ely M. speaks of, an estrangement not only from her mother, but also from her own youthful self.

This sense of alienation appears with great intensity in the testimony of Zezette L., born in Belgium in 1929 and hence only ten years old at the outbreak of the war. She begins by saying, "looking back on my family, and fully cognizant of the fact that you idealize what you don't have any more, we had a very good family." But the notion of a good family disintegrates in a single night after her parents receive a notice to report for "resettlement" and decide instead that they must go into hiding. There were no rules, however, for how "a good family" should behave under such circumstances. Zezette L.'s parents sent her to a Catholic convent under an assumed name and told her to forget her parents and to act like all the other Catholic girls. They sent her brother to hide with some Trappist monks. But during the Easter vacation in 1943 the old family feeling reasserted itself, with disastrous consequences. Human responses are often fatal in an inhuman milieu such as the one that reigned during the Nazi era, but decent people were loath to embrace this principle at the time, and many students of the period today continue to resist its unsettling impact. Simply put, Zezette and her parents missed each other, and since the convent was closed they resolved to take a chance and have her come to their hiding place. And to celebrate the reunion, since it was Easter Sunday, they thought it might be safe to go on an excursion into the country. Zezette L. never knew whether they were followed or deliberately betrayed, but while returning to the hiding place they were arrested by the Gestapo and sent to the transit camp of Malines. Whether they were reckless or brave remains a debatable issue, but in any event their yearning for normality proved to be their undoing. A few days later, they were deported to Auschwitz. Zezette L. was barely fourteen years old.

Upon arrival, Zezette joined those selected for work in the camp, while her mother was sent to the left. The daughter's solemn comment is that she hopes her mother didn't know where she was going. She saw her father twice in the camp, but they didn't dare speak; soon after, he vanished among the mass of anonymous dead. We are now left to imagine how a fourteen-year-old orphan might experience the daily ordeal of Auschwitz. An odd dialogue ensues between interviewer and witness, the former needing to put a hopeful twist on the experience and the latter determined not to falsify her account. Asked what she did in Auschwitz, she replies, "I was dehumanized." Asked if she ever sang songs in Auschwitz, as some child survivors report, she stares with disbelief at the question. She has *no* good memories. Her most vivid one is of standing at roll call, endlessly, in the freezing cold, ill-clad, often barefoot. Asked if she had any friends, she responds that she was alone and could never understand people remembering their "friends" at Auschwitz. Maybe older people had them, she says, but not younger ones like her. "You had no one to rely on?" "No." "You had no one to relate to?" "No." "Did you have a sense of being entirely alone?" "Yes." And then she adds, "Strangely enough, I still do." Reluctant to accept the dismal vision that Zezette L. depicts, the well-intentioned interviewer persists: "Some people say that the only way to survive Auschwitz was if you had someone." Reply: "I had no one."

What Zezette L.'s testimony demonstrates is the futility of searching for an exemplary version of the adolescent experience in a place like Auschwitz. We must respond to a series of solo performances rather than a musical ensemble or a chorus, appreciating each one separately and accepting nuances of difference rather than fixed categories of similarity. There is little to celebrate about a tainted childhood, even though it need not necessarily lead to a poisoned future. Zezette L. is saddened and even embittered by her memories, but not disabled. When she reached her mother's age, she returned to Auschwitz to say Yizkor for her parents, the memorial prayer for the dead. "One can talk about it in a positive way," she concludes, "if, if, if, if . . ."—but she never finishes her sentence, as the whole negative burden of her testimony intervenes to silence her latent thought, or wish. She makes a conscious statement about needing to live for the future, but when she describes her ruined childhood, she does not say "I live with it," but "It lives with me." Her verbal assertion about living for the future stumbles against her dismal account of the past, and her consciousness of this tension is a vivid indication of her determination to restore continuity to her life. She has had the number on her left forearm erased not as a gesture of amnesia, which is impossible in any case, but to cast off the public identity of Auschwitz survivor decreed by her oppressors and to choose her own useful role in the present. She balances the dignity of her present life against the memory of a dehumanized adolescence. How well she manages internally is a private matter, whose fluctuations remain hostage to reminiscence and time.[12]

The issue of transmitting the effects of damaged childhood from one generation to the next is difficult to assess. Neither the Fortunoff Video Archive for Holocaust Testimonies at Yale University nor Steven Spielberg's Shoah Foundation has taken detailed testimony from children of survivors. There is no archive of such accounts comparable to the thousands that are available from the parents. Perhaps the most powerful statement about this potentially burdensome legacy appears in Carl Friedman's brief novel *Nightfather,* whose survivor protagonist cannot suppress the need to recount his camp experiences to his wife and three young children. He does this relentlessly, transforming the most benign occasions into analogues of his horrendous past. His memories of the camp surge uncontrollably from inexhaustible depths to wash over his children's lives and leave a touch of pollution in their wake. When the children ask their mother what is wrong with Papa, she replies succinctly, "He has camp." Unfortunately, the "illness" is contagious, like the persistent tuberculosis he brought back with him. The only cures are silence and love, but the former eludes him, and the latter, which he genuinely feels, is contaminated by the narrative impulse that, fifteen years after the war, he still cannot suppress.

Friedman's narrator is one of the victims of this impulse, the middle child of unknown age, but surely less than ten, who tells her family's story with a mixture of innocence and dismay. She captures the confusion of any child trying to make sense of the anecdotes that survivor parents brought back with them after their release. Her father's influence is infectious in ways that reflect the spread of disease rather than enthusiasm; because the naïve children never really understand this, however, the reader is left to feel and interpret the devastating impact of family interaction. The young narrator is shrewd enough to realize, as she says, that "Max, Simon, and I are different from ordinary children," but she has no audience to help her digest the significance of her father's camp legacy. An episode in school illustrates the hermetic dilemma that enfolds her:

> "A man flying through the air!" The teacher smiles, as she bends over my drawing.
> "He isn't flying," I tell her, "he's hanging. See, he's dead, his tongue is blue. And these prisoners have to look at him as a punishment. My father is there, too. Here, he's the one with the big ears."
> "That's nice," says the teacher.
> "It's not," I say. "They're starving and now they have to wait a long time for their soup." But she's already moved on to the next desk.[13]

Overheard memories pursue the children throughout their daily adventures. On a drive into the country, the father suddenly stops the car by a ditch backed by a grove of trees:

> "Great woods," he says. We nod. He clicks his tongue. "Great woods to escape into. So thick and so deep. They'd never find you there, not the ghost of a chance."
> He gets out. We stay where we are and watch him jump across the ditch. The woods swallow him up.
> "What's he up to?" Simon wonders nervously.
> "The usual," I say, "just a little escaping." Simon winds down the window.
> "I can't hear a thing. Only birds."
> "You can't hear escaping," I whisper. "Escaping has to be done very quietly, otherwise it doesn't work."
> "And what about us?" he says.
> I start sucking my thumb. What does Simon know about such things?[14]

Unlike most memoirs, fiction gains its effects through omission as well as inclusion. In *Nightfather* we are obliged to brood on an anxiety of influence that has nothing to do with the literary tensions that Harold Bloom wrote of. The narrator suffers from a different stress, an insecurity resulting from the net of reminiscence that her father inadvertently casts over *her* when contending with his own unpacified past.

The narrators' siblings are also caught in the father's web of remembering. "Tell us a story," the younger brother Simon asks his father, a legitimate request from the world of normal childhood. Instead, he is barraged by a series of barbarous anecdotes about camp life until Simon grumbles with disappointment, "That isn't a story. . . . That really happened." But there is no escape into the imagination from the Holocaust; its reality ruthlessly pursues its survivors, and indeed all future generations, with a pitiless intensity that Friedman captures in her narrative:

> "Do you want a story then? Okay, have it your way!" says my father. "Little Red Riding Hood is walking with her basket through the woods. Suddenly a vicious dog jumps out of the *Hundezwinger* [dog kennels]. 'Hello, Little Red Riding Hood, where are you going?' 'I'm going to see my grandmother,' says Little Red Riding Hood. 'She's in the hospital with typhus.'"
> "No," says Simon, "that's not how it goes."[15]

But for the children of this father, that *is* how it goes. His past permeates their thinking and taints their games. The narrator buries her toys in a garden so that when the SS come for *them* they will not take the toys too. One day the narrator finds her older brother Max sitting on a chair in the kitchen, his socks on the floor and his bare feet in the refrigerator. His reply to a request for an explanation is "I want to know what they feel like when they freeze." "I want to be one of them," he adds. "And you can only be one of them if you're half-starved or if you've had typhus. Being gassed a bit helps, too. Anyway, you have to have suffered damage in some way." This is the same son who earlier had broken under the strain of his father's dogged reminiscences and exploded at him, "Just don't keep coming to me with stories about that stupid camp of yours. It served you right!"[16]

The tension between the need to incorporate the horrors of their father's Holocaust past into the rhythms of their daily life and to repel that past in order to make way for the future remains an unresolvable dilemma for the children in Carl Friedman's vignettes. All Holocaust victims were sentenced to die, but many of those lucky enough to survive found themselves sentenced to live, a prospect that few were prepared to face with equanimity. The anguish of the heirs to atrocity in Friedman's *Nightfather* resides less in the words of her children than in what remains unsaid. The art of her fiction complements and complicates the more straightforward statements that energize the memoirs and testimonies that we have examined. As the forms of representation of the experience of children during and after the Holocaust grow more imaginative, greater demands are made on the interpretive faculty. Finally, a total collaboration is required between audience and artist if the implications of a work are to be reclaimed from the silence that surrounds it.

A classic example of this summons to collaboration is the painting of Samuel Bak. He is a child survivor of the Vilna ghetto; his four grandparents were murdered at Ponary woods and his father was shot by the Germans a few days before the arrival of Soviet troops. Only he and his mother survived. In a large canvas called *Self Portrait* (1995–1996) Bak captures the interlocked destinies of the living and the dead as he divides the "self" into juxtaposed alter egos, illustrating one of the deepest impulses of Jewish consciousness after the catastrophe: no one's survival can be separated from the death of someone else. For the child in this canvas life and death are no longer opposites or alternatives, but coexist in the imagination with a painful intimacy that changes our way of viewing the self in relation to history and time. Although the boy who was Bak occupies the foreground of this picture, the center is dominated by a fragmented version of the most famous photograph to emerge from the Holocaust—another boy with his hands raised being rounded up with other Jews from the Warsaw ghetto. The face of the living boy is permanently bonded to the replica of the murdered one; the self-portrait of one *includes* a self-portrait of the other. For the artist, the Holocaust has shattered the notion of an independent and unified self, as it has destroyed the possibility of remembering an untroubled childhood. The dead youth peers at the living one as if to say, with the ghost of Hamlet's father, "Remember me." In other words, the rhythms of creation must somehow absorb the jagged heritage of loss.

The boy who grew up in prewar Vilna is not the same as the one who survived the catastrophe remembering a murdered father and a ruined community. The sack in which he sits is a reminder of the sorrow from which he has not yet fully recovered. In a labor camp on the outskirts of Vilna, Bak's father put him in a sack, like this one, that was supposed to be filled with wood, and when no one was looking he dropped him from the ground-floor window of the warehouse where he was working, enabling his son to escape and thereby saving his life. Thus the life of the son is tightly entwined with the death of the parent. Here history and autobiography merge as private references fuse with allusions to public moments of atrocity, creating an aftermath of distraught reminiscence that invites us to inquire into its complex origins.

The staring eyes solicit us to share a silence that is flooded with melancholy memories, while the paintbrush in the boy's hand reminds us that the task of making art from all this devastation still lies before him. On his left are stacked cutouts for future renditions of child victims, a cue to Bak's habit of painting multiple versions of the same theme, as if to confirm the absence of a definitive interpretation of crimes of such magnitude. The pale figure with raised hands has stigmata on his palms, and if he were to stretch out his arms, they would be cruciform. One of the muted themes of Bak's paintings is the role of Christian responsibility for the unfolding of Holocaust history. The viewer is also urged to reflect on a pair of empty shoes, once occupied by the vanishing feet of the boy from the Warsaw ghetto. Who will wear them now, and how will he or she carry on the tradition of Jewish memory once transmitted by their former owner? This issue is deepened by the small stones in the right foreground holding down blank sheets of paper, indicating how the Holocaust has disrupted the familiar Jewish custom of placing such stones on the tombs of the dead. Are these empty pages part of a Torah scroll at the boy's feet, and with what text will they be re-inscribed to include the story of the disaster? We cannot tell whether the skies are warmed by a glowing sun or heated by the fires of destruction, but the distant vista hints at a community in flames, while belching smokestacks summon us to a voyage of sinister intent. These tensions have etched themselves on the internal vision of the boy, who throughout his life as an artist will seek forms to capture the paradoxical fusion of life with death and creation with decay that will become major motifs of his work. The large blank canvas in the upper left-hand corner of the picture awaits its destiny with patient expectation.

Bak extends the incentive in a painting like *Group* (1997), where the face of the living boy peers over the shoulders of the ghostly figures, some of them faceless, of the murdered children. Together with the brick wall, they seem to form a barrier to locating a space of his own, separate from theirs. Identified by their inmate garb, they have already entered the realm of extinction. How does a child move from spectator to participant in this lifeless terrain, where prior to cremation human flesh has already been converted into the more flammable material of wood? The blockade of the dead serves a reciprocal purpose, since it also prevents us from reaching the living boy until *we* have found a way of crossing through the crowd of approaching victims. The mock blessing of the pierced palm offers little assistance or consolation. Bak's world of visual images mirrors the betrayed hope of a million murdered Jewish children. But it also highlights for the thousands of surviving ones and their descendants the immense difficulty of creating a future out of childhoods like his, still intermittently flinching from insurgent memories of a wounded past. Bak's art raises testimony and memoir to its most universal heights, soliciting us to join in repeated visitations to unbearable burdens that must nonetheless be borne. He implicates his audiences in the chore of wresting form, if not meaning, from the debris of a ravaged civilization, much as the God of Genesis shaped our world from the "waste and wild" of a seething chaos. History, however, will not allow Bak *or* us to fashion a new Paradise for our times. The age of innocence is over. His more modest goal is challenging enough: To rescue from oblivion the remnants of Jewish memory and to represent honestly the contradictions between the forlorn and the promising conditions for its continued existence.[17]

NOTES

1. See the documentary *Diamonds in the Snow,* written, directed, and produced by Mira Reym Binford, 1994. Available from The Cinema Guild, Inc., 1697 Broadway, Suite 506, New York, NY 10019-5904 (tel. 1-800-723-5522).

2. Nechama Tec, "A Historical Perspective: Tracing the History of the Hidden-Child Experience," in Jane Marks, *The Hidden Children: The Secret Survivors of the Holocaust* (New York: Ballantine, 1993), 287.

3. Nechama Tec, *Dry Tears: The Story of a Lost Childhood* (New York: Oxford University Press, 1984), 109.

4. Ibid., 144, 145.

5. Yehuda Nir, *The Lost Childhood: A Memoir* (New York: Harcourt Brace Jovanovich, 1989), 26.

6. Ida Fink, *A Scrap of Time and Other Stories,* trans. Madeline Levine and Francine Prose (New York: Schocken Books, 1989), 37.

7. Ibid., 37-38.

8. Interview with Rachel G., Fortunoff Video Archive for Holocaust Testimonies at Yale University, Tape T-139.

9. Interview with Edith H., Fortunoff Video Archive for Holocaust Testimonies at Yale University, Tape T-47.

10. Interview with Ely M., Fortunoff Video Archive for Holocaust Testimonies at Yale University, Tape-1170.

11. Charles Taylor, *Sources of the Self: The Making of the Modern Identity* (Cambridge, Mass.: Harvard University Press, 1989), 36.

12. Interview with Zezette L., Fortunoff Video Archive for Holocaust Testimonies at Yale University, Tape-100.

13. Carl Friedman, *Nightfather,* trans. Arnold and Erica Pomerans (New York: Persea Books, 1994), 5.

14. Ibid., 26.

15. Ibid., 33-34.

16. Ibid., 114, 115, 83.

17. For a more extended discussion of Bak's Holocaust paintings, together with numerous reproductions, see *Landscapes of Jewish Experience: Paintings by Samuel Bak,* essay and commentary by Lawrence L. Langer (Hanover, N.H.: University Press of New England, 1997).

26 Dealing with the Holocaust
"After Auschwitz" in Germany

Edna Brocke

THE TITLE I chose for this chapter was meant to be a pun, but it definitely does not come through. By formulating it as I did, I wanted to draw attention to two points: "Dealing with the Holocaust" and "'After Auschwitz' in Germany." On the one hand, there is as yet no word in the German language for "Holocaust," so this foreign term is often used. On the other hand, Germans do not want to use the foreign term "Holocaust," because they feel they should have a name for it in their own language. So they are compromising in a way when they say *Nach Auschwitz,* meaning "after Auschwitz." This is an indication of time and space, but it makes no mention of what really happened, to say nothing of naming the actors.

It points to a place in Poland called *Oswiecim* and, in terms of time, to the "break in civilization" caused by Auschwitz. One might say that it is only a matter of language and communication; but I think it indicates something much deeper: it pinpoints an obvious speechlessness on the part of the Germans, who have not found a term in their own language for what happened in their own history—not even after fifty years.

I am the director of a memorial site in Germany. It is located in a former synagogue that was not destroyed in the so-called *Kristallnacht* of November 1938 or by the Allies' severe bombing of Essen; rather, it was destroyed from within in 1960 by the city of Essen so that a museum for industrial design could be installed. In 1988 it was restored and reconstructed. Thus you might easily guess my approach to the question of education after the Holocaust.

This memorial site was opened in 1980 with a permanent exhibition dedicated exclusively to the resistance (mainly the communist one) in Germany between 1933 and 1945. It was no easy task to incorporate themes connected not only with Jewish history of the Nazi era but with Jewish history in general.

This memorial site is financed by the municipality of Essen. The staff consists of two full-time and two part-time workers who are engaged in research, and two full-time and two part-time workers in administration. I am the only Jew working there, which will give you a sense of how complicated the structure is.

One of the most interesting consequences for me, having worked there for almost eleven years, has been my observation that the work done by historians in the last twenty or thirty years has neglected, or even rejected, the fact that the study of the Holocaust can be viewed in terms of three intertwining yet distinct themes: (1) What was the National Socialist regime, and where did it come from? (2) What were the goals of World War II? and (3) What were the interests of those in Germany who set out to destroy the Jewish people?

I am convinced that these are not a single theme but three separate themes. While they fall together in time, and to some extent in space, how they are approached by an academic engaged in research will very much depend on his or her motivation for a particular study. The first theme, which focuses on the National Socialists, includes in my view all the questions concerning their attitude toward other minorities besides the Jews—Gypsies, gays, people with mental disabilities, and the other groups that were excluded from German society by this regime. I would not include in this first point their interest in eliminating the Jewish people. The second theme, pertaining to the diverse goals of World War II, needs to be researched from the point of view of both German and Russian interests. In addition to continental Europe, Japan was an interested party, as was Italy; both countries were deeply involved politically as well as economically. The third theme traces the question of the regime's motivation for attempting to annihilate the Jewish people throughout Europe. For example, what compelled people such as Eichmann to organize the trains and railways so that they could most efficiently transport large numbers of Jews from areas as far away as Greece and the Isle of Crete to Poland in order to kill them there? Keeping part of the military out of battle in order to meet this other goal was obviously counterproductive for the Germans in World War II.

German historians who study this period tend to tie these three segments together. They are not motivated to differentiate them. Other scientists are primarily interested in the research being done in their own scientific field. On the other hand, it is astonishing to see how many "normal citizens" in Germany are preoccupied with learning the negative aspects of their own history. An amazing number of people are seeking more knowledge and more information about their history, realizing that these were their own people. In no other country would I have expected either academics or ordinary people with an interest in politics to confront their own history. I know of no comparable interest on the part of the Japanese in, for example, their involvement in Manchuria. I know of no parallel interest among Russians; neither the gulags nor other periods of their history are a central topic of research or general interest. In Germany, however, especially in Western Germany, many are interested.

After 1968, which marked a break of sorts, historians seem to have branched off in two main directions. On the one hand, there are people such as Professor Nolte of Berlin, who tried to draw parallels between the Soviet regime and the Nazi regime. His attempts were not accepted by most of his fellow historians. He was seen not as having tried to compare the systems, but as having tried to make them equal. On the other hand, there is another group of historians, the most famous among whom is Professor Hans Mommsen (not to be confused with his twin brother Wolfgang, also a professor of history), whose research is basically different. Mommsen was mainly interested in tracing the hierarchies within the Nazi system on both the political and the military level.

* * *

The common denominator between these two groups of historians is that neither is interested in the Holocaust. Yet bear in mind that these two schools of historians were established after the war and are still the leading schools in historical research even now, though both named protagonists are retired.

For many of us who work at memorial sites, it has become clear that real help in our work, including our everyday work, will not come from historians. The primary fields from which we can draw support are the social sciences, sociology, and, first and foremost, psychology. Historians tend to refuse even to reflect on their own motivation for the subject.

Among circles of religiously motivated people, there are some who are deeply concerned with the part played by the churches in paving the way to Auschwitz. A number of parishes contain impostors who are trying to renew their relationship with the Jewish people.

In short, there are many people in Germany who are being forced to confront the Holocaust, not just World War II, and not just the Nazi regime. This is true of the media as well, where I sometimes get the impression that people are being given more than they really can cope with. It might be *too* much, because it leaves people with a question mark. Most films on the subject are accompanied by a documentary film or a panel, so that spectators can share their insights and emotions about their own national identity. Sometimes it seems that the media present too much about all three themes—so much so that even people who know very little about Judaism automatically associate Jews with World War II and think of them as "victims."

The same is true of the education system. Depending on the school system, students are generally taught about the Holocaust (that is to say the extermination of the Jewish people in Europe, and not primarily World War II) in several grades during their school career, and not just in different grades, but in different courses as well. They study the Holocaust in religion, in political science, and in German literature and language, among others. My impression is that students are sometimes subjected to so much information about the Holocaust that they cannot emotionally cope with it.

Until the Iron Curtain came down in Eastern Europe, there were around thirty or forty thousand Jews in Western Germany who were affiliated with a synagogue yet were not religious. And very few of them were particularly concerned with Halakah. It was the only way for Jews in Western Germany to meet other Jews. Most of them were survivors, first generation so-called displaced persons who had remained in Germany, in the American or the British zone, rather than follow friends and relatives to such countries as Israel, Australia, and the United States. Those who stayed—for a variety of personal reasons—gave birth to their children in postwar Germany. These children grew up not knowing why their parents had remained in Germany, but often accusing them for having done so. This underlying problem has rarely been discussed within the communities, let alone been the subject of an open discourse between the two generations. Nor has it happened with the grandchildren. Thus there is a Jewish population of thirty to forty thousand synagogue-affiliated Jews and between twenty and thirty thousand Jews who are not synagogue-affiliated, living primarily in the big centers such as Frankfurt and Berlin, who are very active in presenting their political opinions in the media. This group of Jews is less concerned with what happens in Jewish circles. The Germany that Professor Gilman describes in his chapter is a Germany that I personally have not known in my twenty-eight years of living there.

At the memorial site where I work, we are currently pursuing two pertinent activities. One is a project for which I lack an adequate word in English, the *Gedenkbuchprojekt*. We ask people—primarily, but not exclusively, young people—to try to write the biography of a person murdered in the Holocaust, be he or she Jewish or not. In addition to the basic material we have collected on each of these murdered people, we try to provide addresses of acquaintances, friends, or relatives around the world, people with whom our participants can correspond in order to obtain more information. Our primary aim is to put young Germans in contact with people whom they otherwise would never meet. Quite a number of friendships have been born out of this work. Among our alumni are students who have written, in their own language, the biographies of murdered people from Essen.

We correct only obvious historical mistakes. The text is then copied in nice calligraphy, so that the documents all have a more uniform appearance. They are entered into a memorial book, which is part of our permanent exhibit. Of the 2,650 names known to us of murdered people from Essen (including more than 2,500 Jews, along with social democrats and communists who were killed by the Nazis), all the biographies for the non-Jews have been completed. The memorial book now contains approximately 350 biographies.

Another project we have tried to establish is a partnership between a school in Essen, Victoria Schule, and a school in Tel Aviv, Wizo-Tzarfat. The partnership between these two schools means that Israeli students regularly visit Essen and vice versa. The exchange, now in its seventh year, has been popular with both the students and the teachers. Even the head of the Israeli school, who survived with his father in Poland, willingly supports the program wherever he can. He welcomes the guests from Germany to his school, but he will not greet them in German, and he will not reciprocate with a visit to Germany. Perhaps this attitude has particularly impressed the children in Essen.

Thus our concern is not really education about the Holocaust in terms of teaching the Holocaust itself, but rather an indirect approach to this period of time and the problems connected with it. We are convinced that the indirect way, the more open way, enables more people to find their own approach and their own individual insight. We do not want to be part of creating a new "dogma" that one has to "believe" in.

27 Video History of the Holocaust
The Case of the Shoah Foundation
Michael Berenbaum

THE SURVIVORS OF THE Shoah Visual History Foundation was established in 1994 by Steven Spielberg with a daunting goal: to videotape-record the testimony of Holocaust survivors and eyewitnesses, so that future generations will have more direct access to their experiences. Spielberg was moved by the power of oral history during his experience creating *Schindler's List*. He was besieged by survivors coming forward to tell their stories, and he undertook a public commitment to record fifty thousand testimonies and to disseminate such testimonies in five initial repositories: Yad Vashem in Jerusalem; the Simon Wiesenthal Center in Los Angeles; the Museum of Jewish Heritage in New York; the United States Holocaust Memorial Museum in Washington; and the Fortunoff Archives of Holocaust Testimonies at Yale University in New Haven, Connecticut.

This was not the first oral history project of the Holocaust. The Fortunoff archive was begun in 1978, and has been recording testimonies ever since. And during the 1980s and 1990s, as video technology evolved, regional and local projects were developed in many communities throughout the United States and Canada: the United States Holocaust Memorial Museum began its oral history project in the late 1980s; and the Hebrew University and Yad Vashem began their projects, which were audio- and not video-recording projects, as early as the 1950s. Still, no Holocaust history project of the size and scope of the Shoah Foundation's had ever been developed, and none was as global in reach, once the project had fully developed.

It was a race against time: survivors were rapidly aging, and within a few years, the last eyewitnesses would be gone. It was the right time: just after the war, many survivors were anxious to tell the world about their experiences, their tragedies, but they were silenced by listeners' disbelief or incredulity; later, in midlife, many wanted to share their stories with their children but didn't for fear of upsetting them. Now, before it was too late, these survivors were invited to give testimony, to ensure that their stories would be preserved. They understood that it was now or never. These memories would have to be shared if they were to reach future generations.

Now was the time. Museums and movies such as *Schindler's List* had heightened interest in the Holocaust. And as this event receded further into the past, it seemed to gain in significance. In classrooms throughout the world we

348

have seen the intense encounter between survivors and students—the transmission of memories, a discussion of values, and a warning against prejudice, antisemitism, racism, and indifference.

Mark Twain once said that there are truths, lies, and statistics. The statistics of the Shoah Foundation as of February 20, 1999 are listed below. As of that date, the Foundation has recorded the testimonies of 50,127 survivors and other eyewitnesses in thirty-three languages and fifty-seven countries. It has amassed 232,906 videotapes, more than 31,978 miles of tape (that's greater than the circumference of the earth!). It has collected more than 116,453 hours of testimony, which would take a viewer thirteen years, three months and twelve days—working night and day—to see in their entirety. The longest interview is seventeen hours and ten minutes, and the average interview is two hours and fifteen minutes. The archive is diverse: it centers on the experiences of Jews but includes testimonies from each of the Nazis' victim groups, as well as rescuers, liberators, and other important eyewitnesses. It does not, however, include perpetrators, as perhaps a complete video record of the Holocaust should.

The Shoah Foundation will complete its task of gathering testimonies within the next few years. This will be primary material for interpretation by historians and for use by documentary filmmakers, educators, students, and scholars. It will provide a visual documentation of the most evil event of our century—and perhaps of all centuries.

Why videotape-record oral testimonies of the Holocaust? The reasons are many. Let the historians tell us why. Without recorded oral histories, what would we know of resistance, but mere dates and events? We would know much of German documents but little of Jewish testimony, for does the Stropp Report tell the full story of the Warsaw Ghetto Uprising? Without oral histories, we would know almost nothing of the death marches—the forced marches of the winter of 1944–45 in which beleaguered concentration camp victims, stretched beyond the limits of human endurance, walked hundreds of miles without food or shelter. Oral testimony fills in the gaps; it gives us a more complete picture of the gestalt; it individualizes and personalizes the event. Without oral histories, how could we learn of the life of a hidden child, too young to write and to record, but still able to remember? History would indeed be impoverished if the Holocaust remained, to our eyes, depersonalized, robbed of the vividness of individual testimony. While its victims may now be nameless and faceless to us, its survivors are not.

Why oral history? Let the poets tell us why. Elie Wiesel has said: "Only those who were there will ever know. And those who were there can never tell." If there is truth to the first part of Wiesel's statement (that those who were there have an unparalleled sense of what it was like to be "there"), we respectfully disagree with the latter half of his statement. Those who were there *can* speak, and their stories can be preserved for coming generations.

Primo Levi has argued that to understand life in the camps, a new language is needed.

> Just as our hunger is not that feeling of missing a meal, so our way of being cold has need of a new word. We say "hunger," we say "tiredness," "fear," "pain," we say "winter" and they are different things. They are free words, created and used by free men who lived in comfort and suffering in their homes. If the *Lagers* had lasted longer, a new harsh language would have been born; and only this language could express what it means to toil the whole day in the wind, with the temperature below freezing, wearing only a shirt, underpants, cloth jacket and trousers, and in one's body nothing but weakness, hunger and knowledge of the end drawing nearer.[1]

It is precisely the testimony of Holocaust survivors that provides a language for understanding their experiences. Lawrence Langer makes this point in his work when he shows how Holocaust video testimonies provide a unique entrée into the life of ordinary men and women who lived through an extraordinary event and hence ceased to be ordinary. Testimony is thus the "literature" of the non-elite.

And so, when we ask "Why an oral history of the Holocaust?" we should most importantly let the survivors and their students tell us why. The conclusion of the permanent exhibition at the United States Holocaust Memorial Museum presented survivors' testimonies because it was the survivors who could effectively bridge the gap between that world and our world. Their testimony was one of the high points of the museum's exhibitions and also created sacred living space within the exhibition. These survivors had heard two commandments in the darkness of the Holocaust: "Remember," and "Do not let the world forget." Now before it is too late they can be assured that their stories will be preserved. In classrooms, the dialogue between students and survivors is electrifying. History comes alive to these students as they hear directly from those who were there. Unfortunately this experience will soon no longer be available to future generations of students. Survivors are dying, and a decade or two from now they will no longer be with us. With video testimony, the possibility remains for student-survivor interactions. This means that each time they meet with students, survivors need not repeat their whole story but must merely be present to clarify and amplify. And when they are no longer available, interactive technology will permit active inquiry of the eyewitnesses by students.

Professional movie makers recognize and respect the profound power and effectiveness of oral history. The two most recent Academy Award winners for best documentary have been based almost exclusively on survivors' testimonies.

Yet some historians are uncomfortable with oral history. They contend that the information is unreliable, or at best far less reliable than documentary evidence or contemporaneous evidence such as diaries and notes. These historians have a point, but at the same time they seem to be *missing* the point: no oral history should be viewed uncritically as historical evidence. It must be evaluated within the context of everything else we know. If some oral histories are self-serving, so too are some documents, speeches, memos, and other accounts of the time. Oral histories should be considered alongside other forms of documentation, and they should at least be considered by historians as subject to verification and classification. However, even historians who most vociferously object to oral history do rely upon it to provide context and texture. They do interview people who were participants in historical events, and they read their memoirs and review court testimony.

The material assembled by these oral accounts from the Holocaust will provide the possibility of a people's history of the Holocaust. It will be of interest to historians, but not to historians alone: sociologists and psychologists, students of literature and language, filmmakers and documentary makers will find this material of interest. It will provide unequaled visual recollections of the world before the Holocaust, vital information about the transition between the Holocaust and the post-war years, and, of course, vivid recollections of the Holocaust.

The Shoah Foundation treats every one of these testimonies as important and precious. We never rush the survivor in an interview. Quality assurance staff work with every one of our interviewers to prepare them for the task at hand. Then each interview is reviewed, and each interviewer is coached in ways for improvement—he or she is shown, for example, how to better phrase a question to better elicit information—to make them equal to the task of being midwives to testimony.

Each testimony is catalogued, moment by moment, in a pioneering way that will allow people not only to see entire interviews, but to explore segments of interviews through a keyword search process which specifies the huge range of historical, biographical, and geographical data, including proper names, offered by the witnesses. A keyword authority has been developed by a team of historians, geographers, and archivists. The keywords emerge from the spoken word. They provide for both lateral and hierarchical classification. They are dynamic rather than static terms, and they reach toward the specificity of experience.

The terms must be specific. For example, if we used "ghetto" as a keyword, we might get five million citations, and the researcher or filmmaker would face the daunting, almost impossible task of sorting through the hits. But if we use the keywords "acquisition of (the) food," and then specify place and means as in the following examples,

> acquisition of the food
> acquisition of the food during deportation
> acquisition of the food during forced marches
> acquisition of the food during transfer

acquisition of the food in forced labor battalions
acquisition of the food in hiding
acquisition of food in prisons
acquisition of food in the ghettos
acquisition of food by resistance groups
acquisition of food in the [place] by smuggling
acquisition of food in the [place] by bartering
acquisition of food in the [place] by rationing
acquisition of food in the [place] by growing, etc.,

the search results will be more specific. We define place in a dynamic rather than a static way, since geographical concepts change over time and in response to situations. For example, Poland is specified according to time, geographical situation, and political conditions. The listing under Poland is:

Poland 1918 (November 3)–1939 (August 31)
Poland 1918 (November 3)–1920 (May 12)
Poland 1920 (October 13)–1926 (May 11)
Poland 1926 (May 12)–1935 (May 12)
Poland 1935 (May 13)–1939 (August 31)
Poland 1939 (September 1)–1945 (May 7)
Poland 1939
Poland 1940
Poland 1941
Poland 1941 (June 21)–1945 (May 7)
Poland 1941 (June 21)–1944 (July 21)
Poland 1942
Poland 1943
Poland 1944
Poland 1944 (July 22)–1945 (January 16)
Poland 1945
Poland 1945 (January 17)–1945 (May 7)
Poland 1945 (May 8)–Present
Poland 1945 (May 8)–1948 (December 20)
Poland 1948 (December 21)–1956 (June 27)
Poland 1956 (June 28)–1967 (December 31)
Poland 1968 (January 1)–1980 (August 13)
Poland 1980 (August 14)–1985 (November 5)
Poland 1985 (November 6)–1989 (June 4)
Poland 1989 (June 5)–Present

Transcribing more than fifty thousand interviews was financially and logistically prohibitive, so rather than prepare transcripts of each interview, a summary is prepared as well as an organization of segments according to keywords. The entire interview is digitized and linked to keywords, thus permitting immediate access to specific points in the interview. There is no need to play the entire interview; no requirement to fast forward or rewind. Keywords can be coordinated with other data such as age or gender, village or town, camps or ghettos, to allow greater access to comparative information. Such a project has never before been undertaken. The system is still evolving and is getting more complete with each catalogued testimony and with the addition of each new language.

To Gather, to Catalogue, to Disseminate

In establishing the Shoah Foundation, Steven Spielberg pledged to make the material available at five repositories. We are not there yet, but the material is now available at two repositories: New York's Museum of Jewish Heritage (according to a review in the *Washington Post,* "it forms the most powerful part of the exhibition"), and the Simon Wiesenthal Center, where data is received from the Foundation over broadband fiber-optic lines. Material may soon be available at the United States Holocaust Memorial Museum and at Yad Vashem in Jerusalem. But one hopes this will only be the beginning. The new university-based broadband fiber-optic closed system known as Internet 2 should allow access to 133 research universities in the United States and some forty more in Canada. Thus, the archive will be accessible in diverse locations by different populations, and this technology should only become more widely available in the coming years.

To Gather, to Catalogue, to Disseminate, and to Educate

Once the painstaking work of the Foundation has been done, History will be incarnated. It will come alive to students! Imagine what we could learn of American slavery if we could listen to the voices and see the faces of former slaves. Stories are transmitted powerfully and emotionally by narrative witnesses. The Passover story of the Jews, the Christians' reenactment of the death and resurrection of Jesus at Easter time—imagine direct access to the testimonies of those who were there as these great religions were formed!

We have already begun to make the contents of our archive available. Three documentaries have been released as well as a CD-ROM. And the Shoah Foundation will not be the only one to use this material. Our task is to share. Our material is already being made available to researchers and scholars, students, documentary filmmakers, and educators. Our methodologies, technology, and experience will in turn be made available to other groups to document their experiences: survivors of Rwanda and Bosnia, cancer victims, those who triumphed over apartheid or segregation, and others.

For the new generation, we will have to find new ways to impart knowledge, to teach values, to speak of our past and to our future. To some traditional scholars, this is a discomforting challenge. But creative education need not be the antithesis of scholarship, precision, and seriousness. Its mission is an urgent one: to forever serve as a resource for the preservation and transmission of the memory of the Holocaust, and to educate *against* hatred and bigotry and *for* tolerance and decency.

NOTE

1. Primo Levi, *Survival in Auschwitz* (New York: Summit Books, 1960), translated by Stuart Woolf, p. 123.

What to Do
Approaches to Post-Holocaust Education

David R. Blumenthal

A Preliminary Linguistic Note

For many years I used the word "holocaust" to designate the destruction of European Jewry during the Second World War. I have since been persuaded that "holocaust" should not be used for two reasons. First, it bears the additional meaning of "a whole burnt offering," which is certainly not the theological overtone to be sounded in this context. And second, the destruction of European Jewry happened to Jews, and hence it is they who should have the sad honor of naming this event with a Hebrew term. The word "shoah" has been used for a long time in Hebrew to denote the catastrophe to Jewry during World War II and has even been adopted by many non-Jews as the proper designation. I now adopt this usage and acknowledge my debt to Professor Jean Halpérin of Geneva and Fribourg for the insight.

It is my practice to capitalize only nouns referring to God, together with nouns usually capitalized in English. This is a theological-grammatical commitment to the sovereignty of God. Thus, I spell "messiah," "temple," and the like. Furthermore, to infuse literature with ethics, I especially do not capitalize "nazi," "führer," "fatherland," "third reich," "national socialist," "final solution," and the like, except in quotations. I am indebted to Hana Goldman, a plucky ten-year-old, who defied her teachers by refusing to capitalize "nazi," thereby setting an example for all of us. The word "shoah" falls in this category and, therefore, I consistently do not capitalize it.

Getting from There to Here

As we approach the end of the century and try to bring some perspective to its most traumatic event, the shoah, the task before us seems overwhelming. Can one really "bring some perspective" to such an event? Is the very attempt to do so a banalization of the lives of those who died, or survived?[1] To a theologian, two questions cry out for answers. First, where was God? How can those of us who are religious people reconcile our belief in the continuous presence of God in the life of the Jewish people with the presence of God in the shoah? How can those of us to whom God's presence is alive and important believe in a God who allowed the shoah to happen? This is, perhaps, the most searing theological question of this *fin de siècle*. The usual answers are inadequate, and, in an attempt to save the doctrine of God for our times, I have ventured another, rather bold, answer in *Facing the Abusing God: A Theology of Protest.*[2]

The second basic question of our times is, where was humanity? Here, the issue is not the cruelty and sadism of the shoah, for, although these were certainly present, cruelty and sadism were not peculiar to the shoah. Nor is the question one of numbers, for there have been other mass murders and even genocides in which large numbers of people have been killed. The issue in the shoah is also not one of state policy, though that certainly sets off the shoah from previous forms of genocide.[3] The real horror of the shoah lies in the compliance of the masses with the final solution. The key question about humanity, then, is, why did so many tens of millions of people go along with the shoah? How did the nazi regime persuade the overwhelming masses of Europe to remain bystanders? to accept passively, if not actively, the extermination of the Jews? Terror was certainly a factor, but it is not a sufficient answer.

An equally puzzling question is posed by those who rescued Jews: Why did they rescue? How did the rescuers manage to resist the persuasion and threat of the nazi regime such that they defied it? If obedience characterized the masses, what describes the resistors and rescuers?

The question, where was humanity, can also be framed as follows: When one interrogates perpetrators, the usual response is, "I was only doing my job," "I was only following orders," "I was only doing that which was expected of me." While this "Nuremberg defense" is not admissible legally, it does express the sense of the perpetrator and the bystander. Similarly, when one questions rescuers, the usual response is, "I did nothing heroic," "I was only doing what any human being would have done," "I was only doing that which was expected of me." While this explanation is routinely rejected by those who have been rescued as well as by those who marvel at the "heroism" of the rescuers, it does express the sense of the rescuer. Why is this so? Why do both perpetrators and bystanders, and rescuers, regard their behavior as "normal," as "banal" in the sense of "ordinary"? (Note: The word "banal" has two meanings in English: "normal, ordinary," which is how it is used here, and "trivial, morally unimportant," which is certainly not its sense in the context of the shoah.) The question, where was humanity, then, revolves around the issue of the banality of both good and evil.

The answer to the question, where was humanity, lies first in careful historical study of the period of the shoah. Extremely useful data, however, can also be found in the field of social psychology. A series of social psychological experiments in compliance, known loosely as "the obedience experiments," were conducted, and the results have been widely discussed. A series of experiments in prosocial action, known loosely as "the altruism experiments," were also conducted, and their results are rather widely known too. Unfortunately, within the discipline of social psychology, experimental work in obedience and in altruism is not usually done together. Nor is analysis of these complementary phenomena usually undertaken as a whole.[4] Similarly, within the discipline of history, systematic social psychological questions are not often asked. To answer the question, where was humanity, however, one must study the obedience experiments and the altruism experiments, as well as the historical literature on perpetrators and rescuers during the shoah and other traumatic human events. Such research generates a unified field theory of antisocial and prosocial human behavior and helps us address the issue of the nature of human responsibility.

It is incumbent upon us as morally serious persons to look at the data from antisocial studies and ask: What have we learned in the fifty years since the end of the shoah about human moral behavior? What lessons, if any, can we draw for humanity from this event as we enter the next century? Especially theologians and religious educators must confront the fact that an overwhelming majority of the perpetrators and bystanders were religious. They were believers, energetic adherents of their churches and active participants in the various praxes of piety.[5] How did church leaders—priests, pastors, theologians, and others—allow themselves and their institutions to be drawn into evil? Why did some religious leaders resist, often taking their followers with them? What was it that religious institutions were teaching that enabled the shoah to happen? Western religion and culture has been discussing the problem of good and evil and preaching ethical behavior for three thousand years. We are not amateurs. Yet in the shoah, we failed miserably, and there is every reason to believe that we will fail again. Why? What *ought* we to be discussing and teaching?

It also is incumbent upon us as morally serious persons to look at the data from prosocial studies and ask: What have we learned about human goodness? What do we know about the basic impulses to do good? And how could we cultivate those impulses? In the century that discovered Auschwitz in the actions and motivations of humankind, what is goodness and how would one shape human society so as to surface goodness and not evil? Especially theologians and religious educators must confront the difficult question: Why hasn't organized religion succeeded in inculcating goodness in humanity? Judging from the history of this century, and indeed the history of organized religion before this century, we have failed to teach goodness, we have failed to so instruct those under our tutelage such that they will, in overwhelming numbers, act in a prosocial manner toward their fellow human beings. What have we done wrong, and what *ought* we to be doing to do it right?

If there are answers to the question of human compliance and resistance in social psychology and history, then it is the responsibility of educators in general and theologians and religious educators in particular, Jews, Christians, and Muslims, to bring these insights back into the school, the university, the church, the synagogue, and the mosque, and to modify what one teaches and how one teaches it so as to increase resistance to evil and to encourage the doing of good.

The problem, where was humanity, then, implies two tasks: first, a descriptive-analytic task rooted in history and social psychology and, then, a normative-prescriptive task rooted in moral thought and theology intended to better humankind's ability to teach resistance to evil and to cultivate doing of good. Elsewhere I have done the descriptive-analytic work, outlining the relevant studies in the fields of social psychology, personal psychology, and history and developing a field theory for the factors that facilitate the doing of good and the doing of evil.[6] I have also done the normative-prescriptive work, identifying eleven affections and twelve value-concepts of the prosocial life, together with the complex linkages between the affections, teachings, value-concepts, and the praxis and socialization patterns of the prosocial life, and making several specific recommendations for inculcating prosocial attitudes and behaviors.[7] Here, I shall address some of these recommendations in detail.

The Failure of Moral Education Creates a Problem

In the course of my work in the field of religion, I have acquired many friends and colleagues in Christian institutions like the Candler School of Theology, the Gregorian Pontifical Institute, Notre Dame University, and elsewhere; in Jewish institutions like the various rabbinical schools, the Solomon Schechter Day School movement, and others; and in secular institutions like Emory University, the Association for Moral Education, and elsewhere. What binds us together is that we share the burdens of life in the post-shoah world and we join in assuming the task of religious and secular moral education toward a better world in the fullest sense of interfaith and intercultural dialogue. For all of us, the past weighs upon the future, and we all sense that this is our watch, that we are the responsible ones at this time in history.

For Jews and Christians, dialogue about the past and toward the future is particularly poignant because the history of prewar Christian antisemitism weighs heavily on all of us. As Jews, we ask: Why didn't more of our Christian brothers and sisters act to protect us? Why didn't the Church, which preaches love of the other, practice it? It pains us to ask, and it pains us to see the anguish of our Christian partners in dialogue when they hear our questions and contemplate their own history. For Catholics the problem is particularly acute since the record of the Catholic Church, particularly of its leadership, is not very "Christian" in the spiritual sense of the word, and because most of the worst killing took place in overwhelmingly Catholic countries. Here, too, the pain of the next generations is clear, but the task is also evident. It becomes, then, all the more important to face our failures squarely and deal with them.

Those of us in the field of moral education, especially those of us in religious moral education, like to think that we are accomplishing something when we teach ethics and morals. We like to think that students, by studying the great classic ethical texts, actually become more ethical; that, by wrestling with deep moral dilemmas, students actually come to be more moral. As a fairly prominent member of the religious and academic establishment, I too would like to believe this. However, it is just not so.

In a famous experiment conducted at the Princeton Theological Seminary,[8] sixty-seven students were asked to study the parable of the Good Samaritan (Luke 10:29–37) and then requested to proceed to another facility where they were to be filmed giving a sermon on the parable or on alternate ministry. Between the two buildings, the experimenters placed a "victim," the goal being to find out how many of these theology students, who had just finished studying the parable of the Good Samaritan, would stop to aid the victim and what kind of help they would give. Only 40 percent stopped to help. While this constitutes a rate above the usual helping rate of 12–25 percent, it is certainly not high enough for those who take the parable, and similar prosocial religious teaching, seriously. The conclusion relevant here, then, is that religious prosocial teaching helps a little, but not enough. Teaching texts and discussing moral dilemmas is just not enough.

The evidence from other sources is even more discouraging for those in both secular and religious moral education. The *social-psychological evidence* indicates that religious affiliation and praxis is not a determining factor in antisocial, or in prosocial, behavior. Thus, religion did not help or hinder subjects, in any systematic way, in the Milgram,[9] Staub,[10] Colby,[11] or other social psychological studies. Subjects who shocked victims with what they believed were lethal doses of electricity were not inhibited from doing so by religious affiliation or conviction. And, conversely, subjects who aided victims in distress did so with no established link to their religious association or belief. Nor do most exemplars of prosocial action attribute their prosocial activity to religion.

In yet another investigation, Batson and Ventis[12] noted, after studying closely three people from very different but actively religious backgrounds, that it was not the religious teaching but the context of social roles, norms, and reference groups that provided the best predictors of religious identity.[13] Further, by asking about people's attitudes and then checking their actual behaviors, Batson and Ventis concluded that seeing oneself as prosocially motivated and actually performing prosocial actions were not the same: "The more religious may *see* themselves as more helpful and caring; they may even be seen this way by others. But when it came to action, there is no evidence that they are."[14] The *historical evidence,* too, indicates that religious affiliation and praxis is not a determining factor in antisocial, or in prosocial, behavior. Thus, religion was not a determining factor among the rescuers for, while some rescuers rescued out of specifically religious motivation, most did not.[15] Nor was it a salient factor in the organized resistance to the nazis, though some activists were certainly moved to resistance by their religious convictions.[16] Those who rescued Jews during the war, and they did that at considerable risk to themselves and to those around them, did it for many reasons, but religious affiliation and praxis is not a key factor except in a small percentage of the cases. Religion also was not a significant factor, in any systematic way, among the soldiers of the German police battalions.[17] Of the hundreds of thousands of soldiers and civilians who participated in the murder of Jews during the shoah, religious association or belief was not a factor that influenced their actions. Further, it must always be born in mind that the shoah took place in the midst of Christian Europe; that is, that Christian religious teaching did not stop, or even seriously hinder, the discrimination against, persecution of, and eventual extermination of the Jews of Europe. No one knows for sure, but I have speculated publicly that had the Pope ordered that any Catholic who participated in the killing of Jews be excluded from communion, perhaps 30 percent of European Jewry might have been saved because Eastern Europe, the site of most of the mass killing, was devoutly religious and such an exercise of papal authority, even if followed half-heartedly by local Church authorities, would have been taken very seriously. Finally, it must also be born in mind, *mutatis mutandis,* that the Jewish resistance in the ghettoes and in the forests was also not significantly composed of people with religious training.[18]

In short, the historical evidence shows that religion was simply not a determinative factor during the shoah, except for the very few—not for the rescuers or the resistance; not for the perpetrators, active or passive; and not for the resisting victims—although the religion of the Jewish victims was always their death warrant.

The case is not better in the least for the *secular humanist tradition,* as Richard Rubenstein has shown in *The Cunning of History*[19] as well as in several other books. The secular state, which was supposed to protect all citizens regardless of race, religion, ethnic origin, and economic status, responded during the shoah by declaring Jews stateless and, hence, without the protection of the secular state. No human or civil rights obtained for Jews, and for some others, during the shoah. Indeed, under all of the totalitarian regimes set up in the tradition of the Enlightenment, the prosocial tradition bearing the values of modernity collapsed; hence, the state-approved, or state-tolerated, persecution of Jews, Gypsies, homosexuals, and others under fascism, communism, and certain types of socialism. The "people's republics" embody the failure of the secular humanist tradition.[20]

Much to the consternation of adherents and advocates of both religious and secular moral traditions, then, the historical and social-psychological evidence is quite clear: the role of religious and of secular moral teaching in prosocial and in antisocial behavior is episodic. Some people, indeed most, use these traditions to justify antisocial behavior while others, a minority, use them to justify prosocial behavior. To put it differently: *There is no overall*

*consistent pattern of prosocial influence in secular or religious moral teaching.
Religious as well as secular moral teaching accounts for very little of humankind's ability to resist evil and do good.*

Finally, the evidence from the world of teaching is equally clear and disturbing. Studying ethics, moral theology, and the intersection of law and ethics, together with work in comparative ethics, is a major goal in intellectual
academic circles. Books are written, conferences are held, dialogue is engaged
in on these subjects. There is a whole field of moral education with a professional organization, conferences, and publications. Sometimes even ethical
grand rounds are held in hospitals. Still, one must ask with the Talmud, *mai
nafka minah,* "What results from all this? What difference does it make?" The
study of ethics and moral theology does *not* make us better people. Analyzing
the teaching of morality and dialogue in comparative ethics do *not,* in and of
themselves, inculcate prosocial values or lead to prosocial behavior. Remember
Hitler's professors, and clergy, and educators, and lawyers—all serious persons and professionals who, despite their personal, spiritual, and professional
concern with the doing of good, ended up doing evil.[21] What, then, is needed?
What do we need to do, as morally responsible people and leaders, to encourage prosocial attitudes and behaviors?

Four Very Strong Recommendations for Encouraging Prosocial Attitudes and Behaviors

Resistant and caring behaviors come from a background of proportionate
and reasoned discipline, combined with modeling, practice, and the teaching
of caring attitudes and behaviors. The following four recommendations, with
specific proposals where appropriate, then, should be incorporated in any program, religious or secular, intended to encourage the doing of good and discourage the doing of evil.[22]

Admit Failure

As noted, the results of social psychological and historical research indicate that secular and religious moral education is not a factor, in any systematic way, in people's choice of good and evil. Bluntly put: Religious and secular
moral education has failed to discourage antisocial behavior or to encourage
prosocial behavior. This, however, does not seem to have penetrated fully into
the minds of secular and religious educators. To put it most simply: If religious
and secular moral education works, why do we not see more prosocial action
in human society? We must, first, admit our failure as moral educators.

Give Formal Instruction

Formal instruction, while not sufficient, is necessary. Content does count,
even if it is not determinative. A plan of instruction intended to educate and
inculcate prosocial values must include the following five areas.

(1) *Teach prosocial value-concepts.* There are a large number of prosocial value-concepts.[23] Discuss the terms: inclusiveness, extensivity, globalism, goodness, kindness, justice, fairness, law, integrity, virtue, uprightness, rectitude, equity, impartiality, righteousness, ethics, caring, morality, protest, resistance, bonding, humanness, and humanity. And the complements: exclusiveness, isolationism, ethnic superiority, injustice, oppression, prejudice, unfairness, uncritical compliance, inhumaneness, and inhumanity. In a religious setting, discuss specifically religious prosocial value-concepts.[24] In Jewish tradition, these would include: *tselem* (image), *brit* (covenant), *tsedek* (justice), *hesed* (caring), and many others.[25] In Christian tradition, these would include: agape, justice, faith, hope, and many others.[26]

(2) *Use the language of justice and caring.* The way we phrase what we want to say forms who we are and who we become. Discuss the words: pity, compassion, concern, affection, love, care, cherish, nourish, protect, understanding, empathy, kindness, mercy, sympathy, attachment, devotion, heart, feeling, respect, awareness, recognition, intimacy, attention, warmth, and consideration. And the complements: pain, sorrow, grief, worry, anxiety, distress, suffering, trouble, sensitiveness, stress, intimidation, persecution, threats, and terror. Be sure to use these words in conversation on all topics and issues.

(3) *Identify and actively teach prosocial texts and traditions.* For the secular tradition, this would include stories and poetry from the American and French revolutions, the period of slavery, the civil rights movement, and the antiwar protest; exemplars from industry and education;[27] and stories of ordinary citizens who have accomplished prosocial tasks.[28] For the biblical tradition shared by Christians and Jews, this would include the stories of: Shifra and Pu'ah, the midwives who resisted Pharoah's genocidal decrees; Rahab, the prostitute, who resisted the Jericho secret police to hide the spies; Nathan, the prophet, who confronted King David forcefully on his adultery with Bathsheba and the murder of her husband; Saul's officers who refused to kill the priests of Nob who had sheltered David; Abraham, who argued with God about the justice of destroying the cities of Sodom and Gemorrah; Moses, who consistently defended the people of Israel against God's unjust threats; and the author of Psalm 44, who protested vehemently against God's desertion of God's people in time of war.

Rabbinic Judaism is particularly rich in prosocial value-concepts, texts, and traditions. Only a list is presented here: *talmud Torah* (study of Torah); *mitsva* (commandedness); *lifnei 'iver* (you shall not put a stumbling block before the blind); *ve-'asita ha-tov veha-yashar* (you shall do what is right and proper); *patur mi-dinei adam ve-hayyav be-dinei shamayim* (exempt in a human court but not in heaven); *tsedaka* (righteousness, charity); *middat hasidut* (the standard of the pious/caring/nonviolent); *gemilut hasadim* (doing good deeds); *lifnim mi-shurat ha-din* (beyond the line of the law); *shalom* (peace); *mipne darkhei shalom* (for the sake of social peace); *tikkun 'olam* (repairing/

restoring the world); *yetser ha-ra'* and *yetser tov* (the impulse to evil/to good); and *pikuah nefesh* (saving a life). There are many more. Prosocial rabbinic texts and traditions also include: norms for proper court procedure and judicial protest; laws commanding one to reprove one another and to rescue someone in trouble; the uses and limits of military disobedience and nonviolence; and the doctrines of "doing good deeds," "going beyond the demands of the law," "honoring God's creatures," and martyrdom.[29]

Christian tradition, too, has a long and distinguished set of texts and stories that encourage and support prosocial action. These include the story of the Good Samaritan, the concern of Jesus for the oppressed and excluded, the model of St. Francis, the civil courage of St. Bernard of Clairvaux in defending Jews during the Crusades, and the many stories of heroism motivated by Christian faith during the shoah, for example, the story of Le Chambon sur Lignon, the miracle at Assisi, and others.[30]

(4) *Teach the nature of social processes.* Social process is the determinative factor in the avoiding of evil and the doing of good. Secular and religious educators must, therefore, provide formal instruction about the social processes within which we live and make moral decisions. Discuss the terms: authority, obedience, disobedience, resistance, protest, heteronomy and autonomy, norms, rules, values, normocentric, agentic shift, salience, permission, ingroup-outgroup, conflict management and resolution, win-win, socialization, identification, modeling, peer support, and incremental learning. Discuss the nature of hierarchies and the effect of excessive versus caring discipline. Read the books by Milgram, Kelman and Hamilton, the Oliners, Browning, and so on. Show the films and discuss them.[31] An understanding, no matter how tentative, of these processes is an important first step.

(5) *Teach critical thinking.* Thinking against the social grain is crucial. People must be consciously taught to ask: How does one identify a lie? What is propaganda? Who is manipulating whom? Whose power is at stake here? Do I agree with the truths being expounded here; and if not, why? What do I think, independent of what I feel? The instinct for truth and good common sense needs to be developed and reinforced.

Teach Prosocial Skills

Intellectual knowledge is not enough; one must learn how to do things. Therefore, religious and secular authorities must teach concrete prosocial skills. I recommend teaching the following seven prosocial skills:

(1) *perspective taking and empathy*—This enables one to understand how the other feels, to appreciate the affective dimension of the other's situation. Ask: "What do you think he or she feels?" "What does she or he feel even if she or he cannot express it?" "How angry, happy, ashamed, proud . . . is he or she?" "What would you feel in that person's place?" "What is empathy? What is sympathy?" Everyone is capable of perspective-taking, and everyone will

need to be the object of perspective-taking by others in the course of life. Being able to empathize is an important prosocial skill.

(2) *identifying and coding one's own feelings*—Our feelings are basic to who we are; they are the ground for much of our being and the agency for much of our action. We need to know our own feelings. Ask: "What did you feel when you saw . . . ?" "Can you recall feeling ashamed, guilty, joyous, powerful, hurt, nurturing, modest, immodest, content?" "What is the difference between anger and rage? Have you ever felt either? What was it like?" "How do you feel when someone threatens you, challenges you publicly, or praises you in front of others?" Almost everyone has experienced every one of these emotional states at one time or another. Being able to recognize and label them is an important prosocial skill.

(3) *identifying authorities, hierarchies, norms, roles, and social processes*— Everyone exists within a series of social hierarchies. Ask: "What is the social hierarchy in this particular situation?" "To whom are you subordinate? To whom are you superior?" "Is there more than one authority at work here? more than one set of subordinates?" "Upon what is the legitimacy of the authority in this situation based?" "What would you have to do to break the rule, the norm? What would you have to do to challenge the authority?" "Are you, as an authority, acting in a responsible way, within the limits of your legitimacy? And, if not, how do you as an authority challenge your own authority and reshape it?" Knowing one's place in various hierarchies and, hence, imagining how one might challenge these hierarchies is a major prosocial skill—and it can be learned.[32]

(4) *externalizing repressed prosocial impulses*—Doing good, as Batson has shown and as rabbinic tradition teaches, is a basic part of being human. All people want to do good to others, even if the motivation for that is, sometimes, egoistic. Yet, many people hesitate to do good. Ask: "What does your impulse to do good tell you to do?" "What act of caring have you done today?" "What can you do that would be really kind?" "Whom do you know who is a really good person? What does she or he do? How do you know he or she is good?" Realizing that one does know good when one sees it, recognizing good impulses in oneself, and realizing that the impediments to doing good are not as formidable as they seem is an important prosocial skill.

(5) *conflict management skills*—Conflict does not need to be "overcome" or "eliminated." Quite the contrary, conflict is a natural part of life. It does, however, need to be managed so that human relationships do not deteriorate into resentment, hatred, and violence. Teach the skills of mediation. Instruct people in the art of finding superordinate goals. Ask: "What is at stake behind the surface issues for each party?" "What are the common goals of these people?" "Why should these persons cooperate with one another? And if they cannot live in harmony, what intermediate relationship could they have?"

(6) *networking*—No person is an island, as the poet says. Everyone needs

support, even those who do good. A network provides moral, as well as tactical, support. Because doing good is contagious, a network also supports increased prosocial action. A broad network also distributes the impulse to do good over a larger number of areas of one's life. Teach how to build and broaden a network. It is not enough for prosocial action to be a "school (or church, or professional) activity"; it must become part of the larger lives of the participants. Teach how to make all participants stakeholders in the activity and how to use participatory democracy to involve everyone—the disadvantaged, the willing, the reluctant, even the opposition. Also, show how to involve legitimate authority figures, because authority does count; it is only a matter of which side it will count on.

(7) *protesting*—At some point, social protest may be necessary in order to effect a prosocial goal. There is a long history of this in the West in this century. Teach the skills of coalition building.[33] Teach the techniques of nonviolent protest: persuasion, social noncooperation, economic noncooperation in the form of the boycott and the strike, and political noncooperation especially with state authorities. Teach how to organize the various types of demonstration—sit-ins, stand-ins, ride-ins, pray-ins, and hunger strikes—as well as the skills of direct action, negotiation, and reconciliation.[34] Familiarize people with how to find the resources for further training in these areas.[35]

Pay Attention to Context and Process

Religious and secular authorities must recognize that it is not only what one teaches but how it is taught that makes the difference. It is not only the content of the teaching but the social psychological context in which it is taught that makes the real difference between successful and unsuccessful moral education. In order to accomplish this goal, I make the following additional five practical recommendations for how to teach prosocial values:

(1) *Establish a means by which authority can be challenged.* All social structures need discipline to give them form. To be as certain as one can that discipline is proportionate and reasoned, set up a mechanism of criticism and appeal within the disciplinary process, and be sure that that mechanism functions fairly. In a school, business, hospital, government, synagogue, church, or volunteer organization, even in a family, I recommend the following, bearing in mind that these mechanisms must be used honestly and in good will, not as ploys to pacify underlings or as shields for superiors:

(a) Set up an *ombudsperson* or an *ombudscommittee* who will hear appeals of disciplinary action taken by the central hierarchy.

(b) Set up a *whistle-blowing mechanism* that will enable criticism of the hierarchy.

(c) Set up a *care team* that will evaluate, not the efficiency with which the task of the organization is being carried out, but the caring quality of the relationships between members of the organization, particularly those relationships that are hierarchical.

(2) *Act. Do. Implement prosocial action.* It is relatively easy to plan and to build programs. It is much harder to make sure that the action one intends to motivate actually takes place. One needs to have some mechanism for checking the efficacy of what one does, even (perhaps, especially) in education for prosocial action. In a school, business, hospital, government, synagogue, church, or volunteer organization, even in a family, I recommend the following:

(a) Undertake a *specific project*: visiting the sick, lobbying for a cause, being part of a watch organization, caring for the homeless, and so on. Do not let prosocial commitment remain vague.

(b) See to it that there is *personal contact with the disadvantaged person.* Salience to the victim is critical to prosocial activity. Do not let prosocial commitment be only financial or administrative.

(c) Create a *feedback mechanism* in the form of a journal or report in which one records what one has actually done. In addition, one should record feelings and thoughts for later sharing and discussion.

(3) *Model prosocial attitudes and behaviors.* People have a very fine instinct for hypocrisy. This comes from an equally fine ability to observe what others do, hear what they say, and then compare the two. It is, therefore, very important to practice what one preaches, that is, to do prosocial acts, for in the doing is the teaching. In a school, business, hospital, government, synagogue, church, or volunteer organization, even in a family, I recommend the following:

(a) Model prosocial behaviors *yourself.* It is easy if one is in charge of organizing or implementing a program in altruistic behavior to forget to actually do altruistic acts. No matter where one is in the organization, a deed of kindness counts.

(b) *Hire staff* who have a record of prosocial action. The criterion of prosocial action is not usually used in hiring professors, teachers, engineers, doctors, business executives, government employees, or hospital staff. It is used more often, but not systematically enough, in hiring clergy and social workers and in engaging volunteers. Make prosocial action a part of the resumé that candidates must submit to apply for a job, and if it is not a part thereof, ask. (Note: I have never been part of an academic search, even in a department of religion or school of theology, where this was so. My own curriculum vitae, which is quite long, does not include my prosocial activities and commitments, nor have I been asked to add them.)

(c) *Evaluate and promote* using prosocial activity as one of the criteria. Prosocial action is not usually used in evaluating and promoting professors, teachers, engineers, doctors, business executives, government employees, or hospital staff. It is used more often, but not systematically enough, in evaluating and promoting clergy and social workers and in engaging volunteers. Rewards do not always work;[36] however, process establishes norms. By making it known that prosocial action is approved and used in professional assessment, prosocial action acquires the sanction of the hierarchy and becomes a norm.

(d) Acknowledge *heroes and heroines.* Set up a publicity mechanism that will highlight the activity of those who do perform prosocial acts. Recognition, too, sets norms and standards, as well as reinforces the impulse to do good.

(4) *Develop syllabi and curricula in prosocial action.* There are texts and methods that inculcate prosocial value-concepts and actions. Identify the questions. Prepare the materials. Find the teachers. Teach the texts. There is no other way.

(a) Find the *texts* in Judaism, Christianity, and other world religions, as well as in the secular tradition and in American and European civilization. Find the material in the media, on the Internet, anywhere it is available.

(b) Be sure to use the *applied learning methods:* study-buddies (small units that prepare and work together), field observation of prosocial organizations, and project-oriented tasks.

(c) Provide a *full-time person* to encourage and supervise the program in prosocial education and action.

(5) *Be intentional about what you are doing.* It is so easy to let matters slide, to drift into complacency. These recommendations demand a great deal of effort. Indeed, doing good requires much energy, thought, questioning, and care. Still, consciousness is what renders us human. Intentionality is what makes us a part of humanity. Especially in doing good, we must be conscious, intentional.

Traditional religious and secular moral education has not been a great success. Perhaps, by paying more attention to the processes at work when we educate and then educating for social process, those of us—Christian, Jewish, and others—who share the burdens of life in the post-shoah world and who join in assuming the task of religious and secular moral education toward a better world in the fullest sense of interfaith and intercultural dialogue will be able to accomplish the age-old goal of educating a generation of human beings who are capable of resisting evil and of doing good.

NOTES

The material here is derived from my book *The Banality of Good and Evil: Moral Lessons from the Shoah and Jewish Tradition* (Washington, D.C.: Georgetown University Press, 1999).

1. On the "use" of the shoah, see D. Blumenthal, "The Holocaust and Hiroshima:

Icons of Our Century," http://www.emory.edu/UDR/BLUMENTHAL (my Web site), and "From Anger to Inquiry," in *From the Unthinkable to the Unavoidable,* ed. C. Rittner and J. Roth (Westport, Conn.: Prager, 1997) 149–155, also available on my Web site.

2. (Louisville, Ky.: Westminster/John Knox, 1993). See also my "Theodicy: Dissonance in Theory and Praxis," *Concilium* 1 (1998): 138–154, also available on my Web site.

3. On both these issues, see S. Katz, "The 'Unique' Intentionality of the Holocaust," in *Post-Holocaust Dialogues,* ed. S. Katz (New York: New York University Press, 1985), 287–317, and S. Katz, *The Holocaust in Historical Context* (New York: Oxford University Press, 1994).

4. For a preliminary attempt, see E. Staub, *The Roots of Evil: The Origins of Genocide and Other Group Violence* (Cambridge: Cambridge University Press, 1989), and E. Staub, "Psychological and Cultural Origins of Extreme Destructiveness and Extreme Altruism," in *Handbook of Moral Behavior and Development,* ed. W. Kurtines and J. Gewirtz (Hillsdale, N.J.: Lawrence Erlbaum, 1991), 425–446.

5. As Elie Wiesel has noted, while not all the victims were Jewish, all the perpetrators and bystanders were Christian.

6. See Blumenthal, *Banality of Good and Evil,* pt. 1.

7. See Blumenthal, *Banality of Good and Evil,* pt. 2.

8. J. M. Darley and C. D. Batson, "From Jerusalem to Jericho: A Study of Situational and Dispositional Variables in Helping Behavior," *Journal of Personality and Social Psychology* 27, no. 1 (1973): 100–108.

9. S. Milgram, *Obedience to Authority: An Experimental View* (New York: Harper and Row, 1974), 62–63, 170.

10. E. Staub, "Helping a Distressed Person," in *Advances in Experimental Social Psychology,* vol. 7, ed. L. Berkowitz (New York: Academic Press, 1974), 293–341. None of the experiments and analyses lists religion as a factor in prosocial behavior.

11. A. Colby and W. Damon, *Some Do Care: Contemporary Lives of Moral Commitment* (New York: Free Press, 1992). In this study of exemplars religion, again, is not a determinative factor.

12. C. D. Batson and W. L. Ventis, *The Religious Experience: A Social-Psychological Perspective* (New York: Oxford University Press, 1982).

13. Ibid., 31–48.

14. Ibid., 289 (emphasis in original).

15. S. and P. Oliner, *The Altruistic Personality* (New York: Free Press, 1988), reviewed by me in *Critical Review of Books in Religion* 3 (1990): 409–411, 155–156, 290–292; P. Oliner et al., *Embracing the Other: Philosophical, Psychological, and Historical Perspectives* (New York: New York University Press, 1992), reviewed by me in *Pastoral Psychology* 46, no. 2 (1997): 131–134, chs. 11–13, esp. ch. 14; E. Fogelman, *Conscience and Courage: Rescuers of Jews during the Holocaust* (New York: Anchor Books, 1994), reviewed by me in *Journal of Psychology and Theology* 23 (1995): 62–63, 169–172.

16. See for example M. Gilbert, *The Holocaust* (New York: Holt, Rinehart and Winston, 1992), index.

17. C. Browning, *Ordinary Men: Reserve Police Battalion 101 and the Final Solution in Poland* (New York: Harper Collins, 1992), chs. 2 and 18.

18. See, for example, N. Tec, *Defiance: The Bielski Paritsans* (Oxford: Oxford University Press, 1993). Religion has also not been a factor in conscientious objection in the Israeli armed forces or in the various Israeli peace movements (though there is one small religious peace movement). See R. Linn, *Conscience at War: The Israeli Soldier as a Moral Critic* (New York: SUNY Press, 1996), reviewed by me in *Jewish Spectator,* Summer 1998, pp. 52–54.

19. R. Rubenstein, *The Cunning of History* (San Francisco: Harper Colophon, 1975).

20. This, in spite of the avowedly secular and atheistic ideology of these totalitarian-

Enlightenment states. The "religious republics" of modern neo-fundamentalist bent do not augur much better treatment of prosocial issues.

21. See Blumenthal, *Banality of Good and Evil,* chs. 2–5 and the Selected Bibliography, for the details.

22. For more on this, see especially S. and P. Oliner, *Toward a Caring Society* (Westport, Conn.: Praeger, 1995). I have tried to arrange these recommendations in a sequence. But it is possible that I am completely wrong about the sequence or that there is no sequence at all. In either case, the order can safely be ignored. The important thing is to get started facilitating good, no matter where one starts.

23. "Value-concept" is a term that has both intellectual and moral dimensions. The intellectual dimension allows one to discuss and analyze the concept, while the moral dimension allows one to understand the concept as normative, that is, as something one ought to do or as an attitude one ought to have. On this see Blumenthal, *Banality of Good and Evil,* ch. 7, and M. Kadushin, *The Rabbinic Mind* (New York: Jewish Theological Seminary, 1952).

24. For more on this, see Blumenthal, *Banality of Good and Evil,* ch. 7.

25. For more on this, see Blumenthal, *Banality of Good and Evil,* ch. 10.

26. It is my fervent hope that Christian colleagues will develop this fully.

27. See, for example, Colby and Damon. See also the Oliners, *Toward,* passim.

28. The Giraffe Project (Box 759, Langley, WA 98260) keeps track of these, prepares press releases, and has prepared syllabi for all ages on "sticking out one's neck" for a prosocial cause.

29. For more on this, see Blumenthal, *Banality of Good and Evil,* chs. 10–13.

30. See the bibliography in Fogelman; the records of Yad Vashem, the Israeli shoah authority; G. Block and M. Drucker, *Rescuers: Portraits of Moral Courage in the Holocaust* (New York: Holmes and Meier, 1992); and others. On Le Chambon, see P. Sauvage, *Weapons of the Spirit* (a film about Le Chambon sur Lignon). It is my fervent hope that Christian colleagues will develop these resources fully.

31. See the Selected Bibliography in Blumenthal, *Banality of Good and Evil.* Consult the Web.

32. The centrality of this issue accounts for its appearance as an area of formal instruction and also as a social skill.

33. See for example The National Coalition Building Institute, 1835 K Street, Washington, DC 20006.

34. See "198 Methods of Nonviolent Action," prepared by The Albert Einstein Institution (1430 Massachusetts Ave, Cambridge, MA 02138; phone: 617–876–0311), reprinted in Blumenthal, *Banality of Good and Evil,* Appendix.

35. See for example The Martin Luther King, Jr. Center for Nonviolent Social Change, Atlanta, Georgia, and "List of Prosocial Resources" in Blumenthal, *Banality of Good and Evil,* Appendix.

36. See A. Kohn, *Punished by Rewards: The Trouble with Gold Stars, Incentive Plans, A's, Praise, and other Bribes* (New York: Houghton Mifflin, 1993).

PART 7

Beyond the Survivor
Aesthetic Representations of the Holocaust

Introduction
The Notre Dame Holocaust Project
John P. Welle

THE HOLOCAUST PROJECT at the University of Notre Dame was a multi-year initiative with many different facets. It began with the "Lessons and Legacies" conference, which Notre Dame hosted in the fall of 1997, and culminated in the international, interdisciplinary conference "Humanity at the Limit: The Impact of the Holocaust Experience on Jews and Christians" in April 1998. These conferences brought to campus a distinguished group of scholars to focus on a wide variety of issues involving the Holocaust, Holocaust studies, and Jewish-Christian relations. In addition to these two major events, a series of distinguished visiting scholars provided lectures and met with classes during the 1997–98 academic year. Notre Dame also hosted a photography exhibit, a concert, a film series, and a symposium entitled "Film, Media, and the Future of Holocaust Education." While the project came to fruition in the major scholarly gathering of which this volume is the happy result, the impact of the varied aspects of the Notre Dame Holocaust Project on the local academic community have perhaps yet to be fully ascertained.

As a faculty member at Notre Dame, a leading North American Catholic university with a predominantly Catholic undergraduate population, I became involved with the project as an interested non-specialist. My own fields of teaching and research include modern Italian literature, film history, and translation studies. In addition to organizing the film symposium mentioned above, I was pleased to serve on a committee charged with forming a panel focusing on film, literature, and the arts. By participating in the project, I became exposed to the current trends, issues, and debates in Holocaust studies, particularly as they relate to aesthetic representations. The contributions to the conference by the arts and literature panelists—John Felstiner, Marcia Landy, Alan Mintz, and Remi Hoeckman—speak for themselves and require no introduction here. In what follows, then, I would like to provide a brief reflection.

In considering any possible future initiatives at Notre Dame, one should begin by attending to the current controversies surrounding Holocaust studies and to the critical voices raised both in favor of, and in opposition to, their proliferation. An article entitled "A Debate about Teaching the Holocaust"[1] raises serious questions about the place of the Holocaust in the university curriculum and frames some of the key issues in the debate. For the affirmative, Steven T. Katz argues that the Holocaust requires the formation of an independent field of study and favors the creation of programs of the highest quality. He writes:

> anyone concerned to understand the modern world—its unprecedented capacity for altering the human condition, and its immense potential for good and evil—must confront, with all seriousness, the events that together make up the whole of what we call the Holocaust. . . . to confront such far-reaching matters in all their complexity, should not lead to denying the Holocaust a special place in the university curriculum, but rather requires that it receive one. Given its monumental significance, the Holocaust must be front and center, taught by experts to students of all ethnic and religious backgrounds whose world has been, in large measure, created by it.[2]

Other scholars, however, warn of the dangers inherent in focusing on the Holocaust, particularly if this attention continues to portray Jews primarily as victims. Ruth R. Wisse, for example, takes issue with those who would utilize the Holocaust for a variety of educational purposes. She writes:

> If the slaughter of the European Jews dare not be forgotten, neither should it overshadow the way of life it tried to destroy. Jewish education and American education ought to have much more to teach about the creative energy of the Jews than the destructive energy of Hitler.[3]

In addition to her point about the need to educate students about Jewish history, culture, and contributions to civilization, Ruth R. Wisse's distinction between the roles of Jewish education and American education in approaching the Holocaust is a useful one.

This distinction leads to the question: What is the role of Catholic education in attempts to teach the Holocaust? I do not wish to suggest that there is a "Catholic" way to treat the subject, nor that those working in Catholic institutions have points of view necessarily different from those working in other educational institutions. Notre Dame's position as a leading American Catholic university, however, with its mission of serving the broader Catholic community, does suggest that it could play an influential role in promoting greater Jewish-Christian dialogue; in educating Catholic students about Jewish history, life, and culture; and in creating a greater awareness of the historical role of Catholicism in the creation and diffusion of anti-Semitism.

The Notre Dame Holocaust Project has succeeded in bringing the local academic community in contact with some of the most important scholars working in the field. Through a variety of initiatives, the project has also created an awareness among various sectors of the Notre Dame faculty and student body of the key issues and controversies in Holocaust studies. Having come this far, the University of Notre Dame might now begin to more aggressively address its responsibility to serve as a leader among Catholic institutions of higher learning. If Catholic education is to play a future role in Holocaust studies, and if American Catholics are to make greater contributions to Jewish-Christian dialogue, then Notre Dame should be one place where these initiatives find support.

Notes

1. *New York Times,* August 8, 1998, pp. A13–15.
2. Steven T. Katz, ibid.
3. Ruth R. Wisse, ibid.

29 | Cinematic History, Melodrama, and the Holocaust

Marcia Landy

T HE QUESTION THAT animates my concern with "Cinematic History, Melodrama, and the Holocaust" is this: What is to be learned about cinematic and televisual representations of the Holocaust—the popular and the unpopular? This question is intended to reopen the controversy over high and low culture as they handle emotion-charged issues of historic dimensions. We continue to be confronted by familiar jeremiads about the destructive effects of what Theodor Adorno dubbed the "culture industry," mainly associated with commercial media. Umberto Eco offers another but related position when he writes:

> It doesn't matter what you say via the channels of mass communication.
> . . . The important thing is the gradual uniform bombardment of information, where the different contents are leveled and lose their difference.[1]

The pendulum also swings the other way, and in response to these negative characterizations of mass culture, some critical writing of the past two decades has regarded mass culture seriously to the extent of locating in these texts positive emotional and educative effects. Some critics have gone further in regarding mass culture as socially transgressive. These divergent positions cannot be reconciled, but they need to be examined if we are to arrive at a critical position concerning media's uses of the past. What is at stake, though, is the need to put aside for the moment our inherited and monolithic conceptions of popular culture.

I am concerned with the impossible but imperative task of producing different forms of thinking about the character and impact of cinema and television, especially in relation to their uses of the past. Too often, we apply commonsensical and, hence, familiar, exegetical and interpretive approaches to the popular media (derived from methods associated with literature and history) rather than analyzing their unique formal properties and their cultural sources. I believe that we ought to be mistrustful of most explanations of what media texts are (both non-fictional and commercial narrative texts) and of how they are received by audiences.

One of the characteristics of the popular media's uses of the past is based on what the Italian philosopher Antonio Gramsci once described as "common sense," a reliance on an uncritical assimilation of past events and on affective, ritualized, and aphoristic responses to pain, injustice, and death. For example, the commonsensical attitude toward history is often epitomized by the aphorism that "those who do not know history are doomed to repeat it," or by the phrase "the act of remembering is an act of resistance, dissent, and challenge." While many serious critics might endorse these positions, they would not generally identify them with Hollywood or mass culture.

Inherited prejudices about Hollywood (extended to television) make many critics immediately doubtful—even before critical analysis—that an event like the Holocaust (or any historic event for that matter) could be treated responsibly or "accurately" by a Hollywood filmmaker or by a television program through the conventions and codes of mass cultural production. For many cultural critics, historians, and scholars of the Holocaust, seriousness is identified with documentary authenticity, with the posing of questions and not with "solutions," and certainly not with the formulaic and, hence, "popular" and "commercial" modes of representation, as exemplified by the genre system and by the contamination of "fact with fiction." At stake in this controversy is the belief that popular representation is not only pernicious but destructive to any viable and creative sense of cultural life.

The common sense that inheres in popular culture is not completely critical but is based on inherited though inconsistent attitudes and values drawn from religion, past moments in history, juridical forms, oratory, proverbs, and truisms about the world. This folklore is not to be denigrated, for it is a traditional, emotion-laden, though not critically informed, way of confronting the incomprehensible, the unknown, and the threatening aspects of economic, social, and cultural life. It is not mindless. At its core is a philosophical and pragmatic understanding of the world, enabling groups to come to some sort of détente with subjugation and oppression.

Such knowledge is not to be rejected out of hand but understood and refined upon within an analytic and pedagogical context based on questioning what we mean by history, the role of memory and of forgetting, and their relation to melodramatic forms of narration, a form of expression that only in recent years has received scholarly attention for offering insight into questions of subjectivity and history. Various articulations of melodrama, all highly affective, have at their core attempts to connect history to an investigation of ethical and epistemological concerns articulated in monumental and everyday forms. I see melodrama functioning as a mode of addressing disjunctions between the public and the private arenas of life, between desire and expectation, and between the horror of meaninglessness and the possibility that forms of justice and injustice can be recognized.

Despite scholarly work that has been done on popular culture in film studies, ethnography, and cultural studies, many cultural commentators continue to inveigh against the popularization of history as being "bad" in and of itself and as "bad for culture."[2] For example, critical commentary on popular texts that recreate historical events, such as the television series *Holocaust* and *Heimat* and Steven Spielberg's film *Schindler's List,* has labeled these works as melodramatic and has, therefore, judged them to be anti-historical. By contrast, *Night and Fog, Shoah,* and the films of Marcel Ophuls are lauded as serious treatments of history. Moreover, the praise for these films is often gained at the expense of denigrating popular texts.

The pervasiveness and vagueness of these judgments should alert critics to the necessity of shifting focus from the classification and, hence, from the isolation of particular texts to the more daunting enterprise of identifying, analyzing, and understanding appeals to history via the media. My objective, therefore, is not to valorize either documentary or feature treatments of the Holocaust but to examine their strategies and the discourses on which they are based. I intend to introduce new questions that serve to break down prevailing misconceptions about avowed differences between these media forms and analyze their common affective strategies.

In the scholarly literature on the cinematic treatments of the Holocaust, Alain Resnais's *Night and Fog* (1955) is identified with a cinema preoccupied with the past not for mere purposes of documentation but as an alternative form of historicizing and as a prod to thought for understanding the workings of memory. But what is it that the films asks the spectator to view, to contemplate, and to understand? In its dispassionate yet engaged voice-over and in its images, the film confronts the audience with documents of a gruesome past. The spectator is given images of the landscape of the concentration camps in the present, filmed in color as in the oft-quoted opening shots and throughout, then shifted to the black-and-white film that has come to be associated with reproductions of the past.

Throughout the unrelenting voice-over commentary, the persons and objects presented are identified with a vast bureaucratic machine for killing. The film provides a poignant image of this bureaucracy especially through the visualization of a registry of names of the people who were "processed" in the camps. The spectator is treated to a lengthy, slow, and elegiac leafing through this document that invites a reflection on and interrogation of the fate of those endless names of people, and the image is emblematic of the film's invitation to experience the meaning and impact of this document.

Of this film, André Pierre Colombat has written that Resnais

> refuses to impose upon his spectator any sentimental or lyrical attitude
> conveyed by the easy use of adjectives, pathetic music, a linear chronology.
> . . . Unlike what happens in commercial cinema.[3]

The key terms in this quotation are "sentimental," "pathetic," and "lyrical," terms that reproduce the conventional complaint that affect is the unique and spurious property of popular culture and that it must be avoided. Also evident in this description is the familiar contrast to and valorization of European art cinema over commercial cinema. By invoking these strategies, the critic can lay to rest any suggestion of contamination by mass culture. I challenge this characterization of the film for its facile assumptions about popular cinema and even more for its misreading of the affective properties of the Resnais film. Throughout *Night and Fog,* the spectator is bombarded with images and a mode of thought that are, in fact, melodramatic, particularly in reiterated preoccupation—endemic to melodrama—of unresolved and haunting questions of responsibility, legality, and judgment. In being confronted with the painful, affectively resonant images of the Holocaust, the spectator is summoned to do jury service and to make judgment. In fact, the image of the Kapo and of the officer at the end of the film, disavowing their responsibility ("I am not responsible") leads to the narrator's question, which is like a charge to a jury: "then who is responsible?"

"Who is responsible" leads to my question: What is responsible for the affective dimensions of the film? Is it melodrama? Or, if not, what is melodrama? I locate the affective appeal of melodrama as parallel with mourning, with their mutual emphasis on the threat (and reality) of violence, death, the loss of belief in any moral order, and the articulated plea for justice and for some form of restitution. As such, melodrama is not confined to the commercial cinema: it plays a major role in the culture of modernity, becoming in the words of Peter Brooks, "the principal mode for uncovering, and making operative the essential moral universe in a post sacred era."[4] Too often, this notion of melodrama has gone unnoticed. Too often, melodrama has been uncritically designated as signifying disingenuous histrionics, regarded as having no substance, no context, and no relationship to the high moral seriousness of existence.

A closer look at melodrama reveals that it has historically addressed suffering, misfortune, and death in the language of theatricality, that is to say, in Brooks's sense, through a "text of muteness." As he writes:

> we encounter the apparent paradox that melodrama so often, particularly in climactic moments and in extreme situations, has recourse to non-verbal means of expressing its meanings. Words, however unrepressed and pure, however transparent as vehicles for the expression of basic relations and verities, appear to be not wholly adequate to the representation of meanings, and the melodramatic message must be formulated through other registers of the sign.[5]

In the confrontation with death and disaster, verbal language is inadequate and the rituals of mourning serve better as a conduit for expressing the inexpressible, for communicating the affect that arises from the impossible quest for answers to injustice.

Similarly, the traditional poetic form of the elegy has grappled with the limitations of verbal language and the need to express powerful affect in the face of the incomprehensibility of death. Moreover, the elegy has sought through myth and/or religion to explain or at least to rationalize suffering, death, and loss. The elegiac form has been primarily identified with the need to make sense of the pain of loss through the ritual of mourning, and mourning has been considered a major psycho-social discourse for addressing the perceived importance of "coming to terms" with the past. This "coming to terms" has been identified with a revisiting of the past, with posing questions of responsibility and guilt, and with confronting the affect of impotence and rage which inevitably accompany this process.

In short, the elegy, the mourning process, and melodrama share common attributes. Furthermore, the language of loss and restitution common to the elegy, to mourning, and to melodrama lends itself to a meditation on mortality and to a questioning of morality. In *Night and Fog*, the elegiac and the melodramatic are evident and cut across questions of crime, guilt, death, responsibility, and the anticipation of enlightenment. We can see in the film's investigative process the moral dimensions of melodrama, its affective sources, its reliance on history, and its preoccupation with judgment.

Shoah, too, has been praised for respecting "History" and for avoiding melodrama. This film, unlike *Night and Fog*, relies on interviews, but, like the Resnais film, it pays scrupulous attention to documentation. A key moment in the film occurs during an interview with Raul Hilberg, a major commentator on Nazi atrocities. Hilberg and the director, Claude Lanzmann, peruse and discuss a printed schedule for the death trains that ran regularly to the extermination camps. The lengthy close-ups of the paper and of Hilberg as he comments on it offer an indication of the film's affective attachment to documents that preserve the memory of the Holocaust and, most expressively, of the links between that piece of paper and the many lives that were destroyed. Hilberg's reactions to the schedules for the trains that he holds in his hand, his verbal commentary, the close-ups of his face, provide a clue to the film's affective investment in summoning the past through exhibits and documents as evidence of crime.

A general examination of the guiding structure of the film reveals that *Shoah*—despite its differing style—is in certain important ways not so far removed from the popular cinema of crime detection and particularly of courtroom drama. The investigative form of the narrative involves a filmmaker who has assumed the dual roles of detective and prosecutor, haunting the scenes of a barbaric crime. His work of crime detection entails the relentless pursuit of the guilty, employing witnesses to, victims of, and perpetrators of the events, marshaling evidence to uncover the offense, and employing any available strategy in the pursuit of the evidence, the facts. In this sense, *Shoah* is "a real detective story," as much as Marcel Ophuls's film on Klaus Barbie, *Hotel Terminus*.[6]

The stylistic strategies of *Shoah*'s investigation of criminality differ from the commercial cinema, but its epistemological concerns situate its investment in a common cultural discourse predicated on legality, guilt, and judgment, the reiteration of characteristics endemic to melodrama. The affect in the film arises too from the lengthy and intense interviews that end in sobbing, particularly striking in the scenes with Abraham Bomba and Jan Karski, where the director relentlessly urges the men to summon their memories of pain, suffering, and the spectacle of annihilation they witnessed. Of this film, Judith Doneson writes:

> *Shoah* . . . is a film that honors its subject. . . . No melodrama; not even archival photographs or film. *Shoah* is art that is memory—of survivors, of the perpetrators, and of the bystanders. Indeed, Lanzmann has created a film at whose very foundation is history.[7]

How in the face of the images presented in the film, its formal structure, the role of the filmmaker and his subjects, can critics such as Doneson assert that the film is not melodramatic?

Doneson's comments indicate, once again, how little understood are the connections between history and melodrama. In fact, the presence of melodrama should alert us to the need to better recognize its pervasiveness and the ways it inflects different styles of narration, including historical forms, suggesting a collusion with the common sense of culture and hence with popular history. Without their taking a look at its presence in so-called historical, anti-melodramatic, and anti-narrative texts, critical reviews of commercial films rush hastily to segregate them, to marginalize them, and scapegoat them for succumbing to the dominant order. Because of this sequestration and name-calling, the valuable opportunity is lost for gaining a synoptic sense of the investment of all modern cultural forms in the melodramatic imagination.

On the other side of the cultural barrier, one of the major mass media cultural events relating to the Holocaust occurred with the appearance of the U.S. television series *Holocaust* (1979) (and with its later German counterpart, *Heimat,* 1984). These programs fueled numerous debates about history, especially about the commercial media's uses of the past.[8] What is important about the debates that ensued is how they sought to gauge the consequences of screening the Holocaust and Nazism for a mass audience. Critical discussions detailed the massive pre- and postpublicity surrounding the telefilm, *Holocaust* in particular, as compared to *Heimat,* and the political problems entailed in its airing on television.

Critics measured the size of the audience for *Holocaust.* They tabulated and analyzed responses to the program, its positive and negative effects. Generally, the negative assessments of the program are located in a familiar claim for or against the aesthetic qualities of the program, its form and stylistic techniques, whereas the positive assessments focused on the "film's *political* implications and *pedagogical* dimensions."[9] The negative critiques also raised predictable objections to mass media, their soap opera quality, commercial context, trivialization of events, and, yes, their melodrama. The positive evaluations countered by stressing the important role of *Holocaust* in reaching a mass audience with a message, its importance for "understanding" and "coming to terms" with the past,[10] and particularly the program's power to create

> emotional identification with the individual members of a family . . .
> with the Jews as Jews [whatever that means] . . . like themselves members
> of a family, united by and conflicting in their emotions, their outlook,
> their everyday concerns.[11]

Holocaust grafted popular melodrama onto history in its strategies of blending documentary footage and fictional narrative, its focus on the emblematic nature of the falling fortunes of the Jewish Weiss family and of the rising fortunes of the German Dorf family, its distinctions between victims and aggressors, and its cataloguing of the events leading to the Final Solution. Since melodrama feeds on folklore and common sense, popular psychology— the exploration of motivation, personal threats, and individual conflicts and differences—is a necessary component in its treatment of the characters and the obstacles they confront. Psychologizing provides a means for connecting the public to the private dimensions of the events. The domestic drama addressed the common-sense imperative of compromise and survival through familiar, middle-class representations of romance, marriage, monogamy, cultural production, physical health, and threats to economic security. In short, the melodrama provided a customary and affective format in which to embed the gruesome events represented. At the same time, the grafting of history and melodrama introduced critical and uncomfortable questions about the specificity and uniqueness of those events and about the mutability of history.

Holocaust was carefully constructed to address representations of the Holocaust in the idiom of the contemporary 1970s television audience by focusing on familial, gendered, and generational conflict. Its blending of fact and fiction, its preoccupation with "memories of justice," and especially its drawing on melodrama's fascination with crime detection and legality are best illustrated in the penultimate moments of the program, in the confrontation between Eric Dorf, the Nazi perpetrator of the crimes against the Jews, and the American officer who interrogates him. The scene is reminiscent of *Night and Fog* in the disavowal of responsibility on the part of the Nazis. Here too, Dorf, the character, when confronted with visual evidence of atrocities, lamely seeks to evade responsibility and judgment.

Despite its similarities to cinema, *Holocaust* is not a film. The program belongs to the televisual medium, with its addiction to information, crisis, investigation, collective catastrophe, and collective mourning. Television appears to be melodrama writ large, twenty-four hours a day. One is, therefore, properly suspicious of those arguments on the part of critics that stress the program's curative effects through the dialogue and the emotional identification it engenders. One is also suspicious of those critics who are quick to condemn it, since in terms of scholarship, there is still a paucity of information and methods to understand the nature and effects of this global and reiterative circulation of melodrama via television. From the perspective of a cultural event, the medium challenges the critic with a multitude of questions—not answers or judgments—about its cultural role. Rather than again rushing to judgment, critics need to carefully evaluate this form of medium as different from cinema and as offering a different sense of melodrama and of its relations to historicizing.

The union of melodrama and history is not limited to cinema and television but has its expression in other aspects of contemporary visual culture, which would include the recent popularity of and contestation over the proliferation of monuments and museums. The representation of the Holocaust in film and television has many affinities with the creation of Holocaust museums, and particularly with the opening of the monumental museum in Washington, D.C., and with the speeches and testimonials accompanying that event apropos of their pedagogical and melodramatic inflection.

The subtitle of an article in *Smithsonian* magazine on the opening of the museum reads: "A new museum in Washington opens to exhibit the lessons of history as testament to the dead and a reminder to the living."[12] President Bill Clinton, in his remarks at the museum opening, said:

> I believe that the museum will touch the life of everyone who enters and leave everyone forever changed: a place of deep sadness and a sanctuary of hope, an ally of education against ignorance; of humility against arrogance; an investment in a secure future against whatever insanity lurks ahead. If this museum can mobilize morality, then those who have perished will thereby gain a measure of immortality.[13]

In contrast to the elegiac words of the president, one visitor described the experience of the museum as follows:

> Violence and the grotesque are central to the American aesthetic and the Holocaust Museum provides both amply. It is impossible to take in the exhibition without becoming somewhat inured to the sheer graphic horror of the display. . . . The Museum courts the viewer's fascination, encouraging familiarity with the incomprehensible, and the unacceptable: one is repeatedly forced into the role of voyeur of the prurient.[14]

Finding the identity cards of victims that each visitor is given upon entrance to the Museum, this visitor concludes, "One way history is doomed to repetition at the Holocaust Museum is that day in and day out, year after year, the *Einsatzgruppen* murderers will play over and over."[15] According to Simon Louvish, painstaking research, capital investment, and reiterated emphasis on the importance of memory and education have seen to it that

The Holocaust will be painfully reconstructed in all its horrors and misery. The transport trains will roll, the Ghetto will be populated and depopulated, even the chimneys of Auschwitz-Birkenau will belch forth anew in the full depiction of that particular hell on earth.[16]

Clearly, these critics are affectively invested in the question of memory, in defending it against the incursions of time and its dulling through repetition. The problem posed by these negative (and melodramatic?) comments is how to understand the changing role of the Holocaust and of the concept of witnessing. James Young, who has written extensively on monuments and memorials to the Holocaust, reminds us that "witnessing" has a very specific meaning beyond merely recording a legal injunction to report an injustice.[17] It is related to the need to lament, to mourn, and to restore dignity to the victims. Sensitive to the inevitability of change over time, he recognizes the need to find a language to evaluate—not merely condemn—how the creation of memorials, whether in stone or wood sculpture, functions so as to "make memory and pedagogy their twin aims."[18]

Significantly, *Schindler's List* appeared a year after the opening of the Holocaust Museum in Washington, D.C., and film critic Thomas Doherty linked the two events. He wrote:

No less than the opening of the Holocaust Museum on the Washington Mall, a site reserved for memorials of the American past, *Schindler's List* is a capstone event in a process that has been called the "Americanization of the Holocaust."[19]

Spielberg's film is not the first Hollywood work on the Holocaust. Earlier, Hollywood was willing to deal with the Holocaust, if only through fiction with *Sophie's Choice*. The formula—use an attractive and popular star as a non-Jewish witness (Meryl Streep)—worked at the box office and set the stage for *Schindler's List*. As commercial cinema, as biopic, as part of the Spielberg canon, and as memorial to the Holocaust, *Schindler's List* participates in discourses identified with popular modes of narration—in its highlighting of the drama of conversion, in its identification of survival with a "just man," a "savior," in its linking of survival to work, in its reenactment of the ritual of mourning, and in its recourse to an elegiac style that mimes the mourning process. The film draws on the folklore and magic of Hollywood in its uses of the past—but in complex terms. Spielberg's film is not ignorant of the history of cinema and of non-commercial forms of filmmaking, which he incorporates into the style of the film. Nor is the film oblivious to the philosophical issues entailed in witnessing and memory.

In its project of linking past and present, *Schindler's List* gives prominence to the importance of memory through naming. As in *Night and Fog* and in Holocaust museums, the visualization of names and the question of identification are central to *Schindler's List*. When we first see Schindler (Liam Neeson), his identity is withheld and the question asked, "Who is that Man?" The identity of the Jews is also highlighted. Early in the film, the Jews are rounded up as a bureaucrat calls out, "Name?" Slowly, elegiacally, the camera lingers on each character. They recite their names. In close-up, a typewriter prints the name for the audience to see, not once but several times. Throughout the film, we see visual identification and documentation through the invocation of names, places, and events, and through a conjunction of the visual image and the printed word.

The reiterative visual role of writing and typing linked to the calling out of the names is an insistent reminder of the film's awareness of the transitoriness of history (and of the visual image) for capturing a sense of the past and of the memory of the people and events that would disappear were they not invoked through name and image. In addition, the visual use of the typewriter (like the camera), the conjoining of printed names to faces, raises the importance of the face in cinema as a reminder not only of the presence of the fictional figures but also of the absence of their "originals." Furthermore, from the outset of the film, the burning candle presented in Technicolor (the film returns to this image later) is another instance of the film's self-conscious (and pedagogically obvious) attempts to create bridges between the present and the evanescent past.

Likewise, the film will play with, complicate, and interrogate the melodramatic dimensions of Oskar Schindler's identity. He is a Nazi, though not of the rabid variety familiar in many film and television representations. He is attached to the Nazi Party through conformity, opportunism, and indifference to ideology, similar to the ways he is attached to the Jews at the outset. He derived profit from his traffic in Jewish workers. He ran a labor camp (albeit beneficently). He was a sensualist, a man of hedonistic temperament. He lacked discipline, was promiscuous, and was unable to intellectualize. The film sets out to examine a figure different from the Eric Dorfs of *Holocaust* (and even from Amon Goeth, the commandant of the Plaszow camp) and to dramatize what accounts for the difference.

The similarities and dissimilarities between Schindler and Goeth (Ralph Fiennes) serve to complicate the portrait of the Nazi and of Schindler, in particular, differentiating levels of cruelty, opportunism, and even compassion. Goeth's behavior is by no means ideologically driven. The crass materialism he shares with other officers (and to some extent with Schindler) is evidence of a certain cynicism rather than of pure fanaticism. His cynicism is most marked by his expectation that Helen Hirsch, the object of his brutal seductive treatment, will, when called upon after the war, testify in his behalf. Goeth's appearance, as played by Fiennes, and his violent behavior bears some resemblance to the conventional image of the Nazi that has been part of the visual iconography since World War II—with an important difference. The film offers little by way of the spectacle of Nazism commented upon by Susan Sontag as "fascinating fascism"—the choreography and sound so prominent in Nazi newsreels and in *Triumph of the Will,* which get played and replayed in films and television.

Goeth, like Schindler (but without any benevolence toward his workers), is inclined toward profit rather than zealous articulation of Nazi positions except when it is convenient. The familiar image of the Nazi ideologue has given way to a more pragmatic, economic, and psychological treatment. In the linking of the two men, the film probes not only the question "Who is that man?" but the question "How could Schindler have turned out so different from the other Nazis?" Other critics have asked similar questions about the film. For example, in addressing certain critical objections that Stern and the other Jews in the film are merely background figures or ciphers in relation to Schindler, Miriam Hansen has appropriately called attention to the ways in which Ben Kingsley as Stern is inserted into the narrative in terms of point-of-view edits and reaction shots that invite a different reflection on the film's style and its designs on the audience. Stern is a witness to the events and a shaper of the events. While his ability to alter events on a grand scale is circumscribed, he does, after all, facilitate Schindler's actions, once again highlighting the film's self-consciousness about the limits imposed on representing the past. Most importantly, Stern's role serves to underline the film's question, "What makes Schindler different from the others?" The reiterated shots of Stern in close-up, quizzically observing Schindler, seem to ask, "Will you do the right thing?"

In seeking to "imagine the film differently," Hansen suggests that one should look to the "film's complex use of sound and its structuring of cinematic subjectivity."[20] For example, she points out how the Nazi Goeth's "Today is History" speech becomes a voice-over as the film moves from his image to different shots of the Jews in the Ghetto, thus creating a disjunction between his speech and actions and their subsequent disastrous effects on the Jews. The uses of voice-over, the breaks between image and sound, and the effacing of dialogue in favor of music have the effect of breaking the narrative flow, making visible (as does the use of names and titles) the film's self-conscious work of memorial reconstruction, in particular, its working at certain points against conventional expectations of continuity and resolution.

If the film is attracted to the legend of Schindler, it is also attracted to images of emotional intensity in the events portrayed and in their capacity for generating an affective response from the spectator in relation to the anticipated concern with justice and restitution. The melodrama is enhanced through the film's operatic uses of music: a melange of popular, religious, and classical forms. The Yiddish folk songs, the chanting of ritual prayers, the singing of Kaddish, the Elgar music played by Isaac Stern on violin and Sam Sanders on the piano, accompany scenes with no dialogue, thus indicating the limits of language at certain moments. The music functions as the mute language of melodrama, heightening affect that cannot be articulated within the constraints of verbal language to encompass the horrors of the Holocaust, striving to express and heighten moments of suffering, giving them religious significance.

The film's reliance on the elegiac mode is strikingly evident in its stress on the images of the threatened children, especially in its focus on Genia of the red coat. Through the contrasting use of black-and-white and color (her red coat), her image is singled out from the others, providing an image of the vulnerability of the victims and a link between that brutal past and the threat of its recurrence in the present if one cannot experience empathy with those who suffered. Genia is also an image of unrealized life, a figure to be mourned. She becomes a synecdoche for the innocence of the children and their destruction at the hands of the Nazis. Her role functions as a vehicle for dramatizing questions of knowledge (including the audience's) concerning human agency, judgment, and memory. Finally, she serves in the narrative as one of the agents for visualizing Schindler's and the Jews' growing knowledge of the Nazi plans to destroy the Jews.

The filmic narrative takes the spectator step by step toward the Final Solution, but then, in the episode where the women's train is sent to Auschwitz, the film relents. Through Schindler's magical intervention, the lethal Zyklon-B gas miraculously turns to water, and the women are "saved," Schindler being the agent of their salvation. However, the images in long shot of inmates arriving and of the smoke spewing forth from the chimney are set in contrast to their rescue. The melodrama presented in this fable is that of the savior hero, which intensifies as the film develops—but again with a twist. The question, "Who is that man?" is tied to the film's central thematic of knowledge, a thematic intrinsic to most examinations of the Holocaust. The spectator as juridical observer is invited to share with the filmmaker-detective the difficulty of arriving at a satisfactory unified explanation of the Holocaust, or, for that matter, of accounting for the existence and behavior of a "righteous" person. The survival of some and the death of so many remains an absent meaning. The concern for knowledge then is tied to Schindler's character, his manipulation of others, and their perceptions of him in their attempts (like Stern's) to manipulate him for their purposes. To the survivors, he emerges as "a minor god of deliverance." To the audience, the troubling question, who he was, remains unanswered. What is evident is that he was different, that he was imperfect, but that in his imperfection he was unique.

The film reveals the porousness and complexity of melodrama. The common sense of melodrama is not simplistic; it is preoccupied with questions of discernment and judgment; and it strikes an affective chord in the viewer in its appeal to the necessity of a moral response. In the elegiac language of melodrama, in its reliance on recollection, the film ends with a scene of mourning at Schindler's grave in Israel. The procession of mourners, survivors and their families, accompanied by the actors who played them or their relatives, files by the grave, each person stopping and placing a stone on it. The last to stand there is Liam Neeson, his head bowed.

Relying again on the memory of *Night and Fog,* this episode, in the present and in Technicolor, serves as the hinge between past and present, between the dead and the living, and between fiction, memory, and documentation. Like ritual mourning, the spectators must shed tears (and according to reports, they do in copious amounts)—but for whom? for what? for the victims of the Holocaust? for themselves? for the affect raised by any moving melodrama?

In its generalized preoccupation with threats to survival, the specificity of the historical event is unstable, capable of being transposed from one set of events to another, antithetical set, and from one group of protagonists to another, perhaps also between victim and aggressor, posing the dilemma of the impossibility of the absoluteness of judgment and of knowledge.

Thus, in both popular and unpopular media texts, we are confronted with surprising similarities in their reliance on juridical forms of discourse and in their search for judgment. The texts turn within the orbit of the melodramatic as a means for weighing and judging the evidence of history and memory. They also remain within the melodramatic orbit in their intensely affective investment in the past, in their memorialization, and in their reliance on the ritual of mourning. The commonsense adherence to the belief that mourning is therapeutic and cathartic—with its emphasis on confronting loss, coming to terms with the past, and the need for knowledge as the appropriate means for addressing history—is common to both high and popular culture. Mourning is central to *Night and Fog* and *Shoah* and to *Holocaust* and *Schindler's List.* But are the films all univalently the same?

It would seem that these works differ in their commitment to different forms of knowing. Spielberg is not Resnais. Lanzmann is similarly not Resnais, nor is he Spielberg. *Holocaust* is not *Schindler's List.* The "serious" historical documentaries and the popular commercial cinema paint different kinds of history, though they paint them with a melodramatic brush. These differing treatments in recreating the Holocaust testify to the need to rethink the meaning of melodrama, to redeem it from monolithic sameness so as to extricate and confront what it reveals about its different forms and ends, in the interests of arriving at new forms of knowledge about the past, and especially the status of popular history.

The pejorative treatment of melodrama, relegating it uncritically to a derided realm of mass culture, situates it outside the critical knowledge necessary to pry open the nature, persistence, differences in, and effects of this form of apprehending the world. In rethinking history, it must be possible to question past events without congealing them, freezing them indelibly out of the fear that they will be forgotten, and, in the process of memorializing, obliterating any possibilities for understanding. Melodrama provides necessary insights into the characteristics and persistence of affective forms of experience that are invested in history. Paradoxically, the melodramatic mode seeks to escape catastrophe and repetition; yet it reveals at the same time that it is trapped in fear and anticipation of the return of the past. In discussing "the uses and disadvantages of history for the present," Friedrich Nietzsche wrote that "life is in need of the services of history. . . . [This] must be grasped as firmly as must the proposition, that an excess of history is harmful to the living man."[21]

The problem of popular history is not accuracy, not "facts" or "evidence" alone, but the questions and answers we bring to bear on our analysis of the various uses of the past. If, as in Walter Benjamin's famous aphorism, "There is no document of civilization which is not at the same time a document of barbarism," then we are obliged "to brush history against the grain," sparing no documents and sparing no means to identify the modes whereby we can fall prey ourselves to barbarism in the spirit of "good intentions."

NOTES

1. Umberto Eco, *Travels in Hyperreality: Essays,* trans. William Weaver (San Diego: Harcourt Brace Jovanovich, 1986).

2. Warren Goldstein, "Bad History Is Bad for Culture," *The Chronicle of Higher Education* (April 10, 1998): 64.

3. André Pierre Colombat, *The Holocaust in French Film* (Metuchen, N.J.: Scarecrow Press, 1993), 162–163.

4. Peter Brooks, *The Melodramatic Imagination: Balzac, Henry James, and the Mode of Excess* (New York: Columbia University Press, 1985), 15.

5. Ibid., 56.

6. Kevin Thomas, *Los Angeles Times* (quoted on back of video box).

7. Judith Doneson, *The Holocaust in American Film* (Philadelphia: Jewish Publication Society, 1987), 208.

8. Andrea S. Markovits and Rebecca S. Hayden, "*Holocaust* before and after the Event: Reactions in West Germany and Austria," *New German Critique* 19 (Winter 1980): 53–80.

9. Ibid., 60.

10. Ibid., 60–62.

11. Andreas Huyssen, "The Politics of Identification: *Holocaust* and West German Drama," *New German Critique* 19 (Winter 1980): 134–135.

12. Michael Kernan, "A National Memorial Bears Witness to the Holocaust," *Smithsonian* 24 (April 1993): 51.

13. William J. Clinton, "U.S. Museum Dedicated," April 22, 1993, *U.S. Department of State Dispatch* 4, no. 9 (May 19, 1993): 322.

14. Philip Gourevich, "Behold Now Behemoth," *Harper's* 287, no. 17/18 (July 1993): 61.

15. Ibid., 62.

16. Simon Louvish, "Witness," *Sight and Sound* 4, no. 3 (March 1993): 12.

17. James E. Young, *Writing and Rewriting the Holocaust: Narrative and the Consequences of Interpretation* (Bloomington: Indiana University Press, 1988), 17.

18. Ibid., 183.

19. Thomas Doherty, *"Schindler's List,"* *Cineaste* 20, no. 3 (1994): 51.

20. Miriam Bratu Hansen, "*Schindler's List* Is Not *Shoah:* Second Commandment,

Popular Modernism, and Public Memory in Spielberg's Holocaust," in *Spielberg's Holocaust: Critical Perspectives on Schindler's List,* ed. Josepha Loshitzky (Bloomington: Indiana University Press, 1997), 99.

    21. Friedrich Nietzsche, "The Uses and Disadvantages of History for the Present Time," in *Untimely Meditations,* trans. J. R. Hollingdale (Cambridge: Cambridge University Press, 1991), 67.

Speaking Back to Scripture
The Biblical Strain in Holocaust Poetry
John Felstiner

NO MORE SAND ART, no sand book, no masters.
Nothing on the dice. How many
mutes?
Seventeen.

Your question—your answer.
Your song, what does it know?

Deepinsnow,
   Eepinnow,
      E - i - o.

Over the past twenty years I have learned so much by translating and writing about Paul Celan, a German-speaking poet from Bukovina who barely survived the European Jewish catastrophe, that I must begin with his voice. "No more sand art" from 1964 runs thus:

KEINE SANDKUNST MEHR, *kein Sandbuch, keine Meister.*
Nichts erwürfelt. Wieviel
Stumme?
Siebenzehn.
Siebenzehn.

Deine Frage—deine Antwort.
Dein Gesang, was weiss er?

Tiefimschnee,
   Iefimnee,
      I - i - e.

The sand initiating this lyric calls up God's covenant with the Israelites: they shall multiply like the sands of the sea. At the same time, Celan's image evokes their long desert wandering. Ambiguity and contradiction, far from disabling his verse, in fact identify his only way of speaking the truth of "that which happened," as he called what we call the Holocaust.

Dein Gesang, was weiss er? "Your song, what does it know?" This single and signal question holds for all of Paul Celan's work, indeed for any lyric poetry *nach Auschwitz* (to borrow Theodor Adorno's dictum: "After Auschwitz, to write a poem is barbaric"). How can song possibly contain or convey a knowledge of what happened throughout Nazi-ridden Europe between 1933 and 1945? The snow that closes Celan's poem appears to be suffocating speech as it goes, actually enacting a stifling of lyric testimony that says more than any putative narrative could. And when we realize that Celan's own parents, deported from Czernowitz to Transnistria in 1942, both perished in the Ukrainian winter, we see that snow forms more (or less) than a metaphor for this poet. Reality preempts poetics.

"*La poésie ne s'impose plus, elle s'expose*," Celan remarked in 1968: "Poetry no longer imposes, it exposes itself." The speaker in "No more sand art" leads himself and his listener toward silence, toward the unmaking of even the most essential vision of *l'univers concentrationnaire*. This volume is aptly titled "Humanity at the Limit"; in the case of Paul Celan and countless other poets he represents, we may well speak of language itself at the limit. If Celan's 1964 lyric were to be translated into Hebrew of all languages—the Holy Tongue, the language of Judaism's founding text, the saving language for some Jews before, during, and after the war—in Hebrew, whose alphabet has no vowel characters, this poem's closing line, *I - i - e,* would vanish into silence!

This volume speaks, in part, of a time or condition "beyond the survivor." My own emphasis here will be on literature, as well as art and music, *by* the survivor—that is, by the victims themselves. I am most drawn to what was created at the core of "that which happened," in the ghettos and camps and in hiding. These works, emerging under duress, form the most acute aesthetic challenge. Since Aristotle, philosophy has inquired into the human "representation" of reality. Paul Celan, perhaps more drastically than anyone since the war, has felt the need not merely to represent reality but to make reality present in his verse: *Tiefimschnee, / Iefimnee, / I - i - e.* His major poem, "*Engführung*" (Stretto, Straitening), contains these lines:

Read no more—look!
Look no more—go!

The poem urges us to move from text to image to act.

At this point a question arises: Has this literature, art, and music a redemptive impulse, a redemptive effect? That depends on whose perspective you are adopting. Certainly for the victims who made a poem or song or drawing, their work was necessary. It embodied a human imperative, involving the twofold impulse of art: to express the self, and to tell another person. Paul Celan in his 1958 Bremen speech described himself as "one who goes toward language with his very being," his *Dasein*, "stricken by and seeking reality." He also said: "A poem can be a message in a bottle, sent out in the (not always greatly hopeful) belief that it may somewhere and sometime wash up on land, on heartland perhaps."

And not incidentally, art in this twofold sense, self-expression and telling another, forms a kind of resistance—not physical resistance as in a ghetto uprising or the derailing of a troop train, but resistance nonetheless: call it cultural or creative resistance, often performed at risk of one's life.

For a momentary and minute example of such resistance, the exclamation of oneself and the urgency to tell, look at this graffito scratched on a wall at Drancy, the transit camp outside of Paris, by one Marcel Chétovy in 1944, on his way to Auschwitz: "Arrived the 1st, departed the 31st of July, in *very very* good spirits and hoping to return soon." Marcel Chétovy, with his father Moïse, did not return, yet in one midsummer moment he made his mark imperishably, as the Thousand Year Reich never could.

Presently I find myself gripped even more by music that emerged from the catastrophe than by literature—perhaps because music, though a universal and immemorial human phenomenon, seems strangely free, a less likely activity under severe duress than the writing of a poem or diary entry. Anyway an entire range of musical expression did emerge: from a Jüdische Kulturbund performance of Handel's *Judas Maccabeus* in 1938 or Verdi's *Requiem* in Terezín to the innumerable ghetto songs whose bitter or humorous satire updated old tunes with new lyrics. My friend Gloria Lyon, at 14 in Auschwitz, composed a song of hope with her companions, in Hungarian, set to the melody of "Hatikvah." While Marcel Chétovy's defiant *very very* good spirits" did not make the difference between life and death in Auschwitz, maybe Gloria's making that song somehow helped sustain her, kept her barely viable.

A little-known Czech Jewish composer, Gideon Klein, intensified his musical activity once he was sent to Terezín: running classes for children, organizing and performing concerts, and composing. One woman remembers Klein playing "so wonderfully that there were tears running down our cheeks." She also remembers an attic concert "with only three chairs, for the string trio . . . the audience stood still as mice. . . . Someone kept lookout from an attic window, and guards stood on the steps. . . . These few hours of spiritual nourishment made many people forget the hunger and misery and long for another concert. . . . Meanwhile for the artists this was a revolt against the regime." And a Czech child, identified as "Anonymous" in the collection *I Never Saw Another Butterfly*, wrote a poem about Gideon Klein called "Concert in the Old School Garret":

> Under closed eyes he seeks among the keys
> As among the veins through which blood flows softly
> When you kiss them with a knife and put a song to it.

One cannot enter unscathed the imagination of a teenager to whom it has been given to see and say such things.

Perhaps Gideon Klein's most telling music is the densely and compellingly beautiful largo from his string trio, variations on a Moravian folk song sung to him in childhood by his nanny. He composed this in September 1944, still in his twenties. The trio was not performed in Terezín (but his score survived). Nine days later he was deported to Auschwitz.

Gideon Klein caught the attention of two artists, Petr Kien and Charlotte Buresova, whose renderings of his face reveal a pure seriousness and—again, not incidentally—constitute in themselves a resistance to the human efface-ment and degradation prescribed by the "Final Solution."

About the matter of visual art under Nazi oppression, two anecdotes come to mind that illuminate the ironic, sometimes bizarre interaction of art and history. In Auschwitz, Dinah Gottlieb came to the attention of Dr. Mengele. At the time he was interested in Gypsy physiognomy, and had her make watercolor portraits. Thanks to her useful talent, she survived. Years later, in the 1960s, she went to the Polish state museum in Auschwitz and asked for her artwork. No, she was told, it is not really "hers"—and she is still trying to recover it.

In 1937, horrified by the Fascist bombing of the Basque town of Guernica, Pablo Picasso painted his tortured twenty-five-foot image of the atrocity. Later, in occupied Paris, a curious SS officer visited his studio and, gesturing toward a photo of Picasso's *Guernica,* asked: "Did you do this?" "No," the artist re-plied, "you did."

One figure in particular has served artists, especially Israeli artists, to imagine what happened to Jews and others in Europe: namely, the binding (or as it's called, the sacrifice) of Isaac. In fact the sacrifice that Abraham was called to offer as an act of faith in God is called in Hebrew *olah*, as is any ritual sacrifice that must be wholly consumed and whose smoke rises to heaven. In the Septuagint's Greek translation, *olah* yielded "Holocaust." Thus that term for a willing offering pleasing in the sight of God is now a terrible misnomer for the Jewish catastrophe.

Still the *akedah,* or "binding," of Isaac has served since the Crusades and probably before as a mythic source and recourse by which to imagine ultimate Jewish peril. The drawings and paintings of Israeli artists, such as Abel Pann's in 1942, show an agony that claims its own distinctive site, even alongside Rembrandt's great representation. The poet T. Carmi singles out the *akedah* as "capable of absorbing the shocks of history."

The poem that best proves this mythic capacity, Amir Gilboa's "*Yitzhak,*" comes from someone born in the Ukraine in 1917 who emigrated to Palestine in the 1930s but had to leave his parents behind. After the war, instead—of course!—of simply recounting the Isaac story under his title, Gilboa recasts it in a child's nightmare, here translated by the American poet Shirley Kaufman (I have changed "father" to "daddy"):

Early in the morning the sun took a walk in the woods
with me and my daddy
my right hand in his left.

A knife flashed between the trees like lightning.
And I'm so scared of the fear in my eyes facing blood on the leaves

Daddy daddy come quick and save Isaac
so no one will be missing at lunchtime.

It's I who am butchered, my son,
my blood's already on the leaves.
And daddy's voice was choked.
And his face pale.

I wanted to cry out, struggling not to believe,
I tore my eyes open
and woke.

And my right hand was drained of blood

Inevitably the very words from the Hebrew Bible's account—"knife," "wood"—recur in these lines. But not only is someone now sacrificed; it is Abraham, the progenitor of a people, here as if cut off at the root—Holy Writ countermanded in the Holy Tongue. And Isaac the son's hand is drained of blood, the poet's hand emptied of life.

With the poetry that emerged from the Shoah, we find ourselves caught between Adorno's dictum and a question and answer Bertolt Brecht once penned: "In the dark times, will there also be singing?" "Yes, there will be singing. *About* the dark times." Brecht's exchange may sound a bit facile in some contexts. But Adorno's stricture, "After Auschwitz, to write a poem is barbaric," vaporizes under the force and art of poetry from the core times and places.

Warsaw's leading Hebrew and Yiddish poet Itzhak Katznelson looks out with crushed visage from a 1943 drawing the artist Lea Lilienblum did on the back of a shoe box. His epic Yiddish "Song of the Murdered Jewish People" echoes what it must, Psalm 137 from the Babylonian exile. Katznelson begins, "Sing! Take your light, hollow harp in hand. . . . Sing of the last Jews on Europe's soil." Later he turns to Ezekiel: "Can these bones live? . . . Not even a bone remains from my murdered people." No despair could be more forcefully, utterly grounded than that generated by gainsaying the Bible itself.

Two thoughts about the poetry emerging from Europe's Jewish catastrophe seem to me germane. First, I find Scripture pervading this poetry. My title, "Speaking Back to Scripture: The Biblical Strain in Holocaust Poetry," embeds a double meaning in the ongoing participle "speaking back": to retort, revise, refute, but at the same time to reach back, to get back, by way of speech. Paul Celan catches the contradiction in a few lines:

You prayer-, you blasphemy-, you
prayer-sharp knives
of my
silence.

And my word "strain" embodies a kindred ambiguity: the well-nigh impossible effort of composing such poems, and yet the presence they generate, the lyric motif.

Early in his memoir *If This Is a Man (Survival in Auschwitz)*, Primo Levi remembers himself and his fellows sitting around in the evening telling stories that came from all over Europe. They were terrible stories, "simple and incomprehensible like the stories in the Bible," Levi writes. "But are they not themselves stories of a new Bible?" Levi's first poem after liberation, from January 1946, advances an equal blasphemy: entitled *"Shema"* (Hear!), it replaces the Judaic watchword and the *ahavah* with new words that thou shalt speak of when thou sittest by the way and shalt teach diligently unto thy children— words now revealing the abandonment and degradation of human beings at Auschwitz.

A second thought or observation about poems emerging from the Catastrophe concerns the language they were written in. To my mind, the most penetrating of them are likely to occur—indeed in some sense must occur—in one of three languages: Yiddish, Hebrew, or German. Yiddish, because it was the mother tongue obliterated in four to five million mouths; Hebrew, because it was the holy tongue conferring peoplehood and was for some Jews the saving tongue of Eretz Yisrael; German, because that language effectuated the genocide—and as Hölderlin put it: *Wo aber Gefahr ist, wächst / Das Rettende auch*, "Yet where danger is, grows / What rescues as well." This is not in the least to discount poems such as Levi's *"Shema"* in Italian, Miklós Radnóti's Hungarian lyrics, or even those of the Pole Tadeusz Borowski, for example. Only to suggest that Yiddish, Hebrew, and German, each in its own way, have a particular grasp, a privileged perspective, on "that which happened."

In Yiddish and in Hebrew (then later in English), the Vilna partisan and poet Abba Kovner liked to tell the story of how they had to defend the ghetto but found they had no sandbags for the bunkers. A people of sand—and now no sand! What could they do? They went to the Strashun library where heavy bulking tomes of the Talmud had been studied for centuries, and took these in place of sandbags to steady their rifles. Avraham Sutzkever, another partisan-poet from Vilna, wrote a 1943 poem, "The Lead Plates at the Rom Press": lacking lead for bullets, they decided to melt down plates used for centuries in printing the Talmud and Bible.

These stories ring with a resolve that not all poems and songs could muster. The Yiddish poet Kadya Molodowsky began one lament with a hallowed Biblical epithet: "O God of Mercy / Choose another people." And Yankev Glatshteyn's "Dead Men Don't Praise God" wrests that utterance from Psalms and begins: "We received the Torah at Sinai / And in Lublin we gave it back," wherein Lublin means the death camp Maidanek.

The Biblical echo chamber that is modern Hebrew, as we've seen in Gilboa's *"Yitzhak,"* makes for a specifically endowed way of speaking back to Scripture. One of the two most striking—I would even say monumental—lyrics to emerge from the Catastrophe is by the Bukovina-born Dan Pagis, who mastered Hebrew in an astonishingly short time after the war.

WRITTEN IN PENCIL IN A SEALED BOXCAR

here in this transport
I Eve
with Abel my son
if you see my older son
Cain son of Adam
tell him that I

Various questions and contradictory answers abound here. What's more, because Hebrew has no present tense for the verb "to be," the sudden muteness at the end of the last line, the absence of a verb, may send us circling back to the opening, "here in this transport," so that the poem repeats into the millions until every "I" has spoken. And in any event, that thunderous silence following "tell him that I," *tagidulo sh'ani*, must resound quite differently after Hebrew than after any other tongue.

For German, my example must be Paul Celan, who unappeasably teaches what it means to write a poem after Auschwitz—indeed, to write a poem at all, in this disastrous century. When Celan returned to Czernowitz in 1944 a raw orphan after nineteen months at forced labor, he had literally nothing left but his native German language. But his mother's tongue, which had given him songs and classics from the minnesingers down through Goethe, Schiller, Hölderlin, and Rilke, had turned brutally into the murderers' tongue. He wrote a couplet to her who he knew must have perished: "And can you bear, Mother, as—oh at home—once on a time, / The gentle, the German, the pain-laden rhyme?"

In its way, this verse enacts a response to the very question it asks, firmly measured as it is and rhymed—*daheim* ("at home") with *Reim* ("rhyme")—in the language at issue. Before the war's end, destitute in Soviet-occupied Czernowitz, Celan made his fateful choice. He composed in German a sort of ballad that gives voice to the people and the language that "had to pass through frightful muting," as he later put it, "through the thousand darknesses of deathbringing speech." *"Todesfuge"* (Deathfugue) nervily adopts the plural "We" of Jewish prisoners, iterating a relentless daily degeneration that annuls the fiat of Biblical Creation itself:

Black milk of daybreak we drink it at evening
we drink it at midday and morning we drink it at night
we drink and we drink
we shovel a grave in the air there you won't lie too cramped

By the end of this fuguelike ballad the premier heroine of European literature, *Faust*'s Margareta, is counterpointed by the Hebraic maiden par excellence, Shulamith, the Song of Song's figure of longing and return from exile:

Black milk of daybreak we drink you at night
we drink you at midday Death is a master from Deutschland
we drink you at evening and morning we drink and we drink
this Death is a master from Deutschland his eye it is blue
he shoots you with shot made of lead shoots you level and true
a man lives in the house you golden hair Margareta
he looses his hounds on us grants us a grave in the air
he plays with his vipers and daydreams this Death is a master from
Deutschland

your golden hair Margareta
your ashen hair Shulamith

Paul Celan's poem quite literally spells an end to the German-Jewish symbiosis attested to from Moses Mendelssohn on down to Martin Buber and Franz Rosenzweig, whose heroic translation of the Hebrew Bible was interrupted by the wholesale murder of much of their audience.

What I call the Biblical strain in Celan's writing shows up most starkly in a poem he titled simply "*Psalm*." In seeking a likely, lively translation, I hold to the King James version, with words such as "earth," "clay," "dust," because Celan's opening lines are refuting human genesis:

No one kneads us again out of earth and clay,
no one incants our dust.
No one.

Then the ritual opening of Hebraic benediction invokes God by a new name, a profanation if it were not couched in blessing:

Blessèd art thou, No One.
In thy sight would
we bloom.
In thy
spite.

The Biblical Psalmist, and Job, and Abraham arguing with God over Sodom remind us that such verbal arraignment of divinity stems from the source of Judaism. *Kvetchen zikh mit got*, the Yiddish saying has it—witness Sholem Aleichem's Tevye along with this century's Yiddish poets.

Could the art of poetry, even so radically contradictive and conflicted a poetry as Celan's, sustain him?

Speak you too,
speak as the last,
say out your say,

he said to himself as "*Todesfuge*" was becoming absorbed—too easily, he feared—into German anthologies and textbooks.

Speak—
But don't split off No from Yes,

Doch scheide das Nein nicht vom Ja.

For this "true-stammered mouth," as he called himself in Moses' prophetic vein, the task of "going with his very being toward language, stricken by and seeking reality" proved too much. Germany's neo-Nazism and recrudescent anti-Semitism in the early 1960s, plus a groundless plagiarism charge, adding insult to the core trauma, brought out a manic-depressive tendency in Celan. Yet in his poems a gleam persists, like the "radiance that streams inextinguishably from the door of the Law" in Kafka's parable "Before the Law."

In the fall of 1969 Celan made his long-deferred journey to Israel, the road not taken, the land that had housed childhood émigré friends and family. His poems after that visit bear witness to a "binding brightness"; to a "shining" at Abu Tor overlooking Gehenna and "a goldbuoy, up from / Temple depths"; to a "glowing / text-void" at the Western Wall, where "text-void," *Leertext*, puns on *Lehrtext*, "Torah-void."

To close this account of "speaking back to Scripture," of the "Biblical strain" in Holocaust poetry, I return to a day in late November 1963 when Paul Celan, emerging from severe depression, composed two brief poems. The first announces a lifelong allegiance:

> With the persecuted in late, un-
> silenced,
> radiant
> covenant.

The other begins with a bleak, tenuous light before Creation and ends with a hope, a pre-vision:

> Threadsuns
> over the grayblack wasteness.
> A tree-
> high thought
> strikes the light-tone: there are
> still songs to sing beyond
> humankind.

Psalm 98 urges, "O sing unto the Lord a new song, For He hath done marvelous things." Although that *shir chadash* voices more praise than Celan could ever manage, in his own voice he found "new song" enough to sing for a while, *jenseits der Menschen*, beyond that people with whom he kept "radiant covenant."

31 | Two Models in the Study of Holocaust Literature
Alan Mintz

FOR PHILOSOPHERS AND THEOLOGIANS, the unprecedented enormity of the Holocaust changed everything. All of the assumptions that we carried with us from the nineteenth century into the present—assumptions about the nature of God and man, the progress of the human endeavor, the sanctity of art and the vocation of culture, the place of the Jews among the nations—all these were shattered or turned inside out by Auschwitz and its crematoria. The Holocaust thus constituted a "tremendum," an event of such awful negative transcendence that it cleaved history into a before and after. That we view the present through a profoundly altered lens goes without saying; but we also cannot escape viewing the past through the medium of this terrible knowledge. All human achievement and aspiration before the event—and for Jews especially, the record of the covenantal relations between God and Israel—must be reunderstood retroactively under the sign of the Holocaust.[1]

Yet if the Holocaust is indeed a "rupture in the very fabric of being," as the philosophers have taught us, then this is a teaching that has been largely ignored for most of the half century since the war. To state this is not to be flip or anti-intellectual but to point to a fundamental truth about how cultures behave. For however persuasively we may posit the Holocaust as a paradigm-shattering tragedy, it is not in the conservative nature of cultures to be easily shattered and reconfigured. It is far more typical for cultures to resist admitting the Holocaust precisely because of this subversive quality; and when the Holocaust is finally let in, and then only gradually, it enters not on its own terms, scorching earth and blazing new ground, but within the terms already set out from within the culture's own dynamic.

During the postwar years, the Holocaust moved from the margins to the center of American culture. Among the factors that encouraged this shift, I count the experience of victory at the close of the war, the new opportunities for integration opened to American Jews, the Eichmann trial, the rise of the civil rights movement and the protest against the war in Vietnam, the response of American Jewry to the Six-Day War, the reception of the stage and movie versions of Anne Frank's diary, the emergence of the survivor as a hero of culture, the broad impact of key media events on television and in motion pictures, the role of the Holocaust as a point of moral consensus between political parties and orientations. Other informed interpreters would doubtlessly give greater weight to some factors and less to others. They might, for example, amplify the role of survivors and their "second-generation" offspring in bringing attention to the Holocaust, or they might demur from the emphasis I would place on the impact of the Eichmann trial. There might be a different valuation placed on works of high culture as compared to those of popular culture.

Yet however the tale is told, one thing remains clear: this is an indelibly American tale. It would be unthinkable to analyze the response to the Holocaust in America without taking into consideration postwar economic conditions, the Cold War preoccupation with communism and the Soviet Union, domestic protest movements, the centrality in America of television and film, the political leverage of the organized American Jewish community, and United States policy toward Israel and the Arab world, among many other factors that are particular to the American scene. In a similar vein, it would be equally unthinkable to examine writing about the Holocaust in Poland without considering Polish self-perceptions as victims of Nazism and the imposition of Soviet communism; or to look at the case of France without considering the mystique of the resistance and the disavowal of Vichy; or the former Soviet Union without an understanding of how the Jewish identity of Jewish victims of Hitler was suppressed in the remembrance of the Great Patriotic War.

On the face of it this would seem to be self-evident: simply a matter of basic responsibility in taking context into consideration in understanding the impact of the Holocaust. Yet behind this question, I would argue, lies a fundamental difference of approach as to how we should evaluate cultural responses to the Holocaust. This is a difference with far-ranging consequences for how we conceive and constitute the enterprise of Holocaust studies generally. In the following pages, I conceptualize this difference as a tension between two models of inquiry. One I call the exceptionalist model and the other I call the constructivist model.

The exceptionalist model is rooted in a conviction of the Holocaust as a radical rupture in human history that goes well beyond notions of uniqueness. The Nazi will to murder all the Jews and the abyss of abasement inflicted upon the victims place the Holocaust in a dimension of tragedy beyond the reach of comparisons and analogies. In the black hole of this concentrationary universe, the very humanness of man was annihilated, along with his rootedness in culture. For the victims who were not killed, life in the aftermath was forever shattered, no matter how successful its outer trappings. The truth about the Holocaust is a horror that few can abide without some palliative. True artistic responses to the catastrophe are rare, and they are necessarily bleak and unadorned and resist the temptation to uplift and to give false comfort in its many forms. Hewn out of the same void, these works of art, no matter their different origins or languages of composition, make up a canon of Holocaust literature with a shared poetics. When it comes to cultural refractions of the

Holocaust, however, the norm is, sadly, vulgarization, especially in works of popular culture. Most disturbing and most prevalent, moreover, is the way in which the Holocaust is traduced by being appropriated to serve purposes— national interests, universalist ethics, personal identity—that are not only un- related to the Holocaust but often antithetical to its memory.

The constructivist model stresses the cultural lens through which the Holo- caust is perceived. Even in accounts of the concentration camps, the place where identity was almost blotted out, such preexisting factors as educational background, religious outlook, and native language fundamentally shaped the ways in which the experience is represented. This is true as well for the surviv- ing victims, whose lives, despite the unspeakable sufferings and losses during the war, display remarkable continuities alongside the inevitable changes. If the cultural lens is operative even for the victims, how much more so is it in the case for bystanders, those who observed the grim transaction between per- petrators and victims but were not directly party to it. Cultures, like individu- als, can of necessity comprehend historical events only from within the set of their own issues and interests; the very willingness to engage an external event must be motivated by an internal exigency. The typical response is first denial and resistance; when the Holocaust is eventually "admitted," it is inevitably in the form of an appropriation that at once connects to the Holocaust and uses it for ulterior motives. The result might be serious or vulgar, but it will always be an appropriation. In the study of artistic responses to the Holocaust, there- fore, language is key, because it is within the set of values and discursive practices embedded in a particular language and its literary traditions—be it Yiddish, Hebrew, French, Italian, Polish, German, or English—that the artist struggles to represent the Holocaust and to communicate with an audience that shares his or her language. Although the artist may seek to subvert those values and practices under the force of the Holocaust experience, the subver- sion can only take place and make sense within the cultural medium in which it is enacted. Similarly, acts of Holocaust memorialization, whether in the form of museums, monuments, or days of remembrance, will always reflect as much about the community that is doing the remembering as about the event being remembered.

These two models rest upon very different theoretical assumptions. For the constructivist model, the point of the departure is the assumption that be- yond their factual core, historical events, even the Holocaust, possess no in- scribed meanings; meaning is constructed by communities of interpretation— differently by different communities—out of their own motives and needs.[2] The exceptionalist model, in contrast, discovers in the Holocaust a dark truth that inheres in the event. To be sure, there may be different versions of this truth among serious students of the event who similarly decline to be seduced by false comfort. But this vision is nevertheless not open to being coopted and constructed for other needs and purposes. Although the vision may be refracted through the lens of different cultures, it is possible to hold these amalgams up to the light of criticism and discern the elements that are true to the Holocaust experience and those that have been wrapped around it for different purposes.

As an argument, the rhetoric of the exceptionalist model has great prophetic appeal. It exhorts us to remain loyal to an authentic but difficult truth and to eschew relativism, false consciousness, and opportunism when they threaten to compromise that truth. I am moved by this rhetoric as much as anyone else who feels deeply about the Holocaust, identifies with the pathos of its victims, and is zealous to preserve its memory. I am also aware that, because it stresses the mediated nature of our perception of the Holocaust, the constructivist model can appear like an accommodation to cultural relativism, which it is not. Yet despite the ostensible moral appeal of the exceptionalist model, I wish to argue in the following pages for the general utility of the constructivist model as a standpoint from which to understand responses to the Holocaust.

I make this argument on two grounds. The first is pragmatic. The constructivist model provides a much more powerful explanatory framework for comprehending Holocaust-related literature because it accounts for both the cultural materials out of which the artwork is constructed and the Holocaust vision it projects. The second is a moral argument. Because the exceptionalist model fixes the meaning of the Holocaust as a message about death and atrocity, it forecloses the process of memorialization, in which human communities, through intentional or unconscious memory, construct the Holocaust in ways relevant to their future. The burden of this chapter will take up the pragmatic issue as it pertains to the study of Holocaust culture; the question of memorialization will be the subject of the concluding thoughts. The pragmatic issue is, admittedly, an argument among academic students of Holocaust literature about method. But the argument is not trivial, and it bears directly on the larger meaning we will assign to the Holocaust in the future.

* * *

The very notion of Holocaust literature, to begin with, did not have an easy time establishing itself. Already by the 1960s there was a significant body of writing relating to the Holocaust, although much of the work had not been translated into English. Yet the same factors that joined together to keep the Holocaust out of the mainstream of American life at that time kept works of literature on the subject on the margins of academic and intellectual discourse. Individual works were read—often read obsessively—by individual readers; and some attained the status of underground classics. But there was resistance to recognizing the phenomenon as a whole, and this came from two sources. The first was an attitude that viewed the very idea of art "based" on the Holocaust with radical suspicion. Adorno's famous statement that to write poetry after Auschwitz is barbaric—despite that fact that Adorno did not mean it in the categorical way it was often taken—represented a widespread contemporary sentiment. No matter how severe, there is no art that does not create, if only at the level of form rather than content, some beauty or pleasure; and beauty and pleasure, it was averred, should not be derived from atrocity. All art, moreover, involves some artifice and rearranging of the facts in the imaginative reworking of reality. Precisely because the horror of the Holocaust was unprecedented, the proper response, it was felt, was to document that horror rather than transfigure it in any way. The second reservation related not to artistic responses to the Holocaust, which were steadily multiplying despite these suspicions, but to their critical study. The dryly analytical methods used in the academy for studying literature should not be applied to works of art that emanate from the dark mystery of the Holocaust. These works are messages from the void that are supposed to create an aura and make an impact on the reader's emotion. To submit them to the apparatus of literary criticism is to trespass upon an unspoken cordon of respect for the dead in the horror of their dying.

Although this resistance continues among some general readers, in the academy the idea of the critical study of Holocaust literature has largely been accepted. The sheer number of serious works of fiction in many languages about the Holocaust that have continued to be produced makes it difficult to avoid it as a body of work. Poetry has always had an easier time of it because it is viewed, rightly or wrongly, as being expressive rather than representational and because the verse of such poets as Paul Celan, Dan Pagis, and Nelly Sachs has manifestly needed glossing and interpretation in order to be understood. The case for taking fiction seriously has been made by critics such as Alvin Rosenfeld, Lawrence Langer, Sidra DeKoven Ezrahi, David Roskies, James Young, and Sara Horowitz, whose strong analytic writing has demonstrated that literary critical acumen need not operate at the expense of outrage and empathy. In the context of Holocaust literature, they have explored strategies of fiction—including humor, estrangement, and the grotesque—and even the "lying" component at the heart of fiction—the license to select, rearrange, and even invent; they have demonstrated how these techniques can be exploited not to take flight or avoid but to sharpen the horror in ways impossible through means that are ostensibly more loyal to the plain historical record. This project of demonstration—largely successful, I believe—was aimed at two audiences at once. One was a general audience that had to be persuaded that imaginative literature and its critical study would not traduce the aura of sacred memory; the other was an academic culture of English and comparative literature departments that had to be persuaded to "admit" works of Holocaust literature into the canon of serious literature meriting critical study.

Although the students of Holocaust literature may be united in their conviction of its importance, they are deeply divided as to what it is and how it should be studied. Which are the most important authors and the most significant texts and in which contexts are they to be read? What, in short, is the canon of Holocaust literature? Canons, we know, are not naive formations, simply the preference of good taste over bad. Even without assuming a militantly ideological stance that views canons as a means of institutionalizing hegemony, we can say, at the very least, that different canons represent different conceptions of what are strong works of art and in which qualities that strength resides. In the case of Holocaust literature, there are two major competing conceptions of the canon. Underlying one of them, I will argue, is the exceptionalist model, and underlying the other is the constructivist model. What is at stake in how they draw the map of Holocaust literature differently is profound. It is not a matter of academic nuance as much as it is a quarrel over the question of what of the Holocaust most needs to be remembered.

The contrastive examples I wish to adduce are two anthologies: Lawrence L. Langer's *Art from the Ashes* and David G. Roskies's *The Literature of Destruction*. Both works are large and ambitious, each containing over 650 crowded pages; and both are written by key figures whose considerable previous scholarly writing gives particular authority to their anthologizing efforts.[3] These volumes, important in themselves, will provide us with two concrete instances for unfolding the assumptions and ramifications of these two models for the study of Holocaust literature. Looking at the Roskies volume first will make the differences between the two most quickly apparent.

By the rubric "the literature of destruction," to begin with, Roskies means something far more extensive than the Holocaust. He begins with responses to the destruction of the first Jerusalem temple in 587 B.C.E. in the biblical books of Lamentations and Psalms and in the classical prophets; he proceeds to the responses to the destruction of the second temple in 70 C.E. in the midrashic writings of the rabbis. He then goes on to Hebrew chronicles, liturgical poems, and consolation literature composed in response to a series of catastrophic persecutions in the Middle Ages. Next is a grouping of modern, secular literary responses to the pogroms in Russia in 1881 and 1903. The World War I period, including the Russian Revolution and the Civil War, saw the virtual destruction of traditional Jewish society in Eastern Europe; these events are the subject of a selected grouping of short stories and poems in Yiddish, Hebrew, and Russian. The remainder of the anthology, except for a short coda on Israel's War of Independence, deals with the Holocaust, emphasizing literature written in the Warsaw and Vilna ghettos rather than in or about the concentration camps. In addition to literary-historical introductions to each of the volume's twenty chapters (there are one hundred entries), each text is accompanied by notes that supply sources, explain literary allusions, and reference historical events. Rather than appearing at the bottom of the page or at the end of chapters or of the volume as a whole, the notes are placed up and down the page in the margin alongside the reference that needs to be explained.

For Roskies, it need hardly be pointed out, the Holocaust literature does not stand alone but must be seen in relationship to a long record of responses to catastrophe in Jewish literature. The context, then, could not be less unambiguous. But the *relationship* between the murder of European Jewry and these earlier destructions is not so evident. Is the Holocaust and its responses only the latest in a series of destructions? Or is the Holocaust the great destruction that overshadows the others? What, in fact, is the shape of the Jewish "literature of destruction"? The answer lies in the way the volume is organized; the anthology reveals its intentions through the disposition of materials from different historical periods. This is the distribution by pages:

First and Second Temples	57
Middle Ages	43
Pogroms in Russia, 1881–1905	87
World War I and Aftermath	177
Holocaust	223

This arrangement makes Roskies's modernity unmistakable. In Jewish religious culture, especially as embodied in the liturgies for the summer fast day on the Ninth of Av, the destruction of the Jerusalem temples is the preeminent and primal catastrophe, while all later depredations, no matter how destructive, remain echoes of the ancient calamities. Roskies has turned this tradition on its head and made ancient and medieval history into a kind of background that leads up through modern times to the Holocaust. So, in Roskies's construct of a Jewish literature of destruction, two things are true: The Holocaust is indeed preeminent rather than being another in a series of catastrophes. Yet at the same time, the responses to the Holocaust can be understood only by reference to responses to these earlier events. The relevance of this contextual background, moreover, increases the closer in time to the Holocaust. It is a striking feature of the anthology that the material on the pogroms in Russia at the turn of the century and during World War I make up together a larger unit (87 + 177 = 264 pages) than the section on the Holocaust itself (223 pages).

Implicit in this inverted structure is the paradoxical assumption that the tradition and the subversion of the tradition are inextricably bound up with one another. It is in the nature of collective memory, Roskies argues, that we meet the present catastrophe armed with the symbols, archetypes, and rubrics supplied by the previous catastrophe, which we then transfigure, invert, or betray because of their inadequacy in the face of the new reality. We can bring to this encounter nothing other than the cultural materials we have been given, though they be unequal to the task; and our encounter can be understood only in terms of how we reshape, deform, or jettison those materials. This is a fierce dialectic that, in a religious tradition that privileges revelation and antiquity, needs to be camouflaged. So, for example, when the rabbis of the midrash faced the destruction of the second temple, they had to do so through the biblical Book of Lamentations, which was written in response to the first destruction. Lamentations was authoritative because it was a canonical text, yet it is so severe in its depiction of God's unmollified rage that the rabbis had nearly to turn it inside out with their hermeneutical techniques in order to make it yield a serviceable message of consolation.

In the modern age after faith the dialectic is more patent. The responses to the successive waves of anti-Jewish violence early in the century were written by Hebrew and Yiddish writers for readers who, like themselves, had turned from traditional faith to nationalism and socialism and the other faiths of modernity. Their rejection of the martyrology and covenantal theology they inherited from the religious tradition was not veiled by the need to vindicate received forms. Yet again, their subversions can only be fully understood in terms of what they were subverting. In some cases they secularized religious categories and appropriated their authority; in other cases they parodied those traditions; in still others they imitated the tradition by focusing on the murderousness of the gentiles. These are enormous changes, but they were so entangled with the traditions that are in the course of being found inadequate that they can only be decoded with a profound awareness of the dialectical nature of the transaction.

This explains why Roskies gives as much space in his anthology to the decades that preceded the Holocaust as to the Holocaust itself. It is in this earlier period that the modern Jewish cultural formations were created that provided the categories through which the victims of the Holocaust strove to grasp their fate. There was Bundism, communism, socialism, Zionism, European humanism, and radical acculturation, together with modernized forms of Hasidism and Lithuanian Orthodoxy, and each with multiple and overlapping variations and inflections. The issue here is not so much ideological doctrine as the way in which these outlooks determined a cultural frame of reference through which individuals and communities understood the world around them. To take examples solely from the Ringelblum archive of the Warsaw Ghetto, there is one writer who experiences his hunger by contrast to an Arthur Schnitzler novel he is reading in German; another whose point of reference for the horrific sight of the ghetto being put to torch by the Germans is the epic scenes of modern cinema; another who inveighs against the ghetto leadership in language borrowed from the prophetic verse of Ch. N. Bialik, the great poet of the Hebrew revival; and still another who, though secular, invokes the image of the Yizkor, the communal prayer for the dead, as an ultimate gesture.[4]

In all of these cases, what is both moving and innovative is the tension between the received cultural frame, on the one hand, and the awful reality that was unfolding in unprecedented ways and what the writer does with this tension, on the other. Even in the death camps, where men and women were reduced to the most primitive level of existence, prisoners viewed their situation through the lens of their upbringing and their commitments. If in the camps, then all the more so in the ghettos. This is the reason why Roskies devotes more space to the latter than to the former. For it was in the ghettos, unlike the camps, that Jews were forced to live without significant internal interference as to the form that their cultural life took. It is this highly circumscribed zone of cultural desperation that Roskies finds more interesting and revealing than the radically individuated and nearly sub-biological regime of the camps.

The roles of language and cultural reference are therefore critical for Roskies. For him, language is destiny—and memory. The choice to write in Yiddish or Hebrew as opposed to Polish, German, or Russian determines not only the audience but also the entire repertoire of sources, allusions, and speech habits that are available to the writer to convey his or her message. So deeply are the cultural practices of earlier eras embedded in the conservative medium of language that leaving them behind is not really possible. The writer who strives to write in a radically dissociated and displaced style that owes nothing to the past and reflects the denuded world of the camps is inescapably stuck with the residual integuments that words bring with them. He or she must work against them, around them, or through them; there is no choice. Translation can only do so much. Even the best literary translators, endeavoring to create vivid English texts rather than literal equivalents, will necessarily have to make immense renunciations. It therefore falls to editors, compilers, and anthologists to provide annotation that will fill in some of the gaps. Short of saturating a text with commentary, no editor can hope to gloss the nuances and associations words bring them. It is possible, however, selectively to note crucial allusions to texts, cultural practices, and historical events. Because Roskies believes that writers inevitably undertake their encounter with the Holocaust with their responses to previous catastrophes in hand, the editor cannot do otherwise.

Lawrence Langer does in fact do otherwise, and for reasons that are consistent with a very different conception of Holocaust literature. The greatest difference between Langer's *Art from the Ashes* and Roskies's *The Literature of Destruction* is the very location of the object to be anthologized. For Roskies, Holocaust literature is situated toward the end of a long—and mostly Hebraic—tradition of responses to catastrophe in Jewish literature; although this belated literature is largely not continuous with the tradition, it remains incomprehensible without it. For Langer, Holocaust literature is a body of work unto itself; what came before is far from irrelevant, but the antecedents pale into insignificance compared with what works of Holocaust art hold in common. The black hole, the *anus mundi,* to which all acts of Holocaust writing refer, is the great, determining fact and not the cultural provenance of the writing, which, in any case, is swept away by enormity of the event. Because the *univers concentrationnaire* was a world unto itself, with its own language and its own laws, which resembled nothing else that man has devised on earth, it then follows that the literature that represents this world should form its own category, with its own poetics.

Langer accordingly organizes his anthology not historically, but rather by genre. There are six genres. In addition to fiction, poetry, and drama, Langer includes sections on documentary writing, journals and diaries, and the painters of Terezín. Langer opens *Art from the Ashes* with the section on documentary writing, which he calls simply "The Way It Was." It includes non-fiction writing (Charlotte Delbo, Christopher Browning, Primo Levi, Jean Améry, Elie Wiesel, and others) dealing with the work of the mobile killing squads and life and death in the death camps. The second section is devoted to selections from the diaries of Abraham Lewin, Jozef Zelkowicz, and Avraham Tory, which describe deportations and *Aktionen* in the ghettos of Warsaw, Lodz, and Kovno, respectively. Langer intends these testimonies to form a kind of a standard, "a ballast for the chorus of fictional, dramatic, and poetic voices that succeeds it."[5] The imaginative literature that follows in the volume has been selected not only because of its "artistic quality" and "intellectual rigor" but also because it remains loyal to this essential vision of atrocity. For Langer, the truth of the Holocaust is about the defeat of hope and the victory of meaningless death. Langer is unrelenting in his contempt for sentimentality and such "safe props" as love triumphing over hate or the romantic rebellion against evil or the cult of Anne Frank. But he is also opposed to writing that casts Holocaust experience within such rubrics as "character and moral growth" and "suffering and spiritual identity."[6] Even a concept like "the tragic nature of experience" is suspect because it implies moral agency; similarly, the common notion of the concentration camps as hell is mistaken because the Christian conception of hell implied a moral universe in which punishments matched misdeeds. Wresting meaning from suffering, Langer admits, is a universal need. Yet in the instance of the Holocaust, it is a false comfort and a temptation to be resisted; Langer assesses the achievement of works of Holocaust literature according to the strength of their refusal to derive meaning. The ways in which Jews have met their deaths under conditions of persecution in the past and the narratives they have constructed to understand, to make sense out of, these calamities have no relevance. "Myth and tradition," Langer states tersely, "are of little use in consoling them [the victims] or us."[7]

Langer's exceptionalist vision also determines the nature of his editorial treatment of the texts he anthologizes. He introduces each author and locates his or her work within the world of the Holocaust, but the texts themselves remain barren of annotation. Absent are the kind of references that stud the pages of Roskies's anthology: verses, sources, and traditional allusions as well as references to the specifics of contemporary events. This is true in part because of Langer's criteria of inclusion. To begin with, he selects *out* all writing that makes extensive use of "myth and tradition," even if these are invoked only to be subverted or parodied. Still, the texts he does bring into the canon display many points that would have elicited annotation if they were being dealt with by a different editorial hand. How then are we to understand his restraint? There can be no question of dereliction on Langer's part; there is no custodian of Holocaust texts more respectful and responsible than he. The implication, I think, is that these references—which, in the end, are the cultural differentiae of their authors—are not essential, certainly not essential for the general reader, in grasping the core experience of the text. That experience is about annihilation of man's humanity and the obliteration of received cultural constructions, and in the margins of this drama of extremity, glosses on those constructions make little contribution.

Langer's position asserts itself most radically when it comes to the question of translation. This issue is not the generally high quality of the translations Langer has selected for his anthology, but the fact of translation itself. All but one or two of the texts in the volume have been translated into English; the languages of the originals span the languages of Hitler's victims: German, Czech, Yiddish, Hebrew, French, Italian, Hungarian, and so on. Yet try as one might, it is only by resourceful detective work that the reader can discover the language in which a given text was written originally. Biographical notes are not a sure enough base upon which to make accurate inferences. Is it so clear that a Jew growing up in Hungary will write in Hungarian and not German? Or a Jew growing up in Transylvania will take on French as a literary language? Or a Jew from Tchernovitz will write in Hebrew? Even with persistence it is still impossible without prior knowledge to discover the original language of at least a half-dozen of the selections. The names of the translators—but not the languages translated from—are listed only in the small print of the copyright acknowledgments in the front matter of the volume and not in the body of the book. Again, this is not negligence, but a kind of principled indifference. If the Holocaust constitutes a separate kingdom—or planet or universe, whatever the metaphor may be—then it has its own language, a language that is displaced and unnatural but at the same time unmistakable. Although there is a price to be paid for reading all of these documents in English, it is a price that is paid equally across the board, and it is far from being the renunciation it would have been in an earlier era, when the echoes and nuances of cultural traditions counted for more.

If one is inclined to be sympathetic when it comes to prose, it is harder to do so in the case of poetry's intricate verbal artistry. Yet Langer is unremitting even here. He includes selections from six poets: Abraham Sutzkever and Jacob Glatstein in Yiddish, Paul Celan and Nelly Sachs in German, Dan Pagis in Hebrew, and Miklos Radnoti in Hungarian. The linguistic situation of each of these poets—the languages they grew up with in relation to the language they chose to write in as opposed to the languages of the milieu in which they wrote—is, to say the least, complicated. For Langer, however, their orientation toward a single, transformative event is the key.

> They are linked by the premise of a people's extermination, and by the need to enter into what Paul Celan called a "desperate conversation" with their audience—a conversation that evidently has already occurred within their own imaginations. *This bond reduces, if it does not elimi-nate, the cultural differences separating poets writing in Hebrew, Yiddish, German, and Hungarian.*[8]

Langer's statement about poetry presents an image of poets in different languages being "linked" together in a common "bond" by the destruction of European Jewry, their separateness transcended by a universal experience. Yet at the same time this is a solidarity that is purchased at expense of the debasement of the linguistic medium that creates the connection. Words may be all that remain after Auschwitz, but their aura, their power, and their difference have been vastly leveled and reduced.

* * *

I have adduced these two anthologizing projects to illustrate in a pragmatic way the differences between the exceptionalist and constructivist models in the study of Holocaust culture. Of the two, Langer's exceptionalist point of departure is the more immediately evident. The constructivist foundation of Roskies's work needs more elaboration. It is important to point out, to begin with, that Roskies's *The Literature of Destruction* realizes only one line of sight among many other possibilities. He has reconstructed a cultural continuum and context from within which Jews from a particular geographical sphere with certain kinds of literacy and outlooks would experience the Holocaust. These tend to be—I generalize but not overmuch—Jews from Eastern Europe who are native Yiddish speakers (as well as being literate in Hebrew), intellectuals and citizens of modernity who identify with Jewish nationalism in its Bundist or Zionists forms. Roskies attempts to reconstruct the relevant Jewish past and present as they would have seen it on the eve of the war and in the midst of the ghettos. In the far distance are the ancient destructions and the archetypal figures and terms of reference they established; more vivid and closer at hand are the pogroms and persecutions of modern memory, which in turn invoke both the martyrologies of the Middle Ages and the ideologies of recent times. This is the cultural lens through which this set of victims experienced their fate—and remembered it as well, for those who survived—and this is also the set of cultural materials out of which and against which they fashioned a response to that fate.

Being specific about the identity of the subjects of Roskies's anthology makes it easier to imagine the many alternative constructions that are possible.

The *metier* of Roskies's subjects is Yiddish; if one shifts the focus to Hebrew, then a related but very different construction looms large. The cultural lens then becomes the Zionist interpretation of history, with its harsh judgment of the exile-ridden passivity of East European Jews. The poetic descriptions of the Kishinev pogrom in 1903 by the national poet of the Hebrew revival Chaim Nachman Bialik will provide the standard stock of images. Survivors will undertake their work of remembrance against the grain of stigma and avoidance in the new, forward-looking society of Israel.[9] An entirely different perspective comes into view if the subject is changed to traditional religious Jews, whether Hasidic or non-Hasidic. Their understanding of the Holocaust, viewed retrospectively or from within the depths of the event itself, configures the past differently, privileging biblical promises and consolations and refurbishing medieval mystical teachings concerning God's concealment as well as His empathy. Their determination to replicate and even surpass the religious institutions that existed before the destruction locates this community within a different continuum. And so the examples of hypothetical anthologies could be multiplied: the anthology of the acculturated German Jews, with their traditions of Enlightenment and belief in civil society and devotion to the German language; the anthology of Soviet Jews, who saw the conflict as part of the great patriotic war against fascism and imagined the past as a time that was divided by the period before the Revolution and after; the anthology of Viennese Jews and Jews from other lands formerly under the Hapsburg Empire. Each of these hypothetical anthologies, and others that could be easily added to them, would constitute a different kind of lens that refracts the Holocaust differently and recalls the Jewish past differently because of the different nature of the Jewish community's relationship to modernity and to the particular gentile society that surrounds it. This would hold true for America as well. Like Israel, America is a bystander community with a survivor minority. How America, whether one speaks of the Jewish community (and its subcommunities) or the nation as a whole, constructs the Holocaust will then necessarily be deeply colored by the issues, long antedating the Holocaust as well as succeeding it, that animate American society.

Langer's position, if I can take leave to imagine what it might be, would regard these various anthologies as interesting and worthwhile but, in the end, beside the point—if the point is the Holocaust itself. Each anthology is at bottom a plotting of the collective memory of a discrete interpretive community; it demonstrates how a group, with its proprietary issues and interests, appropriates the Holocaust and reconfigures the past, both the pre-Holocaust past and the more recent post-Holocaust past, to make sense of the present. It is the act of appropriation that, in addition to being offensive to Langer on moral grounds, points in a direction away from the core experience of the Holocaust. That experience is about "the way it was" in the eye of the storm as experienced by individuals, stripped of their family and community, facing their fate without the consolations of "myth and traditions." The temporal extensions backward and forward, the retrojection of the Holocaust and the solvent action of present memory, are not unimportant; to the contrary, they can be revealing as cultural data, but they belong to something other than the representation of the Holocaust as such.

The quarrel between the exceptionalist model and contructivist model is, in the final analysis, not a small one. Even within the circumscribed area of the academic study of the Holocaust, the differences between the two have profound implications for how the field is constituted and how students should be trained. Should Holocaust Studies stand as an enterprise unto itself, or should it be embedded in Jewish Studies or French Studies or German Studies or English Studies? How crucial is it for students to undertake the hard work of learning Hebrew, Yiddish, German, and Polish, not to mention several other languages? According to which set of criteria should canons, lists of readings, and syllabi be set up? Is the literature produced in the ghettos during the war to be the main object of scrutiny, or accounts of the concentration camps written shortly after? Are works of art composed in a realist mode to be preferred over those that employ allegory and symbolism? When it comes to survivors, is the goal to extract from their testimony true reflections of the war years or to study the reconstruction of their lives and the shaping of their memory subsequent to the war? I do not mean to imply that affirming the exceptionalist model over the constructivist one, or vice versa, supplies a key to answering these questions, or that by virtue of such an affirmation the questions dispose themselves in some consistent and aligned way. It is evident, nevertheless, that these two models provide the contrastive terms in which the clarifying discourse around these questions is undertaken.

It would be convenient to think that a larger truth could be obtained by simply combining both models or by working them into a flexible dialectic. But there is a fundamental asymmetry between the two. The exceptionalist model posits a displaced Holocaust literature with its own poetics and studies the shared strategies used to represent the horror of the experience. There are, to be sure, insights to be gained from these kinds of investigations, and the student of responses to the Holocaust in, say, American culture or French culture can only benefit by applying them to the analysis of particular works. Yet it does not necessarily work the other way around. The exceptionalist model draws a tight cord around the Holocaust canon, excluding works that stray in time or place from the "core experience" or are too culturally fraught or are too embedded in their original language. In the case of the works that are included, the residual entanglement of the work with its cultural origins is relegated to the background as accidental information.

One needs, in the end, to take a stand. I have endeavored to be fair in presenting the assumptions and the claims of both models, although I stated my own sympathy at the outset. Now that the differences have been laid out more explicitly and practically, I wish to demonstrate what is to my mind the greater utility of the constructivist model for understanding three critical components of Holocaust writing: the literature of the concentration camps, the literature of the ghettos, and the testimony of the survivors.

* * *

The account of death and survival in the concentration camps is what we know to lie at the center of Holocaust literature. It is a story about the systematic annihilation of the individual's humanity before the final act of extermination. The process began with the wrenching apart of families and continued with the shaving of the head, crushing labor, progressive starvation, random terror, and death. Fundamental to the Nazi design of the camp regime was the dismantling of the inmate's civilized and socialized self and his or her reduction to a cowed, animal-like state of isolated self-interest. The balance of starvation, exhaustion, and fear was calibrated to hold human existence, for an interval, just above the threshold of death and just below the threshold of memory and thought. It is here, in the nethermost darkness of a horror never before devised, that Langer and others locate the normative Holocaust experience. It is an experience in which man is stripped of all the integuments of identity, culture, solidarity, and belief that clothe his nakedness.

This is a presumption, I would submit, that is at odds with a fundamental aspect of the greatest writing on the camps. Tadeusz Borowski's *This Way for the Gas, Ladies and Gentlemen,* Primo Levi's *Survival in Auschwitz,* and Elie Wiesel's *Night* stand, by most all accounts, at the center of the Holocaust canon and can hardly be said to shrink from the representation of atrocity. Yet for each of these writers it is cultural identity that provides the essential lens through which they focus their vision and by which we can best gain access to their work. Borowski was a humanistically educated non-Jewish Pole; Levi was a chemist from an acculturated Italian Jewish family; and Wiesel was a Talmud student from a traditionally religious family in Transylvania. Rather than simply being points of departure that are swept into the dark hole of the Holocaust, these identities—though they be assaulted, rent, and transfigured— remain fundamental ways of seeing the world and organizing experience. These narratives are inverted *Bildungsromanen* that recount the story of how the hero *unlearns* what his culture has taught him and learns the ways of death and survival on the new, concentrationary "planet." Yet the process of reeducation is never fully completed for the retrospective narrator who, more dead than living, has survived to write now, in the immediate aftermath of the war, about the young man he was then. It is through this residuum of identity that the experience is most tellingly refracted.

Take the case of Borowski, the author of some of the most searing writing about the camps. Borowski was born in the Soviet Ukraine in 1922 to parents who were both transported to Siberian labor camps when he was a child.

They were released in a prisoner exchange, and the family settled in Warsaw, where Tadeusz was sent to a boarding school run by Franciscan monks. After the German occupation, Borowski attended underground university seminars and published a book of poems. Both he and his fiancée were arrested and sent to Auschwitz in the spring of 1942. Spared the gas chambers as an "Aryan," Borowski lived the life of a slave laborer whose "privileges" allowed him a degree more mobility and sustenance than Jewish inmates. The fact that Borowski's situation was located adjacent to the fate of the Jews but not within it provides his fiction with a powerful opportunity for observation. The way he exploits this distance is made all the more credible by his refusal to spare scrutiny of himself and the prerogatives enjoyed by non-Jewish prisoners. One of these was the possibility of occasional communication with his fiancée, who was an inmate in the women's camp at Auschwitz. To illustrate the issue of cultural identity, I have chosen a passage from "Auschwitz, Our Home (A Letter)" in *This Way for the Gas, Ladies and Gentlemen,* which describes camp life in the form of a letter to his fiancée.

> Do you really think that, without the hope that such a world is possible, that the rights of man will be restored again, we could stand the concentration camps even for one day? It is that very hope that makes people go without a murmur to the gas chambers, keeps them from risking a revolt, paralyzes them into numb inactivity. It is the hope that breaks down family ties, makes mothers renounce their children, or wives sell their bodies for bread, or husbands kill. It is hope that compels man to hold on to one more day of life, because that day may be the day of liberation. Ah, and not even the hope for a different world, but simply for life, and life of peace and rest. Never before in the history of mankind has hope been stronger than man, but never also has it done so much harm as it has in this war, in this concentration camp. We were never taught how to give up hope, and this is why today we perish in the gas chambers.[10]

Borowski's narrator/correspondent addresses an issue that has disturbed many observers of victims' behavior in the camps. How is it, given the virtual inevitability of death as well as the tiny number of captors relative to prisoners, that there was so little resistance and rebellion? The answer, it turns out, lies not where we would be most likely to look for it: in man's essential animality and his reduction to monstrous self-interest under conditions of absolute extremity. Rather it lies in what is ordinarily counted as an admirable human impulse: the ineradicability of hope. Whether it is a primitive hope that surviving another day may bring deliverance tomorrow or an idealistic hope that a better world will be built on the ruins of the concentration camps, the effect is the same kind of denial of reality, the reality of the Nazi's programmatic intention to murder all Jews after having exacted from them the last measure of labor. Had the victims been able to admit this truth, they might have realized that they had nothing to lose in resisting, or at least in preserving the "family ties" that would otherwise be betrayed. It was hope, then, that paradoxically abetted the implementation of the extermination program. Borowski's speaker, it should be noted, offers this analysis not as a judgment censuring the victims for collusion in their fate. He is a victim, and the lover he is writing to is a victim as well; he writes as part of a communal "we" in an effort at collective self-understanding.

Now, if we read this passage with the commonsense understanding of the term "hope" in mind, it is persuasive enough on its own terms. But it becomes immensely more powerful if we understand hope in relation to Borowski's background and education. For when the speaker says at the end that we "were never taught to give up hope," he is stressing a concept of hope that derives not from instinctual biological survival but from a set of values that a culture consciously transmits to its young. For a young Pole whose parents were imprisoned by Stalin, who was educated by monks and who then studied literature in the university (or its equivalent under the occupation), "hope" is one of the most ideologically fraught terms in the modern lexicon. In the Christian tradition, it signals the hope for salvation, which will be the lot of the faithful if they believe perfectly enough despite the wickedness of the world. In Marxism, hope signals the conviction that the contradictions of capitalism will inexorably lead to its collapse and to the ascent of a just social order and that, in the name of the unfolding of this certain hope, all means are sanctioned. In the liberal tradition of the Enlightenment and the university, hope signals the belief that the realization of man's perfectibility can be nurtured by the right kind of sentiments and social institutions. Borowski is the heir to all of these traditions, which are knotted together under the tangled signifier "hope"; so when he makes this term the prime agent of the victims' submission to their victimizers, he is making a rejection whose enormity resonates mightily. We can strive to understand this thing called hope that must be unlearned only if we succeed in understanding, in all its overdetermined cultural specificity, what was once so diligently acquired.

Not all that is learned is unlearned. Primo Levi takes the habit of scientific observation with him into Auschwitz and takes it with him after the liberation. The awareness of the scientific voice of the narrator of *Survival in Auschwitz*[11] was heightened by the later publication of *The Periodic Table,* which used the schemata of chemistry even more explicitly, and by Levi's postwar work as the manager of a Turin chemical factory. There is simply no more persuasive example than Levi's for the argument that even the concentrationary experience is inevitably viewed through the lens of culture. Levi was raised in an acculturated Jewish family whose ancestors had come from Spain in the 1500s to settle in the Piedmont. The scientific training Levi chose for himself in the university was an expression not only of his own temperament but of the commitment of Italian Jewry as a whole to the traditions of liberal rationalism and the inheritance of the Enlightenment.

Levi was trained in his profession to observe the properties and interactions of physical substances. In Auschwitz, however, the object of Levi's observations becomes, of necessity, the moral behavior of human beings. Levi thus recapitulates in reverse the development of Enlightenment rationalism, which began expansively with the measure of man and society and narrowed into the methods of the exact sciences. The force of experience compels Levi to apply these observational methods to the chaos of human terror; and the enormous power of his book derives from the tension between the techniques of rationality and the eruption of radical evil embodied in the camps. Levi carries this off by making a fundamental distinction between the minds and motives of the perpetrators, whose evil can never be penetrated by reason, and the behavior of the victims, which can indeed be understood empathically as adaptations to the unspeakable conditions in which they were condemned to exist. Levi's description of the Nazis' "gigantic biological and social experiment" is governed, as Philip Roth puts it, "very precisely, by a quantitative concern for the ways in which a man can be transformed or broken down and, like a substance decomposing in a chemical reaction, lose his characteristic properties."[12] Levi's laboratory notes are not a vindication of reason but a method of coping. Through the lens of science that he acquired from his culture he is forced to see things that had never fallen within the purview of science to observe. But instead of abandoning the tools of reason, Levi clings to them in the service of memory and clarity.

In the case of Elie Wiesel, the lens of culture is bifocal. Although *Night* covers much of the same territory as other memoirs of Auschwitz, its distinctiveness lies in the way in which experience is focalized through the perceptions of the author's young autobiographical persona. When the Germans occupy Sighet, Eliezer is a sixteen-year-old Talmud student from a comfortable home who has been free to immerse himself in his studies and pursue a covert passion for the mystical lore of the kabbalah. The transport to Auschwitz, the breaking apart of the family, and the torments of camp life are all presented as chapters in a process of compulsory reeducation in which the young man unlearns what he believes about God and man. The climactic moment of apostasy is reached in the famous scene when Eliezer is forced to watch the hanging of a beloved little boy with the face of a "sad angel"; to the question "Where is God now?" the narrator hears a voice within himself responding, "He is hanging here on this gallows."[13]

The fact that Wiesel frames his experience as a theological crisis at once sets him apart from writers like Borowski and Levi and makes his story understandable only in terms of who he was and where he came from. The complexity of *Night* as a phenomenon derives in part from the two different ways in which this crisis was refracted retrospectively. *Night* was first written in Yiddish and published within survivor circles in Argentina; Wiesel then revised and rewrote it in French with the encouragement of the Christian existentialist François Mauriac, who contributed a foreword, and it was the French version that served as the basis for the English translation. There are significant differences between the two, as Naomi Seidman has pointed out, and the differences have a great deal to do with what it meant to write in Yiddish or to write in French in the 1950s.[14] To write in Yiddish meant to write for a small survivor audience that would feel at home with expressions of high pathos and share the writer's outrage at the nations of the world for standing by silently. To write in French meant to envisage a different audience and to work within the sensibility of another language. It meant to rein in the urge to accuse, to contain pathos and sentiment, and to frame the central crisis in more universal terms as the young believer's discovery of radical evil. Whether the discursive practices of one language are to be preferred over those of the other is beside the point. The point is that a constructivist approach to Wiesel's *Night* and other concentration camp literature heightens our awareness of how the "Holocaust experience," even in its most unspeakable precincts, is built up out of the materials of language and culture and focused through one among a number of possible lenses.

The very notion of the concentration camp as the prototypical site of Holocaust literature is put in question by the constructivist model. Both critical discourse and the popular imagination have long been drawn to representations of the death camps because of their ultimacy. The camp as a mechanized death factory, along with comprehensive genocide, was the Nazis' most infamous contribution to the history of persecution. In the perverted sense of a "final solution," it was also the culmination of various earlier means devised to commit mass murder. As the most extreme instance of evil, the camp—or to be more precise, one camp—became a metonym for the Holocaust as a whole. To begin a statement with the words "After Auschwitz" is not to make a specific reference but to invoke the catastrophe in its totality. Terrence Des Pres's seminal study *The Survivor: An Anatomy of Life in the Death Camps*[15] and much of Lawrence Langer's writing are only two examples of a large body of critical work that examines the world of the camps in writers such as Charlotte Delbo, Jean Améry, and Primo Levi and finds in it, even if in different ways and for different reasons, the essence of the Nazi assault on the Jews and on the idea of man. The camp has become a kind of telos, an ultimate end case, by which all proximate experience is measured.

In its critique of this notion, the constructivist model asserts that, although the world of the camps does indeed occupy the ultimate model on the continuum of horror, what it has to tell us about Jewish behavior during the Holocaust is contingent and, in a number of crucial respects, less interesting than behavior in other venues. Whether it was starvation and sleep deprivation, the kapo system, collective reprisals for individual deviation, or any of the other components of what Des Pres calls the "excremental assault on man," the camp regime was effectively geared to obliterating consciousness and individuality and reducing human beings to submissive, half-dead automata. That some inmates were able to hold on to shreds of their humanity should not, Langer insists, distract us from the kind of fate that awaited almost all, nor should it lead to an idealization—and here Langer dissents from Des Pres—of the impulse to survive. The scope of human agency remained radically delimited and radically isolated. Despite the masses of inmates who were forced to live an insufferably thronged life, literally one atop the other, each individual faced the daily ordeal of survival in a state of deep isolation while ceaselessly pursuing his or her self-interest, often at the expense of others. Instances of unselfishness, solidarity, and expressions of group identity did exist, to be sure, but the modal nature of existence in the death camps remained cut-off and self-involved.

It is the literature of the ghettos that provides a crucial supplement to the literature of the camps. There were many ghettos in Eastern Europe; the situation of each was somewhat different, and the kind and volume of literature and other cultural artifacts produced in them were also different. Much of what was produced did not survive and could be recovered only in accounts by survivors. The most famous instance is the Oyneg Shabbes archive in the Warsaw ghetto, organized by Emanuel Ringelblum and buried in the rubble of the ghetto in tin boxes and milk canisters. The archive consisted of about six thousand documents, including "eye-witness accounts and diaries; letters and postcards; sermons and songs; epic and lyric poems; novels, short stories and plays; essays, questionnaires and autobiographies; and issues of the underground Jewish press."[16] The reason why there exists such a vast literature derives from a startling difference between the ghetto and the camp: within the ghetto Jews were free to conduct their own collective life. At this stage of the war, the Nazis sought to concentrate the Jews and strip them of their wealth; they did not seek to control the organization and expression of internal political, social, spiritual, and cultural life, choosing instead to administer the ghettos through the intermediacy of the *Judenräte*. Although terror and starvation stalked their daily lives, the Jews of the ghetto were free to organize their own forms of social welfare, put on political cabarets, hold concerts, publish uncensored newspapers, and give public sermons.

What sets the camps apart from the ghettos is not necessarily the quantum of suffering and atrocity. The camps were admittedly worse, but this is a dreadful calculus that can be figured in many ways. The difference lies in the question of control. In the camps, individuals were wrenched out of their familial and communal bonds and placed under a regime that dominated and scrutinized their every waking and sleeping moment. The discovery of the least individual expression, whether a sketch of camp life or a written document, could be grounds for punishment or death. The accounts of camp life that we have are necessarily recollections and reconstructions written at different removes after the war, and their authors, again by definition, are survivors. The ghetto documents, by contrast, are written during the actual duration of the ghetto, reflecting on and responding to events that changed with enormous rapidity. They were written overwhelmingly—it need hardly be said—by authors who did not survive the war. Most importantly, this literature was written from within a tightly circumscribed yet essentially free cultural space that allowed for the expression of the collective in a variety of ways. Jews could identify themselves with political parties and ideological movements, express their theological struggles, adopt the role of the social scientist and study behavior in the ghetto, compose folk and cabaret songs for public performance, write stories about life in the ghetto, keep diaries, or undertake any of a number of other forms of activity or expression, and they could do so in Yiddish, Hebrew, or Polish at different times for different purposes and audiences.

The enormous claim this literature makes on us is that it opens a window onto the experience of Jewry in real time rather than in recollected time. It is a commonplace of writing on the Holocaust to say that time has to pass, perhaps even a generation, before words can be uttered about so awful a trauma. Yet this conception is challenged by the contentious and articulate voices of the ghetto writers as they argue, document, analyze, and imagine. The contribution made by the growing profusion of survivor memoirs and videotaped testimony is invaluable, but it is necessarily subject to the selective and harmonizing operations of memory, and it is written with a global and retrospective understanding of parallel developments and final outcomes. This was precisely the kind of knowledge that actors in the drama could not have; the inhabitants of an individual ghetto could know with only very imperfect certainty what was happening at the same time to Jews elsewhere, not to mention what would be the next moves of the German administration. A ghetto like the Warsaw Ghetto, was, after all, not a suspended moment but an extended duration in which the situation changed, as Ringelblum put it, "with cinematic speed." The Warsaw Ghetto was established soon after the German invasion of Poland in 1939; the Great Deportation of 300,000 Jews took place in the late summer of 1942; the uprising and the liquidation of the remaining 70,000 Jews took place in the spring of 1943. Stories and reportage by such writers as Simon Huberband, Leyb Goldyn, and Peretz Opoczynski describe a complex mosaic of individual and communal responses—denial, flight, lamentation, mutual aid, documentation, political organization—to a pattern of events whose unfolding was unknown.

Writing about the Warsaw Ghetto in 1942, David Roskies illuminates the multiple strands of ghetto life in a single critical moment:

> It began erev Tisha b'Av and ended on Yom Kippur: *di oyszidlung,* the Great Deportation. First the Germans demanded that 6,000 Jews be delivered to the Umschlagplatz each day, then 10,000 a day. Adam Czerniakov, head of the Judenrat, took his own life rather than sign away the lives of the children; the children—the only hope of regeneration. Dr. Janusz

Korczak went to his death leading all the children of his orphanage behind him. At the end of July, the Hechalutz Youth movement organized
the first combat unit. At the end of August most of the ghetto shops were
closed down, thus dooming the dream that productivization would guarantee survival. The first couriers sent by the Bund and the Zionists returned from Treblinka and confirmed the rumors about the final destination of the cattle cars. At the same time, Israel Lichtenstein and a few
assistants buried the first part of the Oyneg Shabes Archive in the base-
ment of the soup kitchen for children at 68 Nowolipki Street.

Ironically, Roskies's synoptic slice of ghetto life illustrates just the kind of
global, retrospective knowledge that no one of the actors could have had in
its entirety at the time. Yet by simultaneously evoking the initiatives of many
sectors of the ghetto at a single critical juncture, Roskies gives us a glimpse
of the deeply textured nature of time as it was experienced by the ghetto's
inhabitants.

One of the key features of the ghetto literature is its uncensored moral
rhetoric, in which collaborators are named and the behavior of Jews toward
Jews is unflinchingly described. The censorship imposed on these realities
came not from the Germans at the time, who did not care what went on inside
the ghetto; rather it was generally imposed by Holocaust survivors in their spoken or written recollections of the war. There is a pronounced tendency in
survivor testimony, the result of a number of motives, to play down the feelings
of accusation and betrayal that were strongly felt at the time. These include
not only the evident indictments of members of the *Judenräte* or the Jewish
police but also the polemics and controversies among political parties and
groupings with rival ideologies. In this, the ghettos were normal Jewish communities, full of contentiousness among opposing political and religious interests. The ghettos were abnormal in that they were swelled by the forced influx
of surrounding communities, concentrated into a tiny space, and submitted to
the pressures of a deteriorating external situation. Under these conditions, the
"normative" divisiveness of communal life could only be exacerbated by an
exponential factor. These are hard truths, but they have to be reckoned with
in any honest understanding of the Holocaust. Ringelblum understood this
and specifically instructed his staff "to write as if the war were already over,
not to fear retribution from those in power because the indictment would not
be read until everyone in question was either living in freedom or already
dead."[17]

Nothing could stand in greater contrast to Ringelblum's charge to his staff
than the urge toward discretion evident in many postwar memoirs. The anger
that was once directed internally because the real aggressor was beyond reach
finds an outward channel after the catastrophe. The memories of the fierce
intra-Jewish conflict fade as the totality of the victims are absorbed into the
aura of martyrdom and as the remembrance of past strife and perfidy seems

increasingly pointless. There is no unworthiness and a great deal of natural-
ness in this way of remembering, and I shall have occasion later on to speak
on behalf of the selective appropriation of the Holocaust past. Yet it is important to point out, as Yosef Yerushalmi has reminded us, that this kind of remembering belongs to the flow of collective memory rather than to the project
of historiography. In our struggle to grasp the Holocaust, we manifestly need
both, and the literature of the ghettos stands as an essential counterpart and
corrective to the gathering sway of memoir.

Finally, there is the issue of cultural density. When survivors write about
the concentration camps, they are usually attempting to explain a radically
foreign experience to readers who are, thankfully, uninitiated in the subject;
this was a world that had been emptied of all received culture and filled with
a new and perverted language and moral code. However, when the inhabitants
of the ghettos wrote songs, broadsides, and stories, they were—Ringelblum's
exhortation aside—by and large addressing each other with words and gestures whose meaning was guaranteed by shared frames of reference. Whether
it was the lexicon of Jewish socialism or Zionism, Yiddish literature, the Hebrew Bible, Hasidism, or contemporary European literature, the cultural codes
in play before the war not only were not abandoned but in many cases were
intensified. So the secular Yiddish writer Rachel Auerbach, in contemplating
the destruction of the Warsaw Ghetto and of her whole family from hiding in
the Aryan side of Warsaw, is thrust back upon, despite her secularity, the image
of the collective recitation of the memorial Yizkor prayer in the synagogue as
the only adequate symbol for expressing her grief.[18] Or take one of the great
diarists of the Warsaw Ghetto, Abraham Lewin, who switches from Yiddish
to Hebrew as the language of his diary entries after the Great Deportation.[19]
When the narrator of Yehoshue Perle's brilliant satire on life in the ghetto after
the Great Deportation chimes up with "I'm all right, I'm a number!," it will
be intelligible to all Yiddish readers as a play on the motto ("I'm alright, I'm
an orphan!") of one of Shalom Aleichem's most famous characters, Motl, son
of Peyse the Cantor.[20] Or when Chaim Kaplan, another of the preeminent diarists of the Warsaw Ghetto, writing in Hebrew exclaims, "Oh earth! Do not
hide my blood!! If there is a God to judge the land—come and take revenge!!!"
no Hebrew reader can mistake the quotation from Bialik's famous poem on
the Kishinev massacre of 1903.[21] Taken together, these are not the sort of re-
condite intertextual allusions intended for the learned; they are signals meant
to be picked up by any literate person. They are simply indicators of what it
means to be part of a culture.

Now, one would think that given the critical importance of this corpus, it
would be the object of intense study, interpretation, and reflection. For where
else in the galaxy of Holocaust writing is there such a revealing body of inter-
related cultural production? In light of the enormous interest in the Holocaust
in America, we might have expected that the disintegrating sheets of paper in

Ringelblum's milk canisters would be accorded the same care as the Dead Sea Scrolls and the fragments of the Cairo Geniza and be preserved, annotated, and translated. The fact is, however, that shockingly little is available to the English reader and that the original documents in the original languages are very unevenly available to scholars. As far as the Warsaw Ghetto is concerned, besides the diaries of Chaim Kaplan and Abraham Lewin, there is little represented in English of Ringelblum's herculean archival effort. How much is there, is indicated by the simple fact that Joseph Kermish's meticulously edited Hebrew translation of the newspapers published in the Warsaw Ghetto runs to six volumes. Moreover, what was available in English until recently did not touch upon the belletristic works in the collection. Until Roskies published translations of texts by Yehoshue Perle, Leyb Goldin, Rachel Auerbach, and Peretz Opoczynski, stories that are by any account masterpieces of Holocaust literature could not be read in English. Again, in light of the intensive publishing activity on Holocaust matters in America, how is one to explain that it is the Poles who are slowly bringing out the Warsaw Ghetto materials in facsimile editions, with annotations in Polish?

The reasons for this relative neglect are not immediately apparent. To be sure, making the ghetto materials accessible to a wider audience is not an easy job. It is not so much the task of translating from several languages as it is the challenge of translating the *context* in which these documents are embedded: the references to personalities, events, places, political groupings, slang, and religious practices and the textual allusions. It is not an easy job, but it is a doable job, and even a partial and selective level of annotation of the sort Roskies employs in his anthology is enough to dissolve the strangeness and allow us to penetrate the drama of ghetto life. All it takes is the individual and institutional will to undertake the project.

The problem, I suspect, lies in the embarrassment of particularity embodied by these documents. The ghetto writers describe lives that are deeply enmeshed in the very particular culture and politics of their times, and to know these lives requires acquiring some familiarity with this tangled knot of time and place and belief. When it comes to concentration camp literature, the "literacy" necessary to master the code of the *Lager,* despite the greater extremity and greater strangeness, is ironically much easier to come by. There is one primitive language and one primitive and unequivocal rule of behavior. By reading a single exquisitely observed and empathic book like Levi's *Survival in Auschwitz* one does not learn all there is to know about the concentrationary universe, but one learns enough to learn more. The life of the prisoner is a life that has been reduced to a biological core that exists before culture or beneath culture. In contrast, it is easy to perceive the embroiled particularity of life of the ghettos as not partaking in the essence of things and not demanding—and demanding it is—our best energies, because it remains penultimate rather than ultimate.

In his discussion of the phenomenon of "cultural resistance to genocide," Lawrence Langer adds another layer of explanation. Langer is uncomfortable with the term "resistance" because it implies "the possibility of an immediately beneficial consequence, a gesture of affirmation or defiance that might alter the condition of the poet, writer, the painter."[22] Avraham Sutzkever's composition of his Yiddish poems in the Vilna Ghetto or the production of Rabindrath Tagore's play *The Post Office,* which was mounted by the orphans in the Warsaw orphanage run by Janusz Korczak before he marched with them to the transports, are admirable in many respects, Langer allows, but they must be seen in perspective. These cultural efforts, and others like them, are to be understood as attempts at self-consolation, even denial, in the face of the nameless terror they were incapable of affecting. Langer writes:

> Cultural traditions furnish a certain security and even sanctity to a life otherwise sundered from the normal props of existence. Few were able to endure on a diet of mere blank terror. The illusion that a familiar past could prepare one for an unknown future never lost its magic appeal to imaginations that had nothing else to rely on.[23]

If the most that can be claimed for culture under the sign of the Holocaust is that it offers the comfort of the familiar, then the artifacts and activities of the ghetto inhabitants cannot count for much in the face of the "blank terror" of the real thing.

* * *

The shape of survivor narratives is the third area materially affected by the divergence between the exceptionalist and constructivist models. As the survivor population has aged and as the acceptability of the Holocaust has grown, memoirs of the war years have been published in recent decades at a dizzying rate. Ambitious projects recording survivor testimony on videotape are creating a vast archive of personal narratives. We are at a stage of recording, gathering, producing, publishing, and preserving. The task of figuring out what it all means is necessarily being deferred for the present, but it is a challenge that will eventually have to be met. For now, we can begin to formulate the questions that we would like to put to this archive once it has completed its task of gathering testimony and is ready to receive our queries. In the meantime, one can make some observations on the general shape of these narratives based on the strong examples that have already appeared. I use the term "shape" purposefully. For if there is one thing that we have learned from contemporary research in the humanities—the excess of jargon-laden theories aside—it is that all narratives, from the personal story to complex novels, are not simply naive and faithful transcriptions of experience but are built around preexisting armatures or schemata or master plots. New narratives may add to, play with, and subvert these story lines, but an appreciation of their uniqueness must begin with an understanding of the preexisting models. Certain of these models are "strong" models in the sense that Harold Bloom uses the term to designate works that exert a powerful influence on subsequent creativity.

In place of an overarching taxonomy of survivor narrative, I will illustrate the differences among master, shaping Holocaust narratives by contrasting two examples: Elie Wiesel's *Night* and David Weiss Halivni's *The Book and the Sword*. *Night* is probably the most influential survivor narrative. A short, accessible, and powerfully written narrative, *Night* was published in English in 1960, at the dawn of Holocaust consciousness in America, which in turn it helped to create. The book's influence was enhanced by the fame of its author, the paradigmatic survivor in our culture, and his increasing visibility in American public life. David Weiss Halivni is a renowned professor of Talmud, who spent most of his adult life on the faculty of the Jewish Theological Seminary, leaving to teach at Columbia University when the Seminary decided to ordain women rabbis. He published *The Book and the Sword* in 1995 after a distinguished record of scholarly publications on the development of the corpus of talmudic literature.

The books are admittedly different in significant ways. Their appearance is separated by thirty-five years; one is the work of a young man, the other the work of an older man; one is written in French, the other in English; one belongs to the category of serious literature, while the other presents itself only as a straightforward personal account. The reason for comparing them lies in a biographical connection that is more than accidental. Both Wiesel and Halivni were born to religious families at about the same time in the Transylvanian city of Sighet, and they both emerged from boyhood to adolescence as promising, full-time students of the Talmud. Lest nostalgia should suffuse the sense of the past, it should be remembered that this vocation was becoming a rare one in a rapidly secularizing and urbanizing East European Jewish community that had been ravaged by World War I.

Yet despite this common background, Wiesel and Halivni shape their stories in profoundly different ways. *Night* has become the classic narrative of rupture. It tells the story of how the spiritual world of such a youth is brutalized and broken down in the death camps. At the center of the narrative is the horrendous scene in which the camp inmates are forced to watch the hanging of a young boy who dies slowly on the gallows because his light weight will not bring his death agony to a quick end. To the question, "Where is God now?" a voice within the narrator answers: "Here He is—He is hanging here on this gallows." When the book concludes three days after the liberation of Buchenwald, the narrator looks at himself in a mirror for the first time since the ghetto; from the depths of the mirror he sees a corpse gazing back at him. Though his first work, *Night* remains Wiesel's most powerfully influential writing because early on it established a norm for what a Holocaust memoir should be. The defining moment is one of negative transformation. In the face of unspeakable horrors, the spiritual and cognitive identity of the victim breaks down, leading to the death of the self. In later autobiographical works, Wiesel brings his narrator into the postwar world and delineates a portrait of the survivor as a man who is living a kind of death in life and who is possessed by the burden of bearing witness to the catastrophe.

In *The Book and the Sword* Halivni stakes out a very different claim as to what a Holocaust memoir can be. He is interested less in representing the destruction of identity—and all the horrors that accompany it—than the persistence of identity. The reason Halivni devotes the preponderance of his book to his life before the war and to his life after the war is because of the essential and deep-running continuity between the two, which revolves around his vocation as a student of the Talmud. There are differences, to be sure. He studies Talmud differently now than he did then, and he is burdened by fears and insecurities he ascribes to the trauma of the war. But the central axis of identity remains unbroken.

The strength of this axis is underscored by the one brief section of the book that deals with events that transpired during the Holocaust itself. (The very paucity of material on the author's time in the camps makes a statement about the relative importance of before and after and during, and it will make the book a disappointment to connoisseurs of atrocity.) Halivni had been transferred to a slave labor camp whose inmates dug tunnels to protect future munitions factories from Allied bombardment. Every night he would pass by a Nazi guard who was eating a greasy sandwich; one night the grease had made the paper the sandwich was wrapped in translucent, and Halivni was able to make out that the paper was actually a page torn out of a Jewish legal code. It was, he writes,

> a page of *Orach Chaim,* a volume of the *Shulhan Aruch,* Pesil Balaban's edition. The Balabans began publishing the *Shulhan Aruch,* the Jewish Code of Law, in Lemberg in 1839. The first publisher was Abraham Balaban, and after his death he was succeeded by his widow, Pesil. Pesil's edition of the *Shulhan Aruch* was the best; it had all the commentaries. . . . As a child of a poor but scholarly home, I had always wanted to have her edition. . . . Here, of all places, in the shadows of the tunnel, under the threatening gaze of the German, a page from [Pesil's] *Shulhan Aruch,* fatty spots all over it, met my eyes.[24]

The paper is coaxed from the hands of the guard and becomes a focus of clandestine study and a rally point for the religious prisoners. This vignette, which is quite beautifully told, does not come across as pious preening; rather, it serves to reveal an unexpungeable connection between the boy and the young man, even under the most unspeakable conditions. The point of the passage is not the appalling sacrilege of the greasy wurst wrapped in the sacred text but rather the young prisoner's familiar, almost caressing intimacy with the text and with its printing history and his excitement over this most peculiar fulfillment of a boyhood wish.

To say that Halivni's faith and vocation survived the nightmare of the Holocaust largely intact is not to say that he is more worthy than others who experienced and wrote about the same events differently. But he may be more representative. There are many survivors who struggled to establish lives after the war that are not the same as but are continuous with the religious, political, or cultural, or even family, values they held before the war. This is especially true in the case of the enormous expansion of Orthodox Jewish life and institutions in Israel and America, which could not have taken place if survivors and their communities had focused on the devastation caused by the Holocaust rather than on restoring what had been lost. Such survivors are more numerous than we think, and their stories have much to teach us, even if they run across the grain of our received notions of what it means to have survived the Holocaust.

Survivors' experiences are varied, yet the dominance of the exceptionalist model led to our recouping their narratives under the sign of rupture. The widespread phenomenon of continuity has been underrepresented and underreported. Continuity does not mean sameness, nor is it necessarily a product of repression, denial, and emotional constriction. Reconstructing a life after the war and striving to incorporate in that new life elements of prewar identity and belief deserve to be seen as a struggle as dramatic as the struggle to survive in the camps, in hiding, or in the forests during the war. To take the reconstructed life seriously does not mean to minimize the infinite suffering that preceded it nor the unending effects of that suffering. What it does ask us to do is to attend to the matrix of identity and society into which the survivor was born and to examine the reconstructed life in relationship not only to the common trauma that intervened but also to the formation of the life that came before.

NOTES

A version of this essay appears in my book *American Popular Culture and the Shape of Holocaust Memory* (Seattle: University of Washington Press, 2000).

1. See, for example, Arthur A. Cohen, *The Tremendum: A Theological Interpretation of the Holocaust* (New York: Crossroad, 1981), and Emil Fackenheim, *Quest for Past and Present; Essays in Jewish Theology* (Bloomington: Indiana University Press, 1968), and *The Jewish Return into History: Reflections of the Age of Auschwitz and Jerusalem* (New York: Schocken Books, 1978).

2. From the point of view of theory, this position would be more properly called a "soft" constructivist position because it assumes a core fact that is beyond dispute.

3. Lawrence L. Langer, ed., *Art from the Ashes* (New York: Oxford University Press, 1995); David G. Roskies, ed., *The Literature of Destruction: Jewish Responses to Catastro-*

phe (Philadelphia: Jewish Publication Society, 1989). There are a number of anthologies of Holocaust literature that can be located on a continuum between Langer's conception and Roskies's. One notable for its breadth and good taste is Milton Teichman and Sharon Leder, eds., *Truth and Lamentation: Stories and Poems on the Holocaust* (Urbana: University of Illinois Press, 1994).

4. These are, in order, Leyb Goldin, Anonymous, Chaim Kaplan, and Rachel Auerbach, as they appear in Roskies, *The Literature of Destruction*, chapter 15, pp. 424–464.

5. Langer, *Art from the Ashes*, 8.

6. Ibid., 6.

7. Ibid., 5.

8. Ibid., 554, emphasis added.

9. This is in fact the lens I attempted to provide in my study *HURBAN: Responses to Catastrophe in Hebrew Literature* (New York: Columbia University Press, 1984; Syracuse, N.Y.: Syracuse University Press, 1996).

10. Tadeusz Borowski, *This Way for the Gas, Ladies and Gentlemen,* trans. Barbara Vedder (New York: Penguin Books, 1976), 121–122. Borowski wrote the stories contained in the volume in the year or two immediately after the war. He committed suicide in 1951. His work was first published in English translation in 1967.

11. Primo Levi, *Survival in Auschwitz,* trans. Stuart Woolf (New York: Collier Books, 1993). The book was written soon after the war; the original title was *Se questo e un uomo (If this is a Man)*. It appeared in English for the first time in 1960.

12. "A Conversation with Primo Levy by Philip Roth," in Levi, 181.

13. Elie Wiesel, *Night,* trans. Stella Rodway (New York: Bantam Books, 1982), 62. *Night* first appeared in French in 1958 and in English in 1960.

14. Naomi Seidman, "Elie Wiesel and the Scandal of Jewish Rage," *Jewish Social Studies* (New Series) 3, no. 1 (Fall 1996): 1–19.

15. Terrence Des Pres, *The Survivor: An Anatomy of Life in the Death Camps* (New York: Oxford University Press, 1976).

16. David Roskies, *The Jewish Search for a Usable Past* (Bloomington: Indiana University Press, 1999), ch. 3, "Ringelblum's Time Capsules."

17. Roskies, *Literature of Destruction*, 391.

18. Originally published in *Di goldene keyt* 46 (1963): 29–39. Translated by Leonard Wolf in Roskies, *Literature of Destruction*, 459–464.

19. Abraham Lewin, *A Cup of Tears,* ed. Anthony Polonsky, trans. Christopher Hutton (London: Blackwell Publishers, 1989).

20. Yehoshue Perle, "4580," trans. Elinor Robinson, in Roskies, *Literature of Destruction*, 450–454.

21. Roskies, *Literature of Destruction*, 437.

22. Langer, *Admitting the Holocaust: Collected Essays* (New York: Oxford University Press: 1995), 57.

23. Ibid.

24. David Weiss Halivni, *The Book and the Sword: A Life of Learning in the Shadow of Destruction* (New York: Farrar Straus and Giroux, 1996), 68.

32 | The Jewish-Christian Encounter
A Matter of Faith?

Remi Hoeckman

HISTORY TEACHES US that where there is no religious space for the other, soon there may be no space at all for the other. That is why I have focused my essay on the religious dimension of the Jewish-Christian encounter today.

* * *

Jonathan Sacks, the British chief rabbi, has written that for the secularist in our society religion is neither the engine that drives society nor the map that directs its driver, but that it is at most a tape played on a mental stereo to while away idle hours.[1] This definition, which unfortunately seems to apply to many people in the West today, including Christians and Jews, does not describe me, however. I am not a secularist but a person of faith, and since the day that I was entrusted with my present task as secretary of the Holy See Commission for Religious Relations with the Jews, I have had no idle hours.

I am a man of faith who does believe in interfaith encounter, but I have a problem with what I feel is an ambiguous use of these words. That which contains great potential in terms of sharing and discovery, growth and promise—especially in the realm of Jewish-Christian relations and dialogue, which provides a space where hearts meet hearts and minds meet minds, and where these can be informed and transformed in the process—is too easily emptied of its religious content and filled with something else.

To me, interfaith without faith is an empty word, and encounter without the other is an empty show. Paraphrasing a statement made by Rabbi J. B. Soloveitchik, I am not ready to meet with another faith community in which I am regarded as an object of observation, judgment, and evaluation, rather than as a person of faith.[2] In my daily dealings with Jewish and Jewish-Christian "interfaith affairs," "interfaith institutes," "interfaith programs," "interfaith relations," "interfaith dialogue," "interfaith groups," and "interfaith directors," I often have difficulty finding religious content in those "affairs," "programs," or "institutes." I may have it wrong, but to me interfaith encounter means experiencing the other on a level or in a space where perhaps only souls can meet, under the gaze of God. To me, it means to meet with one who might not be in my image but who is nonetheless in the image of God. It means to meet with one whose face I can see "as one sees the face of God" (Gen. 33:10) and feel blessed by it.

I say these things because of something that Rabbi Sacks has said recently, which has stayed with me. In September 1997, addressing a conference of the International Council of Christians and Jews at Rocca di Papa, near Rome, on the topic "The Other—Jews and Christians," Rabbi Sacks spoke about the story of Jacob and Esau and the strange encounter that Jacob had with The One who gave him his new name. Sacks explained:

> At that moment, Jacob is cured of wanting to be Esau. For the first time he can meet Esau without aggression or deception or fear. He says to Esau, "I have seen your face as one sees the face of God," meaning I have recognized your otherness, and I have let it go. You are not me. I am not you. It is in our mutual otherness that we can have relationship. If I am I and you are you, we no longer threaten one another, for we each have our own blessing. We are affirmed in our otherness by Him who is ultimately Other. The Torah signals that this was not an easy discovery. It took many years, it took a deep inner struggle; after it Jacob limped. But after it Jacob became Israel—he who is content to be different, not to be Esau.

> Judaism and Christianity, in their different ways, have had to undergo that inner struggle, and we still do. At times, Christians sought to take their brother's blessing—to be Israel, to carry its name, to take hold of its covenant, to displace it from its relationship with God. At times, Jews faced the opposite temptation—*not* to be Israel, to be Assyrians, Greeks, Romans, to assimilate, become anonymous, no longer different; to be, in Ezekiel's words, "like the nations, like the other peoples of the earth." In Christianity the temptation is supersession. In Judaism it is secession. In both it is a failure to be ourselves and not another. Yet it is only by being ourselves and not another that we create space for the other to be himself and not us. Only when I-am-not-Thou and Thou-are-not-I can there be a relationship, each affirming the other in his or her difference. And because God lives in relationships, he lives in difference.

> We are others. We are also brothers. We have been so for a long time. . . . When we look back on our past, we find much that we have in common. We trace our ancestry through the prophets and back to Abraham and Sarah, the first people to hear the call. We share many of the same texts, though we read them through different traditions of interpretations. We have shared origins, though our paths diverged. . . .

> It took a long inner struggle, and the darkest night of all, for Jews and Christians to reach the moment when we could meet without fear, each secure in our own blessing, each faithful to our particular truth. . . . We have reached that stage today, and we must never regress. For it is only if we are true to our separate vocations, if Christians are not Jews, and Jews are not Christians, that we bring our respective truths to the world, and live, as brothers, in peace.

* * *

Rabbi Sacks's phrases are spoken by a person of faith. They are in a language that I can identify with and that is understood by people to whom I relate every day, my students, the people in my church, people who are open to what I have to say. It is a language that springs from a soil that nourishes us Christians and that both communities, Jews and Christians, revere. It is a language that creates a healing space that allows me to realize how utterly sad it is that it took such a long time to reach this moment, and above all that it took the "darkest night of all," the Shoah, to hasten its coming. This moment counts, and, as Rabbi Sacks has put it with force, "we must not regress."

We must not regress, indeed; rather, we must join forces and work together in order to let it become a blessed moment for ourselves and humanity. We have work to do, and "none of us can do it alone."[3] This is not a time to celebrate in forgetful euphoria, but a time to let memory, healed of its wounds, become our teacher and the teacher of our children, in order to "ensure that evil does not prevail over good as it did for millions of the children of the Jewish nation."[4] These are the words of the Pope, which, as he told the Jews in Poland, "my faith and heart dictate."[5]

When I listen to these words and to those of Rabbi Sacks, when I listen to the words—often spoken with hesitation, yet with hope—of the Jewish men and women whom I have the privilege to relate to as fellow human beings who, just like me, want to reach out and want to be reached, I hear the language of an encounter in which both parties are, from the start and at the same time, neighbors and strangers who, in the very experience of encounter, discover that, in spite of their differences, they are also brothers.

Jonathan Sacks has reflected on this point too. "A neighbor is one who is like us," he said. "A stranger is one who is not like us. . . . Our neighbor is one we love because he is like us. A stranger is one we are taught to love precisely because he is *not* like us. That is the most powerful command of the Torah. I believe it to be one of the great truths of all time, and in a century of mass destruction, the most urgent. It is why Jews were commanded to be different."

Sharing his Jewish self-understanding, Sacks pointed out that "throughout history . . . Jews were different to teach that God lives in difference, [that] they were strangers to teach that God loves the stranger, [that] they were not like other people, and yet [that] God set on them His special love, to teach humanity the dignity of difference." This is the language of faith and of interfaith dialogue. Cardinal Edward Idris Cassidy, president of our commission, in his keynote address to the same ICCJ Conference at which Chief Rabbi Sacks spoke, stated: "Much of the progress accomplished so far in our relations has been the result of dialogue, but our dialogue has tended to remain at a rather superficial level. We have spoken together about our problems, but not about ourselves!" Jonathan Sacks did speak about himself: "I speak as a Jew," he said:

And surely no people has suffered more, or longer, for its faith than ours. Many times our ancestors from Egypt to Auschwitz asked the great question of the book of Psalms, *Keli Keli lamah azavtami,* "My God, my God, why have You forsaken me?" They suffered because they were different. At all times, even at the cost of suffering and death, the majority of Jews refused to assimilate to the dominant culture or convert to the dominant faith. They were different . . . because they alone had been commanded to be different, to be holy, because "I am the Lord your God who have separated you from other peoples" (Lev. 20:24). Why does God make those He chooses suffer? Why was there a chosen people? Today, in this century of Auschwitz, we begin to understand the answer.

This language does not threaten people; instead, it opens their ears and eyes. It touches their hearts, penetrates their minds, and helps to shape their concerns and attitudes. It qualifies their perception. It invites them to come near, to become partners in a struggle that, ultimately, both have to face, although for different reasons. It is a language that not only respects the differences but provides the space that is necessary for a genuine interfaith encounter. "Those who persecuted Jews showed that they could not tolerate difference," Sacks affirmed; "a civilization that does not tolerate difference fails the basic moral requirements of humanity." Auschwitz has shown this to be true.

Today the otherness of the other is still a motive for cruel indifference or savage treatment, not only "out there" but also in your continent and in mine, and elsewhere. As Cardinal Cassidy commented, "In the recent past, in the very heart of Europe, in fact not far distant from the death camps of the *Shoah,* children have been starved to death because they belonged to *the other;* women were raped because they were part of *the other;* men and boys were murdered and buried in mass graves because they were from *the other* ethnic group."[6] That is why the words of Jonathan Sacks are relevant: "We are others. We are also brothers." They provide us with a program. They set the agenda of Catholic-Jewish dialogue. In the words of the Pope: "Surely the time has come for us, Jews and Christians, to go beyond the dialogue of the past, and to move ahead in common witness to the religious values that we share, the moral principles placed in our hands by the One who created this world and which are set down in Holy Scriptures that both Jews and Christians revere. That is where the new agenda for Catholic-Jewish relations lies."[7]

* * *

In the introduction to their book *Our Age,* on "the historic new era of Christian-Jewish understanding," Rabbi Jack Bemporad and Rabbi Michael Shevack stated that they wrote it "for those who dare to believe; for those who dare to believe that the past need not condemn the future, that enmity can be transformed into trust, that good can be chosen over evil, that people can change."[8] That is true, people can change, but the question is *how,* and change takes time. "The issue is to reach the conscience of the faithful, an effort which is under way," said Tullia Zevi, head of the Union of Italian Jewish Communities; "these things take time. We are a patient people, and the Church is a patient institution. We move in slow times. The issue is to move in the right direction."[9]

To move in the right direction is our concern, too. Can we not meet as communities of faith, or must we meet as organizations and structures that carve out spheres of interest and develop separate agendas? Are we trapped? On both sides? I am afraid we are. We are trapped by history and memory, by our perceptions and expectations that are shaped by them, and, on both sides, by an inability to cope with them. I listen to my Jewish friends. I refuse to suffer what Jonathan Sacks calls "the strange contemporary blindness to Jewish history—a history that could be written in terms of wanderings and expulsions, inquisitions and pogroms, martyrdom and exclusion, the powerlessness and homelessness of 'the wandering Jew.'"[10] I realize that "we cannot understand where we are unless we first understand how we came to be there," and I quote Sacks again: "Israel cannot be understood as simply a secular democratic state on the European model, or American Jewry as a typical version of American pluralism and denominationalism. These are part . . . of the Jewish story. The Israeli and American Jewish communities still carry within them the pains and tensions of the European Jewish experience, and even today they are shaped by what they were created to forget."[11]

We have come a long way, yet we have a long way to go. However, as Tullia Zevi says, "the issue is to move in the right direction," and we will do that as long as we are willing to move together, step by step, making sure that the past illuminates the path instead of obscuring it. Knowledge and respect illuminate; contempt, fear, or arrogance obscures. However, knowledge can obscure as well when it is partial, unilateral, or polarized around certain issues. As far as Jewish knowledge about Christians is concerned, the Jewish community has the right to know not only what we are or what we have done, but also *who* we are and what we are doing. The same is true of Christian knowledge about Jews, in this country, in Israel, in Europe, and indeed everywhere. "We well know the abyss of ignorance in *both* our communities concerning the other, which includes dangerous myths, and prejudices," Geoffrey Wigoder admitted in his address at our International Catholic-Jewish Liaison Committee meeting in Jerusalem in May 1994.

In February 1997 I participated in an excellent symposium on the future of Catholic-Jewish relations in Israel/Palestine/The Holy Land.[12] It took place in Jerusalem. At the symposium a Jewish voice spoke up, that of Daniel Rossing, an educator who has been involved in Jewish-Christian dialogue in the West for more than twenty years and who is now living in Israel, where he is deeply involved with the various Christian communities. Rossing realized, as did all of us present, that we were dealing with an extremely sensitive and difficult topic, yet he was determined to speak his mind on it. "I think it is obvious to all who have labored in the vineyard of Jewish-Catholic relations that nearly all of the changes which have brought about the vast improvements in relations have taken place on the Catholic side," he said, and "in the light of the historic record of the Church's relations with the Jewish people, it is fully understandable that the dialogue in the West has for the most part been a one-way street, at least in terms of the re-examination of traditional attitudes."

However, Rossing expressed sincere hope that today the "historic changes in the attitudes of Christians towards Judaism and Jews" that have occurred since the Second Vatican Council, "will also enter the consciousness of the inhabitants of this land [Israel], and most especially the hearts and minds of Jews . . . , among whom the changes are little known." "We have to honestly admit that there are virtually no indigenous Jewish-Catholic interfaith relations or dialogue in this land," he said:

> [T]oday, in and around Jerusalem, there is hardly any contact between Jews and local Christians. . . . In Galilee, where one finds a majority of the Christians in the land living alongside a minority of the Jews in the land, there is some contact, both in daily life and in the framework of the many organizations whose activities are designed to promote Arab-Jewish co-existence and cooperation. However, these contacts and activities are for the most part characterized by, indeed premised on, a conspiracy of silence with regard to anything that touches upon religious faith and identity.

Although in that part of Israel there is fruitful cooperation between the many Catholic educational, medical, and social welfare institutions and the Jews working in these fields, Daniel Rossing pointed out that "important as these cooperative relations are, *they cannot be counted as interfaith.*"[13]

Rossing realizes, as I do, that interfaith means something else. Moreover, he seeks to understand why even the limited number of Jews who are open, indeed committed, to interfaith relations have not entered into an interfaith dialogue with the Christian communities in Israel. "The task is complex and difficult," he said, "but the path is clear. . . . There will be no significant breakthrough in this country in the area of interfaith relations in general, and Jewish-Catholic relations in particular, until there is a similar change of heart and mind, and a sincere reaching out, on the part of the dominant Jewish Community in this land."[14]

Rossing then indicated some preliminary steps that he considered necessary to lay the foundations for the possibility of honest interfaith relations in Israel. The measures he emphasized reflected similar steps taken by the Catholic Church to pave the way for constructive dialogue with Jews and Judaism. These steps should be viewed as "a mandatory cleansing of the heart and mind before entering the sacred space of dialogue." "The temptation will be great to focus on our own deep pain, or on the injuries caused to Christians by another faith community, rather than to honestly confront the very tangible, as well as many subtle, ways in which Christians in this land [Israel] are hurt and offended by Jews," he said, "but although there are elements of a 'teaching of contempt' in our [Jewish] tradition, we do not bear the burden of a 2,000-year history of persecuting Christians."

These words convey the pain of the "inner struggle" to which Chief Rabbi Jonathan Sacks also referred. It is the pain of a person and a people that a long and tragic history has left severely wounded. It is the pain of one who seeks both to be healed himself and to heal the other. Therefore, Rossing affirmed, "it is vitally important to us [Jews] that the Catholic Church continue to reach out to us where we are and as we understand ourselves." I would like to add that it is equally important to us Christians that the Jewish community seek to gain the strength and the wisdom to reach out to us, too, for the benefit of both our peoples and indeed for the benefit of all peoples. Both our communities are in need of healing, and both need the help of the other for it. Whoever is able to see this, Jews and Christians alike, will perform the "mandatory cleansing of the heart and mind before entering the sacred space of dialogue," the sacred space in which Jacob turned to his brother and said, "I have seen your face as one sees the face of God."

* * *

Eugene Fisher, in an article entitled "Catholic Grapplings with the Shoah and Its Theological Implications," has written: "If there was a temptation to silence in the dialogue between Jews and Catholics in the face of the intractable realities of the Shoah that silence has been shattered by the increasingly vocal controversies between our two communities in recent years."[15] Although much of what I have written here comes from this experience, it is my deepest wish that these controversies should come to an end. In spite of them, the dialogue goes on. "Despite the rhetoric, the fabric of our relations has not torn," Eugene Fisher states, and to the question "what, exactly, are Jews saying to us underneath the often hurtful rhetoric thrown at us via the Media?"[16] he answers: "What Jews are saying in essence is no more and no less than what the prophets and Jesus said to the world in earlier generations: 'Repent and sin no more!' It is a timeless and timely message. For Christians to speak of reconciliation with Jews in this, as the Pope has rightly called it, 'the century of the *Shoah*,' we must take the first step, repentance, a *heshbon ha-nefesh,* an accounting of the soul."[17]

In the Catholic community we are doing this by implementing the Council's mandate (*Nostra Aetate* n. 4). Pope John Paul II is leading us in this effort. I will emphasize just a couple of points that are expressed very clearly in his teaching: "No dialogue between Christians and Jews can overlook the painful and terrible experience of the *Shoah*";[18] "The days of the *Shoah* marked a true night of history, with unimaginable crimes against God and humanity";[19] "We Christians approach with immense respect the terrifying experience of the extermination, the *Shoah,* suffered by the Jews during World War II";[20] "Joint collaboration and studies by Catholics and Jews on the *Shoah* should be continued."[21]

Furthermore, in his greeting to the new ambassador of Germany to the Holy See, he said:

> It was really the Second World War which . . . made many people aware of what fate and guilt mean to all peoples and individuals. We think of the millions of people, most of them totally innocent, who died in the war. . . . In this context we should also mention the tragedy of the Jews. *For Christians the heavy burden of guilt for the murder of the Jewish people must be an enduring call to repentance;* thereby we can overcome every form of anti-Semitism and establish a new relationship with our kindred nation of the Old Covenant. The Church . . . "deplores the hatred, persecutions, and displays of anti-Semitism directed against the Jews at any time and from any source" (Second Vatican Council, Declaration *Nostra Aetate,* n. 4). Guilt should not oppress and lead to self-agonizing thoughts, but must always be the point of departure for conversion.[22]

This reminds me of what Rabbi Awraham Soetendorp, a survivor of the Shoah, told us at the Eisenach Conference of the International Council of Christians and Jews in 1995. He then said: "The real meaning of repentance (*teshuva*) is not to be burdened with guilt but to learn from experiences and to turn the mistakes and the transgressions into a passion for a new future."[23] Rabbis Jack Bemporad and Michael Shevach say the same thing: "No one should be so obsessed with the past that they prevent themselves from moving into the future. No one should *live* in the past." Yet, they rightly point out, "the past is not just something you should ever toss away and forget." "Quite to the contrary, it must be remembered, heeded, learned from, so that it will never repeat itself."[24] That is why the Holy See's Commission for Religious Relations with the Jews has recently published *We Remember: A Reflection on the Shoah,* a document that is addressed to the Catholic faithful throughout the world, and not only in Europe where the Shoah took place, and where several Catholic bishops' conferences (in Germany, Poland, the Netherlands, Switzerland, Hungary, and France) have courageously and responsibly taken their stand in this regard.

The numerous reactions to this document are mixed, since one's evaluation very much depends on the expectations one has. I think that the reaction that we received from the Tanenbaum Center for Interreligious Understanding in New York written by Judith Banki, program director, sums it up well: "This long-awaited document does not break new ground," Banki states:

> It incorporated much that has been said before. However, augmented by a historical overview and molded into a single statement addressing the most traumatic and painful events in Jewish history, it adds the Church's

moral authority to the need to understand what gave rise to the greatest crime of the twentieth century, and to remember it — "for there is no future without memory. . . . " When *Nostra Aetate . . .* was promulgated in 1965, it was immediately criticized by Jewish leaders as a compromise, an insufficient and over-cautious document. Later Vatican documents, including the catechetical *Notes* of 1985, were similarly criticized. Yet these very documents laid the groundwork for a new relationship between the Church and the Jewish people. Key elements are now routinely invoked by Catholic and Jewish leaders alike. Implementation made the difference. The Church's expression of human solidarity should guide our footsteps as we seek to implement the teaching and preaching opportunities inherent in this document, which lays out a challenging agenda for the future.

The Pope seems to have anticipated *We Remember* when he told Jewish leaders in Budapest in 1991:

> Today, after the period of darkness when it seemed as though the Jews would be completely exterminated, you are here once more and making a significant contribution to Magyar national life. I rejoice at your active presence, which reveals the new vitality of your people. But, at the same time, I recall each and every one of the Jews — women and children, old men and young — who, though they lost their lives, kept their faith in the Lord's promises. . . . Our gaze now turns from the past to a future of reconciliation in justice. Once again, I deplore and condemn, together with you, the wickedness which made you suffer and which brought about the death of so many others. Of course, we must try to "purge the evil from our midst" (cf. Deut. 17:7), but what concerns us now is not desire for revenge on the wicked, since it is fitting to leave the supreme judgment to God, but a commitment to ensure that never again can selfishness and hatred sow suffering and death. . . . The hard quest for justice, love, and peace must begin with ourselves. . . . Therefore, with God's powerful help, true liberation from evil is a continuous crossing of the Red Sea, and involves a patient struggle, through which we have to progress by means of a daily conversion of heart, or *Teshuva*. In repentance, fasting, and works of mercy. . . . Knowing our weakness, and trusting in the strength of God who works in us and delivers us from evil, let us have recourse to the Lord who sets us free.[25]

* * *

Such is the Holy Father's vision, totally realistic and totally anchored in faith. It accords with the vision of the person of faith with whom I started my story, Rabbi Jonathan Sacks, who wrote in *The Tablet*:

> There are two quite distinct challenges to religious leadership as this century and this millennium draw to their close. One challenge is very simple. We have to restate for a new generation a compelling sense of the sheer beauty and majesty of the Judeo-Christian ethic. And we can do it. We have to repeat again for children who have not heard it and need to hear it, our belief in the sanctity of human life as bearing God's image

and his likeness. . . . And there is the second challenge that we must as religious people face fairly and honestly. For the real secular challenge to religion does not come from any scientific world view. It comes from the voice of conscience itself, from the claim that religion has sometimes made us passive in the face of human suffering, has even itself contributed, God forbid, to human suffering. Until religions can live at peace with one another, they will not command the respect of our young people. They will be seen as part of the problem, and not as part of the solution. Those are the two great challenges. Let me here and now pay tribute in both regards to the work over these last few decades of the Catholic Church itself, which in recent years has been both an extraordinarily powerful moral voice, reminding us of those eternal truths that we have been in such great danger of forgetting, and which has shown, especially in the field of Catholic-Jewish relationships, that religions can learn to live at peace with one another, that we can begin to heal the pain of centuries and meet in understanding and mutual respect.

It is not easy to be a person of faith. But let us realize that every single word of faith that you or I speak touches and strengthens the faith of other people . . . and that it is by sharing our faith, even where our faiths differ, that we recreate a world of faith for our children.[26]

Indeed, in our age it is not easy to be a person of faith. Neither is it easy for us, Christians and Jews, in this post-Holocaust era to let our encounter be truthfully an interfaith encounter. Yet our relations not only involve (and I borrow the words of Rabbi Leon Klenicki) "persons of flesh and blood, but also continents of faith." "God is our common ground and sense," Klenicki says in an article on the need for a *theological* discussion in the interfaith dialogue between Christians and Jews, "our faith commitments are areas of sacredness," which can meet in the sacredness of God's Presence.[27]

It is in this sacred space that the past ought to be remembered, that memory can be healed, and that present challenges that both faith commitments face in today's world should be discussed.[28] It is in this space that we should ask our questions beyond contempt, triumphalism, or self-righteousness. Where else can Christians overcome the triumphalism of power and Jews the triumphalism of pain?[29] Where else can we believe, trust, and be changed? Where else can we repent, forgive, and be forgiven? In the words of Jonathan Sacks, where else can Jacob meet his brother without aggression or deception or fear? It took them many years. It took a deep inner struggle. After it Jacob limped. But after it Jacob became Israel.

The Pope sees the basis of our encounter not merely in reciprocal respect, but in our faith in the one, true God.[30] Or, as he put it in addressing the Anti-Defamation League of B'nai B'rith:

[T]he respect we speak of is based on the mysterious link which brings us close together, in Abraham and, through Abraham, in God who chose Israel and brought forth the Church from Israel. . . . All of us, Jews and Christians, pray frequently to Him with the same prayers, taken from the

Book which we both consider to be the word of God. It is for Him to give to both religious communities, so near to each other, that reconciliation and effective love which are at the same time His command and His gift (cf. Lev. 19:18; Mk. 12:30).[31]

"In spite of this [nearness], our respective religious identities have divided us, at times, grievously, through the centuries," he told the Jewish community in Sao Paolo, Brazil, on 3 July 1980. But "this should not be an obstacle to our now respecting this same identity, wanting to emphasize our common heritage and in this way to cooperate, in light of this same heritage, for the solution of problems which affect contemporary society, a society needing faith in God, obedience to His holy laws, active hope in the coming of His kingdom." In other words, the Pope does not think of Catholic-Jewish relations in merely secular terms, but in religious terms, in terms of faith.

Shmuel Hadds, the first ambassador of Israel to the Holy See, was well aware of this when he addressed the Pope on the occasion of the presentation of his credentials on 29 September 1994. "Your Holiness," he began, "The Holy See and the State of Israel, mindful of the unique character and universal importance of the Holy Land and aware of the unique nature of the relations between the Catholic Church and the Jewish people, and of the historic process of reconciliation and growth in mutual understanding and friendship between Catholics and Jews. . . ." These eloquent and meaningful words introduced the preamble to the Fundamental Agreement between the Holy See and the State of Israel, which on 30 December 1997 paved the way for the normalization of relations between the Holy See and Israel, overcoming an obstacle to progress in Jewish-Catholic *rapprochement*. "Obviously," said the ambassador, "this is not the conventional language of international diplomacy. It could not be otherwise."

* * *

I conclude by quoting from an address by Cardinal Joseph Ratzinger at a conference held in Jerusalem a few weeks after the signing of the Fundamental Agreement between the Holy See and the State of Israel: "After Auschwitz, the mission of reconciliation and acceptance permits no deferral. . . . Jews and Christians should accept each other in profound inner reconciliation, neither in disregard of their faith nor in its denial, but *out of the depth of faith itself*. In their mutual reconciliation they should become a force for peace in and for the world."

NOTES

1. Jonathan Sacks, *The Perspective of Faith: Religion, Morality and Society in a Secular Age* (London, 1991), 3.
2. Cf. Leon Klenicki, "The Need for a Theological Discussion in the Interfaith Dialogue: A Proposal," *Atonement* (March/April 1994): 1.

3. A. J. Heschel, "No Religion Is an Island," *Union Theological Seminary Quarterly* 21, no. 2 (January 1996).

4. Pope John Paul II, Address given on the occasion of a concert held in the Vatican on 7 April 1994 to commemorate the *Shoah*.

5. 9 June 1991.

6. Cardinal Edward Idris Cassidy at the ICCJ Conference cited above.

7. Pope John Paul II, Address to the International Catholic-Jewish Liaison Committee, 26 March 1998. Cf. my paper "Catholic-Jewish Relations after World War II: A Catholic Assessment" (presented at the Symposium on The Fundamental Agreement between the Holy See and the State of Israel, the Catholic University of America/Columbus School of Law, Washington, D.C., 8–9 April 1997).

8. Jack Bemporad and Michael Shevack, *Our Age* (New York: New City Press, 1996), 10.

9. Cf. Celestine Bohlen, "The Pope's in a Confessional, and Jews Are Listening," *New York Times,* 30 November 1997, p. 12.

10. "Love, Hate, and Jewish Identity," in *First Things,* November 1997, p. 27, n. 77.

11. Ibid.

12. At the Van Leer Institute, 10–11 February 1997; the symposium was co-sponsored by the Rabbi Marc H. Tanenbaum Foundation, FAITH, ICCI, IJCIR.

13. My italics.

14. Rabbi Henry Siegman, "Ten Years of Catholic-Jewish Relations: A Reassessment," in *Fifteen Years of Catholic-Jewish Dialogue 1970–1985* (Rome: International Catholic-Jewish Liaison Committee, 1988), 27–45: "Taking full advantage of the prerequisite of the injured party, Jews have successfully managed the dialogue so that it has focused entirely on what we consider to be Christian failings; we have not been compelled to examine ourselves and the problematic of our own theology and traditions—at least not within the context of dialogue. I suppose that Christian forbearance with this one-sided situation is compounded of a sense of guilt and of *noblesse oblige*. However, it is a situation which cannot persist for long . . . because our Christian partners are not likely to continue the dialogue on these terms. . . . We have been forthright in calling Christianity to account, but we have been somewhat less than daring in initiating a process of self-examination. . . . I have come to the conclusion that there is something particularly distortive of the relationship, and misleading of its genuine character and depth in the frenetic efforts in which we engage with such monotonous regularity to extract public statements from Christian officials at every turn in Jewish affairs. Indeed, it seems to have become a major industry of American Jewish life, whose major beneficiaries, insofar as I can tell, are the advertising agencies and metropolitan newspapers. Of course, Jewish existence continues to be fragile and vulnerable, and we need understanding friendship and public support as desperately as we ever did. But if these are to have any meaning and particular consequence, then they must be spontaneous expressions rather than ritualistic responses to heavy-handed pressure exerted by Jewish organizations, including my own."

15. Eugene Fisher, "Catholic Grapplings with the Shoah and Its Theological Implications," in *The Holocaust Now: Contemporary Christian and Jewish Thought,* ed. Rabbi Steven L. Jacobs (East Rockaway, N.Y., 1996), 237.

16. Ibid., 238–239.

17. Ibid., 241.

18. Pope John Paul II, Address to the International Catholic-Jewish Liaison Committee, 6 December 1990.

19. Pope John Paul II, Sunday prayer of the *Regina Coeli,* 18 April 1993.

20. Pope John Paul II, letter to Archbishop John L. May, then president of the National Conference of Catholic Bishops in the USA, 8 August 1987.

21. Pope John Paul II, Address to Jewish leaders in Miami, 11 September 1987.

22. 8 November 1990. My italics.

23. Cf. *Towards a Europe of Compassion,* in *Common Ground* (the Journal of the Council of Christians and Jews in Great Britain) (1995): 24, n. 11.

24. Ibid., 64.

25. 18 August 1991.

26. Jonathan Sacks, "From Slavery to Freedom: The Journey of Faith," *The Tablet* (10 June 1995): 734–735.

27. Klenicki, 1.

28. Pope John Paul II, Message to the Jews from around the world gathered in Poland in April 1993 on the occasion of the 50th anniversary of the Uprising of the Warsaw Ghetto, 6 April 1993: "We remember, and we need to remember, but we need to remember with renewed trust in God and in his all-healing blessing." "As Christians and Jews, following the example of the faith of Abraham, we are called to be a blessing for the world (cf. Gen. 12:2ff). This is the common task awaiting us. It is therefore necessary for us, Christians and Jews, to be first a blessing to one another. This will effectively occur if we are united in the face of the evils which are still threatening: indifference and prejudice, as well as displays of anti-Semitism."

29. Cf. Klenicki, 2. See also Siegman, who already in 1976 outlined his perception of what was then happening in Jewish-Catholic relations: "It seems reasonably clear that the process is an irreversible one. The capacity to hurt one another is still there, and—more likely than not—will not remain unexercised. The areas of misunderstanding still remain vast. But the notions of an earlier Christian triumphalism of the Jewish people as role-players in someone else's Passion play is a thing of the past, and that is a far-reaching change indeed. It also frees the Jewish people to shed its own peculiar kind of triumphalism, the definite triumphalism of the persecuted and the abused, and to relate in a more open and creative way to the world about it." I hope so.

30. Pope John Paul II, Address to Jewish leaders in Brasilia, 15 October 1991.

31. Pope John Paul II, Address to Representatives of Jewish Organizations, 12 March 1979.

Contributors

Monika Adamczyk-Garbowska	Marie Curie-Sklodowska University, Lublin, Poland
Rachel Adler	University of Southern California, Hebrew Union College—Jewish Institute of Religion, Los Angeles
Arnold J. Band	University of California, Los Angeles
Victoria J. Barnett	United States Holocaust Memorial Museum
Michael Berenbaum	Richard Stockton College
Doris L. Bergen	University of Notre Dame
Roberta M. Berry	Georgia Tech
David R. Blumenthal	Emory University
Gerhard Botz	University of Vienna, Austria
Edna Brocke	Alte Synagoge, Essen, Germany
Sidra DeKoven Ezrahi	Dartmouth College
John Felstiner	Stanford University
Saul Friedländer	University of California, Los Angeles, University of Tel Aviv
Sander L. Gilman	University of Chicago
Hanspeter Heinz	Universität Augsburg, Augsburg
Hans Hermann Henrix	Bischöfliche Akademie, Aachen
Remi Hoeckman, OP	Holy See Commission for Religious Relations with the Jews
Daniel J. Kevles	California Institute of Technology
Bertold Klappert	Kirchliche Hochschule, Wuppertal
Robert A. Krieg	University of Notre Dame
Marcia Landy	University of Pittsburgh
Lawrence Langer	Simmons College
Jonathan Marks	University of California, Berkeley
Alan Mintz	Brandeis University
Peter Ochs	University of Virginia
John T. Pawlikowski	Catholic Theological Union
Peter C. Phan	Catholic University of America
Didier Pollefeyt	Catholic University, Leuven, Belgium

Joan Ringelheim   United States Holocaust Memorial
                                           Museum

John K. Roth   Claremont-McKenna College

Michael A. Signer   University of Notre Dame

Phillip R. Sloan   University of Notre Dame

Michael C. Steinlauf   Gratz College

Peter von der Osten-Sacken   Institut Kirche und Judentum, Berlin

J. Robert Wegs   University of Notre Dame

Peter Weingart   Universität Bielefeld, Bielefeld

John P. Welle   University of Notre Dame

James E. Young   University of Massachusetts, Amherst

Index

Abraham, David, 294

Absender, Der (Ganzfried), 262, 295

Adamczyk-Garbowska, Monika, 259, 260, 262

Adler, Rachel, 107, 109–10

Adorno, Theodor, 27–28, 327, 376; on anti-Semites, 304; negative dialectics of, 99; on poetry, 46, 392, 395, 403–404

Age of Atrocity, The (Langer), 328

agency, 260, 261, 387

Aleichem, Sholem, 300, 398, 422

Allowing the Destruction of Life Unworthy of Living, 213

Almosts: A Study of the Feebleminded, The (MacMurchy), 183

Alphabet des Juda Liva, Das (Stein), 299–300

Althaus, Paul, 89

altruism, 72, 247, 356–57

American Eugenics Society, 194, 244

American Indians, 292–93

Améry, Jean, 409, 418

Anguish of the Jews, The (Flannery), 23

Anschluss, 269, 270, 282

anthropologists/anthropology, 178, 209, 210, 259; Christology and, 21; criminal Nazi experiments and, 214; Diversity Project and, 247; eugenics and, 205, 206, 209, 224–25, 244; Nazi ideology and, 17; physical, 205, 206, 220n7, 241, 291; significance of blood, 246; UNESCO Statement on Race and, 215

Anti-Defamation League of B'nai B'rith, 438

anti-Judaism, 91, 92, 110, 252, 266, 268; anti-Semitism and, 80–81, 130n6, 252; Asian Christianity and, 114–18; Christology and, 123

anti-Semitism, 4, 9, 23, 70, 91, 211; anti-Judaism and, 80–81, 130n6, 252; in Austria, 260, 267–69, 274–75, 280–85, 298–99; Christian renunciation of, 436, 441n28; creation and diffusion of, 374;

economic, 264; "eliminationist," 259–60, 302n17; eugenics and, 208, 209; in France, 320; gender and, 261; in Germany, 205, 302n17, 305; Jewish identity and, 269; levels of, 175; in Poland, 260, 312, 323, 331; racial and religious, 261–62, 264, 267, 268, 280, 302n17; redemptory, 47; social Darwinism and, 176–77; stereotypes and, 292; understanding of, 304. *See also* pogroms

anti-Zionism, 312, 314, 315, 317n18

Appelfeld, Aharon, 259

Aqiba, Rabbi, 164–66

Arabs, 32, 34, 401

Arendt, Hannah, 9, 37, 167, 304; on evil, 6; on incomprehensibility of Holocaust, 39–40, 43n20; on limits of law, 5; on Nazism and Communism, 10

Armenian genocide, 88, 327

Aron, Raymond, 9–10

Art from the Ashes (Langer), 405, 408, 409

artificial insemination, 197, 198, 216

artists, 44, 45–46, 48–59

Aryan Laws (1933), 142

Aryan race/Aryanism, 16, 17, 205, 206, 269, 272

Asian liberation theology, 110–11

assimilation, 430, 432; in Austria, 265, 281; in Germany, 304–305, 306; in Poland, 321, 322

Association for Moral Education, 358

atomic bombs, 38, 41, 127, 202

Atwood, Margaret, 197

Auerbach, Rachel, 422, 423

Augstein, Rudolf, 5, 291

Auschwitz, 9, 20, 70, 163, 329, 335; accounts of, 154, 415–18; "break in civilization" and, 343; Carmelite convent at, 4; "concentric circles" of memory and, 31; critical theory and, 28; Jews and Polish national memory